*The Economic History
of Iran
1800—1914*

Publications of the Center for Middle Eastern Studies
Number 8
William R. Polk, General Editor

# The Economic History
of Iran
1800–1914

Edited by
CHARLES ISSAWI

THE UNIVERSITY OF CHICAGO PRESS

CHICAGO AND LONDON

PUBLICATIONS OF THE CENTER FOR MIDDLE EASTERN STUDIES

1. Beginnings of Modernization in the Middle East: The Nineteenth Century
   Edited by William R. Polk and Richard L. Chambers
2. The Mosque in Early Ottoman Architecture
   By Aptullah Kuran
3. Economic Development and Regional Cooperation: Kuwait
   By Ragaei El Mallakh
4. Studies in the Social History of Modern Egypt
   By Gabriel Baer
5. Conflicts and Tensions in Islamic Jurisprudence
   By Noel J. Coulson
6. The Modern Arabic Literary Language: Lexical and Stylistic Developments
   By Jaroslav Stetkevych
7. Iran: Economic Development under Dualistic Conditions
   By Jahangir Amuzegar and M. Ali Fekrat
8. The Economic History of Iran: 1800–1914
   By Charles Issawi

International Standard Book Number: 0–226–38606–6
Library of Congress Catalog Card Number: 70–153–883
The University of Chicago Press, Chicago 60637
The University of Chicago Press, Ltd., London

©1971 by The University of Chicago
All rights reserved
Published 1971
Printed in the United States of America

*To Mohammed Yeganeh*
*in sincere friendship*

# Contents

## Chapter 4: Transport 152

# Chapter 6: Industry     258

# *Preface*

This book is a companion volume to *The Economic History of the Middle East* (University of Chicago Press, 1966). Like its predecessor, it springs from the belief that, in the present state of knowledge, the best way to study the economic history of the area is through a collection of documents; it therefore presents a selection of articles and extracts from documents, reports, and books dealing with various aspects of the Iranian economy. Like it, too, it is neither raw material nor a fully finished product, but the degree of processing has been carried further than in the previous volume. I believe that this kind of preliminary work has to be carried out before a coherent history of the Iranian economy can be written, and I hope it may prove useful not only to students of Iran and the Middle East but also to those in the general area of economic development. It is presented essentially as an aid to teaching and research. If it serves to arouse interest in a much-neglected subject and stimulates further research, it will have fulfilled its main objective.

As in the previous volume, the primary aim in selecting the material has been to include the best and most interesting texts available, but with emphasis on the less accessible sources. Within this framework, five criteria have been applied: First, no passage from any book in English has been reproduced. This has led to the exclusion of important writings by Malcolm, Kinneir, Fraser, Curzon, Lorimer, Shuster, Sykes, and others and of works by such contemporary scholars as Avery, Banani, English, Entner, Farman Farmayan, Greaves, Kazemzadeh, Keddie, Kelly, Lambton, and Ramazani. Second, preference has been given to unpublished over published material. Third, texts in non-Western languages have been given preference over texts in Western languages, and within the latter group, non-English texts over English. Fourth, priority has been given to reports and articles over books and to older books over more recently published ones. Last, since the main laws, treaties, and concessionary and other agreements have been reproduced in J. C. Hurewitz, *Diplomacy in the Near and Middle East*, or are available in C. U. Aitchison, *Collection of Treaties*, and E. Hertslet, *Treaties*, no attempt has been made to include such documents here.

Of the eighty-three selections, thirty-five are published here for the first time, and one of them was written especially for this book. They cover two centuries, the first having been written in the 1780s and the latest in the 1960s, and they are drawn from English, Russian, Persian, French, German, Italian, Hebrew, Arabic, Armenian, and Dutch. Three of the Persian texts were translated by Miss Malihe Sattarzadeh, the Armenian text by Mr. Krikor Maksudian, the Hebrew by Mr. Eugene Rothman, and the Dutch by Mr. Warren Weinstein, all of Columbia University. All the other passages were translated by me. Each chapter of the book is preceded by an essay, and most selections by an introductory note, with bibliographical references. The selections and introductions have been arranged to provide a more or less consecutive narrative and bring out the salient features of the branch of the economy studied in the chapter. A few explanatory words or sentences and cross-references, inserted in the text or footnotes, are enclosed in square brackets. Otherwise, except for some omissions—which are indicated—no attempt has been made to edit the texts.

I have used the pound sterling as the basic unit of account, partly because most of the source material is British but mainly because the pound was by far the most important currency in international trade and finance. For purposes of conversion, during most of the period under review the pound was equal to about five dollars, ten gold rubles, twenty marks, or twenty-five francs. The rates of exchange of the Persian kran are given in chapter 8, selection 1, and those of other currencies where they are mentioned in the text.

No book on the Middle East can avoid a mention in the preface of transliteration—indeed, the fourteenth century historian and sociologist, Ibn Khaldun, found it necessary to devote a couple of pages to this subject in his preface. I have made no attempt to change the fanciful spelling of Arabic, Persian, Turkish, or Russian words and names used by some of the authors. In the translated passages and introductions I have used a reasonably consistent system, omitting diacritical marks and paying due respect to usage; in these passages Persian, Arabic, and Turkish words have been italicized, except terms for weights and measures and currencies.

I should like to thank the following for permission to reproduce various texts: Controller of H.M. Stationery Office, for the dispatches taken from the Public Record Office and India Office. Ministère des Affaires Etrangères, for the dispatches taken from their archives. Professors A. K. S. Lambton and Nikki R. Keddie for the two articles in chapter 2. The Dvir Company for the extract from Hanina Mizrahi's book, also in chapter 2. Thomas Y. Crowell Company for the extract from Paul English's article, also in chapter 2. Dr. Ziya al-Din Sadrzadeh, for the extract from his book in chapter 3. The Royal Geographical Society, for the extract from the paper by Lord Curzon in chapter 4. The Royal Society for

India, Pakistan and Ceylon, for the article by Frechtling, in chapter 4. Wolters-Noordhoff Publishing, for the extract from the book by Brünner, also in chapter 4. The editor of *Orient*, for the article by Goblot, in chapter 5. The Royal Central Asian Society, for the extract from *The Melville Papers* in chapter 6. Dr. Mustafa Fateh, for the extract from his book, in chapter 7. The Institute of Bankers, for the article by Rabino, in chapter 8. Professor Shamseddin Jazayeri, for the extract from his book, also in chapter 8.

In preparing this book, I have received help from more persons than I can mention, but I cannot omit thanking Professor Lambton, Dr. R. W. Ferrier, and Professor Kazemzadeh, for indicating to me several interesting sources, my father-in-law, who clarified for me some of the more baffling German and Russian passages, and my colleague Ehsan Yarshater, for similar help with Persian, and, above all, my wife, without whom I certainly could not have completed the book. I should also like to thank the courteous and efficient librarians at the Public Record Office, India Office, London University, School of Oriental and African Studies, and Columbia University, and Mrs. C. Wheeler, who typed part of the manuscript.

Last, I wish to express my gratitude to the John Simon Guggenheim Memorial Foundation, which granted me a fellowship in 1968–69, to the American Philosophical Society, which granted me one in 1967, and to the School of International Affairs at Columbia University, whose financial assistance made it possible for me to carry out much of the work that went into this book.

# *Abbreviations*

| | |
|---|---|
| FO | United Kingdom, Public Record Office, Foreign Office Series |
| IO | United Kingdom, India Office Records |
| A and P | United Kingdom, Parliament, *Accounts and Papers* |
| AE | France, Ministère des Affaires Etrangères, Correspondance Commerciale |
| DSP | United States, Department of State, *Papers Relating to the Foreign Relations of the United States.* |
| CHI | *Cambridge History of Iran* |
| EHME | Charles Issawi, *Economic History of the Middle East* |
| EI | *Encyclopedia of Islam* |
| EI (2) | *Encyclopedia of Islam* (New Edition) |

For works listed in the bibliography, only the author's name and the page are indicated in reference footnotes; where, however, more than one work by the same author is listed, a shortened title is added in the reference.

# Geographical and Historical Background

## GEOGRAPHICAL

The geography of a country molds its history and society, and in Iran the influence of the geographical factors has been strong.[1] There is, first of all, the huge size of the land; even within its present reduced frontiers Iran covers 1,645,000 square kilometers (628,000 square miles), an area larger than that of Italy, France, Switzerland, Western Germany, the Netherlands, Belgium, Luxembourg, Denmark, Great Britain, and Ireland combined. Second, there is its mountainous nature; by far the greater part of Iran lies at an altitude of over 3,000 feet, and mountain chains with many peaks of 10,000–14,000 feet—and some higher—close in the central part of the country from the surrounding lands and seas. There is the aridity of its climate; most of Iran receives less than 10 inches of rain a year, and its center consists of a huge desert where precipitation is below 5 inches and most forms of life are excluded. Last, there is Iran's location, situated as it is near the heart of the Eurasian land mass, between the Fertile Crescent and Central Asia and between India and the Black Sea and Caspian regions.

The imprint of these forces on Iran's economic, social, and political structure has been clear. The huge size of the territory and its ruggedness have prevented the emergence of a high degree of centralization and the political and economic fabric of Iran has generally been more loosely knit than that of, say, Egypt, Iraq, or even Turkey. The absence of large, smooth-flowing rivers has also worked in this direction. On the one hand, Iran has lacked the splendid means of internal communications provided by the Nile, Tigris-Euphrates, Indus, and Ganges. And on the other, the scarcity of large-scale irrigation has greatly reduced the force of one of the main factors making for centralization in the neighboring lands and producing what Wittfogel calls "hydraulic societies" with strong governments, large standing armies, and vast and complex bureaucracies. Save for brief periods, as

---

[1] For an excellent survey of Iran's geography, see CHI, vol. 1, and the sources cited therein.

under Shahpur I and Abbas I and their immediate successors, Iran has always been more "feudal" and "tribal," and less "bureaucratic," than other Middle Eastern countries.[2] And it has no monuments to the exploitation of subjects by rulers comparable with the Great Pyramids or the temples of Baalbeck.[3]

Yet at the same time the aridity of the climate makes agriculture impossible over most of the country, except under irrigation. The paucity of large rivers has deprived Iran of the inexpensive and reliable method of flood irrigation practiced in the Nile valley, and—except in Khuzistan—even of the more elaborate and fragile system of perennial irrigation by canals and weirs traditionally used in Mesopotamia. Instead Iran has had to rely mainly on small-scale, costly, underground tunnels (*qanat*), carrying water from the foothills to more level areas and irrigating little patches of land (see chap. 5, sel. 1); these *qanat* require constant upkeep and can easily be destroyed, as has repeatedly happened in the country's long history.

Aridity has also created a huge breeding ground for nomadism, since there are vast areas where livestock raising constitutes the most economical—or even the only possible—use of the soil. Nomadic tribes have always played an important part in Iran's history, both enriching its economic and social life and posing serious problems for its government. The mountain chains have played a similar role, by providing summer pasture for tribes that practice "vertical" rather than "horizontal" seasonal migration. And, as elsewhere, the mountains have served as a refuge for various minority groups, which helps to explain Iran's high degree of ethnic, linguistic, and religious diversity.

The combination of mountains and lowlands, and the fact that the center of Iran is, so to speak, a "hollow," uninhabitable desert, has led to a heavy concentration of population on the country's rims. This has meant that the capital city was always necessarily peripheral, which partly accounts for the frequent shifts in the center of government. Thus, during the last six hundred years, not only in Western Europe (Paris, London, Edinburgh, Vienna, Copenhagen, Lisbon) but also in the Middle East (Constantinople, Cairo, Baghdad, Damascus, Delhi), the political center has remained in the same city. But during this period the whole or the greater part of Iran has been ruled from no less than nine cities: Tabriz, Sultanieh, Ardabil, Herat, Qazvin, Isfahan, Shiraz, Mashad, and Tehran. Tehran, which is now more than six times as large as the next biggest cities, Isfahan and Tabriz, did not outstrip these two places in population until the past hundred years. And it was these hundred years that saw the birth of political centralization.

---

[2] For the Achaemenid period see Olmstead, pp. 239–48, 291–301, and Frye, *Persia*, pp. 127–42; for the Parthian period see Frye, 218–24, and Ghirshman, pp. 263–66; for the Sasanian period see Frye, *Persia*, 244–46, 263–65, Ghirshman, 309–13, and Christensen, 97–140, 206–8, 367–69; for the Safavid period see Minorsky, *Tadhkirat*, introduction. The relevant sections in Pigulevskaya et al. contain much useful information on this subject for the whole period down to the end of the eighteenth century, and an interesting discussion is to be found in Coulburn, chaps. 5 and 8.

[3] The only exception is the palace of Ctesiphon, in Babylonia—a province long inured to the discipline imposed by irrigation and strong government.

Last, the size, structure, and location of Iran help to account for its relatively great isolation from the mainstream of history during the past two or three hundred years. Thanks to its huge area and great range of altitude, it enjoys a wide variety of soils and climates—from the drenched jungles of the Caspian coast to the dusty, windswept central plateau, and from the Alpine peaks of Azerbaijan to the torrid shores of the Persian Gulf. And thanks to its great geological diversity—ranging from the sedimentary Khuzistan plains and central plateau to the more recent folded mountain chains—Iran also contains a large variety of minerals, including oil, coal, iron, copper, sulfur, and salts of many kinds. This, and the relatively high development of its handicrafts, meant that the country was essentially self-sufficient not only in the basic necessities of life but also in a wide variety of crops and products. Its impulse to look out into the world and engage in large-scale commerce was to that extent weakened.

During most of Iran's history, this was offset by a very powerful factor: its location on the great overland trade route joining the Near East to Central Asia—the famous "silk road" to China. Starting in the Mesopotamian lowlands, near Baghdad, "the road headed for the Iranian plateau through modern Kirmanshah, Hamadan, Tehran, and then north-east to Merv, Bukhara, Samarkand and on to China, or turning south to Seistan, east to Qandahar and over the mountains to the plains of the Indus river." [4] However, the shift of world trade to the sea routes since the sixteenth century has deprived this ancient road of most of its importance. And in an era of sea trade, Iran was under severe handicaps. Not only is its coastline short and inhospitable, but it is cut off from the heart of the country by high and rugged mountain barriers. It is not fortuitous that Iran did not have any large seaport on the Persian Gulf until the development of the oil fields began in this century. And the remoteness of Iran from Europe by sea, until the opening of the Suez Canal, its inward location, and its isolation left it outside the influence of the currents of trade and ideas that were flowing over the other parts of the Middle East.

## HISTORICAL

One of the clearest leitmotivs of Iranian history, the repeated submergence of the country by foreign invaders and its constant reemergence, invigorated, resilient, and with renewed vitality, has been described, in words too eloquent for translation, by a distinguished French journalist:

Quand on a dompté le conquérant grec, triomphé de la puissance romaine, assimilé son vainqueur arabe, survécu au Mongol, contenu l'empire ottoman et, cas presque unique dans les annales contemporaines, desséré l'étreinte de l'Armée rouge sur une province pratiquement perdue, que peut-on craindre de l'avenir? Le meilleur argument en faveur de l'existence de ce pays, c'est qu'il ait pu exister jusqu'à ce jour. [5]

---

[4] Frye, *Persia*, pp. 27–28.
[5] Edouard Sablier, preface to Inge Morath, *De la Perse à l'Iran* (Zurich, 1958).

An excellent example of Nietzsche's saying, "That which does not destroy me strengthens me," Iran not only survived such onslaughts but was enriched by them. The Greeks brought with them seeds of art and science which came to bloom under the Parthians and Sasanians. The Arabs gave Iran a noble religion and a rich and flexible language on which Persian was to draw as freely as English did on French and Latin, and with equally beneficial results. The Mongols cleared a channel through which Chinese influences poured in to vivify the arts and crafts.

Another less inspiring theme has been the dynastic cycle which often, though by no means always, ended with a foreign invasion. Again and again the vigor shown by the founding monarchs and some of their immediate successors—a Cyrus and a Darius, an Arsaces and a Mithridates, an Ardashir and a Shahpur, a Tughril Beg and a Malik Shah, an Ismail and an Abbas, a Nadir Shah and a Karim Khan—flickered and died down among their more distant descendants. One cannot help surmising that the absence of a firm principle of legitimate succession, and the consequent killing, mutilation, or confinement of sons, brothers, and other possible aspirants to the throne which mars so much of Iranian history, must have greatly weakened the royal houses after the first two or three generations. Only the Sasanians, whose reign of over four centuries is almost unmatched in Persian annals, produced a long line of able and energetic kings.

Still another theme, again connected with the two preceding ones, is the interaction between nomads and farmers. In Iran, as in other parts of the Middle East, only strong governments could stave off the constant danger posed by cohesive, predatory, and well-armed mounted tribesmen. Again and again the Sown has been invaded by the Desert, from the south by the Arabs and from the north by the Scythians, Ephthalites, Khazars, Turks, Mongols, Tatars, Uzbeks, and Afghans. In addition Iran has another reservoir of tribesmen in its highlands—Kurds and Lurs and Turkomans and others—who until very recently defied the strongest governments in their mountain fastnesses and could usually raid at will and with impunity.

The nomadic invasions provide a further, and deeper, explanation of the dynastic cycles. Several of Iran's royal houses, including the Saljuqid, Il-Khan, Timurid, Safavi, Zand, and Qajar, were carried to the throne by tribal power. Then followed the pattern which has been analyzed, in the Arab context, with consummate skill and penetration by the fourteenth-century historian and sociologist Ibn Khaldun.[6] In its early days, the new dynasty relies on the kinship solidarity of the dominant tribe, which provides the armed force required for internal coercion and external defense. But several parallel forces sap the basis of this order. Sedentary life, civilization, and luxury undermine the solidarity and martial

---

[6] For Ibn Khaldun's views on this subject see Charles Issawi, *An Arab Philosophy of History* (London, 1950), pp. 10–13, 98–130; the complete text of Ibn Khaldun's *Introduction to History* was translated and annotated by Franz Rosenthal, *Ibn Khaldun : The Muqaddimah*, 3 vols. (New York, 1958).

qualities of the dominant tribe. At the same time, the monarchy seeks to reduce its dependence on its tribal kinsmen by building up a civilian bureaucracy and a standing army, recruited from slaves, retainers, or other subjects. Last, the granting of estates, or of taxing power, to tribal or other notables, in lieu of salary payments, substantially reduces the source from which the crown draws its revenues, and leads to increasing financial stringency. The tensions and dissatisfactions thus created usually weaken the state sufficiently; to open a breach for a new invasion or rebellion by other tribes.

The cycles which mark Iran's political history have naturally had a profound effect on its economic life, with periods of prosperity succeeded by decline or breakdown as governments weakened or became more oppressive. But in one respect there was cumulative growth, since the institutions, techniques, products, and cultural advances introduced in one period were seldom abandoned in the next. Thus under the Achaemenids (559–330 B.C.) Iran developed closer ties with Babylon, an ancient commercial center, and acquired from its Near Eastern provinces the use of coinage and banking, royal routes and posts, and standard weights and measures. The currents of trade flowed through it much more strongly than ever before, necessitating the building of new ports. Agriculture also made some progress: *qanat*, subterranean canals carrying water from springs or mountain slopes to the surrounding plain, had been used in Iran from much earlier, but many new ones were built under the Achaemenids, as were small dams and other kinds of irrigation works. Lucerne was introduced as a fodder crop, and the cotton plant was brought in from India, probably in the eighth century B.C.[7]

Alexander and his Seleucid successors founded many cities, with a nucleus of Greek soldiers which was soon surrounded by Iranian and other layers. Two main patterns are discernible: a string of towns along the great road from Seleucia on the Tigris to Bactria, which was important both strategically and because of the nascent silk trade with China; and a cluster on the shores of the Persian Gulf, presumably for purposes of trade. These towns, and others, were linked by new or restored roads. The vigor and skills brought in by the Greeks and other colonists, the diffusion of Greek and Aramaic which opened new horizons to Iranians, the roads, canals, and other public works, the further standardization of currency, weights, and measures, and possibly also the rise in prices caused by the dishoarding of the huge Persian treasures following their seizure by Alexander, seem to have had a stimulating effect on the economy. Agricultural techniques were markedly improved and several plants and farm animals seem to have passed during this period from Iran to the Mediterranean area, while others, such as the apricot and peach, may have come to Iran from China at this time. The handi-

[7] See Olmstead, pp. 83–85, 185–94, 240, 292, 299–301; Ghirshman, pp. 25, 93, 181–88; and Wulff, pp. 61, 178, 246–50. "The German archeologist Bergner in 1936 discovered three gravity dams in Iran near Persepolis, which date from the Achaemenid period, 558 to 331 B.C. The best preserved is 25 m. long and 25 m. high (about 80 ft.)" Raymond Furon, *The Problem of Water* (London, 1967), p. 59.

crafts, particularly textiles and carpets, also developed. The volume of trade seems to have expanded considerably, and its content became much more diversified, including manufactured goods, such as textiles, pottery, and glassware, raw materials—for example, wood and metals—and goods in transit, notably drugs from India and silk from China. There is also some evidence of wider use of money, a trend no doubt facilitated by the greater uniformity of coinage and by the increased availability of gold from Siberia and silver from Asia Minor.[8] The collapse of the Seleucid monarchy, and the international and civil wars that ravaged the Mediterranean world, adversely affected the Iranian economy. But the consolidation of Parthian rule (247? B.C.–A.D. 227?) shortly before the beginning of the Christian era, coinciding with the establishment of the Empire in Rome and the apogee of the Han dynasty in China, whose dominion extended to Central Asia, ushered in a new advance. Trade between the Far East and the Mediterranean increased considerably, and the Parthians, who derived much revenue from taxes on goods in transit, stimulated it by improving roads and providing wells and caravanserais. The introduction of the horseshoe at this period also facilitated communications. Greater international contacts led to the development of the handicrafts—thus metal work was improved under Chinese influence and glassware under Syrian. New crops were also brought in from the East, including sugarcane and rice.[9]

The first half of the Sasanian period (A.D. 222?–651) was very prosperous, but the dynasty ended in political breakdown and economic retrogression. The communist revolution of the Mazdakites, at the beginning of the sixth century, was both a symptom and a further cause of social disintegration. Nevertheless many advances made during this period proved enduring. Thus numerous towns founded by the first Sasanians survived and grew. The prisoners captured during the increasing wars with Rome were settled in Fars, Khuzistan, and other provinces; they brought with them precious skills, and the bridge and dam they built on the Karun, near Shushtar, still stand; other dams were built on the Karkheh and Dez rivers. The breeding of silkworms may have been introduced at this time, and silk and brocade weaving made much progress, in part thanks to the Roman prisoners, and other handicrafts also flourished; there is some evidence that the handicraftsmen were organized in guilds.[10] Irrigation works were carried out in Mesopotamia[11] and elsewhere, the water wheel—which had been introduced earlier from Greece—passed into general use, and the windmill seems to

---

[8] See Ghirshman, pp. 219–40; Frye, *Persia*, pp. 161–70; Wulff, pp. 172–78, 244; and Rostovtzeff, pp. 447–62, 1258.

[9] See Frye, *Persia*, p. 224; Ghirshman, pp. 283–86.

[10] Pigulevskaya, pp. 71–73.

[11] Adams, *Land behind Baghdad*, p. 115, has compiled population estimates for Lower Diyala starting around 2000 B.C. The figure given for A.D. 500, slightly under 700,000, was surpassed only in the early Abbasid period, and again in the 1950s. See also idem, "Agricultural and Urban Life," where it is estimated that the population of Khuzistan reached its peak in Sasanian times.

have been invented in Sistan, at the end of the Sasanian period or the beginning of the Muslim.[12]

Commerce and finance developed. The overland trade with China continued, but Persian merchants also used the sea route, competed with the Romans in the Indian Ocean, and may have reached China in their own ships. Both internal and foreign trade were facilitated by the standardization of silver and copper coinage and the development of bills, checks, and letters of credit issued by banking houses. Commercial, religious and other contacts with neighboring civilizations led to the introduction of a large body of Greek and Indian science and medicine, the translation of numerous foreign works and the founding of medical schools. Last, in the aftermath of the Mazdakite upheaval, and probably influenced by the system used in Byzantium, land taxation was reformed by Chosroes I (A.D. 531–79). Following a land survey and agricultural census, the previously prevailing practice of taking part of the crop was replaced by a fixed sum per unit area, which was determined according to the type of crop grown. Poll taxes were also reorganized. This system of taxation, and the bureaucracy that was set up at the same time, continued to form the basis of government in Iran for many centuries.[13]

The Arab conquest and some of the subsequent conquests of Iran, such as the Saljuq, had a disruptive effect on certain provinces, but on the whole the country flourished economically and culturally during the first six centuries of the Muslim era.[14] Iran contributed more than its share to the development of Islamic culture and institutions, but it also profited greatly from inclusion in a vast, vigorous, and prosperous civilization which was making notable advances in such fields as irrigation and hydraulics; cultivation of high-value crops like cotton, linen, silk, rice, sugarcane, and citrus and other fruits; sugar refining; steel production; ceramics and glassware; distillation; the making of soap, nitric acid, sulfuric acid, and other chemical products; and many branches of the textile industry.[15] Above all, Iran was one of the first producers of paper in the Muslim world.[16]

But it was not only through the transmission of ideas and techniques that Iran benefited. In the words of the leading authority, the Muslim Mediterranean area was, in these centuries, "a free-trade community." Persian silk and other fabrics enjoyed a high reputation and were exported as far west as North Africa, and "many persons in Egypt and Tunisia bore Persian names, as attested by the Geniza."[17] Financial transactions between the eastern and western halves of the Muslim world were also frequent, and often covered huge sums.[18] This was

---

[12] Wulff, pp. 280–88; see also Singer, 2:594, 608, 614–17.

[13] See Frye, *Persia*, pp. 240–42, 257–60; Ghirshman, pp. 292–93, 301–4, 312, 336, 341–46; Christensen, pp. 126–28, 366–67; Hadi Hasan, pp. 64–79; Hourani, pp. 46–50; and Manandian, pp. 76–115.

[14] For this period see Le Strange; Schwarz; Minorsky, *Ḥudūd*; Pigulevskaya, pp. 93–96, 104–7, 130–40, 154–56; Adams, *Land behind Baghdad*; and CHI, vol. 5.

[15] Singer, 2:57, 191, 199, 285, 327, 356–57, 372, 738; Wulff, pp. 50, 142–48, 172.

[16] See Carter and Goodrich.

[17] Goitein, pp. 50, 60–61, 81, 103, 164, 400.

[18] Ibid., pp. 229–66; Mez, chap. 26.

facilitated by the extension to Iran, at the end of the ninth century, of the gold standard used in other parts of the Middle East and North Africa.

Trade in the Indian Ocean area was far greater than in the Mediterranean, and here too Iran played a leading part. As early as Sasanian times Persian trade with East Africa was considerable. The first mention of Persians in Chinese sources dates from A.D. 671, and by 758 Muslim navigation had increased so much that "Ta-shi (Arabs) and Po-sse (Persians) together reached and burned the city of Kwang chou (Canton) and went back by sea." Conversely, in the 878 revolt, the number of Muslims, Jews, Christians, and Parsees massacred was put by an Arabic source at the improbably high figure of 120,000. Thereafter, and partly because of the troubles afflicting both the Abbasid and the Tang dynasties, two important shifts seem to have occurred in the China trade: first, Muslim ships generally sailed no farther than Malaya, where they exchanged goods with Chinese junks; and second, the Gulf Arabs seem to have taken an increasing share of the Indian Ocean trade, at the expense of the Persians. In the meantime, the migration of Zoroastrians to India may have forged new commercial links between Iran and the subcontinent.[19]

The development of agriculture, the growth of the handicrafts, and the expansion of trade greatly stimulated urbanization. Several important towns, including Shiraz, Kashan, Qum, and Maragheh, are known or believed to have been founded during this period, and many more increased severalfold in size and wealth. Among them were Kermanshah, Savah, Ray, Simnan, Damghan, Hamadan, Nishapur, Tus (Mashad), Sarakhs, and Marv, on the great road connecting Baghdad with Central Asia; Tabriz, Ardabil, and Zanjan in Azerbaijan; Amul, Gurgan, and Astarabad in the Caspian region, which was already becoming famous for its silk; Ahwaz and Shushtar in Khuzistan, the leading producer of sugar; Siraf on the Persian Gulf; and Qazvin, Isfahan, Yazd, Kirman, Zarang, and Herat in the central and eastern parts of the country.[20] And it was in these towns—as well as in Baghdad and Cairo—that Muslim science and philosophy produced its finest work, at the hands of such men as Ibn Sina, al-Biruni, Omar Khayyam, and al-Ghazzali.

The countryside was, naturally, much less affected by these developments. Here the most important change was the emergence, by the tenth century, of the *iqta*. In the previous century permanent tax revenues had already become insufficient to pay the troops and, to an increasing extent, land taxes were assigned "not to the tax-farmers, but to the military themselves."[21] Gradually, the right to collect land taxes was transformed into "rights over the land itself," with accompanying

---

[19] See Richards; Toussaint, chap. 4; Hadi Hasan, pp. 76–106; and Hourani, pp. 62–83; the quotation is from the *History of the Tang*.

[20] For a description of these towns, their main products, and the roads linking them, based on the medieval geographers, see LeStrange and Schwarz.

[21] Lambton, in CHI, 5:231; see also idem "The Evolution of the *Iqta*"; Cahen, "L'évolution de l'iqta"; and Lokkegaard.

powers of local administration. In principle, *iqtas* were granted for life, and were conditional on performance of military service or administrative duties, but they soon became hereditary and their holders became largely independent of the central government. The system was further transformed during the Mongol and Safavid period, but, under such names as *soyurghal* and *tuyul*, assignment of land taxes and rights over land continued to be the dominant form of land tenure in Iran until the nineteenth century.[22]

This prosperity was abruptly ended by the Mongol invasions of 1220–58—for Iran, as for so many other parts of the Middle East, perhaps the greatest calamity suffered in the course of a very long history. The horror of contemporaries can still be felt in the deeply moving account by Ibn al-Athir.[23] Even discounting heavily the figures given in the Persian and Arabic sources, it seems certain that several millions were massacred or died of famine or epidemics, and many towns were either obliterated (e.g., Ray) or remained in ruins for decades or even centuries, for instance Marv, Herat, and Nishapur.[24] In addition to the direct devastation of war, other forces caused great economic dislocation, notably the large increase in the nomadic population following the migration of Mongol and Turkish tribes, which disrupted agriculture, and the fiscal policy of the Il-Khans, which reduced the peasants to destitution. Perhaps the best single index of the decline in the economy is that—even after the recovery initiated by Ghazan's fiscal and other reforms—total tax receipts in the first half of the fourteenth century were only a fifth of what they had been under the Saljuqs.[25]

The fourteenth and fifteenth centuries were a confused and troubled period. The petty dynasties that ruled over different parts of Iran were often at war, and the invasions of Timur Lenk inflicted great damage on such large cities as Isfahan and Zarang, and also on smaller places such as Sus.[26] But some economic recovery seems to have taken place. In particular the output of silk—which in the thirteenth century had already attracted Genoese merchants from the Crimea, across the Caspian, to Gilan[27]—seems to have increased. Persian navigation in the Indian Ocean was also active, from Malabar and Ceylon to Malacca and Sumatra, and important Persian colonies are mentioned in Bengal and other countries.[28]

The irruption of the Portuguese into the Persian Gulf in 1506 was fatal to Muslim shipping. Albuquerque forbade "any native vessel to trade in the Gulf without a pass,"[29] and a few years later he told the ambassador of Shah Ismail, "Should any merchant from Persia be found in another district of India save the port of Goa, they should lose their merchandise and be made subject to the

[22] See chap. 5, sel. 2.
[23] Translated in Browne, 2:427–31.
[24] For a detailed account of economic and social conditions in 1220–1340, see P. Petrushevsky in CHI, vol. 5.
[25] Ibid., pp. 497–500.
[26] LeStrange, p. 335; Adams, "Agricultural and Urban Life."
[27] See Marco Polo, *Travels*, book 1, chap. 4.
[28] Hadi Hasan, pp. 141–46, quoting Barros and other sources.
[29] Wilson, *Persian Gulf*, p. 116.

greatest penalties we could inflict."[30] As a result, Barros could say without much exaggeration: "This busy trade [to Malacca] lasted until our arrival in India, but the Moorish, Arabian, Persian and Gujarati ships, fearing our fleets, dared not in general now undertake the voyage and if any of their ships did so it was only by stealth, and escaping our ships."[31]

It is true that the Portuguese attempt to monopolize the spice trade broke down partly because of insufficient naval power, but it was also because their officials were corrupt and entered into various open and illicit agreements with local merchants and shippers in the gulf.[32] And during the first half of the seventeenth century the Portuguese were expelled from the gulf. But the beneficiaries were not the Persians but, on the one hand, the British and Dutch, and on the other, the Arabs of Muscat and the Trucial Coast. Nadir Shah's attempt to restore Persian seapower was unsuccessful,[33] and parts of the Persian coast and islands were occupied by Arabs until the nineteenth century and the Persian government was completely powerless to deal with piracy in the gulf.

However, these changes in navigation had relatively little impact on Iran's economy, which continued as in the past to rest on bases far removed from the open seas. Here, the main event was the unification of the country under the Safavis. Although the frequent wars with the Uzbeks and Ottomans caused much devastation in the border areas, particularly Tabriz, the economy seems to have made significant progress. Thanks to a long period of peace and the enlightened rule of Shah Abbas—and also to his policy of favoring the central provinces of the country at the expense of such outlying parts as Armenia, Shirvan, and Luristan —the seventeenth century was a period of great prosperity; however, in the opinion of the leading authority, on the whole it failed to regain the level attained in the pre-Mongol period.[34]

Hardly any technical progress was made at this time. New methods of glassmaking were introduced from Italy, and Shah Abbas invited three hundred Chinese potters to instruct the Persians, which seems to have led to a distinct improvement.[35] But the English and Swiss clockmakers employed by the shah came to a sad end,[36] and Chardin stated that there was not "one single native that knows well how to mend a watch," described the failure of his own scheme to set up printing presses, noted the lack of paper mills, and judged the Persian craftsmen to be "soft and lazy" and "not desirous of new inventions and discoveries."[37] But some branches, notably carpets and other textiles, reached a very high level

[30] Hadi Hasan, p. 147.
[31] Ibid., p. 146.
[32] Toussaint, p. 114.
[33] Lockhart, *Nadir Shah* pp. 93–94, 182–84, 212–22; idem, *Fall*, pp. 66–69; see also Moyse-Bartlett, and Lorimer.
[34] Petrushevsky in Pigulevskaya, pp. 276, 285. Other indispensable sources on this period are Minorsky, *Tadhkirat*, and the works of the European travelers, especially Chardin, du Mans, Tavernier, Herbert, Kaempfer, Olearius, and Mandelslo, listed in the bibliography.
[35] Wulff, p. 149.
[36] Olearius, pp. 280, 299; his journey was made in 1636–38.
[37] Chardin, 2:97–99; his account refers to the 1660s.

of craftsmanship. Chardin and other observers describe the guild system prevailing (see 6:5); he also mentions the thirty-two royal workshops, employing some five hundred persons each and with an annual expenditure of 5,000,000 [écus?].[38] In transport, "they have neither carriages, nor carts, nor litters, nor sedan-chairs."[39] But, along with other travelers, Chardin was much impressed by the security of the roads and the presence of numerous caravanserais. Attention was also paid to upkeep, and in Mazandaran a 270-kilometer road, paved with stone, was laid down by Shah Abbas.[40]

As for agriculture, although some of the more ambitious schemes such as the diversion of the Karun River into the Zayanderud, to water the Isfahan plain, were abandoned, both the developed irrigation system—based on wells and *qanats* (see 5:1)—and the variety of crops—including silk, cotton, opium, tobacco, and a wide range of fruit trees—were favorably noted by European travelers.[41] As regards land tenure, the cultivated area continued to be mainly owned by the crown or the holders of *tuyuls* and *soyurghals* and worked by peasants, who in the vicinity of cities paid cash rents and in other parts surrendered varying shares of the crop.[42] Chardin's opinion was that the peasants "are quite well off, and I can assert that there are, in the most fertile countries of Europe, people who are incomparably more wretched."[43]

But perhaps the most striking feature of the seventeenth-century Iranian economy was the development of trade, particularly with Europe. In the words of Olearius: "There is not any nation in all Asia, nor indeed almost of Europe, who sends not its Merchants to Isfahan, whereof some sell by Whole-sale, and others by Retail"; he mentions over 12,000 Indians and "Tartars, Turks, Jews, Armenians, Georgians, English, Dutch, French, Italians and Spaniards."[44] Iran's trade with Europeans was described as follows by Mandelslo:[45]

The Hollanders and the English bring thither ready money, and some certain commodities which they either take up in Europe, or goe to the Indies for, and sell them there to very good profit. The Dutch are the better settled there of the two, and do furnish in a manner all Persia with Pepper, Nutmegs, Cloves and other Spicery, though they also expend very much ready money in their trading as we said before, and especially Spanish Ryals, and Rixdollars, which the Persians prefer before all other mony, because they melt them, and make into their own coins with great advantage.

The English do either sell or truck their English cloaths, Tinne, Steel, Indico, silk stuffs and Cottons out of the Indies; for though there are excellent good ones made in Persia, yet are those of the Indies more esteemed, because they are finer and closer woven.

[38] Ibid., 2:18.
[39] Ibid., 3:55.
[40] Pigulevskaya, p. 277.
[41] Ibid., pp. 283–85; Olearius, pp. 305–24; LeBrun, 1:226–31, mentions the abundance of food crops, poultry, and game and quotes the price of several goods, which struck him as being very low.
[42] Minorsky, *Tadhkirat*, pp. 21–23; for fuller details see Lambton, *Landlord*, pp. 105–28.
[43] Chardin, 3:343–44.
[44] Olearius, p. 299.
[45] Mandelslo, pp. 11–12.

They buy of the Persians Satins purfled with gold or silver, silk-stuffes and the Cottons of the Country, Persian Tapistry, which those of the Country call Kalichey, and the Portuguese Alcatifer, raw silk, Cotton, Rhubarb, Saffron, and Rose-water.

Muslim Persian merchants handled Iran's internal trade, but religious inhibitions and other factors made them reluctant to travel to Europe. Hence the most important single segment of Iran's foreign trade, exports of silk, and some of its imports, came to be monopolized by the Armenians, who had been deported by Shah Abbas to Julfa, near Isfahan, in 1604 (see 2:8). Armenians settled in the Ottoman Empire and various parts of Europe and had agents as far afield as Sweden and China.[46]

The silk crop was estimated by Olearius at 4,300,000 pounds, which, at a price "not above 2s. 6d. or 2s. 8d. the pound," would give a total domestic value of some £550,000. But in 1620 the East India Company had estimated Persian exports of silk to Europe alone at 1,350,000 pounds, and the cost price at the gulf port of Jask at 8 shillings a pound, which would imply that exports to Europe alone fetched £540,000. In 1670, Chardin put the crop at 6,072,000 pounds; at that time, the Dutch Company was paying 4 to 5 florins a pound, which would imply a total value of £2,000,000 to £2,500,000.[47] Since the bulk of the Persian silk crop was sent abroad, and since Iran also exported many other articles in significant quantities, Iran's total exports were perhaps between £1,000,000 and £2,000,000, a figure that may be compared with £5,000,000 for England and Wales in 1688 and £4,800,000 for France in 1715.[48]

The route used for the export of silk to Europe shifted with the vagaries of international politics, particularly Ottoman-Persian relations. Generally speaking, the overland route to the Mediterranean was preferred to the Persian Gulf, except during hostilities with Turkey. Tabriz became the main starting point in Iran, and first Bursa and then Smyrna and Aleppo were the main western terminals. In addition to international rivalries, there was also competition between the various companies, the Levant Companies favoring the Mediterranean route and the East Indian the gulf. Efforts by the British Muscovy Company to open a route through Russia in 1561–81, and again in the eighteenth century, failed, as did the British attempt to trade with northern Iran through Trebizond in 1609, which was stopped by the Ottoman government.[49] Silk was also sent to Russia, overland or across the Caspian.[50]

The splendid Safavid structure began to show signs of strain in the latter half of the seventeenth century, and in the 1720s it collapsed.[51] In the next few years

[46] Chardin, 3:121–23; see also Olearius, p. 324.
[47] Chardin, 3:123; EI(2), s.v. Harir; Glamann, pp. 115–21; this book contains valuable information on Iran's foreign trade.
[48] Deane and Cole, pp. 2, 28; Sée, p. 124.
[49] EI(2), s.v. Harir; Curzon, Persia, 2:532–54; Glamann, pp. 114–27, 281–85; Masson, pp. 371–75; Wood, pp. 48, 75–76; Foster; Inalcik, "Ottoman Economic Mind," in Cook.
[50] See articles by Kukanova.
[51] For the causes, see Minorsky, Tadhkirat, pp. 23–24, and Lockhart, Fall, pp. 16–34; the best eyewitness account is that of Father Krusinski.

Iran was invaded by the Afghans, Russians, and Turks. Isfahan, Shiraz, Qazvin, Yazd, and Tabriz—as well as many smaller places—were sacked, and it is estimated that these cities lost over two-thirds of their inhabitants.[52] The population of Isfahan, which had been put at 600,000 or "as populous as London" by Chardin, was reduced to a few tens of thousands and that of Tabriz, estimated by him at the improbably high figure of 550,000, to some 30,000.

In the 1730s, the foreign armies were expelled by Nadir Shah, whose conquests culminated in the capture of Delhi, with a booty of 700 to 800 million rupees (£70 to 80 million).[53] But these campaigns imposed a further strain on the already exhausted country. Hanway quoted a Persian merchant as saying that Qazvin "had then twelve thousand houses inhabited, and now it has only eleven hundred . . . nor is Isfahan much better; that city had formerly a hundred thousand houses well inhabited . . . but incredible as it may seem to you, I am assured that only five thousand houses are now inhabited."[54]

One measure of the economic decline of Iran in the eighteenth century is the sharp fall in output of silk. Hanway estimated the Gilan crop at only 360,000 pounds, a figure that may be compared with one of 2,760,000 by Chardin and 1,728,000 by Olearius; a Russian observer had put Gilan's exports of silk to Turkey and beyond, before the outbreak of the troubles, at about 1,400,000 pounds, worth some 3,200,000 rubles.[55] Another measure is the drop in the trade carried on by the British and Dutch Companies in southern Persia.[56] The latter was affected not only by the reduction in the country's productive and purchasing power and the general insecurity—checked only partially under the rule of the Zand dynasty in Shiraz from 1750–94—as well as by the increase of piracy in the gulf, but also by the emergence of rival centers of silk exports, especially Bengal. Bengali silk was more profitable than Persian, partly because it was in greater demand in the Japanese market, hence Dutch and British purchases in Iran dropped sharply.[57]

The civil wars that marked the last years of the Zand dynasty inflicted further sufferings and hardships, notably on Kirman. And although the first decades of Qajar rule saw a relatively rapid recovery, the accounts of all travelers visiting Iran at the beginning of the nineteenth century agree in depicting a country suffering from depopulation, poverty, and economic exhaustion, and largely isolated from the mainstream of world politics, trade, science, and culture.

[52] Pigulevskaya, p. 318.
[53] Lockhart, *Nadir*, p. 156; see also Sykes, *Persia*, 2:261.
[54] Hanway, p. 156.
[55] Lockhart, *Fall*, p. 238. At that time the silver ruble was worth about 3 shillings and 6 pence.
[56] Ibid., pp. 388–423; Glamann, pp. 161–65, shows the sharp decline in Persian imports of sugar through the Dutch Company; as for British sales, they soon shrank to negligible amounts. See Curzon, *Persia*, 2:552, and chap. 3, sel. 4.
[57] Glamann, pp. 117–27; Boxer, p. 200.

# I

# *General Introduction: 1800–1914*

Perhaps the best way of bringing out the peculiar features and trends of the Iranian economy in the nineteenth century is to contrast its evolution with that of the rest of the Middle East. In the countries bordering the Mediterranean—Turkey, Lebanon, Palestine, Syria, and, most markedly, Egypt—the direction and pace of economic development were largely determined by a set of forces which, in Iran, were either absent or much less powerful.[1] There was, first, the need for swift communications between Europe and India. This led to the establishment of regular steamship lines in the Mediterranean and Red Sea in the 1830s, and to the building of railways across Egypt in the 1850s. By 1914 there were 10,300 kilometers of railway line in the Ottoman Empire, Egypt, and the Sudan, and work was proceeding rapidly on such important projects as the Baghdad Railway. Several modern ports had been built, notably those of Alexandria, Beirut, Constantinople, and Port Sudan, and steamers were sailing on the Nile and the Tigris.

Improved transport was required for, and in turn facilitated, greater trade. In most of the countries mentioned above trade increased thirtyfold in the period 1800–1914, and in some, such as Egypt, the growth was even greater. Imports rose because of vastly increased purchases of such European manufactured goods as textiles, metal products, and glassware and of colonial goods like sugar and tea. Exports, which more or less kept pace with imports, consisted mainly of agricultural produce.

This points to another change in the structure of the Middle Eastern economy: agricultural output rose severalfold and there was a shift from subsistence to cash crops, for example, cotton and tobacco. This was accompanied by a fundamental change in land tenure: the traditional communal or tribal forms of ownership

---

[1] For the latter see EHME and the books by Hershlag, Cook, and Polk and Chambers, listed in the bibliography.

were gradually superseded by individual ownership and vast estates were concentrated in the hands of large landlords, often city dwellers.

Agricultural expansion presupposed greater inputs of the factors of production: labor, land, capital, and enterprise. Labor was provided by the rapid growth in population stimulated by improved hygiene, the elimination of famines, and, in many regions, a rise in the level of living. Land—with adequate rainfall—was, in most countries, readily available and could easily be brought under cultivation by enterprising landlords or peasants provided two conditions were met: that the government assured security from nomad depredations and that improved transport reduced the cost of sending the crop to market. In some places however, notably Egypt, expansion of cultivation and the shift to cash crops necessitated the building of costly irrigation works.

The capital needed for modern transport, public utilities, irrigation works, and other overhead came partly from domestic sources, but largely from foreign. The Middle East attracted a huge amount of European funds, in the form of loans to governments or investments in the private sector. By 1914, Egypt's foreign debt, public and private, was around £200 million ($1,000 million) and the Ottoman Empire's was slightly higher. The financial system required by the Middle East's rapidly expanding trade was set up by Europeans, and many parts of the regions were quite adequately supplied with banks and other facilities.

The driving force, enterprise, and skill which transformed the Middle Eastern economy were mainly provided by Europeans or members of the large minority groups—Greeks, Armenians, Jews, Christian Lebanese, and Syrians. The Muslim majority played a minor part in the economic development of the region. As for the governments, their main contribution was the establishment of security, the removal, under foreign pressure, of some of the main obstacles to foreign trade, and the setting up of a political and legal framework within which European and local capitalist enterprise could operate. In Egypt and some other countries this was achieved by the middle of the century. In some parts of the region, British occupation carried this process much further than had the previous national authorities.

In all these respects Iran differed markedly from its neighbors. Throughout the period under review, the government enjoyed less authority than did those of Turkey and Egypt, and was far less able to enforce its will on recalcitrant subjects, especially tribesmen. Its military forces were far weaker, its administration less efficient, its fiscal system much more archaic, and its educational institutions far less developed. To a large extent this was due to Iran's social and political structure, which frustrated the efforts of such early modernizers and reformers as Prince Abbas Mirza and Amir-i Kabir and allowed them far less success than was achieved by Muhammad Ali in Egypt or even Mahumud II in Turkey. But an important factor was the stultifying effect of Anglo-Russian rivalry. Of course the Ottoman Empire and Egypt were subjected to great pressures from the Powers, and many schemes, notably railways, were frustrated or delayed by them. But there was a certain safety in numbers, and the multiplicity of contenders often reduced the total impact of the pressure. In Iran, on the other hand, the competition of Britain and Russia meant that each was determined to thwart any scheme proposed by the other, and was generally in a position to do so.[2] Hence the absence of railways and the smallness of the scale of the British, Russian, and other enterprises in Iran; one of the few exceptions, the British oil concession, seems to have been secured owing to Russian inadvertence, and a Russian counterthrust, in the form of a kerosine pipeline, was stopped by Britain.

Another unfavorable factor relates to social composition. Unlike its neighbors, Iran did not have large non-Muslim minorities whose contact with Europe had started centuries earlier and who had, as a consequence, acquired a substantial amount of Western education and knowledge of Western commercial methods. As was mentioned before, these minorities were responsible for a good portion of the economic advance achieved by Turkey, Egypt, Lebanon, Palestine, and Syria. Iran, too, had Armenian, Jewish, Nestorian, and Zoroastrian minorities, but their number was very small, their cultural isolation was great, and their influence was too limited for them to play a major part in the economic and social development of the country.

Iran's geographical position was also, in the nineteenth century context, distinctly unfavorable. Unlike Egypt, Syria, and Iraq, it did not lie on Britain's direct route to India, and therefore offered far less attraction to railway and canal builders. Until the opening of the Suez Canal, it lay more than 11,000 miles from Western Europe. Its productive regions were shut off from the sea by high mountain ranges. And its richest part, the northern, was still farther removed from the center of world activity. Moreover, the fact that Iran was adjacent to India meant that the British authorities inevitably thought of it as a glacis, to be kept denuded of any facilities which might make it easier for the Russians to advance through it to the subcontinent, while the Russians were most reluctant to expose their southern flank to British economic or political penetration.

The combined result of all these factors was the comparative neglect of Iran by European capital and enterprise and its far slower rate of development. Whereas Egypt alone had some 250,000 European residents in 1914, those in Iran were numbered in hundreds. Foreign capital investment was negligible until the turn of the century and even in 1914 was below £30 million ($150 million), including the national debt. Not one modern port had been built, and there were less than a dozen miles of railways. The banking system was still rudimentary. And although trade did increase considerably, its rate of growth was far smaller than that of Egypt, Lebanon, and Syria and below that of Turkey and Iraq. In 1913 Iran's total trade (imports plus exports) was estimated at $93 million, compared

---

[2] On this subject see the excellent study by Firuz Kazemzadeh, *Russia and Britain in Persia*.

with $291 million for Egypt and $273 million for Turkey; on a per capita basis the figures were about $9, $24, and $15, respectively.[3]

This relatively slow rate of development of financial and commercial links with the advanced countries had internal consequences, not all of them wholly adverse. Population grew, but at a rate which was surely far below that of Egypt, Syria, Lebanon, and Iraq, and possibly below that of Turkey. The area under cultivation expanded, but again almost certainly to a far lesser extent than in other parts of the Middle East, and the shift to cash crops was on a more limited scale. The combined result of the last two developments was that, today, Iran has a more favorable land/man ratio than other parts of the region, and is distinctly less close to having reached the limits of its agricultural potential. Iranian handicrafts, like those of its neighbors, suffered greatly from the competition of foreign machine-made goods, but, owing to poor transport, the process started later and made less headway. And it is just conceivable that the absence of a large body of skilled and enterprising foreigners and members of minority groups may have stimulated the growth of a native entrepreneurial bourgeoisie, although this is only a tentative surmise.

Even where the general trend is clear, lack of accurate information makes it almost impossible to trace fluctuations during the subperiods. The rule of the first two Qajars (1796–1834) was one of rapid recovery from the devastations of the previous century. Except for the two humiliating but brief wars with Russia in 1813 and 1826, the country enjoyed peace and a large measure of internal security. The population, and the handicraft production, of some of those towns that had suffered most once more increased. The government lived within its means, and indeed a sizable reserve accumulated in the shah's treasury. But the outstanding feature of this period was the rapid growth in international trade, caused by two factors. First, there was the opening of the country to foreign merchants by such treaties as the apparently inoperative one with Britain in 1801, the Gulistan and Turkmanchai treaties with Russia in 1813 and 1828, and the Anglo-Persian Commercial Treaty of 1841; these agreements imposed low and uniform duties on imports and exports and banned the use of monopolies or prohibitions in foreign trade. And second, there was greater security in the adjacent areas: the Persian Gulf, thanks to the British efforts to suppress piracy; the Caucasus, because of the firmer Russian hold on the area; and eastern Anatolia, which was being increasingly brought under the control of the Ottoman government. In the 1870s, the extension of Russian rule to Central Asia also served to protect Iran's northeastern provinces from the depredations of tribesmen.

The next thirty years (1834–64) saw a continued growth of foreign trade, due on the one hand to increasing exports of agricultural produce, including such new

[3] League of Nations, *Statistical Yearbook, 1928* (Geneva, 1929).

items as opium, and on the other to rising imports of European textiles and other manufactured goods, which caused great harm to Iranian handicrafts. Attempts by the modernizing prime minister, Amir-i Kabir, to establish factory industries ended in failure, but some of his administrative and educational reforms were more enduring. Returning to Iran in 1862, after an absence of four years, the French minister Arthur de Gobineau noted signs of progress, such as greater construction, some road building, improved posts, and a service for transferring funds between the main towns. "To sum up, the country is not in the same state as before—on the contrary. Progress is slow, doubtless it is strongly opposed, businessmen are below average in ability and well below average in scrupulousness. Nevertheless, very evident progress has been made and nothing leads one to predict that this ascending movement has to stop."[4]

But in fact the advance was halted, and even reversed, in the late 1860s by two disasters that struck Iran in quick succession: the muscardine disease that sharply reduced the silk crop, and a series of droughts resulting in the famine of 1872 (see chap. 2, introduction). A further disruptive factor was the rapid devaluation of the currency, due partly to debasement but mainly to the fall in the price of silver from the late 1860s on. This naturally raised the price of commodities and inflicted much hardship on large sections of the population. And the sharp fall in world prices of raw materials in the 1870s also had adverse effects on the exports and economy of Iran.

In the meantime, Iran's communications with the outside world were being greatly improved by the establishment of a telegraph service to Europe and of steam navigation on the Caspian and the Persian Gulf. The opening of the Suez Canal, in 1869, brought the country within easy reach of Europe by steamer. And although all the railway schemes—beginning with the Reuter Concession of 1872—proved abortive, some improvement in Iran's internal transport was made with the opening of the Karun river to steam navigation, in 1888, and Russian road and port construction in the north and some British road building in the south, in 1890–1914.

Improved transport was only one of many factors drawing Iran more closely into the international economy in the years 1890–1914, and subjecting it to rapidly increasing foreign financial and political influence. Trade once more expanded rapidly, thanks to greater output and exports of cash crops such as silk, cotton, and rice and to increased imports of manufactured and colonial goods. The establishment of British and Russian banks facilitated financial transactions. A sizable amount of British, Russian, and other capital was invested in petroleum, fisheries, and certain branches of manufacturing. Most important, the budget began to show rising deficits—mainly because of the increasing extravagance of the shahs—and, starting in 1892, loans were contracted abroad by pledging certain

[4] Hytier, pp. 169–70.

revenues and making other concessions which decreased the country's independence.

Matters came to a head after the revolution of 1906. On the one hand, the new government, with the help of American, Belgian, and other experts, undertook sweeping reforms in administration, taxation, and other fields. The emerging Persian bourgeoisie also began to show more courage and awareness, and founded several relatively large industrial, commercial, and financial enterprises. Trade continued to grow and the discovery of oil gave promise of future wealth. But, on the other hand, the increasing turmoil afforded an excellent pretext for foreign intervention, mainly Russian but also British.[5] The Anglo-Russian Agreement of 1907, partitioning the country into spheres of influence, was followed by a rapid loss of government control over the most productive parts of the country. At the outbreak of war in 1914, both the economic and the political future of Iran seemed very much in doubt.

[5] For a detailed account see Shuster, Millspaugh, Wilson, Kasravi, and other works. For an example of interference by the British in the south, see memorandum by the Belgian Financial Agent at Muhammarah, dated 5 May 1914. This was forwarded by the British minister in Tehran with a covering note stating: "In sending me this report M. Mornard [the treasurer-general] has made no complaint against the British consular officers concerned, but it serves to underline one of the reasons given for his recent resignation, namely, that it is impossible for the Belgian financial Administration to carry out its work so long as it cannot feel sure of the genuine support of the British and Russian Consular officers." Townley to Grey, 6 July 1914, FO 371/2078.

## 2

## *Social Structure*

The study of social change, as indeed of other aspects of the history of Iran before the First World War, is greatly impeded by the absence or unreliability of statistics. As the British consul K. E. Abbott, one of the best-informed students of the Iranian economy, pointed out in 1848: "It seldom happens in Persia that two statistical accounts on one subject, even when derived from official sources, are found to correspond."[1]

Nevertheless, on the basis of several estimates of varying degrees of accuracy, a few general observations may be made. First, the population seems definitely to have increased—from perhaps 5 or 6 million in 1800 to about 10 million by 1914 (see 2:1–3).[2] This implies an annual compound rate of growth of a little over 0.5 percent, compared with 1 percent in Egypt; in view of the far lower degree of economic development in Iran during the period and of the distinctly worse hygenic conditions prevailing, this discrepancy is not unreasonable, and it should be noted that the Iranian figure is very close to the estimated Indian rate of growth. It is possible that the rate of increase during the second half of the period was higher than during the first half.[3] Second, several towns—notably Tehran and Tabriz—grew considerably, partly through immigration; and although others probably declined, the overall rate of urbanization seems to have risen (see 2:2). Third, the proportion of nomads fell from perhaps a half to about a quarter of the total population.

[1] Report on Journey to the Caspian, FO 60/141.
[2] See Hambly, and Bémont, *Villes*, p. 65, who quotes the following estimates: 5 million in 1812, 6 million in 1838, 5 million in 1858, 5 million in 1869, 7.5 million in 1894, and 8 million in 1910.
A very rough check on the 1914 figure is provided by extrapolation. In 1956, when the first Iranian census put the population at 18,954,000, that of Egypt was 23,532,000. Assuming the same ratio to have prevailed in 1907 would indicate a figure of 9,000,000 for Iran, compared with 11,287,000 for Egypt. However it is highly unlikely that in 1907 to 1956 the Iranian rate of growth was as high as the Egyptian, and a figure of 10,000,000 for 1914 does not seem unreasonable.
[3] In 1890, Curzon, *Persia*, 2:493, estimated annual population growth at 0.75 percent, at a time "free from both war and famine."

No firm statement can be made regarding changes in the regional distribution of the population. At present, some two-thirds of the inhabitants occupy about one-quarter of the area, in the northwestern corner of the country that enjoys abundant rainfall,[4] and there is every reason to believe that a similar concentration prevailed during the period under review; since, however, both urban and agricultural growth seem to have been higher in that region than in the rest of the country, it is possible that in 1800 or even in 1850 its share of the total was somewhat smaller.

Of the Malthusian checks, war had a minor effect in the nineteenth century, but pestilence and famine were frequent and devastating. A Persian scholar lists nine cholera epidemics in 1851–61.[5] The British consul in Tabriz gave an equally depressing account, stating that outbreaks had occurred in that town in 1835, 1846, 1847, 1853, 1856, 1857, 1860, and 1861.[6] In 1861, deaths totaled 2,487 (excluding the garrison and strangers in caravanserais), compared with 6,077 in 1846 and about 5,000 in 1847.[7] In 1866, Abbott put mortality in Tabriz at 5 percent of the population (that being the proportion of deaths among Christians), or 6,500, and there was another epidemic in 1872.[8] Outbreaks of plague seem to have been less common than those of cholera, but in 1876 one was brought over from Iraq and killed about 1,800 of the 8,000 inhabitants of Shushtar.[9]

After that the incidence of epidemics seems to have decreased, thanks to improved international quarantine and the efforts of the Council of Health, which was founded in 1868 and included representatives of the British, Russian, and French legations, to impose quarantines along Iran's frontiers and within the country.[10] Moreover, medical facilities in Iran were slowly increasing and improving, mostly because of clinics and hospitals set up by foreigners.[11] But the country continued to be subject to epidemics, such as the cholera epidemic of 1892, brought over from Russia, which killed 10,000 persons in Gilan and was also severe in Khurasan and Tehran.[12]

---

[4] See figures and maps in Bémont, *Villes*, pp. 68–76.

[5] Behnam, chap. 3.

[6] Report on Azerbaijan, 19 April 1864, FO 60/286.

[7] Dispatch by Abbott, 31 December 1861, FO 60/259; for descriptions of earlier epidemics in Tabriz see dispatches of 2 November and 6 December 1846, FO 60/126, 4 September 1847, FO 60/133, and also one of 28 July 1852, published in *Middle East Journal* (Washington, D.C.), Spring 1969; in the 1848 epidemic in Tehran, 4,760 deaths were "registered by the Body-washers," but this was regarded as an underestimate; see Abbott to Palmerston, 23 December 1848, FO 60/141.

[8] Abbott to Stanley, 28 December 1866, FO 60/300, and "Tabriz," A and P 1872, 58.

[9] Memorandum of 14 January 1877, FO 60/400.

[10] See dispatches in 1872–78 in FO 60/382, FO 60/400, and FO 60/414; "Rasht," A and P. 1878, 74, and AE Téhéran, vol. 2, dispatch of 23 November 1868.

[11] For example, the British dispensary in Bushire treated 20,000 patients in 1873/74 and 13,500 in 1874/75—see FO 60/375; a medical mission was set up by the Church Missionary Service in Julfa in 1879, and transferred to Isfahan in 1904, and a free dispensary was also available in the British consulate—see "Isfahan," A and P 1914, 93; British consular hospitals were established in Mashad and Kirman, and in 1906/7 the former treated 14,000 inpatients and 38,000 outpatients—see "Isfahan," A and P 1908, 114.

[12] "Rasht," A and P. 1893–94, 95, and "Mashad," A and P 1894, 87. The French physician Tholozan stated that in the period 3 to 17 August 1892 the body washers in Tehran had reported 1,037 deaths from cholera; he added: "in the thirty three years I have spent in Persia, this is the first epidemic I have witnessed which is so severe and so widespread"—report of 21 August 1892, AE, Téhéran, vol. 4.

In addition to, and sometimes conjoined with, pestilence there were frequent famines, generally due to drought. The most serious was perhaps that of 1871/72, caused by five successive years of low rainfall in several parts of the country, which killed off first the livestock and then the inhabitants. A British observer stated:

taking into consideration that half the population at least were unaffected by the famine, I do not think that the actual deaths from disease and starvation can have exceeded half a million, though from the disproportionate mortality of women and children, the ultimate loss to the country will be far higher. One of the immediate effects of the famine was to let loose bands of robbers, generally half-starved Iliats, all over the country.[13]

A British Legation official reported: "The destruction of life must have been fearful; and many doubted whether, had the dryness continued for another season, the country would have been habitable."[14] Local famines continued to be experienced, for example in the Urumiya district in 1880,[15] but no such general disaster recurred until the First World War, in part, presumably, because of the rise in agricultural production and the slight improvement in transport.

But even in normal times, the mass of Iranians lived at a very low level. The lack of data makes it impossible to measure the level of living, or even to state whether it improved or deteriorated over the years (see 2:5, 7). Most foreigners were struck by the great misery prevailing, and even a Russian observer could state in 1908: "Compared to it, the mournful Russian picture pales completely."[16] This judgment may be contrasted with that of Chardin, in the 1660s (see historical background). The discrepancy may well indicate a deterioration between the seventeenth and twentieth centuries, but it also surely reflects the new attitude and standards of Europeans, arising from the progress achieved in the West.

At the same time that it was growing in numbers, in spite of these various checks, Iranian society was becoming somewhat more complex and differentiated. To the traditional classes of landlords, military, officials, merchants, craftsmen, and peasants (see 2:4, 6, 7, and 11) the country's economic development added the nucleus of two new ones: an industrial, commercial, and financial bourgeoisie and an industrial working class (see 2:5). Both of the latter remained very small until the First World War, but were to play an increasingly important part after it, and a still larger one after the Second World War. Another group whose influence increased was the minorities: Armenians (see 2:8), Jews (see 2:9), and Parsees or Zoroastrians (see 2:10).[17] The members of these groups were

---

[13] St. John, 1:98; the author gives a vivid and detailed account of the famine.

[14] "Persia," A and P 1872, 59; two censuses in Qum showed a decrease from 25,382 in 1867/68 to 14,000 in 1874/75—Lambton, *Landlord*, p. 153.

[15] FO 60/431.

[16] Yevgenii Ilin, quoted by Abdullaev, p. 25.

[17] Estimates of the size of the minority groups vary. In 1868, Thomson put the number of Armenians at 26,000, Jews at 16,000, and of Zoroastrians at 7,000 (see chap. 2, sel. 2). General Houtum-Schindler gave the following for 1884: Armenians, 43,000, Jews, 19,000, Zoroastrians, 8,000; his figures are criticized by Curzon (*Persia*, 2:493) as being too low for Armenians and Jews. According to Curzon, there were 29,000 Armenians in Azerbaijan (1:548); on the other hand, Curzon regarded another figure, of 65,000, for the Jews as exaggerated (1:510). Aubin's estimates for 1908 were: 65,000 Armenians, of whom 34,000 were in Azerbaijan, 50,000 Jews, and 10,000 Zoroastrians (p. 177).

able to seize many of the opportunities afforded by the growth of international trade and the increasing penetration of the country by foreign political and economic influence.

The number of foreigners remained very small. In 1860, there were only twenty-five Britishers in Iran—as distinct from Indians and others enjoying British protection, who numbered eighty-six.[18] Of course their number grew over the next fifty years because of such enterprises as the Telegraphs, Anglo-Persian Oil Company, consulates, hospitals, and various trading firms, but it is unlikely to have exceeded a few hundred by 1914. The number of Frenchmen in 1863 was fifty, of whom thirty-one were men, sixteen were women and three were children; one may presume that most of them were connected with religious missions or schools.[19] Their number must have grown much more slowly than that of the British.[20] Russians were much more numerous, thanks to their various enterprises in the north of the country, which imported labor. On the eve of the First World War, some 5,070 Russian subjects worked in such enterprises,[21] but this figure naturally includes many Azerbaijanis, Armenians, Georgians, and other "nonethnic" Russians. As for the Germans, there were sixty in Tabriz in 1913.[22] All together, Iran had a very small number of foreign residents compared with such countries as Egypt, Turkey, Palestine, and Lebanon.

The influence of the minority groups arose not only from the contact they had with coreligionists living abroad,[23] but from their superior level of education, acquired in American, French, and other missionary schools or in communal schools founded by themselves. The Muslim majority, on the other hand, was very poorly provided for. As in Egypt and Turkey, student missions were sent to Europe, but the scale was far smaller. In 1811 two young Persians, and in 1815 five others, were sent to England "to be educated and instructed in various branches of Science and Mechanics."[24] In 1844, another five were sent to France, followed by forty-two in 1861. Several others went on their own, and in 1911 a group of thirty was sent to Europe by the government. By 1918, "there were in Europe about 500 Iranian students, 200 of whom were in France, 34 in England, 9 in Germany."[25] No less important was the founding of Dar al-Funun, the country's first modern school, in 1851, and the creation of the nucleus of Tehran University, starting in 1901. Skilled workers were also sent to Russia and other

[18] Figures cited in dispatch in 1885, FO 60/474.
[19] Report of 1863, AE Téhéran, vol. 1.
[20] The number of Frenchmen in the Tabriz consular district, where many of the missions were located, was given as twenty-six in 1879—AE Tauris, vol. 2.
[21] Abdullaev, p. 210. In 1894, ten of the eleven leading firms of Sabzavar belonged to Russian subjects, and only one to an Iranian—Glukhoded, p. 66.
[22] Ibid., p. 151.
[23] In 1857, Gobineau reported that the Zoroastrians of Tehran had been too poor to undertake any "speculations," but that one from Bombay had been residing in that city for a year and "has had some influence over them"—Dispatch of 20 July 1857, AE Téhéran, vol. 1. (See chap. 2, sels. 8–10.)
[24] Memorandum respecting Persian Youths, February 1826, FO 60/19; for previous correspondence see FO 60/8, FO 60/11, ad FO 60/15.
[25] Arasteh, p. 29.

countries for training, and various foreign technicians were brought in, starting with British engineers in Azerbaijan in 1812. But the very limited extent of educational advance is shown by the fact that as late as 1922 there were only 44,000 students in all Iranian schools, figures distinctly lower than those of other Middle Eastern countries (see epilogue).

A still more striking index is the very low degree of literacy. No exact figures are available before the 1956 census, which showed that 15 percent of those over ten years old were literate, but the following estimates, made by Soviet observers in the late 1920s, are of considerable interest; it should be borne in mind that they cover only districts in the north, the most advanced part of the country.[26]

*Daregaz-Kalat* district, population 21,000—overall literacy 10 percent; among traders 51 percent, clergy 15, craftsmen 13, landowners 12, officials 7, and peasants 2.

*Astarabad* district, population 200,000—"hardly 5 percent"; all clergy and most landowners and traders literate, but among craftsmen not more than 2 percent and among peasants practically none.

*Gilan*, population 381,000—overall literacy 5 percent; among landowners 60 percent, merchants 60, small merchants 25, craftsmen 10, peasants 5, workers 2, townswomen 2.

*Maku-Khoi* district, population 230,000—in the towns 30 percent and in the villages 2.

*Urumiya* district, population about 65,000—among officials 100 percent of the men and 70 percent of the women, among landowners 100 and 30, clergy 100 and 20, merchants 90 and 5, workers 3 and 0.5 and peasants 1 and nil. A breakdown by ethnic groups put literacy among Assyrians at 80 percent for men and 80 for women, among Armenians 70 and 70 and among Jews 90 and 20, whereas the Kurds and Muslim Persians, who constituted two-fifths of the population, were almost totally illiterate.

In a way, such figures are misleading, for they underestimate the extent of the penetration of new ideas in Iran. Those two remarkable phenomena, the Bahai Movement and the Constitutional Revolution, showed not only the scope of Iran's spiritual and moral resources but also the amount of fermentation arising from the introduction of Western ways of life and thought. But from the point of view of economic development, which is the subject of this book, the small size of the school population and the low degree of literacy do point out the fact that Iran's human resources, like its material resources, remained almost wholly untapped.

## Gardane Mission

In 1807 Napoleon sent General Gardane at the head of a military mission to Iran (see text of instructions in Hurewitz, 1:78–81). The small size of the mission

---

[26] *Severniya Persiya*, pp. 19–39, 65–73.

—eighteen persons, including three dragomans and a chaplain—its short stay, and its exclusive interest in diplomatic and military matters, precluded its producing any valuable economic or social studies of the country.[1] The two following extracts are not, however, without interest. The first is from "Note sur certains détails fesant [sic] suite aux idées sur une expédition aux Indes adressées par le Géneral Gardane le 24 X^{bre} 1807 à S.E. le Ministre des Relations Extérieures,"[2] and the second from a note on the trade of Persia written a few months later.[3]

(See also works by Hambly, Malcolm, Fraser, Ouseley, Porter, Dupré, Drouville, and Joubert, listed in the bibliography.)

[1] See "Etat des Travaux executés pendant la durée de ma mission en Perse," 23 April, 1809. AE Correspondance Politique, Perse, vol. 11.
[2] Ibid., vol. 10.
[3] Gardane to Minister of Interior, 28 May 1808, ibid.

## Selection 1. Iran in 1807
Gardane dispatches, AE, Correspondance politique, Perse, vol. 10, 24 December 1807 and 28 May 1808

GARDANE TO MINISTER OF EXTERNAL RELATIONS, 24 DECEMBER 1807

*The troops of Persia*—they may amount to 180,000 men, of whom 70,000 to 75,000 are known as imperial troops (*Qushuni rekabi*) and are paid by the imperial treasury. The rest, known as provincial troops and put under the command of various princes, are paid from the treasuries of these governors, depend on them, and are more particularly charged with defending these provinces; should one of these provinces be attacked, the king sends some of his imperial troops to support those of the province and meets their expenses.

The troops are, in general, paid very badly, because of the spirit of avarice prevailing in the court and among the great men of the realm.

*Statistics of Persia*—The present area of this country, up to the limit of the Yazd-Mashad line, may be 40,000 to 45,000 square leagues. Its population is, at most, 9 million inhabitants.[1] Its revenues amount to 2

[1] The league referred to was probably the kilometric league of 4,000 metres; Gardane's figure for the area, say 650,000 square kilometers, is far too low, even bearing in mind that he excludes a large part of Iran's eastern provinces; that for the population is probably much too high, although it includes the transcaucasian provinces lost to Russia in 1813.

million tumans (40 million francs). The subjects pay about one-tenth of their income, in cash or kind; the *hakim* (village chief) converts payment in kind into cash, according to prevailing prices, and this money is paid into the king's treasury.

The payments in kind made to the court by the provinces, as well as the supplementary taxes and extortions with which the governors of the said provinces burden the people, may be put at 1 million tumans (20 million francs); this figure is not included in the one given above.

As for His Majesty's private treasury, it must be very great, for one does not see how it could have been dissipated. It was constituted by Nadir Shah and the Zand successors of Karim Khan, as well as by Agha Muhammad Khan Qajar, the predecessor of the reigning monarch, all of whom were very clever and miserly. An exception must, however, be made for Karim Khan, who had a generous character; at his death his private treasury contained only 75,000 tumans of that period, which may be estimated at nearly 3 million francs [sic].

GARDANE TO MINISTER OF INTERIOR, 28 MAY 1808

Here, Excellency, as announced in my previous dispatch, are the names of various merchants who enjoy the highest credit in Persia:

In Tehran, Mirza Taqi, who has the title of *malik al tujjar*, or dean of the merchants of the realm. He may be presumed to be worth 30,000 tumans—public opinion credits him with 50,000. His trade consists only of precious stones, which he buys from foreigners and sells to the king, at a profit of 20 percent. Second, Mirza Muhammad Ali, brother of Mirza Taqi. His wealth is small, compared with that of other merchants, but as he has protectors, foreigners do business with him; however, whether because of blunders or bad luck, he has not made great gains.

In Isfahan, the richest and most trustworthy persons are: Hajji Muhammad Ali, son of Hajji Affin (?), who is credited with one and half million [francs]; Ibrahim, a goldsmith;

Hajji Muhammad Ali Adahi; and Hajji Mulla Ali Naki, who deals in shawls and trades with India.

In Shiraz, Hajji Muhammad Ibrahim, of Dekhti, agent of Nabi Khan, whom I had the honor to mention to Your Excellency in my last letter; he also trades on his own account. Agha Muhammad Ali, son of Hajji Abdullah, who enjoys the reputation of being very wealthy but does little business. In Bandar Bushire, Hajji Ismail of Khurasan.

All these merchants hide their goods and feign poverty, because of the court. They are very much afraid of being called to Tehran, where they would surely be made to pay [mis à contribution].

## Population and Urbanization

Compared with most European countries in the preindustrial period, Iran—like other parts of the Middle East—was rather highly urbanized.[1] Hambly estimates the population of the six largest cities at about 500,000, and Bémont puts the total urban population at some 800,000.[2] If the total population is assumed to have been about 5,000,000, it will be seen that about one-seventh of the inhabitants lived in cities. The figures compiled by Thomson and given in the following selection would imply that there was no substantial change in either total population or overall urban population in the first half of the nineteenth century, whereas the estimates shown in Chapter 2, Selection 3 indicate a sharp rise in both in the second half. In view of the unreliability of all the earlier estimates, no firm conclusions can be drawn, but a slight rise in urbanization may well have taken place.

In the individual towns, the most remarkable growth was that of Tehran, from about 50,000 at the beginning of the century to around 90,000 in the 1850s[3] and 150,000 in 1910, to 200,000 in 1920 and over 500,000 in 1939. According to Malcolm, the population of Isfahan doubled, from 100,000 to 200,000, between 1800 and 1815; if so there must have subsequently been a sharp decline, since most estimates for the second half of the century range between 60,000 and 80,000; the 200,000 mark was not passed until the 1950s. Similarly, Shiraz may have had as many as 50,000 inhabitants in 1780 but had distinctly less in the nineteenth century. Yazd, which had suffered little in the wars of the eighteenth century, may have had a population of 60,000–70,000 in 1800—indeed some sources put

[1] For an analysis of this question see Charles Issawi, "Urbanization and Economic Development," in *Middle Eastern Cities*, ed. Ira Lapidus (Berkeley, 1969).

[2] Hambly; Bémont, *Villes*, p. 67; the figures on individual towns are based on the sources cited in these two works and on those given in Curzon, *Persia*.

[3] The report on the trade of Tehran for 1847 gives this figure, FO 60/141.

it as high as 100,000; its population seems to have declined to 40,000 in 1850-60[4] but to have recovered to 60,000-80,000 by 1890. Tabriz, which became the leading commercial center, showed a steady growth from 30,000-50,000 in 1800 to around 100,000 at the middle of the century and 170,000-200,000 in 1890;[5] however, the diversion of trade from the Trebizond route to the Persian Gulf route (see 3:11) reduced the prosperity of the town, and the population seems to have stagnated during the next fifty years. The population of Mashad, Kirman, and Kermanshah seems to have remained broadly unchanged, at 40,000-50,000.

A striking feature of Iran's urban history in the nineteenth century is that no seaport attained a considerable size; in this Iran presents a sharp contrast to the other Middle Eastern countries. Neither Rasht[6] nor Bushire, the main ports on the Caspian and the Persian Gulf, had passed the 20,000 mark by 1870, and although Rasht may have doubled its population by 1914, Bushire showed almost no growth. It was only with the coming of the oil industry that Iran got a really large port, Abadan.

(See works by Hambly, Curzon, Balfour, Bémont, Lockhart, and Foreign Office Handbook, *Persia*, listed in the bibliography; *Statesman's Yearbook*, EI(2) s.v. Abbadan, Ahwaz, Ardabil, Bandar Abbas, Bandar Pahlawi, Bushahr, Damghan, and Harat; and EI s.v. Isfahan, Kashan, Kazwin, Kirman, Kirmanshah, Khoi, Lahidjan, Maragha, Meshed, Muhammara, Nishapur, Resht, Shiraz, Shuster, Tabriz, Teheran, Yazd, Zandjan.)

[4] See Abbott's report of 1850 in FO60/165 (see chap. 6, sel. 2), and Curzon, *Persia*, 2:240.

[5] A figure of 200,000 is given in the report on the trade of Azerbaijan for 1859, FO 60/253. In 1868 the French consul stated that a few years earlier a census had shown that there were 32,000 Muslim households, implying a population of 160,000; adding 3,000 Armenians and 2,000 for the garrison, and allowing for the growth of the population, he put the total at 180,000 and perhaps as much as 200,000; Tabriz had 270 mosques, 70 baths, 70 khans, 40 caravanserais, and 4,500 shops—report of 10 May 1868, AE Tauris, vol. 1.

[6] In 1844 Abbott put the population of Rasht at 15,000-20,000; figures for other towns in the Caspian provinces are to be found in his report on his journey, FO 60/108.

## Selection 2. Population, 1867
["Report on Persia," A and P 1867-68, 19, pp. 247-50, 255-58]

MR. THOMSON TO MR. ALISON
Sir,                    *Tehran, April 20, 1868*
I submit herewith, for your information, a report which I have prepared on the population, revenue, military force, and trade of Persia.

POPULATION
The population and general resources of this country have always been over estimated. Extending for 700 miles from north to south, and 900 miles from east to west, Persia contains an area of 648,000 square miles; but an immense extent of its superficies is absolute desert, and the population is everywhere so scanty that it only gives about seven inhabitants to the square mile. In some parts it is even much less than this. Taking Kerman, for instance, which is one of the largest provinces in the south of Persia, we find that it contains about 73,000 square miles, with a population of only 207,000, which gives something less than three inhabitants to the square mile. It is a difficult matter to reconcile the extravagant statements made by natives and the conflicting opinions advanced by Europeans respecting the number of inhabitants in any given district. To those who have travelled through Persia, and especially in such parts

as are removed from the ordinary lines of traffic, it must be obvious, however, that great misconception exists on this subject. The calculations made by natives are for the most part worthless. They range from 10,000,000 to estimates which are preposterous. Malcolm mentions that, in a manuscript which it was pretended had been compiled from State Papers, the population of Persia was stated to be 200,000,000. Chardin estimates it at 40,000,000, and in geographical works it is usually given at from 9,000,000 to 15,000,000. Even Fraser, who is generally so accurate in his descriptions of Persia, places it at from 8,000,000 to 10,000,000. Pinkerton appears to have arrived at a nearer approximation to the truth, as he estimates the population of Persia and a portion of Afghanistan at 10,000,000, of which 4,000,000 belonged to the latter country, leaving 6,000,000 for the territory now included in the Shah's dominions. Under the Tuffanean [Safavid] Kings, and even when the reigning dynasty came into power, it is probable that Persia was more populous than at present, for she had, especially at the former period, attained a comparatively high state of prosperity. The ravages frequently made by plague and cholera, with continued misrule and extortion, may account for the condition to which the country is now reduced. Certain it is, that according to the best information I have been able to collect on journeys performed in nearly every province of Persia, which is corroborated in a great measure by the opinions of others, who have given attention to the subject, the population of Persia does not at present exceed 5,000,000, while it is probable that it is not much over 4,000,000.

The population of the principal cities in Persia may be estimated as follows, at about 850,000 souls.

| | |
|---|---|
| Tehran . . | 85,000 |
| Ispahan . . | 60,000 |
| Yezd . . . | 40,000 |
| Kerman . . | 30,000 |
| Sheeraz . . | 25,000 |
| Bushire . . | 18,000 |
| Shooster . . | 25,000 |

| | |
|---|---|
| Disfool . . | 15,000 |
| Booroojird | 10,000 |
| Kermanshah | 30,000 |
| Hamadan . | 30,000 |
| Sennah . . | 20,000 |
| Maragha . | 15,000 |
| Oroomiah . | 30,000 |
| Khoi . . . | 20,000 |
| Tabreez . . | 110,000 |
| Ardebeel . . | 10,000 |
| Zinjan . . | 20,000 |
| Cazveen . . | 25,000 |
| Resht . . . | 18,000 |
| Saree . . . | 15,000 |
| Barferoosh . | 10,000 |
| Amol . . . | 8,000 |
| Asterabad . | 18,000 |
| Bestam . . | 7,000 |
| Shahrood . | 8,000 |
| Nishapore . | 8,000 |
| Sebzawar . | 12,000 |
| Koochan . . | 10,000 |
| Boojnoord . | 8,000 |
| Toorsheez . | 10,000 |
| Cashan . . | 10,000 |
| Koom . . . | 12,000 |
| Meshed . . | 70,000 |
| Gulpaizan . | 10,000 |

These numbers cannot, of course, be ascertained with perfect accuracy; but the figures here given are rather over than under the mark. Allowing 150,000 more for the other small towns, we have 1,000,000 as the total population of all the cities and towns in Persia. More than half of the remaining population belongs to the Turkish, Lek, Koordish, and Arab tribes, which are spread over the whole of the Persian territory. In some provinces, such as Khorassan, and in the districts contiguous to the Turkish and Russian frontiers, nearly the entire population belongs indeed to one or other of these numerous tribes. A full account of them is given in Sir Justin Shiel's published "Notes on Persian Eelyats"; and, according to that paper, they amount to about 340,000 families, or 1,700,000 souls. This is a liberal computation of their numbers, as Persians themselves admit; and if for the rest of the inhabitants we add an equal number, we have for the whole population of Persia:—

| | |
|---|---|
| Inhabitants of cities . . . . . | 1,000,000 |
| Population belonging to tribes | 1,700,000 |
| Remaining inhabitants . . . | 1,700,000 |
| Total | 4,400,000 |

The general accuracy of this calculation may be tested thus:—The population of the Province of Kerman is known with tolerable certainty. In an official return lately furnished to the Persian Government by the local authorities there, a full report is made on the condition of the province. It is divided into twenty-five districts, and each district is described in detail with reference to its position, climate, produce, and population. According to this document, the total number of inhabitants, not including Persian Beloochistan, is 207,000. The amount of revenue paid annually is 210,000 tomans, which gives about 1 toman for each individual. It may reasonably be assumed that the rate of Government taxation is pretty much the same all over Persia, though the amount actually raised in different localities by illegal exactions, doubtless varies considerably; but in order further to verify the above estimate, I have made inquiries respecting the authorized taxes collected from several villages in different provinces, and I find that they average from 500 to 600 tomans in cash for 100 families, which allows about 1 toman for each person. The

aggregate revenue of Persia paid in money being about 4,361,000 tomans, it would therefore appear that the entire population cannot be much in excess of 4,250,000, as stated above. It is true that the majority of the inhabitants of the principal towns in Persia pay no taxes. These may be reckoned at 500,000; but the amount of revenue derived from the Customs, which is 536,000 tomans, has to be deducted on the other hand, as it is not levied from the provinces by direct taxation.

REVENUES

During the reign of the present Shah, the revenues of Persia have been increased by nearly 3½ crores of tomans, or 694,000*l*. They now amount to 4,361,660 tomans, or 1,744,664*l*. in money, besides payments in kind, consisting of barley, wheat, rice, and silk, valued at 550,840 tomans, or 220,336*l*., making the total revenue of Persia, equal to 4,912,500 tomans, or 1,965,000*l*.

The following return shows the revenue demanded from each province during the present year:—

| | Tomans |
|---|---|
| Ispahan | 420,000 |
| Fars | 380,000 |
| Kerman | 210,000 |
| Yezd | 170,000 |
| Mazanderan | 110,000 |
| Ghilan | 440,000 |
| Cazveen | 70,000 |
| Khemseh | 180,000 |
| Azerbijan | 620,000 |
| Koordistan and Gerroos | 50,000 |
| Khorassan, with Shahrood and Bestam | 220,000 |
| Asterabad | 25,000 |
| Kermanshah, with Looristan and Nehavend | 200,000 |
| Arabistan | 215,000 |
| Booroojird | 60,000 |
| Gulpaigan | 60,000 |
| Cashan | 70,000 |
| Koom | 15,000 |
| Tehran and adjacent districts | 210,000 |
| Hamadan | 30,000 |

|  | Tomans | £ |
|---|---|---|
|  | 3,825,000 | 1,530,000 |
| Customs, given in separate Table | 536,660 | 214,664 |
| Persian Revenue in money | 4,361,660 | 1,744,664 |

The income received in kind is as follows:—

| | | |
|---|---|---:|
| 247,000 kherwars of barley and wheat, valued at. . . . . . . . . . . . . . . | | 494,000 |
| 8,500 kherwars (650 lbs. each) of rice . . | | 25,500 |
| 58,500 kherwars of straw . . . . . . . | | 29,250 |
| 75 kherwars of nokhood (peas) . . . . | | 300 |
| 71 mans of silk . . . . . . . . . | | 1,790 |
| | 550,840 = | 220,336 |

Total Persian Revenue, in money and kind   £1,965,000

The payments in kind are mostly reserved for the use of the army, the Shah's own expenses, and extraordinary disbursements.

The Shah does not, however, receive the whole of this revenue. From Khorassan, for instance, nothing is paid to the Royal Treasury, owing to the heavy disbursements made in that province for military service, and for the protection of the line of frontier by a large body of irregular troops employed in repelling the inroads of Turkoman marauders; and during the last year, in consequence of the failure of the silk crop in Ghilan, the revenue of that province has been reduced by more than 100,000 tomans. The provincial governors, moreover, are frequently defaulters to a larger amount. When appointed, they undertake to account to the central government for the sums specified above; but it often happens that at the end of the year's tenure of office there is a large deficit which they declare they have been unable for some reason or other to collect from their districts. A fee is then paid to the financial authorities in Tehran, and the Shah is persuaded to remit a large portion . . . .

The irregular exactions amount to a sum equal to the legal assessments, and there does not appear to be any reason for supposing that this is an exaggeration. An idea may be formed of the extent to which they are carried with the connivance of the Government, from the fact that the Governor of Fars is authorized to demand over and above the usual revenue, for his own use, 75,000 tomans a year, and the Governor of Ispahan, 60,000 tomans, as "Hek el Hekoomeh" or Governor's fee. The former likewise pays 60,000 tomans, and the latter 40,000 tomans under the name of "Peeshkesh," or an offering made to the King for their appointments, and by these payments they no doubt consider that they have purchased the right to reimburse themselves by means of arbitrary taxation. The same system is pursued with respect to the appointments of all the other Governors, and so long as they pay to the King's Treasury the stipulated amount of revenue and keep the inhabitants from rising in open rebellion, few inquiries are made as to how their duties are discharged.

REVENUE PAID BY MAHOMETANS

Nearly all the revenue of Persia is contributed by the Mahometan subjects of the Shah. The whole amount collected from the Christian population, Jews and Guebres, is very trifling.

REVENUE PAID BY NESTORIANS

The Nestorians of Oroomiah and Telmass (including both Protestants and those who have joined the Roman Catholic Church, about 3,500 and 600 families respectively), who number 25,000 souls, are all engaged in agriculture. Their taxes are comparatively light, so far as they are authorized by government, but they suffer great wrong and oppression at the hands of the Afshar Chiefs, who own most of the villages in which they reside.

REVENUE PAID BY ARMENIANS

The entire Armenian population in Persia is estimated at about 4,660 families, or 26,000 persons. The following statement shows the districts where they reside, and the nature of the taxes levied from them:—

ARMENIANS

| DISTRICTS | FAMILIES | PERSONS | REMARKS |
|---|---|---|---|
| Bushire . . . . . . . | 14 | 80 | ⎫ |
| Sheeraz . . . . . . . | 4 | 30 | ⎪ |
| Hamadan . . . . . . | 40 | 200 | ⎬ Pay no taxes |
| Tehran . . . . . . . | 120 | 800 | ⎪ |
| Tabreez . . . . . . | 400 | 2,200 | ⎭ |
| Julpha near Ispahan . | 350 | 2,000 | Pay 1,075 tomans, assessed on house and garden property |
| Peria . . . . . . . . | 1,042 | 6,500 | ⎫ |
| Chetrar Mehel . . . . | 390 | 2,100 | ⎪ |
| Boorwaree . . . . . | 260 | 1,300 | ⎪ |
| Kamareh . . . . . . | 390 | 2,450 | ⎪ |
| Kazaz. . . . . . . . | 340 | 2,050 | ⎪ |
| Gapleh . . . . . . . | 220 | 1,100 | ⎬ Pay taxes as cultivators of the soil |
| Shevereen . . . . . . | 75 | 370 | ⎪ |
| Melayer. . . . . . . | 190 | 950 | ⎪ |
| Karraghan. . . . . . | 136 | 700 | ⎪ |
| Villages near Tehran . | 70 | 350 | ⎪ |
| Oroomiah and Selmass | 439 | 2,415 | ⎪ |
| Miandoab . . . . . . | 80 | 440 | ⎭ |
| Total | 4,660 | 26,035 | |

The Armenian inhabitants of Tabreez pay no taxes. When the Russian troops withdrew from that city in 1828, the Christians resolved to accompany them to Georgia, but the English Envoy persuaded them to remain on the promise of exemption from all taxation. A Firman to this effect was issued by Abbass Meerza, which has been renewed by the present Shah and the heir apparent.

REVENUE PAID BY JEWS

There are about 16,000 Jews residing in different parts of Persia. They are mostly very poor, and excepting in Tehran, and some of the principal cities, are much persecuted and oppressed by the Mahometans. The towns and districts where they are permitted to reside are shown at the foot of the following page.

In all the provincial districts the Jews are more or less persecuted, and in places where the taxes are light, it is owing more to their extreme poverty than to the forbearance of the authorities. As a general rule all over Persia, as much is taken from the Jews as can possibly be extorted from them. In Meshed, twenty-five years ago, the Jews were all forcibly converted to Islamism, and many were massacred in the struggle which then took place; and in Barferoosh in 1866, a number of Jews were cruelly massacred, and an attempt, which was nearly successful, was made to force them to become Mahometans. In places where they are not protected by the presence of European officials, they are liable at any time to be subjected to similar acts of violence and outrage.

REVENUE PAID BY GUEBRES

The Guebres, or Parsees, in Persia number 1,200 families, or 7,193 persons. They reside in Yezd and Kerman, where they are well treated by the inhabitants and authorities. A sum of 907 tomans is paid annually to the Government in Tehran by their agent for the taxes due by the whole community, and no other demands are made upon them.

The Christians, Jews, and Geubres in Persia are exempt from all military service.

EXPENDITURE

Small as is the revenue of Persia it is in excess of the expenditure. As will be perceived from the following statement of disbursements, a surplus of at least 1 crore of tomans, or 200,000*l*., is left annually, which is paid into the Shah's own Treasury.

As explained before, the payments in kind, valued at 200,000*l*., are employed for the use of the army, the Shah's private establishment, and other purposes, and do not appear in this Table, which only shows the expenditure of the revenue received in money.

Besides the surplus noted above, a considerable sum is paid into the Shah's Treasury annually for presents.

ANNUAL EXPENDITURE

| | Tomans | £ |
|---|---|---|
| For the army and equipment of troops . . . . . . . . . . | 3½ crores = | 700,000 |
| Salaries of princes, Ministers, and government employees . | 1½ crores = | 300,000 |
| Pensions to priesthood and syeds | ½ crore = | 100,000 |
| For Shah's private expenses . . | 1 crore = | 200,000 |
| Extraordinary disbursements . | 1 crore = | 200,000 |
| Surplus paid into shah's treasury | 1 crore = | 200,000 |
| Total | 8½ crores = | 1,700,000 |

JEWS

| DISTRICTS | NO. OF PERSONS | TAXES, AS FAR AS THEY ARE KNOWN | REMARKS |
|---|---|---|---|
| | | Tomans | |
| Tehran . . . . . | 1,500 | 150 | Taxes extremely light. The Jews are not molested here; but they are not allowed to open shops in the bazaars |
| Hamadan . . . . | 2,000 | 600 | Double the amount is extracted |
| Kermanshah . . . | 250 | 30 | |
| Kerrind . . . . . | 80 | .... | |
| Toosirkan . . . . | 150 | .... | |
| Nekavend . . . . | 200 | .... | |
| Booroojird . . . | 200 | .... | |
| Khorumabad . . | 250 | .... | |
| Gulpaigan . . . . | 500 | 50 | Much more is extracted, but they are miserably poor |
| Khonsar . . . . | 200 | 40 | |
| Shehrinow . . . | 250 | .... | |
| Cashan . . . . . | 750 | .... | |
| Ispahan . . . . . | 1,500 | 150 | |
| Yezd . . . . . . | 1,000 | 500 | |
| Sheeraz . . . . . | 1,500 | 1,200 | Said to be much oppressed |
| Kazeroon . . . . | 100 | 50 | |
| Bushire . . . . . | 350 | .... | |
| Oroomiah . . . . | 1,000 | 600 | Much more has been exacted for many years, but last summer their condition was improved |
| Selmass . . . . . | 400 | .... | |
| Miandoab . . . . | 250 | 60 | |
| Gerrooss . . . . | 300 | .... | |
| Sekkez and Baneh | 450 | .... | |
| Ghilan . . . . . | 150 | .... | |
| Barferoosh . . . | 350 | .... | |
| Demavend . . . | 150 | .... | |
| Borazjoon . . . . | 100 | .... | |
| Gerghoon . . . . | 150 | 25 | |
| Jehroon . . . . . | 300 | 50 | |
| Laur . . . . . . | 300 | 50 | |
| Feeroozabad . . . | 300 | 30 | |
| Darab . . . . . | 100 | 25 | |
| Gohab . . . . . | 100 | .... | |
| Koordistan . . . | 600 | .... | |
| Gellehdar . . . . | 150 | .... | |
| Novendegan . . . | 100 | .... | |
| Total | 16,030 | .... | |

## Selection 3. Population, 1913

[L. A. Sobotsinskii, *Persiya: Statistiko-ekonomicheskii ocherk* (Saint Petersburg, 1913) pp. 11–18]

. . . It is very difficult to determine the size of the Persian population and on this point the figures given by various students of the subject diverge sharply. This is due to the fact that no general census has been taken in Persia—unless one counts the attempt made in 1860. This ended in complete failure, because of opposition from the uncultured and fanatical people which hindered every effort to enumerate the population, and also because of the inviolability of the harem and other obstacles, leaving no real results behind it except for its cost. Even the administration itself had an interest in impeding the governmental enumeration of the population and the introduction of registers of births and deaths. For the amount of taxes levied by the central government is based on the number of inhabitants and the local governments were interested in transferring to the treasury as little as possible of what they had extracted from the people. The extent to which the data given by different writers on the Persian population diverge is evident from the following comparison of the estimates of its size given by various students of this question.

POPULATION OF PERSIA
(in thousands)

| GROUPS OF POPULATION | HOUTUM-SCHINDLER 1884[a] | ZOLOTOLIV 1888[b] | CURZON 1891[c] | CONTEMPORARY BY MEDVEDEV[d] |
|---|---|---|---|---|
| Settled . . | 5,744 | 4,500 | 6,750 | 7,500 |
| Towns . | 1,984[e] | 1,500 | 2,250 | 2,500 |
| Villages . | 3,780 | 3,000 | 4,500 | 5,000 |
| Nomadic . | 1,910 | 1,500 | 2,250 | 2,500 |
| | 7,654 | 6,000 | 9,000 | 10,000 |

[a] Sir A. Houtum-Schindler, general in the Persian army, quoted in Curzon, *Persia*, 2: 493. See also his article in *Encyclopaedia Britannica*, 11th ed. (1910) s.v. Persia.
[b] *Sic*—General A. M. Zolotarev in *Proceedings of the Russian Geographical Society*, quoted in Curzon, 2:493.
[c] Curzon, 2:493.
[d] Colonel A. I. Medvedev, *Persiya* (Saint Petersburg, 1909), p. 390, on whose figures Sobotsinskii draws heavily in this section.
[e] *Sic*—read 1, 964.

Accepting the last figure—since it was estimated by such an expert on Persia as Lord Curzon, who studied the country for three years—and adding the annual growth of 0.75 percent established by him, we see that the present-day population of Persia consists of 7.5 million (or 75 percent) of settled people, of whom 25 percent live in towns and 50 percent live in villages, and 2.5 million (or 25 percent) of nomads. Since we take the area of Persia to be 29,986 square miles,[1] the overall density of population is 367 inhabitants per square mile, or 6.8 per square verst.[2] In density of population, Persia is therefore very close to Russia, where we have 7 persons per square verst, or to the United States, where 8 persons live on each square verst. The above-mentioned density of population is far from being the same everywhere, as may be expected from the data given in our natural-historical sketch. The worse and less fertile the province and the more difficult are

[1] The Russian mile was equal to 7 versts or 7.468 kilometers, i.e., about 4.67 statute miles.

[2] A verst was 3,500 feet or 1,067 meters; a square verst was, therefore, very slightly larger than a square kilometer.

living conditions, the sparser is the population; conversely, the more humid the climate, and the more generous nature is, the thicker is the population. The province of Kirman—which includes a significant portion of the barest part of the interior of Persia, the Lut desert—is the least populated section of the country, with a density not exceeding 2 persons per square verst. In Farsistan, Khuzistan, Khurasan, and Iraq-i Ajami the density of population is about 7 per square verst, a figure close to the national average. In Gilan, Mazandaran, Astrabad, Azerbaijan, and Luristan, which are distinguished by more favorable climatic conditions, the density reaches 14 and even 20 per square verst. In these conditions, for each person in Persia there are 5 desyatins,[3] in Russia in similar conditions there are about 10 desyatins, in England 0.87, and in China 0.42 (note: a hectare = 0.9 desyatin).

The nomadic population is mainly concentrated in the southern and southwestern portions of the country. The total number of urban centers in Persia reaches 100, but there are hardly any large cities, as may be seen from the following list of the most important towns and their inhabitants.

| | |
|---|---:|
| Tabriz | 300,000 |
| Tehran | 350,000 |
| Isfahan | 80,000 |
| Mashhad | 70,000 |
| Yazd | 50,000 |
| Kirman | 50,000 |
| Kirmanshah | 50,000 |
| Hamadan | 50,000 |
| Khoy | 50,000 |
| Qazvin | 40,000 |
| Qum | 30,000 |
| Senne | 30,000 |
| Shiraz | 30,000 |
| Rasht | 25,000 |
| Urumiya | 20,000 |
| Bushire | 15,000 |
| Nishapur | 10,000 |
| Shahrud | 10,000 |
| Muhammarah | 10,000 |
| Shushtar | 10,000 |

The small size of the urban population is accounted for by many factors. In Persia there are no factories which, being con-

[3] A desyatin equaled 2.7 acres or about 1.1 hectares.

centrated in towns, could provide earnings to the incoming population and cause the gathering of inhabitants in such towns; in addition Persian towns do not offer, as regards services and amenities, any advantages over village life. Nor is there in Persia that powerful factor of growth of European towns, credit banks advancing loans on urban real estate. Last, for Persia, the time has not yet come when the production of food requires a smaller percentage of the labor force in the villages, thanks to the introduction of various kinds of improvement. Thus, at a time when in several countries a quarter or more of the total population is concentrated in towns, in Persia the urban population does not exceed 12 percent of the total.

As regards villages, in Persia the prevailing type is small units. Most villages consist of only a few houses, though at times one finds a large village, such as Taft (near Yazd), where some 10,000 persons of both sexes live. In spite of the patriarchal structure of Persian life, we do not find there the extended family which, until recently, existed in European Russia and which now survives only in Siberia. Moreover, in contrast to Russia, the Persian urban family is larger and more numerous than the rural; the average in towns may be put at six persons and in villages at five.

This phenomenon, which at first sight may seem strange, is explained by the fact that the propertied, well-to-do classes live mainly in towns, and consequently the structure of the urban family is, on the average, larger than that of the rural. The difference would be even more significant were it not that the very unsanitary conditions of Persian towns make of them constant breeding grounds of epidemics and lead to an extremely high mortality rate. Even the rate of annual growth of the Persian population, estimated as we have said by Lord Curzon at 0.75 percent, bears witness to the unfavorable living conditions of the Persian people and of the high death rate.

The ethnic composition of Persia is

extremely diverse. Serving for many centuries as an arena for numerous invasions by various peoples, Persia retained within its borders part of these diverse newcomers, who were rarely assimilated by the indigenous population, and in most cases have retained their physical and moral characteristics down to this day. The main lines of the ethnic composition of the Persian population may be seen from the following table, which gives a breakdown by main groups.

The motley pattern is further variegated by the fact that, except for the Persians, all the tribal groups are divided into tens of tribes and stocks, often differing from each other in manners and customs and living in constant enmity. This diversity represents one of the main causes of the disorder of the Persian monarchy—breaking it into separate pieces—of the absence of firm cohesion in the state, and of the constant internal disturbances. Thus the Turco-Tatar group is subdivided into ten large tribes (of which one, the Qajar, living mainly in Mazandaran, gave Persia its present ruling dynasty) and many smaller ones. The Lurish group—to which belong the Bakhtiari who have in our time played such a leading part in the historical destiny of Persia—is broken down into many clans (kaitul), subject to different leaders (kand and tushmal) and only partly brought together by the personality of that tushmal who, at any given time, enjoys most influence among them. . . .

| Ethnic Type | Number of Both Sexes | |
|---|---|---|
| | Absolute Figures | Percentage of Total Population |
| Persians . . . . . . . . . | 5,500,000 | 55 |
| Turco–Tatar . . . . . . . | 2,000,000 | 20 |
| Lurish tribes . . . . . . . | 1,000,000 | 10 |
| Kurds. . . . . . . . . . | 800,000 | 8 |
| Arabs. . . . . . . . . . | 350,000 | 3.5 |
| Turkoman and other tribes | 350,000 | 3.5 |
| | 10,000,000 | 100 |

## Social Classes

The following four selections sketch some features of the main social classes in Iran. The first is by Arthur de Gobineau, the celebrated writer who served as first secretary of the French legation in Tehran in 1854–58 and again as minister in 1862–64; it describes the traditional merchants and handicraftsmen, whose situation was only beginning to be affected by the impact of external economic forces (see 6:2, 3, 5). The second, by a Soviet scholar, shows the emergence of two new classes as a result of the transformations the Iranian economy underwent in the course of the nineteenth century: a commercial, financial, and industrial bourgeoisie and an industrial working class; both groups remained very small and weak until the end of the period under review. The third selection, by the leading authority on the subject, stresses those characteristics of the Persian landowning class which differentiate it most markedly from the feudal nobility of Western Europe. The last selection, by an American scholar, traces the changes in the conditions of the peasants brought about by the gradual shift from a subsistence to a market economy, by the change in land tenure, and by the decline of the village handicrafts.

## Selection 4. Merchants and Craftsmen, 1850s

[Arthur de Gobineau, *Trois ans en Asie* (Paris, 1859), pp. 392–404]

. . . After the *mirzas* [a mirza is approximately what the English call a gentleman] come the merchants. I have stated elsewhere what the manners of merchants and their behavior should be, and have nothing to add on this subject. In this respect, things in Persia are what they are in Egypt, Arabia, and India. But in Persia merchants are, perhaps, the most respectable part of the population. They are regarded as being very honest. Since they do not take unnecessary risks, and as merchants are more often than not sons of merchants who have inherited a more or less substantial fortune which they will transmit to their sons, they are devoid of worldly ambition and above many forms of intrigue. They need public esteem and carefully cultivate it. As a result, this witty, skeptical, mocking, and distrustful people does not hesitate to entrust merchants with its money for investment; in this respect, merchants play the same part as European credit institutions. They therefore hold most of the capital of Persia, which gives them great importance in the eyes of the government, which is always harassed by financial obligations and which would not know what to do if they were not there to help it out. The government borrows from them, but as the merchants lend it funds which do not belong to them and for which they are responsible, they can advance money only on sound security; hence they often take over monopolies, or assignments for the revenues of certain provinces, or precious stones or similar assets.

It has happened that the court, ruined and not knowing where to turn, could think of nothing better than bankruptcy. But such arbitrary acts [*coups d'état*], which are resorted to in extreme crises, are very infrequent, for their certain outcome is to rule out any further loans. I do not therefore think that there have been any recent examples of such bankruptcies. What does happen is that the security is left forever in the hands of the lender, but in such a case the only person who is despoiled is the borrower. For the same reason, it is very difficult to inflict a serious injury on merchants; for a man from whom one has taken a hundred francs by force will refuse, later on, to lend a thousand in a case of urgent need—and not only will he give nothing, but his fellow merchants will do likewise, out of esprit de corps.

The Persian merchant does not pay a penny in taxes. He sells all sorts of things: silks, cotton fabrics, porcelain, crystal ware, spices, goods from Europe and Asia. He carries out banking and brokerage, and no taxes or duties are levied on such operations. He is regarded as a capitalist. What he has to pay is rent on his shop to the bazaar owner; nothing else.

The horror in which Oriental nations hold precision strongly marks commercial usage. I have already said that the Persian merchant is almost always strictly honest. No doubt—but he does not feel obliged to pay a bill of exchange when it falls due. If this does happen occasionally, it is because of a certain feeling of self-respect. In fact, such action is not regarded as an obligation, and the soundest and most respectable people do not feel committed to it, unless they have given an oral or written promise which binds their conscience. In such circumstances, the creditor easily grants a delay, merely raising the interest rate. As this rate is almost always 24 percent, it is raised to 30—I have seen debts on which the interest rate has thus reached 60 percent. Often, in such circumstances, the debtor declares that he is incapable of repaying the capital and of meeting such high interest. It is true that the law authorizes expropriation, but as it does so with repugnance, and imposes many restrictions, this is an extremity to which one cannot resort without damaging one's reputation. One does it, so to speak, only as an act of vengeance, if one has personal reasons for complaint against the behavior of the debtor. Most frequently, however, payment is put off once again, without increasing the interest rate; or else the creditor is satisfied with one more payment [*une somme une fois payée*] which, added to what has already been recovered, is equal to the original capital plus a reasonable profit. This kind of agreement does not spot the reputation of either party, and does honor to the creditor.

From the point of view of morality, it would perhaps be wrong to judge this mode of behavior with the rigor of our commercial principles. This kind of easy-going behavior does not stop Persian merchants from acting in good faith in their business dealings. As proof, I would adduce the trust with which these same merchants act. I have seen one of them, following an oral request, send 18,000 francs in gold, in a sealed silk bag, and tear up the receipt he was given, declaring that he was offended by this way of doing things. When I was in Tehran, I received from Hamadan—which is seven days' journey away—through a muleteer, a parcel containing 3,000 francs' worth of old medals. I had never heard of the man who sent me that parcel. In other words, he did not distrust either his muleteer or an unknown European, which to me seems to be the most convincing proof of his own honesty.

Thus the merchants live within Persian society with almost no obligations toward it, in an environment marked by a fairly great degree of liberty. The same is true, in many respects, of the main handicrafts. The latter are grouped in corporations, *Esnafs*, which have their officers, as the merchants have theirs. These officers are elected by and from their members. They have assemblies to discuss matters of interest. They have

funds and a treasurer. The master craftsmen are designated after examination. In a word, it is Saint Louis's organization, or rather the organization which Saint Louis had found and which he regulated, and which our merchants owed to the Romans, who in turn owed it to Asia, where it has remained, as everything remains. The handicrafts pay nothing to the government, and the only tax levied on craftsmen is raised by the craftsmen themselves, and its proceeds go to their fund. As a matter of fact, they do pay a duty designed to meet the common expenses of the bazaar, but it is only a small sum. It is clear that these organized corporations are backed, on the one hand, by the merchants for whom they work and, on the other, by the *mullahs* who, their prestige requiring that they be surrounded by the masses, are glad to take up the interests of apprentices, craftsmen [*artisans*], and even master craftsmen. In normal times, the Persian craftsman lives very quietly: the laws protect him and demand nothing from him. The government and administration can hurt him only by acting in an illegal way.

The Persian worker is able, ingenious, skillful and, in his way, even hard-working. I say in his way because he has no intention of letting his work impose on him the much greater labor to which his European counterparts subject themselves. The idea of spending twelve to fifteen hours on the job does not appeal to him, and no one would, anyway, think of imposing on him such pains. Moreover, subdivision as known to us does not exist, and each craftsman completes, by himself, both the constituent parts of the product and the product itself. As a result, he has some of the whims, the pleasure, the imaginative activity, and, it must be admitted, the carelessness common to artists. For our part, we obtain immense commercial results by dividing the making of a pin—and still more that of a watch—between a large number of workmen, each of whom has a speciality which he never forsakes. All of them acquire astonishing faculties of precision and speed of work;

they produce in incomparable abundance and with mechanical perfection; but they become a kind of machine themselves, and neither their intelligence nor their real and reflective liking for the craft they exercise gains anything from this system. Speculation and production may make great profits, but man certainly loses by it. Nothing surprises and disconcerts a European more than asking him to do something which falls ever so little outside the habits of his daily routine. He almost gets indignant at the thought, and his first answer is that it is impossible. I know I am going against the current view, but anyone not seized by systematic admiration for the working class and who has tried to get something unusual done, will agree that the Parisian workers (who nevertheless are regarded as paragons of skill) show both ill will and clumsiness—a double obstacle which can be overcome only by dint of patience, repeated attempts, and money.

The Persian workman, on the contrary, is always attracted by the thought of a kind of work he has never done before. He eagerly gets down to work, quickly gathers what is wanted of him, and carries it out with an astonishing amount of intelligence and promptness. He is particularly fond of copying European products: I have seen tables, chairs, armchairs, wardrobes, and windows perfectly made by men who were almost at their first try. In Shiraz and Isfahan, the English type of knives are made—a common, very low-priced product which is so well turned out that even the word London is not missing on the blade. I have seen a locksmith for whom this was a completely new kind of work make spurs with screws [éperons à vis] after a British model put before him; his copy was so good that, except for the quality of the iron, the Persian product was at least as good as the English, and moreover was one-third cheaper.

But for things to be done this way satisfactorily, they must either be rushed through or not take too long. Anything that demands continuity, sustained work, and persistence devoid of the excitement caused by novelty is almost certain to be given up long before completion. The Persian worker enjoys his work—which ours does not—but he is also liable to get bored with it, and in such cases it is extremely difficult to hold him down to it and to make him see it through. I hardly need say that if, by misfortune, he has been paid in advance, one can be almost certain that the work will never be completed.

It would seem that formerly—I mean a hundred or a hundred and fifty years ago—the industrial population of Iran was very considerable. At that time there was a large production of silks, velvets, taffetas, and brocades in Kashan, Isfahan, Rasht, and Yazd. Weapons were made in Kirman and Shiraz, calicos [*indiennes*] were woven almost everywhere, and beautiful copper ware, famous throughout the East, was turned out. Last, there were many other branches of manufacture, among which one cannot fail to mention many kinds of carpets. Today, all this is far from having survived, but nevertheless a little remains of everything. [See 6:2, 3.] This little keeps a certain number of craftsmen, and could be easily increased were it not for the factors which operate, in all the various countries of Asia, to destroy industrial activity. But these factors, which I shall discuss later, are so strong that it is not sufficiently profitable to become a workman and, consequently, people of this class often prefer to take up a profession which is the usual refuge of all penniless adventurers, of all unemployed domestic servants, and, to tell the truth, to a certain extent of everyone at some time: brokerage.

This occupation seems to be admirably suited to the Persian spirit. It requires sharpness, cunning, a kind of eloquence, and a persuasiveness of sterling quality, patience, and some knowledge of the human heart. It is a school of experience, and hence of wisdom. All Persians, but especially those of Isfahan and Shiraz, are born *dallals*, or brokers. Everyone sells or pawns what he owns. When I say everyone I mean everyone. The king pawns his jewels, his wives pawn their ornaments; the scholar borrows on his books and the landowner on his estates.

There are no men or women who are without debts, and there is perhaps nobody who is so indebted that he in turn does not have his debtors. When people buy any object—a suit, a jewel, a pot—they ask themselves, no doubt, whether it is suitable for the use to which it will be put, but above all they are careful to see that it is fit for pawning or selling. During the year there are certain distinct occasions when half the town lends money to the other half, or gives it money in this way. The high point is the feast of Nawruz, the New Year's day; the second is Muharram, when theatrical presentations are given. And all occasions of joy or mourning, whether public or private (and God knows they are not lacking), especially the former, are, for a people whose main and constant occupation is enjoyment, circumstances in which we see everyone setting about to get money. Brokers run here and there, carrying large parcels and accosting people in the streets or in their houses with a look which is half important, half confidential, which is peculiar to them and which would lead one to believe that, out of sheer philanthropy, they are selling at a miserable price the riches of the universe.

I have had dealings with *dallals*, which have surely not always been good for my purse. But the truth compels me to confess that they have their uses for devotees of curios, and that no one could be more amusing. I would like to express to two members of this corporation—who will surely never read these pages—my gratitude for the pleasant moments I have spent with them. May Nasrullah always find easy-going buyers and may his crony, Ustadh Agha, find undemanding sellers. The first is from Isfahan, but the second is from Shiraz, and it is difficult to know which of these clever fellows deserves the crown. I have had a few minor misunderstandings with Ustadh Agha, whereas not the slightest cloud has ever marked my relations with Nasrullah. One day, when we could not easily agree over a deal, I suspected him—no doubt wrongly— of taking more than usual advantage of my credulity and called him by the current "son of a burnt father." This expression, which is widely used, means that the father of the person one is addressing is burning in hell because of his misdeeds. "Sir," replied Nasrullah with a sweet look, "do me the honor to call me what you choose, I shall feel honored by it, but not in that way because it makes me sad. If my father were alive, I would say nothing, but he is dead, and you understand. . . ." I admired Nasrullah's delicacy and, in return for the favor I was making, asked him to bring down his price a little, which he did not.

One can say that the whole nation has had a taste of, is tasting, or will taste the broker's calling, and is none the worse for it. Thus, as I have already said, people are as quick to lend money as to borrow. The sovereign lends to the government, notables lend to subjects, merchants lend to notables, servants to their master, masters to their servants, officers to soldiers, soldiers to officers, the bazaar crowd lends to and borrows from itself—in a word, it is Panurge's ideal. This state of affairs seems at first inexplicable, when one realizes that in this pandemonium no one is in the least inclined to honor his debt. Signatures, as we say, or seals, as they use, are handed out as long as there are people willing to take them; but to withdraw from circulation these witnesses of a debt is something to which little attention is given. The result of all this is, no doubt, much disorder but little misery. A creditor who forces the sale of his debtor's furniture is regarded as a monster. The whole quarter bands against him and he can no longer enjoy any peace. It is therefore better to lose what one has lent than to recover it by violent means. Hence, it is easy to see that a man covered with debts in Tehran is far removed from the difficult and unfortunate situation of his counterpart in Paris. His friends and neighbors pity him; his creditors seek to improve his situation, so that he can earn something and hand them part of it; in a word, he bears the day's burden quite cheerfully. . . .

The habits of frenzied usury, of constant

debts, of expedients, of lack of good faith, and of prodigies of skill provide much fun to Persians but do not contribute to raising their moral level. The life of all this world is spent in a movement of perpetual intrigue. Everyone has only one idea: not to do what he ought. Masters do not pay their men, who rob them as best they can. The government does not pay its officials, or pays them in paper, and the officials rob the government. From top to bottom of the social hierarchy, there is a measureless and unlimited knavery —I would add an irremediable knavery. This pleases everybody, benefits each one in turn, makes it possible to avoid much trouble, allows everyone to indulge in much idleness, and constitutes a game which, keeping active minds alert, accustoms them to an excitement they could not easily do without. The Amir-i Nizam [Mirza Taqi Khan, see 6:6], as I said previously, paid officials regularly, but strictly forbade corruption. There was general discontent. What proportion is there between, on the one hand, being paid one hundred tumans with great regularity and, on the other, catching only sixty, with unimaginable trouble but at the same time having, perhaps, the prospect of picking up, here and there, two hundred more, by means of many fine and skillful tricks? That is the hope; as for the reality, after having taken ten times as much trouble as would have been necessary to be honest, it usually happens that the clever official only just manages to make, by the end of the year, the hundred tumans to which he is legally entitled. But are we to reckon as nothing the hopes, the castles in Spain, the thousand intrigues he has enjoyed the whole year round and the knaveries which made him laugh so much when he related them to his friends? As imagination plays an enormous part in the happiness of Orientals, two equal sums, one acquired by lawful means and the other picked up here and there, are to them incomparable. All schoolboys, the whole world over, would agree with them. . . .

## Wages and Standard of Living

References to the standard of living in Iran are scanty and inconclusive. In 1840, a French report on Azerbaijan put the daily wages of a master craftsman (*maître ouvrier*) at 1.29 to 2.90 francs, or about 1 kran 12 shahis to 3 krans 13 shahis; that of an unskilled laborer (*manoeuvre*) was 40 to 60 centimes, or $\frac{1}{2}$ to $\frac{3}{4}$ kran, "i.e., twice as much as their expenditure on food."[1]

In 1878, the British consul in Rasht stated:

In India it has been calculated that the income of the native peasantry is, on an average, £2 a year. In Ghilan it is no less than from £5 to £9. The principal food of the peasantry is rice, of which they produce an abundance of a very fair quality, and at a very low price. The women are mostly employed in the cultivation of this grain. Meat is cheap, 3d. being paid per pound for mutton, and 1½d. for beef. The clothing of the villager in summer is scanty, consisting in dyed cotton wares and no shoe leather; in winter he wears a homespun woollen cloth of a very coarse but substantial quality.[2]

It should be remembered that Gilan was an exceptionally prosperous province.

As regards wages, in 1872, in Rasht day laborers were paid 8 to 10 shahis (4–5d.), and carpenters and masons 2 krans (1s. 8d.).[3] And in 1878, agricultural

[1] Report dated 29 January 1840, AE Téhéran, vol 1.
[2] "Rasht," A and P 1878, 74.
[3] W. G. Abbott, "Report on the Condition of the Industrial Classes in Resht," A and P 1872, 62.

wages were "on an average 3d. a day, but they are entitled to rations and other advantages which, in money value, make up an income of 6d. a day"[4]—or say $\frac{3}{4}$ kran. In 1893, laborers in Rasht earned 1 kran (6$\frac{3}{4}$d.), tilers 1$\frac{1}{2}$ and masons and carpenters 2$\frac{1}{2}$.[5] This would imply a slight rise for unskilled and a slight decline for skilled labor. In the next five years prices rose very sharply (see 8:1), and the British consul in Rasht estimated that "expenses have risen by at least 100 per cent," but he also stated that "carpenters', masons', and labourers' wages that were 2$\frac{1}{2}$ krans for the two former and 1 kran for the latter have increased by just 100 per cent."[6]

On the other hand the consul in Tabriz reported:

The prices of the prime necessaries of life have increased by bounds since my last report, and at the death of the late Shah, the lower classes in Tabreez were at starvation point. . . . Their wants are few, a little "sangak," a native bread, and a bit of cheese will satisfy them, but their power to procure these must be decreasing day by day.[7]

A figure of 1 kran per day for unskilled labor seems to have been fairly widespread in Iran around 1890. It is quoted for both the Ahwaz area and Mashad in that year.[8] On the other hand, in Sistan, where "the necessaries of life are cheap," labor was "also at most seasons of the year very cheap, the latter due to there being no factories or other employment beyond that of agriculture," and as late as 1908, common laborers earned only $\frac{1}{2}$ to $\frac{3}{4}$ kran per day, masons 2$\frac{1}{2}$ to 4 krans, carpenters 3 to 4, blacksmiths 2 to 3, and children in carpet factories 1 kran 2 shahis. Wages in neighboring Birjand were somewhat higher.[9]

For the period 1890–1906 the following information on wages in Mashad is available (in krans).[10]

In the interval, prices had risen sharply and the consul's opinion was that "the rate of wages has also risen, but not to the same extent."

Some data on wage rates shortly before the First World War, gathered by Abdullaev from Russian archives, may also be quoted:[11] In a silk reeling factory in Rasht, wages were 1$\frac{1}{2}$ to 3 krans a day for men, $\frac{1}{2}$ to $\frac{3}{4}$ for women and 7 shahis for children. Among weavers, men earned around 1$\frac{1}{2}$ krans, women 1 kran, and children $\frac{1}{2}$ kran; miners earned around 3 krans. The Caspian fisheries paid Persians

---

[4] "Rasht," A and P 1878, 74.
[5] Ibid., 1893–94, 95.
[6] Ibid., 1898, 97.
[7] "Tabriz," A and P 1897, 92.
[8] Gordon, "Report," A and P 1890–91, 84; "Mashad," A and P 1890, 76.
[9] "Sistan and Qain," A and P 1908, 94.
[10] "Mashad," A and P 1890, 76; ibid., 1892, 83; ibid., 1906, 127.

|  | 1890 | 1902/3 | 1905/6 |
|---|---|---|---|
| Mason . . | 2 | 4 | 7$\frac{1}{2}$ |
| Carpenter | 3 | 3 | 6 |
| Blacksmith | 1$\frac{1}{2}$ | 2 | 5 |
| Laborer . . | 1 | 1 | 2 |
| Writer . . | 10 tumans a month | | |

[11] Abdullaev, pp. 224–30.

about 2 krans and Russians 5 and the lumbering industry 3–5 and 10 krans, respectively. Unskilled workers on the Enzeli-Qazvin road received 2 krans.

These figures may be supplemented by others taken from British consular reports. In Shiraz, "it ranges from $1\frac{1}{2}$ krans (7d.) to 4 krans (1s. 7d.) for skilled day labour."[12] In Kermanshah, the rate of unskilled labor was 1 to $1\frac{1}{2}$ krans.[13] In Bushire, in 1907, "except during the months of harvest, April and May, the current rate of hire of labour was from $1\frac{1}{2}$ krans ($6\frac{1}{2}$d.) for a labourer to $3\frac{1}{2}$ krans (1s. 3d.) for a mason."[14] However, by 1913, the greater demand for labor because of the extension of cultivation, building in the town and increased navigation, as well as the "exodus of large number of the labouring class made labour expensive." Masons earned 3 to 5 krans, carpenters 3 to 4, laborers on shore 2, and coolies on board ships $1\frac{1}{2}$ plus food.[15]

Last, two judgments by British missions that visited Iran in 1904 may be quoted. Labor was said to be "dearer than Indian,"[16] and one may presume that the level of living in Iran was above that of India. As regards the trend

I believe there is, on the whole, a distinct improvement in the condition of the people. . . prices having risen, the cost of living must have increased. But prices of labour and produce appear to have risen in proportion. Information obtained at the various places visited usually tended to show that the peasant is somewhat less hardly treated by landlord and taxgatherer, and is better clothed and better fed than formerly, and that more land has been brought under cultivation. Of course these circumstances have varied in different localities: in parts of the south, elsewhere referred to, extreme hardship has been reported, and in Ghilan and Khorassan unusual prosperity.[17]

To draw a general conclusion is almost impossible. One may presume that, as in other countries, craftsmen (more particularly weavers) suffered a decline in real wages because of machine competition, and the wage rates for 1840, quoted above, lend some support to this view (see also 2:7). One also gets the impression that, on the whole, the wages of unskilled labor failed to keep pace with the very sharp rise in prices, but this can only be presented as a tentative surmise.

[12] "Shiraz," A and P 1909, 97.
[13] "Kermanshah," A and P 1911, 94.
[14] "Bushire," A and P 1908, 114.
[15] Ibid., 1913, 71.
[16] Gleadowe-Newcomen, p. 12.
[17] MacLean, A and P 1904, 95, p. 9.

## Selection 5. Bourgeoisie and Working Class, 1900s

[Z. Z. Abdullaev, *Promyshlennost i zarozhdenie rabochego klassa Irana v kontse XIX-nachale XX vv.* (Baku, 1963) pp. 32–42, 158–60, 183–92]

. . . Traders and merchants, who constituted a significant part of the urban population, played a major role in the life of Iranian towns. Small and medium traders represented a force which brought into being commercial relations between town and village. The process of class stratification of Iranian society, notwithstanding its slowness, promoted the further development of the local merchant class. In addition, the years of famine and increased demand for certain agricultural products accelerated this development by centralizing capital.

Not infrequently the trading functions were performed by rich landlords settled in towns. As Atrpet points out: "In the shortest time many owners of villages appropriated almost all the riches of the country and became large capitalists" (he means landlords—Z.A.). "Until 1880," he continues, "there were few millionaires and rich property owners but in 1900 one could count them in hundreds."[1] Such landowners, by constantly accumulating produce in storehouses, artificially raised prices and made huge fortunes.

High government officials also carried out similar operations. "Until now not one of the governors of Kirman had made such a fortune as did Bahjat-al-Mulk. . . . All local products—starting with wheat, barley, peas, lentils, cotton, wool, butter, etc., and including poppy seeds and opium plantations —were bought by him and kept in storehouses to be sold in winter at three times the price."[2] Kosagovskii [sic] gives convincing examples of the buying up of grain by the representatives of notables (*volmozh*), closely connected with court circles, and also by the clergy of Azerbaijan.[3]

As a result of such machinations the price of agricultural produce rose every year. According to Atrpet, whereas until 1870 a Kharvar of wheat (*khleb*) cost 2 tumans, by 1895 it cost 4 tumans. The evidence indicates that at the end of the nineteenth century and the beginning of the twentieth prices rose faster than before. In 1895–1905 the price of wheat rose sixfold.[4]

With the development of trade the role of local merchants gained importance in operations dealing with such valuable products as silk, rice, and opium. The merchants

of Gilan, trading in silk, by the beginning of the twentieth century competed with West European and Russian merchants.[5] Among the most powerful Iranian merchants one may mention Hajji Mamed Hasan Amin az-Zarb, whose business was carried on after his death, in 1896, by his son Hajji Mamed Husain. The fortune of this family was put at 25 million tumans. The family also carried out banking operations and showed much interest in investing capital in industry and in other commercial enterprises. Amin az-Zarb engaged in a widespread trade in many foreign markets. In all the main towns of Iran he had agents both for the purchase and sale of goods and for the taking of deposits, transfer of money, and other banking operations. He owned real estate not only in Iran but also in Moscow and Nizhni Novgorod. Amin az-Zarb had a large trading office in Marseilles, agencies in London, Paris, and China, and correspondents in many cities of Europe, Asia, and America.[6] Kosagovskii states that most of the large money transactions involving foreigners were concluded directly with the elder Amin az-Zarb.[7] Ten years before the expiration of the Imperial Bank's concession, Hajji Mamed Hasan already had proposed to the shah the creation of a government bank, in which both government and private capital would participate. But this wise suggestion met with no official response from court circles.[8]

We do not know of any other representative of national capital comparable to Amin az-Zarb. In the large commercial-industrial towns there were also big merchants who carried out substantial commercial and even banking operations. Among them was Hajji Mamed Ismail Magazi of Tabriz, who exercised very great influence in Tehran and took an active part

---

[1] Atrpet, *Mamed Ali Shah* (Alexandropol, 1909) p. 141.
[2] Ts. G.V.I.A. (Central State Military-Historical Archives) f. 76, d. 190. l. 14.
[3] [V. A. Kosogovskii], *Iz tegeranskogo dnevnika polkovnika V. A. Kosogovskogo*, [G. M. Petrov. ed., Moscow, 1960] p. 169.
[4] Atrpet, pp. 138–40.

[5] S. Olferev, *Shelkovodstvo v Gilane v 1904–1905 gg.*, SKD, [*Collection of Consular Reports*], 1905, vyp. 6, p. 454.
[6] Ts. G.I.A.L. (Central State Historical Archives in Leningrad), f. 560, op. 28, d. 362, l. 9; ibid., d. 206, l. 12.
[7] Kosogovskii, p. 119.
[8] *Tarikhche si saleh Bank-i Milli Iran*, (1307–37), (Tehran), p. 65.

in uniting the richest and most influential merchants and bankers.[9]

The financial king of southern Iran was Hajji Agha Mohamed Muin-Tujjar, whose real estate around Ahwaz and on the Persian Gulf coast was put at one million tumans. He invested part of his capital in ocher mining, carried on a large business in India and London, and was closely connected with the British.[10] Another merchant, Hajji Mamed Tagi Shahrudi, was also reputed to be very rich, had a large import and export business with Russia, and showed interest in participating in various industrial and other entrepreneurial activities.[11] The representative of Iranian Zoroastrians, Arbab Jamshid, who raised himself from an apprentice tailor to become one of the biggest bankers in Tehran, carried on commercial and banking business in the whole of Iran.[12] Hajji Malik-Tujjar, a leading merchant not only in Tehran but in the whole of Azerbaijan, carried much influence and weight in the commercial world of Iran.[13]

As a result of the increasing involvement of Iran in the world capitalist market at the beginning of the twentieth century, the number of the representatives of large Iranian traders in the various world capitals rose appreciably. In this period the process of specialization among traders was accentuated; whereas an Iranian trader had usually dealt at the same time in cotton, grain, and cloth, his commercial business now began to be limited to separate specialized fields. Each one handled either cotton or other products which played an important part in the country's commercial life.[14] The capital of large merchants did not usually exceed 50,000–100,000 tumans,[15] and in local markets medium and small merchants were clearly predominant.

In spite of the dominance of feudalism, objective conditions furthered the development of an internal, common, national [obshchenatsionalnogo] market. This process was accentuated by the impoverishment of the peasants, the ruin of the small producers, the development of market and monetary relationships in the country, and the specialization of various regions. Economic links existed between the various provinces, in spite of serious obstacles. A. Miller wrote, "Sistan could not survive without imported goods."[16] However, the dominance of subsistence [naturalnogo] economy in the villages, the slow separation of industry from agriculture, and the weakness of capitalist forms of production seriously impeded the formation of an internal market. This in turn adversely affected the process of capital accumulation in industry and of production on a large scale [rasshirennogo vosproizvodstva].

The formation of an internal market, although slow, had immense importance for both the development of the economy and the further involvement of Iran in the system of the world capitalist market. It is significant that, starting in the 1880s, various national companies and societies began to appear in Iran, carrying on a vast business in internal and foreign markets. Thus in 1882, on the initiative of Mashadi Kazem Amin, the "Aminie" company was formed, and came to enjoy a high reputation.[17] Around 1886, the "Commercial Company of Iran" was formed, with a capital of 350,000 tumans.[18] In 1892 the "Mansurie" company was formed in Yazd.[19] Approximately four years later the "Fars" company was founded in Shiraz, under the direction of Hajji Abd al-Rahim Shirazi; it continued to function until the end of the period under study.[20]

In 1897 the well-known merchant Hajji Mahdi Kuzekunani, with the help of his brothers and with the participation of Hajji

[9] Ts. G.I.A.L. f. 560, op. 28, d. 362, l. 29.
[10] Ibid., f. 560, op. 82, d. 362, l. 35; Ahmad Kasravi, Tarikh-i pansad saleh Khuzistan, 3d ed., (Tehran, 1330), p. 253.
[11] Ts. G.I.A.L., f. 560, op. 82, d. 362, l. 36.
[12] Ibid., f. 560, op. 28, d. 362, l. 58.
[13] Kosogovskii, pp. 140–42.
[14] Ts. G.I.A.L., f. 560, op. 28, d. 362, ll. 23–24.
[15] AVPR (Archives of Foreign Policy of Russia). f. "Persidskii stoll," d. 1899, ll. 27–28.

[16] A. Miller, Proshloe i nastoyashchee Sistana, ocherk. (Saint Petersburg, 1907), p. 15.
[17] Jamalzadeh, Ganj-i Shaigan, p. 98.
[18] Tarikhche, p. 52.
[19] Ganj-i Shaigan, p. 98.
[20] Tarikhche, p. 52.

Sayyid Murtaza Sarraf, founded in Tabriz the "Ettehad" company, which survived for about fifteen years.[21]

In 1898, on the initiative of the well-known merchant Hajji Muhammad Husain Kazeruni, the "Masudie" company was constituted in Isfahan; it undertook commercial and banking operations. At the same time, those same entrepreneurs founded, also in Isfahan, the "Islamie" company, with a capital of 150,000 tumans; its functions included widespread distribution of native textiles [22] In 1899, seventeen Tehran merchants and *sarrafs* (money changers) founded the "Omumi," whose capital was one million tumans. This company carried out internal and external trade and banking operations; five years later it broke up, owing to discord among its members.[23] In Kosagovskii's diary there is an entry concerning the formation by a group of influential capitalist-*sarrafs* and banking houses of Tehran including the Tumaniants brothers, Hajji Lutf Ali, Etade, Hajji Bagir, Malik Tujjar, and others of a similar syndicate designed to counteract the British Imperial Bank.[24] This syndicate succeeded in taking advantage of the dissatisfaction of the masses with the activities of the Imperial Bank, and gave the British a serious fright.

On the basis of the above-mentioned facts, one may state that the 1880s saw the appearance of the first national, united, merchant capital investment, engaged in large-scale internal and foreign trade. In this period the first attempts were made by the nascent national bourgeoisie to restrict the dominance of foreign capital in Iran.

The rise of trading and banking companies and societies was not accidental; they began to appear even in the smaller towns. Thus in Soujbulag there was the "Soujbulagi" firm and in Shahrud there were six local firms dealing exclusively in trade with Russia.[25]

Along with this, merchants engaged in the same line often formed a syndicate and thus subjected the market to their own interest. For instance, in Gilan cocoon prices were set in each locality by the syndicate of silkworm breeders.[26] According to Atrpet, in Azerbaijan the large landowners formed a syndicate and set the prices for wheat (*khleb*).[27] During the First World War, a committee "Ittihad-i tujjar" was active, headed by the above-mentioned Amin az-Zarb.[28]

In this period, merchant capital no longer played the part of a simple intermediary, exchanging the goods made by small producers and participating in the realization by landowners of part of the surplus product appropriated by them. Iranian merchants more and more actively took part in buying up goods from small producers and reselling them.

National capital was an indispensable source for the financing of large commercial operations. In this respect a definite part was played by the *sarrafs*, who represented an original banking institution, carrying out banking operations within their region, over the whole country, and sometimes even in foreign lands. Several of the above-mentioned trading firms and companies simultaneously performed the functions of *sarrafs*. In addition, the trading house of "Jahanian," founded in Yazd in 1890, also carried out banking operations. The history of this firm is a clear example of the transformation of merchants—engaged in farming and trading in cotton—into modern bankers, to whose services even the central government resorted.[29] The trading house of Tumaniants, along with import and export business and farming, was engaged in large banking operations. This enterprise, which played an important part in the economic life of Iran, arose out of the small shop of Haratun Tumaniants [an Armenian], founded in the

[21] Ibid., p. 53; in *Ganj-i Shaigan*, p. 98, the date of foundation is mistakenly given as 1887.

[22] *Ganj-i Shaigan*, p. 98; AVPR, d. 3869, ll. 51, 52, 109.

[23] *Tarikhche*, p. 53.

[24] Kosogovskii, pp. 139–41.

[25] Benderev, *Astrabad-Bastamskii raion Persii* (Ashkhabad, 1904) p. 193; AVPR, d. 1899, l. 27.

[26] A. Shritter, *Shelkovodstvo v Gilane v 1906*, (SKD 1907), vyp. IV, p. 317.

[27] Atrpet, p. 141.

[28] Ts. G.V.I.A., f. 13185, op. 3, d. 4, l. 67.

[29] *Tarikhche*, p. 50.

middle of the nineteenth century in Tabriz, which exported dried fruits and cocoons and imported metal wares.[30] The activity and development of this firm, as also that of Jahanian, shows that significant amounts of capital could be concentrated by entrepreneurs engaged in trade in dried fruits, cocoons, silk, cotton, and other goods, the demand for which rose constantly on world markets. The Tumaniants (there were four brothers), understanding the importance of trade in these goods, established their own farms, which gave them further possibilities for getting rich. The success of Tumaniants enabled them to acquire a fortune approaching 3 million tumans, to spread their activity in Russia, and even to compete with the Imperial Bank.[31] In order to secure normal conditions for the development of their enterprise, the Tumaniants brothers became Russian subjects, which played a not unimportant role [in their success].

The above-mentioned trading house of "Jamshidian," representing the Zoroastrians of Yazd, enjoyed considerable influence. Its head, Arbab Jamshid, began in textile trade, soon set up business as a sarraf, established branches in Shiraz and Kirman, and had representatives in Baghdad, Bombay, Calcutta, and Paris. He was elected a member of the First Majlis and, in his capacity of large banker, had business dealings with the government and representative notables. Like other trading enterprises, "Jamshidian" also invested a certain amount of capital in agriculture, and bought large plots of land around Tehran and also in Khurasan and Fars. However, this firm did not take account of its limitations, and as a result, being unable to meet its commitments to the Discount and Loan Bank and the Imperial Bank, went bankrupt in 1915.[32]

Alongside the above-mentioned large sarrafs, who were at the same time engaged in trade, there were in the large towns groups of small and medium sarrafs, whose activity was more limited. Thus for example, according to Curzon, in Mashad there were 114 sarrafs and moneylenders, whose aggregate capital was 931,000 tumans. Among them only two had 100,000 tumans, five had from 30,000 to 50,000, and the capital of the others was insignificant.[33]

Notwithstanding the fact that the institution of sarrafs continued to develop in the face of serious obstacles, it could not meet the needs and demands of the Iranian economy. The Imperial Bank and the Discount and Loan Bank constituted the main and fundamental obstacles in their path. In addition, the struggle between Britain and Russia for domination over the financial system of Iran, which took place mainly with the help of these banks, had adverse effects on government finance and the rate of the rial.

The attempts of the Iranian bourgeoisie during the first years of the Constitutional Period (the revolution of 1905–11) to found a national bank of Iran expressed the desire to create a native bank for the financing of trade and industry, in order to break the constantly increasing domination of the foreign banks over the Iranian economy.[34]

The absence of normal conditions for the development of a national bourgeoisie and the situation created by the increasing penetration of foreign capital and the dominance of feudal relationships made it seem expedient for the bourgeoisie to invest in farming, whose products (cotton, opium, etc.) were in great demand in world markets. Thus, as a result of the dominance of foreign banks, the resources of the nascent Iranian bourgeoisie became a powerful instrument of the colonial policy and were directed to the production of agricultural raw materials required by the industry of capitalist countries. Through loans and banks, foreigners subjected the whole financial system of Iran to their control, and Iranian national capital itself was put in a dependent position. This had a disastrous effect on the process of

[30] Ibid., p. 47.
[31] Ibid., pp. 49–50.
[32] Ibid., pp. 51–52; Ts. G.I.A.L., f. 560, op. 28, d. 362, l. 58.

[33] Curzon, Persia, 1: 167–68.
[34] Tarikhche, pp. 75–81.

primitive accumulation of capital, and more generally on the character of the bourgeoisie. Nonetheless, the period between the 1880s and the First World War saw definite progress in the process of primitive accumulation of capital in Iran, conditioned by the drawing of the country into the orbit of the world capitalist market and by other factors.

Regarding the foreign bourgeoisie and its position, it is necessary also to consider the place and function of foreign capital in Iranian trade. The main factor accounting for the successful penetration of foreign capital in the sphere of trade was the privileges and possibilities which arose out of the system of capitulations forced upon Iran and which opened wide the door to foreign capital. At the same time, native merchants were subjected to numerous arbitrary taxes, which constituted serious obstacles to the formation of a national market. For instance, between Enzeli and Isfahan, road tax (*rahdari*) had to be paid in Rasht, Qazvin, Tehran, Qum, Kashan, and Isfahan, that is, six times. There were also other dues, which were in the nature of direct taxes (*kapandari*—weighing tax, etc.). Being exempt from internal duties and taxes of all kinds, foreign goods penetrated unhindered all towns and regions of Iran [see 3:2]. Thus, in the markets of that country foreign capital held a dominant position. For instance, the fate of such important local products as cotton, rice, cocoons, opium, tobacco, gum tragacanth, dried fruits, and carpets was mainly dependent on foreign firms. And if in this field local capital played only an auxiliary part, in the import trade, where foreign capital had undivided power, the situation was still more critical. Nevertheless the noticeable participation of Iran in world commodity exchange, although slow, had a positive influence on the transformation of the country's economy.

The needs of trade and economic development in Iran required the immediate destruction of feudal dispersion and the surviving medieval partition. The overcoming of feudal dispersion proceeded very slowly and entailed great difficulties. The

centralization of the government of the country at the hands of the feudal aristocracy, which had sold out to foreign capital, greatly limited the potentiality of the Iranian bourgeoisie and constituted an important obstacle in the path of its development.

In all parts of Iran the merchants suffered oppression at the hands of the governors and their officials. . . .

After 1911 the already slow rate of development of national industry in Iran slowed down even further. The enterprises that were started could not be counted even as medium industries, as regards their scope or importance. According to S. M. Jamalzadeh, in 1915 a brewery was founded in Tehran.[35] In the same year a cartridge factory was opened in the capital.[36] In Sabzevar, in 1912, a cotton ginnery belonging to Hajji Muhammad Ali Isfahani was in operation, in Barfurush the factory of Hajji Sayyid Husain, in Sari that of Amin az-Zarb; in 1915, in the Nishapur district, a cotton ginnery belonging to Ibadzadeh and Herati was built, with two 10 horse-power petrol engines and two gins.[37] According to certain indications, during the war a sugar refinery started operating in Mazandaran, but we have not been able to get confirmation of this.

The rapid course of political developments in Iran, the transformation of its territory into a war zone and the further loss of state sovereignty because of the venality of the ruling classes caused great damage to industry. A clear example of this is furnished by the fate of Amin az-Zarb and his enterprises. Hajji Muhammad Husain Amin az-Zarb was the richest and most influential Iranian merchant, with offices or representatives in Moscow, Nizhni Novgorod, Marseilles, London, and Paris, and with correspondents in numerous countries of Europe, America, and Asia. His fortune

[35] *Ganj-i Shaigan*, p. 95.
[36] Ts. G.I.A. F. Gruz. SSR (Archives of Georgian Republic) f. 521, op. 5, d. 487, l. 15.
[37] *Ganj-i Shaigan*, p. 95; Ts. G.I.A.L. f. 600, op. 10, d. 202, l. 61; Archives of MID (Ministry of Foreign Affairs) SSSR, f. 94, p. 15. d. 32/7, ll. 78–79.

was put at 25 million tumans.[38] Yet that very powerful merchant-banker-industrialist was deprived of the means of developing his enterprises by the dominance of feudalism and the sway of the imperialist powers. Already at the end of 1908, under the extortionate pressure of the shah, who constantly demanded large sums from him, Amin az-Zarb was forced to declare himself bankrupt. There were rumors that Amin az-Zarb had previously transferred his capital to a London bank. In addition, his business had been so bad that he owed the Discount and Loan Bank about 5 million rubles.[39]

On the eve of the First World War, Amin az-Zarb sold his silk reeling factory, which had cost him 300,000 tumans, to Muin Tujjar for 90,000. By the summer of 1916, the new owner no longer had the means and possibilities of exploiting the enterprise. With this objective, Muin Tujjar started negotiations with the Discount and Loan Bank, but we do not know the outcome.[40] The important point is that neither Amin az-Zarb nor the new owner of the silk factory was capable of assuring its operation. In the words of the then manager of the Discount and Loan Bank, on 18 July 1916: "For two months already the electric power station (of Amin az-Zarb) has not been functioning."[41] Around the same time another of his enterprises, a brick-making factory near Tehran, was closed down.[42] As Kucherbaev, the manager of the Barfurush branch of the Discount and Loan Bank, remarked, the younger Amin az-Zarb "did not extend, but on the contrary appreciably reduced the property left to him by his father, Hajji Muhammad Hasan."[43] This observation also holds true for the other properties of Amin az-Zarb, scattered in Gilan and other regions.

The example of Amin az-Zarb serves to trace the descending curve in the destiny of the nascent bourgeoisie which strove to invest part of its capital in national industry...

WORKING CLASS

In the sources and literature there are many direct references to the fact that the peasantry was the main source of the nascent Iranian proletariat. The history of the formation of the British oil monopoly in the south shows that the settled—and to a certain extent the nomadic—population of that area, as well as that of some of the inner regions, was the main source of hired, unskilled labor in the oil industry. Already in 1903, when work was confined to drilling, the Russian consul in Kermanshah reported: "Simple earthwork and various kinds of unskilled labor are carried out by the peasants of a certain Aziz Khan Badilian, whose horsemen are charged with the duty of guarding the whole camp."[44] The said peasants did not work as hired employees of the company—they evidently carried out the obligations imposed by Aziz Khan. This is quite possible, in view of the survival at that time of kinship-tribal relations among Iranian nomads. Nevertheless the involvement of nomads and seminomads as unskilled workers in an industrial enterprise was an objectively positive phenomenon in the development of Iranian society. But this process operated from above, without taking into account local conditions and the interests of the working people. Thus the author of *Naft va Khuzistan*[45] was right when he accused the British imperialists of having, by their activities, thwarted the development of the productive forces of Khuzistan, as a result of which the main parts of that region declined, forcing the inhabitants to seek some kind of work with APOC. Afshin states that even some peasants engaged in market gardening gave up farming and went to work in the English enterprise.

At the outbreak of the First World War, the Bakhtiaris, Arabs, and Persians constituted the mass of workers in such important

[38] Ts. G.I.A.L. f. 560, op. 28, d. 362, l. 9; ibid., d. 206, l. 12–12 ob.
[39] Ibid. f. 600, op. 9, d. 1,049, ll. 71, 78, 79, and 89.
[40] Ibid. f. 600, op. 10, d. 340, ll. 162, 167.
[41] Ibid., l. 162.
[42] Ganj-i Shaigan, p. 95.
[43] Ts. G.I.A.L. f. 600, op. 10, d. 324, l. 5.
[44] Ibid., f. 560, op. 28, d. 206, l. 47.
[45] Kazim Afshin, *Naft va Khuzistan* (Tehran, 1333) pp. 69, 117–21.

centers of the oil concession as Abadan, Masjid-i Sulaiman, Nasiri, Mamatain, and Muhammara.

Another document underscores the fact that the Abadan workers "have been constituted by the peasants of the inner provinces, who were unable to continue farming because of incessant oppression by the administration and, particularly, by the feudal leaders, who treat their peasants worse than did the barbarian, feudal Czars."[46] This valuable document shows, in addition, that before the establishment of the oil company, these peasants usually migrated to Basra and other Persian Gulf ports. The document also shows that, as the feudal yoke became heavier and peasants increasingly lost their lands, the movement of farmers to industry gained in strength.

A third document[47] shows that in the villages around Isfahan a large percentage of peasants were landless, and that these villages supplied unskilled labor to the oil industry in the south. According to that document, the Isfahan region provided over fifteen hundred oil workers. It is, however, necessary to draw attention to the following important aspect of the matter: not all the workers, and perhaps not even the majority, severed their ties with their village. As a rule, the families of these workers remained in the village and their members kept some relation with farming. This is understandable, for in a country like Iran, where the rise of industry had its own specific characteristics, one should not expect a speedy liquidation of the ties between the worker and his village. In addition one should note that part of the working force was occupied in industry only seasonally (e.g., in sugar refining and fishing). Thus, according to P. Rittikh, during the period of sugar refining (*varka*), which lasted two months, the Belgian factory in Kahrizeke engaged up to three hundred workers.[48] The seasonal

character of work in some branches impeded the formation of a regular cadre of workers. Nevertheless, bearing in mind the socioeconomic structure of Iranian society and the fact that the working class was just beginning to be formed, one must observe that seasonal work by peasants in industry represented a long step forward in the tearing away of the backward, oppressed, peasant from farming and his transfer to a new, progressive branch of production. The greatest calamity for the toiling masses of Iranian villages arose from the disproportion between the process of immiserization, on the one hand, and the absorption in industry of peasants ready to sell their labor, on the other. This disproportion, which was the real social catastrophe of Iranian society at the end of the nineteenth century and the beginning of the twentieth, can be explained by the strength of feudalism in the country and by the low level of development of productive forces and the slow formation of a local bourgeoisie, which determined, in the last analysis, the fate of the industrial buildup of Iran.

The second most important source for the formation of a working class was the handicraftsmen, who constituted the most highly qualified section of Iranian workers. In view of the increasing penetration of foreign goods in Iranian markets, native crafts could not escape the destructive influence exerted by the dominance of foreign capital in the country. Thus the production of various cotton, silk, and woolen textiles felt most strongly the competition of foreign goods [see 6:2,3]. Only carpet making, the production of opium, and a few other branches, in which foreign capital was interested, did not face dangerous competition [see chap. 6]. The other branches, passing through a great crisis due to foreign competition, constantly threw thousands of toilers onto the streets. Of course their number was incomparably smaller than that supplied by the villages, since peasants constituted 75 to 80 percent of the population. Moreover the very character of relations in the villages is distinguishable from that in the towns, for in the villages the

---

[46] Archives of MID SSSR, f. 94, op. 4, a.d. l, papka 10105, l. 302.

[47] Ibid., f. 94, op. 7a, d. 2, papka 107, l. 1.

[48] Rittikh, *Otchet*, part, p. 121.

process of immiserization proceeded more swiftly. . . .

Another source from which the working class drew its cadres was the mass of urban poor, who constituted an important part of the town population. Travelers' accounts abound in material showing that the streets and bazaars of Iranian towns, especially the large commercial centers, were overcrowded with poor and unemployed persons, ready to sell their labor for a piece of bread.

These facts show that, in the period under study, there were certain conditions favoring the birth and growth of an Iranian working class. It is another matter altogether that this process was not brought about by the development of the necessary and appropriate conditions for the right process of formation, qualitatively and quantitatively, of the working class of Iran. This led to the tragic situation in which, each year, hundreds of thousands of migrants in search of work were forced to go to other countries.

It seems to us that, without studying this question of migrants, it is impossible to understand correctly the essence of the birth of the working class in Iran. The increase in the force of migration from Iran to Russia was the result of the limited growth of the capitalist elements in Iran itself, together with the rapid development of capitalism in Russia, with its demand for a huge mass of cheap labor. This process acquired such a scope that the migration of tens of thousands of peasants, workers, and handicraftsmen to various parts of the Russian Empire, in search of work, became a common occurrence.

Let us consider the question of nonfarm migration within Iran itself. Unlike many European countries where capitalism grew rapidly, in Iran we do not see nonfarm workers migrating from one district to another not only because they do not find work in their own village but because they are looking for better conditions elsewhere. In Iran, where capitalism developed in very complex and difficult circumstances, the demand for labor lagged far behind the supply. In the period under study, poor peasants did not,

as a rule, find work in villages, and moved to the towns in search of a job. At that time, the demand for labor came from the oil industry in the south, the fishing industry on the Caspian, and from construction on roads, bridges, ports, and irrigation works.[49] It is known that among the fishermen of the southern Caspian shores many came from the Khalkhal district of Iranian Azerbaijan. Not a few workers on the Caspian and Persian Gulf coast came from the interior regions. A certain number worked as longshoremen, as employees in trading firms, or as servants in enterprises, institutions, or private houses. But such occupations were far removed from industrial production.

The complex of conditions prevailing in Iran caused a mass movement of Iranian poor to the southern parts of Russia. In addition, there was a migration from northeastern Iran to Herat and from the southeast and south to Karachi, Muscat, and even the Zanzibar islands.[50] There was also some migration to India and Turkey. The majority of Iranians going to these countries (except for Russia) did not find work in industry, for no significant industrial development had taken place there.

Migration to foreign countries from the northern provinces was on a much larger scale than that from other regions. This is explained by the fact that the bigger part of Iran's population was concentrated in the northern provinces and, what is very important, that the population of these provinces was at a higher economic and social level than that of southern and southeastern Iran. Hence migration acquired a massive character in these northern provinces. The available data and the interesting article of N. K. Belova show that a large part of migrants from the northern provinces went to Trans-

---

[49] On the causes of migration see the interesting document "The movement of population in the town of Maranda in Transcaucasia in search of work as a cause of rural crisis." AVPR, f. "Persidskii stol" d. 535, ll. 68–74.

[50] Ts. G.V.I.A. f. 2,000, op. 1, d. 3,760, l. 29; ibid. f. 76, d. 392, l. 9.

caucasia, especially to Azerbaijan.[51] The statistics on migration from Iran are very incomplete, for they covered only these who paid a tax at the consulate for an exit permit. A large number of poor people crossed the frontier secretly and naturally were not counted.

But even the fragmentary data point to the massive, and growing, scale of migration from Iran to Russia. For example in 1891, in Tabriz alone 26,855 visas were granted and by 1903 this figure had risen to 32,866. Of the visas given in 1904 in Tabriz and Urumiya, 54,846 went to unskilled workers.[52] According to L. Sobotsinskii, 193,000 persons left Iran for Russia in 1911.[53] We agree with N. Belova's estimate that, in 1905, the total number of Iranians crossing the border was not less than 300,000.[54]

Although a large number of migrants returned home—for example, in 1911, there were 193,000 emigrants from Iran but also 160,000 returning[55]—the process was so steady and advanced that, in Transcaucasia, there was a constant Iranian population of some hundreds of thousands, who in certain branches or enterprises already constituted the mass of workers. Consider the oil industry in [Russian] Azerbaijan: in 1893 there were 7,000 workers in that industry, of whom Iranian immigrants accounted for 11 percent; ten years later, the number of oil workers had risen to 23,500, of whom the Iranians formed 22.2 percent.[56] And by 1915 the Iranian share had risen to 29.1 percent (13,500 persons), and the Iranian immigrants occupied first place among the national groupings in the Baku oil industry.[57]

The clear rise in the Iranian component of the Baku proletariat shown by these figures is confirmed by the quite interesting study of I. V. Strigunov, *From the History of the Formation of the Baku Proletariat*. In the province of Elizavetpol, Iranians constituted the main working force in copper mining, and in 1912, in the copper-smelting plant of Kedabek, Iranian migrants accounted for 27.5 percent of permanent workers.[58] In G. Arutiunian's study, in connection with the strike which took place in 1906 in the copper mines and plants of Alaverdi, in Armenia, it is stated that about 2,500 Iranian Azerbaijanis constituted the basic core of strikers.[59]

Tens of thousands of Iranian poor found work in Tiflis, Batum, Ganje, and other towns and ports of Transcaucasia. For instance, in Tiflis the number of unskilled workers from Iran was 5,000 to 6,000.[60]

The number of migrants seeking work in the various parts of Central Asia was also significant. We cannot agree with N. Belova, who seeks to deny the mass character of migration from northeastern Iran to Central Asia. Of course migration from northwestern Iran was on a much larger scale than that from northeastern, but the fact remains that the latter also had a mass character, although it was impeded by certain forces: the difficulty of crossing the desert border regions, the danger of capture by the Turkman khans, the relatively small demand for labor in Central Asia, and so on. The evidence shows that Iranian workers also went to Central Asia by way of Transcaucasia. For example, A. M. Nikolskii reported in 1886: "In Baku our ship took on three hundred Persian workers, on their way to work on the Transcaspian railway."[61] We also have other data pointing to the movement of migrants from northwestern Iran to Central Asia. In Colonel Kosagovskii's papers there is a "Note on the Kurds"

[51] N. K. Belova "Ob otkhodnichestve iz severo-zapadnogo Irana, v kontse XIX—nachale XX veka," *Voprosy istorii*, 1956, no. 10, pp. 112–21.

[52] V. Minorskii, "Dvizhenie persidskikh rabochikh na promysly v Zakavkaze," Consular Reports of Ministry of Foreign Affairs, vyp. 3, Saint Petersburg, 1905, p. 206.

[53] Sobotsinskii, pp. 288–89.

[54] Belova, p. 114.

[55] Sobotsinskii, pp. 288–89.

[56] K. A. Pazhitnov, *Ocherki po istorii bakinskoi nefte-dobyvayushchei promyshlennosti* (Moscow, 1940), pp. 95–97 and tables 18 and 19.

[57] A. G. Rashin, *Formirovanie rabochego klassa Rossii* (Sotsekgiz, 1958) p. 516.

[58] Belova, p. 116.

[59] G. S. Arutiunian, *Iranskaya revolutsiya 1905–1911 gg. i Bolsheviki Zakavkaza* (Erevan, 1956), pp. 27–28.

[60] Belova, p. 116.

[61] A. M. Nikolskii, *Letnie poezdki naturalista* (Leningrad, 1924) p. 129.

which states that some Kurds of the Kaka-bend tribe, dwelling around Zanjan, "go to work in Gilan, Turkestan, to Herat, Marv, Bukhara and Samarkand."[62] The Caspian provinces attracted the poor even from distant Sistan. For example, in his report for 1900, the Russian vice-consul in Sistan, Miller, reports that the inhabitants of the village of Sikuhe "maintain relations with the Transcaspian region" and that each year 10,000 to 15,000 go to Marv and Ashkabad, where they work as repairmen on the railways. In this interesting report it is stated that in Marv there were people from the above-mentioned village who played the part of contractors and found work for their fellow villagers on the railway.[63] In the spring of 1903, Almazov, the physician of the Trubetskoi medical-observation post, brought to the attention of the chief of staff of the army of the Transcaspian region the depressed condition of the Iranian migrants in the Transcaspian regions.[64]

We agree with the conclusion of B. Mannanov regarding the mass character of migration from Khurasan to the Trans-caspian region.[65] Basing his ideas on archival material, Mannanov declares that the influx of people seeking work in the Transcaspian region in 1909 increased so fast that the number of villages in Khurasan with offices for the granting of external passports rose from ten to twenty-five.[66] In Belova's article, it is stated that in 1905 there were 5,150 male Iranian subjects in Ashkabad.[67]

Impoverished peasants, handicraftsmen, and persons from other strata of the Iranian population year by year increasingly flooded the Caspian ports and the towns of the Volga region. They were particularly numerous in Daghestan and Astrakhan. We have found a document showing that Iranian workers got as far as the mines of Krivoi Rog and the coal basin of the Don. It is known that in 1915 Prince Shah-Kuli Mirza, an engineer by training, brought over from Iran 118 Iranians for work in the Krivoi Rog iron mines and in the coal mines of the Don.[68]

The outflow of the mass of ruined inhabitants from Iran was so deep and steady that the Persian government was not in a position to impede this ever accelerating movement of the population. . . .

## Selection 6. Landlords, 1900s

[A. K. S. Lambton, "Rural Development and Land Reform in Iran," in *Symposium on Rural Development* (Central Treaty Organization, 1963), pp. 112–15]

. . . There has, in spite of the variety, nevertheless been an astonishing continuity in some fields, notably the land system, over a period of some thousand years. Although throughout this period there was a close connection between the land revenue system and the land assignment on the one hand and the levy of troops on the other, the land system was basically a bureaucratic, not a feudal, system. Broadly speaking the feudal system in western Europe arose out of the prevailing need for protection. It is true that the element of "protection" was not absent from the land system which developed in Persia, but the dominant need of the state at the time when this system began to emerge in its medieval form, which in its essentials prevailed until the beginning of the twentieth century, was for money to finance its operations; and the crucial problem was the payment of its civil and military officers. Hence, it was the financial and administrative institutions of the state that this need seized upon and transformed. From this stems a fundamental difference between the feudal institutions of western Europe and the land assignment of Persia, namely that, whereas a contractual relationship was an essential characteristic of the former, the

[62] Ts. G.V.I.A. f. 76, d. 392, l. 9.
[63] *Sb. materialov po Azii*, 76: 59.
[64] Ts. G.V.I.A. f. 400, op. 262/919, d. 74, l. 50.
[65] B. Mannanov, "Sotsialno-ekonomicheskii ocherk Khorasana na rubezhe XIX i XX vv." Lenin University, Tashkent, 1958, p. 153.
[66] Ibid., p. 154.
[67] Belova, p. 117.

[68] Ts. G.I.A. Gruz. SSR, f. 13, op. 12, d, 409, ll. 6, 7, and 21.

element of contract never became a feature of the latter.

I do not intend to bother you with the history of the development of the land assignment, but would merely point out that in the course of time the functions of the provincial governor, the provincial military commander, the tax collector, the tax farmer, and the man to whom the land assignment was made tended to be combined in one person. This led to the emergence of large landed properties virtually independent of the central government. The crucial difference between the holder of a land assignment in Persia and the European feudatory was that the former held his assignment solely at the will of the ruler and as a matter of grace. Those features of the Persian land system which are often loosely described as feudal derived not from feudalism but from the arbitrary nature of power. It is important, I think, to remember that all power in medieval Persia was essentially arbitrary. This has profoundly affected social conditions and has also been an obstacle to economic growth; and still, perhaps, lies at the base of many of the problems of the present day.

In medieval times if the central government was strong the land assignment was closely controlled (and involved, in fact, centralization and not decentralization); but more often the central government was weak and those holding the land usurped control and carried out most of the functions of government. The relationship between the peasant and the landholder was based on crop sharing and the provision of certain dues and services. Agriculture was predominantly subsistence agriculture. Prior to the adoption of western techniques of government and military organization it was possible to administer the state in this way; but in the 19th century when changes in the administration of the state began to take place it was no longer possible to finance the much wider operations of the administration on the basis of subsistence farming. Agriculture, nevertheless, continued to be predominantly subsistence agriculture. This

was one of the factors at the root of the perennial financial crises which occurred in the 19th century. Today, also, although there has been a much greater diversification of economic activity and revenue is not any longer mainly derived from the land, one of the fundamental problems facing the country is to carry out, or to complete, the transition from subsistence agriculture to intensive farming, and to raise the level of agricultural productivity.

Another point I should like to make because it has considerable social implications is that land ownership in Persia for a variety of reasons has been largely an urban rather than a rural phenomenon. Landowners tended to be concentrated in the town and not, as in western Europe, in castles and manorial estates. This in the course of time has resulted in a lack of understanding and contact between the landholding classes (who belonged thus rather to the urban population) and the rural population. The gulf between them has in modern times been further widened by the growth of amenities in the towns relative to the countryside. No one, I think, would deny the great evils of absentee landlordism or the unfortunate nature of the gulf between the urban and the rural population. One, indeed, of the great social problems in the field of rural development is the establishment of understanding and respect between the different sections of society. As long as urban society regards the countryman with contempt—as is all too often the case—there can be no real integration of the two sectors, vital though this is to the well-being of the country. The problem is further complicated by the fact that the rural population itself is split into two main groups, the settled and the semi-settled, between whom, also, there is an absence of understanding. Again it is essential to the well-being of the country that there should be mutual understanding and respect. The rural population, both settled and semi-settled, have acted in the past, and still so act, as a kind of population reservoir. Quite apart from the flight into the towns in modern times for a variety of political, social and economic reasons, there has always been an almost continual seepage into the towns from the countryside and from the tribes into the villages and towns.

There is one other feature of society to which I would like to draw your attention as being relevant to the assessment of the problems and difficulties of rural reform, namely two trends running through society, mutually opposed, though in fact seldom coming into conflict: the "equalitarian" theory of Islam and the social, but not functional, pre-eminence of "old" families. There was, however, nothing in the nature of an hereditary aristocracy. Repeated conquest and the inheritance laws of Islam effectively prevented the emergence of such a class. The Sayyids, admittedly, occupied a special position deriving from hereditary descent; but this was not combined, except by coincidence, with land ownership. The only other class, which had perhaps some claim to be regarded as an hereditary aristocracy, was that of the tribal leaders. But their authority was essentially personal, and derived from the possession of flocks and their tribal followers, not from the possession of land (though tribal leaders often eventually acquired land). It is true that the land owning classes and tribal chiefs held an immensely privileged and influential position but the vicissitudes of conquest, invasion, and economic pressure resulted in periodic changes in the composition of the land owning class (though not in their privileges and functions), the frequent dispersal of tribal groups, and the disappearance of dominating families.

Geographical and political conditions in the past fostered provincial particularism. Time and again the central government has been overthrown and the state destroyed. Society has nevertheless shown an astonishing recuperative power, due, I think, in part to the semi-autonomous nature of the local communities. In times of crises these have taken over under local leaders and carried on the administration, the religious classes in particular playing an important part in the handing down of the traditions of society.

There has thus, in the past, from time to time been recourse to self-help by the local communities. Given favorable conditions there is, I think, no reason why a similar tendency should not manifest itself again.

## Selection 7. Peasants, 1900s
[Nikki R. Keddie, *Historical Obstacles to Agrarian Change in Iran* (Claremont, 1950), pp. 4–7]

... Although the periods of anarchy and war were hard on the peasants, in periods of peace before the mid-nineteenth century the peasants were apparently better off than they are today (although probably never at a level of comfort). That the period of Western impact has seen a worsening of peasant conditions and not simply a maintenance of traditional standards is indicated by comparing Western travelers' reports before the mid-nineteenth century with present conditions. Jean Chardin, an observant and thorough reporter on seventeenth-century Iran, spoke of the comfortable standards of Iranian peasants, which he compared favorably with those of the West.[1] As late as 1833 another perceptive observer, the Englishman James Fraser, noted:

> The cultivators of the soil ... are those on whom the tyranny of their rulers falls the most heavily. Yet their houses are comfortable and neat, and are seldom found without a supply of good wheaten cakes, some mast or sour milk, and cheese,—often fruit makes its appearance, and sometimes a preparation of meat, in soup or pilau. Their wives and children, as well as themselves, are sufficiently though coarsely clad; and if a guest arrives there are few who cannot display a numed or felt carpet in a room for his reception. In fact, the high rate of wages proves that the profits of agriculture are high, while food is cheap; and we may be satisfied that in despite of rapacity, enforced by torture, no small share of the gain is hoarded by the farmer.[2]

Even allowing for possible exaggeration, it is difficult to imagine such a description of peasant conditions being made now. Since the late nineteenth century descriptions show nearly all peasants living on the bare edge of subsistence, with the poorest kind of food and lodging. The best recent study of

[1] Chardin, 5:391.
[2] Fraser, p. 204.

Iranian agrarian history, A. K. S. Lambton's *Landlord and Peasant in Persia*, also points out that the condition of the peasantry was better in the early nineteenth century than it was later.[3]

Why the Western impact encouraged large landholdings and a decline in peasant standards is a question which has not been studied thoroughly, but an attempt can be made here to summarize the outlines of an answer. In general, feudal and nomadic leaders took advantage of economic changes brought by Western contacts to enhance their position, and new groups were encouraged to invest in large estates run for profit.

Already in the second half of the nineteenth century a reinforcement of landlord power may be noted beneath the apparently static Asian facade. In this period the central government was in constant and acute need of money, partly in order to buy Western goods, including arms to defend itself. This need led to the systematization of the sale of offices. Local governorships were sold to the highest bidder every year, so that governors were most concerned with raising enough taxes to keep up their bids and make a good income. The governors also recruited lower officials on the basis of promised monetary returns. Since officials at all levels retained a profit from collected taxes, the peasants were forced to support an increasingly oppressive official hierarchy whose main duty, in turn, was to fleece them. Similar sales of office had appeared in periods of feudal breakdown before the Western impact, but they now coincided with other trends strengthening landlord power and so had a more permanent harmful effect on peasant standards than before.[4]

Nineteenth century wars with European powers put a strain on the central government which weakened its control over tribal

areas and over some of the areas given out as fiefs. This meant a loss of tax revenue from these areas, as some landlords and tribal khans pocketed all the local revenue, and the government had to raise taxes or insist on higher bids for governorships elsewhere. Peasants in the areas freed from central control did not profit, since landlords raised their feudal rents and dues to equal the increased government taxes. When the central government, in the 1920s, reestablished firm control over tribal leaders and independent landlords and set up an efficient paid bureaucracy and army, the pattern of high rents and taxes was continued.

The late nineteenth and early twentieth centuries saw the inauguration of a number of economic trends which have continued until today. The government began to ask for cash taxes, and to pay these the peasant had to sell his crops at artificially low exchange rates, often giving profits to middlemen who could resell the grain on the open market elsewhere.[5] Then as now the peasant had to sell grain right after the harvest, or even pledge his crop before the harvest, and often had to repurchase grain in the season of high prices to keep himself and his family fed.

Western influence brought a gradual development of modern private property in place of the various forms of feudal tenure which had previously existed. Traditionally, peasants and lords might have had certain rights to a given area without either being considered absolute owner. Now rights of peasants and nomad commoners to certain areas or flocks began to be abrogated, as the wealthy used their superior power to assert absolute property right on the Western model. Feudal dues on the peasants were not removed, and although individual peasants could not be sold as serfs, whole villages were freely sold, with implied rights to the labor of their inhabitants.

Loss of land by the peasants took place not only through such expropriation, but also through the new use of land to secure loans.

[3] Pp. 143–45. Miss Lambton believes that the control of landlords and fief holders over local land jurisdiction was the main cause of the decline, and does not stress the Western impact in this regard.

[4] On nineteenth century economic trends see F. Mochaver, *Evolution*, pp. 148–83.

[5] Ibid., p. 161.

The government's preference for cash taxes and the landlords' increasing demands led to the growth of moneylending to peasants. The peasant often had to borrow for food or implements, and inability to repay might mean loss of land. Unpaid debts could also tie the peasant to a landlord's property, since landlord and moneylender were often one and the same.

The Western impact favored investment in land and a more thorough exploitation of land and peasants than had been traditional in Iran. Foreign demand for certain crops turned parts of Iran into areas of specialized raw material production, dependent on the foreign market. Opium, for example, began to be cultivated widely after the decline in silk production in the 1860s. The English encouraged the growth of opium, which they transported and sold in the Far East. Much opium was also consumed in Iran once its cultivation became widespread. In the North cotton became a speciality because of Russian demand. As had happened in Eastern Europe in previous centuries, landlord income and power were increased by the growth of a profitable Western market for agricultural goods. The sale of crown lands in the late nineteenth century resulted in more intensive exploitation of the peasants there than had been traditional.

Another continuing trend which began in the late nineteenth century was the replacement of Iranian handicrafts by Western manufactured goods. Peasants, nomads, and city artisans gradually lost the employment and income which home industries had provided. Unlike the West, Iran did not compensate for the decline in handicrafts by developing manufacturing industries which could provide both employment and capital growth. The West had a formidable head-start in producing cheap manufactured goods, Iranian tariffs could not be raised to protective levels because of Western treaty limitations, and there was no capital readily available for launching competitive industries. What capital there was went into the more quickly profitable fields of land and moneylending. Although some handicrafts, notably carpets, were actually in greater demand than before due to Western interest, the general trend was in the opposite direction, particularly in articles of mass consumption like textiles. The former, almost self-sufficient village economy was undermined, without any satisfactory modern replacements being created.

The drain on Iran's economy caused by its dependent economic relation to the West is indicated, in the best available figures, by the fact that in the late nineteenth century Iran was exporting a volume of raw materials five times larger than the volume of finished goods it imported, and was paying three times more for its imports than it received for its exports.[6] The increasingly adverse trade balance was ultimately paid for by increased exploitation of the agriculturalists.

Certain groups benefited directly or indirectly from the Western impact. Among these were landlords, who strengthened their hold on the land and peasants who profited if they owned land producing goods for exports. Various middlemen moneylenders, traders, and lower officials also found new opportunities of enrichment, sometimes leading to landownership, and a small proportion of the peasants profited by lending tools and goods to others.

The ruling feudal classes increased their local political power as well as their economic position in the nineteenth century. There was an end to an earlier relative division between landownership and the administration of law and taxes, whereby village administration, land and central government representation had not been entirely in the same hands. Local administration and judicial processes increasingly became the monopoly of the same men who owned villages and received feudal dues. Village headmen and other local officials were appointed by the landlords, and the peasants rarely had recourse to any outside authority.[7]

The Western impact not only indirectly increased the power of the old landlords but

[6] Kia, pp. 87–88.
[7] Lambton, *Landlord*, p. 143.

added new families to their ranks. The growth of trade with the West brought an increase in the merchant class, and merchants invested in land. Land became freely alienable as buyers increased, the shahs sold state land to meet fiscal needs, and peasants lost their traditional land rights because of unpaid debts and the registration of land as private property by landlords and tribal leaders. Some moneylenders, village headmen, and prosperous peasants also succeeded in becoming landlords after their wealth increased.

If the Western impact helped the wealthier groups it harmed most peasants. Although the influence of the West was felt only indirectly by the peasants, through the actions of the wealthier classes, and although some of the features of their worsened position might have occurred even without a Western impact, the total picture of peasant conditions in this period cannot be separated from Western influence. Traditional land rights of the peasants were abrogated, the majority of villages fell under landlord ownership, debt grew, and most peasants eventually became landless sharecroppers. The late nineteenth and early twentieth centuries saw the creation of that destitute peasantry now associated with Iran, with peasant prosperity found only in areas inaccessible to the ruling hierarchy:

> Everything in Persia depends on whether a village is brought into direct intercourse with the Government or not. In the more retired valleys, where grasping khans do not penetrate, fertility and contentment reign, but if the Shah or the Governor of a province cannot pay inferior officers they give them a village or villages to do their worst with, and woe to the village thus given— nobody therein can call anything his own.[8]

Bent, like many observers today, regards poor peasant conditions as an outcome of traditional feudalism and upper class selfishness. Although these factors certainly contributed to low peasant standards, it seems impossible to account for an actual decline in the peasant's position in the late nineteenth and early twentieth centuries without considering the indirect impact of the West.

[8] J. T. Bent, "Village life in Persia," *The New Review* (1891): 366.

## The Armenians

The Armenians rose to a position of great economic influence in Iran in the seventeenth century. Shah Abbas deported several thousand families to Gilan and other places, and an important colony was settled in New Julfa, a suburb of Isfahan. Thanks to royal patronage and to their great industry, skill, and business acumen, the Armenians soon gained control of the silk trade and "dominated the Persian external trade and much of the internal commerce." In the south, the Portuguese, Dutch, and British found it necessary to conclude their business through Armenians. In the west, Armenians "established, from the silk producing provinces of Persia to the ports of the Mediterranean at Aleppo and Smyrna, an efficient supply and distribution network both for the export of silk and for the import of cloth."[1] This led to increasing contact with Europe, and thriving colonies were soon set up in Leghorn, Marseilles, and Amsterdam, and Armenian metal workers in Poland enjoyed a high reputation.[2] In India, Armenians conducted an active trade, from the beginning of the seventeenth century; this greatly increased in the 1680s, when the East India Company encouraged them to settle in Bombay, in order to develop the entrepôt trade. Similarly, Armenian trade with Russia

[1] R. W. Ferrier, "British Persian Relations in the Seventeenth Century," doctoral diss., Cambridge University.
[2] Very fine weapons and other objects made by Armenians were shown at the exhibition of Polish art in Paris, May 1969.

expanded considerably, especially after Peter the Great tried to develop the Volga route to Iran and India.[3]

But at the very moment when their power seemed at its height, it was being sapped at the base. Religious schisms divided and weakened the Armenian community, causing various groups to turn to France or Russia for support. Growing religious intolerance in Iran led to increasing pressure and discrimination. Deteriorating conditions in Turkey sharply reduced the volume and profitability of trade with Europe. Finally, there was the collapse of the Persian economy in the eighteenth century. This caused a considerable exodus of Armenians from Iran to Turkey, Russia, and India.[4] In India, they took advantage of the changing conditions created by the expansion of British trade and came to play an important part during the eighteenth century,[5] and some also succeeded in business in Russia and Turkey.

Matters improved very little in the first half of the nineteenth century, and travelers' accounts of Julfa show a population of three to five hundred families, living in poverty.[6] Nor were conditions better in the north. In 1844, the British consul in Tabriz reported:

Last year several thousand Armenians and Nestorians from Khoeh, Salmas, and Ooroomieh have received passports and gone into Russia; of these however the greater portion return after working as labourers for a few months; a few only whose families succeed in reaching the boundaries of the Aras by stealth, whence they are allowed to cross without question by the Russian authorities, permanently remain. If passports are granted to these Armenians in question, it is probable that the whole body of the Armenians now residing in Sooldooz, Sooghboolak and Maragha will seek passports and emigrate to avoid the oppression to which they are now subjected in this country.[7]

The following selection, written in 1858, shows that the Armenian community in Julfa was living in modest conditions, and was heavily dependent on remittances from India and Java. But it also shows stirrings of new life and awareness of the opportunities available. In Tabriz, too, the British consul in 1851 reported that building had begun on an Armenian school; teachers were to be Russian and the languages taught Russian and Armenian.[8] By 1868, the French consul put the Armenian population in Tabriz at five thousand and said that numbers had increased because many who had gone to Russia in 1827 had returned. Armenians had profited from the long period of peace and prosperity; they monopolized wine-making, played a leading part in foreign trade, and traveled on business to Tiflis, Astrakhan, Nizhni Novgorod, Moscow, and even France. However, he

[3] See articles by Kukanova.
[4] Malcolm was told "that an enumeration of the Armenian population of Iran, undertaken by the Bishop of Julfa, resulted in the figure of 12,383—one-sixth of the Armenian population before the Afghan invasions"; Hambly.
[5] Holden Furber, *John Company at Work* (Cambridge, Mass., 1948); and Mesrovb Seth, *Armenians in India* (Calcutta, 1937).
[6] See estimates cited in Curzon, *Persia*, 2:52–53.
[7] Bonham to Sheil, 12 March 1844, FO 60/107.
[8] Stevens to Sheil, 18 July 1851, FO 60/166.

commented on their low degree of education and the social discrimination from which they suffered.[9] By the turn of the century, a French official could state: "Trade in Persia is entirely in the hands of Persians and Armenians"[10] and another French observer judged that "Armenian business houses in the bazaar [of Tabriz] hold a large share of trade with Russia."[11] Armenians also found employment in British banks, the Telegraphs and other foreign enterprises.[12] More important, some of the largest new commercial, financial, and industrial enterprises established in the years preceding the First World War were owned by Armenians (2:5).

Although their share has declined, Armenians continue to play a significant role in the economy. Thus a list of merchants receiving foreign exchange in 1335/36 (1957/58) shows 44 Armenians out of a total of 1,074.[13] And a report by a Japanese mission on the textile trade in Tehran in 1965 estimated that Armenian merchants were about 10 percent of the total number.

[9] Crampon to Ministry of Foreign Affairs, 16 August 1868, AE Tauris, vol. 1.
[10] Report on Trade in Northern Persia, 1900, AE Téhéran, vol. 4.
[11] Aubin, p. 44.
[12] Ibid., p. 293
[13] Figures taken from Majlis reports and supplied by Dr. E. Abrahamian, of Columbia University.

## Selection 8. The Armenians, 1850s
[I. P. Yarutiwn Ter Yovhaneanc, *Patmutiwn Nor Julayu u Aspahan* (New Julfa, 1881, 2:285–91)]

### THE ECONOMIC CONDITION OF THE PEOPLE OF JULFA, AND SPECIFIC REFLECTIONS ON THAT MATTER

*a.* According to statistical data given in the previous chapter, the population of Julfa is composed of 371 families—1,204 males and 1,382 females. The people of Julfa are divided into four classes according to their economic status. The first class is made up of people who lead a worthy and suitable manner of life. The priests occupy the foremost place in this first class, for they become priests with the expectation of having parishes in India, and after having served as parish priests in the cities of India for four or five years, they return, each one having earned enough money inasmuch as he can. The number of priests now in Julfa is thirty-six, of whom twenty always attend to duties in the parishes, and sixteen remain in Julfa. There is also a distinction among the priests in economic status; for some are poor, yet, in my opinion, the cause of their poverty is their ignorance of how to put

to use the opportunities of fortune. The second place in the first class is occupied by those who in particular are employed in commercial transactions, and whose number is hardly six. Approximately thirty-five or forty households of families receiving an annual subsidy from members of their families and relatives in India and Java are reckoned among the numbers of the second group of the first class. The foremost source of income of Julfa is the subsidy that India and Java grant both to the parish priests and to families and friends in Julfa. The sum total of this, according to my calculations, is not less than 6,000 tumans per year. The livelihood of monks, nuns, schoolmasters, and teachers is financed by that sum. According to my reckoning there are one hundred families in Julfa of the first class, some being of the first group and others of the second.

The second economic class is that of the artisans, who earn as much as they can and support their families in a modest manner. The artisans in Julfa are: peddlers 10, buyers and sellers of socks 30, goldsmiths 10, carpenters 6, blacksmiths 4, grocers 5, butchers 6, buyers and sellers of wheat 8, weaving and linen manufacturing factory

130. A great majority of the women weave socks, and many men are employed in weaving. Some ten years ago the gain from the weaving industry was plentiful, to the extent that weavers not only supported their families moderately, but also amassed riches in addition to necessities. However, now the earnings of a diligent weaver are not more than 10 shahis per day. Annually 130,000 or 140,000 sheets of linen are produced in Julfa, and 25,000 to 30,000 pairs of socks. The second class numbers as many as 140 households.

There are also landowners in Julfa, approximately twenty in number, who possess vineyards, orchards, and crop-producing lands. However, because lands in Julfa are unprofitable and costly,[1] and because vineyards are constantly attacked by frost, the people who are landowners, not having great profits, are economically of the same class as the artisans.

The third class is composed of the toiling laborers and tillers, namely the bricklayers, stonecutters, bath keepers, barbers, wine dealers, shoemakers, saddlemakers, and others who are occupied in tilling land and secure their livelihood by means of daily earnings. The number of these must be as high as eighty [households].

Finally, the fourth class is that of the poor and the needy, who live in misery and woeful affliction, and their number is not less than fifty or sixty households.

b. As everywhere, more so in Julfa, wise household management, which particularly depends on women, is essential. Consequently, the house with a zealous mistress is secure in its management. As it is customary in Julfa to buy the year's provisions and to store them in the house, the first duty of prudent management is to buy everything at its proper time; for if one should not buy something at the right time, there would be a difference of 25 to 30 percent in expenditure.

After buying the year's provisions, in accord with the amount necessary per day, a diligent housewife would make use of them, with no need to buy anything from the store except for meat. In the house they bake *losh* bread, and having dried it for two to three months, and sprinkled it with water, they enjoy it with good appetite. Each house has a well with crystal-clear sweet water, which decreases in the extreme [heat of the] summer, but does not dry up. Thus, in so far as water is concerned, no one is in distress, or compelled to build reservoirs in order to preserve water.

Generally, there is no need for male or female servants in Julfa; for whatever work there may be outside the house is attended to by the men, and the household management is carried out by the women, who only on necessary occasions call hired women to come and bake bread, wash the laundry, and perform certain heavy tasks. The women have no need for wet nurses, because each woman tends to her own child with motherly care. Consequently, the parents of Julfa care greatly for their children, and the children love their parents.

c. Even though earnings and labor in Julfa are cheap, the low cost of all provisions[2] balances the lack of earnings; for each tiller whose daily earnings are 10 shahis can survive modestly with his wife and three children. There is no demand for housing or need to rent a house, as there are houses which are given for the purpose of residence without any rent to whoever may ask either because of the great size of the house or because of the lack of inhabitants.

d. Wine and other liquors are not bought at a high price, but each house has its own wine press, barrel, and wine storage; hence at vintage time each household, to the extent it needs, buys grapes and prepares wine

---

[1] In the summer when the water dries up, it is necessary to draw water out of the wells by means of oxen and to water the vineyards and all the crops, for which reason expenditure on the land increases and gain decreases. For each vineyard it is necessary to take water out of the well three or four times. Hence, all the vineyards of Julfa have wide wells for the purpose of irrigation.

[2] One liter of flour is worth now 10 shahis; a loaf of bread 8 shahis; butter $4\frac{1}{2}$ to 5 krans; rice 18 to 20 shahis; olive oil 2 to $2\frac{1}{2}$ krans; wood $1\frac{1}{2}$ to 2 shahis; meat 32 to 48 shahis.

and raki, which quickly disappear because of the master of the house. The good quality of the wine depends on the prudence of the household manager; for he who does not spare any effort in the important task of the management prepares wines, if not superior, at least not inferior to European liquors. Four kinds of wine are prepared in Julfa, of which the first, made out of *kishmish* or *sorek* grape, is by nature warm, white in color, and easily goes to the head of the drinker and gives a headache.

The second, made out of *alvand* or regular grape, is temperate by nature, red in color, and more popular. The third is *rang*, which is made out of black grapes; it is light in nature, but to most people in Julfa it is undesirable for drinking. The fourth is *natjabadi*, so called because the grape is brought from the village of Natjabad, whose wine is like that of *alvand*, but stronger and more delicious. Except for *kishmish*, grapes must be laid out for forty days so that the juice may dry out, and then they must be cast into the wine press; the must and the wine yeasts are all put together into the barrel and fermented every day until the wine is prepared. The older the wines get in Julfa, the better they become, as they receive a strong and delicate taste; they emit the fragrance of age. The drinker of these wines feels their effect for two days. The writer of this history had wine preserved for thirteen years, which was superb to the taste in quality and also in potency.

*e.* The costumes of the modern men of Julfa are in all respect similar to the Persian garments, but according to the testimony of pictures, their forefathers had costumes differing from the Persian and similar to those of the Georgians, with a wide belt on the waist and headgear. The costumes of women, according to the testimony of many, is the one they brought from Armenia. The upper garment of women is called *takalay*, whose flank and bottom front are open, and a skirt covers them. Their heads are covered with four pieces of cloth, upon which they put the *kot*, and tie the face veil; they wear a flank cover which they call *mandil*, and in the summer *torn*, and they cover their heads with a veil.

*f.* Even in the olden days, when Julfa flourished in riches, there was no more profit there than the livelihood that each working man made. Therefore, it is clear that in Julfa, both formerly and now, it is possible to earn only as much as the inexpensive necessities of a household may demand. The abundance of the former riches of Julfa was from the profits made from commerce, whose hands reached various far off lands, and about which we have spoken a little in the pamphlet on commerce.

*g.* The firm anchorage of Julfa is the Amenaprktchean Monastery, and the welfare or misfortune of the inhabitants is dependent upon the administration of the primates. The people of Julfa now, by the grace of God, are in no distress from the government, but rather they enjoy abundantly its grace, as free citizens. Occasionally, there are oppressions from particular quarters, both from the government and from certain foreigners; for this reason if the primate is attentive to the people and devoted to the welfare of the public, and protective of his flock (as is the present primate Taddeos), the pressures from these same particular oppressors are banished, and the people will not lose their state of well-being. However, if, on the contrary, the primate is timid and careless of the welfare of the people, and only mindful of his personal glory, the distress of the people of Julfa will not cease from the particular oppressors, who are neighboring foreigners, or minor officials of the government.

*h.* According to many wise thinkers, Julfa would be fortunate if it should have in the service of the government a few authentic representatives (interpreters), or other officials who would come from the inhabitants of Julfa; for they, at the appropriate time, could draw the merciful grace of the government on Julfa, and render no small service to their fatherland. With such intentions, the primate sent two youths from Julfa to the college of the Noble Lazarean Lords in Moscow so that, having become versed in different disciplines, they might also be of use to the government and to the fatherland. Now by the grace of God there are four people from Julfa in the service of the government. These are: the brothers Hakob Khan and Abraham Khan, Melkum Khan, son of Hakob Khan, and Harutiwn Eliazarean, interpreter.

## The Jews

All accounts written during the last few centuries, including the following selection, give a very depressing picture of the condition of Jews in Iran (see also 2:2). In the words of Curzon:

As a community, the Persian Jews are sunk in great poverty and ignorance. They have no schools of their own, except in the synagogues, where they are only taught to repeat their prayers, which the majority do not understand. Except in Tehran, Hamadan, Kashan, Khonsar, and Gulpaigan only Hebrew is taught, and not Persian. Such as can read or write the language of the country have studied it privately. In Hamadan, about a hundred young men receive tuition in the school of the American Mission; in Tehran, about fifteen study foreign languages under similar auspices. In Isfahan, a converted Jew of Tehran, Mirza Nurullah by name, who has been educated in England, has recently started a school where he instructs about twenty young men in Hebrew, Persian and English. . . .

The majority of Jews in Persia are engaged in trade, in jewellery, in wine and opium manufacture, as musicians, dancers, scavengers, pedlers, and in other professions to which is attached no great respect. They rarely attain to a leading mercantile position.[1]

However, thanks to contacts with other Jewish communities in Europe, India, and Iraq, the Jews were able to improve their condition. They came to play a significant part in the Persian Gulf trade: "Taking Persia as a whole, Jews do not occupy a very important position in the trade of the country, but this statement is not equally true of all parts: at Bushire, for instance, there is a prosperous Jewish element."[2] And MacLean's report shows that the Jews were prominent in the import of cotton textiles from Manchester through Baghdad; thus "at least 80 per cent of the [Kermanshah and Hamadan] trade is in the hands of Jewish traders" and "the business in Muhammarah is largely in the hands of small Jew traders."[3]

As for their educational level, it was greatly raised by the schools founded by the Alliance Israélite Universelle, starting in 1898; by 1908, there were eleven such schools, with 2,225 pupils.[4] The restrictions from which they suffered were gradually relaxed, and in recent years they have come to play a significant part in the country's commercial life. Thus a Japanese mission estimated that in 1965 Jews constituted about 30 percent of the total number of textile merchants in Tehran. The 1966 census put the number of Jews in Iran at 61,000.

[1] Persia, 1:510.
[2] Foreign Office Handbooks, Persia, p. 105.
[3] MacLean Report, A and P 1904, 95, pp. 36–39.
[4] Aubin, pp. 295–300.

## Selection 9. The Jews, 1900s

[Hanina Mizrahi, *Yehude Paras* (Tel-Aviv, 1959), pp. 110–11]

... The Jew is ritually unclean (*najas*) in the eyes of the Muslim. If he touched something he was forced to purchase it. The Jewish customer had to stand at some distance from the merchant. On a rainy day the Jew was forbidden to pass by the Muslim merchant, because water and moisture transferred his uncleanliness, while during the hot season his sweat transferred his impurity. The Jew's coins and money, however, were never suspected of being unclean. The Jew bought from the Muslim, but the Muslim did not buy from the Jew. Because the Muslim considered the Jew to be unclean, the latter was prevented from participating in the country's commerce and economy and was forced to confine his activities to small trade with other Jews. He therefore lived a miserable life of want and poverty. A small number were craftsmen: glaziers, shoemakers, builders, tailors, and barbers. These too eked out a living with difficulty. A few were gold- and silver-smiths or moneylenders.

The members of the middle class—householders—were mainly small tradesmen or chemists [perfumers], and a small minority dealt in goods of considerable substance: cashmere scarves, precious stones, pearls, and the like. Here the Jew's wife was of assistance. Wrapped in a *chadur, chakchul*, and veil she could not be distinguished from a Muslim woman. She therefore was able to enter freely the most important places, the harems of princes, wealthy men, and dignitaries, to trade or to lend money for interest or surety. One such transaction and she earned her livelihood for several months or even an entire year. Several have become wealthy. There are almost no men of enormous wealth, although a small number are well off and constitute, with the few doctors, the upper class of the Jewish community. Along with such are also those living in the provinces who succeeded in establishing commercial ties with various parts of the world, particularly India and England. After the new constitution many entered the wholesale trade and became rich. ...

## The Zoroastrians

In the course of the two or three centuries following the Arab conquest, the vast majority of the population of Iran embraced Islam. The adherents of the old religion were further reduced by the exodus, at some time during this period, of Zoroastrians to India, where they are known as Parsis. By the nineteenth century the number of Zoroastrians (or Guebres, as they were usually known) in Iran had fallen below 10,000. In 1854, the Society for the Amelioration of the Condition of the Zoroastrians in Persia gave a figure of 7,200, of whom 6,660 were in Yazd, 450 in Kirman, and 50 in Tehran. By 1892, according to the same source, the total had risen to 9,300, of whom 6,900 were in Yazd, 2,000 in Kirman, and 300 in Tehran.[1]

Foreign observers, from the seventeenth century to the end of the nineteenth, agree that the Zoroastrians suffered from both great poverty and severe discrimination. In common with other minorities, they were subject to the *jiziya*, or poll tax, which was levied in an arbitrary and extortionate way. Most of them seem to have earned a modest living in silk cultivation and weaving.[2]

[1] Murzban, pp. 108–9.
[2] Ibid., pp. 114–20; Katrak, pp. 120–21.

The growing trade between southern Iran and India during the nineteenth century had a doubly beneficial effect on the Zoroastrians. On the one hand, many became prominent in the trade of Yazd—"Their role is similar to that performed in the open ports of Japan by the *compradores* and the Chinese agents, into whose hands nearly all business passes." [3] This in turn was due to increasing contact with the prosperous, enterprising, and highly educated Parsis of Bombay. The latter not only had mutually profitable business dealings with the Iranian Zoroastrians, but also helped them in numerous ways, mainly through the above-mentioned society, founded in 1853. By 1882, thanks to repeated interventions by the society, which eventually secured the support of the British embassy, a *farman* was issued exempting the Zoroastrians from payment of poll tax. [4] More important, in 1856, two schools were founded, in Yazd and Kirman, and additional ones were opened later. These contacts, and the general changes in Iranian society, have enabled the small Zoroastrian community (20,000 according to the 1966 census) to play an increasingly important role in the economic and cultural life of Iran. The impact of these changes on Kirman is described in the following selection.

[3] Murzban, p. 115.
[4] See text in Katrak, p. 283.

**Selection 10. The Zoroastrians in Kirman**
[Paul Ward English, "Nationalism, Secularism, and the Zoroastrians of Kirman," in *Cultural Geography: Selected Readings*, ed. Fred E. Dohrs and Lawrence M. Sommers (New York, 1967), pp. 275–82]

THE ZOROASTRIANS OF KIRMAN IN THE NINETEENTH CENTURY

In the nineteenth century, Kirman was a traditional, preindustrial Muslim city. The heart of the city was occupied by three institutions aligned on an east-west axis—the Friday-prayer mosque, the bazaar, and the citadel. The Friday-prayer mosque near the eastern wall of the city was the pivot of social and religious life in Kirman. The bazaar with its covered stalls and associated caravanserais was located adjacent to the mosque and formed the commercial center of the town. The citadel, which was the center of political power in Kirman, was accorded a secondary position in the town plan and was located on the western edge of the city, ringed by walls to protect governmental leaders both from external attacks and internal uprisings.

The remainder of the city was divided into five residential quarters (*mahalleh*) in which the population of Kirman was segregated on the bases of race, religion, and occupation. These quarters were characterized by the pronounced irregularity of their street patterns. Except for the wide avenues which connected the bazaar with the city gates, the lanes in these sections formed a maze of dark, twisting passageways, alleys, and culs-de-sac. Most were less than twelve feet in breadth and were enclosed by the high outer walls of the household compounds. Four of these quarters were Muslim—Kutbabad, Mahalleh Shahr, Maidani Qualeh, and Shah 'Adil—and were occupied by the merchants, gardeners, artisans, and craftsmen of the city. To some degree the preindustrial principle stressing central location was operative and the richest and most powerful people lived near the center of the city, the poorest on the outskirts near the city walls. The fifth quarter was occupied by a small community of Jews, who, by dint of tribute money paid regularly to local officials, were able to achieve a position of relative security inside the walls next to the citadel.

The Zoroastrian quarter of Kirman was located beyond the eastern wall of the city. The precariousness of life in such a location is evidenced by the ruins of the ancient Zoroastrian quarter to the north of the city which was leveled by an Afghan invasion in the eighteenth century. All Zoroastrians lived within their own quarter, and were forbidden to live inside the city walls. As a result, the fire temples, shrines, baths, and schools of the Zoroastrians were located here. A community council (*anjuman*) represented members in dealings with the Muslims and as late as 1960 it was still possible to find older Zoroastrian men and women who had never ventured beyond the walls of the ghetto and could not speak the Persian tongue.

Shi'ah Islam was extremely intolerant during the nineteenth century and, because of concern with the ritual impurity of nonbelievers, imposed many restrictions on the Zoroastrians to emphasize their inferior status. First and foremost, as non-Muslims, the Zoroastrians had no legal rights in Muslim courts because law was based on the Muslim religion. Any case brought before the courts, therefore, would automatically be decided against them. Zoroastrians could not ride a horse on the main streets of the city, and if when riding a donkey they met a Muslim of any age or sex, they were forced to dismount and bow. Zoroastrian houses and even their fire temples could not be built taller than one story because Muslims allowed no rivals to the beauty and majesty of their mosques. In addition, Zoroastrians were forced to wear mustard-colored robes, could not wear eyeglasses or stockings nor carry umbrellas, and were not allowed in the city on rainy days. In commercial matters, they were forced to pay higher prices for property, were restricted to a limited number of occupations, and had to conceal their wealth for fear of exciting hostile attacks. Furthermore, there was the constant drain of conversion on the community, particularly after the "law of apostasy" was enforced, and any Zoroastrian newly converted to Islam could claim the property of all of his relatives however distant. Above all, the Zoroastrian community feared the alternatives of enforced conversion to Islam or massacre.

In this atmosphere, the Zoroastrian community developed the characteristics of a closed, introverted, and static society. An endogamous priest class wielded increasing power as religion became the prime focal point of Zoroastrian reality. Unfortunately, many of these priests failed to maintain the theology of their faith, though they continued to tend the sacred fire and practice the ritual. Zoroastrian apartness from the Muslims was emphasized and cherished so that practices such as the exposure of the dead in "towers-of-silence" (*dakhmeh*) located outside the city came to have an exaggerated importance not found in earlier Zoroastrianism. By the end of the nineteenth century, the spiritual decay was so apparent that the Iranian Zoroastrians were forced to look to their coreligionists in India, the Parsis, for religious leaders and leadership. . . .

## NATIONALISM, SECULARISM, AND THE ZOROASTRIANS OF KIRMAN IN THE TWENTIETH CENTURY

. . . The impact of nationalism and secularism on the city of Kirman and its Zoroastrian community was immediately felt. The central government ordered that wide avenues be constructed in Kirman and a radial pattern was superimposed on the old city, which shifted its center of gravity to the north and east. The ancient walls of the city were leveled and many old cemeteries and shrines, which previously had restricted urban expansion, were destroyed. And this expansion was substantial. Kirman's population increased from 40,000 to 60,000 in the first half of the twentieth century, despite a sizable emigration of landlords and traders to Tehran. New suburbs spread beyond the old city walls and in these newly constructed quarters land values were low and houses were less crowded. As a result, the labyrinth of twisting lanes so characteristic of pre-industrial Islamic cities is not found in the suburbs.

Certain functional changes were also stimulated by these forces. The mosque declined in importance and no longer acted as the focal point of Kirmani social life. Industry, commerce, and crafts were liberated from their previous concentration in the bazaar and new shops sprang up on the new avenues. With increased communication facilities and increased security, location of the upper class at the center of the town was no longer critical, and, one by one, wealthy families moved to the suburbs.

Most important for the Zoroastrian community was the decline in power of the Muslim clergy and their replacement by secular judges, bureaucrats, political leaders, and government teachers. The many restrictions on Zoroastrian activities were eliminated, they were recognized in civil law, one Zoroastrian was appointed to the Iranian Senate, and a general atmosphere of religious tolerance replaced fanaticism in Kirman.

These social changes were immediately reflected in the distribution of Zoroastrians in Iran and in its cities. Zoroastrian sin nearby rural settlements migrated to the provincial capital; those in Kirman migrated to Tehran—all searching for areas of increased tolerance and opportunity. The tide of these migrations steadily increased, with the exception of a short period after Riza Shah's abdication in the early 1940s. Now there are no longer any Zoroastrians in villages such as Jupar, Mahan, and Qanaghistan, though ruins of fire temples remain in these places. In Tehran, the Zoroastrian community which numbered in the hundreds in 1930 now numbers in the thousands, and the trend suggested by a count of graves in their cemetry and children in their schools indicates that this community is continuing to grow at the expense of other smaller places.

In the city of Kirman, the impact of secularism was even more definite. The Zoroastrian ghetto and the walls which separated it from the city have disappeared. The map showing the religious affiliation of each household in the Zoroastrian quarter of Kirman documents the degree to which integration has replaced segregation in the urban and social organization of Kirman. At present families of both religions live side by side. Only 65 percent of the dwellings in the Zoroastrain quarter are still occupied by Zoroastrians; 30 percent are Muslim homes. The remaining houses are unoccupied, representing Zoroastrian families who migrated to Tehran but still own homes in Kirman. Nor have the Zoroastrians moved into a ghetto in Tehran; they are widely scattered throughout the capital and their distribution represents accommodation to land values and economic status, not to religion.

But this physical integration of religions and the movement of the Zoroastrians into the liberalized society of twentieth-century Iran has not been without cost. A Zoroastrian cemetery, for example, has replaced the traditional Zoroastrian "tower-of-silence." This represents a radical departure from Zoroastrian belief and was spurred by modern debates on hygiene. Countless other customs, traditions, and rituals are disappearing as members of the community are assimilated into the mainstream of Iranian life: the "sacred thread," once as important to Zoroastrians as the cross was to Christians, is no longer worn by most modern Zoroastrians; there are fewer ceremonies at the fire temples and fewer people attend; indeed there are few candidates for the priesthood, as most young men are drawn into more lucrative pursuits. In the words of their leader "Zoroastrians no longer have time to celebrate their faith," which may well mean that the destruction of Zoroastrian ghettos may be shortly followed by the disappearance of the community....

## Habl al-matin: Iranian Bourgeoisie

*Habl al-matin*, the newspaper from which the following selection is taken, was a weekly published in Calcutta in 1893/94. It was described as follows by Browne:

"It is the oldest regular Persian newspaper which still survives, and holds an important position, especially amongst men of learning and in religious circles, in which it has a special weight and influence. Some portion of it is always devoted to religious matters, and it is the champion of Pan-Islamism."[1] But, as the extract shows, it also represented the views of the trading community and advocated a program that was both liberal and nationalistic. It continued publication for some time after the First World War.

To an overwhelming extent, the Iranian bourgeoisie at this time consisted of merchants, some of whom also engaged in small-scale banking or moneylending. The decline of the handicrafts and the almost complete absence of modern factories (see chap. 6) meant that there was practically no native industrial bourgeoisie. On the other hand, there was a rather dense network of retail shops. Thus in 1905, in the town of Ardabil, which had 12,000 to 15,000 households, there were 1,165 shops, of which 250 dealt in textiles and 170 in foodstuffs. In Marandeh, which had 2,500 households, there were 469 shops, of which 104 handled textiles, 112 food-stuffs, and 157 groceries.[2] And on the other hand, there were large Iranian firms, mainly engaged in foreign trade, including some very big enterprises such as that of Tumaniants, whose holdings in Russia alone were estimated at 24 million krans in 1917.[3]

A good index of the composition of the bourgeoisie is the list of the clients of the Russian Bank. On 1 January 1908, this included 813 persons engaged in trade or finance and only 6 in industry; the figures for 1 January 1909 were 1,060 and 9, respectively.[4]

[1] Browne, *Press and Poetry*, p. 73; I owe this reference to Dr. Ervand Abrahamian.
[2] Ivanov, *Iranskaya revolutsiya*, p. 35.
[3] Glukhoded, p. 65.
[4] Arabadzhyan, cited by Glukhoded, p. 62.

## Selection 11. Complaints of Persian Merchants, 1906
[*Habl al-matin* (Calcutta), 18 May 1906]

Honorable merchants: ... After several thousand tests and experiments, now is the time to give up the inauspicious course of flattery and adopt vigilance and unity and proceed so that you may catch up with your friends. Today the world of commerce is linked together like a chain and is like a single factory. If even one part in this factory is damaged the supervisor will have to replace it. If you do not carry on your trade according to contemporary practices and if you continue with the habits and customs of the tent dwellers of a thousand years ago, the supervisor of the trading machine—whose esteemed name is Science—will replace you. In fact he has already begun replacing you, without your being aware: you take his dreadful alarm for a lullaby. Let me give you a good example: The minister of customs in Tehran found that the superintendent of Tabriz was a broken piece in the apparatus of governmental regulations, and replaced him immediately.

Today the world is rotating on the pivot of science. In Europe there are schools for every position, high and low. Let us leave aside commerce—even for coachmen and cart drivers there are schools; they are required to pass a test on the layout of the city, and the name of every street and section, before they can obtain a permit. How much more regrettable, then, that you merchants do not yet have a school of commerce! To this day to you trade means drudgery for foreigners. You do not yet know that even tanning is a part of commerce! Whenever there are a few Frenchmen, Germans, or other foreigners in a city, each group has a council. They meet once or twice a week, discuss the advancement of their trade and the improvement of its market, and make certain decisions.

You have not as yet established a chamber of commerce in Tehran and are not aware of its benefits. It is owing to the lack of a chamber of commerce that you are steadily regressing and have become a broken part in the apparatus of commerce, and the supervisor is busy replacing you. Look: in Tehran, Tabriz, Isfahan, and other cities European businessmen are constantly setting up shops, obtaining concessions, and opening bank branches—and trade is slipping from your hands. I am not old enough, but when I ask my elders they confirm that if fifty years ago there were ten Christian merchants in the whole of Iran, their number now exceeds five thousand. It is owing to the lack of a chamber of commerce that the export of 300,000 bags of Isfahan tobacco has been reduced to 5,000 (and that in foreign hands). It is owing to the lack of a chamber of commerce that opium from Yazd and Isfahan, because of the guile and cheating of ignorant merchants, has lost its market in China and other countries and is sold at a reduced price. Why is it that the sale of Kirman and Isfahan shawls, one of the important sources of wealth of the Iranian government and nation, has steadily diminished and that European cashmere has taken its place? Because we do not have a chamber of commerce. The cashmere trade had been in the hands of a few simple-minded, inexperienced, and uneducated merchants; a crafty foreigner by deceiving them has monopolized the trade. Thus the market for Persian cashmere has stagnated, which in turn has increased the demand for European cashmere.

European merchants, in competition with each other, are constantly trying to supply less expensive goods to the world market and thereby increase the number of their customers. Owing to our ignorance we do just the opposite. There is no one to ask you gentlemen who, in the question of the Tobacco Régie [see 5:13], took refuge in the mosque and regarded monopoly as detrimental, why it is that now, ignoring the state of the poor in Kirman and Mashhad, you committed a crime of such enormity against yourselves and your nation. Until a few years ago all the trade in carpets that came to Istanbul from all parts of Iran and then proceeded to Europe was in Iranian hands. It is owing to the lack of a chamber of commerce that now two-thirds of it is in the hands of Christian merchants. For the past five hundred years lemon juice has been coming from Shiraz. Why do they not make bottles for it that can stand properly? Because we do not have a chamber of commerce. Why have the cotton textiles made by the people of Isfahan disappeared? Because we do not have a chamber of commerce. So far ten to twelve big companies and trade channels have been founded in various Iranian cities. Why is it that like the morning star they have vanished before rising and thus have made people lose all initiative and interest? Because we lack knowledge and a chamber of commerce. We assume that a bulky physique and abusive talk in the Majlis [Parliament] are the basis of greatness and commerce. Why is it that the government, which is the axis of commerce, like the present-day Russian and Ottoman bonds, plays a different game every moment, fluctuates, and impoverishes the nation? Because the blood in the veins of our merchants has become cold. They are not blind; they see, but discord and disunity have taken away their hearts. The merchants in Azerbaijan, for instance, hear that people in Tehran are revolting and demanding their rights from the government, but they do not consider themselves among those oppressed. Passengers between England and America during their six-day cruise can talk by wireless to their people whenever they want. Why is it that the honored post office of the eminent government of Iran is still conveyed by asses and camels as it was centuries ago? Because we lack knowledge and a chamber of commerce. Reason, common sense, and divine law have instructed us to appoint a guardian for a person when he loses his senses and is unable to attend to his gains and losses. . . .

# 3

## Foreign Trade

The volume of foreign trade of Iran grew steadily between 1800 and 1914, with occasional setbacks. Exports were from time to time reduced by crop failures, notably that of silk in the 1860s (see 5 : 6–8), and imports by temporary overstocking of local markets, or failures of local firms, as in 1852 (see 3 : 12), while both were affected by such outside events as the periodic financial crises in the world's leading markets, the American Civil War and the Russo-Turkish War, and the decline in prices in the last quarter of the century. Over the whole period, the increase in real terms may have been about twelvefold (see 3 : 19). This expansion, though appreciable, was far from matching that achieved by either the industrial countries or the main Middle Eastern ones. Thus between 1800 and 1913, world trade is estimated to have risen about fiftyfold, in real terms.[1] As for the Middle East, Egypt's trade increased fifty- or sixtyfold and Turkey's fifteen- or twentyfold, and the available figures for Iraq and Syria also show a much higher rate of growth.[2]

Little can be said about the movement of the balance of trade. It would seem that in the first half of the century, exports, by and large, covered imports; the heavy deficit in trade with India seems to have been offset by a surplus in trade with Turkey, Russia, and Central Asia (see 3 : 19 and 6 : 1). But from the 1860s on, all observers agree that there was an appreciable deficit in overall trade, and this is confirmed by the customs returns for 1901–14 (see 3 : 20), which, however, do not allow for exports smuggled from Persia to Russia. It is quite impossible to say whether the balance on invisible items was positive or negative (see 3 : 18, 23), but in any, case it does not seem to have been large enough to cover the import surplus, and one gets the impression that there was a considerable outflow of specie in the fifty years preceding the First World War (see 8 : 2). It was not until

[1] Imlah, pp. 97–98, 189.
[2] EHME, pp. 30, 132, 208–9, 363–64; between 1813 and 1913 India's trade rose about fiftyfold, in real terms.

the 1920s that petroleum began to make a significant contribution to Iran's balance of payments (see epilogue).

The composition of Persian trade changed significantly (see 3:20). As in so many countries, textiles, which had been an important export item (in this case to Russia and Central Asia), became the leading import, since the local handicrafts were unable to compete with machine-made European goods (see 6: 2, 3). Another significant change on the import side was the sharp rise in "colonial goods"— especially sugar and tea—a phenomenon also observed in many Middle Eastern countries.[3] It is also possible that, over the period, Iran's position changed from that of a net exporter of cereals to a net importer. Imports of machinery and other capital or producer goods remained negligible until after the First World War (see 3:20).

As regards exports, the most striking change was the sharp rise in cash crops. Opium found ready markets first in China and then in Europe, and both production and exports rose greatly. Cotton production, stimulated as in so many Middle Eastern and other countries by the "cotton famine" caused by the American Civil War, was further encouraged by the rapidly rising demand and favorable tariff policy of Russia. Rice also benefited from Russian demand and tariffs. Silk, formerly Iran's staple export, lost its place in the 1860s (see chap. 5). On the other hand, carpets, previously exported in very small numbers, were gradually made in much larger quantity for sale to Europe and the United States and by the turn of the century constituted a significant export item (see 6:9). The balance of exports continued, as in the past, to consist of such products as dried fruits and livestock products, as well as pearls (see 3:23).

There were also marked shifts in the direction of Persian trade. Malcolm's estimates (6:1) indicate that, around 1800, Iran's main partners were Afghanistan and the principalities of Central Asia, Turkey, and India. Trade with India consisted mainly of native products on both sides, the East India Company's exports of British goods to Iran being very small (see 3: 4, 5). Trade with Afghanistan and Central Asia included a large amount of European goods reexported from Iran, and that with Turkey also comprised a substantial amount of such goods, coming through Constantinople or Baghdad.

The main change in the first half of the nineteenth century was the sharp rise in trade with Britain, both through Turkey and through the Persian Gulf, by way of India (3: 4–14). It seems likely that in the 1850s and 1860s Britain accounted for at least half of Iran's total trade, and for imports the proportion was probably distinctly higher. In the second half of the period, the most dramatic change was

---

[3] In 1901–2, Iran imported some 25,000 tons of sugar through the Persian Gulf and 50,000 from Russia, figures more than twice as high as those of 1897–98. Imports of tea through the gulf and Sistan were 2,400 tons and through Trebizond 9,000 cases, but the latter was offset by an export of 9,000 cases to Russia, where prices were much higher (MacLean, pp. 28–32). By 1912/13, imports of tea had risen three times in value, to £723,000 and those of sugar doubled, to £2,521,000 ("Persia," A and P 1914, 93). However, a large part of the rise in sugar was due to the Russian export bounty which made sugar one-third cheaper in Iran than in Russia, and resulted in substantial smuggling back to Russia—see Entner, p. 67.

the sharp rise in Russia's share, especially after 1880; between the 1860s and 1913–14, total trade with Russia multiplied twelvefold, in gold rubles (see 3:21). By the First World War, Russia took some 70 percent of Iran's exports, supplied over 50 percent of imports, and accounted for almost two-thirds of total trade. The share of the British Empire had fallen to a little over 25 percent of imports, 12 percent of exports, and 20 percent of total trade; of this somewhat under half was accounted for by India. The third place was held by Turkey, with about 5 percent of total trade. (See "Persia," A and P 1914–16, 74).

The rapid rise and relative decline of British trade forms part of a worldwide trend. By 1850, Britain accounted for about 40 percent of the world's industrial output and trade.[4] Thereafter its share slowly declined, to 32 percent of output and 40 percent of trade in 1870, as other countries developed. But although complaints about the quality of British goods, and their unsuitability to the Iranian market, were made as early as 1848 (see "Remarks to Accompany the Returns of the Tabriz Trade," FO 60/147), and increased in number and vehemence throughout the period, British trade continued to expand slowly, in absolute terms, thanks to the commercial, transport, and financial links that had been established. In the fifteen or twenty years preceding the First World War, however, Britain found it increasingly difficult to withstand Russian pressure, especially in the northern and central regions (see 3:16, 20).[5]

In most parts of the world Britain had taken the lead in forcing reluctant governments to open up the trade of their countries to foreign capitalist enterprise by removing prohibitions on exports and imports, abolishing or greatly restricting monopolies, and replacing a haphazard and arbitrary system of duties by uniform low ones. This took place, for instance, in the Ottoman Empire in 1838 (see EHME, pp. 38–40), China in 1842, and Morocco in 1856. But in Iran, although Malcolm secured, in 1801, a treaty which gave English merchants the right to settle anywhere in the country, to recover debts, to build, sell, or rent houses, and to leave without obstruction, the pace was set by Russia—first by the Treaty of Gulistan of 1813 and then by that of Turkomanchai of 1828 (texts in Hurewitz, 1:68, 84, 96). In addition to imposing an indemnity of 20 million tumans and providing extraterritorial privileges for Russian subjects in cases of litigation, the Treaty of Turkomanchai established a framework for foreign trade. Consular and commercial agents were to be appointed, subjects of each country could trade and travel freely in the other, in Iran documents were to be registered with the Russian consul and local authority, and all goods (both exports and imports) crossing either

---

[4] E. A. G. Robinson, in *Economic Journal*, September 1954; H. Heaton, *The New Cambridge Modern History*, 10:36.

[5] As early as 1875, "I was informed Russian importations [of copper sheets, iron bars and refined sugar] were shutting out those from England. Iron in the same way." (Mackenzie, "General Remarks on the route from Ispahan to Mohamerah," August 1875, FO 60/375). In 1878 it was stated that "lately Russian manufactures are, through cheap production, driving those of Manchester out of the field, even in the Tehran Bazaars" (Mackenzie to Thomson, 10 September 1878, FO 60/414); among the reasons given were poor transport in the south and insufficient protection to British merchants for debt collection.

border were to be subjected to a single, uniform, 5 percent ad valorem duty. Britain soon sought the same privileges and after prolonged negotiations (see, for example the 1837 correspondence in IO, LP and S/9, vol. 56) obtained the 1841 Treaty (see text in Hurewitz, 1:124). The Iranian desire to protect domestic industries and safeguard the balance of payments was dismissed as a fallacy not worth discussing (see 3:1). Other countries then demanded equal treatment—for example, France (see 3:22) and the United States, which signed a commercial treaty with Iran in 1852, putting its citizens "on the same footing as the subjects of the most favoured nations" (Stevens to Malmesbury, 1 June 1852, FO 60/174).[6] Sometimes the Iranian government proved difficult, as in 1850 with the Dutch, who levied at Batavia duties of 5 to 12 percent on Persian goods and yet claimed the privilege, enjoyed by Britain, of being exempt from all additional inland and transit duties upon payment of the 5 percent custom duty (Hennell to Sheil, 7 February 1850, FO 60/150).

The result of this system was that Iranian merchants, being subjected to road taxes and various imposts from which Europeans were exempt, were put at a disadvantage (see 3:2). But European merchants also found much to complain about regarding the arbitrariness or incompetence of Persian officials (see 3:3).

It was not until 1903 that Iran's tariff was changed. In that year a new treaty was signed with Russia, followed immediately by Britain and then by other countries (see text in Hertslet, 23:1213–39 and 24:819–926). Its main feature was the replacement of the general ad valorem duty of 5 percent by specific duties. On some imports duties were levied according to weight. This favored Russian cotton goods, which were lighter than British, and on the latter the rate rose to 8 percent; similarly, the duty on tea (imported mainly from the British Empire) rose to 100 percent, while those on kerosine and sugar (mainly Russian) fell to 2 percent and 4 percent respectively. Duties on exports going mainly to the British Empire, such as opium, wheat, and linseed, were also raised, while those on goods going to Russia, for example cotton and rice, were were either eliminated or reduced.[7]

The more favorable tariff contributed to the rapid expansion of Russian trade with Iran. Other factors were the extremely rapid growth of Russian industry; the bounties granted to exports, especially on sugar (see above); the great improvement of transport on the Caspian, in Transcaucasia and in the Transcaspian provinces; the financial services offered by the Discount and Loan Bank (see 8:2,3); and the growing number of Russian subjects (mainly from the Transcaucasian provinces) engaged in trade and other activities in Iran (see 8:4). The latter competed successfully with such British firms as Gray, Paul and Company, established in the Persian Gulf area and in the southern provinces.

The shift in the direction of Iran's trade was accompanied by a shift in the

---

[6] For a list of the commercial treaties between Iran and other countries, see Lorini, pp. 507–9, and Jamalzadeh, pp. 191–92.

[7] Entner, pp. 53–55; and Gleadowe-Newcomen, p. 34.

channels through which such trade passed. The problem was very clearly posed by Colonel Pelly:

The greatest consumers in Persia, area for area, are to be found within an obtuse angled triangle, of which a line drawn from Tabreez on the West, along the Southern shore of the Caspian to Meshed on the East, would form the base; and of which lines drawn from Meshed and Tabreez respectively to Ispahan, would form the other two sides. Now trade must reach these consumers along one or more of the following routes:

1st.—*Via* Turkish Armenia from Trebizond to Tabreez
2nd.—*Via* the Russian Caucasian Provinces from Poti to Tabreez
3rd.—From the line of the Volga across the Caspian to Resht or Asterabad.
4th.—From Kurrachee *via* the Candahar line to Furrah, and thence either through Herat to Meshed, or through Ghayn to the Nishapoor portion of the Teheran road.
5th.—From Bundar Abbas through Yezd or Kerman.
6th.—From Bushire *via* Shiraz, and thence through Ispahan or Yezd.
7th.—From some port on the Persian Gulf other than Bushire and Bunder Abbas; or
8th.—Along some line between the head of the Gulf and Baghdad, and thence continuing either into the plateau of Persia *via* Kermanshah, Shuster, or else keeping Northward through the Kurds.[8]

At the end of the eighteenth century, the Baghdad route was perhaps the most important one. After the Napoleonic Wars, with the establishment of British naval power in the Persian Gulf and increasing anarchy in Iraq (see EHME, pp. 135–36), trade through Bushire expanded very rapidly (see 3:5). A few years later, a new route was opened in the north—between Tabriz and Trebizond, which in the late 1830s was connected by steamship with Constantinople (see 3:10). A third route was developed in the 1860s, with the inauguration of a steamer service between the Caspian ports of Russia and Iran (see 4:1, 2).

Traffic on the Persian Gulf and Caspian routes continued to grow rapidly until 1914. The Trebizond route, however, was subjected to great competition from both the route through the Russian Caucasus and, after the opening of the Suez Canal in 1869, from the Persian Gulf route. The opening of the canal, and the establishment of a steamer service on the Tigris (see EHME, pp. 146–53), also led to a revival of the trade through Baghdad and Kermanshah (see 3:15). Russian overland trade with Azerbaijan also increased. The British attempt to open a route for trade through Sistan, in order to meet Russian competition in Khurasan, met with only limited success (see 3:16). Table 1, based on customs returns, shows the magnitude of the flow through the various channels on the eve of the First World War. After that war, thanks to the great expansion of petroleum production, the improvement of the gulf ports, and the building of roads and then railways, the bulk of Iran's trade shifted to the Persian Gulf.

[8] Lewis Pelly, "Remarks on the Tribes," p. 58; see also chap. 4, introduction.

## TABLE 1
WEIGHT OF GOODS AND CUSTOMS RECEIPTS, 1909/10

| | WEIGHT (THOUSANDS OF TONS) | | GROSS CUSTOMS RECEIPTS (THOUSANDS OF POUNDS STERLING) |
|---|---|---|---|
| | Imports | Exports | |
| Azerbaijan (Julfa). . . . . . | 23 | 18 | 124 |
| Caspian ports | | | |
|   Astara . . . . . . . . . | 14 | 7 | 32 |
|   Gilan (Enzeli) . . . . . . | 65 | 54 | 136 |
|   Mazandaran (Mashad-i Sar) | 13 | 10 | 51 |
|   Astarabad (Bandar Gez) . | 12 | 12 | 31 |
| | 104 | 83 | 250 |
| Khurasan . . . . . . . . . | | | |
|   Mashad . . . . . . . . | 8 | 3 | . . . |
|   Qushan . . . . . . . . | 6 | 9 | . . . |
| | 14 | 12 | 60[a] |
| Gulf ports | | | |
|   Bandar Abbas . . . . . . | 12 | 5 | 33 |
|   Lingah . . . . . . . . . | 9 | 3 | . . . |
|   Bushire . . . . . . . . . | 20 | 6 | 82 |
|   Muhammarah . . . . . . | 19[b] | 6 | 41 |
|   Ahwaz . . . . . . . . . | 3[c] | 1 | |
| | 63 | 21 | 156 |
| Baghdad route | | | |
|   Kermanshah. . . . . . . | 12 | 5 | 114 |
|   Qasr-i Shirin . . . . . . | 1 | 1 | . . . |
| | 13 | 6 | 114 |
| Tehran parcel post . . . . . | . . | . . | 20 |

SOURCE: "Persia," A and P 1910, 94; "Persia," A and P 1910, 101.
[a] 1908/9.
[b] Including 8,900 tons for Anglo-Persian Oil Co.
[c] Including 1,700 tons for Anglo-Persian Oil Co.

## The Legal and Administrative Framework of Trade

The three following selections illustrate some of the main aspects of the legal and administrative framework within which foreign and Persian merchants operated in Iran: negotiations preceding the 1841 Anglo-Persian Commercial Treaty; the *rahdari*, or road tax; and methods of valuation used by the customs authorities.

British policy in Iran, as in so many other countries (see chap. 3, introduction) aimed at establishing a system which, by giving them the same legal and fiscal rights and duties as those enjoyed by native and foreign merchants, by abolishing monopolies and administrative restraints, and by reducing government interference, would enable British merchants to use their greater economic power to compete successfully.

Apart from questions relating to safety of life and property—ranging from the insecurity of the Erzerum road (see 3:8) to the plunder of the British India Steam Navigation Company's steamer *Cashmere* off Muhammarah as late as 1873 (see dispatches of 21 October 1873 and 14 August 1874, FO 60/365), three matters seem to have caused most concern: prohibitions on exports or imports; arbitrary taxes; and the difficulty of collecting debts.

As regards prohibitions, in 1841 the British consul complained of a ban issued by the Persian government on the consumption of tea in Tehran and Tabriz. The ostensible reason was that the Chinese mixed poison in their tea, but the real cause was that the merchants wanted to embarrass the Russian Georgians "who have the principal traffic in that article, whereas native merchants have none" (Bonham to Bidwell, 13 March 1841, FO 60/82). Six months later, however, it was reported that, after a vain attempt at enforcing the ban, the Iranian authorities had stopped interfering and inconveniencing, though they had not formally withdrawn the prohibition (ibid., 28 August 1841, FO 60/82).

Three years later the same consul reported that the Persian merchants had asked the government to prohibit imports of European manufactures "on the ground principally of the ruin Persian manufacturers are reduced to by the constant and immense importation of foreign goods." This attempt was, however, unsuccessful, and the combination formed by the merchants for that purpose was dissolved (Bonham to Sheil, 28 June 1844 and 29 July 1844, FO 60/107). Similar, and equally fruitless, attempts were made by "the traders and manufacturers of Cashan" (Abbott to Aberdeen, 31 March 1845, FO 60/117—see also 6:2) and other manufacturers and traders.

Prohibitions on exports were no less resented, and were successfully opposed. In 1853, the consul protested strongly against a sudden embargo on exports of rice from Tabriz (Stevens to Prince Hamza Mirza, 28 July 1853, FO 60/185). The following year a ban on exports of wheat and barley evoked similar protests (Stevens to Thomson, 2 April 1854, FO 60/196). In 1855, the consul complained that the prohibition on exports of wool was hurting British Indian merchants in Kirman and Yazd (Stevens to Murray, 31 December 1855, FO 60/205). In 1875, the complaint was about the "interdict imposed by the Persian government on the exportation of grain from Bushire, fifteen days' notice of the interdict having been given." This had caused difficulties for Malcom and Company, who had chartered ships to carry grain (Thomson to Derby, 28 January 1875, FO 60/373). In all these instances the British consuls recognized the right of the Iranian government to stop exports in times of scarcity, but insisted on due notice or the taking of measures which would minimize the disruption of contracts made by British merchants.

The extent to which the British—and other—consuls were prepared to go in their opposition to any form of monopoly was illustrated by their prolonged struggles in 1881/82 against the government's grant of a concession to an Iranian of the exclusive right to cut boxwood in the Caspian provinces. They maintained that this infringed the 1841 treaty (Thomson to Granville, 2 September 1882, FO 60/448). In this case, however, the Persian government seems to have remained unmoved.

As regards taxation, selection 2 shows that Iranian merchants were subjected to higher taxes, which put them under a severe handicap.[1] But, as is brought out by selection 3, European traders also had much to complain about. A memorandum addressed by the India Office to the Foreign Office (18 March 1875, FO 60/375) lists some of the grievances. "Attempts have occasionally been made to impose an additional tax [i.e., above the 5 percent levied at entry or exit] on the goods during transit even when still in the hands of British subjects." Moreover, when goods are "sold at the seaport to a Persian purchaser for transmission into the interior, they are subjected to transit dues as if they had not already paid the 5 percent customs duty." As a result, "in reality our imports are taxed 10, 20, or 30 percent, and Persian produce for exportation the same." The memorandum goes on to suggest that two privileges enjoyed by Persian merchants in Bombay should be granted to British merchants in Iran: a drawback on goods reexported from Persian ports and exemption from duty of goods transshipped in Persian ports. Drawbacks, such as were granted in the Ottoman Empire, had been urged in 1871 (26 July 1871, FO 60/337). In 1874, the British merchants in Bushire complained that they were being made to pay the *rahdari* tax on beasts of burden. The Persian authorities argued that the tax was one on Persian muleteers, levied all over the country, and had nothing to do with customs duties. Strong representations were made (Thomson to Derby, 3 April 1874, FO 60/365). And in 1876, the British consul complained about the reimposition of the *rahdarlik*, or road tax (Taylor to Derby, 15 June 1876, FO 60/382).

The recovery of commercial debts was always a prolonged and expensive matter (see 2:4, and 3:11). A *farman* of 27 *shawwal* 1259 (20 November 1843), issued at the request of the Russian government, provided for registration of bonds and attempted to regulate bankruptcies in a manner more satisfactory to European creditors (see translation and accompanying comments by Bonham, 19 December 1843, FO 60/100). But this did little to improve matters and in 1873 the British consul in Tabriz pointed out that "all expenses attending the recovery of debts fall on the creditor—consequently the debtor, having nothing to lose by delay, is the less inclined to meet his engagements with punctuality." Indeed many merchants made a practice of buying on credit, selling for cash at any price, lending the proceeds at 1.5 to 3 percent a month, and delaying repayment. Another abuse was "the impunity which is suffered to attend the crime of forgery" (Jones to Thomson,

---

[1] A list of the provinces where the *rahdari*, or road tax, and customs duties were levied in 1861 is given in a dispatch dated 27 July 1861 (FO 251/39).

Neither duty was levied in Qum. The *rahdari* only was levied in Kashan, Tuyserkan, Qazvin, Zanjan, Kurdistan, and Khoi. Customs only were levied in Mashad, Astarabad, Burujird, Shiraz (at the rate of 1/40), Bushire, Bandar Abbas, Yazd, Rasht (at the rate of 1/20 or 1/10), and Shushtar. Both *rahdari* and customs were levied in Kermanshah (on exports only), Isfahan, Kirman, and Tabriz.

26 September 1873, FO 60/354). In 1874, Gray, Paul and Co. complained of the great delay in recovering a debt in Isfahan, and asked for consular support (Thomson to Derby, 3 August 1874, FO 60/365). And in 1881, because of the difficulty of collecting debts, "the English merchants of Bushire have entered into a mutual agreement to sell only for cash or produce. This arrangement may cause inconvenience but at any rate it behoves European traders to exercise great caution in giving credit to natives in their mercantile transactions" (Thomson to Granville, 15 April 1881, FO 60/448). If to all this be added the fact that foreigners could own land or houses only with great difficulty, it will be seen that Iran was far from presenting the conditions required for successful capitalist enterprise, native or foreign.[2]

[2] For a detailed account of the difficulties met by British merchants in the Persian Gulf area in such matters as recovery of bad debts, embargoes on exports of grain, payment of *rahdari*, double imposition of customs duties, and, especially, purchase of land or houses, see Lorimer, 1:2088–99.

### Selection 1. Treaty Negotiations, 1836
[Ellis to Palmerston, 16 January 1836 and 1 September 1836, FO 539/3]

. . . I subsequently, in my interviews with the Persian Ministers, discussed the commercial intercourse between the two countries as a general question, but was always met by the assertion of the same dogma, that as the balance of the money trade was against Persia, any measure that encouraged the extension of the trade with manufacturing nations would be injurious; the only exception admitted was the import of arms and military stores.

The Persian Ministers seemed wholly insensible to the claim which England had to a participation in the commercial security and privileges enjoyed by Russia. In truth, the Commercial Treaty with Russia bears such intrinsic proofs of having been imposed by force of arms, that it is calculated to create a prejudice against all formal stipulations on the subject of trade.

As my instructions prohibited me from bringing forward the proposition for a renewal of the negotiations formally or distinctly, I never pushed the discussions with the Persians beyond an exposition of general principles and a refutation of the erroneous views taken of the consequence of increased commercial intercourse. I do not deem it necessary to trouble your lordship with the details of the reasoning used by the Persian Ministers in support of their principles. The main points urged were—the scarcity of coin in Persia; the want of mines of the precious metals; the impossibility of making returns in produce, and the discouragement of domestic, from the influx of foreign, manufactures. It was, however, scarcely to be expected that errors not yet eradicated in Europe should readily yield to mere argument in Persia, and the result has been that I have not found myself in a condition to make any formal proposition with that confidence of success required by your Lordship's instructions.

Although I throughout cautiously avoided any language that could be construed into a formal proposition, or an official proceeding, I conveyed to the Persian Ministers a very strong opinion that His Majesty's Government would not permanently desist from the renewal of a negotiation for the conclusion of a Commercial Treaty, which, in point of fact, would do little more than give form and stability to the privileges already enjoyed under the Ruckum (or order) of His Royal Highness Abbas Meerza.

The Shah takes every means to check the consumption of European manufactures, and to encourage those of Persia; to effect the latter purpose he has recently advanced money, and offered rewards to the makers of chintz, and he has insisted that the courtiers shall gradually substitute Persian woollens and Kerman shawls for the broadcloth now used in their dresses. These attempts to compel the use of inferior, and, in fact, more costly articles of home production, in lieu of the superior and cheaper manufactures of foreign countries, find no support beyond the circle of the Court, and will fail in attaining their object; but the principles by which they have been suggested prevented the fair operation of the motives upon which I had relied for inducing the Shah to grant that of his own accord, which I was not authorized to bring forward directly or officially.

I have reason to know that the Russian Minister has been informed of the indirect overtures made by me towards the renewal of a negotiation on the Commercial Treaty, and that his influence has been exerted to prevent them from being accepted.

An increase of the British trade with Persia is, *pro tanto*, a diminution of the commerce of Russia, which she cannot be expected to tolerate, and although the unjust privileges that have been secured to her by the Commercial Treaty of 1827 give Russian subjects an immense advantage in their transactions with Persians over the merchants of all other nations, yet the skill, enterprise and superior capital of British merchants have already succeeded in obtaining a command in the markets of Persia, that bids fair to place the supply of European manufactures almost entirely in their hands.

I am far from conceiving that the Shah or his Ministers will refuse to conclude a Commercial Treaty, when the proposition is brought forward formally and authoritatively, supported as the demand may be by the strong argument of right, derived by the stipulation contained in the preamble to the Treaty of Tehran, namely, "what relates to commerce, trade, and other affairs will be concluded and drawn up in a separate Commercial Treaty." These words undoubtedly amount to a substantive engagement, and may be considered to have the force of an Article. If this be true, it may, upon the authority of Vattel, book 2, chap. 13, sect. 202, be contended that as the violation of one Article in a Treaty may cancel the whole, so the refusal of the Persian Government to conclude a Commercial Treaty on fair and reciprocally beneficial conditions renders the Treaty of Tehran itself null and void.

A conviction that such might be the consequence of continued refusal would command the assent of the Shah, for it would outweigh his prejudices against European trade generally, as well as his apprehension of giving offence to Russia by doing justice to Great Britain. But if it be deemed inexpedient or inconsistent with a fair interpretation of the declaration in the preamble of the Treaty of Tehran, to use so stringent an argument as that just stated, I have little doubt that a serious demonstration of displeasure on the part of the British Government will force the shah to abandon his commercial dogmas, and, though reluctantly, to conclude such a treaty as will give the sanction of public faith to the present rate of duty, and permit the establishment of British consuls at Tabreez and Bushire, and Vice-Consuls, being native merchants of Persia, in the other trading cities of the empire.

I express this opinion from a conviction that, had I not been precluded by the character of the Embassy with which I have been charged, from taking up the negotiation as it was left by the Firman of the Shah brought to England by Mr. Fraser, I should have succeeded in concluding a Commercial Treaty; and I infer that the future Minister at this Court cannot fail, if entrusted with sufficient powers, to obtain that result.

MR. ELLIS TO VISCOUNT PALMERSTON.—(RECEIVED OCTOBER 27, 1836)

(Extract)          *Erzeroum, September 1, 1836*

Mr. McNeill informed me that it was proposed to apply the *ad valorem* duty of five per cent., not as at present, to all goods imported by British Subjects into Persia, but to goods being the growth, produce, or manufacture of the British dominions, by whomsoever imported. I ventured to suggest a doubt of the expediency of the alteration for the following reasons:—First, that as cargoes to Persia are assorted from the produce and manufactures of different countries, the British subjects might lose the advantage of the Treaty on all that was not of British origin; and therefore would not be in as good a situation as other European Merchants not so restricted. Secondly, that the determination of the country of the goods would, from the irregular manner of conducting all business in Persia, prove a source of cavil, which the Russians would not fail to encourage, as embarrassing to our trade and beneficial to theirs; and, thirdly, that as far as British Merchants are concerned, there can be no doubt of their bringing staple goods, of British origin, while those goods as at present, from their cheapness, find a readier sale than those of any other country.

It is quite true that Persian Subjects are the chief importers of British manufactures, and they pay a duty of only three per cent.; the proposed terms of the Treaty would undoubtedly prevent the duty paid by them from being raised *eo nomine*; but if the object of the Persian Government were to discourage the importation of British manufactures, exactions under a different name might be imposed, and the Treaty would scarcely be a protection for Persian Subjects, who would not venture to appeal for redress to the British authority against the acts of their own Government. British Merchants, at present paying the duty of five per cent., are not undersold by the Persian Importer; and there can be little doubt that as our Merchants gain confidence in the stability of the Commercial relations with Persia, the direct Trade will so increase as to reverse the proportion between the imports of British manufactures made by them, and by Persian Merchants. In fact, there are actually other causes in operation tending to this result. I do not, therefore, see

much advantage in the proposed change; and I do see no inconsiderable objections to introducing a new principle to the notice of the Persians. I have always thought that two Articles—the one placing the trade of British Subjects on the footing of the most favoured nation, and the other giving a right of establishing Consuls, where absolutely necessary, would answer every purpose. The Russian Treaty, forced upon Persia at the point of the bayonet, would, as the general rule, give sufficient protection to the British Trade; and we have no occasion to press for the establishment of Consuls, being British Subjects, in more than two or three places. The more we introduce novelty of principle, or variety of detail, into our commercial propositions, the more we provoke discussion and create difficulties; for the Persians more readily yield a principle with which they are familiar, than agree to settle by positive stipulation the terms in detail, according to which the principle is to be applied.

### Selection 2. Taxes on Persians, 1851
[Stevens to Sheil, 26 February 1851, FO 60/166]

*Tabreez*
*26 February 1851*

Great discontent prevails in the Bazaars of Tabreez in consequence of the duties on goods imported by Persians having been increased; the mode of levying them is also greatly and very justly complained of.

A Tax of 5 Kerrans per Horseload on all goods arriving at Tabreez, and which was abolished during the reign of Feth Aly Shah, has been re-established. Certain articles such as Sugar, Tea, paper and spices, hitherto entirely exempt from Customs duty are by the new regulation to pay not 2 per cent like all other goods but 4 per Cent. The position now of the Persian Merchant compared to that of the European may be understood by the following statements;

The European importing a load of Sugar of the value of 10 Tomans—pays his 5 per

Cent once for all and may re-export it to Tehran.

The Persian pays for the load

| | | |
|---|---|---|
| Rohdarlik at Khoi . . . | S.K. | 3.15 |
| —Ditto—Haft Tcheshme | S.K. | 3.15 |
| —Ditto—Tabreez . . . | S.K. | 2.10 |
| New duty 4 per cent . . | S.K. | 4.00 |
| | in all S.K. | 14.0 |

or 14 per Cent and if he re-exports to Tehran is charged Rohdarlik at Meeana, Zenjaun, Kazveen and Tehran.

In regard to Manufactures the relative positions are as follows: We will suppose an importation of a horseload of British Cotton piece goods of the value, at 5 Kerans per piece, of 30 Tomans.

The European pays 5 per cent once for all, and can transport his goods to any part of Persia without extra duties.

For Persians, the new customer [customs official], Meerza Abd-oollah, values precisely the same goods at 8 Kerrans the piece = for the horseload 48 Tomans on which is charged:

| | | |
|---|---|---|
| Rohdarlik at Khoi . . . . . . . . | K | 3.15 |
| —Ditto—Haft Tcheshme . . . . . | K | 3.15 |
| Import duty 2 per Cent. . . . . . | K | 9.12 |
| Old duty recently revived. . . . . | K | 5.00 |
| | in all K | 22.2.0 |

$= 7\frac{1}{2}$ per Cent, and, if re-exported, the Persian Merchant is taxed with Rohdarlik at every Town between Tabreez and Herat, or Tabreez and the Persian gulf.

Unless these duties are not [sic] considerably reduced the natives must abandon Commercial pursuits, and the Trade will then be reduced in amount, and remain entirely in the hands of Europeans. British Commerce will especially feel the effects of any such result for the withdrawal from the market of Native Merchants must produce a great diminution in the amount of British Goods now imported.

The Customer places his own valuation on goods greatly exceeding the market price, or that to which Europeans will submit—he also insists on opening and examining every package previous to delivering it, while the Custom House

affords no accommodation for such a purpose. The consequence is the goods remain for several days exposed to rain and snow, and this has already caused the partial destruction of a parcel of loaf Sugar, and serious damage to manufactures. When remonstrated with Meerza Abd-oollah threatens to report the parties to the Ameer-i-Nizam, and thus compels them to submit to every sort of injustice and vexation.

Several who are of Karabagh origin are endeavoring, through relatives in that Country, to obtain Russian passports. Many are talking of retiring from Trade, while others are hoping to form partnerships with Foreign subjects, and thus escape the hardships to which they are subjected, and all these evils are likely to occur because the Ameer hopes to increase the Customs Revenues by 8 or 10,000 Tomans—an important sum no doubt for an impoverished Treasury, but surely not worth obtaining at the sacrifices it will probably entail.

### Selection 3. Levying of Customs Duties on Europeans, 1860

[Abbott to Alison, 10 September 1860, FO 60/253]

*Tabreez*
*10 September 1860*

I have the honour to report to Your Excellency that the Custom House Authorities of Tabreez have for some time past acted in a very arbitrary and apparently unjust manner towards the European Merchants established here, in seizing and detaining their goods under the plea of their not having hitherto obtained the full rate of duty amounting to 5 per Cent ad valorem stipulated by Treaty—whilst the European Merchants declare they have acquitted themselves of as much as they are bound by Treaty to pay. The difficulty has arisen from a defect in the Commercial Treaty of Toorcoman Chai between Persia and Russia the terms of which have been confirmed to the English and some other European Governments, it not being described in that

Document by what Rule the valuation of Merchandise imported into Persia is to be taken and there being no Tariff of Prices. The Custom House Authorities claim 5 per Cent on the value of Foreign Goods *on the spot* whilst the European Merchants proclaim this to be unjust and bring forward in support of their assertion the example of Turkey which allows 20 per Cent off the prices laid down in the Tariff as representing the probable Expenses incident on the importation from a foreign Country—and that of Russia which at the neighbouring frontier of the Arras is understood to levy duties on the value the goods may bear at Tabreez when coming from thence.

Until comparatively a recent date the Merchants had entered into arrangements with the Custom House to pass their goods at a certain rate per package or per Horse Load—this was very advantageous to them as it precluded the necessity of opening out the packages in a place which affords very little convenience for an operation of the kind on a large scale and where to disturb the expensive and beautiful English packing was a matter of serious consideration as purchasers here are in the habit of taking goods on sample and transporting them into the interior when it is of importance that the original secure mode of embaling should not be disturbed.

There is nothing at present however to prevent the Custom House from interpreting the Treaty in the sense most favorable to itself and doubtless it has a right to take the utmost the Treaty admits of—but the custom having prevailed for so many years of permitting goods to pass at so much per mule load it appeared to me to be an unjust and arbitrary proceeding to detain the Merchants' goods without giving any formal notice either to the Owners or to the European Consulates of their intention of altering the rule hitherto observed—custom being

of as much force as Law itself in this Country. On these grounds therefore I have supported the cause of those of the European Merchants here who enjoy English protection, insisting that it is not in the competency of the Custom House Master to augment at will the rates established for so long a period and stating it as my opinion that as any such measure would require the sanction of the Foreign Missions at Tehran the matter should remain over until a reference to the Capital could be made.

This view of the case was also taken by the Russian Consul General who has entered into a compact with Meerza Abbas Khan the Maaven el Vezareh that Merchants trading here under Russian protection shall be allowed to withdraw their goods from the Custom House on paying duties as heretofore pending a reference of the case to the Persian Government and to the European Missions—and the Maaven has communicated to me officially this arrangement which as it is what I had already proposed I accept of course for British subjects.

The European Merchants here having lately memorialized Your Excellency and the other European Ministers at Tehran on the subject of the Customs Duties demanded of them I have only to add the expression of my hope that the matter may be taken into Your Excellency's consideration and settled once for all by some fair convention with the Persian Government by which whilst the rights of Persia are fully secured, English subjects trading to this Country may not in future be exposed to any arbitrary and injurious dealings such as have lately taken place here. I think some medium between the extreme expectations of the adverse parties in the question might be adopted without injustice to either—but Your Excellency's greater knowledge and experience in such matters render any further observations on my part unnecessary. . . .

## Persian Gulf Trade

By the end of the eighteenth century, trade in the Persian Gulf had dwindled to a trickle. Tables annexed to the following selection show that in 1780/81–1789/90, inclusive, only 667 bales of woolens of all kinds were sold at Bushire by the East India Company.[1] Their original cost in England was £23,420; the addition of 4 percent interest, 3 percent insurance, and freight of £10 a ton brought the cost at Bushire to £26,793, and a total net loss of £1,232 was incurred over the ten years. For Basra, sales totaled 1,391 bales, costing £52,204 in England, and the net loss was £11,305. No wonder the company wanted to close down its establishments in the gulf.

The establishment of order by the Qajars and the consequent revival of the Persian economy, together with the increasing security in the gulf provided by the British navy, led to a rapid growth of trade. Malcolm estimated total Iranian imports from India, including those brought in by the company, at 3,000,000 rupees, or £300,000, and exports at 1,500,000 rupees (6:1). Imports of the whole Persian Gulf from Madras and Bombay in 1805 were 2,191,000 rupees, and exports were 2,935,000; direct trade between Britain and the gulf (imports plus exports) averaged £3,000.[2]

As selection 5 shows, by 1817 total imports through Bushire may have been as high as £300,000 and by 1823 they had more than doubled, to £670,000. In 1824, imports fell sharply, to 3,344,000 Persian rials, or about £476,000 (dispatch by Willock, 30 December 1825, FO 60/25). No figures are available on the trade of Bushire in the next few years, but trade between the whole gulf and Bombay, Madras, and Calcutta leveled off in the years 1822/23–1827/28 (see "Appendix to Report from Select Committee," A and P 1831–32, 10, part 2). After that there may have been a slight increase; Bombay's total trade with the gulf rose from an average of 7,225,000 rupees (about £723,000) in 1821/22–1827/28 to 7,925,900 rupees in 1844/45. As selection 6 shows, progress in the next fifteen years was swift, to 13,143,000 rupees in 1860/61. The American Civil War acted as a strong stimulant, and trade with Bombay increased nearly threefold, to 34,437,000 in 1865/66. In 1866/67 the volume of trade fell by half, then recovered slightly, leveling off at a little over 20,000,000 in the next two years. The gulf's main imports from Bombay were cotton goods (accounting for two-fifths or more of the total), sugar (about one-tenth), grain, and metals. Its exports were not so clearly broken down: fruits and dates were important items and so were wool and silk; grain was exported in good years and so was cotton during the "famine" caused by the American Civil War.

The establishment of steam navigation (see 4:3, 4) and the rapid increase in exports of opium (see 5:10, 11) further stimulated trade, and in 1885 the British consul estimated that, in the previous ten years, the trade of Bushire had about doubled, from 10,000,000 to 20,000,000 rupees, and that of Bandar Abbas had risen from 3,000,000 to 8,000,000. In 1884 the Bushire customs revenue was farmed out for 800,000 krans, "being double the amount realized 10 years back.

[1] I owe this reference to Mr. R. W. Ferrier.
[2] MacGregor, 2:389.

Customs revenues of Bandar Abbas were let in 1884 for 701,500 krans, showing a similar increase. The Customs lease of Lingah has been raised in the period from 65,000 to 160,000 krans" (Bushire," A and P 1888, 78; see also ibid., 1883, 74; ibid., 1880, 73; and "Muscat and Persia," A and P 1876, 74). Table 1 shows the situation in 1874/75, in thousands of rupees; the rate was 10 rupees to the pound.

TABLE 1

VALUE OF PERSIAN GULF TRADE, 1874/75
(IN THOUSANDS OF RUPEES)

|  | TOTAL TRADE | | TRADE WITH INDIA | |
|---|---|---|---|---|
|  | Imports | Exports | Imports | Exports |
| Bushire merchandise . . . | 3,473 | 2,646 | 1,972 | 535 |
| Bushire treasure . . . . . | 125 | 446 | 50 | 148 |
| Bushire total. . . . . . | 3,598 | 3,092 | 2,022 | 683 |
| Bandar Abbas merchandise | 1,691 | 1,459 | 1,060 | 1,174 |
| Bandar Abbas treasure . . | 47 | 306 | 24 | 294 |
| Bandar Abbas total . . . . | 1,738 | 1,766 | 1,084 | 1,468 |
| Total gulf merchandise . . | 13,047 | 10,000 | 6,210 | 5,039 |
| Total gulf treasure . . . . | 789 | 752 | 174 | 442 |
| Total gulf total . . . . . | 13,836 | 10,753 | 6,384 | 5,481 |

SOURCE: Report by Government of India, Department of Revenue, Agriculture and Commerce, no. 23 of 1875, FO 60/375.

A further piece of evidence is worth quoting: "When I first came here [i.e., to Bushire, ten years previously] there was one European firm; now there are three, some with European agencies at Shiraz and Ispahan. There are also agencies of other European firms both in Bushire and up country." Imports of piece goods from Britain had risen from £668,000 in 1873/74 and £435,000 in 1874/75 to £3,100,000 in 1882/83 and £4,000,000 in 1883/84; those from India had risen from £1,090,000 and £1,050,000 to £1,730,000 and £2,000,000 respectively (Ross to Arundel, 2 April 1885, FO 60/475).

A very important factor contributing to this increase, in addition to the great increase in steamers calling at the gulf ports (ibid.), was the diversion of trade from the Trebizond and Caucasus routes by the Russo-Turkish War of 1877 and the abolition of exemption on goods in transit through the Caucasus (see 3 : 7–10 and 4 : 5).

Table 2 shows subsequent developments. Trade rose fairly rapidly until the end of the century, and then leveled off.

Thus, at the outbreak of the First World War, imports through the gulf ports were around £2,300,000 and exports were £1,200,000, or about 20 and 15 percent, respectively, of total Iranian trade.[3] Assuming that in 1817 exports were

---

[3] It is possible, however, that these figures are inflated by some double counting. For, as was pointed out by the French minister in Tehran, "not infrequently merchandise consigned to a business firm in Bushire, having failed to find a buyer there, is redirected to Lingah or Bandar Abbas, and is naturally included once more in the statistics relating to these ports" (De Balloy to Minister of Foreign Affairs, 30 October 1884, AE Téhéran, vol. 3).

## TABLE 2

TRADE IN PERSIAN GULF PORTS, 1895–1913
(IN THOUSANDS OF POUNDS STERLING)

|  | 1895 | 1900 | 1905 | 1909/10 | 1913/14 |
|---|---|---|---|---|---|
| *Bushire* |  |  |  |  |  |
| Imports . . . . . . | 1,017 | 1,323 | 762 | 676 | 826 |
| Exports . . . . . . | 529 | 710 | 470 | 349 | 602 |
| *Bandar Abbas* |  |  |  |  |  |
| Imports . . . . . . | 477 | 339 | 384 | 340 | 459 |
| Exports . . . . . . | 325 | 103 | 152 | 202 | 267 |
| *Lingah* |  |  |  |  |  |
| Imports . . . . . . | 463 | 501 | 103 | 132 | 180 |
| Exports . . . . . . | 511 | 470 | 67 | 194 | 126 |
| *Muhammarah* |  |  |  |  |  |
| Imports . . . . . . | 138 | 202 | 224 | 917[a] | 812[a] |
| Exports . . . . . . | 43 | 103 | 93 | 218 | 313 |

SOURCE: Great Britain, Foreign Office, Historical Section Handbooks,
*Persia* (June 1919), pp. 82–86.
[a] Includes imports by Anglo-Persian Oil Company.

two-thirds of imports,[4] giving a total trade for Bushire of about £500,000, and adding another £100,000 to £200,000 for the other Iranian ports, it would seem that total trade rose about five- or sixfold in the period between the Napoleonic War and First World War.

(See also works by Curzon and Lorimer, and Foreign Office Handbooks, listed in the bibliography.)

[4] In 1821/22–1827/28, inclusive, the whole gulf's exports to Bombay and Madras aggregated 25 million rupees and its imports 29.4 million—see "Appendix to Report." On the other hand, Malcolm believed that Iran's exports covered only half its imports.

## Selection 4. Trade of Bushire, 1780s
[*Three Reports of the Select Committee Appointed by the Court of Directors* (London, n.d.), pp. 113–20]

### PERSIA

Your committee will, in the next place, offer such information and observations as relate to Persia, in compliance with their lordships request.

That Empire is most happily situated for trade, almost surrounded by Arabia, Turkey, the Tartars, and countries whose commerce is imperfectly known to the North and North East, and also by India; it has moreover a very considerable tract of sea coast, and communicates at the same time with Aleppo and Constantinople, through Bussora and Bagdat, and with Russia by means of the Caspian sea. If to these circumstances are added its former state of prosperity,

affluence, and splendour, with the fertility of soil, and its numerous natural productions, it is reasonable to form great expectations from such a combination of circumstances. Persia, however, adds another melancholy instance of those found in the annals of history, that every blessing which nature can bestow is of no avail, unless accompanied by that peace and tranquility which alone results from a steady well-regulated government.

During the time of Nadir Shaw's usurpation, the Company found themselves exposed to repeated instances of oppression; notwithstanding the Shaw directed that the loss which Mr. Jonas Hanway sustained by the seizure of his woollens should be made good to him. From the assassination of Nadir Shaw until the establishment of Kerim Khan, the empire was plunged into the deepest confusion and distress. The result of this (as stated in the First Report) was, that the Company could place no reliance whatever, nor obtain any solid protection from a Persian phirmaund [*farman*]. Under the last-mentioned prince, commerce had begun to revive, and very considerable progress had been made at his death, which happened early in the year 1779. The confusion occasioned by that event did not subside until Jaffer Khan (the nephew of Kerim) assumed the government of the southern provinces, Schyras and its dependencies, in the year 1784. His conduct with regard to trade was similar to that of Kerim Khan; and at the time he was assassinated in the year 1789 a considerable degree of confidence had appeared in the stability and equity of his government.

The present ruler of Schyras, Lutf Ally Khan, has already manifested the same disposition to protect and encourage foreigners in their trade.

If, in addition to the political convulsions before mentioned, we consider the havock made by maladies, which in some places, and upon some occasions, in the confines of Turkey, are stated to have destroyed one third of the inhabitants; the emigrations which have ensued; the few in number now left to enjoy ease and affluence, whence trade derives its best support; the comparison between the past and present state of Persia, in every respect, will be found truly deplorable.

The trade of Ormus has been long since lost. It is the same with regard to Gombroon whence the Company withdrew their establishment, in consequence of the heavy expence; but it ought to have been abandoned long before, upon a principle of humanity. Further up the Gulph is Bushire, where a Resident is now fixed. Beyond that is Bundanck [Bandar Rig], formerly a place of some note, where the Dutch had an establishment, upon the Island of Carrick [Kharg], but which was abandoned when they withdrew from the Island. At the head of the Gulf, and about 70 miles from the sea, is Bussora; which, although situated in Arabia Deserta, on the banks of the Arab

river, formed by a junction of the Tigris and Euphrates, yet as it forms more or less the centre of the Company's commercial concerns in those parts, it becomes absolutely necessary to be introduced in the present report.

At one period the Company had abandoned Omnus [Ormus], Gombroon, Bushire, and Bunderick; but, at the request of Kerim Khan, an establishment was made at Bushire, which has remained ever since.

The result of the annual sales, both at Bussora and Bushire, have been already comprised in the First Report, under the Presidency of Bombay; but for the purpose of complying in the fullest manner with the request of their Lordships, your Committee now state them separately.

The particulars of the sales of woollens at Bussora will be found in the Appendix, No. 2.

The particulars of the sales of woollens at Bushire will be found in the Appendix, No. 3.

In this account of the sales at Bushire, no duty nor expence paid towards the government of the country is charged.

And your Committee will have occasion to offer their observations relative to the very considerable expence which attends those establishments hereafter.

When patterns of the Norwich and Manchester manufactures were sent to Bussora and Bushire, in 1788, some of the qualities and colours were well adapted to the taste of the Persians; but the invoice price was so high that the loss must have been very considerable, and therefore they were returned. The manner in which Persia has been drained of its gold and silver for a long period of years, has compelled the natives to establish manufactures of coarse cotton, and other articles, for common wear; and with which the southern parts of Persia are at present supplied.

Yet your Committee entertain no doubt but that the European articles, and woollens in particular, may be sold, and readily consumed, in Persia.

There are, however, other points necessary for consideration:

1st, The profit and loss resulting therefrom.

2dly, The means which Persia possesses of paying for those sales.

3dly, The competition to be expected from European foreigners.

Enough has been already said with regard to the first; and it is presumed, that a discussion of the second and third will ascertain how far individuals, the subjects of Great Britain, have a prospect of extending the sale of her manufactures and produce into Persia, beyond what the Company have done, independent of the heavy loss which they must sustain in the first instance from the sale.

Before your Committee proceed to the investigation of those points, it becomes necessary to consider the expence arising to the Company from their establishments at Bussora and Bushire. For no trade can be carried on with those places from the sea without a regular establishment of persons constantly residing there, to cultivate the protection of those fluctuating arbitrary governments, by making presents, at times, to a considerable amount, whenever a revolution may take place in the country.

| | | |
|---|---|---|
| The average amount of sales at Bussora is | £5,047 | |
| And the average annual loss is. . . . | . . . . . | £1,130 |
| Besides which, the expence of the factory at Bussora amounts annually to . . . | . . . . . | 4,276 |
| Total loss arising from the sale of woollens, and from the establishment. . . | . . . . . | £5,406 |

The duties to the Turkish government are included in the estimate of profit and loss on the sale of woollens; but the presents which the factory have been obliged to make, from time to time (the average annual amount of which is £630) are included under the expence of the factory of Bussora, and must be paid by those who carry on the trade.

The Company have no other emolument or trade whatsoever resulting from their establishment at Bussora, by which any part of the expence of £4,276 per annum can be recovered: and they incur a further annual expence at that place of £2,311, for supplies furnished to the Bombay cruizers, and for the charge of receiving and forwarding packets to and from Europe.

| | | |
|---|---|---|
| The average annual amount of sales at Bushire is . . . . . . . . . . . . | £2,608 | |
| The annual loss resulting therefrom is . . | . . . . . | £ 123 |
| Besides which, the expence of the factory at Bushire amounts annually to. . . . | . . . . . | £1,375 |
| Total loss arising from the sale of woollens and from the establishment . . . . . | . . . . . | £1,498 |

There are no presents to the government of Bushire, nor to the superior government at Schyras, for reasons already mentioned; but should the trade with Persia improve, those presents will be expected hereafter, and must be made.

The advances to the Bombay cruizers, at this residency, amount to about £340 per annum.

Although it is impossible that a complete cargo of Europe goods could be formed capable of being sold in all or in any parts of the Gulf, yet, as your Committee have made their calculation upon a freight of £10 per ton, they do not charge additionally for the freight from Bombay to Bushire and Bussora nor do they include some other charges, which would fall heavy upon individuals.

We must observe, however, that the Bombay cruizers are a great expence to the Company, but absolutely necessary to the intercourse with the Gulph of Persia from the vexations of pirates; and consequently some part of that expence must be commercial. . . . .

But this is not the whole inconvenience. In a country where the exchange is nominal, (which is the case with Turkey as well as Persia) the proceeds of goods sold must be invested in the produce of the country.

The usual prices, at which such produce will sell at the place of their destination, is always below (and sometimes considerably below) the nominal course of exchange, unless in the case of accidents and consequent speculations. If individuals shall prefer to receive gold or silver in such countries as Turkey or Persia, instead of produce, there is an additional, and sometimes considerable, loss arising therefrom.

As it is evident therefore that returns cannot be made in bills, and that gold and silver will augment the loss, it becomes necessary to take a short review of what Persia affords, in order to ascertain whether any other means exist of making returns for the sale of European articles.

The manufactures and produce of Persia are silks, brocades, carpets, manufactures of steel, sword blades, spear heads, gun barrels, glass, rose water, attar of roses, cotton cloths, some shawls, sheep skins dressed in a very superior manner, raw silks, some indigo and tobacco, rhubarb, irak, drugs of different sorts, dried fruits, cotton, mines of iron and copper, wool of the Kerman sheep, in small quantities, wines, marble and some trifling articles; to which must be added Persian and Turkish coins, Venetian chequins, German crowns, and gold and silver in bars.

As those individuals who carry on the whole of the trade with Persia, except in woollens, are not actuated by the same liberal principles as the Company, it must be enquired what are the articles which Persia regularly demands, and which must be paid for at their full value. For until those demands are satisfied, the proprietor of British woollens, etc. cannot expect payment for his goods without a further addition to the heavy loss which has been stated.

The imports into Bussora and Bushire from the sea consist of Bengal piece goods, chintz from the coast, long cloth, Porto Novo blue cloth, Malabar, Surat, and Guzarat piece goods, Cuttanees, Cambay, Chanders, Broach and Sundy cotton, cotton yarn, shawls, bamboos, China ware, sugar, sugar candy, pepper, ginger, cardamums, cloves, nutmegs, cinnamon, cassia, clowers, musk, lack, camphire, turmerick, indigo, tootenague, red lead, coffee, tobacco, British woollens, iron, lead, steel, tin, and a variety of drugs.

A considerable part of the importations into Bussora is no doubt for Turkey, and probably for Arabia, as well as Persia; but as most of those articles are also imported into Bushire (the Indian manufactures however, in small quantities, but the others in a much larger proportion) it must be admitted that some of those necessary for the supply of the empire of Persia (under such a climate) must be of considerable value, and naturally entitled to a preference over woollens or other European articles; whilst, on the other hand, the products of Persia are not suitable for the Indian markets.

It has been found indeed by experience, that notwithstanding the loss, India is a constant drain upon Persia for its gold and silver. This loss is made good to the Indian merchant by a proportioned advance upon the price of the goods which he sells; but that loss, so far from being compensated to the European merchant, would become an addition to a burthen which is already too great. When your Committee state, that the products of Persia are not suitable to the Indian markets, they beg to be understood in a comparative sense only. The exact proportion cannot be ascertained, although great pains have been bestowed for the purpose; but there is reason to believe, that not one fifth part can be returned to India in the produce of Persia. The remainder, or balance, must therefore be paid in the precious metals; for the rich and most valuable product of silks is in no demand.

In addition to this constant drain upon the country must be mentioned the pilgrimages made by the Persians to Kuballey [Karbala] and Mecca, to which at least 10,000 annually resort; and it will be found, that if merchants require payment in gold or silver for articles which constitute, in the most favourable point of view, a *forced trade*, such payment must produce an enormous loss, or deduction, from the current course of exchange.

Having thus stated the difficulties which occur relative to the very slender means which Persia possesses of paying for her imports from India, and which apply still more forcibly to Great Britain, your Committee will proceed to the 3d point, *viz.* the competition to be expected from European foreigners.

In the year 1681, the Turkey merchants [Levant Company] remonstrated against the East India Company in particular for interfering with them in the sale of woollens in the northern parts of Persia. At that period silks, carpets, etc. were [sold] in England, by which means returns could be secured. But the contest on the part of the Company, even at that time, was not for a beneficial market, being compelled by their charters to export manufactures and produce to a certain amount; and which, as they could not sell in India, they were compelled to send woollens to Persia, for the purpose of avoiding a total loss. If the Turkey merchants could procure returns, and sell the silks in the same proportions as formerly, they would be equally capable of extending their exports of woollens, etc. for the expence of carriage across the deserts, including the insurance from risk, and the duties paid to the wandering tribes, etc. is very moderate.

Unfortunately the silk manufacture has never been deemed an object worthy the protection of government in this country. The heavy duty paid on the importation of the raw material will always prevent the manufacturers from contending upon equal ground with those of foreign nations; whilst the produce of India and China, with a small quantity from Italy, precludes the necessity of importing any from Persia, and very little from Turkey, as heretofore, for our domestic consumption, and for the little proportion of the export trade which we enjoy.

France has pursued a different course; and the manufacture at Lyons, which owes its establishment to one of the ablest ministers that country ever boasted, employs silk of every country and of every description. The Persian and Turkey silks are purchased from the merchant of Marseilles, who receives them in return for the woollens and manufactures of France, which he had previously exported.

In the north, Russia is making rapid strides towards commercial pre-eminence; and at Moscow, Persian silk is sold in large quantities, whilst it is seldom, if ever, seen in London.

It is in vain to contend against such competitors; and therefore, under all the circumstances stated, your Committee are decidedly of opinion, that the export of British manufactures and produce to Persia by sea cannot be increased, either by the Company or by individuals, until that empire, or the countries which surround it, shall obtain the blessings of a regular and established government.

And even if that event should ever happen, doubts must still remain whether Russia, but more particularly France, will not be enabled to supply Persia with European goods upon better terms than British subjects, for reasons which have been fully stated in the present Report.

### Selection 5. Persian Gulf Trade, 1817–23
[Willock to Canning, 7 July 1824, FO 60/24, and IO, LP and S 9/37]

*Sultanieh*
*July 7, 1824*
Sir,

In my dispatch No. 5 of 1823 I stated that I had requested The Hon'ble Company's Resident at Bushire to afford me such information as he possessed on the state of trade between India and Persia.

I have now received from Colonel Stannus the result of his enquiries, and I have the honour to transmit a Copy of his report.

In the year 1817, the Imports on British bottoms of British, Indian, and China merchandize to the Port of Bushire amounted in value to the Sum of Persian

Rupees 3003947 or about £ Sterling 225,296 and continued to increase yearly, with the exception of 1821, till in 1822 they amounted to the sum of P.Rs. 7769530 or £582715. In 1823 the imports on British Bottoms amounted only to P.Rs. 3115806 or £233685. But in this year the Imports on Ships and boats belonging to the Port of Bushire, and Native boats of the Gulph amount to the additional Sum of P.Rs. 5811830 or £435887, giving a gross import for 1823 of P.Rs. 8927636 or £669572.

Although the Imports on British bottoms are smaller in 1823 than in previous years, yet as we are not possessed of any returns showing the Imports on Asiatick vessels, prior to 1823, we have not the means of ascertaining whether the gross Imports have advanced or declined.

Were we to suppose that the vessels of the Gulf have for some years brought to Bushire merchandize equal in amount to that shown on this first return of their trade it would give us as the gross importation of 1822 the Sum £1018602, which would show a reduction of £349030 in the amount for 1823.

I am inclined to believe that so great a reduction has not actually taken place in the gross amount, and that the security with which small vessels now navigate the Gulf, as well as the increased industry of the Inhabitants of its shores mentioned by Colonel Stannus have caused a considerable part of the carrying trade to pass from the hands of Europeans to those of natives who can do it cheaper. It is probable that the same causes will continue to operate and to diminish the share which the European Shipowners still have in this trade without producing any unfavourable effect on its actual extent.

Colonel Stannus has been informed that the trade of the minor Ports on the Persian Coast of the Gulph amounts collectively to about half of that of Bushire. If we calculate by this estimate, the total amount of merchandize imported from India annually will be from one Million to fifteen hundred thousand Pounds for which India is paid principally in bullion, specie, and pearls. Of this large sum it would appear on an average of four years that about £233023 is imported in the shape of European articles as chintz, broad cloth, etc. which are British Manufacture,—and we may suppose that a considerable quantity of goods of the same description is also carried to the Arabian Coast and to Bussora for the consumption of the interior of Arabia, and of a part of Turkey and the South West Provinces of Persia and Curdistan.

Colonel Stannus states that Persia has lately begun to furnish a return for her imports which promise to be highly advantageous to her. The opium now grown in Persia is brought to market at Bushire for half the price at which Malwa opium of the same quality is sold at Bombay.

The following table shows the Imports at Bushire from the 1st of January 1817, to the 31st of December 1823 on British and Asiatick vessels, in New Persian Rupees.

This is independent of any Imports on Asiatick bottoms previous to the year 1823.

| Years | Indian & China goods | European goods | Total each year |
|---|---|---|---|
| 1817 . . . . . | 2,369,652 | 557,915 | 2,927,767 |
| 1818 . . . . . | 2,520,842 | 685,243 | 3,206,085 |
| 1819 . . . . . | 3,659,471 | 1,221,278 | 4,880,749 |
| 1820 . . . . . | 6,298,987 | 353,287 | 6,652,274 |
| 1821 . . . . . | 2,070,805 | 1,483,624 | 3,554,429 |
| 1822 . . . . . | 5,921,008 | 1,848,530 | 7,769,538 |
| 1823 . . . . . | 6,736,245 | 2,191,391 | 8,927,636 |
| Totals . . . . | 29,577,010 | 8,341,268 | 37,918,278 |

If we add to this one half for the minor ports it gives a Total of Persian Reals. . . . . . . . . . . . . . . . . . . . . . . . . . . . . . 56,877,417

If we state that the Native vessels have been in the habit of importing as much as they bought last year, which however I am inclined to doubt, it would give us with the Minor ports a grand total of P.Rs. 109,183,887 or about £8,188,791.

Having given a table of the Imports at Bushire for 7 years, I shall also show the amount of bullion, specie, and pearls exported from that Port for India and Arabia during the same period in New Persian Rupees.

| Years | India | Arabia | Total of each year |
|---|---|---|---|
| 1817 . . . . . | 1842672 | 149182 | 1991854 |
| 1818 . . . . . | 2985947 | 117371 | 3112318 |
| 1819 . . . . . | 2921195 | 108270 | 2029465 |
| 1820 . . . . . | 3312487 | 24890 | 3337377 |
| 1821 . . . . . | 3142174 | 83500 | 3225674 |
| 1822 . . . . . | 2187471 | 21875 | 2209346 |
| 1823 . . . . . | 3510291 | 35265 | 3545556 |
| Totals . . . . | 19902237 | 540353 | 20442590 |

Total in English Money. . . . . . . £1533194

To this remains to be added one fourth to cover the deficiencies arising from the practice of understating the amount of treasure shipped which making allowance for a still greater concealment in shipping pearls will give about two Millions Sterling paid by Persia in cash and pearls in that space of time, and almost the whole of it for British and Indian commodities. Add for the minor ports 1000000, total—3000000 Sterling.

I am indebted to Colonel Stannus for the whole of the interesting information I now lay before you regarding the Trade of Persia with India; and I cannot allow the opportunity to pass of expressing my acknowledgements to Colonel Stannus for the cordiality with which he has co-operated with me in the discharge of my official functions, or of stating the advantage the publick service is likely to gain by the nomination of a Gentleman of his character and attainments to the important office he has lately been called to fill.

I have the honour to be with the greatest Respect,

Sir,
Your most obedient,
devoted, humble Servant—
Henry Willock

## Selection 6. Persian Gulf Trade, 1840s and 1860s

["Report by Colonel Pelly to the Indian Government," A and P 1871, 51, pp. 1–2, 5]

. . . 4. His Excellency in Council will perceive that this commerce has developed rapidly and largely. It appears, for instance, that in 1844–45 the trade with Bombay showed a gross total of 79,24,609, rupees that in 1860–61 it amounted to 1,31,42,602 rupees; while in 1865–66 it amounted to 3,44,37,408 rupees. In other words, that between the years 1845 and 1865 the trade quintupled itself, while it nearly trebled itself during the five years between 1861 and 1865.

5. From the statement of trade with the port of Bombay, concluding with the year 1869, it will be seen that the trade, as compared with 1865–66, being the highest year of the American war, had apparently fallen off, but this is accounted for by the fact that the cotton trade was abnormally large down to the conclusion of the American struggle; while, on the other hand, successive disturbances on the Arab coast between 1866 and 1869 have, of course, been injurious to trade; so that it may fairly be assumed that, under ordinary circumstances,

the general trade would have continued to show a steady increase.

6. As regards Calcutta, it will be observed that the increase as between the years 1864–65 and 1868–69 was as follows: 27,32,681 rupees.

I am unable to include the year 1844–45 in my comparison of this trade, since at that period it was not shown separately from the trade between Calcutta and the Red Sea.

7. As regards Kurrachee, the increase as between 1847 and 1867 has been as follows: 8,33,731 rupees.

8. The appended statement (E) shows the most favourable total of trade with the above-named three ports for any one year has been as follows: 4,05,55,796 rupees.

9. I have not inquired into the trade with Madras, because although I believe that trade to be considerable, I understand that a large portion of it is indirect through Bombay, and thus were the Madras trade shown it might appear twice. It has seemed to me preferable to be rather under the mark than run the risk of exaggerating in statistical statements.

10. But the trade with these principal British ports by no means represents the total of trade with the gulf, although I am unaware that there are any reliable statistics in regard to trade with other ports. But from the testimonies of numerous native merchants, I think I am safe in submitting that the subjoined items do not over-estimate the export and import trade with miscellaneous ports:

|  | Rs |
|---|---|
| Malabar Coast . . . . . . . . . . . . . . . . . . . . . . . . . . . . . . . . . . . . . | 10,00,000 |
| Cutch and Kattiawar . . . . . . . . . . . . . . . . . . . . . . . . . . . . . . . . . | 10,00,000 |
| Jedda and Red Sea . . . . . . . . . . . . . . . . . . . . . . . . . . . . . . . . . . | 12,00,000 |
| Opium trade with China, 2,500 chests, at 1,200 rupees per chest of 136 lbs. . . . . . . . . . | 30,00,000 |
| Average annual value of Pearl Trade . . . . . . . . . . . . . . . . . . . . . . | 75,00,000 |
| Trade with Busreh, Baghdad, and Mesopotamian line in general . . . . . . . . . . . . | 3,00,000 |
| Trade with Zanzibar and African Coast . . . . . . . . . . . . . . . . . . . . . . . | 3,00,000 |
| Trade with Mauritius (irregular) . . . . . . . . . . . . . . . . . . . . . . . . . | 4,00,000 |
| Trade with England and America in square-rigged vessels unknown, but unquestionably above | 20,00,000 |
| Trade with Java . . . . . . . . . . . . . . . . . . . . . . . . . . . . . . . . . . | 20,00,000 |
| Total, one crore and seventy-eight lacs . . . . . . . . . . . . . . . . . . . . . . . Rs | 1,78,00,000 |

11. Thus the gross total of the export and import trade passing up and down the Gulfs of Persia and Oman appear to have totaled 5,83,55,796 rupees, or nearly 6,000,000 *l.* sterling, exclusive of the trade carried on in small coasting craft. . . .

## Trade through Trebizond

The diversion of the trade of northern Iran from Constantinople and Smyrna to Trebizond, in the 1830s, was an event of capital importance in the country's economic history.[1] As the following three selections show, this was brought about by two factors: British desire for a shorter channel, which would not only facilitate the inflow of British goods but also make it possible to export silk and other Persian products by reducing their cost of transport; and the establishment of steam navigation between Constantinople and Trebizond. Further factors were the levying by the Russian government of duties on goods in transit through Georgia between 1831 and 1846 and the growing difficulties on the Baghdad route (see 3:21).

As regards the first, already in 1812 Sir Gore Ouseley was pointing out to the East India Company that if Gilan silk were shipped from Trebizond instead of

---

[1] For fuller details, and tables, see Issawi, "Tabriz-Trabzon Trade."

Bushire, overland transport costs would be reduced from 2.5 percent of the cost of the silk (5 tumans on a mule load of "20 Shahi Maunds, of 200 Tumans value") to 1 percent, bringing down the f.o.b. price per pound to 8s. $5\frac{1}{2}$d. at Trebizond compared with 8s. $6\frac{1}{2}$d. at Bushire; in addition, freight from Trebizond to Britain would be lower than from Bushire (5 August 1812, FO 60/7).

In 1831, the consul in Tabriz took up this subject in connection with the establishment of a British consulate in Trebizond. He referred to Persian conservatism: "Wedded as the Persians are to ancient usages, the Merchants manifest a repugnance to embark into business through a new channel, till some one of their community shall, after a trial, have ascertained the certainty of success." He recommended the opening of a British consulate in Erzerum, to facilitate trade (Campbell to East India Company, 10 August 1831, FO 60/32). Two years later he suggested sending British arms to the Prince Royal at Tabriz through Trebizond instead of Bushire, since this would save about 22 shillings per musket (Campbell to Grant, 1 October 1833, FO 60/35).[2]

The British consul in Trebizond, James Brant, in an appendix to his Report on the Trade of Persia, written in 1834 (FO 78/241), also calculated the advantage of "direct trade" with Tabriz through Trebizond over "indirect trade" through Constantinople. Not only would freight rates be lower but, by buying the goods at Trebizond instead of Constantinople, Persian merchants would lock their capital for a much shorter period of time.

Once the trade through Trebizond had been established, its progress came to depend on three factors: the adequacy and cost of steamer transport on the Black Sea; the adequacy and cost of port facilities in Trebizond and of the Trebizond-Erzerum-Tabriz road; and the degree of competition offered by the alternative route through Russian Transcaucasia.

Steamer transport did not present any serious problem. By the 1860s four companies—the Austrian "Lloyd," the French "Messageries Impériales," the Russian "Black Sea Company," and the Turkish "Osmaniyeh"—each had a weekly service to Trebizond, and an occasional British steamer also called at the port. These steamers accounted for "at least four-fifths of the trade" and "have formed, to their own great advantage, and to the no less detriment of trade in general, a monopoly which they have disguised under the seemlier name of a 'Convention.'"

[2] In the meantime, "an enterprising Persian Armenian merchant of Tabreez, 'Sittik-Khah,' early in 1826 recognized the profits likely to accrue from a direct trade between this his own country and England, and therefore was the first to introduce it by importing a valuable consignment of English goods he had bought himself in London and Manchester for disposal at Erzeroom and his native place. . . . Previous to this [1830, when the first English ship, chartered by Consul Brant, reached Trebizond] our wares found their way to Trebizond and so here, by two little miserable coasting craft of Italian origin—all that remained of the old glories of Venetian and Genoese commerce with these ports; or by the round-about land route from Scutari. The commercial connection, too, that has long existed between Smyrna, via Kaiserieh, and Aleppo with Erzeroom served also, as the periodical caravans from those places arrived, to swell the indirect supply for the Armenian market, that was further augmented by similar importations once a year from England by the circuitous route of India and Baghdad." "Erzerum," A and P 1873, 67. This report contains much useful information.

Another pioneer attempt should also be mentioned: "The Trebizond trade route was first initiated about the year 1830 by Abbas Mirza, the son of Fath Ali Shah and Heir Apparent to the Persian Throne, who despatched a vessel laden with English goods for Persia from Constantinople to that port." Curzon, *Persia*, 2:563–64.

As a result, freightage of passengers and goods between Trebizond and Constantinople was "about half that between Constantinople and Marseilles, though the distance is scarcely one-fourth." The other fifth of trade was carried by sailing ships and coastal craft. The Russian company had the largest share of business, a fact explained by the British consul in Trebizond as follows:

This remarkable excess of the Russian steamer export accounts, whether for goods, specie, or passengers, over those of the other companies, is chiefly due to an exceptional contract made between the Russian steamer agents of the Black sea and the bulk of the Persian merchants at Tabreez and Trebizond, whereby the Persians have engaged themselves to employ Russian transport exclusively on these seas; while the Russians, in their turn, allow the Persians a considerable reduction on the ordinary fares.

The Consular rank of the Russian steamer agents on these coasts, the active support given by the national embassies at Constantinople and Tehran, and the peculiarly Russian singleness of tenacious purpose which makes all their external relations, even the commercial ones, subservient to political and perhaps to territorial aggrandisement, have determined and still maintain this engagement.

It needs scarcely be added that all the attempts made by the Turkish and French Companies to break up the Russo-Persian "convention" have hitherto failed, the former being easily overridden and the latter outwitted; while the Austrians, content with their own traffic—one, as we have already seen, by no means inconsiderable—have hardly made an effort at interference. The ulterior tendency of the contract in question is, however, no less evident than its actual effect on Black Sea trade.[3]

However, the service was

inadequate in winter to meet the requirements of commerce. The Russians having seldom available stowage, owing to the quantities of goods embarked at Batoom in transshipment from Poti, and the Ottomans proceeding only so far as Constantinople, the steamers of the two remaining companies not only find full cargoes along the coast, but are very often compelled to refuse merchandize.

In summer, affairs although slack are perhaps still sufficient to cover expenses, more especially when there is demand for grain.[4]

But by the 1880s, this complaint is no longer heard. In 1883, 378 steamers aggregating 368,000 tons called at Trebizond, and in 1884 the figures were 411 and 392,000; the value of the merchandise and specie loaded and landed was £2,400,000 in each year. To this should be added 20,000 to 25,000 tons of sailing ships and coastal craft, carrying £124,000 to £150,000 worth of goods.[5]

No significant improvements were, however, made in either the port or the road. As regards the port:

The construction of a jetty to protect the roadstead of Trebizond has been projected long ago, the engineering plans have even been made, but the works have not yet begun,

---

[3] "Trebizond," A and P 1870, 64; this report contains much information.
[4] Ibid., A and P 1874, 67.
[5] Ibid., A and P 1885, 79; these figures may be compared with those given by MacGregor (2:110) for earlier years. In 1837, 131 ships aggregating 22,000 tons entered Trebizond, loading and landing goods worth £1,503,000; in 1841, these figures were 189 ships, 34,000 tons, and £2,099,000. MacGregor supplies useful information on the years 1832–42.

and are not likely to be begun soon. In the way suggested at present for carrying them out the funds required are estimated at 150,000 *l*.[6]

As for the road, the following statement seems a fair summary: "*Public Works—* Under this head there is nothing to mention but the Erzeroom road, and that in deprecatory terms."[7] That wagon road had been begun in the late 1860s,[8] but the construction was faulty in many ways and "I was told by people travelling usually between this and Erzeroom that, with all its deficiencies, the old road was still preferable, the reason alleged being that they could always reckon on finding hard soil underneath, while now they can never guess how deep they may immerge in mud."[9] To this should be added both the insecurity of the road (see chap. 4, Introduction) and the steadily mounting cost of fodder. Thus in 1865 the consul at Erzerum complained of "new difficulties" and stated that the number of pack animals was gradually diminishing, because the price of fodder had doubled."[10]

While the Ottoman government was thus failing to make any improvement on the Erzerum road, and in addition levying a "duty nominally of 1 per cent, but which, by vexatious practices and frontier impediments, never falls short of 2 per cent, and is even frequently raised to 8 per cent,"[11] the road was meeting new and intense competition. On the one hand, the opening of the Suez Canal diverted much trade, especially British, to the Basra-Baghdad-Kermanshah-Tehran route. And on the other, the Russian route through Georgia became increasingly effective.

Competition from the Russian route sprang from two sources: better transport and new fiscal policy. Already in 1823 a British report described the road from the port of Redutkaleh to Tiflis as "very good, a military road having just been completed."[12] By the early 1870s Russia had crushed the rebellion in Daghestan, established steamship lines on the Caspian (see 4:1, 2) and pushed its railways to Tiflis and linked the latter to Poti and, in 1883, to Baku.

Secondly, the Tiflis Railroad Company has already made and put into execution arrangements for conveying each bale of goods, weighing on an average 1 cwt., from Poti to Tabreez itself, at a total charge of 5 fr. (4*s*. English). Now the transport cost of the same bale, per caravan, for the same distance viâ Trebizond, is about 30 fr., or 1 *l*.4*s*. English.[13]

---

[6] "Trebizond," A and P 1874, 67.

[7] Ibid.

[8] For details see ibid., A and P 1870, 64.

[9] Ibid., A and P 1874, 67.

[10] "Transit Trade between Erzerum and Persia" (in French), A and P 1866, 72; see also reports on Erzerum for 1864 and 1865, A and P 1866, 70.

[11] "Trade of Turkey," A and P 1874, 66.

[12] "Notice on the Trade of Georgia by the Port of Redutcale," 20 December 1823, FO 60/24.

[13] "Trade of Turkey," A and P 1874, 66. Even before the building of the railway, the Russian government had succeeded in diverting much traffic. Goods went from Trebizond to Poti by steamers, up the Rioni river by steamboats, then by wagons or carts to Tiflis and by wagons or caravans to the Persian border. The journey took not less than 50 days, or slightly more than from Trebizond to Tabriz, but offered two main advantages: merchandise was better protected from rain on wagons than on pack animals; and insurance was provided by the Nadezhda Company. As a result, traffic on the Russian transit route to Tabriz rose from 5,118 packages in 1863 to 13,688 in 1864, to 20,802 in 1865 and 30,374 in 1866. Crampon to Minister of Foreign affairs, 12 June 1868, AE Tauris, vol. 1.

Russian fiscal policy oscillated. The above-mentioned 1823 report listed numerous advantages of trading with Tabriz through Redutkaleh rather than through Trebizond. In addition to better roads and the possibility of selling goods in Tiflis, it stated that duties on the Russian route were fixed and known, whereas on the Turkish "he is never sure of what the amount of Duties will be—as every Pasha's charges are almost entirely regulated by the state of Politics, at the Moment."[14] To this one may add that, in order to encourage trade in Georgia, the government gave significant tax exemptions to Russian and foreign merchants.[15]

In 1831, however, European goods passing through Transcaucasia were subjected to Russian customs duties, a fact that increased the pressure to open the Trebizond route.[16] Moreover, there was much smuggling, which the Russian government was unable to control. Hence

in 1846 the Viceroy, Vorontsov, prevailed on the government to reopen passage and in 1865 the conditions under which European goods were admitted were greatly liberalized and a postal service from Tiflis to Julfa was created. In 1877 conditions were made more difficult—Russia required the payment of deposits equal to the amount of customs that would have to be paid on imports into Russia; these were repaid when passage of the goods into Persia was verified by customs. In 1883 free transit [for imports to Iran but not for exports from that country] was abolished altogether. In 1881 Russia's exports to Persia totaled 3.9 million rubles; during this same year European goods to a value of 7.8 million rubles entered Persia through Russian territory [compared with under 100,000 until 1865]. This seemed grossly wrong. So it was stopped, and by 1885 the value of such transit goods fell to 50,000 rubles.[17]

Duties had been reimposed because of pressure from Russian industrialists.[18] These duties, and a considerable tightening of formalities and administrative regulations,[19] practically put a stop to transit of European goods through Georgia. Already in 1878 the Ziegler firm had complained about the caution money demanded by the Russian government, which amounted to 2,240 rubles per bale; "as we import yearly about 5,000 bales, it would require about 12,000,000 roubles for this caution. Only Rothschild could do such a business."[20] The repeal of exemption in 1883 was followed by a sharp drop, and a rise in trade through Trebizond for imports from Europe, but not in exports to Europe.

However, the main beneficiary of this change was not Trebizond but the Persian Gulf. As the consul in Tabriz pointed out in 1885, "the Persian Gulf is now the great connecting link with England . . . whereas ten years ago, the average value of the commerce between Europe and Persia by the Trebizond-Erzeroum

[14] "Notice," 20 December 1823, FO 60/24.
[15] See ukase of 8 October 1821, annexed to ibid.
[16] See "Remarks on the Trade of Tehran," 27 November 1845, FO 60/107, and "Remarks on Trade of Tabriz," 15 April 1849, FO 60/147.
[17] Entner, p. 22.
[18] idem, p. 23; and Abbott to Secretary of State, 26 February 1883, FO 60/457; Finn to Granville, 25 June 1883, FO 60/457; and Finn to Salisbury, 10 October 1885, FO 60/475.
[19] For details see "Gilan," A and P 1878, 74.
[20] Quoted in Abbott to Salisbury, 12 June 1878, FO 60/415.

route represented annually £2,400,000, the most recent statistics show that in 1883–84 the same trade amounted to only £1,018,081..... whilst in 1884–85 the total value was £1,092,617."[21] Twenty years later, a British report on Persia's trade made the following observations:

> The route from Trebizond *via* Erzeroom and Khoi is used by imports of British and Continental goods, but exporters now send many articles of merchandise in transit through Russia to Batoum, which no doubt decreases the quantity of freight available for caravans returning to Trebizond, and may, therefore, affect transport rates in both directions. The caravan must pay keep and profit to its owner for the year, and if it earns no freight in one direction must charge more in the other.
>
> The average rate of freight from Trebizond to Tabriz for the three years 1891–93 was krans 113 (£T 3.42) per kantar, and for the three years 1900–02 krans 205 (£T 4.36) per kantar, a rise of 80 per cent in silver, but of only 28 per cent in gold.[22]

According to Entner, "an estimated 15,000 pack animals made three round trips annually on the route to deliver about 500,000 puds [8,200 tons] of goods."[23]

Trade continued, more or less at this low level, until the outbreak of the First World War (see 3:12).

[21] Memorandum on Azerbaijan, 25 September 1885, FO 60/475.
[22] MacLean, "Report" A and P 1904, 95:61.
[23] Entner, p. 24—see sources cited.

## Selection 7. Search for Trade Route through Trebizond, 1820
[Willock to Castlereagh, 30 October 1820, FO 60/21]

Tabriz
October 30, 1820

My Lord,

Many articles of British manufacture formerly found their way to the Persian market: the difficulties attending the transportation of goods by land from Constantinople, and the more moderate price which is borne on Russian merchandize from Astrachan has nearly annihilated this branch of commerce.

A trade established direct between England and Trebesond although it would be attended with difficulties in the commencement, and although the first investments might meet a heavy sale from the port not being a general resort for merchants, yet I conceive the advantages of its situation are so great that in a short time a considerable commerce might be carried on particularly if it was supported by the presence of a British Consul.

The Persian Merchants at present residing at Constantinople would readily remove to Trebesond from considerations which I shall state.

1. To avoid the danger of infection from the plague.

2. A residence so much nearer home would be highly desirable to Persians who are not adventurous travellers.

3. They would be able to convey British goods to the City of Tabriz by a land carriage of twenty two days, and avoid the duties exacted at the many Cities through which they at present pass.

The Eastern Provinces of Turkey would likewise consume a considerable quantity of merchandize.

The exchange for Europe goods from Persia to Turkey is now specie and Cashmeer Shawls. A great quantity of cotton is grown in the district of Erivan which is partly carried to Turkey, and partly to Tiflis, but I do not know whether it could be delivered at Trebesond sufficiently reasonable to render its exportation advantageous.

The extension of this branch of commerce might in the course of time bring to the port a part of the silk produced at Gilan.

I have collected patterns of the various manufactures brought from Europe which meet a sale here, and have also made a list of articles suited to the wants of the people.

I have begged Mr. Frere to submit this dispatch to the inspection of His Majesty's Consul General at the Porte, whose experience will enable him to judge how far the suggestions I have offered are worthy of consideration.

## Selection 8. Search for Trade Route through Trebizond, 1823
[Willock to Canning, 4 March 1823, FO 60/22]

*Grosvenor Square*
*March 4, 1823*

Sir,

The favourable report made by His Majesty's Consul General at Constantinople on the suggestions I offered in my dispatch No. 40 of 1820 for the improvement of our commerce with Persia has induced me since my arrival in this Country to extend my inquiries on this subject, and the information I collected on a late visit to Manchester confirms the opinions which I formerly offered, and imboldens me again to call them to the attention of His Majesty's Government.

The South East Provinces of Persia were formerly supplied with printed cotton by [?] Sadras and Masulipatam; small ventures of English cottons were introduced, and were much approved—both on account of their quality, variety of patterns, and small cost; the demand for them gradually increased, the Indian chintzes have now scarcely any sale, and one house of Manchester annually sends to Persia cottons to the amount of £100000. The trade is protected by the Hon'ble East India Company's Resident at Bushire, and requires no further aid of Government for its improvement which is progressive.

In the North West provinces of Persia, as I have elsewhere observed, we are undersold by the Russians, but I find by calculations made by an intelligent merchant at Manchester, that we can land our printed cottons at Trebesond at as low or perhaps a lower price than a Russian Merchant can pack his goods from Moscow for Persia, seeing that the Russian pays a large impost on the twist provided by England. We therefore can furnish the Persian market at as low price as the Russians, and our goods from their superior quality and taste will always find a preference.

Russia has of late paid great attention to this branch of commerce, and has nominated a Consul General to reside at Resht for its protection—the late dissensions between the Turks and Persians have discouraged the trade with Constantinople, and the Persian merchants have increased their commercial relations with their Northern neighbours to the exclusion of the small quantity of our merchandize which formerly found its way to the Persian market from the West.

The success of our merchants in the South East of Persia encourages an attempt in the North West; the field is wide, and offers the prospect of a large market not only for our cotton goods, but for woollens, cutlery, glass ware, crockery, imitations of Cashmere shawls in cotton, silk, and wool, and in fact for our manufactures of all description, which by the port of Trebesond would find their way not only into Persia, but into the Eastern Provinces of Turkey, and be spread on the Southern Coast of the Black Sea.

Our merchants are ready to commence their experiments, but they look for protection, and if this is afforded by the nomination of a Consul to the Port of Trebesond, I feel confident that our commercial interests will derive much benefit by the opening of this new channel for the introduction of our manufactures into Asia.

My dispatch No. 40 of which I enclose a copy was submitted I believe by the late Lord Londonderry to the notice of the Board of trade.

## Selection 9. Search for Persian Export Products, 1840

[McNeill to Backhouse, 29 October 1840, FO 60/75]

*Edinburgh*
*October 28, 1840*

... The importance of finding in the productions of Persia some available return for British manufactures is daily becoming more evident, not only because the deficiency of bullion, in which the returns have up to this time chiefly been made, has lately become a serious impediment to commerce, but also because of the extreme jealousy with which the Government regards British Commerce in consequence of the great quantity of the precious metals which it yearly carries out of the Kingdom.

Mr. Abbott's statements of the advantage to Commerce which may be expected from an improved method of preparing and reeling the silk of Gheelan are in accordance with opinions which Sir John McNeill has long entertained and which he has on various occasions brought to the notice of the Shah and of the Provincial Govt. of Gheelan.

There is reason to believe that the value of the Silk produced in that Province might by the introduction of such improvements as would make it suitable for the English market be at once advanced about twenty five per cent and that with an increasing demand the quantity produced in that and the adjoining provinces might be almost indefinitely augmented. That thus a very valuable return would be furnished to such an extent as might very considerably enlarge the British Commerce with Persia to the obvious advantage of both parties.

Mr. Abbott's opinion that the residence on the spot of some one capable of directing these improvements, and from his connexion with trade able to hold out inducements to make the experiment, would be necessary to its success, appears to be well founded.

It is probable that a commercial agent residing in Gheelan would be able to obtain from Mariners and Traders information of occurrences on all parts of the shores of the Caspian, and especially on its Eastern Shores, which it might be difficult or impossible to procure at Tehran or Tabreez.

For these reasons Sir John McNeill is of opinion that if it were practicable to establish a British Consular officer in Gheelan for the purposes proposed by Mr. Abbott, public advantages more than commensurate with the expense incurred might be anticipated from the arrangement; and he is not aware that he could point out any one better qualified than Mr. Abbott himself to discharge the duties of that office. ...

## Selection 10. Trade of Trebizond, 1840s

[Rudolf Gödel, Ueber den pontischen Handelsweg und die Verhältnisse des europäisch-persischen Verkehres (Vienna, 1849), pp. 2–3, 43–51, 64–66]

... It was steam navigation that stimulated afresh the great, ancient, commercial relations with the distant inland regions and spread new life over these lands, benumbed for centuries. The first steamer appeared here in 1836, carrying the British flag. So shrunken was the traffic of Trebizond at that time, that even that ship had to abandon this route for lack of business. Later came the Austrian ship Ferdinando. The Donau-Dampschiffahrts-Gesellschaft, the owners of that ship, boldly continued its service, and soon earned the reward for their perseverence. Hardly a decade has passed since then, and already this coast is visited six times a month by steamers. Three lines, Lloyd, Compagnia Ottomana, and Peninsular and Oriental Steam Navigation Co., participate in the business and all find it worth their while. In addition to Sinope, Samsun, and Trebizond, all steamers call regularly at Inebolu. The Turkish company is taking steps to run a steamer which would connect with the main lines at Constantinople and serve, on the one hand, the ports between Trebizond and Samsun and, on the other, Rizeh, Choppa, and Batum. Last, the Liverpool "Levantine" line made trial trips with screw steamers, on the basis of which three ships were chosen for a direct connection between Trebizond and England during the fair season. . . .

## TRADE RELATIONS BETWEEN CONSTANTINOPLE AND TABRIZ

The bulk of trading business between Europe and Persia is concentrated in Constantinople and Tabriz, which can be considered as the two commercial poles. The European (*frankische*) establishments in Constantinople, which directly handle Persian trade, all have subsidiaries in Tabriz and, conversely, the Armenian and Persian merchants in the latter city have their business agents in Constantinople. European business houses and factories do not have direct dealings with Persia. Their trade with Persia is solely indirect, and is conducted in Constantinople through the firms established in that city and engaged in Persian trade. The latter import goods on their own account and either sell them in Constantinople to Persian merchants or send them to their agents in Tabriz, whose business it is to handle further distribution.

Similar conditions prevail in Persia regarding articles exported to Europe. These goods flow in from the various corners of the country, are gathered in Tabriz, and from there are sent to Europe, the operation being conducted by the Tabriz firms. Thus Constantinople and Tabriz are the great emporia for the trade in question; all towns in Persia and Europe lying beyond them partake in this trade only through their intermediation.

## PERSIAN COMMERCIAL TRAVELERS

Along with the above-mentioned kind of large-scale exchange of goods, a sort of retail trade grew up and continues to subsist, carried on by Persian travelers. These men, some of whom are real Persians, some Armenians, and some Turkomans from the Khanates of Bukhara and Khiva, undertake their long journeys not always out of commercial interest but in order to make the pilgrimage to Mecca or for some other reason. They always pick up, within their financial means, goods in the Persian pro-

ducing towns through which they pass, usually weapons, lacquer work, marquetry, shawls, rugs, and silk fabrics. With these they trade during the whole of their journey. Part of their stock is sold in Erzerum and Trebizond, the greater part in Constantinople, and the rest in Smryna or Alexandria. The proceeds serve for the purchase of European manufactures, which they sell in the remote towns of Asia from which they came. The amount of goods carried by each person often is worth only a couple of thousand piasters.[1] But in view of the large number of travelers, the amount of goods thus handled amounts to a not insignificant sum.

Among the travelers coming from Persia are some who carry on a considerable business and regularly visit European markets. To this class belong, especially, Armenians from Tabriz, Tiflis, and Erivan. They mostly bring shawls, precious stones, and pearls, and take back European manufactured goods. Their business is usually transacted in Constantinople, but not seldom they also visit the fairs of Vienna, Leipzig, and Moscow and, more recently, have gone as far as Lyons and Manchester to make their purchases. Before the development of the above-mentioned trade relations between Constantinople and Tabriz, the Perso-European trade was entirely in the hands of those Armenians, and the trade in cloth, glassware, and fancy goods is still almost exclusively handled by them.

## THE FORWARDING TOWN OF TREBIZOND

Together with Constantinople and Tabriz, Trebizond plays an important part in Persian transit trade; indeed it is often regarded as the staple market of that trade. Since, however, no trade, whether buying or selling, is carried out in Trebizond for the Persian market, and since Trebizond does not have the required stocks of goods, it is not really entitled to that name. However, it plays an important part as a forwarding place. It is the meeting place of the caravan

[1] One hundred piasters equalled a Turkish pound, which at that time was worth about 18 shillings.

route and the Black Sea steamship route, and all the goods exchanged between Persia and Europe by way of the Black Sea are forwarded and transshipped there. All the Constantinople and Tabriz firms engaged in Persian trade here have their correspondents or business agents. Instead of participating directly in Persian trade, these firms prefer to deal only in forwarding business, which secures them a more reliable source of profit the whole year round. Relations with Persia are very active in Trebizond. The numerous travelers who come and go there from every country have led to the opening of numerous *khans*, or inns, where they find accommodation. Thousands of mules and horses are employed in the transport of people and goods. Porters, boatmen, and jobbers work in large numbers in the forwarding and transshipping business, earning much money for the town. Although Trebizond also transacts a significant amount of business with neighboring provinces on its own account, it owes its swift recovery and present well-being to the Persian transit trade.

TRADING FIRMS

The trading firms in whose hands European-Persian trade is mainly concentrated are
I. In Constantinople
A. European firms: T. Ralli & Co., G. Stefanovich, Ionides & Co., E. Manuelovich & Radocanachi, Ralli & Mavroyanni, E. Novico, N. Negroponti, P. Mavrocordato, Ienidunia Bros.

The first three of these firms are in direct relations with Persia and have in Tabriz the branches mentioned below. The others do not have direct links with Persia, but have a large stock designed for trade with that country, which they sell to Persian traveling merchants and agents.
B. Persian firms: Hajji Ali Akbar, Hajji Sayyid Husain, Hajji Mahmud Nur.

In addition to these houses, which are connected with Tabriz firms, there are also in Constantinople many other Persian traders and agents who spend a longer or shorter time in that city and buy or sell either on their own account or for that of their Persian principal.
II. In Trebizond, European forwarding agents:
T. Gerst, Charnaud Marcopoly & Co., Calimachi; Persian agents: Hafiz Agha, Sayyid Murtaza, Rahim Agha, and others.
III. In Erzerum, European forwarding agents: F. Garibaldi, R. W. Calvert; Persian agents: Hajji Husain, Hajji Ali Rahim, Mulla Hasan.
IV. In Tabriz, Greek firms under Russian protection:
Ralli & Agelasto, a subsidiary of T. Ralli & Co; Stavrachi Calduvachi & Co., subsidiary of G. Stefanovich; L. C. Sgutta & Co., subsidiary of Ionides & Co., in Constantinople.
Austrian, also under Russian protection: F. A. Gelalenz.
Russian subjects from Armenia and Goergia: Garabet Shankuzadov, Agob Hajjiadankov, Mardiros Hakunkov, Th. Masuneov, G. Guliov.
Armenians from Erzerum: Artin Hajjiadunian, Kazar Artin, Garabet.
Persian wholesalers who deal directly with Constantinople are: Hajji Mir Muhammad Husain, Hajji Sayyid Husain, Hajji Rasul Damat, and others,
V. In Tehran, Russian Armenians: G. Manikonov, Garabet Sarafoghlu, A. Kuzinov.
Austrian, under Russian protection: A. Töpner.

In addition there are many Persian merchants, who, however, do not get their goods directly from Constantinople but through Tabriz.

COMMERCIAL AND FORWARDING METHODS

Of the firms mentioned above, the Greek and Persian houses of Constantinople and Tabriz deal exclusively in cotton textiles. The Armenian firms, and the two Austrian, on the other hand, trade mainly in cloth, silk and wool stuffs, glassware, hardware, and fancy goods.

Purchases by Persians in Constantinople used to be on a cash delivery basis, but are increasingly being made on credit. Armenian and Persian buyers and sellers who do not trade on their own receive from their principals either fixed monthly salaries or varying percentage commissions (*Provisions-Gebühren*). In Trebizond, European forwarding agents take 15 piasters, and Persian agents take 100 paras,[2] as a commission on every package sent to or received from Persia, except for Persian silk bales, on which Europeans take 40 piasters. In addition, their principals reimburse them for all shipping charges and other expenses incurred by them; for imports these amount to 70 paras a bale and for exports, $4\frac{1}{2}$ piasters, including the quarantine duty.

Forwarding agents in Erzerum act only on instructions from the Trebizond agents, who usually hand over to them one-third of the commissions they receive. Neither European nor Persian forwarding agents take a commission on goods from Persia, and are merely reimbursed for their expenses.

In Tabriz European firms take 3 percent in commission, 1 percent in *sensarie*, and 1 percent in storage fees, or in all 5 percent on Persian products which they buy for foreign principals. The sales of European goods are on credit, the period varying, according to the prevailing practice for different articles, from twelve to eighteen months. Nevertheless, purchasers often pay cash, or on short term, in which case a discount of 1 percent per month is granted to them.

[2] A piaster was worth 40 paras.

Accordingly, a bale of textiles (*Manufacturen*) weighing 60 ockes [about 77 kilograms] and worth 2,000 piasters sent from Constantinople to Tabriz costs:

|  | PIASTERS |
|---|---|
| Turkish transit duty, arrangement (*verglichen*) . . . . . . . . . . . . . . . | 30 |
| Transport by steamer to Trebizond . . . . | 23.10 |
| Charges in Trebizond . . . . . . . . . . | 1.30 |
| Commissions in Trebizond . . . . . . . . | 15 |
| Land freight to Tabriz, average for 1/3 cantar | 133 |
| Persian import duty, arrangement . . . . . | 50 |
| total | 253 |

A bale of silk weighing 60 ockes and worth 8,000 piasters sent from Tabriz to Constantinople would require the following outlay:

|  | PIASTERS |
|---|---|
| Persian export duty, arrangement . . . . . | 200 |
| Land freight from Tabriz to Trebizond . . | 33 |
| Quarantine dues in Trebizond . . . . . . | 2.20 |
| Charges in Trebizond . . . . . . . . . . | 1.30 |
| Commissions . . . . . . . . . . . . . . | 40 |
| Steam transport to Constantinople. . . . . | 37.20 |
| Turkish transit duty, arrangement . . . . . | 120 |
| Total | 434.30 |

Customs charges are, in the above estimate, reckoned at only 50 percent of the amount specified by the tariff, for the settlements made with both the Turkish and the Persian customs officials seldom amount to more. . . .

IMPORT AND EXPORT TABLES

The volume of Persian-European trade passing through Trebizond is shown by the following tables, in which, for lack of data, no values are given before 1843.

| YEAR | IMPORTS TO PERSIA (NUMBER OF PARCELS) | EXPORTS FROM PERSIA (NUMBER OF PARCELS) |
|---|---|---|
| 1831 . . . . . . | 4,500 | . . . . . |
| 1832 . . . . . . | 6,750 | 5,302 |
| 1833 . . . . . . | 8,975 | 8,040 |
| 1834 . . . . . . | 11,250 | 12,660 |
| 1835 . . . . . . | 15,525 | 15,800 |
| 1836 . . . . . . | 20,615 | 23,278 |
| 1837 . . . . . . | 16,710 | 16,031 |
| 1838 . . . . . . | 22,360 | 16,618 |
| 1839 . . . . . . | 21,095 | 10,891 |
| 1840 . . . . . . | 25,830 | 16,770 |
| 1841 . . . . . . | 27,092 | 17,483 |
| 1842 . . . . . . | 30,985 | 17,493 |

| YEAR | IMPORTS | | EXPORTS | |
|---|---|---|---|---|
| | Parcels | Value (Florins)[3] | Parcels | Value (Florins) |
| 1843 . . . . . | 31,690 | 10,140,800 | 14,879 | 2,518,000 |
| 1844 . . . . . | 33,100 | 10,432,000 | 16,900 | 3,684,360 |
| 1845 . . . . . | 40,028 | 13,239,574 | 17,012 | 3,708,742 |
| 1846 . . . . . | 38,980 | 12,892,592 | 13,615 | 3,165,390 |
| 1847 . . . . . | 34,850 | 11,522,738 | 12,130 | 2,784,500 |
| 1848 . . . . . | 50,277 | 16,623,804 | 10,456 | 1,813,782 |

[3] At that period the prevailing rate was 10 Austrian florins or gulden to the pound sterling.

The table begins in 1831, the first year in which large amounts of goods for Persia reached Trebizond. Since that year, imports to Persia have been increasing rapidly and the prospect is for this progress to continue. For European goods are beginning to be popular in Khiva, Bukhara, and other parts of Central Asia, and traders from these regions are coming to the Persian market more frequently to buy such goods. Persian exports have also increased since the opening of the Black Sea route, although in a less striking proportion. Their culminating point was in 1836, when significant amounts of raw silk and *tumbak* [water-pipe tobacco] passed in transit. After that they remained almost stationary until 1846, when a gradual decline became noticeable; this is mainly attributable to the fact that several Persian staple exports, like raw silk, gallnuts, and buckthornberries (*Kreuzbeeren*) are less in demand in Europe than they were formerly.

One can estimate, in round sums, imports to Persia through Trebizond at that time at 16 million gulden and exports at 2 million, leaving a deficit of 14 million, which is covered by an outflow of money. According to the declarations made by the shipping agents, the latter amounted to:

In 1843 . . . . . 36,000,000 Turkish piasters
1844 . . . . . 45,000,000 Turkish piasters
1845 . . . . . 63,000,000 Turkish piasters
1846 . . . . . 58,500,000 Turkish piasters
1847 . . . . . 78,750,000 Turkish piasters
1848 . . . . . 72,060,000 Turkish piasters

The figures shown above, however, give only an incomplete picture of actual cash remittances. For, on the one hand, the goods, which are sealed, are declared at a value below the real one when handed to shipping agents, in order to lower freight charges. And, on the other, a not insignificant amount of goods carried in travelers' luggage is not declared. . . .

## Foreign Firms in Tabriz

The following selection, taken from the travel book of a Russian who visited northern Iran in 1842, describes both the commercial practices prevailing at that time and the entry of Greek and other foreign firms enjoying Russian or British protection. Selection 14, from a British consular dispatch of 1844, adds further information on this subject and describes the unsuccessful attempts made by Iranian merchants to oppose these firms. However, most of the trade remained in Persian hands. In 1858, 44,846 packages were handled by Iranian subjects and 34,318 by foreigners; in 1859 the figures were 51,339 and 35,552 respectively (report by Dickson of 14 February 1860, FO 60/253).

In 1864 there was another unsuccessful

combination of the native merchants against European trade, the pretext for which was found in imprudent transactions entered into by a Greek firm, which, by suddenly and very materially lowering prices, brought heavy losses on the whole of the commercial community of the place. For about four months great excitement and irritation was manifested; business was interrupted; a feeling of distrust and uncertainty of the intentions of the foreign merchants here seems to have succeeded to the confidence in which business with them had previously been conducted; and though the mischief done was attributed to the conduct of only one house, the consequences fell upon the European merchants generally. Prices which had been high and remunerating having been so suddenly reduced by the transaction alluded to, all who possessed stocks of goods purchased at previous rates found themselves obliged either to retire from the market for a time or to submit to ruinous losses. For some months, therefore, there was a great stagnation of business; but ultimately the reduction in prices appears to have led to an increased activity in the demand which, continuing for the remainder of the year, enabled the merchants very generally to clear off their stocks of goods at somewhat improved rates.[1]

The remarks on this subject by Abbott in his account of his journey to the Caspian are also revealing.

At present there is not a single Russian Mercantile Establishment on the Persian Coast of the Caspian, nor indeed in any town in Persia.—The Commerce between the two Countries is entirely in the hands of Persians, Georgians, Armenians, and the Natives of Bâkou and Dâghestân small Traders who are seldom Stationary in any part of the Coast. It has already been explained how indisposed the people of Isterabad are to the establishment of Russian Merchants amongst them—this is not the case in Gheelân and Mazanderan but the climate of those Provinces is much against the permanent residence of people from any other Country.

There is not the least reason to think that the Trade of Russia with the Southern Shores of the Caspian is at all on the increase. The value of English goods consumed there is probably nearly equal to that of the Importations from Russia [Report dated 29 June 1844, FO 60/108].

It is not clear whether further attempts were made by Iranian merchants to prevent the expansion of European trading houses. What is certain is that, well before the end of the century, the latter had grown greatly in number and power, and controlled the bulk of Iran's foreign trade (see 8:4).

The Ralli and Agelasto firm mentioned in the following selection was, presumably, connected with Ralli Brothers, established by two Greeks in London in 1818; three other brothers worked, in partnership with the London firm, in Marseilles, Odessa, and Constantinople. Business was mainly in silk, grain, and cotton piece goods. In the 1850s the firm began opening offices in India, and in the 1930s in Africa.[2]

As regards Iran, in 1860 the firm asked for and obtained British protection (dispatches by Abbott of 30 May and 20 September 1860, FO 60/253; see also 3:13). It played an important part in developing silk production and trade in Gilan, and helped producers by importing silkworm eggs from Japan, but in 1871 it withdrew from business in Iran.[3]

---

[1] "Tabriz," A and P 1865, 54.
[2] *Ralli Brothers* (privately printed, London 1951), p. 9.
[3] "Gilan," A and P 1871, 65, and Jamalzadeh, p. 27.

## Selection 11. Foreign Firms in Tabriz, 1830s
[L. Berezin, *Puteshestvie po Severnoi Persii* (Kazan, 1852), pp. 58–66]

The bazaar of Tabriz deserves attention because of its extent and the number of its shops, and for a Persian bazaar it is fairly broad. The variety of goods available in it is hardly matched in any other Persian town except Tehran; as for the quantity of goods, in this respect Tabriz has undoubtedly no rival in Persia. As regards commercial relations, this town is an important center in Persia: for the bigger half of the country it serves as the main fair and it is primarily from there that European goods, received from Constantinople through Trebizond, are distributed over Persia. The annual turnover in the trade of Tabriz is put by the Persians at fifteen crores, which is nearly equal to eighteen million assignat rubles;[1] these figures, however, refer to the past, and at present the trade of Tabriz is not going too well in all respects and the turnover does not exceed five thousand crores [*sic*].

The table given in the appendix to this book shows the total imports of Tabriz. From it one can see that the trade of Tabriz flourished until 1836. In that year there was a sharp increase in imports of goods in which the Persians were motivated not by considerations regarding the needs and means of their country but only by the possibility of getting goods worth large amounts without having to make cash payments. This led to a crisis in trade and a decline in credit in Persia; European goods filled up all storehouses in Tabriz and for a long time could not be sold; meanwhile there was no reason to import new goods and nothing to pay with.

Until 1837, the largest share of import of goods, which was constantly and rapidly increasing, was undertaken by the Persians themselves from Constantinople. In that year their imports fell from 33,488,000 assignat rubles to 2,000,000 and total imports declined from forty to twelve million. Thus the trade of Tabriz, in which the dominant factor was Persian imports of goods from Constantinople, falls into two sharply defined periods: until 1837 the Persians themselves were predominant and after that date foreign merchants, including Russian, were preponderant.

It should not be thought that the shift of trade to other hands caused a complete change in the nature of the goods handled. As before, English goods prevailed over all others, but the difference was that other nations, taking advantage of the decline in the credit of the Persians, took the trade into their own hands. In 1837, Russian subjects imported from Leipzig 1,352,700 assignat rubles worth more than in the previous year, and their purchases in Constantinople rose from 19,000 to 1,736,000 assignat rubles. Imports from Russia also increased so that 1837 was one of the most advantageous for Russian trade in Persia. Foreigners, exporting practically nothing from Constantinople, imported goods for 700,000 assignat rubles. Even the Persians themselves turned to Russia and bought from us in that year goods worth 729,600 assignat rubles, whereas in the previous year they had not taken a kopek's worth. In spite, however, of this possibly advantageous change in the agents of the trade of Tabriz, total imports fell by more than half and since then have not recovered; Russian exports also decreased and, as has already been pointed out, in general the trade of Tabriz is not doing too well.

The main European articles imported into Tabriz are cotton, calicoes, broadcloth, metal and glassware, sugar, muslins, velveteens, velvet, mirrors, and various products of small industry. In return, Tabriz sells significant quantities of silk, gallnuts, which grow in Hamadan and Kurdistan, dyes, shawls,

---

[1] In Iran the crore usually equals 500,000; Occasionally, however, it equals 1,000,000; see J. J. P., Desmaisons, *Dictionnaire persan-français* (Rome, 1908–14) s. v. Krur. Here the author must be presumed to mean 15,000,000 krans, which, at the current rate of exchange, would equal about £750,000.

The rate of the assignat ruble at that time was about 23 to the pound sterling, so that 18,000,000 rubles would equal £780,000.

This estimate seems reasonable; see chap. 3, sel. 12.

tombak (tobacco for water pipes), weapons, among which are the famous Khorasan wedges, wax, dried fruits, and a few minor silk or other manufactures. The balance of trade is always unfavorable to Persia.

The quantity of the main goods imported to Tabriz is as follows: 10,000 parcels of English cottons and calico, with a value of two and half million silver rubles;[2] and up to 10,000 boxes of sugar. English sugar is sold at 6 assignat rubles per batman in Tabriz, at 7 in Tehran, and at 9 in Qum. It is said that foreign goods were cheaper here eight years ago, but now only cottons are inexpensive. The prices of weapons are also disproportionate: thus pistols worth 150 assignat rubles cost 600 rubles in Tabriz and weapons with English barrels [rifles?] are sold for 300 assignat rubles and more. Up to 5,000 parcels of silk are exported from Tabriz, and also gallnuts worth 150,000 silver [rubles]. Among the various kinds of cottons, the Persians like particularly those known as *bandarguli* or *gul-i bandar*, in four or five colors; next follows in general appreciation *zillek*, a six-colored cotton cloth.

Formerly, Persian trade went from Smyrna to Iran overland, then followed a period in which goods went from Constantinople to Tabriz, also by land. Now they go over the Black Sea from Constantinople to Trebizond, and from there overland through Erzerum to Tabriz on pack animals, but not camels. In addition to sailing ships, four steamers ply regularly between Constantinople and Trebizond—two Austrian and two Turkish—taking three or four days for the journey. Goods reach Erzerum from Trebizond in ten days and go from there to Tabriz in two or three weeks. Overland transport faces many difficulties and dangers from robber tribes; by sea, however, goods are almost completely secure, the more so as there is a company that insures them. . . .

Goods exported from Constantinople to Tabriz pay a customs duty of 3 percent in Turkey. In Persia they pay another 5 percent

if they are sent under the name of a non-Persian subject; Persians pay only a *rahdarlik* [road tax] of two rials per package and in addition the transport of goods is cheaper for them. In spite of that advantage, however, the Persian merchants are slowly losing control over trade in European goods. What factors can explain this revolution, knowing as we do the capacity of the Persian nation for commercial speculations—if not for far-sighted calculations at least for very complex operations? To answer this question we must cast a general look at the structure of Persian trade.

Traders in Persia, as everywhere else, are divided into wholesalers and retailers. The first group includes, in addition to traders of the first rank, merchants trading with a small capital; but even Persian merchants of the first rank do not have a capital of over 150,000 silver [rubles] and there are only five such wealthy persons in Tabriz. Given this insufficiency of capital, the Persians strive to make gains through credit, but internal credit, being based on very unstable rules, is exposed to frequent losses, from which merchants engaged in foreign trade suffer along with others. Internal trade in Iran is carried on either a cash basis or by means of bills: no loan transaction may be effected without the approval of a high clergyman, and moreover, in cases of dispute, witnesses are required (one man or two women).

In view of the variety of terms included in Persian contracts, continuous deceptions in trade are very common. Thus the same object, for instance a house, may be mortgaged several times: some *mujtahids* in Tabriz, by various subterfuges, authorize the mortgaging of the same house nine times, to nine different persons. In addition there are many other temptations to deception: thus a Persian trader may, without danger, declare himself bankrupt, *muflis*, because he can take refuge, *bast*, in the house of a *mujtahid* or in any place of pilgrimage, *ziarat*, where he can quietly stay on as long as he pleases and later on, when the danger has passed away, emerge and again engage

---

[2] The silver ruble was worth about 3s. 2d. at that time.

in trade with capital which he has concealed. These last circumstances caused much harm to trade and fraudulent bankruptcies were extremely frequent in Tabriz up to my arrival, at which time the revolution took place which will be mentioned later in order that our narrative on the decline of Persian trade should not be interrupted.

At the death of Fath Ali Shah, the new shah could not devise anything for the straightening of the disordered financial affairs of his empire other than the useless and unprofitable Herat campaign. The loss of government credit and the insufficiency of money in the shah's treasury gradually made themselves felt among the people too. But during that time no attention was paid in Constantinople to the credit situation in Persia, unnecessary goods continued to be acquired on credit, and the year 1837, which was to prove so fatal for Persian traders, arrived.

Many agents of Tabriz firms live permanently in Constantinople, as do also some Persian merchants. In addition a not so significant number of merchants make frequent journeys from Tabriz to Constantinople and back, carrying on their trade and accompanying their merchandise. The blindness of everybody reached such a point that neither the capitalists nor their agents saw the abyss toward which the Tabriz trade in European goods was moving; only when huge stocks of manufactured goods had been imported to Tabriz—for which there was absolutely no demand in Persia—did the Tabriz merchants realize their error, but too late and when there was no way of rectifying it. Many bankruptcies followed in Tabriz, engulfing a few firms in Constantinople, but the most seriously affected was the credit of Persian traders in Constantinople. To the actual bankruptcies in Tabriz were added the intentional ones, so that a certain amount of confusion in business dealings was unavoidable.

In these circumstances, so favorable for a newly arrived capitalist, the trading house of Ralli was founded in Tabriz. Its head, whose permanent residence was in Constan-tinople, could dispose of large means since he had offices in Manchester, Marseilles, Odessa, and other places. Taking advantage of the privileges enjoyed by Russian subjects,[3] the trading firm of Ralli soon established itself firmly in Tabriz, regardless of the fact that the Tabriz capitalists neither themselves brought goods to it nor allowed them to be brought by small traders, *bazzaz* and peddlers, *dallal*. The advantageous conditions offered by Ralli and the influence of the Russian consulate changed the attitude of the Persians within a month, and English manufactured goods—which were the only ones stocked by Ralli—soon flooded the caravanserais of Tabriz and from there also Tehran, Qazvin, Qum, Kashan, and many other towns. When I was there the firm, which was housed in the Hajji Sayyid Husain caravanserai, sold three million assignat rubles' worth of English cottons and broadcloth. In order to develop their trade further, the managers of that firm in Tabriz were generous in the credit they offered and the concessions they made. In order to satisfy the Persian taste, they ordered designs from Persian artists and had cloth printed in England according to them. Such accommodation was necessary because Persians do not like some of our colors and in general do not agree with European taste.

In order to recover the capital supplied by Constantinople, the Tabriz office of Ralli sent back silk, raw silk, and Russian rubles—the latter because the customs authorities forbid the export of Persian coins. In addition to its main office in Tabriz, Ralli has an agency in Rasht.

Besides Ralli, there are in Tabriz a Greek firm and two English shops. Before the establishment of Ralli, the Russian firm of Callouste sold, with a fair measure of success, a significant amount of European goods, but during the absence in Germany, on a buying trip, of the eldest Callouste brother, their affairs in Tabriz fell into disorder and at present the firm is insolvent and claims 280,000 assignat rubles from the Persian

[3] Later Ralli, a Greek, became a British subject.

government. The latter has stated in reply that the debt was incurred not by it but by the late Kahraman Mirza, the brother of the shah. To meet the claim made by the Calloustes, a small copper mine has been handed over to them, as an interim arrangement. . . .

IMPORTS OF GOODS TO TABRIZ
(THOUSANDS OF ASSIGNAT RUBLES)

| YEAR | RUSSIAN SUBJECTS | | | PERSIANS | | FOREIGNERS | | TOTAL |
|---|---|---|---|---|---|---|---|---|
| | C | R | O | C | R | C | O | |
| 1833 . . . . . | 263 | 1,088 | 432 | 13,040 | . . . | . . . | 523 | 15,347 |
| 1834 . . . . . | 21 | 1,506 | 478 | 14,976 | 176 | . . . | 780 | 17,938 |
| 1835 . . . . . | 39 | 601 | 2,125 | 28,286 | 86 | . . . | 1,812 | 32,954 |
| 1836 . . . . . | 19 | 905 | 2,960 | 33,488 | . . . | . . . | 2,718 | 40,090 |
| 1837 . . . . . | 1,736 | 1,038 | 4,313 | 2,000 | 730 | 688 | 2,352 | 12,856 |
| 1838 . . . . . | 1,423 | 235 | 3,838 | 6,720 | 270 | 789 | 1,464 | 14,739 |
| 1839 . . . . . | 933 | 196 | 1,067 | 4,500 | . . . | 243 | 467 | 7,407 |
| 1840 . . . . . | 951 | 404 | 783 | 3,360 | . . . | 960 | . . . . | 6,458 |
| 1841 . . . . . | 636 | 130 | 5,979 | 3,500 | . . . | 960 | 560 | 11,035 |

C = Constantinople.    R = Russia.
O = other (England, Leipzig, France, etc.).

## Trade of Tabriz

For the reasons given in the two following selections, Tabriz was the leading trading center of Iran, and remained so until the development of the Persian Gulf and Caspian routes (see 4:1–4).

Two breakdowns of the trade of Tabriz in the 1840s are available, one by origin and destination and the other by commodity. In 1839/40, exports to Constantinople amounted to £218,000 and to "Tiflis and beyond the Aras," £246,000; imports were £595,000 and £38,000 respectively. Thus Tabriz may have handled a quarter to a third of Iran's total trade. The apparent deficit of £173,000 was partly covered by "the value of Pearls, Diamonds and Cashmere shawls sent down to Constantinople without passing the Custom House Accounts" and by exports of gallnuts "direct from Songboulak, both to Constantinople and Lenkeran." "A considerable quantity of manufactures also, sent from the South of Persia, is imported into the Russian territory by way of Ardebeel, the amount of this does not appear in the enclosed accounts." If to this be added increasing exports of silk from Gilan to Russia, paid for in gold and silver, "the heavy drain of gold on this country to supply the deficiency of returns on the Constantinople trade is yearly diminishing" (Bonham to Bidwell, 16 November 1840, FO 60/75).

As regards commodities, a breakdown for 1848 is available (Stevens's dispatch no. 17, 1849, FO 60/147). On the import side, by far the leading supplier was Britain, with £772,000 out of a total of £831,000; of this, printed cottons accounted for £559,000, bleached calicoes for £153,000 and sugar for £14,000. Germany followed with £33,000, of which £24,000 was woolen cloth, Russia with £12,000 and France with £8,000. Exports amounted to £344,000, of which £190,000 went to Russia and £154,000 to Turkey, the latter mostly for reexport. Raw silk totaled £144,000 (£84,000 to Turkey and £60,000 to Russia). Cotton

manufactures amounted to £79,000 (Russia £65,000 and Turkey £14,000)—
"the native Cotton Manufactures sent to Russia are, with a few exceptions,
British cloths—dyed or printed in the Country, a fact proving that the restrictions
to which our Commerce is subjected by that Government do not prevent us from
participating to some extent in the advantages of its Trade with Persia" (ibid.).
Exports of silk manufactures were £43,000 (Russia £41,000 and Turkey £2,000)
and of woolen manufactures £40,000 (Turkey £30,000 and Russia £10,000);
presumably both were handicraft products. Tobacco exports totaled £12,000,
almost all to Turkey.[1]

Three factors stimulated the development of the trade of Tabriz: the increase
in output and exports of silk (see 5:6–9); the channeling of trade through Trebizond (see 3:7–10); and the influx of Greek and other merchants (see 3:11). In the
period covered by the following selection the trend was upward, but with sharp
fluctuations caused by natural disasters—such as droughts, locust attacks, and
epidemics—political disturbances, or financial crises. Thus on 1 June 1852 the
British consul in Tabriz reported:

> I have the honour to inform Your Lordship that the Trade of Tabreez is just now in a
> very unsatisfactory state, and that failures to a considerable amount are expected to occur
> among the native Merchants who import British Manufactures. One Trader has already
> declared himself Bankrupt—his liabilities in this place amounting to about £25,000,
> Sterling.
> The cause of the expected crisis is attributed to the large deposits of Manchester goods
> —the increased difficulty of passing them into Georgia, where the Custom house guards
> are more than usually vigilant, and to the entire stoppage of the Trade formerly carried
> on with Meshed for the supply of Herat, Bokhara, Khiva etc. The Merchants cannot sell,
> and are in consqeuence unable to meet their engagements at Constantinople [Stevens to
> Malmesbury, FO 60/174].

The American Civil War, and the consequent "cotton famine" also had marked
repercussions:

> English commerce at Tabreez has suffered in common with that in other countries
> during 1862–3 from the failure in the supply of raw cotton to the European markets.
> During the years 1858–9 and 1860 an unusual amount of cotton manufactures was imported
> into the north of Persia. In 1861 there was a marked decline in the quantity of such im-
> portations, arising principally from local causes in this country alluded to in a previous
> report, which had lessened the demand for foreign produce. Then followed the scarcity
> of raw cotton in the European markets, and consequent rise there in the value of manu-
> factures produced from that article; but Persia being already overstocked by previous
> importations, no improvement in prices occurred until the autumn of 1862. A temporary
> rise then took place, which was presently checked by false intelligence of the probability
> of peace being restored between the contending parties in America, and so things con-
> tinued until the termination of the Persian financial year, 20th March, 1863.[2]

---

[1] A rough breakdown of trade in 1844–45, by commodity, is also available—see dispatch by Abbott, 27
November 1845, FO 60/117.
[2] "Tabriz," A and P 1864, 61.

The relief given by the end of the Civil War was offset by the combined effects of the 1866 financial crisis, the failure of the silk crop, and a cholera epidemic.[3] Further reasons were "the Russian conquests in Turkestan which closed that market to foreign manufactures" and the "systematic bad faith of native traders," encouraged by "the interested indifference of the authorities" (Jones to Secretary of State, 9 July 1871, FO 60/337). In 1872 the consul reported: "During the past year the trade of Persia fell to the lowest point known since the commerce of the country first seriously attracted the attention of European merchants" ("Tabriz," A and P 1872, 58).

Little improvement was shown in subsequent years, and the Russo-Turkish War of 1877 further disrupted trade:[4]

|  | Imports (£) | Exports (£) |
|---|---|---|
| 1872/73 | 1,267,000 | 634,000 |
| 1873/74 | 1,176,000 | 531,000 |
| 1877/78 | 526,000 | 271,000 |
| 1878/79 | 1,082,000 | 298,000 |

The relative decline in the trade of Tabriz during this period may be judged from the fact that whereas in 1868 its customs were farmed out for 2,350,000 francs, out of a total of 5,366,000 for the whole country—or 44 percent—in 1880 the figure was 2,340,000 out of 6,064,000 or 38 percent.[5] By 1892/93 imports had declined to £854,000 and in 1893/94 they fell to £412,000; exports were £390,000 and £200,000 respectively. Under the subheading *Reasons for the Gradual Decline of Trade and Commerce in Azerbeijan*, the consul stated:

In the past Tabreez enjoyed the privilege of being the "entrepôt" for European produce coming to the northern provinces of Persia. The opening of the Suez Canal came as the first blow to its supremacy in this line and the stopping of transit through Russia put an end to it.

Goods now find their way to the southern provinces principally through Bushire and Baghdad.

Ispahan and Shiraz have now become the "entrepôts," Teheran drawing the greater part of its requirements from Russia. The capital in former years used to provide itself almost exclusively from Tabreez.

The provinces of Ghelan and Khorassan are furnished by Russia.

The rates of transport on the Bushire route are considerably cheaper than those of Trebizond-Erzeroom, where for the last year they have ruled at $3\frac{1}{2}l.$ per kanter (500 lbs. weight) as against half the amount merchants were accustomed to pay.

Another, and, I say, a most important cause of the very unsatisfactory state of trade of this year, is the great depreciation in the price of silver, which from 3s. 2d. per ounce in 1893 has now fallen to 2s. $3\frac{1}{2}d.$ per ounce, or a decline of almost 30 per cent.

Goods being sold here on a long credit, merchants who calculated their cost on the exchange ruling on the day of sale, found themselves when the time came for remitting, faced by large differences, owing to the constant decline of the white metal ["Tabriz," A and P 1894, 87].

---

[3] "Tabriz, 1866," and "Tabriz, 1867," A and P 1867–68, 68.
[4] "Tabriz," A and P 1875, 75; ibid., A and P 1878, 75; ibid., A and P 1880, 73.
[5] Stolze and Andreas, p. 43.

Some improvement took place after that, and in 1902/3 imports amounted to £1,236,000 and in 1903/4 to £1,797,000, while exports were £722,000 and £575,000 respectively. But this was largely due to increased trade with Russia, which supplied one-half of the imports and took well over half of the exports. ("Tabriz," A and P 1905, 99). Thus Tabriz accounted for some 25 percent of Iran's imports and 15 percent of its exports.

After the First World War Tabriz suffered further from the decline in trade with the Soviet Union, and from the general shift in the course of trade to the Persian Gulf. By 1924/25, its share of imports had fallen to 7 percent, compared with 20 percent in 1913/14, and of exports to 8 percent, compared with 14 percent;[6] and the decline has continued since then, except for a brief recovery in 1939–41.

[6] Sventitski, "Transport Routes."

**Selection 12. Trade of Tabriz, 1837**
[Abbot to Aberdeen, 30 September 1840, FO 60/107]

... Until the Year 1837 there were no Greek Establishments in this Country—up to that time, Greek and other European Merchants had carried on a large traffic at Constantinople for the supply of Persian Traders to that City—but the latter people having run themselves greatly into debt to the European Merchants a crisis in the Trade occurred in which several of the Greek Houses were ruined. Finding that the Persian Merchants were not prepared to carry on the Trade with Constantinople on a safer basis than before, some of the Greeks determined on establishing for themselves Agents in this Country that they might thus be in a manner brought nearer to the consumers of their Goods, rendering the Trade also a more direct one. This step met with considerable opposition at first from the Native Merchants and there was a combination amongst them to abstain from purchasing any thing of the Greeks or other European Merchants—in this measure they endeavoured to include all the smaller Traders, but the scheme proved impracticable and the Trade of the Greeks has continued to prosper and increase until now. The large share of it which they at present possess and the late arrival of other Greeks has naturally alarmed the native merchants for

what remains to them of the Commerce of Tabreez—but the Person who brought the Petition told me he had several other subjects of complaint in what he terms the oppressive and unjust conduct of the Russian Authorities in prosecuting the claims of, and in the protection afforded to, their own Traders and to people not subjects of Russia to the detriment and ruin of Persian Merchants. One of his Arguments is that as Russia will not permit Persians to import into her Territories the Manufactures of England etc. she can have no right to encourage and protect in Persia other than her own subjects bringing hither English and other Foreign Produce—but he pretends that this is only a secondary matter of complaint—that Russian violence and oppression is what he is chiefly bent on representing. I told him that as to the protection afforded to Greeks his representations would be of no avail, as if Greek subjects were excluded from Tabreez their Principals in Europe would replace them by English or Russian Agents against whom no objection could be made. He replied that they would never complain of Englishmen whose just dealing they had seen nor of Greeks if placed under English protection, as they would then be sure of fair play. On my expressing a doubt of this he declared that if it were necessary he and all the rest of the Merchants would sign a paper to that effect—that the oppression of the Russians had now become past all endurance though the Merchants had little hope of redress from their own government which is completely subservient to that of Russia. I believe this man to be much inclined to exaggerate the sufferings of his Countrymen from Russian violence and that notwithstanding his assurances to the contrary, jealousy of the Greeks interference in the Trade would be transferred to any Merchants who might come in their stead—though there might be less to object to in English subjects and Protégés than in those of Russia.

In regard to the suggestion of the Merchants for the Prohibition of European Merchandize; though this cannot be carried against our Trade in the face of Treaties, I would remark that it was the Persians themselves who first introduced English goods into this Country from Constantinople and who now complain only because they cannot have the Trade entirely to themselves. It must doubtless be very distressing to them to find Foreigners superseding them in the Commerce of this Country, but had they acted honestly in their previous dealings the Greeks might never have given them trouble at Tabreez and were they possessed of more enterprize they would still endeavour to maintain their position as Merchants by having Agents in England to purchase supplies on the same terms as their Competitors.

It is understood that the Merchants appeal met with no favor either from the Prime Minister or the Shah to whom it was taken. The former is said to have remarked that he had once wished to see a stop put to European Trade and people were told not to purchase European goods but that they did so secretly notwithstanding. The Shah is reported to have said that he had in vain endeavoured to encourage Manufactures in this Country and that now he must be content with the encreased Duties which the European Trade brought to the State however much the Country suffered by that Trade.

Persia has unfortunately but few articles to offer in exchange for the produce of England otherwise the Trade might be profitable to both Countries. She has no navigable Rivers or Canals, and much of her Produce can never reach a Port from whence it could be shipped to Europe, on account of the expense of land Carriage. It is the general belief therefore that the Country is becoming drained of its wealth but still the consumption of our manufactures has experienced no decline as yet—and their introduction has so greatly diminished the production of many articles of native industry that Persia must now depend on us chiefly for her supplies of such goods. The people also acquired a taste for our Manufactures which nothing but positive inability to purchase can diminish the demand for, and their cheapness enables the Consumers to gratify the hankering which all Persians have after change and novelty of Pattern which could not be the case were they confined to their own Manufactures. There is therefore every reason to think that our Trade here will continue as long as the people have the means of purchasing of us—and in time the resources of the Country may perhaps become better known and turned to better account than they have been.

### Selection 13. Trade of Tabriz, 1837-71
[Tabreez—Report by Consul-General Jones. "Tabriz," A and P 1873, 67, pp. 364-71]

The city of Tabreez has been from the beginning of the present century the depôt of the European trade with Northern Persia, and, until the year 1868, with Central Asia likewise. It is situated at the junction of the high roads leading to Teheran, from Tiflis on the north, and Trebizond on the west. It contains about 200,000 inhabitants, and is by far the largest and most important city in Persia.

The earliest importers of British merchandize into Northern Persia seem to have been the Armenians of Georgia, who made their purchases for this market at Constantinople. When the prohibitive tariff of Russia was extended to the Caucasian provinces, the greater number of the Russian merchants engaged in the Persian trade established themselves at Tabreez, and monopolised there, in a great degree, the trade with Europe.

The importance of the silk trade of Ghilan at length attracted the attention of some enterprising Greek traders, who in the year 1837 commenced business at Tabreez under Russian protection; and as British manufactures have always held the first place in the Persian markets, this firm, afterwards Ralli and Co., established direct relations between itself and the Manchester manufacturers.

Their command of capital and systematic method of trading quickly gave them the advantage over their Oriental rivals, and until the retirement of this house from the Persian trade in 1871, it continued to occupy the first place in commercial importance.[1]

During the Crimean war the East in a great degree engaged the attention of Europe, and when peace was re-established between Russia and the Porte, many European houses, chiefly Greek, had already made arrangements to take part in the Persian trade.

At the present time British commerce is represented there by three firms, having their head-quarters at Manchester. The chiefs of these houses are naturalised British subjects, and their agents and employés in Persia have invariably been foreigners, for the most part Greeks or Germans.

Obstacles and drawbacks have continually occurred to impede the development of European commerce in this country. Of these I shall speak afterwards in detail. Those, however, which were apparently insurmountable, and which no forethought could guard against, were—the successive failures of the silk crops in Ghilan from 1863 up to the present time; the increased price of cotton goods, consequent on the civil war in the United States; and the visitations of cholera and famine, which have so frequently devastated this country, but more especially during the last three years.

It is at all times difficult to obtain even an approximate estimate of the real value of the Persian trade, from the following causes:— The natural disinclination of those who farm the Customs-revenues to publish the annual amount of their gains; the practice of keeping count merely of the number of horse-loads of each article entered, without stating the intrinsic or declared value of the same; and the extended contraband trade which is carried on here with the adjacent provinces of Russia and Turkey.

In the following Schedule of the European trade of Tabreez from the year 1837 to the present time, the estimates are taken from the Reports furnished from time to time by this Consulate to the Foreign Office, and are calculated in each case to the 20th of March in the succeeding year. I have no means of supplying the deficiency where, from the absence, sickness, &c., of the Consul, these Returns are wanting.

As silk is probably the sole export which finds its way to England, I have given in a separate column the value of the amount sent westward from Tabreez in each year.

. . . Many of the changes in the form, pattern, and quality of the cotton goods are due, no doubt, to the caprice of the purchasers. At the present time novelty of design is much sought after, and indeed each season requires a fresh variety. The patterns and qualities, however, which have altogether disappeared or fallen into disuse are those which found a special market in Turkestan, Bokhara, and Khiva, formerly supplied indirectly from Tabreez, but since the Russians have consolidated their conquests in Central Asia, it is found easier and safer to supply these provinces with the manufactures they require direct from Moscow.

I may here remark that a large proportion of the grey calicoes imported into Tabreez are afterwards dyed or printed here, and sent to the Russian provinces in the Caucasus, where they are admitted on payment of five per cent. duty as Persian manufactures.

Broadcloth, which formed an important

[1] The Persian branch of this house became entitled to British protection in 1860, which it continued to receive up to the time of its retirement from the country in the year above stated.

| Year | Total Imports | Of British Manu-factures | Total Exports | Of Silk | Contingencies and Casualties influencing the Trade in each Year |
|------|------|------|------|------|------|
| | £ | £ | £ | £ | |
| 1837 . . . . . | 985,000 | 600,000 | 105,000 | . . . . . . | |
| 1839 . . . . . | 591,825 | 450,000 | 464,219 | 214,180 | Roads in Kurdistan very unsafe after death of Sultan Mahmoud. Heavy falls of snow and great scarcity of provisions, rendering transport very expensive |
| 1844 . . . . . | 703,204 | 562,000 | 369,057 | 131,418 | Increased contraband trade with Georgia consequent on the weakness of the frontier guards |
| 1848 . . . . . | 830,773 | 771,943 | 343,738 | 144,030 | Rebellion in Khorassan. Disturbances following the death of the Shah. Destruction of crops in Persia and Turkey by locusts |
| 1850 . . . . . | 882,175 | 762,003 | 607,128 | 236,434 | |
| 1858 . . . . . | 1,639,225 | 1,368,300 | 974,942 | 389,300 | Several new trading firms established at Tabreez. Goods imported considerably in excess of the demand |
| 1859 . . . . . | 1,786,488 | 1,518,207 | 965,140 | 409,582 | Ditto, ditto |
| 1863 . . . . . | 1,460,000 | 815,000 | 534,000 | 351,000 | Excess of imports in two preceding years. Increased price of cotton goods consequent on the American war |
| 1864 . . . . . | 1,800,000 | 1,575,000 | 600,000 | 502,000 | Combination of the native traders against Europeans |
| 1865 . . . . . | 1,669,231 | 1,242,516 | 886,883 | 499,322 | Failure of the silk crops in Ghilan. Uncertainty of prices during the American war |
| 1866 . . . . . | 1,699,712 | 1,107,441 | 516,626 | 374,400 | Cholera appeared in Azerbijan. Failure of silk in Ghilan. Large surplus of goods remaining unsold |
| 1867 . . . . . | 1,432,069 | 946,672 | 643,093 | 65,000 | Failure of silk crops. Scarcity of money. Frequent failures among native dealers |
| 1868 . . . . . | 1,351,005 | 1,017,285 | 683,885 | 80,000 | Markets in Central Asia supplied from Russia. Increased export of cotton from Persia |
| 1869 . . . . . | 1,575,776 | 1,123,211 | 901,218 | 136,400 | Ditto, ditto |
| 1870 . . . . . | 1,094,717 | 864,000 | 422,632 | 116,000 | Famine devastating the entire kingdom |
| 1871 . . . . . | 789,559 | 611,280 | 340,790 | 119,440 | Famine and cholera. Frequent bankruptcies among the native merchants |

article in the early trade of the East India Company with Persia, is now altogether supplied from Germany. The petty Armenian traders alone import it. The profits are small, as long credit is required. The higher classes among the Persians prefer to wear the fabrics of Kerman or Baghdad, and the lower classes make use of the produce of their domestic looms. The customers for European broadcloth are generally found among the minor employés of the Government and the servants or retainers of the higher classes, who being badly and irregularly paid, are seldom in a position to purchase with ready money what they require.

Hardware is supplied chiefly from the foundries and manufactories of Tula, in Russia. It is of a very rude and inferior description, indeed very little better than that made here; its cheapness, however, recommends it to Persian buyers.

Sugar and tea were formerly imported from England; but Marseilles has at present the monopoly of the former and Holland apparently, of the latter article. The sugar of Marseilles is light, porous, of bad colour and inferior quality; but it can be sold here at a price with which no other can compete. These two articles form the principal item in the contraband trade with Georgia.

As early as the year 1849 Mr. Consul Stevens called the attention of the Manchester Commercial Association to the inferior quality of the British cotton goods exported to Persia, and represented that unless the manufacturers discontinued supplying such, British prints would gradually fall into disuse, and be superseded by the fabrics of the country. In reply it was stated:—"That no deception whatever was practised with reference to the true character of the goods in question, it being a matter of perfect notoriety to the trade generally, that the printed and other cotton goods supplied to the Persian market were of a most inferior quality, and that they must continue to be so was equally obvious, unless remunerating prices were paid to the manufacturers where better articles were required." A merchant of the highest respectability, largely engaged in the Persian trade, remarks at the same time,—"The exporters of goods from Manchester for the Persian markets formerly sent out good qualities both in cloth and printing, say up to the year 1844–45; since that period, however, some exporters commenced sending out inferior goods, and the Persian buyers gave them the preference on account of their cheapness, heavy losses being sustained by holders and parties continuing to ship good qualities;—the buyers refusing to pay the difference in proportion to the relative value of the goods, all importers were forced to unite in sending out goods of inferior qualities, and prints of loose colour. The consequent low prices having produced increased consumption, the exports have been proportionately augmented to a very considerable extent. Notwithstanding the very low prices, the Persian buyers are still wanting the goods cheaper and cheaper, and exporters, in order to meet the demand, have been obliged to send out worse and worse qualities every year. It follows, therefore, that so long as they refuse to pay the value of better qualities of goods the existing evil cannot be remedied."

I may add, that the quality of imported manufactures has in no way improved since the above complaint was made, and that the same causes are still in force to produce inferior articles; cheapness is above all the characteristic which finds favour with Persian customers, and to this they are prepared to sacrifice every other consideration.

The share taken in the trade of Persia by the other nations of Europe is comparatively unimportant. France ranks second, and under very favourable circumstances and in prosperous seasons may supply Persia with silk brocades, porcelain, and sugar, to the amount of about 200,000*l.* annually. Germany (including Austria) sends broadcloth, glassware, gold, lace and embroidery, to the amount of about 100,000*l.* in ordinary seasons. The imports from Russia amount to about 80,000*l.* annually, and consist of hardware, candles, paper, naphtha, iron, and copper. The imports from Turkey are chiefly coffee, leather, woollen fabrics (coats and cloaks), drugs and dyes, and rarely exceed the value of 30,000*l.* in favourable years.

EXPORTS

Few Persian products can support the expense of carriage to the European markets. There can be no doubt that with improved means of transport a very extensive export trade would be developed. At the present time the neighbouring provinces of Turkey and Russia offer the only market where the produce of this country can be profitably disposed of. According to the returns of the Custom-house at Tabreez, silk, tobacco, shawls, carpets, dyed leather, galls, safflower, tallow, orpiment wax, and dried fruits, form the chief exports to Turkey. To Georgia are sent British calicoes dyed in Persia, carpets, silks, drugs and dyes, fox and martin skins, dried fruits, and whatever cotton is produced in this province, besides which a considerable trade is carried on in horses, sheep, and black cattle by the wandering tribes on the frontier. The average value of the exports to Georgia from Persia is in ordinary seasons about 260,000*l.*, and to Turkey 400,000*l.* This, however, does not include the contraband trade, which probably equals the above amount in each case.

The following list of the products and manufactures of the different provinces and chief towns of Persia, is taken from the Return of the Custom-house at Teheran. . . .

British manufactures intended for the Persian market are generally shipped from Liverpool to Constantinople and from thence to Trebizond, or from London, by the Russian Company's steamers, to Poti, in Georgia. Freights by the former route vary from 4s. 6d. to 5s. per bale, by the latter from 5s. to 5s. 6d. The cost of transport to Tabreez from Trebizond, by way of Erzeroum, is from 30s. to 45s. per bale; from Poti, by way of Tiflis, 30s. to 34s.

Merchandize sent from England to Tabreez by way of Trebizond will reach its destination in from fifty to sixty-five days; by way of Tiflis, in about eighty-five days. As the railway from Poti to Tiflis is now completed, the time and money saved will be about twenty days and 8s. in each bale.

It is impossible to insure goods sent by way of Turkey, but the Russian Company is willing to undertake this risk from Poti to Tabreez at 1½ per cent.[2]

[2] A bale of merchandize sent through Turkey must not weigh more than 200 lbs.—about half an average horse-load. Bulky articles, or those of inconvenient shape, should not exceed 150 lbs., otherwise there is difficulty and delay in finding a muleteer to transport them.

Transport through Turkey is much more rapid during

Notwithstanding the advantages offered by the Russian route, the merchants here still prefer to have their goods brought by way of Trebizond, although the Turkish Government levies a toll of one per cent. on goods in transit. The negligence and indifference of the Russian Company agents frequently cause great loss and delay to the importers. It is to be hoped that the officials of the new railway company will take measures to insure punctuality and despatch in the transmission of goods destined for Persia.[3]

the autumn and winter months than in the spring and early summer, as during the latter seasons the pack animals are chiefly fed on the grass and herbage in the neighbourhood of the road. When this fails, the muleteers are obliged to purchase straw and grain for the subsistence of their beasts, and are thus interested in reaching their destination as speedily as possible.

[3] I forward the Tariff and Regulations of the Poti-Tiflis Railway, and a list of merchandize classified according to the charges for transport. It will be seen that the articles likely to be of foreign origin are generally placed in the highest one whereas those which are the productions of Russia are carried at a much reduced rate.

## Trade of Tehran

In the nineteenth century, Tehran owed its commercial importance not to its industrial or agricultural production but to its location and the presence in it of the royal court. The network of its trade with the northern, southern, and western provinces is clearly brought out in the following selection.

Over the next few years trade increased, mainly because of greater imports of Belgian and German manufactures (Thomson to Bidwell, 30 November 1843, FO 60/100). Imports of European goods through Tabriz rose to 4,391 horse-loads (8,782 packages) in 1843/44, while those from Baghdad were 120 horse-loads; of these 3,371 horse-loads were reexported. Using a figure of "not less than 100 or 120 Tomans per Load," imports from Tabriz were estimated at 483,000 tumans, or £217,354. Local consumption (1,020 loads) was put at £50,490, "which would be at the rate of 15 shillings per man—but as the Peasantry around supply themselves also in Town the real consumption is probably not so much per head though it may not be perhaps a third less." The consul adds: "The valuation of European Imports given in my Table for 1841, I have reason since to think was much too high but it is impossible accurately to determine" (Abbott, "Remarks to Accompany Two Tables on the Trade of Tehran," 25 October 1844, FO 60/107).

In 1844/45, imports of European goods through Tabriz rose further to 4,957 horse-loads (9,913 packages) worth 545,216 tumans or £247,825, "and after deducting 25 per cent for Expenses on the way out from Europe the original cost may be taken at Tomans 408,912 or £185,869." Of these, 3,573 loads were reexported. There was also an import of 10,283 loads of Russian goods—mainly metals—against 8,753 in 1843/44. A rough estimate of their value was £109,000, "a great part of which is sent to other parts of the country." (Abbott, "Observations to accompany a Table for the Trade of Tehran," 1 July 1845, FO 60/117).

In 1847/48, imports of European goods through Tabriz were given by the customs authorities as 5,215 horse-loads (10,430 packages) worth about £260,750, "but I do not feel confident of the accuracy of this Document and the Native Merchants estimate the quantity at about one-Half more." Reexports to "Mazendaran, Asterabad, Koom, Arak, Khorassan and other parts of the country" were put at "1,453 Horse loads, valued about £72,650, exclusive of what is carried to and consumed in the Villages around Tehran of which there is no account."

The report adds that "the trade with Khorassan in European goods, for the present interrupted by the state of that Province, has greatly increased during the last few years and is now become of considerable importance—the quantity of such Merchandize passing to Khorassan either by or through Tehran (only the latter is included in the Custom House Return) amounts probably to 5,000 Horse Loads a year, (value about £250,000). From Meshed considerable supplies are sent to the Principalities of Khiva and Bokhara where the consumption appears to be yearly augmenting" (Abbott, "Remarks on the Trade of Tehran," 8 November 1848, FO 60/141).

Later figures are not available, but it may be assumed that the upward trend continued, because of the growth in Tehran's population and wealth and also because of increasing centralization. However, there were important changes in both the national origin of the goods and that of the merchants handling them in Tehran. As to the first, in the 1840s the predominance of Britain was overwhelming. "It may be safely reckoned that full Two-Thirds of the Importations of European Goods through Constantinople into Persia are from England—they consist chiefly of Plain and Printed Cottons" (Abbott, FO 60/107). But imports from Russia were on the increase. By the end of the century British consular reports are full of complaints about Russia's predominance in the Tehran market. To take one example: "A Russian institution is now flooding Tehran with goods obtained from Russian manufacturers on the advantageous terms which a big trade and unlimited means command."[1]

As regards the merchants, in the 1840s they seem to have been almost wholly Iranian—including, no doubt, members of minority groups. In 1848 the British consul reported:

As yet, since the first establishment of this Consulate at the close of 1841, no English merchants have resided here permanently though two have during that period visited Tehran for a short time on commercial speculations and at present [there is] no English

[1] MacLean, "British Trade in Persia," A and P 1904, 95, p. 66.

house of commerce. . . . The only Traders here under British Protection consist of two or three Natives of India who have resided here for many years past, and a Maltese more recently established here [Abbott to Palmerston, 2 August 1848, FO 60/141].

A few months later he added: "The Trade in English merchandize is in the hands of Natives of the Country who make their purchases at Tabreez and Constantinople." There were no regular houses belonging to French or United States citizens except for "two French subjects, small Traders, who are in the habit of bringing trifling Investments of French and other goods from Europe to dispose of at Tehran" (Abbott to Palmerston, 25 April 1849, FO 60/147).[2] By the turn of the century, however, the number of foreign—especially Russian—firms established in Tehran had grown considerably (see 8:4) and it may be presumed that they handled a great part of the city's trade.

[2] In 1887 the United States minister reported: "There are no American houses doing business here" and suggested that agents be sent to Iran, where several kinds of manufactured goods could find a market—Pratt to Bayard, 25 April 1887, USDSP, 1887.

### Selection 14. Trade of Tehran, 1840s
[Abbott, "Report on Trade for 1841," 31 December 1841, FO 60/92]

*Tehran*

Tehraun although the present residence of the Court of Persia, is only the Second or Third City of the Empire in respect to Commerce. The number of its Inhabitants probably amounts to about Sixty Thousand. It owes its Trade to the presence of the Court and to its Central position with reference to Mazanderaun on the North—Astrabad and the populous part of Khorassaun towards the North-East and East—Koom, Kashaun, Isphahaun and Shirauz on the South—and Yezd and Kermaun towards the South-East—all which Countries and Towns receive supplies of European and other produce from hence. But with the Districts to the West, Tehraun has only a limited trade principally confined to importations of Grain and other provisions, for those parts are more conveniently supplied with European Produce from Tabreez and Casvine— the latter a town which may be considered to rank equally with Tehraun in the extent of its commerce and which possesses perhaps as many thriving and wealthy Merchants, Natives of all parts of the Country, as any other City in Persia. Tabreez still ranks as first, for it is not only the chief Emporium of the most populous province of the Empire, but it is that from which Casvine, Tehraun and some other Cities derive their supplies of European goods almost entirely, distributing them in their turn over a vast extent of Country.

It is quite impossible to obtain any accurate and detailed official Return of the Trade of this Place, for no such account of it is kept—there is no regular Custom-House Establishment, but every package entering the City is subject to an impost called Road-due amounting to about Two Shillings per package. No distinction however is made in levying this due, between one denomination of goods and another, except that a trifle more is charged on European Merchandize (imported by Natives) than on the produce of the Country. No enquiry is made as to the particular contents of the packages and there is therefore at present no means of obtaining a true Return of the Import and Export Trade. As well as I can ascertain, however, the imports from Tabreez of European goods (principally English) for the last Three Years, have been as follows.
In the Years (according to the Mohammudan style) ending early in
1840—
3,913. Packages—value about £235,000.

1841—

3,187. Packages—value about £191,000.
whilst in the latter 10 Months of 1841, about

6,000. Packages—value about £360,000.
are stated to have been imported. The falling off in the Imports in the Year ending the early part of 1841 is attributed to the absence of the Court at Isphahaun, whither goods, would have been forwarded direct from Tabreez without passing through Tehraun. During the last Year the Importations exceeded the quantity required and there was a temporary check to business in consequence—but I should think there must be a decided encrease in the demand for European produce, otherwise the Native traders would not have been induced to import so much more than the usual quantity.

In the annexed Table I have endeavoured to give a sketch of the nature of the Import and Export Trade of this Place—what I have already stated will explain why I am not able to give a more particular account of it at present.

The traffic between this City and Baghdad has for some time past almost ceased. A few years ago English Produce reached this part of the Country from Baghdad, but the difficulties and delays encountered in conducting supplies to that Quarter either from Bombay or Aleppo, gradually drove the Trade into the Channel of Trebizond and Erzeroum. Things are now changed and would seem to open out a prospect of Baghdad again becoming the Depot for this part of Persia—for the transit of English goods through Egypt to Bombay and thence to Baghdad would be comparatively rapid to what it even has been before—and should the navigation of the Euphrates answer the purposes of Commerce, I think there can be little doubt but that supplies for the Central and Southern parts of Persia may be advantageously imported through Baghdad. The distance from thence to this place is about 23 Caravan Marches and the road is as secure as most other roads in Persia. Baghdad would therefore be the point to which Traders from these parts

would naturally look to supply themselves with English Produce. Returns for any such Trade might be made in the Silk of Ghilaun.

Traders from the Principalities of Tartary Bokhara and Khiva are few in number to this place—the insecurity of the Roads, the great distance and the deficiency of Products in those parts of sufficient value to bear the expense of so long a land Carriage would seem to be the obstacles in the way of Commerce with them from hence. Nevertheless the high estimation in which British Manufactures are held, and the enormous prices sometimes obtained for them at the places I have mentioned, induce some adventurous Merchants to send them thither from hence. Thus Russia finds us competing with her even in those distant Markets bordering on her own Empire although our produce has to penetrate to them by very long and expensive routes.

From Cauboul and Candahar a few traders make their appearance here each year, bringing Cashmere Shawls and carrying back certain descriptions of European Manufactures—but it is not probable that this trade will much encrease whilst supplies can be brought from India.

Though hitherto there have not been any permanent Establishments of British Merchants in this City, those who have occasionally conducted adventures of European goods hither have I believe found a favorable mart for them. The presence of the Court creates a demand for many articles not of general sale in other parts of the Country. I have little doubt but that the establishment of British Merchants here might lead to an extension of the trade which I consider is capable of considerable improvement, and the security and confidence which the recent Treaty of Commerce affords, may I hope lead eventually to the formation of some such establishments here. British produce still maintains the preference, generally speaking, over that of any other Country, and the Trade in Cotton goods which Russia once possessed with this part of Persia, is now extinct—it has given way before the importation of goods of British and other European Manufacture through Constantinople and Trebizond. She still however retains a trifling trade with this place in articles of Hardware, Glassware and Earthenware, of an inferior kind, and in Iron and Copper, although both these articles are abundant and of excellent quality in the Mountains of Azerbaijan.

I trust that the circumstance of my recent arrival here and the very limited means within my reach of obtaining accurate information regarding the Trade of this part of the Country will be considered a sufficient apology for the very imperfect nature of the present Report.

[The annexed table put imports of British and other European manufactures, sugar, and tea through Tabriz at £360,000, and of Russian iron, copper, hardware, and glassware through Gilan at £15,000. Tehran imported sugar, tea, spices, cashmere shawls, and printed cottons from India through Isfahan and Shiraz. It imported lambskins and cashmere shawls from Bukhara and Khiva and cashmere shawls from Afghanistan. It also drew on the produce of other parts of the country, e.g., carpets, leather, and grain from Hamadan and Kermanshah, copper utensils from Kashan, silk and silk fabrics from Gilan and Mashad, and textiles, sugar, and opium from Yazd.

Exports were put at only £75,000–85,000, since Tehran "has no manufactures or produce of its own for exportation." Most traffic between northern and southern Iran bypassed the capital, but £20,000 worth of European goods were reexported to Qum and Kashan and £50,000 to 60,000 to northern Khurasan and Afghanistan.]

## Selection 15. Persian Trade with Iraq, 1860s–1914

[Muhammad Salman Hasan, *Al-tatawwur al-iqtisadi fi al-Iraq*, (Beirut, n.d.), pp. 128–29, 253–56]

EXPORT MARKETS

The most important change in Iraq's export trade during the period under study

was the absolute and relative increase in the value of goods exported to Europe and the absolute and relative decline in trade with neighboring Middle Eastern countries.

Available information does not allow an exact and comprehensive estimate of these changes in direction during the period before the beginning of this century. But it is possible to given an approximate and incomplete indication of the shifts in the relative importance of exports from the *vilayets* of Baghdad, Basrah, and Mosul to Europe, India, the United States, and the Middle Eastern countries, especially Iran. Thus the average value of total exports from the *vilayet* of Baghdad in 1864/65 and 1865/66 was 5.8 million Ottoman piasters, or the equivalent of 52,000 dinars, based on the current exchange rate of 110 piasters to the pound sterling or Iraqi dinar.[1] Normally, two-thirds of exports went to Iran and consisted chiefly of hides, dates, and gallnuts but also included small quantities of local manufactures such as shoes, turbans, and soap.[2] The remaining third was exported to India and Europe in the mid 1860s; it included wool, sent to Europe and more particularly France, and horses sent to India; the amount of grain exported to these countries was still insignificant.

The shift in Iraq's trade from the Middle East to Europe was facilitated by the improvement in river and sea transport—especially after the opening of the Suez Canal in 1869—by the growth of European companies, and by the expansion of European demand for raw materials and foods. Hence, in 1877/78–1878/79, exports of local goods to Iran amounted to only 13,000 dinars, or 5.5 percent of total exports of local goods from Baghdad.[3] The remainder, amounting to 222,000 dinars a year, was

[1] "Baghdad Consular Trade Report, 1867/68–1868/69," p. 383 [A and P 1870, 64] . . . .

[2] Among exports of manufactures from Baghdad to Iran in 1867/70 were 1,803 pairs of shoes, 137 turbans, and [about 200 kilograms] of soap; idem, 1869/70, p. 383 [A and P, 1872, 57].

[3] However, transit trade to Iran through Baghdad in cotton textiles, sugar, tea, and metal products amounted to about 125,000 dinars in that year—see ibid., 1878/79.

sent to India and Europe. Wool continued to be a leading export item to these countries, but grains and pulses (chickpeas and beans) came to account for more than a quarter of exports.[4]

By the beginning of the present century, exports from Baghdad went chiefly to Europe, especially to Britain. Thus in 1903 Baghdad's exports of horses, mainly to India and China, amounted to only 70,845 dinars, whereas Europe took over 752,390 dinars worth.[5] As for the Iranian market, it lost all importance except for transit goods. . . .

Baghdad has always been the center of distribution of trade in Iraq and the changes in the markets from which it imported its goods are representative of the country at large. Although imports of European goods to Iraq began before direct exports from Iraq to Europe, imports of Iranian products to Baghdad were very important at the time of the opening of the Suez Canal. Total annual imports to Baghdad amounted to some 20 million Ottoman piasters, or about 182,000 dinars at the exchange rate prevailing in 1869–70.[6] Of this more than half, namely, 11.7 million piasters, came from Iran. The main items were cotton textiles, silk textiles, tobacco, carpets, foods, saddles, etc., part of which was undoubtedly reexported to the neighboring lands or to Europe. As for the remaining imports, most of them came from India and England, in varying proportions. The chief items were textiles and metal products from England and dyes from India. But it is important to note that they also included clocks, printing presses, agricultural implements, and the cars used on the Kazimiya tramway, which functioned until 1941. To this should be added some 30,000 dinars worth of pearls from Bahrain.[7]

By the end of the 1870s, imports from Europe and India accounted for about three-quarters of the total to Baghdad. As for Iranian goods, not only did they drop to a quarter of their previous value, but they were mostly for reexport. Baghdad's total imports in 1878/79 were 463,000 dinars. Imports from Europe and India amounted to 360,000 dinars and consisted of textiles, tea, coffee, sugar, dyes, and metal goods.[8] The remainder came chiefly from Iran and consisted of wool, which was mostly reexported to Europe, and also of tobacco and some Persian silk manufactures.[9]

Goods imported to Iraq from Iran and the Arabian Gulf through Basrah were of limited importance at the beginning of the period under consideration, amounting to less than one-fifth of Basrah's imports in 1864/65 and 1865/66.[10] The trend that set in Baghdad's import trade, that is, the increase in the proportion of European and Indian goods, was also evident in Basrah. . . .

Mosul's imports show a similar change, with Indian and European goods gaining in importance relative to those from the Middle East. Imports from Great Britain and the European Continent amounted to about 200,000 dinars and accounted for two-fifths of the total in 1884/85.[11] More than three-fifths of imports, with a value of 360,000 dinars, came from India and the neighboring Middle Eastern lands, especially Syria and Iran. By the beginning of the present century, two-fifths of Mosul's imports came from European sources. Total imports in 1909–12 amounted to about 158,000 dinars; of this over 90,000 were provided by Great Britain and the European Continent, in roughly equal proportions, 37,000 by India and the rest by Syria and Iran.[12] Needless to say, this import trade consisted of the same kinds of goods as were sent to Baghdad and Basrah. . . .

[4] Ibid.
[5] Ibid., 1902, pp. 6–7 [A and P 1904, 101].
[6] Ibid., 1869, pp. 309–11 [A and P 1872, 57].
[7] Ibid., p. 310.

[8] Ibid., 1878–79, pp. 1734–35.
[9] Ibid.
[10] "Basrah Consular Trade Report, 1864," pp. 260–62 [A and P 1867, 67].
[11] "Mosul Consular Trade Report, 1884," p. 1477 [A and P 1884–85, 79].
[12] Ibid., 1910 and 1911, pp. 4–7 [A and P 1913, 73].

## Trade of Khurasan

The report from which the following selection is taken was written at a time when Britain was increasingly feeling the strain of Russian competition. Russian goods, coming across the Caspian or on the Transcaspian railway, easily undersold British goods, transported over long caravan trails, and for the same reason Russia was a more accessible market for exports from Khurasan. The Russian government also gave bounties to exporters. Moreover, it was easier for the Russians to meet the needs of the Persian market since they supplied the consumers of Muslim Central Asia "who are, more or less, in the same scale of civilisation, and who all desire cheap and, generally speaking, similar articles." [1]

The British tried to shorten their lines by exporting goods from the Indian railhead through Sistan. In 1901/2, British trade with Khurasan was estimated at over £138,000, of which £35,000 passed through the Sistan route. Russia's trade in the same year was £646,000, and that of Afghanistan £88,000. [2]

In the following twelve years there was a large growth in both Russian and British commerce. By 1912/13, Khurasan's imports from Russia had risen to £1,104,000 and its exports to £1,403,000. Britain's total trade had increased in a similar proportion to £521,000; an average of £100,000's worth of imports passed through the Sistan route and it was estimated that about one-eighth of British goods imported through the Persian Gulf ports—Bandar Abbas and Bushire—found their way to Khurasan. Imports from Afghanistan averaged £100,000 and exports to it £70,000. [3]

[1] "Khurasan," A and P 1914, 93.
[2] Ibid., A and P 1902, 109.
[3] Ibid., A and P 1914, 93.

### Selection 16. Trade of Khurasan, 1890

[Consul-General MacLean, "Report on the Trade of Khorassan for the Year 1889–90." "Meshed," A and P 1890, 76, pp. 1–4]

The information contained in this, the first trade report that has been compiled since the establishment of a British Consulate-General in Khorassan, does not pretend to absolute accuracy, but the figures given, procured with considerable difficulty from the most reliable sources available, may, however, be considered as approximately correct.

There are only two main routes by which British goods are imported into Meshed. The first is by the Black Sea, Trebizond, Tabriz, and Teheran, entailing a caravan journey of about 1,600 miles. No transit dues are levied by the Turkish Government on goods coming this way, and 5 per cent. only is paid on arrival at Tabriz. The goods are then bought by Persian merchants, and despatched to Khorassan, where a further duty of 2½ per cent. is levied. An English firm, with an agent in Khorassan, would not pay this latter sum, as, by treaty, English goods only pay 5 per cent. on entering Persian territory, and no further dues can be levied on them in any part of the kingdom. The camel hire from Trebizond to Meshed is about 27½ tumans (7l. 17s. 2d.) a load, and the journey at the best season of the year would take about four months. The second route is by the Persian Gulf, Bander Abbas, and Yezd, or Kirman,[1] entailing also a caravan journey which can be traversed by a mule in 40 days, but which takes a camel,

[1] By Kirman, Ab-i-Bed Rahwar, Naiband, and Tun = 940 miles.

on an average, about 75 days. Camel hire from Bander Abbas to Meshed is about 9 tumans (2*l.* 11*s.* 5*d.*). The Kirman route is shorter, and the Yezd dues are avoided by traversing it; yet merchants often use the latter route, as Yezd is a busy mart, and they may obtain a sale for their goods there. Transport, too, is more easily procured there than at Kirman, though it is cheaper by the latter route. As above stated, according to treaty rights, British goods need only pay an ad valorem duty of 5 per cent. on entering Persian territory, and after that no further duties or tolls may be levied on them in any part of Persia; but the privilege has not yet been secured for our subjects in Khorassan, and the Persian authorities still levy sums amounting in all to about 7½ per cent. on goods coming to Meshed viâ Kirman, and over 9 per cent. on goods coming viâ Yezd. The merchants complain that receipts are not given by the custom officers at Bander Abbas for the customs dues paid there. Consequently on arrival at Meshed, having no vouchers, they are at the mercy of the customs officers there, who, instead of charging only the difference between the amount levied at the coast, take 4 and even 5½ per cent. By an official decree of the Council of the Russian Empire, dated February 5, 1889, goods from Europe, India, and Persia imported into Trans-Caspia are subject to an ad valorem duty of 2½ per cent. Exceedingly heavy duties are again levied on all British goods which are a necessity (such as tea and indigo) on arrival at Samarcand; and piece goods, &c., are rigidly prohibited.

The shortest and best route for Indian goods coming to Meshed would undoubtedly be that viâ Kandahar and Herat, a journey of only 800 miles, or 30 stages from our own railway terminus, but the exorbitant duties levied by the Amir (2*l.* 2*s.* a cwt.) have caused its entire abandonment. The hire per camel load would be 33 rupees (2*l.* 6*s.* 9*d.*).

Russian goods come to Khorassan almost entirely by the Trans-Caspian Railway, a small quantity only finding their way by Tabriz or by Astrabad. The total value of British goods imported into Khorassan during the year viâ Trebizond and Tabriz was about 82,000 tumans (23,429*l.*), and of British goods, viâ Bander Abbas, 213,050 tumans (60,871*l.*). This last total does not include the value of Chinese tea, the larger proportion of which should, however, be fairly included, as there is no doubt that most of it was purchased and brought from China by English merchants. No less than 415,000 tumans (118,571*l.*) worth of China green tea, and 18,000 tumans (5,143*l.*) worth of China black tea came from Bombay, while the value of the Indian green tea was only 25,000 tumans (7,143*l.*), and of the Indian black tea, which is universally drunk in Khorassan, 42,000 tumans (12,000*l.*). Thus the total value of Chinese tea was 433,000 tumans (123,714*l.*), against 67,000 tumans (19,143*l.*) of Indian. Nearly all the green tea (430,000 tumans worth = 122,857*l.*) went on to Bokhara, Khiva, &c. A Peshawar tea merchant, just arrived here to arrange to forward his goods by this route in future states that the Amir of Afghanistan levies 80 Indian rupees (5*l.* 13*s.* 4*d.*) on every camel load of goods passing through his territory (viâ Kabul) to Bokhara. The Amir of Bokhara also levies 2½ per cent. He further states that a pound of tea, costing 12 annas in India, will cost about 16 annas when it reaches Meshed, 18 annas when it reaches Bokhara by this route, and 21 annas by the Kabul route. He says two-thirds of the green tea imported into Bokhara is Chinese, and one-third Indian. If this is so, a great quantity of Indian tea must travel there by Kabul, the most expensive route, and the Indian merchants must be unaware that the Persian route is the cheapest. India supplies all the indigo used in these parts, and 18,000 tumans (5,143*l.*) worth passes on to Russian territory by Persia. The total value of British goods, omitting Chinese tea, imported into Khorassan was 295,050 tumans (84,300*l.*), and of Russian goods 386,420 tumans (110,408*l.*). All articles of English manufacture are considered infinitely superior, and are much preferred to Russian goods, but, being of better materials, and having to be brought a longer distance, they cannot be sold so cheaply. At the present moment English and Russian chintzes are selling at the same price in the bazaars. The Russians are trying to force the English article out of the market, by the importation of large quantities of their own chintz, which they are selling at a very small profit. The English chintz, on the other hand, must be got rid of, and so it, too, is being sold at a loss, or at no profit. It is obvious that with the Trans-Caspian Railway at Ashkabad, only 150 miles from Meshed, and with both towns linked, as they shortly will be, by an excellent macadamised road, British goods having to cross the seas and traverse the long, rough land routes above indicated, cannot hope to compete with Russian goods, and must eventually be driven entirely out of the market, even in these provinces of Persia, unless our own railway is extended in this direction. English broadcloth is preferred to all others, but the cheaper material from other parts of Europe, brought by Tabriz, finds a readier sale. There is a good demand for what is called Russian imitation broadcloth, a thick cotton coloured material with a nap which, however, has very little wear, and soon looks extremely shabby.

Russian sugar has entirely driven Indian and all other sugars out of the market. It is sold in the bazaars at about $4\frac{1}{2}d.$ per lb.

The wholesale price of sugar in India is $3\frac{1}{3}d.$ per lb.; so, under any circumstances, even if the bounties granted by the Russian Government to Russians for exporting sugar were withdrawn, it would be difficult to undersell them in Khorassan. Yet Indian sugar, being made from sugar-cane, is far better, sweeter, and easier to melt than Russian sugar, and is looked upon as a sweet-meat by the Khorassanis. None came last year, but there is still a little remaining in the market from former years. There is no reason why sugar should not be manufactured here, as most excellent beets are grown and are largely consumed by the people.

The chief exports of native produce from Khorassan are opium, cotton, wool, turquoises, dried fruits, almonds, carpets, and shawls. A very large proportion of the goods from Europe and India pass on to Russian territory and to Afghanistan. Opium is the only native article exported in any quantity (130,000 tumans, or 37,143l. worth) towards India, its destination being China. 50,000 tumans, or 14,286l. worth, also went to Constantinople viâ Teheran. Of other native goods only about 6,350 tumans, or 1,814l. worth, found their way to India. Wool, cotton, dried fruits, turquoises, &c., to the value of 390,050 tumans (111,442l.) were exported to Russia. . . .

## The Slave Trade

It has been estimated that, in the fifteenth through the nineteenth centuries, Europeans were "responsible for the removal from Africa of at least 12 million Africans. . . and certainly a great many more, perhaps an equal or even higher number, perished in the process."[1] The slave trade across the Sahara, which lasted for over a thousand years, carried a roughly equal number—as late as the nineteenth century, the annual average was about 20,000.[2] But the East African trade began "before the Christian era and it did not stop till some fifty years ago"[3] and the total number of slaves exported must have been considerably greater than in the other two.

Leaving aside the caravans from the Sudan to Egypt (see EHME, pp. 473–76), two main flows may be distinguished: from Ethiopia through the Red Sea or the

[1] Reginald Coupland, *East Africa and its Invaders* (Oxford, 1938) p. 35.
[2] Leon Carl Brown, "Race and Color in North Africa," *Daedalus*, Spring 1967, and sources cited therein.
[3] Coupland, p. 35.

Somali coast; and from the area between the Great Lakes and the coast, through Zanzibar, which gained greatly in importance after the Umani conquest of Zanzibar and Pemba at the end of the seventeenth century. These have been thoroughly studied by Professor J. B. Kelly, in *Britain and the Persian Gulf, 1795–1880*, on which the following account draws heavily.

Estimates of the numbers carried vary widely, which is not surprising since the trade must have shown sharp fluctuations. In addition to those given in the next selection, the following may be quoted. In 1811 Smee put annual exports from Zanzibar at 6,000 to 10,000.[4] In 1831, according to Wilson, 1,400 to 1,700 were sent from East Africa to Muscat and 300 to Bahrain; these figures do not take account of shipments to Persian ports, or to Basra.[5] In 1832-33, Blane put annual exports from Zanzibar at 12,000; in 1835-38, according to Fontanier, Muscat imported 4,000 slaves a year, and Basra and Bushire 300 to 400 each; in 1839, Cogan estimated Zanzibar's total annual exports at 20,000, a figure confirmed by Mackenzie in 1840. In 1842, Hamerton estimated exports from Zanzibar at 10,000 to 15,000, a figure confirmed by Brucks, who stated that 5,000 went to the Red Sea ports, 4,000 to 5,000 to Muscat, and the rest to Arabia, Persia, India, and Iraq.[6]

In 1842, Kemball estimated the number landed at Persian ports at 1,080 and at Basra at 1,217. He also added that Muscat and Sur were the main importing centers from Zanzibar and the Red Sea and that slaves were sent from there to Turkey, Persia, Scinde, the Arab states, and the west coast of India. Of these, "Turkey consumes by far the largest proportion, Bussorah and Bagdad being the largest marts; none of the Persian ports send vessels direct to Zanzibar, with the exception of Lingah, whence three or four boats are annually despatched each returning with about 70 slaves."[7]

In 1842, Robertson put total exports from Zanzibar at the rather high figure of 30,000. And in a letter dated 4 March 1842 it is stated that a slave dealer "informed me that the annual importation of slaves to Muscat and Soor is never under twenty thousand and is more often near thirty thousand souls"; estimating "other Eastern Coast of Arabia and Persian Gulf" at 4,000 raised the total to about 30,000 which, at an average of 50 Bombay rupees, gave a value of 1,500,000 rupees or £150,000.[8]

Estimates on the trade from Ethiopia also vary, but in the early 1840s the total seems to have been about 2,000 to 3,000 a year.[9]

As regards the share of the Persian ports, in 1842 the number "in Bushire and other Persian ports" is given by Kemball as 1,080. The number of boats arriving at Kharg in August-October 1841 was put at 117, with 1,217 slaves. And an answer to a questionnaire stated that some 3,000 slaves (two-thirds male and

[4] Kelly, p. 414.
[5] Robertson to Sheil, 9 July 1842, FO 84/426.
[6] Kelly, pp. 415–16.
[7] Kemball to Robertson, 8 July 1842, FO 84/426.
[8] Letter to Willoughby, FO 84/426.
[9] Kelly, p. 418; see also the extensive Report on Slave Trade of Abyssinia," by L. C. Harris, FO 84/444.

one-third female) arrived in Bushire each year, of whom only 170 or 180 were sold in that town, the rest being sent on to Muhammarah and Basra; Bandar Abbas took about one-quarter as many as were sold in Bushire and a small number was also sold in Lingah and Congoon.[10]

The trade in Ethiopian slaves, *habshis*, was extremely profitable; a girl bought at Shoa at 12 to 20 Maria Theresa dollars (£2.8.0. to £4) could be sold for 85 to 100 in Mocha, and one bought for 40 at Berbera could fetch as much as 90 in Muscat, 50 to 150 at Bushire or Bahrain, and 100 to 150 on the Pirate Coast. Profits on African slaves, *sidis*, were not so high; "the importer at Muscat in the early eighteen-thirties could reckon on a margin of 20–35 per cent over the selling price at Zanzibar." A slave purchased for 20 to 35 Maria Theresa dollars would fetch 25 to 40 at Muscat and 40 to 50 at Sharjah and Bahrain.[11] Kemball stated that the profit on Africans "at Muscat is 20 per cent, and at Bussorah and Bushire never less than 50 per Cent."[12]

It remains to add that almost all sources agree that the transport of slaves from Africa was relatively humane, and that the hardships endured by them were not appreciably greater than those of the crew and other passengers. And once they had reached their ultimate destination, their condition was little worse than that of the free population around them.

The suppression of the slave trade by the British government is described in detail by Kelly (chapters 9 and 13). The first steps were taken in 1821 and in the next twenty-five years various agreements were concluded, most importantly with the Sultan of Muscat, and negotiations were carried on with the rulers of Turkey, Egypt, and Iran. But "the volume of slaves imported into the Gulf between 1848 and 1850 was almost as great as it had been before the conclusion of the 1845 and 1847 treaties," the decline in exports from Zanzibar being offset by the rise from Ethiopia.[13] After that, increased British pressure on the Middle Eastern rulers and more intensive naval patroling began to have some effect, but it was not until the 1870s that the traffic was seriously restricted and not until the end of the century that it was reduced to a trickle. But the following testimony, among many, shows that it went on until this century: "In Sistan they sell slaves, white and black, delivered openly in Baluchistan and other regions. Almost every village headman in Sistan has a male or female slave. The price of a strong young male slave in Sistan is on average 50 to 80 tumans. The female slaves are cheaper. Relations with slaves are humane."[14] Even today there is evidence that a small number of slaves are still being carried across the Red Sea.

(See also works by Kelly, Lloyd, and Colomb, listed in the bibliography.)

[10] Dispatches dated 8 July 1842, 4 March 1842, and 13 July 1842, FO 84/426.
[11] Kelly, p. 418.
[12] FO 84/426.
[13] Kelly, p. 602.
[14] Dr. A Miller, *Proshloe i nastoyashchee Seistana* (Saint Petersburg, 1907) quoted by B. Skladanek, in *Przeglad Orientalistyczny*, no. 4, 1963. Miller had served as Russian consul in Sistan; see Kazemzadeh, p. 412.

## Selection 17. The Slave Trade, 1840
["Reports of Guards," 21–30 September 1840, FO 84/387]

*September 21st, 1840*

Nacodah [nakhuda, i.e., captain] states "that from the Gulf altogether (that is to say belonging to the Imam of Muscat, the Chiefs of the Arabian coast and their subjects and the different Merchants on the Persian coast) there are about 100 boats annually employed in the slave trade to Zanzibar, some carrying as many as 200 and few if any less than 50 slaves.

In the Burbura slave trade there are not above 20 boats carrying each from 10 to 15 of the Abshee caste (meaning I emaging [imagine] Abyssinian). The slaves are all taken either in petty wars, or by stratagem, and then sold to the slave Merchants on the Coast.

From Muscat direct not above 100 are sent to the Upper part of the Persian Gulf, but belonging to Zoar or Soor the principal port that supplies Bussorah and Bushire there are now 40 small and 4 or 5 large boats on there (*sic*) way up.

The Imam receives a duty of 1 Dollar per head on each slave embarked from Zanzibar, and the same for every one landed at Muscat.

The price of slaves at Zanzibar

| | | |
|---|---|---|
| A. Boy of 7 years of Age | . . . . . | 7 Dollars |
| Do. of 10 years of Age | . . . . . | 20 Dollars |
| A full grown man. | . . . . . . . . | 17 Dollars |

the profit at Muscat is 20 per cent, and at Bussorah and Bushire 50. . . . . . .dº

The Imam has two boats of his own and the Merchants of Muscat 4 four employed in this traffic.

Children born in Muscat although of slave parents are few, but the owner of the parents still feels it incumbent upon him to provide for their offspring.

*September 26th 1840*

His Highness the Imam of Muscat's Buggalah [sailing boat], Ulumarah from Muscat, Nacodah states, Merchants employed on this traffic are all Musselmen.

The slaves are never seized by the crews of the boats, or, by the slave Merchants, but by men, employed for that purpose, or in the petty wars.

The number of boats employed in this trade between the Gulf and Zanzibar is, as follows.

| | |
|---|---|
| Rasel Khyma . . . . . . . . . . | 17 of sizes |
| Bahrein . . . . . . . . . . . | 3 large |
| Grane [Kuwait] . . . . . . . . | None |
| Soor . . . . . . . . . . . . . | 40 small |
| Do. . . . . . . . . . . . . . | 12 large |
| Muscat . . . . . . . . . . . | None |
| Abothabee [Abu Dhabi] . . . . . | 7 small |
| Shargah . . . . . . . . . | 7 small |
| Debai . . . . . . . . . . . | 6 Dᵉ |
| Bussorah . . . . . . . . . . . | 2 large |

The Imam's own vessel or those of his subjects do not bring slaves to Muscat, but the people of that place procure slaves for their households, from the Rasel Khymah and other boats that touch there. Duty upon slave paid to the Imam is 1 Dollar per head.

| | | |
|---|---|---|
| Price of boys of 8 years of age | . . . . . | 10 Dollars |
| Price of boys of 16 years of age | . . . . . | 21 Dollars |
| Price of full grown men | . . . . . . . | 17 Dollars |

profit at Muscat is uncertain, but at Bussarah and Bushire even less than 50 per Cent.

Buggalah Turgerbi from Muscat
September 26th 1840 *Nacodah on Shore* Commanding Officer.

States.—Forty boats have left Zoar this year with slaves on board each boat averaging about 22 slaves.

Belongs to Zanzibar has seen at least 100 buggalahs from the different ports of the Persian Gulf, at the former port employed in the Slave trade is certain that 2 or 3 of them belonged to Lingar [Lingah]—some carry as many as 200 slaves.

IMAMS DUTY 1 DOLLAR PER HEAD

*September 27th 1840*

Buggarah [*sic*] Futtah El Kair and Buggalah Futtey El Kair from Jingah [*sic*], Ahmed, Hussain Omanee (Owner residing at Yesha) the former Vessel has six and the latter 10 female slaves on board.

States the slaves were brought from Zanzibar, by a Lingar boat.

Only one Lingar boat went to Zanzibar, this year. She brought back 150 slaves.

Last year, 2 boats, and the year before three; they brought back from 150, to 160, slaves each. Lingar is a free port for the slave trade no duty being laid upon it.

Price of a boy of 8 years of age . . . . . 17 Dollars
Price of a young Man without a beard full grown . . . . . . . . . . . . . . . 21 Dollars
Men about 30 years of age beard full grown 10 Dollars
A Woman stoutly made . . . . . . . . 35 Dollars

The ports on the Persian side of the coast, have no regulated number [of] boats employed in this traffic, with the exception of Kishm, which sends two large buggalahs

annually carrying in all about 350 slaves.

The slaves brought by these Lingar boats appear picked persons superior to those brought by the other boats.

*September 30th 1840*

Buggalah Hashems from Kishim Syed, Owner (residing at Mocha) Mahomed ben Hamed; Nacodah and Agent for the Owner.

States, no boats are employed in the slave trade direct from Kishim, so this specise [sic] of traffic has been discontinued for the last 5 years, nor do any other boats bring slaves to that port, in fact there is no slave trade carried on at Kishim whatever.

## Balance of Payments

Almost nothing is known about the invisible items in Iran's balance of payments before the First World War. The following selection gives some information on what was probably the largest single debit item for many decades, expenditure by Persian pilgrims in the Shii holy places of Iraq (see also 6:1). The selection also mentions the steps taken by the Qajars to divert this flow to the holy cities of Iran, Mashad, and Qum, a policy that met with much success and was continued after the First World War.[1]

Another large debit item, which grew rapidly toward the end of the period under study, was the servicing of foreign loans (see 8:7). In 1912/13 this amounted to 20.7 million krans, or about £400,000.[2]

Against that must be set several credit items. First, there was the expenditure of foreign pilgrims visiting Mashad; this was estimated in 1904 at 7 to 8 million rubles a year, or £700,000 to £800,000.[3] Second, there were the funds sent to foreign missions and charitable and educational institutions in Iran; in 1905 the British consul at Tabriz put the amount spent in Azerbaijan at £40,000 to £50,000.[4] Third, there were the remittances sent by Persian workers in Iran, Turkey, and India; in the years immediately preceding the First World War over 200,000 went to Russia each year and the amount they sent back has been estimated at some 14 million rubles, or about £1,400,000.[5] Fourth, there were the royalty payments made by the British and Russian enterprises working in Iran; royalties from the Anglo-Persian Oil Company alone amounted to £1,325,000 in 1912/19.[6] Finally,

[1] According to the Ottoman quarantine statistics, 95,000 pilgrims from Iran passed through Khaniqin in 1905 and 55,000 in 1910. Report by A. T. Wilson on railway, enclosed in letter from Greenway to Foreign Office, 11 August 1911, FO 371/1186. In 1800, Malcolm estimated Iranian pilgrim expenditure in Iraq at about £100,000 and in Mecca at about £60,000—see chap. 6, sel. 1.
[2] Jamalzadeh, p. 156.
[3] Entner, p. 59.
[4] A and P 1906, 127—see also chap. 8, sel. 4.
[5] Entner, pp. 59–61. See also chap. 2, sel. 5.
[6] Fateh, *Panjah*, p. 274. See also chap. 7, sel. 1.

it should be remembered that a large amount of goods was smuggled out of Iran, and that the value of such goods should be added to the official export returns when estimating Iran's balance of payments (see also 3 : 23).

After the Bolshevik Revolution the flow of pilgrims and workmen between Iran and Russia was interrupted. The service charges on Iran's foreign debt also declined sharply. This left oil royalties, and the local foreign exchange expenditures of the oil company, as by far the largest items in the balance of payments apart from merchandise trade. By the late 1930s oil accounted for almost one-fifth of Iran's foreign exchange earnings and in the late 1940s and 1950s its share rose to around 60 percent.

### Selection 18. Iranian Pilgrims in Iraq, 1870s
[Thomson to Derby, 30 September 1875, FO 60/373]

... The towns visited by the Pilgrims within the Turkish Territory are 1st Kauzemein in the immediate vicinity of Bagdad, 2nd Samara about sixty miles North of Kauzemein, 3rd Kerbella about sixty four South of the same place and 4th Nejjeff about thirty five miles from Kerbella.

An idea of the importance of the traffic arising from this pilgrimage may be formed from the following details which although not given as positively exact are sufficiently approximate for that purpose.

The number of persons making the pilgrimage annually may as an average be stated as one hundred thousand and those may be divided into three classes, the rich, the middle class and the poor. It is calculated that the rich expend on the round journey, that is from Khanekeen the frontier town of Turkey and back to Khanekeen from two to three hundred Tomans each, and the average expenditure of the three classes for living alone is computed at twenty Tomans a head or two millions of Tomans in all.

The pilgrim as a rule conveys his articles of merchandize to the Holy Places, but on his return every pilgrim however poor sets aside a certain amount of his funds to be expended on articles of little intrinsic value, (but yielding a profit to the local trader of probably fifty per cent) the manufacture of the shrine cities, not as a trading speculation but solely to be distributed among his relations and friends on returning to his native place. The total amount thus invested may be also estimated at two millions of Tomans, and to this adding Two hundred and fifty thousand Tomans as an average amount of mule hire on the round journey from Khanekeen to Khanekeen, the total amount expended by Persian Pilgrims annually may be estimated at four millions and two hundred and fifty thousand Tomans equal to one million and Seventy thousand pounds sterling, exclusive of pontage at the bridges of Bakooba, Bagdad and Moosayb and the Sums levied by the Turkish Government on passports and Customs dues on articles exported by the Pilgrims.

That the cessation of the annual influx of so large a Sum should have seriously damaged the trade of Turkish Arabia and that it has increased the wealth and prosperity of the two shrine cities in Persia—Meshed and Koom—and more particularly the former, does not admit of doubt. It is much to be regretted that British merchants established for sometime at Bagdad should suffer therefrom; but from what I have stated above the responsibility for this state of affairs would appear to rest more with the Turkish than the Persian Government, and I fear there is no help for it, while Turkey continues to remain blind to her material interests and while the consciences of Persian devotees are gradually becoming more reconciled, by improvement in their material interests by the less expensive pilgrimage obtainable in their native country.

This would appear to be however a question not of British commerce so much as of local trade, which has diminished in Turkish Arabia and had been increased in Eastern Persia. In proof of this I may mention that the large firm of Ziegler and Co. only a few days ago obtained from me a recommendatory letter for the Mission Agent at Meshed for a European Agent whom they are establishing in that city; and that in all my reports from Meshed allusion is made to the great increase of pilgrims who since the Kerbella and Najjeff pilgrimage was suspended, visit that shrine, and have added so much to the Wealth and prosperity of the city.

## The Volume of Trade, 1800–1914

Data on Iranian trade in the nineteenth century are conjectural, but they may be used as a basis for estimating the trend in total value and quantum. Malcolm's estimate for 1800 (see 6:1) is the only available one for the early part of the century, and may serve as a starting point. He put total trade at £2,500,000; this figure is the sum of imports, exports, and reexports, and, according to Malcolm, the last item accounted for over half the total.

On the basis of official reports and information given by merchants, Fraser estimated total exports in 1820/21 at roughly £1,225,000. The main components were: exports to India from Bushire, £305,000; exports from Barfurush, £215,000; exports to Tiflis and Georgia, £200,000; exports to Baghdad £200,000; exports to the rest of Turkey £200,000; exports to Bukhara and states eastwards, £50,000.[1] Fraser's figures would imply that there had been no increase in trade since Malcolm's time, which seems unlikely. The explanation for the discrepancy may lie in the fact that all reexports are included in Malcolm's figures, and account for over half the total, whereas Fraser's seem to consist almost wholly of exports of Persian goods.

In 1834, the British consul in Trebizond, James Brant, wrote a Report on the Trade of Persia (FO 78/241). According to him, in 1830 goods imported through Bushire amounted to about £750,000 and through Trebizond £350,000. Assuming Russia sent in goods and bullion worth £600,000, and other places "Baghdad, Kurdistan and the countries East of Persia £300,000," the total was put at about £2,000,000. Brant stated that he had used the 1830 figures because he had returns for Bushire and

at that period the Russian trade was in all its activity. Since then both the Bushire and the Russian trades have fallen off, the one on account of the insecurity of the roads, the other from the restrictive system adopted in Georgia by Russia, but I see no reason to suppose that the same means of consumption do not still exist and although the trade has changed its channels, its collective amount I do not think is diminished. What British trade has lost on the side of Bushire it has gained on the side of Constantinople.

For 1857, Blau put total trade at about £6,000,000 (see following Selection).

[1] Fraser, p. 290, cited by Lambton, in Richards, *Islam*.

These figures were criticized by Stolze and Andreas,[2] who contrasted them with the estimate of £4,000,000 (imports £2,500,000 and exports £1,500,000) for 1868 given by R. F. Thomson, secretary of the British Legation.[3] Part of the discrepancy between the figures given by Blau and Thomson is due to the sharp decline in silk exports following the disease of 1865 (see 5:6–8), which according to Thomson reduced the value of exports by £1,000,000.[4] But there is every reason to believe that there was a marked rise in Iran's foreign trade in the first half of the century. Sir Harford Jones, who knew the country well, had observed that trade "had increased with extraordinary rapidity during the early part of the reign of Fath Ali Shah," because of both greater security and the greater attention paid by the government of India to Persian Gulf trade. Thus, whereas around 1784 annual imports of Indian chintz through Bushire averaged 60 to 70 bales, by 1811 they had risen to 500 to 600 bales.[5] The available evidence also shows a rapid growth in Persian Gulf trade between the 1780s and the 1820s and perhaps a doubling again by 1860 (see 3:4–6). The trade of Tabriz also increased considerably (see 3:12, 13). Russian trade with Iran, expressed in gold rubles, about doubled between the early 1830s and mid 1860s (see 3:21). All together, it seems unlikely that total trade around 1860 could have been much below £5,000,000.

For the 1880s several estimates—based on customs revenues and adjusted in various ways—are quoted by Lord Curzon, who opted for a figure of £7,000,000 to £7,500,000 "of which the imports constitute about two thirds, and the exports the remainder."[6] Stolze and Andreas, also starting with customs receipts and assuming an average duty of 2.5 to 3 percent, put total trade at 272 to 332 million francs, or £10,920,000 to £13,280,000, which seems too high.[7] On the other hand a French estimate for 1875 of 64.1 million francs, although claiming to be based on "sure sources," is far too low.[8]

There was little increase in values over the next fifteen or twenty years, the figure for 1901/2 being £8,982,000 (imports £5,469,000 and exports £3,780,000) (see also 3:20). However, the next ten years saw a very rapid rise, to £18,253,000 in 1912/13 (imports £10,320,000 and exports £7,933,000) and £20,055,000 in 1913/14 (imports £11,767,000 and exports £8,288,000).[9]

In other words, total trade at current prices about doubled between 1800 and the 1860s and quadrupled between the 1860s and 1913. Needless to say, no price indexes are available for estimating the growth in quantum. Since, however, all the figures are expressed in sterling, and since Britain constituted by far the largest

[2] p. 45.
[3] "Report on Persia," A and P 1867–68, 69 (see 2:2).
[4] A French consular report stated that, until 1866, Persian imports were about 45 to 50 million francs and exports 36 to 40 million; the failure of the silk crop had reduced exports by 12 to 15 million francs—Crampon to Minister of Foreign Affairs, 26 June 1867, AE Tabriz, vol. 1.
[5] Lorimer, 1: 1955.
[6] *Persia*, 2: 562–63.
[7] p. 45.
[8] Balloy to Minister of Foreign Affairs, 1 February 1876, AE Téhéran, vol. 2.
[9] "Persia," A and P 1910, 94; ibid., 1914–16, 74.

market in international trade, it is permissible to use the British index of export and import prices as a very rough deflator. Taking 1880 as base, export prices stood at 300 or over in 1800–15 and import prices at 200 or over. In the 1850s both indexes stood near 100, and did so again in 1913.[10] It is probable that the Revolutionary and Napoleonic wars affected prices in Iran much less than in England, and a deflator of 150 for 1800 may perhaps be appropriate. This would imply that, in real terms, trade rose about threefold between 1800 and the 1850s and quadrupled again by 1914, a total rise of about twelve times during the whole period under review.

[10] See tables in Imlah, pp. 97–98.

**Selection 19. Iranian Trade, 1850s**
[Ernst Otto Blau, *Commerzielle Zustände Persiens* (Berlin, 1858), pp. 164–68]

1. Persian imports from Europe through Trebizond:

| | |
|---|---|
| 1847 . . . . . | 8,681,000 thalers, prix courant[1] |
| 1850 . . . . . | 11,825,000 thalers, prix courant |
| 1852 . . . . . | 9,642,000 thalers, prix courant |
| 1854 . . . . . | 8,743,000 thalers, prix courant |
| 1856 . . . . . | 12,393,000 thalers, prix courant |

or an average figure for imports through this route of 10,250,000 thalers

2. Imports from Russia into Persia were, according to statistical declarations:

| | |
|---|---|
| 1852 . . . . . | 897,600 rubles |
| 1853 . . . . . | 795,046 rubles |
| 1855 . . . . . | 866,270 rubles |
| 1857 . . . . . | 750,310 rubles |

or an average of 850,000 thalers, prix courant, which, as mentioned above, being doubled[2] gives 1,700,000 thalers

[1] The rate of exchange during that period was about 7 thalers to the pound sterling.
[2] As Blau pointed out on page 162, Russian figures were based on those of the customs houses of Tiflis (handling trade through Julfa) and Astrakhan, i.e., they covered caravan trade over the Arax and sea trade across the Caspian. However, smuggling was widespread on both routes and the "most judicious Russian authorities in Persia themselves admit that these figures represent hardly half the real turnover in Russo-Persian trade" and that they should therefore be, confidently, doubled.

3. Total imports from Turkey in Asia were approximately: 1,000,000 thalers
From which the average value of the annual imports of Persia from Western trading regions can be safely taken as 12,960,000 thalers

The value of exports from Persia to these same regions is as follows.
1. Via Trebizond, [estimated] from the number [of packages] [*aus den Zahlen*]

| | |
|---|---|
| 1847 . . . . . | 2,894,000 thalers |
| 1850 . . . . . | 4,148,000 thalers |
| 1852 . . . . . | 3,487,000 thalers |
| 1853 . . . . . | 3,770,000 thalers |
| 1856 . . . . . | 4,202,200 thalers |

an average export figure of 3,700,000 thalers

2. From the Russian import returns:

| | |
|---|---|
| 1852 . . . . . | 2,782,847 rubles |
| 1853 . . . . . | 3,033,695 rubles |
| 1855 . . . . . | 3,642,723 rubles |
| 1857 . . . . . | 4,128,000 rubles |

an average of 4,500,000 thalers [*sic*; 3,500,000?], prix courant; therefore the probable amount of exports across the Russian frontier is 7,000,000 thalers

3. Exports from Persia across the frontier of Turkey in Asia are, according to all reports, somewhat more than

twice as large as imports, and may therefore be put at about          2,500,000 thalers
So that, in this [westward] direction Persia's exports amount on average each year

to some                                13,200,000 thalers
which compared to the value of imports from these same countries, given above as        12,950,000 thalers

Leaves a favorable balance, with a surplus of about                          250,000 thalers
In spite of the unreliability of some items, one can state with confidence that both Persia's imports from and its exports to, the group of Western countries exceed twelve million thalers' worth, and that they are about equal in value. In order to evaluate these results in the light of historical development, it may be mentioned that in 1834 Fraser estimated the turnover [*Gesamtumsatz*] of European trade in Persia, including Russian, at one million pounds sterling, and that in 1848 Gödel[3] put the average value of imports through Trebizond alone at the round figure of 16,000,000 gulden, and exports through that route at 2,000,000.[4]
The values given by us under heading 3 [*sic*, read 2], which contradict the Russian official figures, and the estimated excess of 5,300,000 thalers in Persia's exports to Russia over its imports from that country, may be justified by quoting in support three authorities, whose results were reached independently. Ely Smith, a very prudent observer, puts Russia's exports to Persia in 1837 at 600,000 tumans, or over 1,800,000 thalers (see Ritter, *Erdkunde* 9:881). Gödel (p. 67) estimates, from good sources, that Persia's annual exports to Russia exceed its imports from that country by about

5,000,000 silver rubles.[5] The Russian merchant community in Tabriz estimates that, every year, 7,000,000 rubles flow from Russia to Persia to cover Russia's import surplus; part of this flow does not originate in direct Russo-Persian trade, but in intermediate trade with Khiva and Bukhara; but the net gain to Persia in Russo-Persian trade can nevertheless be certainly put at a minimum of 5,000,000 rubles.

No similar data are available on Persia's Eastern trade; in default of such information, the following estimates—which tend to err on the low rather than the high side—can be used to complete our tables.
4. Imports of goods and produce of Tartary, Bukhara, and other lands of Inner Asia amount to at least                3,000,000 thalers
5. Imports from the East Indies [*Ostindische*—meaning here, primarily, India], although smaller than during the previous centuries, have still a value of about            5,000,000 thalers

giving a total for Eastern trade of              8,000,000 thalers
As against that, Persia exports to this region:
4. to Tartary, Bukhara, etc., about              5,000,000 thalers
5. to the East Indies at least                     2,800,000 thalers

                                               7,800,000 thalers
leaving a deficit of                         200,000 thalers
The surplus in Persia's Western trade is sufficient to cover this deficit, which is paid for mostly in silver to India (see the following chapter). Persia's surplus in trade with Central Asia is paid for in gold, partly Russian and partly of domestic origin.

---

[3] Rudolf Gödel, see 3:10
[4] The rate of exchange during that period was about 10 gulden to the pound sterling.

[5] The rate of exchange during that period was about 6 silver rubles to the pound sterling.

In summary, the total figures on Persia's foreign trade are:

| | |
|---|---|
| Imports from Western regions | 12,950,000 thalers |
| Imports from Eastern regions | 8,000,000 thalers |
| Total imports | 20,950,000 thalers |
| Exports to Western regions | 13,200,000 thalers |
| Exports to Eastern regions | 7,800,000 thalers |
| Total exports | 21,000,000 thalers |

From this then—if one does not simply take it that exports and imports are in balance— one can say that Persia enjoys a small annual surplus of 50,000 thalers. Still, the result which has been discovered—that the total turnover of goods in foreign trade amounts to about 42,000,000 thalers—may be considered relatively favorable when compared with that of other Asiatic states with approximately the same population and trading under similar conditions, which show:

| | |
|---|---|
| Burma | 12 million imports, 12 million exports, total 24 million thalers, |
| Afghanistan | 8 million imports, 9 million exports, total 17 million thalers, |
| Annam only | 3 million imports, 3 million exports, total 6 million thalers. |

(See Hübner, Statistical Tables)

Since we discuss in chapter 22 the question of the share of the individual European countries in the total import and export figures given above,[6] it remains for us to attempt to determine the proportion of individual items in the total import and export trade of Persia.

[6] On pp. 238–39, Blau puts imports through Trebizond at about 12,000,000 Reichsthalers, and breaks them down, roughly, into: Great Britain 7,930,000, Switzerland 2,800,000, Prussia and Zollverein 350,000, Austria 250,000, Turkey and Danubian Principalities 180,000, France 170,000, Italian states 150,000, Belgium and Netherlands 170,000, America 100,000, undetermined 250,000.
Exports through Trebizond totaled 4,250,000 Reichsthalers, broken down: France 1,300,000, Turkey 1,250,000, England 1,000,000, Switzerland 300,000, Austria 150,000, Prussia and Germany 100,000, Holland, Belgium, and other 150,000.

## A. IMPORTS

*a)* Manufactures

| | |
|---|---|
| Cottons | 8,600,000 thalers |
| Woolens | 2,877,000 thalers |
| Silks | 1,775,000 thalers |
| | about 13,252,000 thalers |

*b)* Colonial goods and dyes,

| | |
|---|---|
| Sugar . . . . . . about | 500,000 thalers |
| Tea . . . . . . . about | 1,800,000 thalers |
| Drugs and dyes . . . . . | 1,311,000 thalers |
| Sundry . . . . . . . . | 1,429,000 thalers |
| | about 5,040,000 thalers |

*c)* Metals and Metalware

| | |
|---|---|
| Crude metals . . . . . . | 195,000 thalers |
| Wrought metals . . . . | 300,000 thalers |
| | about 495,000 thalers |

*d)* Porcelain, glassware, precious stones . . . . about | 163,000 thalers
*e)* Hardware, various kinds . . . | 2,000,000 thalers

Total 20,950,000 thalers

## B. EXPORTS

*a)* Raw natural produce

| | |
|---|---|
| Sheep, horses, leeches, etc. . . . | 1,800,000 thalers |
| Wheat, rice, barley, etc. . . . . | 2,214,000 thalers |
| Tobacco . . . . . . . . . | 780,000 thalers |
| Cotton . . . . . . . . . . | 216,000 thalers |
| Sundry . . . . . . . . . | 200,000 thalers |
| | 5,210,000 thalers |

b) Semiprocessed natural produce

| | |
|---|---|
| Hides and Skins. . . . . . | 341,000 thalers |
| Butter, tallow, wax . . . . . | 122,000 thalers |
| Raw silk. . . . . . . . . | 6,578,000 thalers |
| Drugs and dyes . . . . . . | 443,000 thalers |
| Dried fruits, grapes, etc. . . . | 850,000 thalers |
| Tea . . . . . . . . . . . | 726,000 thalers |
| Sundry . . . . . . . . . | 150,000 thalers |
| | 9,210,000 thalers |

c) Industrial products

| | |
|---|---|
| Silk manufactures . . . . . | 1,061,000 thalers |
| Woolen manufactures . . . . | 2,304,000 thalers |
| Cotton manufactures . . . . | 2,345,000 thalers |
| Metal products . . . . . . . | 412,000 thalers |
| Leather goods . . . . . . . | 208,000 thalers |
| Starch . . . . . . . . . | 20,000 thalers |
| Sundry . . . . . . . . . | 230,000 thalers |
| | 6,580,000 thalers |
| | Total 21,000,000 thalers |

## Composition of Trade, 1850–1914

The following selection, taken from the report of a British trade mission to Iran, gives an account of the country's main imports and exports at the beginning of this century. The broad trends in the composition of trade are brought out by the following two tables, based on figures provided by Blau (see 3:19), Curzon (*Persia*), and the trade returns.

On the import side, the main shift is the great increase in the import of cotton and other textiles, which continued until the First World War; however, as a percentage of total trade, textiles fell off sharply in the last two decades of this period. Tea and sugar expanded greatly (see chap., 3, introduction). Toward the end of the century, Iran began to import cereals in significant quantities, and kerosine also became an important item (see chap. 7, introduction, and sel. 2). Metals and metal goods continued to form a very small fraction of the total.

On the export side, the most striking feature is the sharp drop in exports of silk (see 5:6) and of textiles. Their place was taken by raw cotton (see 5:12) and carpets (see 6:9), which increased both absolutely and relatively. Dried and fresh fruits and rice also advanced rapidly (see 5:11, 13), while opium and tobacco reached a peak and then leveled off (see 5:9, 13).

MAIN IMPORTS
(percentage of total)

| | 1850s | 1880s | 1911–13 |
|---|---|---|---|
| Cotton cloth . . . . | 43 | 48 | 30 |
| Woolen and silk cloth | 23 | 15 | 5 |
| Tea . . . . . . . . | 9 | 2 | 6 |
| Sugar . . . . . . . | 2 | 8 | 24 |
| Metal goods . . . . | 2 | 2 | 2 |
| Cereals . . . . . . | .. | .. | 4 |
| Kerosine . . . . . . | .. | 1 | 2 |

MAIN EXPORTS
(percentage of total)

|  | 1850s | 1880s | 1911–13 |
|---|---|---|---|
| Silk and products . . . | 38 | 18 | 5 |
| Cotton and woolen cloth | 23 | 1 | 1 |
| Cereals . . . . . . . . | 10 | 16[a] | 12[a] |
| Fruit . . . . . . . . . | 4 | 6 | 13 |
| Tobacco . . . . . . . | 4 | 5 | 1 |
| Raw cotton . . . . . . | 1 | 7 | 19 |
| Opium . . . . . . . . | .. | 26 | 7 |
| Carpets . . . . . . . . | .. | 4 | 12 |

[a] mainly rice.

## Selection 20. Trade of Iran, 1900s

[H. W. MacLean, "Report on the Conditions and Prospects of British Trade in Persia," A and P 1904, 95, pp. 2–9]

The total trade of Persia with foreign countries, as shown by Persian Customs Statistics, now exceeds 8,000,000*l.* sterling per annum, of which over 5,000,000*l.* are imports, and 3,000,000*l.* exports. These figures do not include specie or bullion.

The Customs Statistics are entitled to confidence as the Department is now properly organised and administered. They omit, however, certain articles of trade, mostly exports, which I venture to estimate at a value of from 150,000*l.* to 200,000*l.* yearly.[1]

The records available for a comparison with trade at former periods are unsatisfactory. Such figures as I can offer confirm the conclusion I have formed from inquiry into a number of different lines of commerce, namely, that foreign commerce with Persia, both import and export, has steadily increased during the last decade, to the extent of perhaps twenty per cent. It is subject, however, to wide fluctuations from year to year, and comparisons of any one year with another may be quite misleading.[2]

The export trade is made up as follows:—

One-half, or more, raw vegetable products:—Dried fruits, 450/500,000*l.*; Raw cotton, 400/450,000*l.*; Opium, 280/320,000*l.*; Rice, 250/280,000*l.*; Gums, 80/100,000*l.*

One-fourth, raw animal products:—Silk cocoons, 200/250,000*l.*; Skins and peltries, 100/120,000*l.*; Pearls, 80/100,000*l.*; Wool, 60/80,000*l.*; &c.

One-fourth, or less, manufactures:—Carpets, 230/260,000*l.*; other textiles of silk, cotton, and wool, 150/180,000*l.*; Leather, 40/60,000*l.*

The import trade may be summarised as follows:—

Six-tenths, or more, manufactures:—Cotton yarns and tissues, 1,800/2,300,000*l.* Other tissues of wool and silk, clothing, &c., 380/420,000*l.*; Metals and their manufactures, 140/170,000*l.*; Glassware and porcelain, 75/100,000*l.*, &c.

Three-tenths, food substances:—Sugar, 1,000/1,300,000*l.*; Tea, 220/240,000*l.*; Grain, 130/150,000*l.*; Spices, 40/60,000*l.*, &c.

One-tenth, or less, raw materials, &c.:—Kerosine, 40/50,000*l.*; Skins and peltries, 30/50,000*l.*; Dyes, 30/40,000*l.*; Tobacco, 30/40,000*l.*; Wool, 20/40,000*l.*

[1] The values attributed to the different descriptions of merchandise are somewhat less, I should say roughly from 10 to 15 per cent. less, than their real commercial values at point of entry into or exit from Persia. There is also, no doubt, some merchandise which still eludes Customs control, but I cannot estimate, with any accuracy, the quantity or value of such contraband. The total foreign trade of Persia might therefore be estimated at quite 9 millions, or 5½ millions imports and 3¾ millions exports.

[2] The exports consist largely of raw produce, and are governed by the accident of good or bad harvests and by prices abroad. Imports consist principally of manufactured goods, of which large stocks in proportion to business have to be held on account of the long time they are on the way. They often arrive at the port of entry with a rush after a good trade has depleted these stocks and encouraged orders, thus swelling the trade statistics of one year at expense of another.

The following is a rough summary of the trade done with Russia, the British Empire, and other countries respectively:—

TRADE WITH RUSSIA

*Total Trade.*—Exports, about 1,500,000*l.* per annum,[3] imports, about 2,000,000*l.* per annum.

*Exports.*—Five-sixths, raw or agricultural products, of which far the most important are dried fruits, raw cotton, and rice, then hides and peltries, wool, cocoon silk, and gums.

One-sixth, manufactures:—Leather, carpets, and various tissues destined for kindred Muhammedan population in Russia.

*Imports.*—One-half, sugar.

One-fourth, cotton tissues.

One-fourth, other manufactures, including some 150,000*l.* value of kerosine, animals, flour, tobacco and other vegetable products.

TRADE WITH BRITISH EMPIRE

*Total Trade.*—Exports, about half a million; imports, two millions, per annum.

*Exports.*—Chiefly raw products:—Dried fruits, opium, gums, pearls, raw hides. Manufactures are carpets and some silk tissues for India.

*Imports.*—Three-fourths, cotton yarns and tissues, which form also quite two-thirds of the total imports of these commodities to Persia.

One-eighth or less, other manufactures; and the rest tea, coffee, spices, &c., from India.

TRADE WITH OTHER COUNTRIES

*Total Trade.*—Exports, about one million, imports, one million,[4] per annum.

*Exports.*—Opium to China, 180/200,000*l.*; cocoon silk to France and Italy, 200/230,000*l.*;

carpets to Turkey, Europe, and America, 150/180,000*l.*; cotton, silk, and woollen tissues to Afghanistan and Turkey, 60/80,000*l.*

*Imports.*—Sugar from France and Austria, 200/220,000*l.*; woollen, cotton, and silk tissues chiefly from France and Austria, 250/300,000*l.*; tea from China and Batavia, 50/60,000*l.*; raw material from Turkey and Afghanistan, 180/200,000*l.*; other manufactures, chiefly from France, Austria, and Germany, 160/190,000*l.*

Russia and the British Empire have consequently a preponderating interest in trade with Persia. Moreover, Russian trade shows a very marked increase in recent years, whilst British trade shows neither marked increase nor decrease.[5]

The fact that the foreign commerce of Persia has developed in recent years, and that Russia has acquired a large share of this increase in trade whilst we have made little or no progress, has been frequently commented on, and may act or may have acted as a deterring influence to British trade and enterprise in Persia. I have endeavoured to ascertain the reasons for this fact, and venture to summarise them as follows:

The most cultivated, populous, and prosperous provinces of Persia in modern times lie nearer to the Caspian than to the Persian Gulf. Ispahan is about equidistant. Our commerce, therefore, has to penetrate far inland to arrive at the best markets.

We long ago established law and order in the Persian Gulf, giving our trade secure access to Bunder Abbas and Bushire, which, on the opening of the Suez Canal, proved better bases for transport to Central and Eastern Persia than Trebizond. British enterprise also established a steamer service

---

[3] Fish, caviare, lumber-wood, not noticed in the Customs statistics, may account for another 100/150,000. of exports.

[4] Allowing for omissions and inaccuracies of classification in the Customs Statistics, the foreign trade of Persia might be estimated as follows:—Russia, 4 millions; British Empire, 3 millions; other countries, 2 millions.

[5] The Consular Reports I have made use of show on examination that quantities are converted into values at somewhat high rates. Thus the Bushire Reports, 1900–1, estimate tea at 9*d.* to 10*d.* per lb.; candles, 10*s.* 6*d.* to 10*s.* 9*d.* per case; loaf sugar, 20*s.* to 21*s.* per cwt.; copper, 95*s.* per cwt. (1901). Values only have been used in this Report, as Customs statistics, based on an *ad valorem* tariff, were more reliable for values than quantities. In future they will be more reliable for quantities than values, but the administration is endeavouring to secure accuracy in this respect.

to Bagdad, opening another trade route to Hamadan. The great impetus given to our trade by these measures was already evident some 10 or 15 years ago, and further facilities for reaching new, or lessening time or cost of transport to existing, markets have not arisen. But it is during the last decade that measures tending to increase Russian trade with Persia have produced results.

The conquest of Transcaspia enabled the Persian province of Khorassan to devote itself in security to the agricultural development of its fertile soil, and the opening of the Transcaspian railway provided an outlet for these products, which could not afford the long and costly transport to the Gulf.

Meantime the manufacturing centres of Russia—formerly more distant in time and cost of transport, through the vast extent of Russia itself, from Persian markets than we were—have been brought gradually nearer by improved steamer and rail communications. Water-borne transport by the Volga and Caspian has long existed, but has been accelerated and cheapened. It is available however for the summer months only. Petrovsk and Baku now afford transport by rail the whole year round at freights only slightly higher than by the Volga route.

The construction of the Batoum-Baku Railway and the Akstafa-Julfa road opened to Odessa and Black Sea ports a trade route to Azerbaijan superior in time and cost of transport to the Trebizond route, from which European merchandise for Persia was quickly diverted to it; but this door was soon barred to imports not of Russian origin.[6] The superiority of this route increases as the railway from Tiflis, now open to Erivan, extends to the frontier at Julfa, which it is expected to reach within two years.

All these measures of improved communication have been justified by the development of the Russian territories which they have penetrated and benefited, but they

have equally served to facilitate both import and export trade with Persia.

The merchandise which can be most quickly supplied to a depleted market reaps the best profit. There is also a saving of interest and a more rapid turn-over of capital when goods take a shorter time in transit. The improvement in communications with Russia has materially reduced the time occupied in transport, and Russian merchandise now arrives in the markets of northern Persia perhaps three months or less from date of order, whilst our goods can seldom reach the same destinations within five or even six months of order.

Russia possesses in the Armenian trader a suitable agent to press trade in the somewhat limited markets of Persia. He is a keen trader, living in the fashion of the country at small expense, and speaking and writing the language of both the Russian Armenian and of the Persian with whom he deals.

For years past Russia has opposed a formidable Customs tariff to the import of many foreign commodities, but Persia has been protected against this tariff by the five per cent. *ad valorem* duties of the Turkomanchai treaty, and some of her products will continue to be protected under the existing Russo-Persian Customs Convention. It is almost surprising that Persian exports to Russia have not increased in greater measure. With a similar advantage we might have competed at Moscow viâ Bushire and Enzeli in those red ground prints now being driven out of Teheran by the Russian article. The most important exports to Russia are fruits, cotton and rice, representing a million sterling annually.

Fruits imported into Russia pay duty at the rate of 25 copecks per poud when coming from Persia, and Rbls. 1.80 per poud when coming from other countries. The Russian market for these products seems insatiable, and the important regions of production in Persia—Azerbaijan, Kazvin, Damghan, Shahrud and Khorassan are more accessible to Russia than to any other market. The trade in Ispahan, equidistant from the Caspian and the Gulf, is divided.

---

[6] Exports to Europe continue to benefit, perhaps at the expense of imports, which have to bear the cost of returning unfreighted caravans to Trebizond.

Raw cotton is a most remunerative product in Khorassan, and is freely exported to Russia from Ispahan and even from Yezd and Kerman, but the exports from the Gulf are precarious and show little sign of increase. Cotton pays in Russia 40 copecks per poud from Persia, and Rbls. 4.15 per poud from other countries. It is quoted in Moscow at about 2 roubles per poud less than American cotton (say 20 per cent.), but is undoubtedly of poor quality, and is said to yield 8 or 10 funts less of yarn per poud than American cotton (40 funts equal one poud). The Russian and Persian production combined is estimated at less than half the annual consumption in Russia. I conclude, therefore, that the Persian producer is very much dependent upon this difference in duty on exports to Russia.

Rice is grown for export in Ghilan and Mazanderan, and could not bear the cost of transport to Trebizond or Bushire. Unhusked rice pays in Russia 5 copecks per poud from Persia and 60 copecks per poud from other countries. I have not obtained evidence as to whether this preference confers any marked benefit on the Persian producer.

An increase in exports, it is said, causes an increase in imports from the same country. The trader becomes familiar with the routine of business, the agent who disposes of his produce serves also to effect purchases, and suitable articles of commerce are brought to his notice. Banking commission on the return of funds is saved.

Russia has taken measures to encourage the import into Persia of her manufactures.

Special through rates for goods to Persia are accorded. I have not been able, in Persia, to compare them with the rates charged to frontier destinations within Russia, such as Erivan and Ashkabad. The steamship line to the Persian Gulf from Odessa has a subsidy of about 20,000*l.* per annum or 4,000*l.* per trip on five trips effected, and refund of canal dues. This expenditure secures to the Russian over the British shipper an advantage of 12 to 15 shillings per ton weight on cotton goods to Bushire.

The Banque de Prêts de Perse is connected with the Russian State Bank. Its manager is also a Russian Government official. The standing of this institution is therefore independent of current profits. For some years past, and especially during the last two years, this bank has devoted its attention to the development of Russian trade with Persia, particularly to imports into Persia, and most particularly to the import of cotton textiles. It delivers goods to clients at such prices as old-established Russian traders in Persia have been unable to compete with. Its operations have had, without doubt, a marked effect in increasing Russian trade with Persia.

Drawback, said to be the equivalent of duties previously imposed, is granted in Russia on certain commodities exported to Persia.

Sugar forms quite one-half of the total imports into Persia from Russia. The peculiar regulations governing the export of this article from Russia have affected only our shipping interests. A decrease in the supply of sugar to Persia from Russia would have given place to an increase from France and Austria, not from British possessions, and the consignments from these countries would have been largely to the Persian Gulf, and would have paid freight to British ships.

Cotton tissues form one-fourth of Persian imports from Russia, and receive drawback on export from Russia to Persia, said to be equivalent to the duties levied on raw material imported over the Russian European frontier. If the Russian and Persian cotton growers are able to obtain all or nearly all the benefit of the duty of Rbls. 4.15 per poud imposed on imports of raw cotton into Russia from other countries, by increasing their prices up to the level of the imported commodity of equal quality, then the drawback on categories A. and B. affords little or no advantage to the Russian manufacturer or exporter as compared with his British competitor. With regard to category C., Turkey reds, at Rbls. 5.40, I have not obtained in Persia information as to the nature or value of the substances employed in this dye from which to calculate the proportion of duty paid on them. The articles falling under this category form an important part of the imports from Russia.

The Russian manufacturer caters for a large population in Russia with requirements similar to those of a large section of the Persian population, and therefore does not need to manufacture cotton prints, common glassware, pottery, paper, hardware and mercery, lamps, candlesticks, and various articles of clothing, expressly to suit the Persian market. This has been suggested to me as conferring some advantage in cheapness of production.

To turn to trade with other European countries.

The export of silk cocoons from Ghilan and Mazanderan, now of some importance, is chiefly to France and Italy, and has not interested British traders.

In imports, cane sugar has not been able to compete in the Gulf with French loaf or Austrian bag sugar. The increased demand in the southern provinces supplied from these countries appears to have more than compensated for any loss of trade in northern markets taken by Russia.

In silk tissues France and in woollen tissues Austria and France take a larger share of the trade than we do. Their imports are nearly all viâ Trebizond, purchased in Constantinople by Persian traders.

In white and grey shirtings Holland has begun to compete with us.

Lastly, I may draw attention to influences which have affected our own trade.

The British Empire has increased its takings from Persia of opium and gums. The grain trade has temporarily disappeared, owing to prolonged agricultural depression in the southern provinces and hampering restrictions which tended to throw land out of cultivation; it has been, in a fashion, compensated by an import of wheat, rice, and other foodstuffs, but that is a questionable benefit to our trade as a whole, as these regions, with good harvests, would have bought manufactured articles from us with their surplus agricultural wealth.

It may be asked why the regions of Southern Persia accessible to our influence should not have developed in the same measure as the northern provinces. Luristan, Bakhtiariland, and Arabistan possess well-watered and fertile districts, but the peoples of these regions are still but little amenable to the authority of the central Government, and until law and order are more firmly established but little agricultural or industrial progress can be expected. Much of the southern and eastern regions has but scant irrigation water and little rainfall. Fars and Kerman might have been expected to make greater progress. But these southern provinces have not the advantage of protected markets in which to sell their produce at artificial prices.

Our imports into Khorassan were formerly destined in part for Transcaspia, to which they entered until a few years ago at an *ad valorem* duty of $2\frac{1}{2}$ per cent. Some of our cotton tissues and tea found a market there which is now cut off. A special concession is still made to Transcaspia in respect of green tea, but in such a manner as to divert this transit trade from Bunder Abbas and Khorassan to Batoum.

I have endeavoured to trace, in the foregoing remarks, the principal causes which have affected the foreign trade of Persia in recent years, and the results arising from them. The agricultural development of Northern Persia, due to greater facilities in reaching Russian and other markets and to protection of Persian products in Russian markets, has certainly increased the wealth of these provinces, and therefore their capacity to purchase commodities. Russia has no doubt obtained the greatest part of this increased import trade, but if we eliminate one commodity, sugar, her relative progress in import trade will appear much less striking, and be found to have consisted in an increase of manufactured articles, principally cotton tissues, glassware, pottery, iron, ironmongery, &c.

No improvement in communications would have sufficed to increase Russian exports of manufactured goods to Persia unless she had been able to supply these articles. It has been constantly pointed out to me that Russia's manufacturing skill has made great progress. Her common pottery now competes not only in price but in appearance and quality with other imports. Her common glassware competes on equal or superior terms with Bohemian and French wares of the same class. Her metalwork— lamps, candlesticks, enamelled-ironware— is stated to be much better in quality and finish at a given price than formerly. It is of course in cotton prints that her competition is most felt by us. Our tissues have to some extent been driven out of the northern provinces, and the fact that our imports do not show a marked decrease must be attributed to the increased consumption in other parts of the country compensating for markets lost further north.

I have formed the conclusion that Russian prints have not established a distinct ascendancy beyond such markets as Tabriz, Kazvin, Teheran, and Meshed. It may be questioned whether the trade really affords a sufficient margin of profit between the cost of production and transport and the price paid by the consumer; but without doubt it has been pressed most vigorously, and competent authorities, both Russian and British, have expressed an opinion that it has been pressed to excess, and that stocks have accumulated beyond the needs of the market.

A Russian firm have been established in Ispahan for some two years past. They may or may not be making present sacrifices in order to establish this business in general cotton prints, and tissues but should they be able to establish a business dependent on ordinary mercantile profits, then there is no reason why Russian manufacturers should not be able to compete with Manchester in all parts of Persia—and even in Mesopotamia and India—for the cost of transport from Moscow to Ispahan viâ Enzeli or viâ Bushire (with State-aided freight) is about the same. Up to the present time our shippers in the Gulf have not found this competition formidable.

It is stated that Russian manufacturers are asking for an increase in the drawback allowed on cotton tissues, on the ground that the present allowance does not cover the taxes levied on the commodities consumed by their workmen. A drawback on woollen tissues is also talked of. Whether the Russian Government will be inclined to give effect to such suggestions is beyond the province of this inquiry. It may at least have to consider the effect on the non-manufacturing population in Caucasia and Transcaspia of increasing the marked contrast between the price of certain commodities in these places and across the Persian frontier. In Persia, tea, sugar, kerosine, prints and calicoes are all cheaper than in the Russian markets from which they are derived.

On a general review of all these circumstances I venture an opinion that the impetus given to trade of other countries in Persia must already have produced nearly its full effect, and that our trade, which has survived this competition without very serious detriment, may expect to share in any extension of markets arising from the increase of wealth and population or from the greater consumption of foreign commodities in Persia.

Statistics kindly furnished by the Administrator-General of Customs for the first quarter of 1903–4, compared with the corresponding period of the previous year, show a considerable increase in trade. They are not encouraging from the point of view of relative increase in our cotton textiles compared with those of Russia. But I do not attach much importance to statistical figures for a short period, and for this period in particular they are of little value to form general deductions from, as they must include much merchandise held over from the previous quarter when the new tariff first came into force.

The population of Persia at the present time approaches ten millions, so that the annual consumption of foreign commodities is little over 10s. per head—a little over 4s. per head from Russia, a little less than 4s. from the British Empire, and 2s. from other countries. As regards classes of foreign commodities the sum might be divided thus—about 4s. 6d. per head for textiles, 2s. 6d. per head for sugar, 6d. per head for tea, and 2s. 6d. per head for other commodities.

I believe there is, on the whole, a distinct improvement in the condition of the people. The question is somewhat obscured by the depreciation in the gold value of the silver coinage of Persia, as the first impression usually is that, prices having risen, the cost of living must have increased. But prices of labour and produce appear to have risen in proportion. Information obtained at the various places visited usually tended to show that the peasant is somewhat less hardly treated by landlord and taxgatherer, and is better clothed and better fed than formerly, and that more land has been brought under cultivation. Of course these circumstances have varied in different localities: in parts of the south, elsewhere referred to, extreme hardship has been reported, and in Ghilan and Khorassan unusual prosperity. This year the southern harvest is more favourably reported on. . . .

## Russian Trade with Iran

The subject of Russo-Persian trade has been perceptively studied by Marvin L. Entner, to whose book the reader is referred. Table 1 summarizes, in the form of five-year averages, the annual figures given by him.

TABLE 1

RUSSO-PERSIAN TRADE RETURNS, 1830–1914
(Millions of Gold Rubles [1896], yearly averages)

| YEAR | FROM PERSIA | TO PERSIA | TOTAL |
|------|-------------|-----------|-------|
| 1830–34 . . . . . | 3.8 | 2.6 | 6.4 |
| 1835–39 . . . . . | 3.6 | 1.3 | 4.9 |
| 1840–44 . . . . . | 4.7 | 1.2 | 5.9 |
| 1845–49 . . . . . | 5.3 | 0.9 | 6.2 |
| 1850–54 . . . . . | 5.0 | 1.2 | 6.3 |
| 1855–59 . . . . . | 5.7 | 1.4 | 7.2 |
| 1860–64 . . . . . | 6.0 | 1.6 | 7.6 |
| 1865–69 . . . . . | 5.8 | 1.8 | 7.6 |
| 1870–74 . . . . . | 5.6 | 2.1 | 7.8 |
| 1875–79 . . . . . | 6.3 | 2.7 | 9.0 |
| 1880–84 . . . . . | 7.5 | 3.8 | 11.3 |
| 1885–89 . . . . . | 9.4 | 6.5 | 15.9 |
| 1890–94 . . . . . | 11.5 | 10.9 | 22.4 |
| 1895–99 . . . . . | 19.7 | 16.0 | 35.7 |
| 1900–1904 . . . . | 24.0 | 24.6 | 48.5 |
| 1905–9 . . . . . | 26.4 | 29.0 | 55.4 |
| 1910–14 . . . . . | 38.5 | 49.2 | 87.7 |

SOURCE: Compiled from Marvin Entner, pp. 8–9.
The original gives annual figures in millions of gold rubles for 1830–1914 and in millions of account rubles for 1830–96.

Russia's proximity to Iran's populous and prosperous northern provinces assured it an important share in the country's trade. Writing in 1800, Campbell stated:

By means of the Wolga and navigable Canals Astrakhan has a communication by water all the way to Petersburgh, so that in fact there is a cheap and easy communication by water from Petersburgh to Persia. At this time this trade is, I am sorry to say, pretty considerable, and the Broad Cloths and other European articles which are in most demand in Persia are the produce of Russia and brought from Astrakhan.[1]

[1] *The Melville Papers* (see Chap. 6, sel. 1).

Russian trade with the north continued on a substantial scale during the following decades (see 3:11–14).

However, the Industrial Revolution greatly improved the competitive position of Britain, and subsequently of other West European countries. And until the 1870s, Russian trade with Iran worked under several handicaps.[2] Perhaps the heaviest was the underdeveloped state of Russian industry, which could not produce goods in sufficient quantities, of sufficiently high quality, and cheaply enough to compete with British and other European wares. Hardly less important was the poor state of transport, until the building of railways to Transcaucasia in the 1870s and to the Transcaspian regions in the 1880s, and the organization of steam navigation on the Caspian (see chap. 4, introduction, and sels. 1, and 2). A further source of competition was European goods crossing the Caucasus free of duty, from Poti or Batum on the Black Sea to Erivan and thence to Tabriz. This exemption persisted from 1821 to 1831, was stopped for twelve years, and was again in force between 1846 and 1883; its final abolition was a victory for the industrialists of Moscow and the Ukraine over the traders of the Caucasus. As the British consul in Tabriz reported, a petition was signed by

the Moscow merchants, representing that the new railway would afford such facilities to foreign traders for the introduction of their goods into the markets of Persia and Turkestan, that the manufacturers of Moscow would be unable to compete with them in that respect. . . . On the other hand, the Tiflis merchants have petitioned the Russian Government in favor of the continuance of the Transit Trade, on the ground that its extinction would reduce the Georgian capital to the level of a village and ruin their commercial prospects [Dispatch of 26 February 1883, FO 60/457].

The latter fact brings out another weakness in the Russian trading position: the reluctance of Russians, as distinct from Caucasian Muslims, Armenians, or Persians, to engage in Russo-Persian trade. This was due partly to the hazards of the latter, partly to the greater attraction and profitability of the rapidly expanding internal Russian market.[3] Last, it should be remembered that the advantages secured by Russia under the Treaty of Turkomanchai were soon extended to other countries (see Chap. 3, introduction).

Russia's position began to change rapidly at the end of the 1870s. Not only did railways greatly reduce costs and speed up delivery, but the government began to promote trade actively, by diplomatic support, the sponsoring of transport projects in northern Iran (see 4:12), and, above all, by help extended through the Loan and Discount Bank (see 8:2). Exports to Iran rose rapidly, thanks partly to export premiums on the two main items, cotton goods and sugar.[4] Imports also

---

[2] For a thorough study, by a Russian government commission, of the administrative, financial, and other impediments to Russian trade in the Middle East, see Lisenko.

[3] It is not clear whether anything came out of the proposal of the Moscow Commercial Company "to form trading establishments at Tabriz and Astarabad as well as Resht" reported by Abbott to Clarendon on 21 December 1857, FO 60/223.

[4] Entner, pp. 67–69.

increased considerably, as Russia became by far the leading market for most of Iran's cash crops (see 5:12–14). Russia was also helped by the Iranian tariff changes of 1903 (see chap. 3, introduction), which favored its goods.

Well before that date, Russian competition was causing serious concern to Britain, and the reports of the British consuls note with increasing alarm the steady movement of Russian goods to markets in central and southern Iran hitherto regarded as secure. In 1875, Mackenzie stated: "Already is the commercial policy of Russia making itself felt even at Bushire," and "we find Russian goods supplying the more distant bazaars of Shuster, Khoramabad etc."[5] And three years later he wrote to Thomson: "I have been informed by a native merchant here, that lately Russian manufactures are, through cheap production, driving those of Manchester out of the field, even in the Tehran Bazaars."[6]

Britain tried to counter this Russian pressure by opening the Karun route in the south (see 4:5, 6) and the Sistan route in the east (see 3:16) but this failed to arrest the steady advance of Russian goods. The report of the British Trade Mission of 1904 (see 3:20) analyzed the forces at work and held out hopes of stabilizing the situation. But in fact Russia's share of the Persian market continued to grow, and in 1912/13 it accounted for 58 percent of Iran's imports, 69 percent of its exports, and 63 percent of total trade.

In the interwar period the Soviet Union continued to be an important client and supplier of Iran, and in the 1930s it accounted for about one-third of Iran's trade (other than oil).

After the Second World War the volume of Russo-Persian trade dwindled, but more recently it has recovered, thanks to the credits extended by the Soviet Union and the construction of a gas pipeline from Iran to the Caucasus.

(See also works by Entner, Navai, Fateh, *Economic Position*, Curzon, Bakulin, Tomara, Sobotsinskii, Ostapenko, and Roshkova, listed in the bibliography.)

[5] "General Remarks on route from Ispahan to Mahomerah," FO 60/375.
[6] Letter dated 10 September 1878, FO 60/414.

## Selection 21. Russian Trade with Iran, 1750–1910
[G. I. Ter-Gukasov, *Politicheskie i ekonomicheskie interesy Rossii v Persii* (Petrograd, 1916), pp. 33–37]

The beginnings of Russia's commercial relations with Persia go back to the time of the subjugation of the kingdom of Astrakhan, that is, to the middle of the sixteenth century. Firm relations were established by the embassy of Prince Bariatinskii, who was sent to Persia in 1618 by Czar Alexei, and from that time friendly relations began to grow; as a result, in 1664 Russians were authorized to trade in Persia without payment of customs duties. But already under Peter the Great, economic rapprochement with Persia ceased to be the slogan of Russian diplomacy, which began to direct the government's efforts, if not always toward full political conquest, at any rate toward political preponderance in that country. Peter's eagerness for the commercial and industrial renaissance of Russia, and his attempt to reestablish the former Indo-

European transit trade through Persia, gave high priority to the question of political hegemony over that country and led him to take advantage of the first available opportunity to send a Russian army to Persia. The result of this campaign was the Treaty of 1723, in which Derbent and Baku and all lands and places appertaining to them as far as the Caspian Sea were ceded in perpetuity to Russia, as were the provinces of Gilan, Mazandaran, and Astarabad. Under the Treaty of Rasht of 1729, Mazandaran and Astarabad were returned to Persia, and article 8 guaranteed to Russian caravans free passage through Persia to India.

In 1732 the Russian government, burdened by the maintenance of a sizeable army in fever-ridden Gilan and Talish to keep them under subjugation, returned these provinces to Persia and in 1735, under the Treaty of Ganje (Elizavetopol) returned Derbent and Baku. These political events did not, however, interrupt the commercial rapprochement between the two neighboring governments; trade relations between them continued to develop and were concentrated mainly in Astrakhan, Derbent, Baku, and Enzeli.

Under the Treaty of 1813, concluded after the Russo-Persian War, the Russians obtained the right to the dominance [*pravo gospodstva*] of a naval and commercial fleet over the Caspian Sea. Customs duties were fixed at 5 percent of the declared value of goods. Thus were laid the international conditions for Russian trade in Persia. Until the middle of the nineteenth century, this trade took on an uninterrupted, regular character.

However in spite of this four-century-long history of relations with Iran, Russia, because of the false belief that trade with Asia was not advantageous for it, did not pay any attention to that country. The Europeans did not fail to take advantage of this, especially the English, who flooded the markets of Persia with their goods, brought over by the cheap sea route to the shores of the Persian Gulf. Germany and Austria, being in no position to compete with England in Persia through the sea route, directed their goods to northern Persia via Batum and from there, in customs-free transit, through Transcaucasia to Baku and Julfa. The result was that Russian goods, squeezed out of the markets of southern Persia, could not hold on to the northern, into which goods from Austria, Germany, and even France came through Batum.

Only with the stopping of free transit through Russia, in 1883, was foreign trade in northern Persia dealt a hard blow; Russian trade was immediately given a great advantage and from that time on began to develop and expand rapidly. Data are available, as from 1758, on regular Russo-Persian trade, registered in figures. Thus, for example, in 1758–60 the total value of goods exported to Persia amounted to 243,454 rubles; in 1792, that is after thirty-four years, exports rose to 325,310 rubles, and in 1815 to 499,532 rubles. In 1827–29 exports, for the first time, reached the level of 1,867,000 rubles, and they remained there through the first half of the nineteenth century.

In the 1860s Russian foreign trade, and consequently that with Persia, was registered much more accurately in the officially published customs returns. In 1862 total Russian exports to Persia were put at 1,116,000 rubles and fluctuated insignificantly until the end of 1877, not surpassing the figure of 1,749,000 reached in 1866. Between 1877 and 1880 annual exports were around 3 million rubles.

From 1879, European goods in Transit to Persia did not lag in value behind Russian exports to Persia, except in periods of war. In 1881, they amounted to 7,772,000 rubles, whereas Russian goods exported amounted to only 3,868,000 rubles; thus, for several successive years, Russia voluntarily gave up two-thirds of the Persian market to European competitors.

In the thirty-year period 1880–1909, the value of exports to Persia rose sevenfold, from 3,944,000 to 28,843,000 rubles. The highest rate of growth occurred in the last fifteen years (1895–1909) when, at length, serious attention was paid to that market, which is so important for the Russian national economy.

As regards imports from Persia in the period under review, we notice that their value throughout exceeded that of exports—in other words, the balance of trade in that period was unfavorable to Russia. In the 1830s, the first place among imports from Persia was held by "raw and semiprocessed materials," the second by "manufactures" and the third by "foodstuffs." From the 1830s to the 1850s, the value of manufactures imported from Persia was three times as great as that of raw and semiprocessed materials. Total imports from Persia in

1758–60 amounted to 321,000 rubles, and in 1827–29 they totaled 3,803,000. Thereafter imports developed more slowly than exports—thus in the five years 1862–66 they reached 5,034,000 rubles and in 1877–81 were 6,612,000. Data for the period 1880–1909 show that the value of imports from Persia during these thirty years tripled, whereas exports rose sevenfold; thus, for example, in the five years 1880–85, the value of imports was 7,916,000 rubles and in 1905–9 it was 26,414,000. Rice and fruits accounted for 50 percent of imports from Persia and the value of imports of raw cotton rose from 848,700 rubles in 1877 to 7,501,000 in 1906–9. . . .

## French Trade with Iran

France, whose cultural influence in Iran was until very recently stronger than that of any other country, played a minor part in its economic life. A dispatch to the minister of foreign affairs (AE, CC, vol. 1, 17 April 1856) stated: "Our trade is nil in Persia today, unable to be born in the absence of a Treaty," but added that potential demand for French goods was great. Such a treaty, treating France as the most favored nation, was signed in 1855, and consulates were established in Tabriz in 1869 and in Bushire in 1889; but in fact, progress was limited. In 1858, French exports to Iran, consisting mainly of silks, were estimated at one million francs (£40,000); in return France bought raw silk and silkworm eggs (ibid., 28 December 1858 and 15 February 1860). Because of the silkworm disease in France (see 5:6–8), the demand for the latter was intense; French growers were even urging the legation to get eggs from Bukhara, "les uns croyant qu'il est aussi simple d'aller à Bokhara qu'à Saint Denis!" (ibid., 10 June 1865).

Some increase was registered in the next few years, and Iran's imports from France were estimated at 3,000,000 francs in the mid 1860s and at 5,000,000 in 1868 (ibid., Tauris, vol. 1, 2 December 1867 and 6 July 1868). This growth was largely due to rising imports of sugar brought about by the rapid spread of tea drinking, a habit introduced by the Russians at the beginning of the nineteenth century. In this field, Marseilles sugar competed very successfully with English and Dutch products (ibid., 8 June 1868).[1] But by the 1880s French sugar exports were being subjected to a double squeeze. On the one hand, the suppression of transit of goods from Europe through the Caucasus (see 3:7) made it more difficult for French sugar to penetrate the markets of northern Iran (ibid. *Téhéran*, vol. 3, 15 November 1888). And on the other hand direct Russian competition was

[1] In 1857 the French consul in Trebizond reported that French sugar exports to Persia were insignificant, in 1861 that they were increasing, and in 1862 that French sugar was the only one demanded (AE, CC, Trebizonde, vol. 7, 1 May 1857, 21 May 1861, and 5 June 1862). For a detailed account see ibid., vol. 10, 20 May 1885.

growing, helped not only by a bounty on sugar exports but also by better packaging (ibid., 27 February 1890). As for the south, French exports were handicapped by the lack of regular shipping lines between Marseilles and the Persian Gulf, and also because the French refineries did not have agents in the main consuming centers of Iran (ibid.). Hence the French were vulnerable to German competition, which began to make itself felt in 1890s (ibid., vol. 5, 5 August 1897). A long and searching report on the trade of Northern Persia (ibid., January 1900) concluded that Persia constituted a very small market for French goods. In the years immediately preceding the First World War, Iran's imports from France averaged about £300,000 out of a total of £11,000,000, and its exports to France £80,000 out of £8,000,000.

As for the number of Frenchmen in Iran, in 1863 there were thirty-one men, sixteen women, and three children (ibid., Téhéran, vol. 1); the number in Azerbaijan in 1867 was seventeen, largely missionaries (ibid., Tauris, vol. 1, 1870). The corresponding figures for 1914 were probably not much higher.

### Selection 22. French Trade with Iran, 1869–70

[Dispatches to Minister of Foreign Affairs Affaires Etrangères, Correspondance Commerciale, Téhéran, vol. 2, 10 February 1869; ibid., 30 October 1869; Tauris, vol. 1, 10 February 1870]

French commercial interests are rather small in Tabriz, being represented by only one firm, that of M. Cassabois; the rest, which is in the hands of Armenians, who are Persian or Russian subjects, does not require French protection. It is to be hoped that French merchants will not establish themselves in Tabriz, or in any other Persian town, since their commercial transactions will not enjoy real protection and guarantees until serious administrative reforms replace the arbitrary ways and corruption that reign in this country. In this respect, I can offer no hope of change in spite of the advice which has been proffered in abundance to the Persian government for the last twenty years, and which I never fail to repeat whenever an occasion arises. Our goods will be sold more readily if they are handled by native merchants, who deal directly with our trading firms; our end would thus be attained with no injury to our trade, which would otherwise be gravely hurt by the absence of laws and administrative regularity in the country and which the legation or the consulate would be in no position to have respected, as we understand the matter in Europe.

I therefore wonder whether the keeping of a French consulate in Tabriz, which is costing the government so much, is really useful after the experience which Mr. Crampon, who has held it for two and a half years, has had and which has led him to the conclusion that our trade has little future in this country. . . .

Only European firms are fit for business dealings with Europe, for Persian merchants, in addition to their dishonesty, are not apt to understand the course of business or to carry it out in the way we do. I would therefore not advise this company [Union Nationale, which was looking for correspondents in Iran] to establish relations with any of them and will name only European business firms with whom it could have business dealings. These are: Espitalier Bros., of Sette, which has an agent here [in Tehran], M. Chanoine: Bravay of Paris, which is similarly placed; Raymond Bros., whose standing and knowledge of the country are perfect; last, Ziegler and Co., of

Liverpool, which has branches in Tabriz, Rasht, and Tehran, and whose turnover runs to several million [francs]. . . .

Persia consumes twenty-five to thirty million francs' [£1,000,000 to £1,200,000] worth of English goods a year, and yet in the whole of the kingdom there is not a single English merchant! We ourselves who, without being quite aware of it, also dispose of some five to six million francs' worth of French products, sell almost the whole lot through foreign hands. The three to four million worth of sugar which we sell is imported exclusively by native merchants, and I have explained elsewhere how and why that was advantageous to us up to a certain point. Our silks from Lyon, which are smuggled into Persia in quantities that cannot be exactly ascertained, are not brought in by French hands. Native merchants—Armenians or Persians—buy those two kinds of goods from intermediate places; that is, Tiflis, Trebizond, Constantinople, and sometimes even in France. When other French products, which they know little or badly, or of which they have never even heard, will seem to them to meet the needs of consumers, they will procure them by the same means. Buying in France directly, or through agents with whom they are in contact, they are forced to submit to the customs of the French market, and to supply the guarantees it demands. But once the goods have been delivered and handed over to them, they can sell them at their own risk, in the way they understand—and they understand things much better than do French merchants.

The Chamber of Paris would like the sale of French goods to be made through French hands; it wishes that French merchants should come here first, and that, M. le Comte, is precisely what is not desirable. In general, and with very rare exceptions, the Frenchman does not make good in Persia. The country's climate and customs do not suit his temperament. The slowness of Persians irritates him, its heady wines go to his head, the lack of women exasperates him. The weakness of the government, which is incapable of maintaining law and meeting justice, makes him inclined to take his rights by violence. He is not sufficiently patient in his transactions. Sometimes he is too generous in opening credits and at other times he tries too hard to recover his debts. He piles blunder on blunder. His travels are expensive, his establishment still more so. He has eaten up his profits before ever having made them. On the other hand, Greeks and Armenians, who are Orientals, and the Swiss, who know how to manage everywhere, carry on their trade with infinitely more economy, skill and success. . . .

## Selection 23. Iranian Exports, 1900–1914
[Ziya al-Din Sadrzadeh, *Saderat-i Iran* (Tehran, 1346) pp. 7–13]

. . . On 27 October 1901 (26 Rajab A.H. 1319) a customs treaty was signed between Iran and Russia. Under Article 1, imports and exports were no longer subject to the duties specified in Article 3 of the treaty of 23 February 1828 (5 Shaban A.H. 1243), but to the rates listed in schedules A, B, and C of the customs treaty. The new treaty raised customs duties on Iranian exports to Russia, whereas those on Russian imports to Iran were sharply reduced and British imports were subjected to heavy duties.

On 9 February 1903 (18 Dhilqadeh 1320 A.H.) a treaty was concluded with Britain, under which that country received the most-favored-nation treatment. A new tariff was drawn on 15 March 1903. The final result of this situation was the division of Iran into spheres of influence, under the 1907 treaty between Russia and Britain.

In addition to the tariff obstacles to the expansion of exports, described above, there were internal obstacles, among which was the levying of road taxes (*rahdari*) within the country on all goods. This made the internal transport of goods very difficult, and hence on 9 Dhilhajjeh 1318 [1901] it was decided to cease levying such duties.

As mentioned before, in the Treaty of Turkmanchai it was decided that all exports and imports crossing Iran's borders would pay a duty of 5 percent. Truly, the levying of such duties on exports by a country like Iran with a passive balance of trade is amazing. The gap between imports and exports was enormous. In addition, at that time the countries of Western Europe, which had passed through the Industrial Revolution and were treading the path of economic expansion, were finding in their own colonies and in such countries as Iran—whose rulers were in no way acquainted with economic and social matters—excellent markets for the export and sale of their goods. But this question, which had adverse economic and commercial effects, received very little attention from the responsible authorities. In the *farman* issued by Muzaffar al-Din Shah, the question is alluded to as follows:

> Imports into the Kingdom are far greater than exports from it; as a result, each year a quantity of gold coins leaves the country in payment for foreign goods and this situation is gradually leading to the diminution of the Kingdom's trade and its shortage of gold. . . .
> Since domestic goods pay a five per cent duty when exported from the Kingdom, how can they compete in foreign markets with goods coming from the countries of Europe, which do not pay one dinar in customs duties when exported from their country of origin? It is evident that this situation causes much damage and injury to national merchants.

It is because of these considerations that on 15 Dhilqadeh 1320 [1903] that is, four years before the *farman* promulgating the constitution, a new tariff was put into effect, under which it was decreed that no export duties would be paid on several articles, such as textiles, carpets of all kinds, cotton, wool, dried fruits of all kinds, gum, medicinal seeds, vegetable dyes, wax, honey, and garments made of skins and hides; it was also decreed that the payment of twenty-two shahis on each parcel at the border should be abolished.

Since Iran is an agricultural country, with an extensive area and a diversified climate, we might imagine that from ancient times the food requirements of its inhabitants would always and fully be met internally, and that if in the last few years a shortage of food and agricultural produce was felt, in the past this was not so. But we notice that the *farman* of Muzaffar al-Din Shah decreed that, because of the shortage of food, imports of the following items were exempt from customs duties: animals of all kinds, wheat, barley, millet, flour, cheese, meat, fresh butter, vegetables of all kinds, eggs, and fresh and dried fish. This shows the backward and immature condition even of agricultural production in this society in earlier periods and proves that at that time this country, although having a smaller population, was not able to feed its inhabitants. The supply of some of the above-mentioned imports may perhaps have exceeded local requirements but, because of the lack of roads, and in some places because of shortage of water, and in the absence of the necessary organization, their distribution was not easy and hence imports of such articles continued.

Gums and tar and certain articles required by industry and public utilities, such as wool and other raw materials, including even bricks and wood used for carpentry, were also exempted from customs duties.

The measures taken to abolish *rahdari* and the 5 percent duty on exports led to a certain improvement and increase in Iran's exports. The table on page 150 shows Iran's exports in the years under study, and also the ratio of exports to imports; it does not include exports of petroleum, which had just made their appearance.[1]

The percentage of exports to imports shows that there was a great difference between receipts and outlays. In the years under study, Iran's exports went mainly to Russia, which usually took from over 50 percent (1901/2) to nearly 70 percent (1910/11) of the total. It was followed by Britain and India, the Ottoman Empire, France and its colonies, Germany, Austria-Hungary, Afghanistan, the United States, China, the Netherlands and its colonies, Egypt, Belgium, Oman, Italy, Indo-China, Muscat, Sweden, and Greece.

[1] *Amari-i bazergani khariji Iran; Ganj-i Shaigan.*

| Year | Quantity of Exports (thousand tons) | Value of Exports (million krans) | Exports as Percentage of Imports |
|---|---|---|---|
| 1900/1901 . . . . . | . . . . . | 147.3 | 36.6 |
| 1901/1902 . . . . . | . . . . . | 150.6 | 33.5 |
| 1902/1903 . . . . . | 163.5 | 186.3 | 40.9 |
| 1903/1904 . . . . . | 220.4 | 254.7 | 39.7 |
| 1904/1905 . . . . . | . . . . . | 248.0 | 41.5 |
| 1905/1906 . . . . . | 283.5 | 293.0 | 43.1 |
| 1906/1907 . . . . . | 327.8 | 353.1 | 45.1 |
| 1907/1908 . . . . . | 331.1 | 316.9 | 43.7 |
| 1908/1909 . . . . . | 347.2 | 326.1 | 46.7 |
| 1909/1910 . . . . . | 254.3 | 371.4 | 45.6 |
| 1910/1911 . . . . . | 273.4 | 375.3 | 43.7 |
| 1911/1912 . . . . . | 311.8 | 420.1 | 42.4 |

Iran's exports consisted of cotton, dried fruits, woolen carpets, rice, raw silk, skins, opium, gum, raw wool, and small quantities of tobacco, medicinal herbs, salts, dyes, and domestic animals. . . .

The constant deficit in the balance of trade arising from the excess of imports over exports compelled merchants to fill the gap by exporting gold and silver, and caused a persistent outflow of those metals, a large part of which came from the booty brought back by Nadir Shah from India in A.H. 1152 [1739]. In some places, the scarcity or complete absence of coins had adverse effects on trade, as was reported by the British consul in Tabriz in A.H. 1297 and the Russian consul in Bushire in A.H. 1294.[2] Doubtless this was one of the reasons for the promulgation of the above-mentioned *farman* of Muzaffar al-Din.

The question is often raised how the balance of payments of Iran was balanced during the constitutional period and before that, when oil revenues were insignificant and the balance of trade showed a deficit. Although this matter requires extensive and separate study, we can briefly answer it by stating that the following factors contributed to the balance:

1. At that time, Iran had a closed economy and the volume of its foreign transactions was small.

2. The booty which Nadir Shah brought

[2] See *Ganj-i Shaigan*, p 157.

from India, and the state treasures, were drawn upon to a certain extent.

3. Foreign loans played a part, at certain times.

4. Invisible exports contributed, and the sums in foreign exchange sent to Iran by the large number of Iranians trading in neighboring countries out of their revenues.

5. The existence of unofficial, compensatory transactions should not be forgotten; thus, part of Afghanistan's trade passed through Iran, and the foreign exchange proceeds thereof accrued to this country.

POSITION OF IRAN'S EXPORTS FROM THE FIRST WORLD WAR TO THE FOREIGN TRADE MONOPOLY LAW

The situation described above continued until the outbreak of the First World War. In the later years of the war, especially in the last two, Iran's exports decreased sharply. Among the reasons for this was the October 1917 revolution in Russia, which established socialism in that country and, in consequence, greatly reduced Iran's exports to it. After the war, the Soviet Union began to develop its heavy industry and, because the purchasing power of its inhabitants was reduced, restricted imports of most Iranian goods which were not essential. This caused a commercial depression in Iran in the postwar years.

Although Iran's exports thus declined sharply, its imports rose: thus in 1921/22, whereas exports totaled 84,441 tons, with a value of 179,405,000 rials, imports amounted to 201,096 tons with a value of 609,775,000 rials; that is, exports were less than three-fifths of imports. And since in those years Iran's oil revenues were insignificant [see epilogue], it will be realized how burden-some this trade deficit was for the country.

During the First World War, the balance of payments was partly balanced by the expeditures incurred by the British army in Iran. . . .

# 4

## *Transport*

Few countries need modern transport as desperately as Iran, with its huge distances, its lack of navigable rivers and its short coastline, far removed from the centers of population and production. And, until very recently, no country of comparable importance was as poorly provided. As the vice president of Anglo-Persian Oil Company stated in 1911: "The chief need of Persia—which today occupies a position I believe unique in being the only highly civilized country unserved by this absolute necessity of modern life—is Railways."[1] And whereas, in the Middle East, Egypt had its first railway in 1853, Turkey in 1867, Lebanon and Syria in 1894, and Sudan in 1898, Iran had to wait until 1938 for a major line. Nor, until the late 1920s, was this lack of railways compensated for by a significant amount of motor transport.

Naturally, steamships had come to Iran much earlier. A few ships sailed in the Persian Gulf as early as 1838, and in 1862 the British India Steam Navigation Company started a mail service between India and the Persian Gulf (see 4:3). Steam navigation across the Caspian began in the 1840s, and a regular service between Russia and Iran was established in 1861 (see 4:1, 2).

At about the same time, the telegraph reached the country. As so often in Iran's recent history, the reason must be sought in India. Thoroughly shaken by the fact that the news of the Indian Mutiny had taken forty days to reach England, the British government resolved immediately to link the Indian network with that of the Mediterranean. In 1859–60 a submarine cable was laid down the Red Sea, from Egypt "to Aden and on, by way of the Kuria Muria Islands and Muscat, to Karachi. It failed at once, owing to the lack of experience in laying and operating undersea cables, and a search was undertaken for an alternative route, which

[1] Speech at Persian Dinner at the Savoy, July 1911, FO 371/1186.

would be land-based for most of the way. That selected was through Turkey and Iraq to the head of the Gulf, and thence by submarine cable or land line, or both, to Karachi. The Turkish Government had already constructed a line to Mosul, and it was expected to reach Baghdad by the close of 1860."[2] Various diplomatic difficulties were overcome, and by January 1865 the Turkish line had reached Fao, at the mouth of the Shatt al-Arab. Meanwhile Britain and Iran had signed, in December 1862, an agreement (formalized on 20 October 1863) for the construction of a Khaniqin–Tehran–Isfahan–Shiraz–Bushire line, 1,100 miles long; Iran was to pay the cost, estimated at about 100,000 tumans, purchase the materials in Britain, and place the line under the superintendence of an English engineer; previously, the Indian government had agreed to advance £20,000 to Iran for its purchases. An agreement was also signed between Iran and Turkey on 28 November 1863.[3]

After that progress was swift, although the British superintendents of the line and consuls were often to complain of damage and robbery.[4] By 1868, Iran's debt to Britain for the purchase of materials for the Khaniqin–Bushire line was £10,000 (21,200 tumans), which it was agreed would be paid in five annual instalments.[5] A second wire on the same line cost £47,217 (115,080 tumans), and in 1872 it was decided to erect a third one.[6] By 1875, the director of the Persian Telegraph estimated the total amount invested in Iran at "at least two millions sterling."[7]

In the meantime telegraphic connections had been established with Russia, starting with a line from Tehran to Tabriz in 1860 which was soon extended to Julfa.[8]

By the 1880s, Iran was well equipped with telegraph lines, connecting it with various parts of the world and linking up its towns:

The telegraph system in Persia consists of 3,966 miles of line, with 6,266 miles of wire, and 84 stations; 735 miles of line, with 3 wires, i.e., 2,205 miles of wire, between Tehran and Bushire, are worked by the British Government under the immediate control of Major Wells, R.E: 415 miles of line, with 1,240 miles of wire, between Tehran and Julfa, on the Russian frontier, are worked by the the Indo-European Company; and 2,816 miles of single wire lines belonging to the Persian Government are worked by a Persian staff.

[2] Kelly, pp. 555–56. The total cost of the Persian Gulf section of the 1864 cable "for its manufacture, transportation and laying—was £411,751 (£292,902 paid by Government in England, the balance paid in India). By 1866, the gross receipts of the Persian Gulf–Makran submarine line were at the rate of £95,000 per annum." See Harris.

[3] See "Correspondence Respecting the Construction of a Telegraph Line through Persia," A and P 1864, 66.

[4] See for example, Thomson to Derby, 14 August 1874, FO 60/364; and Smith to Thomson, 17 May 1875, FO 60/373.

[5] Translation of letter, July 1868, FO 60/321.

[6] "Convention . . . Telegraphic Communications between Europe and India through Persia," 2 December 1872, A and P 1873, 75.

[7] Smith to Thomson, 17 May 1875, FO 60/373.

[8] Medvedev, pp. 385–86.

These latter are—

|  |  | MILES |
|---|---|---|
| 1. | Tehran-Meshed-Sarakhs . . . . . . . . . . | 677 |
| 2. | Shahrood-Asterabad-Meshed-i-Sher . . . . . . | 255 |
|  | (There is a Russian telegraphist stationed at Asterabad, and the section from Bunder-i-Gez to Shahrood is kept in repair by the Russian Government.) | |
| 3. | Semman-Firuzkuh . . . . . . . . . . . . | 43 |
| 4. | Resht-Kazvin-Enzeli . . . . . . . . . . . . | 132 |
| 5. | Tabreez-Ardebil-Namin (near Astara) . . . . . | 136 |
| 6. | Tabreez-Sanjboulak . . . . . . . . . . . | 125 |
| 7. | Merend-Khoi-Oroumiah . . . . . . . . . . | 132 |
| 8. | Tehran-Hamadan-Khanekin (on Turkish frontier) | 440 |
| 9. | Hamadan-Sinnah-Genous . . . . . . . . . . | 107 |
| 10. | Hamadan-Burujird-Sultanabad . . . . . . . | 121 |
| 11. | Burujird-Nihavend . . . . . . . . . . . | 24 |
| 12. | Burujird-Khoremabad-Shuster. . . . . . . . | 240 |
| 13. | Ispahan-Yezd-Kerman . . . . . . . . . . . | 396 |
| 14. | Local lines near Tehran . . . . . . . . . . | 18 |
|  |  | 2,816 [sic][9] |

By 1913, Iran had 9,730 kilometers of line (6,000 miles) and 15,562 kilometers (9,726 miles) of wire.[10]

Telephones were installed in the few years preceding the First World War; by 1914 "the Société anonyme des Téléphones persans" had nearly one thousand subscribers, in twelve towns.[11] A telephone service also linked the Anglo-Persian Oil Company's offices in Masjid-i Suliman, Shushter, Khurramshahr, and Abadan[12] and another was used in the Lianazov fisheries on the Caspian.

Steamers and telegraphs constituted a great advance in Iran's connections with the outside world. This became even more marked after the opening of the Suez Canal, in 1869, had considerably reduced the distance between Western Europe and the Persian Gulf, thus making it possible for the steamers of that time to sail between those two areas without incurring excessive fuel costs (see 4:4).[13] A similar effect was produced, in the north, by the extension of the Russian railway system to the shores of the Caspian—Baku being connected in 1884 and Astrakhan in 1909; for although steam navigation had begun on the Volga as early as the 1840s, its benefits for both Russia and Iran were very much reduced because Russian rivers freeze in winter.[14] By the 1870s, the bulk of goods exported from or to Iran was probably being carried on steamers sailing on the Persian Gulf and Caspian.

But steam navigation, although a great help, left many problems unsolved. For,

9 "Report on the present state of Persia," A and P 1886, 67.

10 See Jamalzadeh, pp. 180–83 for details. In June 1914 an attempt was made by the Italian Marconi Company, working with a German syndicate, to install radio telegraphy in Iran. This was opposed by the British government, which wanted to have the service installed by the Indo-European Telegraph Department. FO 371/2075.

11 Jamalzadeh, p. 184.

12 Melamid in CHI, 1: 556—see also "Isfahan," A and P 1913, 71.

13 Max E. Fletcher, "The Suez Canal and World Shipping," *Journal of Economic History*, December 1958.

14 See *Bolshaya Sovetskaya Entsiklopediya* s.v. "Astrakhan, Baku; *Entsiklopedicheskii Slovar* (Saint Petersburg, 1892), s.v. "Volga." The first company for steam navigation on the Volga was founded in 1843; the Merkur Company, which played the leading role in navigation on the Caspian, started operations on the Volga in 1849.

in the first place, the very poor condition of Persian ports made the loading and landing of goods a slow, hazardous, and expensive operation. The only serious port improvement before the First World War was that carried out at Enzeli (Pahlavi) by the Russians (see 4:1). Second—and more important—of Iran's main productive regions, only the Caspian provinces lay along the coast; all the others were separated from it by mountain chains and large stretches of sparsely populated land. The situation is well described in the following passage:

There are five greater arteries for trade in Persia:—
1. From Tabriz and Resht through Kasvin, eastwards and southeast.
2. From the Caspian through Shahrud into Khorassan.
3. From Baghdad northwards to the provinces of Hamadan and Kermanshah and on to Tehran.
4. From Bushire northwards to Ispahan.
5. From Bender Abbas northwards to Khorassan.
The routes from Resht through Kasvin, and from the Caspian through Shahrud, are the main channels for Russian commerce, as those from the Persian Gulf and Baghdad are the main channels for British and Indian trade.

Tabriz is the point of junction of three routes: the one from Trebizond, by which alone European goods can be profitably delivered into northwest Persia; and two from Tiflis and Astara on the Caspian, by which, and especially by the latter, Russian goods are delivered into the same provinces.

As regards advantages of transport, Kashan appears to be the present meeting ground of British and Russian goods coming respectively from the Persian Gulf and Caspian. The English have a slight advantage in cost of carriage to Ispahan, and Russian goods have a considerable advantage to Tehran.

The Russian routes from Ashkabad through Meshed into Khorassan, and from Meshed-i-Sar via Amol and Demavend to Tehran, are at present of minor importance. The English route from Baghdad is the only one which is at present fairly practicable for wheeled vehicles, and by which merchandise in heavy pieces can now be comparatively easily delivered from the Persian Gulf.

In addition to the above-named routes, a very profitable channel for forwarding English and Indian goods into Khorassan would be by the Indian frontier railway, and from Kala Abdullah Khan through Herat. This route is, however, unfortunately, at present, completely blocked to any through trade by the exorbitant exactions of the Afghan local authorities at Herat and other places.[15]

Attention naturally turned to railways, and various schemes for a line linking India to the Mediterranean and passing through Iran, Iraq, and Syria were put forward in the 1850s but, being completely uneconomical and not meeting any strong political or military need, failed to materialize (see 4:10). The next step was taken in the 1860s, with rather shady attempts by European concession hunters and the shah and Iranian officials seeking to push such concessions, but these too did not make headway.[16] Then, in 1872, came the famous Reuter concession, the most important part of which was the project for a railway linking the Caspian

---

[15] "Notes by E. F. Law on British Trade," A and P 1889, 77: 8–9.
[16] See Kazemzadeh, *Russia*, pp. 101–3.

with the Persian Gulf (see 4:7). Faced with both Persian and Russian opposition—and having received no British backing—Reuter was forced to withdraw after having prepared one kilometer of railway bed; but the Russian diplomatic thrust generated by his intrusion pushed through another concession, that of Falkenhagen, in 1874, for a line from Julfa to Tabriz (see 4:8). This too, however, did not bear fruit, because of the Russian government's failure to supply the necessary capital, and no better fate attended the concessions given to, or schemes presented by, various French, British, American, and Belgian promoters between 1878 and 1888. The only concrete result of all these attempts was the six-mile railway from Tehran to the shrine of Shah Abd al-Azim, built by the Belgians in 1888.[17]

The next two years constitute a landmark in Iranian railway history. In 1888, a group of Russian businessmen came forward with a scheme for a line from the Caspian to the Arabian Sea and preliminary agreement was reached with the French Banque d'Escompte, which undertook to raise 300 million francs. The following year the shah made an agreement with the Russian government "that it should grant to a Russian Company the construction in Persia of railways to anywhere where it may be advantageous to the commercial interest of both Governments. . . ." But in 1888 he had already conceded "the priority of the English Government over others in the construction of a southern railway to Tehran." The British government seems to have intended to use this agreement, and the still-undisposed-of Reuter concession, either to restrict the Russian railway to the northern part of the country—with the possibility of building a British line in the south—or to insist on the line's being made an "international one," "in which English capitalists should have a share." But the whole situation was changed by the Russian government's decision, on both political and economic grounds, to refrain from backing the projected line and by the agreement of 11 November 1890 in which "the Persian Government engages for the space of 10 years . . . neither itself to construct a railway in Persian territory nor to permit nor grant a Concession for the construction of railways to a Company or other persons." This agreement, which the British rightly termed "sterilizing," although they welcomed the fact that it removed a threat to the defenses of India, was renewed in 1900 and put an end to all schemes until 1910—whether British, such as the projected Sistan railway, German, such as the line from Baghdad to Tehran, or Russian, such as the Sakhanskii project.[18]

In the absence of railways, some means had to be found to move the growing volume of goods shipped to or from Iran. The British turned to rivers and the Russians to roads. Already in 1862 a British firm, Lynch Brothers, had started a regular steamer service on the Tigris, between Basra and Baghdad, considerably

---

[17] Ibid. pp. 157–75, and "Memorandum on Persian Railways," India Office, 20 June 1911, FO 371/1186.
[18] Ibid., and chap. 4, sels. 8–10.

reducing both time and cost (see EHME, pp. 146–53). From Baghdad, goods were transported to Tehran, by way of Qasr-i Shirin and Kermanshah, a distance of 520 miles, taking some 35 days.[19] In 1888 British pressure led to the opening of the Karun river as far as Ahwaz, a distance of 120 miles, to ships of all nationalities, and a steamer service was immediately started by Lynch; shortly afterward the upper stretch of the river—between Ahwaz and Shushtar, a distance of 60 miles— was also opened to navigation (see 4:5, 6). From Ahwaz to Isfahan, a distance of 270 miles, the journey by pack animals took 20 to 25 days.

For their part, the Russians concentrated on road building; indeed the Soviet scholar A. Popov has called 1890–1910 "the Paved Road Period." Between 1893 and 1914 they laid down nearly 500 miles of very good roads connecting Tehran with Enzeli (379 kilometers), Tabriz with Julfa (135 kilometers), and Qazvin with Hamadan (243 kilometers).[20] Other roads were built by a British firm between Tehran and Qum (147 kilometers) and Qum and Arak (135 kilometers) and by an Iranian in Khurasan (see 4:12). Shortly before the First World War, automobiles began to circulate in various parts of Iran. But the cost of transport within the country remained extremely high (see 4:11). It should be added that repeated attempts to persuade the Ottoman government to improve the road between Trebizond and the Iranian frontier, along which a considerable amount of trade moved, remained fruitless.[21]

In the years immediately preceding the First World War, it looked as though some railways would be built in Iran after all. Russia's defeat by Japan, and the ensuing 1905 revolution, temporarily weakened its position. The Anglo-Russian Agreement of 1907 made it possible to envisage joint projects in Iran. Above all, there was the challenge posed by the strongest economic power of that time, Germany. By 1905, the German-built Anatolian railway was proving a financial and economic success,[22] and pressure was building for its prolongation to Iraq

[19] Jamalzadeh, p. 58.
[20] Gorelikov, p. 295.
[21] Complaints regarding this road are frequent in British consular reports from Tabriz and refer to both the insecurity prevailing and robberies committed (e.g., Abbott to Aberdeen, 23 November 1841, FO 60/82; Abbott to Wodehouse, 20 September 1860, FO 60/253; Abbott to Russell, 30 June 1861, FO 60/259) and the lack of interest shown by the Ottoman government in road improvement. The danger of the transit trade's being diverted to Russia was pointed out: "But the Turkish Government will only have to thank themselves for a loss of which they have repeatedly been warned, and which they might have avoided by constructing a cart-road between Trebizond and the Persian frontier,"—Dickson to Malmesbury, 1 December 1858, FO 60/234 —see also Abbott to Russell, 7 May 1862, FO 60/271. These sentiments were echoed by the British consul in Trebizond: e.g., "There is nothing to mention but the Erzeroom road, and that in deprecatory terms" ("Trebizond," A and P 1874, 67).

But as late as 1871, "Generally speaking, the European traders prefer receiving their goods by way of Turkey, as although the cost of carriage is somewhat higher than by the route through Russia—the former averaging 50s. and the latter 43s. the 160 lbs.—the journey is performed more speedily and with greater regularity." ("Azerbaijan," A and P 1871, 65). The building of the Tiflis railway made the Russian route much more competitive, the cost of a bale weighing about 100 lbs. from Poti to Tabriz being 4 shillings, compared with £1.4.0 from Trebizond to Tabriz ("Turkey," A and P 1874, 66). This diversion of traffic was, however, soon stopped by the abolition of free transit through the Caucasus in 1883, but the poor state of the Trebizond road prevented any substantial increase in traffic, and the main result was an increase in imports to Iran through the Persian Gulf (see 3:12).
[22] See Brünner, appendix.

and Iran (see 4:9). A line from Baghdad to Tehran would open the Persian market to German trade and influence; it would also be welcome to Iranian nationalist circles, eager for a counterweight to the British and the Russians.[23]

In these circumstances, it seemed unlikely that the "sterilizing agreement" could be prolonged beyond 1910. The British, well entrenched in southern Iran, put forward a number of schemes, and in 1911 secured concessions for lines running from Muhammarah and other Persian Gulf ports (see 4:10). For its part, Russia, opposed as ever to the building of railways in Iran and particularly alarmed by the prospect of a German incursion, started negotiations with Germany which led to the "Potsdam Agreement" of 19 August 1911. The German government declared that it would seek no railway, road, navigation, or telegraph concessions for itself or others north of the Qasr-i Shirin–Isfahan–Yazd–Khakh line. In return the Russians undertook not to oppose the construction or financing of the Baghdad Railway and, upon the latter's reaching Khaniqin, promised to build within four years a connecting line from Tehran to Khaniqin. Germany also secretly promised not to construct branch lines toward the Caucasus or Iran. The Russians seem to have acted on the assumption that the railway would not reach Baghdad for another ten or fifteen years;[24] judging from subsequent developments, this greatly underrated German dynamism; but events proved them right.

One more rather grandiose scheme was seriously considered for a Trans-Persian line linking the Russian and Indian railways. Elaborated in Russia in 1910, it originally proposed the following alignment: Rostov–Baku–Tehran–Nushki. The time taken for the 5,156 mile journey from London to Bombay was reckoned at seven to eight days; the cost was put at £21,850,000—on the basis of £13,500 a mile—and net revenue at £1,250,000. Later, the stretch across Iran was put at 1,400 miles, the cost, including rolling stock, at £15 to 18.7 million, and net revenue at £709,000.[25] The reaction of the India Office was skeptical and reserved; the losses to Indian revenue and British shipping, as well as the strategic dangers, were stressed, and safeguards such as a break of gauge and a certain alignment were insisted upon.[26] On the latter question there was a divergence of views between the Russians and the British. The British wanted the line to pass through Isfahan, Shiraz, and Bandar Abbas. The Russians objected that this would be too close to the Baghdad railway and would bypass too many towns; instead they proposed a line through Yazd, Kirman, and Bampur; to meet British objections they were willing to divert the line from Bampur to Chahbar, on the Arabian Sea, instead of to Nushki.[27]

As regards the ownership of the proposed company, it was soon agreed that a

---

[23] See Martin, p. 203.
[24] Kazemzadeh, pp. 595–96.
[25] Memorandum on Railways, pp. 33–46.
[26] Ibid. and India to Foreign Office, Memorandum respecting the Trans-Persian Railway, 6 January 1913, FO 371/1709.
[27] Buchanan to Grey, 20 February 1913, FO 371/1710, and idem, 25 March 1913, FO 371/1711.

French group would be associated with the British and Russian. It was also urged that

the Trans-Persian Railway, from Astara to the sea, be one concession, but let the actual line be constructed and operated in two sections by two companies working in cooperation, Russian interests predominating on the northern section, British on the southern, while the relative interest of the three Powers in the enterprise as a whole are maintained on a basis of absolute equality.

For example, in the northern section the ratios would be Britain 1, France 3, Russia 5, and in the southern Britain 5, France 3, Russia 1.[28]

However, by then the project had lost its appeal to the British group, who did not find the scheme "commercially attractive" and seemed decided to let it "lapse." The Russian government, however, still favored a railway across Iran. In these circumstances, the India Office advocated the following:

It would thus appear that the policy of His Majesty's Government should be to adhere firmly to the alignment already required by us for a railway traversing Persia diagonally, and to revive the project of a north to south line to be effected by a junction of the Mohammerah-Khoremabad and the Julfa-Tabriz lines at, say, Hamadan. Lord Crewe has some reason for thinking that this would be more attractive to the British group than the Bunder Abbas-Ispahan line, while it is not certain that the Persian Railways Syndicate have the necessary funds to exploit their concession. Russian opposition would, of course, be strong, though it is not clear why, if they are willing to admit British goods to Northern Persia viâ Chahbar and Yezd, they should object to doing so viâ Mohammerah and Hamadan. But, as has been observed above, if the Astara-Tehran line is of sufficient importance to Russia, and can be secured so easily in no other way, it is not impossible that she may be willing to pay the price; the history of the Potsdam Agreement, at all events, shows that she is willing to pay a high price for far less tangible advantages, if asked with sufficient firmness to do so.[29]

No further action seems to have been taken on the scheme and no railways were built in Iran until the First World War. During that war, the Russians laid a line from Julfa to Urumiya, passing through Tabriz. The British, who had linked Quetta to Nushki in 1905,[30] extended the line to Duzdab (Zahidan). The whole question had to be reopened in the late 1920s, this time by a government concerned with Iranian, not foreign, national interest. In the meantime, perhaps the best commentary on the state of internal transport is that

in 1914 the journey from Khurramshahr to Tehran took three weeks to a month, and personnel of the oil company in Khuzistan discovered that it was quicker and much more convenient to travel by boat from Khurramshahr via the Suez Canal and Istanbul to the Russian Black Sea port of Batum, from there by railway to Baku, and then by ship across the Caspian to Bandar Pahlavi [Enzeli], and finally by road to Tehran![31]

[28] FO to Garstin, 24 February 1913, FO 371/1710; see also Errington to FO, 3 March 1913, FO 371/1711, and Memorandum respecting Trans-Persian Railway, 19 March 1913, FO 371/1711.
[29] India Office to FO, 30 April 1913, FO 371/1711.
[30] Greaves, p. 213.
[31] Melamid in CHI, I: 556.

As regards merchandise:

Basing oneself on average speed, it may be estimated that one could not make more than 30 kilometres in one day, and that transport costs ranged from 1 to 2 krans per ton-kilometre [0.45 to 0.90 francs]. At that time (1912) in France, the speed of transport of merchandize varied from 35 to 40 kilometres an hour, and the cost was 0.20 to 0.30 francs.[32]

## Navigation on the Caspian Sea and Lake Urumiyah

Lying next to Iran's richest provinces, including its silk producing districts, the Caspian Sea forms an obvious trade route with Russia. But the natural obstacles referred to in the following selection, the fact that the Russian rivers freeze in winter, and above all the insecurity caused by piracy and war, greatly limited its use for navigation. Hence, although sporadic attempts were made, for example by the Genoese in the thirteenth century and by the British in the sixteenth, "regular commercial navigation appeared only at the beginning of the 18th century, under Peter I. The first steamer made its appearance in 1846."[1] However, already in November 1833 Campbell had noted a Russian decree that the "mouths of the River Kaor which empties itself into the Caspian should be cleared out, and that steam boats should be established on that sea," ostensibly for trade with Georgia, "though the real motive must be evident" (FO 60/35); and on 30 November 1843 Thomson reported: "Russia also appears to be making great exertions to establish a mart for her goods at Asterabad... she has already begun to establish steam navigation on the Caspian" (FO 60/100). And even earlier, when Humboldt visited Astrakhan in 1829, he noted four wood-burning steam boats, used to pilot the sailing ships into the harbor.[2]

This increasing use of the Caspian by Russian ships was accompanied by a decline in its use by Persian ships. In a report on his journey to the Caspian dated 29 June 1844, Abbott states:

Ships are now seldom if ever built at Enzelee because the Russian government has prohibited the exportation of planking from Astrabad and that which the Persians have is badly sawn and difficult to procure. Boats are built there with flat bottoms and equally sharp at both ends.

I do not believe there are Five vessels on the Caspian belonging to Persian subjects and any there may be are managed by Russian sailors or natives of the coast belonging to Russia [FO 60/108].

Writing in 1849, Gödel stated; "Hardly 25–30 ships sail on the Caspian Sea under the Persian flag, and these are all commanded by foreign captains."[3] This was echoed by Blau: "Hardly 20 ships sail on the Caspian Sea under the Persian

[32] Djazaeri, p. 121.
[1] *Bolshaya Sovetskaya Entsiklopediya*, s.v. "Kaspiiskoe More."
[2] L. Kellner, *Alexander von Humboldt* (London, 1963), p. 137.
[3] Gödel, p. 68.

flag, and only under foreign command, mostly Russian captains, and subject to the strict control of Russian warships."[4]

By 1857 steam navigation had become sufficiently frequent for Abbott to note, quoting the Persian consul at Astrakhan: "The Russian steamers on the Caspian have been very irregular in their voyages this year—next year the number will be increased. Six are building and three are nearly finished—two or three others will be sent from above" [i.e., up the Volga]; he adds in footnote: "It is not clear whether six only or nine are alluded to as building—it is thought the latter" (Dispatch dated 29 October 1857, FO 60/223).

In 1861 the Kavkaz-Merkur Company was formed (see 4:2), and by 1867 the British consul at Rasht listed in his report fourteen Russian steamers "measuring 3,430 tons and propelled by engines of 970 horsepower (nominal)," the biggest being of 400 tons and the smallest of 100. He notes:

Twelve of these boats belong to the Mercury and Caucasus Company, and the two last to a company lately established at Astrakhan. The competition between them has had a very beneficial effect, the rates of freight being fully 25 per cent lower than they were when the former company monopolised the carrying trade between the ports of the Caspian.

The Mercury and Caucasus Company receives from the Russian Government, one of its largest shareholders, an annual postal subsidy of 300,000 silver roubles, equivalent to £47,500. For this sum the company has undertaken to transport troops and military stores at a low rate of freight, and to run a fortnightly mail boat during the period the navigation of the Volga is open from Astrakhan to Gez, the port of Astrabad, calling at the intermediate ports of Petrovski, Derbend, Bakou, Lenkoran, Astara, Enzelli, and Meshedee-Sir. The steamer calls at the same ports on the return voyage. The first mail boat of the season generally leaves Astrakhan on the 15th April, and the last on the 15th October. Besides this boat another weekly steamer goes exactly the same round for cargo. During the winter only one boat a month plies between Baku and Gez. [Report on Gilan, A and P 1867–68, 68.]

The previous year his predecessor had listed 10 steamers aggregating 2,630 tons and stated:

These steamers are all built in England or Sweden and conveyed to Russia in pieces. They are put together at Tver on the Volga by English and Swedish engineers in the dockyards of the Sparki-Selo Company, and are floated down the Volga into the Caspian when the ice breaks up in spring. The "Caucasus and Mercury Company" has also eight steamers in the northern ports of the Caspian, for the purpose of facilitating the navigation at the mouths of the Volga; and two new screw boats are expected this year from England for the same Company.

Another Company has been recently formed, but has as yet only two steamers in the Caspian; two others will, however, be soon completed. By reducing its rate of freight, this Company hopes to be able to compete with that of the "Caucasus and Mercury."

---

[4] Blau, p. 232.

The freight by the steamers of the latter Company from Enzellee to Bakou is 1 rouble 80 copecks per poud of merchandise, or about 2¼d. per lb.; whereas the new Company has made a reduction of 15 per cent. in its rates of freight. The distance from Enzellee to Bakou is 200 miles and there are two good places of anchorage, one at the island of Saro, near Lankoran; the other at the mouth of the river Kur. The voyage can be accomplished by a direct steamer in 24 hours, but as the steamers generally touch at Astara and Lankoran, they do not perform it in less than 72 hours. [Report on Gilan, A and P 1867, 67.]

By 1879 the Russian merchant marine on the Caspian aggregated 4,150 tons of steamers and 64,500 of sailing ships (Report on Gilan, A and P 1907, 91). In 1883, in order to assure a faster mail service, the Russian government asked the Caucasus Mercury Company "to supply a mail steamer which, besides being thoroughly seaworthy, shall be able in all weather, summer and winter, to cross the bar and enter the port of Enzeli" on a weekly run (Finn, dispatch of 28 January 1883, FO 60/457). But the closing of the Caucasus transit route in that year (see 3:21) reduced traffic, and the same consul reported that the company "have found it necessary to stop their steamers running to Meshedi Ser and their ships will now only run to Enzelli and back to Baku, and on the other side from Baku to Gez and back" (Dispatch of 11 April 1884, FO 60/464). A year later he reported, "My Russian colleague informs me that where ten steamers used to come two years ago and bring or take up cargo only two now arrive at Enzelli" (Finn to Salisbury, 10 October 1885, FO 60/475).

By 1883 the number of Russian steamers had risen to 49, with an aggregate tonnage of 16,600; of these 17, aggregating 7,700 tons, belonged to the Caucasus Mercury Company; 12, aggregating 3,100 tons, to Yagoubov and Company; and the others to nine other companies (see list in A and P 1893–94, 95). Tomara put the Russian fleet on the Caspian, around 1893, at 139, aggregating 74,345 tons,[4] and by 1907 the total had risen to 265 steamers, aggregating 118,347 tons, and 544 sailing ships, aggregating 64,500 tons (Report on Gilan, A and P 1907, 91). The total traffic entering Iranian ports on the Caspian in 1328/29 (1907/8) consisted of 2,171 steamers aggregating 803,000 tons and 584 sailing ships aggregating 15,000 tons.[5] Imports through Enzeli and Astara aggregated 4,878,000 pouds in 1909/10 and exports 3,746,000, a total of 8,624,000, or 141,000 tons.[6]

Litten[7] gives full information on timetables and fares on the eve of the First World War. The Mercury-Caucasus line listed five routes: Baku-Enzeli, twice a week; Baku-Astara, weekly; Astrakhan-Mashad-i Sar, weekly (in summer); Baku-Krasnovodsk, daily; Baku-Mashad-i Sar, weekly (in winter). On the first route, the journey took eighteen hours and the fare was twenty rubles in first class and twelve in second, "including meals and bed linen."

[4] Tomara, pp. 156–57.
[5] Jamalzadeh, p. 65.
[6] Sobotsinskii, p. 84.
[7] Litten, pp. 182–84.

A great impediment to navigation was, however, the poor condition of Iranian ports, especially in winter. This was the more serious because the Russian companies, having much business between Baku and Astrakhan in summer, preferred to do most of their carrying to Iran in winter. This resulted in the accumulation of merchandise in Baku, delays at the Persian ports, and an appreciable rise in costs. To remedy this, "Between 1905 and 1913 Russia invested 1.3 million rubles in improvements at Enzeli," and a further program costing 2 to 5 million was interrupted by the First World War.[8]

After the disruption caused by revolution and war, services were resumed by the Soviet "Kaspar" Company, which in the mid-twenties had three weekly services.[9] But

sailings were gradually reduced to one per week without an increase in the size of vessels: the same ships, built in the nineteenth century in British or German yards and assembled in Caspian ports, still provided this service. After World War II the number of sailings was reduced; e.g. during 1957 there were only two or three sailings per month, and no passengers were carried.[10]

As regards Lake Urumiyah (Rezaiyeh), an attempt was made, around 1850, by some Americans—presumably connected with the missionary and educational activities in that area—to establish a shipping service, but these proved fruitless.[11] Later, navigation rights were granted, as a *tuyul*, to Prince Imam Quli Mirza, who, with the help of a German captain, launched some small ships on the lake. In the words of the British consul at Tabriz:

The great salt lake of Urumiah which might be made into a cheap and efficient means of transport between the wealthy districts around it and Tabreez, still floats but three 20-ton sailing boats, which belong to the Governor of Maragha, who farms the monopoly of the transport and allows of no competitor in the lists.[12]

Russian attempts to secure a concession were unsuccessful, but in 1912 the prince gave a subconcession to an Armenian who was a Russian subject. By 1914, his ships sailed under the Russian flag.[13] Three crossings of the lake were made each week, by sailing ships, and the freight rate was 20 krans per kharvar.[14] The total carrying capacity of the ships was about 60,000 pouds (about 1,000 tons).[15]

(See also the works by Litten, Tomara, Ter-Gukasov, and Jamalzadeh listed in the bibliography.)

[8] Entner, pp. 52–53.
[9] Lingeman, p. 7; in 1924/25, the tonnage of ships entering the Persian ports was 462,000, compared with 798,000 in 1913/14—Sventitski.
[10] Melamid, in CHI, 1:562.
[11] Blau, p. 232.
[12] A and P 1894, 88, p. 4.
[13] Litten, p. 168.
[14] Jamalzadeh, p. 65.
[15] Sventitski.

## Selection 1. Navigation on the Caspian, 1844–94
[A. I. Medvedev, *Persiya: Voenno-statistich-eskoye obozrenie* (Saint Petersburg, 1909), pp. 165–67]

Navigation on the Caspian Sea is determined by the following factors:
1. Prevailing winds: northwest and southeast. In addition, in winter north winds often blow on the southern shore and northeast winds on the eastern shore.
2. Shoals in the northern parts of the sea, the absence of good roadsteads in the southern and western parts, and the abundance of rocky shoals and islands on the western shore.
3. Many ships sail from Astrakhan, Petrovsk, Derbent, Baku, and Krasnovodsk to one or other of these ports and also to the Persian ports of Astara, Enzeli, Mashad-i-Sar, and the bay of Astrabad. The most important ports, as regards freight traffic, are Astrakhan, Petrovsk, and Baku in Russia and Rasht (Enzeli) and Astrabad in Persia.
4. Transport facilities on the Caspian Sea are indicated by the data on the number of steamers and sailing ships making voyages on that sea. These ships were:

| YEAR | NUMBER | TONNAGE (THOUSANDS OF POUDS)[a] | AVERAGE TONNAGE (POUDS) |
|---|---|---|---|
| 1844 . . . . . | 103 | 496 | 4,774 |
| 1854 . . . . . | 362 | 868 | 4,836 |
| 1864 . . . . . | 625 | 3,986 | 6,324 |
| 1874 . . . . . | 735 | 5,952 | 8,122 |
| 1884 . . . . . | 1,431 | 23,312 | 16,306[b] |
| 1894 . . . . . | 799 | 13,144 | 15,996[c] |

[a]) A poud was equal to 16.38 kilograms or 36 lbs.
[b]) War in Turkestan.
[c]) Cholera in Persia.

From this table it is clear that both the number of ships and their tonnage grew very rapidly in each decade, and that a huge army could be sent over to Persia on board the ships now sailing on the Caspian. Moreover, in case of need, the number of ships could be significantly increased; this may be seen in the table as regards the year 1884, when a large number of ships was brought over from the Volga because of the threat of war in Turkestan.

As regards the speed of travel, the distance from Astrakhan to Enzeli is 766 [nautical] miles and represents a journey of 9–10 days; from Astrakhan to Astrabad 875 miles and 12–13 days; from Baku to Enzeli 197 miles and 2–3 days; from Baku to Astrabad 396 miles and 5–6 days, and Baku to Krasnovodsk 190 miles and 2–3 days.

In conclusion it may be mentioned that the Caspian is open for voyages from Baku and Krasnovodsk to the Persian ports the whole year round, and from Astrakhan during eight months. . . .

## Selection 2. Navigation on the Caspian
[Abbott to Russell, 22 March 1861, FO 60/259]

*Tabreez*

I have the honor to state to Your Lordship that a prospectus in the Persian language had been sent sent to this Country setting forth that a Russian Company (the same I believe which has established Steam vessels for the navigation of the Black Sea) is forming or is ready to extend itself for the carrying trade between Persia and Russia by way of the Caspian and Volga. The Principal Director of this Company appears to be one Nicholai Alexander Oobich Novisuliski.

Pilgrims to Mecca from the South-Eastern and Southern Coasts of the Caspian are invited to proceed in the vessels of the Company by the Volga, 400 versts, as far as Tzaritzina—thence by Railway in process of construction, 80 versts, across to the Don down which River Passengers will be conducted to Taganrog on the Sea of Azof and so on to Constantinople where they will be shipped to Alexandria in Egypt—the whole distance to be performed in forty days.

Facilities are offered for the transport of goods from the Western Coast of the Caspian to the Black Sea for shipment to Trebizonde and Constantinople—also from Tabreez to these places—and offers are made by the Company to undertake the Insurance of all goods entrusted to it for transit.

I learn from the Persian consul of Astracan, who was formerly a Persian writer in my service, that the Russian Government has made over some of its vessels in the Caspian to the above-mentioned Company which is also building other vessels at Astracan for the service alluded to. Two Iron steamers, each of 80 Horse Power, are in course of construction at that Port to be employed as Troop-ships.

The Persian Consul by no means confirms the report which was some time since circulated of the Russian Government having a great many Steam vessels (some of large size) in course of construction for service on the Caspian. He thinks that the present number of Steamers of all sizes and descriptions possessed by Russia in that Sea may be about Seventeen—most of them being of small draught to admit of their crossing the Bar at the mouth of the Volga where at certain seasons there are only about two feet of water.

The trade of the Caspian is at present I believe, a very limited one and would not support the expense of many or large Steam-vessels—but the establishment of a regular Communication by Steam may in time render it more important, a result which would become the more certain should the Government of Russia finally determine on carrying out the Scheme so long agitated of diverting the Persian trade now flowing through Trebizonde and Erzerum to the route through Georgia.

## Steam Navigation in the Persian Gulf

Steam came to the Persian Gulf in 1836, when Colonel Chesney's *Euphrates*, which had sailed down the Mesopotamian river (see EHME, pp. 146–47), went on to Bushire.[1] This initiative was not, however, followed up, and for twenty-five years the gulf's trade continued to be carried in sailing ships. A list compiled in 1824 (Stannus to Willock, 3 June 1824, FO 60/24, copy in IO, LP and S/9 vol. 37) gives the size and ownership of the gulf's merchant fleet. Ten ships, aggregating

[1] See various memoranda and letters by Blosse Lynch and others in 1838 (IO, LP and S/9, vol. 60). The same year two steamers, *Semiramis* and *Hugh Lindsay*, participated in the British landing at Kharg (ibid., vol. 61), and in 1839 the *Hugh Lindsay* anchored off Ras al-Khaima, (ibid., vol. 65). From 1830 on, several British officials and merchants in Baghdad and India tried to persuade the British government to choose the Persian Gulf route, rather than the Red Sea one, for the mail service to India. Among the arguments adduced were the possibility of coaling at Muscat, which was much closer to India than was Aden, and the strengthening of British influence in the Gulf area which a steamship service would provide—see memorandum by J. Bowater, 17 June 1830, and other correspondence (IO, LP and S/9, vol. 46); minute by Lord Auckland, 12 April 1837, and other correspondence (ibid., vols. 57 and 60). In a flight of wishful thinking, Lynch went as far as to say: "My information goes on to say that it is the intention of the Danube Steam Navigation Company, to whom these vessels [the Austrian steamers sailing down the Syrian coast] belong, to extend their line along the Euphrates to the India seas" (Lynch to Boyd, 5 April 1839, ibid., vol. 64). However, the greater security of Egypt, and the successful voyage of the *Hugh Lindsay* to Suez in 1834, proved convincing arguments in favor of the Red Sea route—see Hoskins, passim.

It should be added that, in 1834, the *Hugh Lindsay* had been instructed to proceed, with dispatches, to Bassadore, at the mouth of the Persian Gulf (Reid to Governor General, 15 May 1834, L/MAR/C/577). I owe this reference to Dr. Christina Harris, who is engaged on a study of the opening of the gulf to telegraphs and steamships in the 1860s.

4,266 tons, belonged to Indian ports (Calcutta 6 and Bombay 4); "the above ships are regular Gulph Traders, but other Ships from India occasionally visit Muscat, Bushire and Bussora." It may be pointed out that these ships had English names and presumably belonged to British owners. The number of boats belonging to Bushire and trading with India, the Red Sea and East Africa was 105, with an aggregate tonnage of 5,120. Other Persian ports had 80 boats, with a tonnage of 2,740 and the corresponding figures for Muscat and Arabian ports were 70 boats and 9,020 tons, but both these sets of figures were stated to be incomplete.

No significant change seems to have occurred until the establishment of a steam line carrying mails between Bombay and the gulf (see following selection).[2] This was due to the initiative of Sir Bartle Frere, Governor of Bombay, who granted a subsidy for a steamer service between Calcutta and Karachi to William Mackinnon, founder of Burmah Steam Navigation Company. Burmah also obtained the contract for a service to the Persian Gulf, changed its name to British India Steam Navigation Company, extended its sailings to East Africa, Australia, and England and by 1894 had eighty-eight steamers.[3] In Lord Curzon's words: "In 1862 not a single mercantile steamer ploughed these waters. A six-weekly service was then started, followed by a monthly, a fortnightly and finally a weekly steamer."[4] The opening of the Suez Canal gave a great stimulus to steam navigation in the gulf (see 4:4), as did the Russo-Turkish War of 1877–78, which diverted some of Iran's trade from the Caucasus to the sea route (see 3:7). A memorandum prepared in the British legation (Thomson to Hajji Mirza Husain Khan, 20 October 1877, FO 60/400) put the net tonnage of ships clearing from the ports of Bushire and Basra for London at 2,388 in 1871; 2,591 in 1872; 6,516 in 1873; 13,146 in 1874; 12,337 in 1875; 15,432 in 1876; and 13,432 in the first six months of 1877. In addition Turkish steamers served the Arabian side of the gulf, square-rigged European ships sailed to and from Batavia, and the "native vessels run everywhere and distribute goods to all ports of the Gulf."[5]

After that progress was rapid: "In 1876 the tonnage of British shipping in the Persian Gulf was returned at only 1,200 tons [sic]. In 1889, 115,000 tons of shipping, of which 113,000 were British, cleared from the port of Bushire."[6] By then, the British India Steam Navigation Company had six ships in service, leaving Bombay and Basra once a week, and touching at Karachi, Gwadur, Muscat, Jask, Bandar Abbas, Lingah, Bahrain, Bushire, Fao, and Muhammarah, a journey of 1,970 miles in a fortnight. In Bombay the ships were in correspondence with those of the Peninsular and Oriental Company and in Basra with the river steamers of

[2] I am indebted for this reference, too, to Dr. Christina Harris.

[3] John Martineau, *Sir Bartle Frere* (London, 1895), 1:297–98.

[4] *Persia*, 2: 466–67; in 1904, in return for a yearly subsidy of 426,00 rupees per annum, the BISN undertook to make the round trip from Karachi in twelve days on the fast service and in three weeks on the slow—Lorimer, p. 2442.

[5] "Muscat and Persia," A and P 1876, 74.

[6] Curzon, *Persia*, 2:557.

the Euphrates and Tigris Steam Navigation Company. Other lines were the British and Persian Steam Navigation Company "officered by Englishmen, but owned and controlled by native merchants and working on a cheaper scale," which sailed "at irregular intervals between Bombay and the Gulf ports as far as Busrah"; a French line of steamers which, "in spite of a heavy subsidy, was compelled to desist"; and Darby, Andrewes and Company, "the only English merchants now running steamers directly from England to Bushire and Busrah, though vessels are frequently chartered for single voyages by business firms."[7]

The next twenty-five years saw a sharp rise in shipping, intensified competition, and attempts to prevent the resulting decline in freights by forming combines.

As regards the volume of shipping, by 1901/2 the number of steamers entering Bushire had risen to 112, with an aggregate tonnage of 130,000, and in 1911/12, 200 steamships, with a total tonnage of 319,000, entered the port ("Bushire," A and P 1902, 109 and ibid., 1913, 71). Most of these ships also called at other gulf ports and "4,051 ships touched at Persian ports during 1913/14, a decrease of about 100 on the total of the foregoing year." Their total net tonnage amounted to "just over 2,000,000 tons, of which just over three-quarters were British and just over one-eighth German" ("Persia," A and P 1914–16, 74).

The British share, though still overwhelming, had declined considerably; as late as 1909/10, it had been 90 percent ("Persia," A and P 1910, 94). The main competition came from the Hamburg-Amerika Line, which inaugurated its service to the gulf in 1906 (see EHME, p. 352). A Russian line from Odessa, which started in 1901, although heavily subsidized, played a much smaller role.[8] The Arab Steamers Limited, registered in Bombay, began sailing to the gulf in 1911 and "caused some competition in freights from Bombay, but freights to India from Lingah have not been affected" ("Lingah," A and P 1912, 98).

The decline in freights caused by competition is reported as early as 1901: "Freight to London for the first six months of the year gradually dropped from 1*l*. 5*s*. to 1*l*. 3*s*; while in July it further fell to 19*s*., at which rate it remained standing until December, when owing to competition with a Russian steamer, it declined to 15*s*." ("Bushire," A and P 1902, 109). Two years later, "the three British lines of steamers plying the Persian Gulf having formed a combine, the freights which had fallen as low as 14*s*. in the previous year, rose to 1*l*. 5*s*. in the beginning of 1903, and continued steady during the first seven months, when they dropped to 1*l*. for a short time, rising at the end of the year to 1*l*. 7*s*. 6*d*. It is said that freights have been fairly remunerative throughout the year, and if the combine continues, will pay all the three lines in the end" ("Bushire," A and P 1904, 100). The course

---

[7] Ibid., 2:467; see also details in "Bushire," A and P 1888, 78, and Gleadowe-Newcomen, pp. 60–61.

[8] The Russian government gave it £4,000 per trip and refunded the Suez Canal dues it paid—Gleadowe-Newcomen, p. 17. In 1914 a plan for a Messageries Maritimes service to the gulf was announced (dispatch from Bushire, 29 March 1914, FO 371/2074).

of freight rates up to the First World War is shown by table 1, which reveals the impact of German and other competition:

TABLE 1

RATES FOR GENERAL CARGO, BUSHIRE TO UNITED KINGDOM, PER 40 CUBIC FEET

| YEAR | £. | s. | d. | | £. | s. | d. |
|------|----|----|----|----|----|----|----|
| 1904 . . . . . . | 1 | 7 | 6 | to | 1 | 10 | 0 |
| 1905 . . . . . . | . . . . . . . . | | | | 1 | 10 | 0 |
| 1906–7 . . . . . | 1 | 10 | 0 | | 1 | 0 | 0 |
| 1907–8 . . . . . | 1 | 0 | 0 | | 0 | 15 | 0 |
| 1908–9 . . . . . | 0 | 15 | 0 | | 0 | 17 | 6 |
| 1909–10 . . . . . | 0 | 17 | 6 | | 1 | 0 | 0 |
| 1910–11 . . . . . | 1 | 0 | 0 | | 1 | 5 | 0 |
| 1911–12 . . . . . | 1 | 2 | 6 | | 1 | 7 | 0 |
| 1912–13 . . . . | . . . . . . . . | | | | 1 | 5 | 6 |
| 1913–14 . . . . . | 1 | 5 | 6 | | 1 | 0 | 6 |

SOURCE: "Bushire," A and P 1910, 101 and ibid., 1914–16, 74; these sources also give considerable detail on rates to India and the Far East.

(See also works by Hoskins, Wilson, Curzon, Lorimer, and Foreign Office Handbooks, listed in the bibliography.)

## Selection 3. Report on Tenders for Service to Persian Gulf, 1862

[Impey to Stewart, 4 July 1862, IO Z/P/3141, vol. 36, range 352]

*Bombay*

I have the honor to submit for the consideration of Government in original as well as in abstract three tenders received by me for the Mail Steam Service between Bombay and Kurrachee, and the Persian Gulf, in pursuance of the notice issued under the orders of Government on the 9th April last, copy of which notice is attached for ready reference.

2. The date and order of receipt of the tenders have been as follows:

From the Steam Navigation Company on 22d May

From the Cowasjee Jeehangeer Company on 10th June

From the Burmah Company on 27th June the last appears to have been lithographed in Calcutta as late as the 11th June last.

3. It is to be observed that with the exception of Messrs McKinnon's tender the others were sent in prior to the receipt by me on the 13th June (under Resolution of Government No. 1042) of the conditions and particulars adverted to in the 5th para. of the Government notice.

4. Before remarking on the different tenders Govt. may deem it satisfactory to have before them Sir Charles Wood's instructions of the 3rd March under which the tenders were invited. I therefore, attach a copy (app$^{dx}$ B). The monetary consideration which Sir Charles Wood expresses himself willing to Sanction is an additional anticipated expenditure of something less than Rs.88,000 a result obtained as follows:

"*Present annual outlay*"

| | |
|---|---|
| 24 trips from Bombay to Kurrachee and vice versa @ Rs. 4,000 per trip . . . . . . | A 96,000 |
| *Proposed Annual Outlay* | |
| 16 trips from Bombay to Kurrachee and vice versa @ Rs. 4,000. . . . . . . . . | B 64,000 |
| 8 trips from Bombay via Kurrachee to Persian Gulf . . . . . . . . . . . . . | 120,000 |
| | Rs. 184,000 |
| Deduct A | 96,000 |
| *Increased Expense*, Rupees | 88,000 |

5. Sir Charles Wood also limited the No. of trips to the Persian Gulf to 8, the vessels to

call at certain ports—and the period of the Contract to 5 years terminable on 12 months notice either by the Government or contracting Company. All the tenders it will be observed (appendix C) are below the above amount and the additional expenditure may be anticipated to be Rupees 80,000 instead of Rs. 88,000.

6. I have for convenience sake tabulated the points of importance in the different tenders. The observations necessary upon them may be divided into three heads.

    1. The Cost
    2. Time of transit rate of speed
    3. Class of vessels to be employed.

7. Two of the tenders viz the Steam Navigation and Burmah Company offer to perform the Kurrachee service

| | |
|---|---|
| *per trip* for Rupees . . . . . . . . . . . | Rs 4,000 |
| and the combined service to the Persian Gulf via Kurrachee per . . . . . . . . . | Rs 15,000 |
| The 3rd tenderer (Cowasjee Jehangeer) undertakes to perform the former for Rupees | 3,500 |
| and the latter for . . . . . . . . . . . . | 14,000 |

8. But the former is without abatement if 4 trips to Kurrachee are required and the latter in reality is not lower than that of the Burmah Company, who also offer for the Kurrachee Service Rs. 4,000 and for the Kurrachee and Persian Gulf service—as a *separate line* Rs. 10,000 or a total of *Rs. 14,000* and if 4 trips to Kurrachee are required, they agree to a reduction of 250 Rs. for each complete trip to Kurrachee—i.e. to take Rs. 3,750 for the single line to Kurrachee.

9. In respect to the time to be occupied in transit, the tender of the Burmah Company is the shortest by 4 hours per voyage to Kurrachee at $7\frac{1}{2}$ Knots (the rate of speed named by them) 66 hours would be the time of transit for the distance of 496 miles.

10. The other tenderers have named 70 hours—to be reduced to 60 hours after the first year, and after larger and more powerful vessels have been built. The Burmah Company alone have also fixed a rate of speed for their vessels for the Persian Gulf service.

11. The time proposed above is 26 hours under that of the former contract for the same service, and is five hours less than the average time in which voyages have been performed by the Burmah Company themselves during their temporary contract since January last. The monsoon season is unnoticed by all the tenderers and no allowance asked for it.

12. As respects the class of vessels the tender of the Burmah Company has a decided superiority while the terms of the other applicants provide four vessels of from 300 to 450 tons, and 100 Horse power which are promised hereafter to be raised to 650 tons and corresponding Horse Power, the Burmah Company have now ready and available vessels of the size required by Government, and agree besides to have a reserved vessel in case of accident.

13. If the tender of the Burmah, therefore is accepted there will be no interruption to the present efficient service to Kurrachee.

14. The size, horsepower, and number of vessels to be employed are points of considerable importance, for it was chiefly the want of a sufficient number of Steamers and the insufficient Horse power to tonnage—of those in the service of the Steam Navigation Company, that led to the delays, interruptions, and enforcement of penalties in the last contract with that Company.

15. In connection with this subject it will be necessary for Government to determine the period at which the Persian Gulf should commence, a question which the Burmah Company have asked to be specified and reasonable time allowed.

16. The Steam Navigation Company in a letter from their Kurrachee Agent have brought to notice that if the contract is made over to the Burmah Company it will give a single Company a monopoly in Indian waters; but this would scarcely be as disadvantageous as the operations of a poor indebted Agency whose performance of their last contract was not on the whole satisfactory and I incline to the opinion (judging from their temporary contract) that the Government and the Public may expect a more efficient service from the

Burmah Company than from either of the other tenderers.

17. I beg to invite the attention of Govt. to the concluding paragraph of Messrs. Nical and Co. forwarding letter attached to their tender in which they state that they have as Agents been instructed to withdraw the vessels of the Burmah Company, should their tender—submitted on the 27th instant —not be approved before the 30: idem.

18. In an interview with one of the partners I was informed that as mere Agents Messrs. Nical & Co. felt they had no option left them in the above respect, but they agreed to postpone acting until it became necessary to provide a Steamer to carry the next Over-land Mail to Kurrachee.

19. Should Government therefore select the Burmah Company's tender they will probably be able to authorize a general consent to it before the arrival of the next Overland Mail, leaving the detail of condi-tions to be settled by mutual arrangements in which I am led to believe there will be no difficulty.

20. These conditions will be submitted for the approval of Govt. on receipt of certain documents which have been telegraphed for from Bombay, and if Govt. desire I can personally arrange them with Messrs. Nical & Co.

## Selection 4. Steam Navigation in Persian Gulf, 1870

"Report by Colonel Pelly to the Indian Government," A and P 1871, 51, p. 16

*Muscat*
*10 July 1870*

Sir,

In supplement of my recent Report on the Trade of the Persian Gulf, I have now the honour to submit a few facts indicative of the development of the steam-borne portion of that trade:—

  1st. A few weeks ago the first steamer arrived direct from England *viâ* the Suez Canal.
  2ndly. The first of an intended line of steamers between Constantinople and the

Gulf arrived. On this subject the Political Agent, Muscat, writes as follows: "The Turkish merchant steamer, 'Babylon,' arrived here from Aden on the evening of the 27th (May) ultimo, and left for the Persian Gulf the next morning. This vessel is, I understand, the first of a line of steamers to run regularly between Con-stantinople and Bussora, and call at the intermediate ports of Jeddah, Aden, Muscat, Bunder Abbass, and Bushire."

  3rdly. Two or more steamers have run with corn and dates for Jeddah.
  4thly. Two Persian companies have commenced running between the Gulf and British India. These vessels run under the British flag.
  5thly. I understand that the British India Steam Navigation Company have it in contemplation to run a weekly steamer between British India and the Gulf.
  6thly. The first of a British line of steamers to run between London and the Gulf *viâ* the Suez Canal is expected at Bushire about three months hence.
  7thly. A steam trade in dates, corn, and dried fish with Mauritius and Batavia is spoken of.

2. As yet all the steamers appear to have found full cargoes at rates which, although lower than those which obtained in former years, still pay.

3. It is remarkable that the native mer-chants, inclusive of those now largely interested in steamers, have from the com-mencement of steam communication, eight years ago, consistently urged the incon-venience and injury that would result to the Gulf trade from the substitution of steamers for native craft.

4. The fact seems to be that the Gulf trade is capable of indefinite development, provided freights be sufficiently low to admit of produce competing with that of other countries in foreign markets; in other words, the Gulf being the only ocean basin for a vast range of territories, the resources of those territories will increasingly seek the ports of the Gulf provided they can be exported at a profit.

## Navigation on the Karun

The growth of Iranian trade (see chap. 3), the establishment of steam navigation in the Persian Gulf (see 4:3), and the need to counter increasing Russian influence turned British attention to the Karun river. As early as 1871, a firm in Bushire,—Gray, Paul and Company—tried, through the British authorities, to obtain a concession for a steamer service on the Karun between Muhammarah and Shushtar; it estimated that this would reduce the delivery time between the coast and Isfahan from thirty-five days to ten.[1] But this and other British attempts to open the Karun to navigation were long frustrated. The shah feared that such a concession would eventually lead to British domination, or even annexation, of Khuzistan. And he could rely on full Russian opposition to any foreign attempt to gain a foothold in the south or to open an alternative to the Caucasus route. The matter was further complicated by the Reuter and Falkenhagen concessions (see 4:7, 8), and by the granting, in 1878, of a concession to the shah's French physician, Dr. Tholozan, which specifically included the Karun.

British interest was not deflected, however, and on 1 December 1881 Captain Henry Welco, assistant director of Persian Telegraphs, prepared a memorandum on Natural Obstruction to the Navigation of the Karun River at Ahwaz.[2] A few months later an Iranian "engineer of some reputation," Mirza Abd al-Ghaffar Najm al-Mulk, made a thorough study of the question. He recommended the purchase of "two steamers of some length but not drawing more than 1 zer [3 feet 6 inches] of water, consuming but little coal and carrying about 12,000 kharvars [nearly four tons] of goods, the cost of each would scarcely exceed 18,000 Tomans [about £6,000]." One steamer would run between Muhammarah and the dam at Ahwaz and the other above the rapids, to Shushtar. "Cargo would be transferred as at present by hand. Two such steamers would amply suffice for for the carriage of the whole of the present trade between Muhammarah and Shuster."[3]

British persistence was finally rewarded when, on 30 October 1888, a decree opened the Karun, as far as Ahwaz, to "commercial steamers of all nations, without exception." The Euphrates and Tigris Steam Navigation Company (Lynch Brothers), which had been running steamers on the Tigris since 1862, immediately detached a ship to sail on the Karun.[4] Chapter 4, selection 6 gives a succinct history of the project and the advantages expected from it; taken from a lecture delivered shortly after the completion of *Persia and the Persian Question*, it provides a good illustration of Lord Curzon's style and manner.

The Lynch firm was soon followed by a Persian firm, Nasiri, and by the Bombay and Persian Steam Navigation Company. The latter soon withdrew, for lack of

[1] "Persia," A and P 1872, 59, and FO 60/375. See also Kazemzadeh, *Russia*, p. 149; chapter 3 of this book contains valuable information on this subject.
[2] FO 60/448.
[3] English summary translations of report, 2 July 1882, FO 60/448.
[4] "The Story of the Euphrates Company"; see also EHME, pp. 146–53.

profits, but the Persian firm remained active. In 1891 a British consul reported that "the Nasery Company have imported a light steel tramway from England, which is being laid at Ahwaz to convey cargo across the rapids."[5] By 1890, a traveler reported a twenty-ton steel launch and a thirty-ton stern-wheeler between Ahwaz and Shushtar (60 miles) and a tug, a steam launch, and the three-hundred-ton *Blosse Lynch* between Ahwaz and Muhammarah (120 miles). He claimed that

the opening of the Karun has already had a marked effect on the well-being of the Arab population. Labour at 1 kran (8d.) a day has put many in the space of a year in possession of sufficient capital to buy a pair of donkeys and a plough (donkeys do most of the plough work in Arabistan), and seed corn wherewith to cultivate Government lands on their own account, besides leaving a small balance in hand with which to live, without having to borrow at robbery rates on the coming crop. The Sheikhs, who before had a full command of labour in return for little more than the simplest food, now find this condition of things rapidly changing, so many of the very poor who depended on them having started as small farmers.[6]

The further development of river traffic is shown by the following account for 1909; the part played by river navigation in the development of the oil fields should be noted.

The E. and T. Steam Navigation Company's passenger steamer "Malmir" made 38 trips; the steam launch "Ishtar" towing a barge, 14 trips; the passenger steamer "Blosse Lynch," 1 trip. The Nasiri Company (Persian) passenger steamer "Nusrat," made about 25 trips. The increased activity of British river steamers was due mainly to the heavy importations of iron by the Anglo-Persian Oil Company but partly also to the greatly increased traffic over the Ahwaz and Ispahan road.

On the upper river (Ahwaz to Shalili for Shushtar) the passenger steamer "Shushan," run by Messrs. Lynch brothers, made 36 trips; the Persian passenger steamer "Mawin" made about 20 trips.[7]

It should be added that, a few years before the First World War, the Wönckhaus firm also ran a steamer service on the Karun. Lynch ran a weekly service, Nasiri a fortnightly service, and Wönckhaus one every ten days.[8]

The new route undoubtedly helped to open up the southern part of Iran to British trade, which "in the Karun region," rose from £16,000 in 1891 to £272,000 in 1902. The impact on the region itself may be judged by the fact that, in this period, the population of Muhammarah tripled. The time needed for the five-hundred mile journey from Bushire to Isfahan, previously a month, was cut by half, and freight rates were reduced.[9] Just before the war, the freight from Muhammarah to Ahwaz was about 14 shillings a ton on general cargo for the upward journey and 13 shillings per ton on general cargo and 7 shillings per ton for grain on the downward journey by Lynch steamers; on the Wönckhaus and

[5] Curzon, *Persia*, 2:334; Report on Bushire for 1890, A and P 1890–91, 87.
[6] Major General T. E. Gordon, "Report on a Journey from Tehran to Karun," A and P 1890–91, 74.
[7] "Arabistan," A and P 1910, 101.
[8] Jamalzadeh, p. 55; see also EHME, pp 350–55.
[9] Greaves, p. 166.

Nasiri steamers freights were one shilling lower. The journey upstream took thirty hours and the journey downstream fourteen. Sailing boats took four to seven days upstream and two days downstream, and charged 9 shillings, 7 shillings, and 5 shillings respectively.

From Ahwaz to Shushtar Lynch's freights were 15 shillings per ton on general cargo for the upward journey and 13 shillings a ton on general cargo and 6 shillings a ton on grain for the downward journey. Here again, the other firms charged one shilling less. The journey took two days up and one down.[10]

(See also "The Story of the Euphrates Company" and works by Kazemzadeh, Greaves, Curzon, Ainsworth, Litten, and Jamalzadeh, listed in the bibliography.)

[10] "Arabistan," A and P 1914–16, 74.

## Selection 5. Need for Opening Karun River, 1878
[Memorandum by R. M. Smith, 1 June 1878, FO 60/414]

*Telegraph Dept. in Persia*
*Teheran*

Sir,

During my recent tour of inspection by Kermanshah, Baghdad, Bussorah, Bushire, etc: I was greatly struck with the marvellously increased commercial activity I found in those parts compared with former years. At Bussorah, for instance, I saw, besides the river Steamers, 7 large ocean going steamers at anchor at one time loading and unloading merchandize. The River Steamers, I was told, were unable to carry all the Cargo offered for shipment between Bussorah and Baghdad. I also observed an unusual number of large caravans between Baghdad and Kermanshah, many of which were going to or coming from Tabreez. Anyone acquainted with Bussorah only a few weeks ago could not fail to be struck with its altered and improved appearance. Instead of the unbroken line of Palm Groves which concealed the Town at some distance behind them and the river in which nothing but a few Buggalows was to be seen, the bank now presents an imposing line of Substantial European looking houses, offices and Godowns while the river itself is alive with boats and barges going to and from the Steamers whence the rattle of the steam winch is heard incessantly. The General bustle and movement are in striking contrast with the still monotony of former years.

Much of the increased Commercial Activity is due to the closing by the war of the Chief Trade Routes in the North of Persia and Armenia, and to the recent application to the Caucasus of the prohibitive Transit regulations of Russia. As you are probably aware the Caucasus has hitherto been open to the free transit of Merchandise between the Black Sea and the Caspian. This exemption from the prohibitive tariffs in force in the rest of Russia was probably granted as a means of developing trade in the Caucasus and of withdrawing as much of it as possible from the rival route through Trebizonde and Erzeroum. By the wholesale destruction and desertion of villages and by other ravages caused by the war, the Erzeroum road, as a trade route, has practically ceased to exist, and many years must elapse before it can possibly be resumed.

The Russian authorities may therefore have thought that the rival route being abolished, the Caucasus would have a monopoly of the transit and consequently that they might safely apply to it their general system of prohibition with a view to shutting all but Russian Merchandize out of Northern and Central Persia. If such were their object, it is quite possible that they have somewhat overreached themselves by overlooking the facilities for the transport of European Merchandize even into the North of Persia offered by the Baghdad route. As a matter of fact much of the increased trade of Bussorah is not Turkish but Persian.

The present time therefore appears an opportune one for the adoption of measures calculated to fix the southern as the main artery of the external commerce of Persia and by its means to secure for England and India the bulk of the import and export trade of the country. The establishment of a subsidized weekly mail service between the Persian Gulf and India and a monthly direct one with the Red Sea ports and London has already done much to this end. The full advantage of these subsidies however and of other efforts of securing Persia as a market for English produce can only be reaped by providing means of communication between the sea and the Interior of Persia that shall be unaffected by any revision of the transit dues in Turkey, the present lowness of which (1 per cent) alone renders the Baghdad route practicable.

The attention of Russia may therefore soon be drawn to this matter and her efforts at Constantinople directed towards obtaining such a revision of Turkish transit dues as to close the best existing road by which English Commerce in these parts can compete with her own.

There remain the roads into the interior from Bunder Abbas and Bushire, the former so long, and the latter so bad that even now exports from the North of Persia (silk from Ghilan for instance) prefer the circuitous road by Kermanshah and Baghdad notwithstanding the high freights of the Tigris River Steamers and the transit dues levied in Turkey. Besides the difficulty of transport over the mountains between Shiraz and Bushire the harbour of Bushire itself with its four miles of uncertain Communication between the anchorage and the shore offers every impediment to the development of an extensive foreign Trade.

One measure however might be taken which, I am convinced, would be most beneficial to British Trade in Persia, and

also to Persia herself, viz: the opening up of the Karun River to steam Navigation, on which subject I spoke with you 2 years ago during your tour of inspection, and on which I believe you addressed a report to the Govt. of India. It is therefore unnecessary to go over again the same ground by pointing out the advantages to England and Persia of the Karun route. My object is rather to call attention to the opportuneness of the present time for pressing the measure on the acceptance of the Persian Govt. The closing of the Erzeroum route by the results of the war, and of the Caucasus one by the application to it of the General Russian Tariff, has already, as above described, caused a great change in the conditions of the commerce of Persia altogether to the advantage of English Trade thro' the South as compared with Russian thro' the North, and it appears to me that the opening of the Karun would not only make that temporary advantage a permanent one by rendering it independent of any alteration of existing Turkish Tariffs, but would develop a new source of trade, the extent of which it is difficult to estimate. With increased Trade would come the more indirect advantage of increased political influence in a quarter where such influence might, in certain circumstances, be of considerable value.

### Selection 6. Navigation of the Karun, 1890
[George Curzon, "The Karun River and the Commercial Geography of South-West Persia," *Proceedings of the Royal Geographical Society*, 1890, pp. 514–15, 526–28]

... I take up the history of the Karun river at the moment when it first concerns ourselves, and when its commercial advantages began to be recognised, not by the British public, who are habitually ill-informed, but by the few pioneers whose invariable fate it is to be snubbed by their own generation and applauded by the next.

It was just fifty years ago that the immense latent value of the Karun trade route, as an avenue of expeditious approach to the great cities and centres of grain cultivation in the west of Persia, and as an opening more especially for British and Anglo-Indian commerce, was first brought prominently before the attention of Englishmen by the united labours and writings of Sir H. Layard and Lieut. Selby. The former of these explorers, from his intimate relations, both with Mohammed Taki Khan, the great Bakhtiari chieftain, and with the merchants of Shushter, was enabled to guarantee Persian reciprocity in any such enterprise; and he penned at the same time a report to the Home Government, and a letter to the Chamber of Commerce at Bombay, urging the prompt utilisation of so favourable an opportunity. Political convulsions in Persia frustrated the further prosecution of the design, and it was not till thirty years later that the opening of the Karun river to foreign commerce appears to have been made the subject of formal official communications between the Governments of Downing Street and Teheran. After seventeen years of diplomatic fencing, with feint and counterfeint, and all the diversified tricks of the Oriental school—in the course of which France at one time appeared as a combatant in the arena, and all but carried off an exclusive concession for the navigation of the river and the development of the surrounding lands—the matter was at last settled by a decree of the Shah, issued in October 1888, by which the Karun river, as far as Ahwaz, was, subject to certain somewhat vexatious conditions, opened to the mercantile marine of the world.

Ten years earlier, Hussein Kuli Khan, the second redoubtable Ilkhani whom the Bakhtiari clans have produced in this century, had made offers of co-operation to Mr. Mackenzie not less cordial than those which his famous predecessor had made to Layard. The independent action, however, and conspicuous authority of these chieftains in each case excited the jealousy of the central government. Layard's friend died in imprisonment at Teheran; Mackenzie's friend was put to death at Ispahan by the son of the present Shah. Hence it arose that when the concession was finally granted, and the firm of Messrs. Lynch detached a boat from their Tigris flotilla, to run at regular intervals from Mohammerah to Ahwaz, no such local assistance was rendered to the British as might in earlier days have been forthcoming, and the subsequent prosecution of traffic has only been continued in the face of obstacles and discouragement which I have elsewhere described. With the remark that by the exercise of patience, and by fortunate appeals to the sincerity of the Persian Government, these impediments are gradually being overcome, and that by the lately accorded permission for a steamboat to navigate the upper river from Ahwaz to Shushter in correspondence with Messrs. Lynch's steamers on the lower river, and by the expected commencement of a wagon road, under the auspices of an English company, from Ahwaz to Teheran, a notable impulse has been given to the chances of success,—with this remark I will take leave of the historical aspect of the Karun question, and will proceed to the main or geographical portion of my paper. . . .

I have thus conducted my hearers from the mouth of the Karun river to the Persian capital, and have shown the points and places between, which the utilisation of the river channel in the first place, and of the land roads about to be constructed in the second, will bring into novel communication both with each other and with the Persian Gulf. Let me state the case, and the advantages possessed by the proposed over the existing system, in terms of miles, regarding Ahwaz as the new maritime base, just as Bushire and Baghdad are the old. Burujird is distant from Baghdad 350 miles, and from Bushire 700 miles. From Ahwaz it is distant 310 miles. Sultanabad is distant from Bushire 700 miles, from Ahwaz 370 miles. Hamadan is distant from Baghdad 320 miles, from Ahwaz 400 miles; but Turkish river, territory, and custom-houses have not in the latter case to be passed between. Kum is 700 miles from Bushire, 450 miles from Ahwaz. Kashan is 640 miles from Bushire, 510 miles viâ Kum from Ahwaz.

These figures serve to show the greater expeditiousness of the new route; but it should further be remembered that the gain is not to be estimated in mileage only, but that the contrast will be between narrow and sometimes perilous mule-tracks upon the old line, and a cart-road with a probable wagon service upon the new.

If I be asked what is the particular use that is likely to be made of the Karun and inland route, and what are the prospects of mercantile return in the shape of traffic, customs, and tolls, I answer that under proper management it ought to result in a fourfold development, each pregnant with future wealth.

In the first place, a great impetus will be given to local production and manufacture. In traversing the Karun country, whether by river or on horseback, I passed through thousands of acres of splendid soil, capable of producing wheat, barley, cotton, rice, maize, tobacco, indigo, opium, sugar-cane, and with every facility for abundant irrigation, but lying naked and desolate, or else encumbered with tangled undergrowth and marshy pools. Further north, vines and fruit of every description can be grown with ease, and medicinal plants of considerable value. There also are to be found pastures for large flocks of sheep and goats, producing wool that fetches a high price; whilst the Bakhtiari country is celebrated for its breed of horses and mules, hundreds of which are even now brought down to the coast and shipped for sale to Bombay. Mineral resources are believed to exist in considerable extent in the provinces thus opened up; and naphtha springs are well known in the neighbourhood of Shushter and Ram Hormuz. All these products are only at present turned out in scanty volume, and there is not one among them whose annual output might not be many times multiplied were communication rendered simultaneously more easy and more secure.

Secondly: there would in time be a large increase of population in the districts affected. The population of Persia has been wofully diminished by the neglect and breakdown of the water-system upon which it depended. But in this corner of the Shah's dominions, and in this alone, nature has not stinted the most generous supplies; and the plains over which the traveller may now roam for hours without encountering a single human soul, ought under altered conditions to teem with busy life and industry.

Thirdly—and this is a consideration which specially affects ourselves—the opening of this route, if vigorously carried out, should result in an enormously increased import into Persia of British and Anglo-Indian goods. As it is, the import trade of the whole of Southern Persia is almost exclusively in British hands. Steamers of two British or Indian companies run weekly from Bombay to Busrah, and there is also a direct though irregular service between Busrah and London. The cities of Southern and Central Persia, as far north as Ispahan, already derive the bulk of their luxuries, and almost the whole of their clothing, from Manchester or Bombay; and each fresh town, we may even say each new village, that is brought into communication with the Persian Gulf, will thereby be drawn into the mesh of the Lancashire cotton spinner or the Hindu artisan.

Fourthly: should the line thus opened be succeeded at any time by a railway, the returns from passenger traffic would constitute no mean item. Asiatics generally are childishly fond of railway travelling; and the Asiatics of Persia, in particular, are addicted to immense journeys, extending over months of time, in order to gratify their pious desire to gaze upon the last resting-place of some departed saint. When they have reached the holy spot and have paid the becoming devotions, they enjoy what in England is vulgarly described as a spree; after which they return home in the odour of accomplished sanctity, and are known ever after as Hajis if they have been to Mecca, as Meshedis if to Meshed, or as Kerbelais if to Kerbela. I am a Meshedi and a Kerbelai myself, though I confess to being still a stranger both to the turbulent sweets of initiation and to the consecrated joys of reminiscence. A railway running between the Karun and Teheran would carry many thousands of such pilgrims to Kum, to Kerbela, to Najaf, to Kazimein, to Samara, and even in the direction of Mecca itself—all of them shrines of extreme sanctity and popularity. It would thus in time be supported by the superstition against which it might at first have to contend.

Such is the commercial geography of south-west Persia, and such are the advantages, both to Persia and to Great Britain, that may be expected to result from the active development of the Karun trade route. If it be asked why I have not laid greater stress upon or devoted more space to railways, I reply that sufficient for the day is the good thereof. There is a natural sequence of events which no diplomatist can revolutionise or invert. Mule-tracks must precede cart-roads; cart-roads must precede railroads. We shall not conquer Persia by lightning, or convert her by steam. It will be time to discuss a Karun railway when we have seen what becomes of a Karun road. In the meantime it rests with British enterprise to make worthy use of an opportunity which we owe to the successful efforts of British diplomacy and to the friendly disposition of an allied sovereign.

## Reuter Concession

Although, as is described in the following selection, the Reuter concession of 1872 was canceled, with considerable loss to the promoter, it stands as a landmark in the modern history of Iran. For one thing, its scope was unparalleled—Lord Curzon describes it as "the notorious Reuter agreement, that literally took away the breath of Europe and handed over the entire resources of Persia to foreign hands for a period of seventy years." [1] For another, it stimulated the Russian government not only to put great pressure on Tehran to cancel the concession but also to secure a counteradvantage, the Falkenhagen concession (see 4:8). Last, through the revised concession which Reuter secured in 1889, it led to the establishment of both the Imperial Bank of Persia and, indirectly, the Anglo-Persian Oil Company.

Having failed to secure British backing for his schemes, Reuter turned to other governments—the German in 1873 and again in 1885, and the Russian in 1888—but with no greater success. [2] But in 1889 Reuter signed an agreement both canceling his previous concession and authorizing him to set up a state bank, the Imperial Bank of Persia, with the exclusive right, for sixty years, to issue notes. The Bank was also granted "the exclusive right of working through the Empire the iron, copper, lead, mercury, coal, petroleum, manganese, borax and asbestos mines which belong to the State, and which have not already been conceded to others." [3] To exploit these rights, Reuter founded the Persian Bank Mining Rights Corporation, which for three years prospected in various parts of the country and, having met with no success, went into voluntary liquidation in 1894. But two of Reuter's associates were largely instrumental in interesting D'Arcy in Persian oil, thus starting the country's petroleum industry (see 7:1, 2).

[1] *Persia*, 1: 614; see also "the most complete and extraordinary surrender of the entire industrial resources of a kingdom into foreign hands that has probably ever been dreamt of, much less accomplished, in history," ibid., 1:480.

[2] See Martin, pp. 24–26, 33–34; Kazemzadeh, pp 201–2.

[3] Translation of agreement, 28 October 1889, FO 60/576 and FO 65/1378, partly quoted in Kazemzadeh, pp. 210–12.

(See also FO 539/10—*Persia Correspondence Respecting the Reuter and Falkenhagen Concessions, 1872–75*, Confidential, and works by Kazemzadeh, Martin, Kulagina, Taymuri, and Lisani, listed in the bibliography.)

**·Selection 7. The Reuter Concession, 1872**
[L. E. Frechtling, "The Reuter Concession in Persia," *Asiatic Review*, 1938, pp. 518–33]

. . . For the origins of the Reuter concession we must go back to 1864, when the Persian Government granted a railway and mining contract to M. Salavan, an Austrian. No work was actually undertaken in connection with this concession, and it lapsed, to be offered and subsequently accepted by French, Prussian, and English interests in succession. The experience of the concessionnaires was much the same: on arriving in Persia they found great difficulty in keeping their materials intact from theft; it was a hard task to obtain labour; co-operation from local officials was not forthcoming until they laid out the inevitable monetary inducements. In fact, it appeared to the British Minister at the Court of the Shah in 1871 that "the projects presented from time to time by Europeans have been entertained principally as a means of profit to the Persian Ministers and the agents employed by them."[1]

When concession hunters appeared less frequently in Tehran, Mohsin Khan, the Persian Minister in London, began to solicit English business men with a view to disposing of an exclusive concession. His approaches to several prominent City figures were unsuccessful, and then he met Baron de Reuter, already becoming well known in London through his news agency. Although by 1872 Reuter's activities covered a wide field, he had no connection either with railway and associated enterprises or with the geographical area known as the Middle East. Despite this lack of experience,

[1] Public Record Office, *Foreign Office MSS. Records*, Series 60 (Persia), vol. 405; Alison to Granville, July 17, 1871, confidential. (Hereafter the series will be cited in this form: F.O. 60/405.)

the Baron listened receptively to the proposals of Mohsin Khan regarding a Persian concession. A preliminary agreement was reached between the two, and Reuter sent an agent to Tehran to arrange the terms of the concession. After several weeks of negotiation, a document entitled "A Concession between the Government of His Imperial Majesty the Shah of Persia on the one Hand, and Baron Julius de Reuter, Residing in London, on the Other," was completed and ratified by the Shah on July 25, 1872.

The original purpose of this remarkable contract was the construction of a railway from the Caspian Sea to the Persian Gulf. This was provided for in Article II., which gave Reuter the exclusive right to such a line for a period of seventy years and also the right to build branch lines "either to join together the provinces and towns in the interior of the Empire, or to join the Persian lines with foreign railways at any points on the frontiers in the direction of Europe or of India." The concessionnaire was offered all the Crown lands necessary for stations, yards and workshops, and a right of way of thirty yards on each side of the tracks. The Government entered a means of control in Article VII., which stated that the actual method of constructing and working the lines should be determined by separate agreements between the parties before work was actually started. When the railway system began operation the Government was to receive 20 per cent. of the net profits.

As evidence of his good faith, Baron de Reuter was asked to deposit £40,000 in the Bank of England, which was to be forfeited to the Shah in the event of "the works not having been commenced" within fifteen months of the signing of the document. On the other hand, the caution money would be returned when it was reported that there had arrived at Enzeli, the Caspian port, enough rails to lay the line from Resht to Tehran.[2]

In addition to all railway rights, the concessionnaire received the exclusive and definitive privilege of constructing tramway lines throughout the Empire, of working all mines of coal, iron, copper, lead, and petroleum (excepting private mines and mines of precious stones and metals), of managing and exploiting all state forests in the country, of executing works for irrigation, dams, dikes, wells, reservoirs, and canals, and of selling the water thus obtained. From all these enterprises the Government's share of the profits was to be 15 per cent. The company might also extend its activities in the future through the exercise of the right of prior claim should concessions for a bank or for such enterprises as gas supply, street paving, road building, postal and telegraphic arrangements, mills, and factories be granted. One of the most essential means of raising revenue possessed by the Government was made over to the concessionnaire when the Customs control was granted for twenty years in exchange for an annual sum which should exceed the amount previously obtained from Customs contractors by £20,000.

In such an extensive and gigantic enterprise, the question of raising the necessary capital was naturally important, and the concession set out the position of the parties in this field very carefully. The contract authorized Reuter to issue stock to the extent of £6,000,000, on which the Persian Government was nominally to guarantee 5 per cent. interest and 2 per cent. for banking charges annually. In reality, however, the guarantee of the Government amounted to nothing, for it was to become effective only after the railway was completed from Resht to Tehran; before that time the company alone was responsible for debt charges. Even after the railway was completed to Tehran, the guarantee was chargeable, not on the Government revenue, but on the profits of the company's operation of tramways, mines, forests, and irrigation works. In essence, there was no guarantee by the Government at all, which left the promoter to raise his capital without being able to promise much security to investors. The clever and careful wording of the provisions relating to finance might have warned Reuter that while the Persian Court appeared to be giving away the Empire with one hand, they had well secured it with the other by making it extremely difficult to execute the concession. From the very beginning the stipulation regarding caution money placed the entrepreneur at great disadvantage. His position was further weakened by obscure but meaningful clauses in the concession through which the Government was able later to win legal skirmishes.

The concession was ratified on July 25, 1872. Three weeks later Reuter deposited £40,000 as caution money in the Bank of England, naturally expecting the delivery of the concession at once to his agent in Tehran. Instead Hussein Khan, the Grand Vizier, came forward with an additional article to be appended to the concession whereby no work could be undertaken under any clause of the concession until the details had been agreed to by both parties in a *cahier des charges*. In negotiating these agreements the Government's representative was to be Malkom Khan, the recently appointed Minister at the Court of St. James. Reuter attempted to resist this article, which was patently designed to delay and complicate matters, and he only gave in when he realized that time was passing and that the caution money might soon be forfeited. He therefore authorized the Tehran agent to accept the addition, whereupon the concession was dispatched to England.

Not even then was the last hurdle cleared, for when Reuter's agent applied to Malkom Khan for a *cahier* authorizing the purchase of railway material and the survey of the route, he was informed that the diplomat would prefer to deliver the document to the

---

[2] Resht is located on the Persian mainland and Enzeli (now Pahlevi) on a bar several miles from the shore. Between them is a shallow lagoon over which all passengers and freight must be ferried to meet the Caspian ships.

Baron personally when he arrived in London in the following spring during his trip to various European capitals in preparation for the expected visit of the Shah. As Malkom Khan proceeded westward in the spring of 1873, he was met and besieged by Reuter at Vienna, Berlin, Brussels, Paris, and London. At the latter city he was eventually cornered and forced to admit that there was yet another difficulty which must be surmounted before the concession could become effective. It seemed that instead of receiving an unencumbered and complete title to the concession, Reuter had obtained only a partial one, and that Malkom Khan held title for a fourth of the concession, which he could use to the great disadvantage of Reuter by disposing of it to any unfriendly party, perhaps even Russia. He was, however, willing to part with it for a consideration, and the consideration came rather high: £20,000 cash and three further annual payments of £10,000. But into the balance he threw a promise to secure from his Government an absolute guarantee for a stock issue, a promise which he failed to keep. With the days and weeks flitting by and still nothing accomplished, Reuter decided to accede to the diplomat's demands and bought the "fourth share" of his own concession. In return he obtained on July 5 a *cahier* which authorized his engineers to begin constructing the Resht-Tehran line. This was nineteen days short of a year since the original concession was signed, and there remained only three and a half months before the caution money would be forfeited....

Nothing daunted by the failure of this ruse, Reuter took the obvious course when he resumed his attempts to secure official Government aid and approval for the concession. As early as September 12, 1872, not more than two months after the concession had been granted, Baron de Reuter had addressed a letter to Earl Granville at the Foreign Office, notifying him that a concession of wide scope had been ratified by the Shah. In undertaking this project, the Baron declared, his purpose was twofold:

to improve the economic and social condition of the Persians and to advance British interests in that country. He represented his concession to be of high value to Great Britain as a counter to the advance of the Russians who were "making great progress with their railway towards the Caspian Sea," and as furnishing a link in the chain of transportation projects between England and India. In the last paragraph he revealed the request which he felt entitled to make: "I ... desire to feel assured that in the event of differences arising between the Persian Government and myself, Her Majesty's Government will recognize the validity of my scheme, and protect my rights, as a British subject, so far as may be within their power."

Before giving answer to this request, the Foreign Office consulted its sister department across the quadrangle, and since the question was intimately connected with the general problem of the protection of Indian frontiers and the extension of transportation routes to India, the India Office was largely responsible for the attitude assumed by the Government. In formulating a reply, the India Office officials already had before them a memorandum on "Railways in Persia," which had been drawn up a year previously by Sir Henry C. Rawlinson, whose long experience in the Middle East as an army officer and diplomat gave him a commanding position on the Council of State for India. This Elder Statesman in Indian affairs expressed a thorough-going scepticism of the commercial value of any transportation scheme in opening up the ancient kingdom of Persia to Western trade, of finding there a source of raw materials or a market for the products of European factories, or of raising Persia to a position of prominence in the social and economic regeneration of the East. "With regard," he wrote, "to planting a 'seed of progress' in Persia from which a rich harvest is to spring up and rejuvenate the country, I look upon all such hopes as visionary. The nation is effete and is even more incapable than Turkey of adopting European habits of vigorous thought or of moral sense. It is only important to us from its geographical position, and our interest in it must be restricted to that sole consideration."

If, however, the Persian railway were to be considered as a link in an overland line from Constantinople or Syria to India, then Sir Henry was willing to give it his support. He had constantly urged the construction of an all-land line from the Mediterranean to the Indus in preference to the highly publicized scheme for a Euphrates Valley railway to the Persian Gulf, which would be linked to India by sea. If his plan were executed, there would be no necessity for trans-shipment at a Persian Gulf port, forty hours would be saved, and troops could speedily be brought from England to repel any threat of Russia to India. When it became apparent that the Reuter concession envisaged a line from the Caspian to Tehran and the Gulf, and that construction was to start at the northern end of the route, Rawlinson lost interest in the project. Such a line, instead of forming a link in the Mediterranean-to-India railway, would cut across Persia in the opposite direction and would benefit Russia rather than England, especially in the early stages of construction before the line reached the Gulf.

The Government of India, dominated by members of the "masterly inactivity" school, demonstrated a lukewarm attitude toward the construction of railways to India, even to the less ambitious projects of a Euphrates Valley route. A similar indifference to a Mesopotamian railway was shown by the authorities in London, and although a Select Committee of the House of Commons designated to study the problem had reported that such a project was within the realm of possibility and desirable for imperial reasons, no definite steps were taken to get the plan under way. This lack of interest in a railway to the Persian Gulf could not fail to affect in a similar fashion any other proposals for railway construction in the Middle East.

In Government offices in Whitehall there was also a large measure of scepticism as to the financial soundness of the Reuter concession. It was obvious that an immense amount of capital would be needed to launch the railway alone, and that for tramway, mining, lumbering, and irrigation projects a large additional sum would be needed. In order to attract sufficient capital, ample security or definite prospects of a rapid return of invested money was needed, but neither existed under the Reuter scheme. India Office officials especially predicted that British capitalists would find the prospects so nebulous that they would refuse to risk money in the enterprise. Sir John Kaye, then Secretary of the Political and Secret Department, noting the high rate of interest offered by Reuter, wrote that "high interest is only another name for bad security."

In view of these disabilities, the Foreign Office replied in a distinctly discouraging tone to Baron de Reuter's request of September 12, 1872. Viscount Enfield notified the concessionnaire that "whilst Her Majesty's Government would view with satisfaction the efforts of the Shah's Government to increase, by means of railways and roads, the resources of Persia, they cannot bind themselves officially to protect your interests whilst carrying out your engagements with that Government."

Still undaunted by this refusal, Reuter made another request for assistance in May, 1873. This time he proposed altering the projected Persian railway to an east-west line to be linked up with a Turkish line which he would construct, the whole forming an all-land route from the Mediterranean to the borders of India. He maintained that the Ottoman Government would grant him a concession and the land required along a right-of-way running from Constantinople by an undefined route to Tehran and thence to India. To make this project feasible, he asked the British Government to give a contingent guarantee covering the Turkish guarantee on a stock issue, or alternately that Britain join with Turkey in a joint guarantee. The shrewd change made in the projected trace of the railway, rendering it more advantageous to Anglo-Indian interests and less to Russian, was calculated to enlist the support of that section of British officialdom which followed Rawlinson in advocating a land line to India. It was well planned, for while Sir Henry had been discouraging before, he now held that Reuter's project "might conduce most essentially to the prosperity of Persia and to the improvement of our political position in the East." Rawlinson believed that a Mediterranean-to-India line would be built "sooner rather than later" and that it was obviously desirable that England should control this railway either directly or indirectly.[3]

With this change of attitude among certain members of the Council for India, the Foreign Office passed the responsibility for answering Reuter's request to the Treasury. They replied shortly and succinctly that it "would be contrary to established rule for H.M. Government to guarantee interest on the cost of work undertaken in a foreign country..." and thus the Baron was refused aid for a second time.

In the meantime, the entrepreneur was having no more success in Persia than in England. After interminable procrastination on the part of the Persian authorities, Reuter had finally received a *cahier des charges* for the construction of a railway in July, 1873. In April of the same year, a party of engineers had been sent out to Persia and had begun to survey the line and prepare the roadbed. By the time that the Shah returned from his European journey in September, the roadbed had been completed for about half a mile southward from Resht. Soon the twenty-fifth day of October arrived, marking the end of the fifteen-month period within which the Baron was bound by the terms of the concession to begin construction. The roadbed had been extended another half-mile, the sleepers were in place, and the ballast laid; the only material lacking were the steel rails. They had been sent off from England on September 11 under contract to be delivered at Enzeli via Russia in five weeks, but the journey was long and difficult

3 F.O. 60/405, Memorandum by Rawlinson, June 5, 1873.

and vague charges were made that Russian officials had delayed the shipment. It was not until March of the following year that the rails arrived in Enzeli.

Not long after the deadline stipulated in the concession had passed, rumours began circulating in Tehran to the effect that the Government would declare the contract void. In a semi-official note the Minister for Foreign Affairs informed Reuter's agent on November 5 that such a step was being considered, and a few days later there appeared in the *Tehran Gazette* an official announcement that the concession was withdrawn since it was "evident that the Baron does not intend fulfilling his engagement or adhering to his concession." Subsequently in correspondence with Reuter, the Government adduced a second reason: the works of mining, foresting, and irrigation had not been commenced within the fifteen-month period.

In annulling the concession on the basis of the concessionnaire's failure to comply with the provisions of Article VII., the Persian Government interpreted the article very strictly, to say the least. According to the relevant clause, the caution money was to be returned to the Baron when a quantity of rails sufficient to cover the distance between Resht and Tehran had arrived at the port of Enzeli. The deposit was to be declared forfeit, however, if within fifteen months the "works" had not been commenced. The Shah's Ministers read the latter phrase as requiring the roadbed to be levelled, the ties in place, and the rails laid. But since the rails had not arrived, it was obviously impossible for the engineers to fulfil this requirement. . . .

With the Russian agent gone from the scene, the British Legation might have expected a respite in the tedious game of frustrating foreign concession hunters. Instead they continued to swoop down upon Persia, one after the other, like hawks after prey. Twice between 1875 and 1878 Dr. Tholozan, the French physician in attendance on the Shah, obtained for French interests a concession for navigation of the

Karun River, for a dam at Ahwaz, and for irrigation, mining, and public works projects in that area. Twice the concession was cancelled. Another Frenchman, M. Alléon, proceeded with the survey of a rail route from Resht to Tehran in 1878 before he was refused a contract. A German engineer presented a scheme for connecting Julfa with Bandar Abbas on the Persian Gulf, but was unsuccessful. A few years later the American Minister in Tehran was disappointed in a similar way. Against each of these proposed concessions the British Legation brought up the same objection: that they could not be valid as long as the Reuter concession was in force. And in each case this was a powerful check to the ambitions of Western commercial interests.

During the whole of the period from 1872 to 1889, Baron de Reuter, who originally obtained the concession, invested in it, and lost the caution money involved, had received no compensation. The British Minister was supposedly supporting unofficially his attempts to obtain satisfaction, but the Foreign Office was firm in maintaining that this support should be the same as that granted to any other British subject with a grievance against a foreign Government, and that in any case no official aid or diplomatic influence was to be employed. To emphasize the extremely distant view which the Foreign Office took of the Reuter concession, Lord Derby wrote in a dispatch that "although Baron Reuter may have suffered disappointment and probably injustice, from the failure to execute the contract, Her Majesty's Government are not prepared to say that the Persian Government were otherwise than well advised in cancelling it, when they came to appreciate its true bearing, at the earliest opportunity which presented itself."

Whilst holding this opinion toward Reuter, the British Government closely identified themselves with the Reuter concession when addressing the Persian Government in Tehran. Eminently satisfactory as this was for British public policy, it was scarcely a just arrangement for Baron de Reuter and his associates. For seventeen years Reuter pressed his claim for recompense and was not able to obtain redress until 1889. By that time it had become impossible for British diplomacy to hold back the flood of Western entrepreneurs. A French firm had obtained a railway concession in 1882 and finally finished a narrow-gauge line from the capital to Shah Abdul Aziz [Azim], a shrine six miles away. The concession was then transferred to a Belgian syndicate, which secured rights for tramway construction also. Sir Henry Drummond Wolff, the new British Minister, himself obtained a firman from the Shah opening to the commerce of the world the navigation of the Karun River.

Thus when the New Oriental Bank opened branches throughout Persia in 1888 and cultivated an entirely unploughed but fertile field, British policy demanded that such an influential enterprise be withdrawn from private hands. The Shah was urged to give Baron de Reuter a concession for a state bank to be known as the Imperial Bank of Persia, which then bought out the New Oriental Bank interests. The Imperial Bank received a monopoly of note issue in Persia and served as a Government depository.

The story of the Reuter concession illustrates in a lucid and concise manner the policy pursued by the British Government toward Persia in the nineteenth century. From the time when Persia was drawn into the realm of European politics until the Anglo-Russian agreement of 1907, the statesmen in London had constantly and consistently conceived that England's interest in the Middle East would be satisfied if the *status quo* was preserved. Such a programme would seem at first sight to be well adapted to the conditions of the area between the Euphrates and the borders of India, for there one found only a sparsely populated land, largely desert, divided into several kingdoms once powerful but now mere shadows. There were forces on the march, however, that would not be stayed by the will of British diplomats. An early forerunner of the approach of commercial and industrial enterprise was the telegraph. Cables were laid in Persian waters and wires strung across Persian plains by promoters who were mainly English.

Although the British Government could be persuaded of the necessity for telegraph lines and of their comparative ineffectiveness in affecting the *status quo*, they took an entirely different attitude toward transportation channels. Only a few years before, the Suez Canal had been opened, and already it had become apparent in inner circles that such an important portion of the new route to India could not remain under non-British control. If another line to India overland through Persia were developed, the drama of the Suez would be played over again with Persia rather than Egypt as the background. This the British Government was determined to forestall, and hence gave no encouragement to a project which in another time and another place would have received full Government approbation and support.

Instead they used the Reuter concession to defeat the attempts of would-be concessionnaires to wring other railway contracts from the Shah. Eventually such a policy became so unreal that it collapsed of its own weight, for even British power could not prevent the introduction of Western economic influences into this attractive undeveloped land. In the late 1880's Whitehall finally realized that they could no longer maintain a wall around Persia high enough to exclude the onward drive of expanding capitalistic states, and, trying to make the best of the altered situation, the Government at last changed their policy and used the Reuter concession as an effective counter in the scramble for control of the development of Persia, which continued at a high pitch until 1907 and even beyond to the Great War.

### Russian Railway Projects

The following selection is taken from the most thoroughly studied railway project made by the Russians, the report presented by the mission headed by V. A. Sakhanskii in 1900. As Professor Kazemzadeh has shown so clearly,[1] Russian policy toward railway building in Iran was influenced by opposing forces. On one hand, Russian industrialists wanted to open new channels, which would reduce the cost of delivering their goods in Iran; and railways also presented strategic advantages. But, on the other, there was the fear that railways in southern or western Iran would enable foreign competitors—first Britain and then Germany—to flood that country with cheaper and better goods and even to compete within the Russian Empire; more serious still, such railways would facilitate political or military penetration by Russia's rivals. To this should be added the scarcity of capital and the pressing need for funds for investment in domestic railways and other schemes. In the end, the negative arguments proved more convincing and the Russian government used all its power—in Iran as in northern Turkey—to block railway projects.

The first Russian project, drawn up in 1870 by a group of businessmen, was for a line from Enzeli to the Indian Ocean. In 1874, the Falkenhagen Concession— the Russian reply to the Reuter Concession—(see 4:7) provided for a railway from Julfa, on the Transcaucasian border, to Tabriz, a distance of eighty-five miles; as was usual in railway concessions at that time, it included mineral rights—in this

---

[1] "Russian Imperialism" and *Russia and Britain*, chaps. 3 and 5; the following account is based on these works.

case for coal lying within fifty miles of the line. As was also usual, Iran exempted the company from taxes and custom duties and guaranteed a minimum return on the capital invested—$6\frac{1}{2}$ percent; this was later reduced to 3 percent, with another 3 percent to be used for repayment of capital, and all further earnings were to be divided between Falkenhagen and the Iranian government in the ratio of 60 to 40. At the expiration of the forty-four year concession, Iran was to take over the line and rolling stock. But the Russian government failed to provide the necessary funds, about 3,500,000 rubles, and the concession lapsed.

The next attempt, in 1888, was made by a group of Russian merchants and manufacturers with a project for a line between the Caspian and the Arabian Sea. Preliminary agreement was reached with the French Banque d'Escompte for raising 300 million francs. But the scheme was frustrated by the Ministry of Foreign Affairs, who judged it in Russia's interest to block all railways in Iran, whether British or Russian, and secured an undertaking from the shah not to grant any concessions before 1900. Various suggestions for a line through Khurasan also failed to materialize, partly because of British opposition.

As is shown in the following selection, the Sakhanskii project recommended immediate construction of lines in northern Iran, but the Russian government continued to adhere to its basic policy and succeeded in preventing any major railway building until the First World War.

There was, however, one exception. On 6 February 1913, the Iranian government gave the Russian Discount and Loan Bank a seventy-five year concession for a railway from Julfa to Tabriz (eighty-five miles), with a thirty-mile branch to Urumiya. The concession included the right to exploit oil and coal deposits within sixty miles on either side of the line. The Company—which was to be exclusively Russian—was exempted from Persian taxes and was to hand over to the Iranian government half its net profits from railway operations and 5 percent of those from mining. By 1916 the line had been completed as far as Urumiya and was being used for military transport.

(See also works by Kazemzadeh, Entner, Martin, Jamalzadeh, Taymuri, Romanov, Lomnitskii, Ter-Gukasov, Popov, and Rittikh, listed in the bibliography.)

### Selection 8. Russian Railway Schemes, 1900
[P. A. Rittikh, *Otchet o poezdke v Persiyu* (Saint Petersburg, 1901), part 1, pp. 18–37]

The approximate cost of the proposed line from Rasht to Tehran through Qazvin can be estimated on the basis of the accurate data worked out for the cost of the line from Alyat Astara to Rasht, and the two lines from Kivrag to Tabriz [see below].

The first section of the line, stretching across 35 versts [a verst equaled 1,067 meters] from Rasht would be built in conditions identical with those of the Astara-Rasht section, and can therefore be estimated at 44,000 rubles a verst.

The second section, from the 35th to the 85th verst, is equal in cost to the Kivrag-Khoi-Tabriz line, and can therefore be put at 56,000 per verst.

The third and most difficult section, from

the 85th to the 150th verst, can be estimated at 80,000 per verst, an amount equal to the cost of the Kivrag-Marand-Tabriz line; to this should be added the cost of 1,750 *sajens* [a *sajen* equaled 2.13 meters] of tunnels at the rate of 2,500 rubles a *sajen*.

The fourth section, from the 150th to 160th verst, can be put at 56,000 per verst.

The fifth section, from the 160th to the 310th verst, that is, to the town of Tehran, can again be estimated at 44,000 rubles a verst of straight line, since its cost is comparable to that of the Astara-Rasht section.

Putting together these data, we get the following total cost for the line from Rasht to Tehran:

| | RUBLES |
|---|---|
| 1) Section in plain | |
| 35 versts at 44,000 = | 1,540,000 |
| 2) Section in foothills | |
| 50 versts at 56,000 = | 2,800,000 |
| 3) Section in mountains | |
| 65 versts at 80,000 = | 5,200,000 |
| Tunnels | |
| 1,750 *sajens* at 2,500 = | 4,375,000 |
| 4) Section in foothills | |
| 10 versts at 56,000 = | 560,000 |
| 5) Section in plain | |
| 170 versts at 44,000 = | 7,480,000 |
| 330 versts at 66,530 = | 21,955,000 |

. . . The length of the line from Tehran to Bandar Bushire and Bandar Abbas is as follows:

Tehran to Bandar Bushire     1,490 versts
Tehran to Bandar Abbas     1,530 versts

To determine the cost of the three above-mentioned lines, to Bandar Bushire, to Bandar Abbas, and to Chahbar [Chahar Bahar], one should bear in mind that all three would be implemented in almost identical conditions in respect to materials and labor force, for all three would be built in a country with a homogeneous culture and with almost identical climatic and topographic features.

Except for earth, stones, and sand, no materials are available locally, and everything else has to be brought in from Russia. One can obtain limestone, alabaster, and clay, but the lack of fuel raises considerably the cost of lime, gypsum, and bricks. The only means of conveyance are pack animals,

and in inadequate amount, for the inhabitants are poor and their donkeys, mules, and horses are sufficient only for their own limited needs. There is no wheeled transport anywhere, although in many places the roads are suitable for carts or hearses.

In northern and central Persia, one may find unskilled masons. In the southern parts, especially on the Chahbar line, workmen would have to be brought in from northern Persia. Supplying the workmen with food raises serious problems, for on the Yazd-Chahbar line wheat for the local population is brought from western Persia.

The terrain is everywhere difficult: pebbles, loess with pebbles, and many stony and rocky soils. Rocks largely consist of shale. Over the whole course, water is very scanty. Large rivers are very rare, and the small streams dry up. One can count only on the waters of *qanats* or *kariz*, that is, underground water collected by means of galleries and wells [see 5:1]. Except for those built over irrigation canals, few bridges and culverts [*iskustvennikh sooruzhenii*] would be needed. On the Bandar Bushire line there are seven large rivers, on the Bandar Abbas line eight, and on the Chahbar line four. Such works would be expensive, because of the high cost of supplying cement and the insufficiency of water.

In order to estimate costs, let us divide the lines into sections with minor and major works, respectively.

1. The Tehran-Isfahan-Shiraz-Bandar Bushire line (following the valley of the Kara Agach river from Shiraz). The entire length is 1,490 versts, of which 740 need minor work and 750 major.
2. The Tehran-Isfahan-Shiraz-Bandar Abbas line. The entire length is 1,530 versts, of which 740 need minor work and 790 major.
3. The Tehran-Kashan-Yazd-Kirman-Chahbar line. The entire length is 1,635 versts, of which 1,000 need minor work and 635 major. . . . The total amount, per verst, is for the lines:

1. Tehran-Bandar Bushire . . . . . . 70,700 rubles
2. Tehran-Bandar Abbas . . . . . . . 70,900 rubles
3. Tehran-Chahbar . . . . . . . . . 68,400 rubles

On this basis, the cost of the lines is:

*a.* Tehran-Bandar Bushire

1,490 × 70,000 = 105,743,000 rubles

*b.* Tehran-Bandar Abbas

1,530 × 70,900 = 108,477,000 rubles

*c.* Tehran-Chahbar

1,635 × 68,400 = 111,834,000 rubles

exclusive of the cost of rolling stock.

Adding to the above figures the cost of rolling stock for four pairs of trains, that is, 14,900,000 rubles, 15,300,000 rubles, and 16,350,000 rubles respectively, and also the cost of the railway and rolling stock from Alyat to Rasht (15,358,250 + 3,450,000) and from Rasht to Tehran (25,100,000), the total cost of the lines and rolling stock from Alyat station on the Transcaucasian railway through Persia are:

1. To the town of Bandar Bushire, with a total length of 2,145 versts                    164,151,250 rubles

or, in round figures, 164,000,000 rubles

2. To the town of Bandar Abbas, with a total length of 2,185 versts                    167,685,250 rubles

or, in round figures, 168,000,000 rubles

3. To Chahbar bay, with a total length of 2,290 versts                    172,092,250 rubles

or, in round figures, 172,000,000 rubles

Adding to the above a sum of 15,000,000, for the construction of naval and commercial ports, the final costs of construction for the above-mentioned lines are:

For the Alyat-Rasht-Tehran-Bandar Bushire line                    179,000,000

For the Alyat-Rasht-Tehran-Bandar Abbas line                    183,000,000

For the Alyat-Rasht-Tehran-Chahbar line                    187,000,000

All the above estimates are based on the assumptions that the lines will be built with government funds. Should they be built by private capital, it is necessary to add 30,000,000 to take account of losses incurred in raising [*pri realizatsii*] the capital and of interest during the period of construction.[1] ...

[1] As is pointed out in the Memorandum on Persian Railways, presented at the India Office on 20 June 1911 (FO 371/1186, p. 14), these estimates of cost are far too low. Thus the cost per verst on the Chahbar line is put at £8,500, whereas the Siberian and Manchurian railways, which were built in much easier terrain, cost £12,285 and £17,850 per verst, respectively.

WESTWARD DIRECTION

The surveys carried out have shown that the most advantageous line, from every point of view, from the western part of the Caucasus (from the Kars branch) is: prolonging the Erivan branch to the customs house of Shah Takhti, the town of Khoi, through the province of Dilman, along the shore of Lake Urmia, and on to the town of Tabriz.

This line captures the most fertile provinces of Azerbaijan, around Lake Urmia, and from the technical point of view is the most convenient for construction and exploitation. The building of that line would finally destroy the supply of European goods to Azerbaijan and southwest Persia from Trebizond; national [i.e., Russian] industry would not only wholly dominate the market of Azerbaijan but would also have the possibility of sending goods from Tabriz toward the south, and there successfully competing with goods coming through the Persian Gulf.

By building a railway to Tabriz, Russia would in fact place Azerbaijan in the same situation as Bukhara; this will more than satisfy the local population, for the general dream of all the inhabitants of Azerbaijan is that Russia should intervene in the government of the country and put it in order.

The length of the Erivan-Julfa line from Kivrag station is 302 versts, of which 290 would be in Persia. The steepest gradient is 0.015. The cost of the line, excluding rolling stock, would be 17,788,465 rubles, or 58,902 per verst.

EASTWARD DIRECTION

For the eastern side, a survey was carried out from the station of Alyat, on the Transcaucasian railway, along the shore to the small town of Salyan, through the district center of Lankoran, to the customs post of Astara and further along the seashore to the Persian town of Rasht.

This line has immense importance for Russian trade, for it would join Persia to the center of Russia, Moscow, directly by the shortest route, through the towns of Petrovsk and Rostov. Moreover, if prolonged to the Indian Ocean, it would have a world significance and could serve as a transit route for passengers and valuable goods to the Far East, India, Africa, and Australia.

Even the building of a line to Rasht would spare our trade the enormous expenses incurred in carrying, and transshipping, goods to Enzeli. Goods arrive at Enzeli on steamers and sailing ships, which can seldom reach the shore because the bar can be crossed only if several favorable conditions prevail [see 4:1]. Usually, unloading is done by means of lighters [*kirzhimy*], which carry the goods to Enzeli. In Enzeli the merchandise is again transshipped, by boats, across the Murdab bay, to the Pir-i Bazar river. For the third time the goods are transferred to small boats, which are towed or rowed up the river to the landing stage, also called Pir-i Bazar, where the Rasht-Qazvin highway ends.

Until recently, all goods were loaded at Pir-i Bazar on pack animals, and only with the completion of the Rasht-Qazvin highway, a short while ago, has wheeled traffic appeared. With the building of a railway to Rasht, all these expenses would vanish, modern means of transport would be provided, and our goods would be predominant not only in Tehran but in all northern Persia, up to and including Isfahan. All the paths used by pack animals in the south, that is, in the direction of the Persian Gulf, by which foreign goods penetrate into the northern and central parts of Persia, are so rough, inconvenient, and expensive, that I am convinced that if we reduce our cost of transport and increase its speed all foreign goods will have to give way to Russian.

The length of the line from Alyat to Rasht would be 345 versts and has only very slight gradients, not exceeding 0.005. The length of the section of that line lying in Persia, that is, from the customs post of Astara to Rasht, is 155 versts and the cost of the whole railway, excluding rolling stock, would be 15,358,250 rubles, or 44,517 rubles

per verst. Assuming that, to begin with, for both lines four pairs of trains would be needed, and assuming their cost to be 10,000 rubles per verst of line, the cost of both railways (302 plus 345, or 647 versts) would be $17,788,465 + 15,358,250 + (647 \times 10,000) = 39,716,715$ rubles. Assuming that both railways could be built in three years, Russia would, at the cost of about 13,000,000 rubles a year, have acquired 647 versts of line and established itself firmly both in Azerbaijan and ,in Iran.

With the completion of the line to Rasht, that to Tehran—with a length of 310 versts and a cost of 22,000,000 rubles, estimated on the basis of detailed reconnoitering—would be only a question of time.

Having control over the two main vital arteries of the country, Russia would acquire a dominant position in Persia and would no longer fear commercial competition from European markets. But to acquire this favorable situation, it is necessary to start work soon, for although competition through the Persian Gulf is not be to feared, owing to the inaccessibility of the terrain, there is the danger of an influx of British goods from India, through Sistan, in the east and of German goods through Asia Minor in the west. Last year, Germany obtained a concession for building a railway in the Tigris-Euphrates valley and, in expectation of an economic struggle with England in the Persian Gulf, German capitalists have begun to turn their attention to the Persian market and are seeking to find a way for their products, through Mesopotamia, to western Persia and even Azerbaijan. *Because of its highly developed industry, Germany is now a more dangerous competitor than Britain; hence the question of connecting our railway network with the Persian centers must be solved as quickly as possible, before the construction of the German railway attains its full development.*

LINES FROM TEHRAN TO THE SOUTH

The prolongation of the railway from Tehran south, to the ports of the Persian

Gulf and the Indian Ocean, is possible but requires the construction of a difficult stretch from Tehran to:

1. Bandar Bushire—1,490 versts, at a cost of 179,000,000 rubles including the construction of a port.

2. Bandar Abbas—1,530 versts, at a cost of 183,000,000 rubles.

The commercial importance of these two lines would not be great, since the annual trade of the main ports of the Gulf—Bandar Bushire, Lingah, Bandar Abbas, and Muhammarah—is £2,091,224 for imports and £1,273,770 for exports, or a total of 3,364,994 pounds sterling. Adding a sum of £130,282 for the goods arriving overland through Sistan to Khurasan, we get an annual turnover of £3,495,976, or about 32,000,000 rubles. One cannot count on the development of local traffic in the near future because of the sparseness of population in these localities, their topographical conditions, and the political situation of the country.

Nor could these lines have any political significance, since an outlet to the Persian Gulf would not give Russia convenient access to the ocean; for, in the first place, there is not a single good natural harbor in the Persian Gulf, and, second, the British completely control the gulf, the Straits of Oman, and the Muscat shore, thanks to the fleet they constantly maintain in these waters and the Indian army they have at their command. An outlet on to the Indian Ocean through the bay of Chahbar, the only natural harbor in Persia, would have more political significance, for it would give direct access to the ocean. But here too one cannot count on local traffic, even in the most distant future, for the country through which the railway would pass consists almost wholly of barren, stony, scantily watered mountain valleys, bordered on east and west by mountain peaks and salty deserts. A line built in this direction could be made remunerative only by the transit of passengers and valuable goods, seeking quick transport between Europe and the Far East, India, Africa, and Australia. The question of transit is so complex that its profitability for the line can be judged only by careful study of the present movement of passengers and goods to and from Europe and the designated directions.

In conclusion, it is necessary to add that, in general, the construction of railways through Persia to the southern ports would be advantageous only if Russia has the right to levy customs duties; for if this cannot be done, those railways would facilitate the entry of foreign goods into Persia, to the detriment of our trade not only in the central but also in the northern parts of the country.

V. A. Sakhanskii

## German Railway Projects

Germany was a latecomer in the Middle East and its efforts were largely concentrated on Turkey (see EHME, pp. 91–106). Indeed, as far as Iran was concerned, German plans "were merely an afterthought to German plans for Turkey."[1]

The first round of German imperialism in Persia took place in 1898. It was concerned with the implementation of a road and railway concession from Baghdad to Tehran—a branch of the Baghdad Railway. The second round took place between 1906 and 1911 when German interest in Persia shifted into the domain of banking and political matters. At this time also, the hope of driving a branch of the Baghdad Railway into Persia was still current. But in the Russo-German Convention of 1911, Germany's drive to the Iranian plateau was crippled by a Russian diplomatic coup, marking a temporary halt in German hopes of gaining influence there.[2]

[1] Martin, p. 200; the following account is based on this book.
[2] Ibid., p. 9.

Both the Iranian government and nationalist circles, in their search for a force to counterbalance Britain and Russia, began to look to Germany as early as the 1870s. But Bismarck, whose policy was based on the necessity of good German-Russian relations, avoided involvement. After his fall in 1890, the German government became more venturesome, but its attempts were frustrated by Russian and British opposition. Railway plans were blocked (see chap. 4, introduction) and those pursued between 1905 and 1910 for establishing a German bank in Iran failed to materialize (see 8:2). At the outbreak of the First World War, Germany's interests in Iran, though growing, were still minor (see 8:4).

(See also works by Martin, Earle, Wolf, Chapman, Kazemzadeh, Jamalzadeh, and Litten, listed in the bibliography.)

## Selection 9. German Railway Schemes, 1903–6
[E. R. J. Brunner, *De Bagdadspoorweg* (Groningen-Djakarta, 1957), pp. 292–95]

... The Germans, however, did not stay waiting with their hands in their lap, but now turned their attention to Persia. Taking advantage of the experience they had had in Turkey, the German engineers felt that the construction of rail lines in Persia could also be undertaken, which meant that the border region of Turkey and Persia stood in the center of their interest. This was not as strange as it first seems.

By the treaty of March 1903, the Germans had obtained the right to construct different branches from the trunk line. As early as 1903 they had set their eye on Arbil and Khaneqin, places in the Turkish border region. This border region had now become more important because of the exploitation of oil sources. Precisely in connection with this, the idea occurred to the German engineers, and to the board of directors of the Deutsche Bank as well, that these branch lines would have a great future, if they succeeded in penetrating into Persia proper by means of a rail line from Arbil and Khaneqin in the direction of Tehran. The major hindrance until then, however, was that they had to await a favorable opportunity to interest Turkey as well as Persia in it. But a ready occasion for this arose when the Persian government, after applying in vain for a loan from England and Russia, in anger turned to the German bankers to solve the financial difficulties of the Persian treasury by means of credit. With this the Germans, who by then had obtained a strong footing in Persia through the shipping communications of the H.A.P.A.G. between Hamburg and South Persia, had the opportunity to capture a place in the financial sphere.

When, at the beginning of June, the Persian foreign minister stated to the German chargé d'affaires in Tehran that there were no objections to the establishment of a German commercial bank and that he would gladly have further discussions about it, the German government responded that it was inclined to comply with the wishes of the Persians. The negotiations were conducted rather hurriedly. An agreement was very quickly reached with the Persian government whereby the Germans would receive permission to establish a bank which would occupy itself with financing different projects that the Persian government wished to undertake in the interest of the country's economic development. There were no difficulties to be expected from the Persian side, then, concerning the cherished German railroad plans, but there were from another side. In connection with this it should not be forgotten that Persia until then had been the economic domain where English and Russian expansion could assert itself without fear of foreign intervention.

It was rather evident from Iswolski's utterances to Schoen in May that Russia continued to follow the economic and political development of Persia with the greatest attention. Therefore, in Berlin, they deemed it better to enter into contact with the Russians before going further. The German ambassador at Saint Petersburg received orders, for that reason, to declare emphatically that the German enterprises, with their activity in Persia, pursued exclusively and only economic aims and that they had no political intentions for the future.

However, in England and in Russia, the action of the Germans had made a profound impression. It gave rise to all sorts of suppositions in the press, and the governments in both countries were also very suspicious of German activities. But, owing to the increasing confusion in Persia, neither of the above-mentioned powers found any opportunity to take steps with the Persian government. However, it was noticeable that Russia did not show itself as worried as England. This was so because, in connection with the Persian Gulf, an internationalization of Persia or of portions of it would be much less pleasant for England than for Russia, as then Germany too would have some control. Since, owing to the revolution which broke out in Persia in July 1906, the German-Persian treaty which was reached with the previous government lost its validity, the British and Russian governments felt it would be best to assume an expectant attitude. . . .

## British Railway Projects

Like the Russians, the British were of two minds about railways in Iran. Britain was the great railway builder of the nineteenth century, and British-built lines had stimulated the country's exports both directly and indirectly. Faced with growing Russian commercial competition in Iran, the British increasingly felt the need for modern means of transport in the southern and central parts of the country. But, by the same token, railways in the north would facilitate Russian economic and political penetration. And, above all, it was feared that railways would enable Russia to threaten Britain's military and naval position in the Persian Gulf, Indian Ocean, and Afghanistan, and to undermine the defenses of India. In the end, British policy, like Russian, blocked railway construction in Iran.

Various schemes, based on wildly optimistic assumptions, were put forward as early as the 1850s for a railway from India to the Mediterranean, through Iran, Iraq, and Syria, but neither they nor somewhat more modest ones for lines from Iraq to the Mediterranean materialized (see EHME, pp. 137–45). The Iranian section of that line was doomed by the report of the Select Committee of the House of Commons of 1872:

As regards the terminus on the Persian Gulf, your Committee are decidedly of opinion that it would be better to carry the line to some point where it might be brought into communication with the steam vessels which are now under Government subvention to carry the mails, and which ply from the Indian ports to Basra [see 4: 4], than to continue it along the coast to Karachi by a very expensive, and probably unremunerative route.

The first serious attempt, the Reuter Concession of 1872, received little official British backing and was defeated by determined Russian opposition (see 4:7).

In 1878, a plan was presented for a British-built line from Tehran to the upper Karun. In 1888, in an attempt to counter Russian railway schemes in the north,the British ambassador obtained from the shah a statement "that our former promise with regard to the priority of the English Government over others in the construction of a southern railway to Tehran continues to hold good; and, certainly, whenever railway concessions in the north, etc., are given to others, immediately a Concession for a railway from Tehran to Shuster, or such a one, will be given to the English Company."[1] The following year a scheme for a line from Quetta through Baluchistan to the borders of Sistan was discussed in British circles.[2] But all these schemes were ended by the agreement between Russia and Iran of 1890 prohibiting railway construction in the country for ten years, a period later extended for another ten years (see 4:8).

By 1908, the approach of the end of this "sterilizing" agreement, the easing of Anglo-Russian tensions produced by the 1907 agreement, and fears of German railway schemes in Iraq and western Iran (see 4:9), combined to revive British railway schemes. Several routes, starting from various Persian Gulf ports, were proposed, as was the extension of the Indian railway from Nushki and even the linking of Karachi with Yazd.[3] British officials and businessmen in Iran pressed for a line starting from the Karun area. The ambassador advocated a Muhammarah-Khurramabad railway, since "a direct route would be provided to the district, of which the distributing centre is Hamadan, from where 40 per cent of British imports into Persia are distributed. This current of British trade now passes *via* Bagdad" and was threatened by the projected German railway to Hamadan. The managing director of the Anglo-Persian Oil Company suggested a line from Ahwaz to Sultanabad, via Shushtar, Dizful, and Burujird "which would give easy road communication to Kermanshah, Hamadan, Isfahan and Tehran . . . the cost would certainly not be more than £2,000,000 to £3,000,000."

The following selection shows the outcome of these discussions. The capital of the syndicate was fixed at £15,000, of which the Euphrates and Tigris Steam Navigation Company group subscribed £5,000, the APOC group £3,000, and the Imperial Bank of Persia group £2,500.[4] The concession had the usual provisions: exclusive rights of mechanical transport within a zone of 50 kilometers on either side, exemption from taxes and customs duties, free provision of land, survey to be carried out at government expense, government guarantee of minimum income to assure the syndicate 5 percent of gross receipts. The gauge was to be either one meter or 2 feet 6 inches.[5]

---

[1] "Memorandum on Persian Railways," India Office, 20 June 1911, FO 371/1186, pp. 4–5; a marginal note adds that the reference to the "former promise" is not clear, and Kazemzadeh, p. 217, denies its existence and suggests it was invented for the occasion.

[2] Ibid., pp. 9–10.

[3] Ibid., pp. 36–43.

[4] APOC to FO, 10 August 1911, FO 371/1186, giving a breakdown; this distribution remained unchanged—see list in FO 371/1710.

[5] Greenway to FO, 11 August 1911, and Greenway to Mallet, 7 September 1911, FO 371/1186.

Some preliminary surveying was done on the Muhammarah line, but the scheme soon became part of a much larger enterprise, the projected Trans-Persian Railway (see Chap. 4, introduction). As a result, no British railways were built in Iran, except for the 104-mile extension of the Indian railways to Duzdab (Zahidan) laid down during the First World War.

(See also works by Greaves, Kazemzadeh, Avery, Jamalzadeh, and Taymuri listed in the bibliography.)

**Selection 10. British Railway Schemes, 1911**
[Anglo-Persian Oil Company to Foreign Office, "Memorandum Respecting Persian Railways," 15 July 1911, FO 371/1186]

*Winchester House, Old Broad Street, London*
Sir,

I beg to enclose copy of a memorandum which, at their request, I have handed to His Highness Prince Ala-e-Saltaneh and to his Excellency the Persian Minister, giving a rough outline of our proposals in connection with the Persian railways.

Should you consider it advisable to modify what has been said in any respect, I shall be glad to hear from you, and I will, if necessary, send His Highness and his Excellency an amended memorandum.

I have, &c.
C. Greenway,
*Managing Director*

Enclosure

MEMORANDUM RESPECTING PERSIAN RAILWAYS

Our group, which will be called the Persian Railways Syndicate, and will be composed of:—

1. The Anglo-Persian Oil Company group, including—
   Lord Strathcona,
   Mr. W. K. D'Arcy,
   Mr. J. T. Cargill,
   Mr. Tarbett Fleming,
   Mr. C. W. Wallace,
   Mr. Frank Strick,
   Mr. R. W. Adamson,
   Mr. C. Greenway, &c.;

2. The Imperial Bank and Persian Transport Company group, including—
   Sir Thomas Jackson,
   Sir Thomas Gordon,
   Mr. H. B. Lynch, &c.;

3. The British-Indian Steam Navigation Company group, including—
   Lord Inchcape,
   Mr. W. A Buchanan, &c.;

4. The British and Foreign General Securities and Investment Trust, including—
   Mr. T. B. Bowring,
   Mr. Alex. B. Williamson, &c.;

5. The Weetman Pearson group, including—
   Lord Cowdray,
   Sir Clarendon Hyde, &c.;

will be prepared to enter into contracts for, and undertake construction of, the following railways in Persia:—

1. From Mohammerah and/or Khor Musa to Khoramabad or Burujird,
2. From Bunder Abbas to Kerman,
3. From Bunder Abbas to Shiraz,
4. From Bunder Abbas to Mohammerah;

with a view to the eventual carrying on of the first three of these lines as below:—

5. (1.) From Khoramabad to Tehran, viâ Burujird, Dowlatabad, and Hamadan, or viâ Burujird, Sultanabad, and Kom,
6. (2.) From Kerman to Ispahan, viâ Yezd,
7. (3.) From Shiraz to Tehran, viâ Ispahan, Kashan, and Kom.

As Persia cannot, obviously, for financial reasons deal with the whole of these systems at once, it is proposed that they should be taken in hand one by one in the above order in accordance with Persia's ability to provide the necessary guarantees, for the capital required.

The line from Mohammerah and/or Khor Musa to Khoramabad is suggested as the first one that should be constructed, because (1) it will give the readiest communication with the Persian Gulf, for the whole of the trade of the north-west of Persia, including Tehran, being connected by caravan routes or roads with Kermanshah on the west; with Burujird, Dowlatabad, Hamadan, Zindjan, and Kasvin on the north; Sultanabad, Kom, and Tehran on the north-east; and with Ispahan on the east; and (2) will, therefore, by attracting the trade of the important districts, of which these towns are the centres, offer the best prospects of remunerative working.

It would also place Tehran within four or five days' communication of the Persian Gulf, instead of the present fifteen to twenty days.

CAPITAL

It is proposed that the capital should be raised by means of "State railway loans," secured by (1) such revenues of the Persian Government as may be available for hypothecation, and (2) the railway and its earnings.

At present the only revenue within sight available for such a purpose is the surplus shown in the southern customs after meeting outstanding liabilities. This, however, is too small for the purpose in view, but it is possible that the Treasurer-General may before long, either by augmenting existing sources of revenue, or by devising new ones, be able to provide the necessary security.

The capital cannot, in the present position of Persia, be obtained without the securities indicated above, because (1) the possibilities of Persia as a field for the remunerative investment of capital in railways are entirely unknown to investors, and (2) even if there were more knowledge on this point investors would not be willing to invest in Persian railways without substantial guarantees, because public information in Europe leads to the assumption that there is great political insecurity in the country.

The bonds issued in connection with the "State railway loans" would be 5 per cent. bonds, and they would be purchased by the syndicate in the same manner as the bonds which are to be issued for the recent Persian Government loan of 1,250,000l., i.e., at say 87½ per cent. for each 100l., and the nett amount provided by the loans must for each line suffice to cover (1) cost of surveys; (2) cost of construction and equipment, including cost of wharves, jetties, &c., that may be required at ports, and administration expenses during construction; and to relieve the Persian Government of this obligation until the railways are working, it would also be well to include (3) interest on the bonds during the period of construction. It might also be necessary to include amortization.

The bonds would be issued for a period of years, say twenty-five to thirty years, with the right of redemption to the Persian Government at par at any time after five to ten years, either out of the amortization fund, and/or out of the Government revenues.

ADMINISTRATION

The syndicate would be willing to undertake the construction of the lines on behalf of the Persian Government as "State railways," but they would stipulate that the construction should be undertaken by themselves, and that the railways should, as in other countries, be worked under their supervision until such time as the Persian Government were in a position to pay off the loans.

To facilitate the latter, it might be arranged that the loan or loans in respect of each complete railway should be earmarked, thus giving the Persian Government the opportunity of taking over and administering each railway as its loan (or loans) is liquidated.

## Transport: Distances, Time, and Costs

As the following table shows, until the First World War the bulk of transport within Iran, as well as that between it and Turkey, Iraq, and Afghanistan, was still made by pack animals.

The only method of transporting goods in Persia is by pack-animals. Camels, mules, ponies, and donkeys are all used in different parts of the country and under different circumstances. The ordinary load for a camel is about 400 lbs., though under favourable conditions as much as 480 lbs. is sometimes carried; 200 to 250 lbs. is a fair load for a mule or pony, and a donkey-load may be reckoned at about 130 lbs. Both loads and prices depend much on the nature of the country and the season of the year. The cheapness or scarcity of forage also naturally affects prices. In summer drivers feed their animals by allowing them to graze for many hours daily by the road and this habit makes the time occupied on a journey longer in summer than in winter.[1]

Additional information on freight rates at that time is also available. Between Ahwaz and Isfahan the rate during 1910 was 3.98 krans per shahman and between Isfahan and Ahwaz 2.37 krans.[2] A rough average was £19 to 20 per ton[3] for the 277 mile, twenty-six-day journey. In 1909 the following rates prevailed:[4]

| | | | |
|---|---|---|---|
| Ahwaz–Tehran. . . .— | 35 to 50 days | —2s. 10d. for | 13 lbs. |
| Rasht–Tehran . . . .— | 14 days | —£3 to 4 for | 654 lbs. |
| Kermanshah–Tehran .—290 miles—20 to 25 days | | —£4 for | 654 lbs. |
| Bushire–Shiraz . . .—178 miles—16 days | | —£2.16.0 for | 733 lbs. |
| Shiraz–Isfahan . . . .—312 miles—16 days | | —£2.4.0 for | 733 lbs. |
| Isfahan–Tehran. . . .—271 miles—16 days (by mule) | | —1s. 3d. for | 131 lbs. |
| Isfahan–Tehran. . . .—271 miles—25 days (by camel) | | —1s. for | 13 lbs. |
| Bandar Abbas–Kirman—289 miles—30 to 35 days (by camel) | | | |
| | 20 to 25 (by donkey) | —£3 to 4 for | 654 lbs. |
| Bandar Abbas–Yazd .— | 35 to 45 days (by camel), | —£5.10.0 to | |
| | 30 to 35 by donkey | £9 for | 654 lbs. |
| Quetta–Nushki . . .— | 1 day | —½d. for | 78 lbs. |
| Nushki–Sistan . . . .—569 miles—30 days | | —10s. for | 78 lbs. |
| Sistan–Mashad . . .—574 miles—30 days | | —10s. for | 78 lbs. |

Freight rates showed sharp seasonal fluctuations. Thus in 1911/12 rates for the journey from Bandar Abbas to Kirman (25 to 35 days) moved between a high of 350 krans in November 1911 and a low of 115 in March 1912.[5] Still more violent fluctuations were caused by such factors as insecurity or shortage of fodder. Thus, on the Bushire-Shiraz road, both seasonal and other factors are reflected in the following table.[6]

| Year | Price per 738 lbs. (Krans) |
|---|---|
| 1902 . . . . . . | 80 |
| 1904 . . . . . . | 80, 90 |
| 1905 . . . . . | 85, 95, 75, 110 |
| 1906–7 . . . . . | 150, 220, 240, 150 |
| 1907–8 . . . . . | 160, 120, 110, 90, 140 |
| 1908–9 . . . . . | 140, 160, 170, 220 |
| | 200, 250, 300, 310, 240, 200 |

[1] "Persia—Notes by E. F. Law on British Trade and Foreign Competition," A and P 1889, 77:10. See also MacLean, p. 52 for somewhat different figures.

[2] "Persia," A and P 1910, 94:23.

[3] "Arabistan," A and P 1914–16, 74:9.

[4] "Persia," A and P 1910, 101:6–7.

[5] "Bandar Abbas," A and P 1912, 98:11.

[6] "Bushire," A and P 1910, 101:9.

An interesting estimate of the total amount spent on transport on the same road is available; the amount carried from Bushire to Shiraz in those years was around 8,000 tons.

In normal years, before the institution of the Persian Constitution, it is reckoned that at least £40,000 was paid for hire between Bushire and Shiraz, only some 185 miles. These rates worked out at about 1¼ krans (5½d.) per ton per mile for the upward journey and for the downward journey about ½ kran (2¼d.) per mile.

During recent years of disorder, however, as much as £70,000 to £80,000 has been paid annually for transport hire. This can well be seen from the figures given for the year under report, where as regards imports up-country alone an average of 20 to 25 tomans per 100 máns was maintained. Reckoning two mules to the 100 máns and an average departure of 3,000 mules up-country every month, we get a total cost of £65,000 to £80,000 paid for mule hire. Cost of downward transport is often only one-fourth or one-fifth that of upward transport, but at least £15,000 to £20,000 cannot be an excessive estimate.[7]

[7] "Bushire," A and P 1913, 71:22.

## Selection 11. Cost of Transport, 1903
[H. W. MacLean, "Report on the Con- ditions and Prospects of British Trade in Persia," A and P 1904, 95, pp. 77-79]

| ROUTE | MEANS OF TRANSPORT | AP-PROXI-MATE DIS-TANCE IN MILES | BALE GOODS | | | | | MER-CHANDISE DE-LIVERED IN DAYS |
|---|---|---|---|---|---|---|---|---|
| | | | RATE OF TRANSPORT (Local Usage) | EQUIVALENT RATE | | | | |
| | | | | Per Khar-war (650 lbs.) | Per Ton (2,240 lbs.) | Per Ton per Mile | | |
| | | | | Krs. | £ stg. | Pence. | | |
| Ahwaz to Ispahan . . . | { Mule, Donkey } | 277 | { Krs. 4 per Shuster man of 15.45 lbs. Krs. 3.75 per Shuster man in 1903. | 167 | 10.54 | 9.12 | | 26 |
| Ahwaz tram . . . . . . | . . . . . | 1¼ | Krs. 3 per ton | . . . | .05 | . . . | | . . . |
| Ardebil-Hamadan . . . | Camel, mule | . . . | Krs. 150 per Kharwar Tabriz | 150 | . . . . | . . . | | 20 |
| Ashkabad-Meshed . . . | Wagon or camel | 160 | Krs. 90 per Kharwar Tabriz; krs. 80 to krs. 100 per Khar-war Tabriz—in winter krs. 140 | 90 | 5.63 | 8.40 | | 12 |
| Astara-Tabriz . . . . . | Horse to Ardebil, camel from Arbebil | 200 | Krs. 45 per load of 450 lbs | 65 | 4.04 | 4.80 | | 15 |
| Astara-Nijni . . . . . . | . . . . . | . . . | Copecks 20 per poud on dried fruits | . . . | 1.32 | . . . | | . . . |
| Bagdad-Hamadan . . . | Mule, camel | . . . | Krs. 120 per load of 70 mans Tabriz; krs. 90 to krs. 160 per load of 70 mans Tabriz | 170 | 10.58 | 8.00 | | 25 |
| Bagdad-Kermanshah, viá Khanikin . . . . . . | Mule; camel May to September | 220 | Krs. 82 per load of 450 lbs.; 1902–03 krs. 70 to krs. 90 per load | 117 | 7.42 | 9.29 | | 15 to 20 |

Note.—The figures given for cost and duration represent approximately the average over a considerable period, and are not quotations at a given date, the rates of transport in Persia being subject to wide fluctuations from time to time.

| Route | Means of Transport | Approximate Distance in Miles | Bale Goods — Rate of Transport (Local Usage) | Per Kharwar (650 lbs.) | Per Ton (2,240 lbs.) | Per Ton per Mile | Merchandise Delivered in Days |
|---|---|---|---|---|---|---|---|
| | | | | Krs. | £ stg. | Pence. | |
| Bagdad-Busreh . . . . | . . . . . | . . . | 12s. per ton weight; 10s. winter, 20s. summer | . . . | .60 | . . . | 7 |
| | | | Gum trag, 14s. 6d. per 20 cwts. | | | | |
| | | | Wool, 1s. 6d. per bale of, say, 350 lbs., 9s. 8d. per 20 cwts. | | | | |
| | | | Skins, 14s. 6d. per 20 cwts. | | | | |
| Batoum-Constantinople . | Steamer | . . . | . . . . . . . . . . . . . . . . . . . . . . . . . . | . . . | 1.40 | . . . | 7 |
| Batoum-London . . . . | Steamer | . . . | . . . . . . . . . . . . . . . . . . . . . . . . . . | . . . | 1.95 | . . . | 25 |
| Batoum-Tabriz. . . . . | Rail, Wagon | . . . | Tea, Rs. 1.45 to Rs. 1.60 per poud | . . . | . . . . | . . . | . . . |
| Bombay-Persian Gulf . . | Steamer | . . . | Rs. 10 per 40 cubic feet of, say, 15 cwts. | . . . | .89 | . . . | 10 |
| | | | Spices and general cargo, Rs. 10 per 20 cwts. (13s.) | | | | |
| | | | Tea, Rs. 10 per 40 cubic feet of, say, 8 cwts. (2l. 6s. per 20 cwts.) | | | | |
| Bunder Abbas-Kerman . | Camel or donkey | 300 | Krs. 190 per Kharwar Tabriz; 1902, krs. 190 to krs. 200 (Consular Reports, 1901, krs. 82 to krs. 164) | 190 ... | 11.90 .... | 9.50 ... | 30 25 |
| Bunder Abbas-Birjand . | Camel or donkey | 600 | Consular Report, 7s. 4d. per man of 80 lbs. | . . . | 10.26 | . . . | . . . |
| Bunder Abbas-Meshed . | Camel or donkey | 970 | Krs. 410 per Kharwar Tabriz; krs. 380 to krs. 430 | 410 | 25.69 | 6.36 | 110 |
| | | | Consular Reports, 1902, krs. 345 | . . . | . . . . | . . . | 80 |
| Bunder Abbas-Yezd . . | Camel or donkey | 520 | Krs. 430 per Kharwar Shah; 1902, from krs. 415 to krs. 450 | 215 ... | 13.38 .... | 6.17 ... | 45 40 |
| Bunder Gez-Shahrud . . | Mule | 85 | Krs. 18 per load of 6 pouds | 54 | 1.00 | . . . | 7 |
| Bushire-Shiraz . . . . . | Mule, donkey | 160 | Krs. 101 per Kharwar Shiraz; 1901–02, lowest, krs. 75; highest, krs. 150 | 90 | 5.57 | 8.36 | 25 to 30 (in grazing season 50) |
| Busreh-Bagdad . . . . . | Steamer | . . . | 37s. per 40 cubic feet on London cargo | . . . | 2.46 | . . . | 40 (owing to delay in Busreh) |
| | | | General London cargo (spices, &c.) 37s per 20 cwts. | | | | |
| | | | On all Bombay and local cargo, 40s. per 20 cwts. (sugar, by Serafina, say, 15s. per 20 cwts.) | . . . | 2.0 | . . . | . . . |
| Calcutta-Batoum . . . . | Steamer | . . . | Rs. 28 per ton of 50 cubic feet | . . . | . . . . | . . . | . . . . |
| Constantinople-Batoum . | Steamer | . . . | . . . . . . . . . . . . . . . . . . . . . . . . . . | . . . | 1.30 | . . . | 7 |
| Constantinople-Trebizond | Steamer | . . . | . . . . . . . . . . . . . . . . . . . . . . . . . . | . . . | 1.25 | . . . | 6 |
| Enzeli-Resht . . . . | . . . . . | . . . | Krs. 3 per load of 70 mans Tabriz | . . . | . . . . | . . . | . . . |
| Erivan-Batoum. . . . . | Rail | . . . | Copecks 65 per poud on carpets. Dried fruits, 40 copecks. | . . . | 4.30 | . . . | 7 |
| Erivan-Julfa . . . . . . | Wagon, camel | 130 | Copecks 25 per poud | . . . | 1.65 | 3.04 | 10 |
| Hamadan-Bagdad . . . | Mule; camel in summer | 320 | Krs. 40 per 70 mans Tabriz; krs. 25 to krs. 50 | 57 | 3.55 | 2.60 | 25 |
| Hamadan-Ardebil . . . | Mule | 340 | Krs. 100 per Kharwar Tabriz | 100 | 6.04 | 4.24 | 20 |
| Hamadan-Resht . . . . | Mule, camel | 280 | Krs. 100 per Kharwar Tabriz | 100 | 6.04 | 5.18 | 12 |

| Route | Means of Transport | Approximate Distance in Miles | Bale Goods | | | | Merchandise Delivered in Days |
|---|---|---|---|---|---|---|---|
| | | | Rate of Transport (Local Usage) | Per Kharwar (650 lbs.) | Per Ton (2,240 lbs.) | Per Ton per Mile | |
| | | | | Krs. | £ stg. | Pence | |
| Hamadan-Tehran . . . . | Mule, camel | 190 | Krs. 100 per Kharwar Tabriz | 100 | 6.04 | 7.63 | 12 |
| Hong Kong-Batoum . . . | Steamer | . . . | 45s. per ton measure | . . . | . . . . | . . . | . . . |
| Ispahan-Teheran . . . . | Mule, camel | 280 | Krs. 115 per Kharwar Tabriz | 115 | 7.16 | 5.37 | 15 |
| Isaphan-Yezd . . . . . | Mule, camel | 150 | . . . . . . . . . . . . . . . . . . . . . . . . | . . . | . . . . | . . . | . . . |
| Julfa-Erivan . . . . . . | Wagon or camel | 130 | Copecks 20 per poud (raisins, 15 copecks); copecks 18 to copecks 25 per poud | . . . | 1.32 | 2.40 | 10 |
| Julfa-Tabriz . . . . . . | Camel or mule | 80 | Krs. 20 per load of 14 pouds; krs. 10 to krs. 25 per load | 26 | 1.60 | 4.85 | 8 |
| Kazvin-Resht . . . . . | Wagon, camel | . . . | Krs. 30 per Kharwar Tabriz | . . . | . . . . | . . . | . . . |
| Kermanshah-Bagdad . . | Mule; camel in summer | 220 | Krs. 35 per load of 70 mans Tabriz; krs. 30 to krs. 40 | 50 | 3.11 | 3.40 | 20 |
| Kermanshah-Hamadan . | Mule; camel in summer | 100 | Krs. 30 per 70 mans Tabriz; krs. 25 to krs. 35 per load | 43 | 2.67 | 6.40 | 8 |
| London-Trebizond . . . | Steamer | . . . | 1l. 19s. per ton weight on piece goods | . . . | 1.95 | . . . | 25 |
| Manchester-Bagdad . . . | Steamer | . . . | 72s. per 40 cubic feet of, say, 15 cwts. General cargo, 64s. 6d. per 20 cwts. | . . . | 4.80 | . . . | 75, delay at Busreh |
| Manchester-Persian Gulf. | Steamer | . . . | 35s. per 40 cubic feet of, say, 15 cwts. Recently, 25s. per ton | . . . | 2.325 | . . . | 35 |
| Meshed-Ashkabad . . . | Camel, wagon | 160 | Krs. 65 per Kharwar Tabriz; krs. 60 to krs. 70 | 65 | 4.05 | 6.0 | 12 |
| Meshedi-sar–Teheran . . | . . . . . | 160 | To Barfrush, krs. 3 per load of 55 mans Tabriz. Barfrush to Teheran, krs. 120 per Kharwar Tabriz. Krs. 100 to krs. 160 | . . . | . . . . | . . . | 10 |
| Moscow-Ashkabad . . . | Rail steamer | . . . | Viâ Petrovsk, Rbls. 1.28 per poud | | 8.46 | . . . | 35 |
| | Railway steamer, and river steamer | | Viâ Nijni, Rbls. .85 per poud during Volga season | . . . | 5.62 | . . . | 60 |
| Moscow-Erivan . . . . | Rail | . . . | Viâ Belazara, Rbls. 1.48 per poud | . . . | 8.60 | . . . | . . . |
| | Rail, steamer | . . . | Viâ Poti, Rbls. 1.17 per poud | . . . | 7.75 | . . . | . . . |
| Moscow-Astara . . . . | Rail, steamer | . . . | To Bakou viâ Belazara, Rbls. 1.27 per poud | . . . | . . . . | . . . | 25 by rail |
| | | | To Bakou viâ Nijni, Rbls. .702 per poud | | | | |
| | | | To Bakou viâ Yaroslav, Rbls. .622 per poud | . . . | . . . . | . . . | 40 by Volga |
| Moscow-Resht } . . . . Enzeli } | . . . . . | . . . | In summer 75 copecks per poud In winter 115 copecks per poud Spring and autumn 90 copecks per poud | . . . | . . . . | . . . | . . . |
| | | | Average 90 copecks per poud | | 5.95 | . . . | . . . |
| Muhammerah-Ahwaz . . | Steamer | . . . | 13s. 6d. per ton weight or measure, including transhipment | . . . | .90 | . . . | 2 (steamers fortnightly) |
| | | | Sugar 10s. 6d. per ton weight Local, krs. 30 to krs. 40 per ton weight | | | | |

| Route | Means of Transport | Approximate Distance in Miles | Bale Goods | | | | Merchandise Delivered in Days |
|---|---|---|---|---|---|---|---|
| | | | Rate of Transport (Local Usage) | Per Kharwar (650 lbs.) | Per Ton (2,240 lbs.) | Per Ton per Mile | |
| | | | | Krs. | £ stg. | Pence | |
| Odessa–Persian Gulf . . | Steamer | | Copecks 25 per poud; copecks 29 to copecks 30 | ... | 1.65 | ... | 30 (quarterly) |
| Persian Gulf–Bombay . . | Steamer | ... | Rs. 10 per ton weight or measure | ... | 9.0 | ... | 12 |
| Persian Gulf–London Manchester } | Steamer | ... | 25s. per ton weight or measure | ... | 2.00 | ... | ... |
| | | | Gum Trag, 25s. per 40 cubic feet | | | | |
| | | | Wool, 25s. per 40 cubic feet | ... | 2.50 | ... | ... |
| | | | Skins, 25s. per 40 cubic feet | ... | 2.50 | ... | ... |
| | | | Opium per case, 1l. 5s. | | | | |
| | | | Carpets, 25s. per 40 cubic feet | ... | 4.00 | ... | ... |
| Quetta–Meshed. . . . . | Camel | 1,050 | Krs. 350 per Kharwar Tabriz; 1902–03, krs. 340 to krs. 360 Consular Report, 1902, krs. 270 | 350 | 21.90 | 4.99 | 150 |
| Quetta–Birjand . . . . . | Camel | 773 | 10s. per maund of 80 lbs., per Consular Report, 1902 | ... | 14.00 | 4.35 | ... |
| Resht–Hamadan . . . . | Mule | 280 | Krs. 140 per Kharwar Tabriz; krs. 125 to krs. 150 | 140 | 8.70 | 7.45 | 15 |
| Resht–Ispahan . . . . . | Camel, mule | 430 | Krs. 3.25 per Shah man; krs. 3 to krs. 3½ per Shah man | 162 | 10.00 | 5.63 | 25 |
| Resht–Enzeli–Teheran . . | Camel, mule, wagon | 200 | Krs. 120 per Kharwar Tab.; krs. 100 to krs. 140 Kharwar Tab. (Consular Reports, 1902, 8l. 9s. by wagon, and 8l. 12s. by camels; sugar 7l. 10s. wagon, 7l. 10s. camels per ton.) | 120 | 7.50 | 9.00 | 15 to 20 |
| Shiraz–Ispahan . . . . . | . . . . . | 310 | Krs. 96 per Kharwar Shiraz; 1901–2, lowest krs. 70, highest krs. 130 | 85 | 5.30 | 4.10 | 20 |
| Tabriz–Astara . . . . . | Horse; camel to Ardebil | 200 | Krs. 40 per load of, say, 450 lbs; krs. 30 to krs. 45 | 58 | 3.60 | 4.35 | 15 |
| Tabriz–Batoum. . . . . | Camel and rail | ... | Krs. 110 per load of 480 lbs.; krs. 100 to krs. 120 in 1902 | ... | 9.33 | ... | 25 |
| Tabriz–Julfa . . . . . . | Camel, mule | 80 | Krs. 18 per load of 14 pouds; krs. 15 to krs. 25 | 24 | 1.49 | 4.45 | 8 |
| Tabriz–Teheran. . . . . | Camel, mule | 360 | Krs. 3.05 per Shah. man; 1902–3, lowest, krs. 2.10, highest, krs. 3.50 | 152 | 9.50 | 6.30 | 20 to 25 |
| Tabriz–Trebizond . . . | Camel, mule | 500 | Krs. 102 per load of 480 lbs.; 1902–3, krs. 80 to krs. 150 per load. Average 1898–1903, krs. 100 | 138 | 8.60 | 4.12 | 50 |
| Teheran–Ispahan . . . . | . . . . . | 280 | Krs. 1.25 per Shah man | 63 | 3.92 | 3.35 | 15 to 20 |
| Teheran–Meshed . . . . | Camel, mule | 560 | Krs. 225 per Kharwar Tabriz; krs. 220 to 250 per Meshed Kharwar | 225 | 14.00 | 6.00 | 35 to 40 |
| Teheran–Resht . . . . . | Camel, mule, wagon | 200 | Krs. 75 per Kharwar Tabriz | 75 | 4.65 | 5.60 | 15 |
| Teheran–Tabriz. . . . . | Camel, mule | 360 | Krs. 152 per Kharwar Tabriz | 152 | 9.50 | 6.30 | 20 to 25 |
| Trebizond–Constantinople | Steamer | ... | . . . . . . . . . . . . . . . . . . . . . . . . . . . | ... | 1.25 | ... | 6 |
| Trebizond–London . . . | Steamer | ... | | ... | 1.95 | ... | 25 |
| Trebizond–Tabriz. . . . | Camel, mule | 500 | Krs. 195 per Kantar of 230 kilos; 1901–03, lowest, krs. 136, highest, krs. 288. Average last 6 years, krs. 190 | 252 | 15.70 | 7.55 | 50 |
| Yezd–Meshed . . . . . | Camel, mule | 500 say | Krs. 170 per Kharwar Tabriz; krs. 160 to krs. 180 | 170 | 10.60 | 5.10 | 50 |
| | | | Mules, krs. 250 per Kharwar Tabriz | ... | .... | ... | 30 |

## Carriage Roads

The following Selection is taken from the description given by M. A. Jamalzadeh of the main roads of Iran; it includes all those shown by him as being used by some kind of vehicle. The author, one of the outstanding Persian men of letters, wrote this book—a detailed account of the economy of Iran—in Germany during the First World War (see also 6:10).

In the northern part of the country, road improvement was carried out by various companies controlled by the Russian government either directly or through the Discount and Loan Bank. On 1 December 1891, Lazar Poliakov, a Russian financier, obtained a concession which gave him a monopoly of transport and insurance business for seventy-five years, in return for an annual payment of 300 tumans, rising to 1,000 tumans at the end of twenty years. Backed by the Russian government, the Compagnie d'Assurance et de Transport en Perse, and its branch the Bureau des Transports Persans, enforced their monopoly rights against all potential competitors, even restricting the scope of the Iranian Post Office.[1] Their own business increased considerably, the volume of goods they transported within the borders of Iran rising from 94,000 pouds in 1905 to 1,060,000 in 1913, while that of goods brought to or taken from the country by them rose from 2,377,000 to 8,384,000 pouds. All the same, critics pointed out that over that period the number of their agencies fell from twenty to twelve, and that the member firms were more interested in the profits made from shipping across the Caspian than from land transport in Iran.[2]

On 7 July 1893, the Compagnie d'Assurance received, under the name of Compagnie de la Route d'Enzeli, a concession for a carriage road from Enzeli to Qazvin; this was later extended to cover the stretches from Qazvin to Tehran and Qazvin to Hamadan. By 1899 the road from the Caspian to Tehran had been completed, and by 1906 that between Qazvin and Hamadan was finished. Meanwhile, in 1902, a concession for a road from Julfa to Tabriz was obtained and the road was soon completed; the concession also provided for an extension to Qazvin, connecting with the Tehran road.

These roads were excellently built, and expensive: the Enzeli-Qazvin section cost about 3,000,000 rubles, the stretches to Tehran and Qazvin another 7,000,000, and the Julfa-Tabriz road 4,700,000, or over £1,500,000 in all.[3] The Caspian complex failed to return a reasonable profit: although tolls were so high that they increased transport costs by 10 percent and induced many traders to use the mountain trail from Mashad-i Sar to Tehran, they barely covered the interest on the 10,000,000 rubles invested.[4] In 1910, tolls brought in 354,000 rubles, but running expenses amounted to 286,000 and road improvements absorbed another 22,000,

---

[1] Litten, pp. 119–22; in 1904, life insurance business was specifically excluded from the company's activities, being regarded as "opposed to the spirit of the Muslim religion"—see Ter-Gukasov, pp. 107–10.
[2] Ter Gukasov, pp. 98–106.
[3] Entner, pp. 50–51; Jamalzadeh, p. 104, puts the cost of the Julfa–Tabriz road at 10 million rubles.
[4] Entner, pp. 50–51.

leaving a surplus of less than 47,000 rubles, or under 0.5 percent of the capital invested.[5] On the other hand, the Julfa-Tabriz road proved both popular and profitable. It should be added that although the Russian government had originally hoped to draw a good deal of private Russian capital into these road ventures, it ended by supplying the bulk of the funds invested.

The concession allowed the road company to run a coach service with relay stations, but the company preferred to sublease the privilege. Until 1910, the service was run by the Baghirov Brothers—one a Russian and the other an Iranian subject—and after that by the Persian firm of Bahman Bahram. Shortly before the First World War automobiles began to circulate on these roads. At first the company discouraged them by prohibitive tolls—levying on each engine horse-power the same amount as on a horse![6] But on 4 April 1913 a Russian subject, Khoshtaria, obtained "the contract for a service of motors till the end of 1919 on the roads from Resht to Kasvin, and from Kasvin to Tehran, and Kasvin to Hamadan,"[7] and some Peugeot cars were put in service in 1914.

As regards the south, in January 1890 the Imperial Bank of Persia bought a sixty-year concession, granted to an Iranian the previous year, for the construction of a road from Tehran to Ahwaz and between Burujird and Isfahan. In confirming the bank's monopoly rights, the government declared "And the aforesaid Company is also granted the right of prohibiting others from carrying passengers and merchandize in carts or carriages or by any other such means of transport over the road." In 1891 the stretch between Tehran and Qum was completed and the company was authorized to levy a toll of 10 krans on every cart or carriage, and on every pack animal, 2 shahis for the whole length of the road and one shahi for any part of it. In November and December 1898, the bank was authorized to extend the road to Isfahan.[8]

An attempt, in 1902, by the Russian Discount and Loan Bank to control the southern road led to the foundation, with official British backing, of a company headed by H. F. B. Lynch. The following year this was transformed into the Persian Transport Company, with a share capital of £100,000. In addition to building the road, the company was authorized to undertake transport and other business on the road and the Karun River.[9] In 1906 the Qum-Sultanabad road was completed and the tolls were successively raised to 2 tumans per vehicle (including automobiles) and 1 kran per pack animal. And in 1908 the company acquired the right, against an annual payment of 7,000 tumans, to a transport monopoly between Tehran and Sultanabad, which was operated in agreement with the Iranian Post Office. As Litten points out, the rates charged by the British company

[5] Jamalzadeh, p. 101.
[6] Litten, pp. 123–27; see also "Rasht," A and P 1907, 91.
[7] G. D. Turner, *An Account of the Major Events in Persia during the Period October 1912 to October 1913* (The Persia Society, London, n.d.).
[8] Litten, pp. 56–57.
[9] See announcement in *Financial News*, 13 May 1903, quoted in ibid., p. 58.

were much more reasonable than those of the Russian—e.g. an automobile paid, in the form of tolls and monopoly tax, 12 tumans, compared with 107.4 on the Russian road.[10]

No other part of the southern road (variously known as the Arabistan, Bakhtiari, or Lynch road) had been built by 1912—the end of the period foreseen in the concession—and an extension was obtained. But caravans circulated between Ahwaz and Isfahan, as also between Bushire and Shiraz and Bandar Abbas and Kirman. Difficulties were created by the insecure state of the country in the years between the outbreak of the Persian Revolution and the First World War and by sharply rising fodder prices.[11] But traffic showed an upward trend, with marked fluctuations: that between Ahwaz and Isfahan (both ways) rose from 12,000 packages (weighing about 800 tons) in 1904 to 24,000 in 1910 and 29,000 in 1912; of these some two-thirds usually went by the Bakhtiari road.[12]

Nevertheless, the balance sheet of the Persian Transport Company showed a deficit of £46.10.6 for 1912.[13] And an unpublished report by the Company's manager, dated 8 July 1914, contains the following remarks:

The state of the Bakhtiari road is unsatisfactory in the extreme. In many places it is little better than a goat track. It was bad enough when I went over the road in 1910 and it has since deteriorated to an alarming degree. Since that year the number of camels plying between Ahwaz and Isfahan has been reduced by 50 per cent, largely due to the fact that they are of little use on a road which abounds in stretches of rough rocky track, and before long we shall be compelled to abandon camel transport altogether.[14]

A survey undertaken in the summer of 1914 estimated that to put this road "into a fit state for caravans" would cost £5,800; and "to make the road fit for motor traffic throughout, from Ahwaz to Isfahan" £132,000; a "light railway from Ahwaz to Malamir" would cost £200,000, "exclusive of rolling stock," and a "cart road from Malamir to Isfahan" £82,000; the cost of a railway from Ahwaz to Isfahan was put at £1,000,000.[15]

During the First World War several roads were built or improved, and the levying of tolls fell into disuse.[16] Since then, Iran has increasingly relied on its roads for both internal transport and trade with neighboring countries [see epilogue].

(See also works by Entner, Ter-Gukasov, Litten, and Sventitski, listed in the bibliography.)

---

[10] Ibid., pp. 60–62.
[11] Thus an unpublished report on roads, for the September quarter of 1913, mentions "a certain amount of insecurity," "robberies," and "the exorbitant price of fodder" as "menaces to traffic" on the Ahwaz Road—FO 371/1709; see also "Persia," A and P 1910, 94.
[12] "Persia," A and P 1910, 94, and "Arabistan," A and P 1914–16, 74.
[13] In FO 371/2077.
[14] Ibid.
[15] Report on Lynch Road, 17 August 1914, FO 371/2077.
[16] Melamid, in CHI, 1:555.

**Selection 12. Carriage Roads, 1914**
[Muhammad Ali Jamalzadeh, *Ganj-i Shaigan*
(Berlin, A.H. 1335), pp. 46–51]

1. Trebizond-Tabriz-Tehran.

A. Trebizond-Tabriz—about 183 far-sangs (1,100 kilometers); from Bayazit to Tehran about 136 farsangs.

Length of journey (average)—in summer 60 days and in winter 45.

Freight rates (average)—for imports: in bales, 28.5 tumans per qintar of 76 mans; in cases, 5 to 6 tumans per qintar more than for bales.
For exports—8 to 10 tumans per camel load of 80 mans.

Within the frontiers of Iran, droshkys can circulate from Khoi to Tabriz and from Tabriz to Tehran.
From Trebizond to Tabriz, the journey on horseback takes 20 days, and a horse can be hired for 25 tumans.

B. Tabriz–Tehran—about 105 farsangs.

Length of journey (average)—by horse 25 to 30 days, by camel 40 days.

Freight rates (average)—by mule or horse, 5 krans per man of 1,280 mithqals; by camel 3 krans and by cart 3.5 krans.

Merchandise takes 2½ to 3 months to get from Trebizond to Tehran, and the freight rate is 7.5 to 8 tumans per 100 Tabriz mans.

There are no relay stations between Tabriz and Tehran where a traveler can change horses, but there are some private droshkys which can get him from Tabriz to Tehran in ten days, for 150 tumans. But the traveler who wishes to get to Tehran more quickly is advised to take the Tabriz-Julfa-Tiflis-Baku-Enzeli-Resht-Tehran route; the fare on this route is not higher than on the direct Tabriz-Tehran route, and the traveler can reach his destination four or five days sooner.

2. Julfa-Tabriz—20 farsangs (84 English miles).

Length of journey (average)—by caravan or cart, 4 days; by truck one and a half days.

Freight rate (average)—for imports, 1½ to 2 krans for 5½ Tabriz mans, which is equivalent to one *poud*; for exports, 1 to 1½ krans for 5½ Tabriz mans. . .

5. Enzeli–Tehran, via Rasht (paved road)—about 64 farsangs (382 kilometers).

Since the Russian Company [Societé du port d'Enzeli] built a port in Enzeli which allows ships to anchor near the customs house, except during storms, the amount of merchandise loaded and landed at that port has shown a constant increase.

The Enzeli-Tehran road is used by both carriages and automobiles. The tolls taken by the company are as follows: A. Enzeli-Rasht—10 krans for a four-horse droshky or carriage; 4 krans for a two-horse droshky; 1 kran for a camel, horse, or mule.
B. Rasht-Tehran—59.50 krans for a four-horse droshky or carriage; 13 krans for a two-horse droshky; 70.55 for a four-horse cart; 4.55 for a horse, mule, or camel; 2.70 for a donkey.
A. Enzeli-Rasht—4 farsangs.

Length of journey—by droshky 2½ to 3 hours; for merchandise, one day.

Freight rate—The Bureau des Transports Persans carries merchandise on the paved road from Enzeli to Rasht for 0.70 krans per 5½ Tabriz mans (one *poud*), provided the package does not exceed 825 [*sic*—82.5?] Tabriz mans (15 *pouds*); if it is over that figure, the freight rate is fixed by agreement between both parties.

There is also a waterway from Enzeli to Pir-i Bazar, and thence by road to Rasht. The journey takes 2 to 3 days (for merchandise); the freight rate varies according to the season and the mode of transport.
B. Rasht-Tehran—nearly 60 farsangs.

Length of journey (for merchandise)—by cart 12 days; by caravan 14 days.

Freight rate—by cart or caravan, 14½ to 20 tumans per qintar of 100 mans (kharvar).

The more swiftly merchandise is moved the lower the cost, and it is therefore desirable to use a broker to secure the services of a *charvadar* (owner of pack animal).

In 1332 (1913), a Russo-Iranian company was founded for automobile transport of passengers and goods between Enzeli and Tehran...

8. Ashqabad-Mashed, via Quchan—about 40 farsangs.

A. Ashqabad-Quchan—about 20 farsangs (76 miles).

Length of journey—by camel 8 to 10 days; by mule or horse 5 to 7 days; by cart 4 to 8 days.

Freight rate—by camel, in summer 3 tumans and in winter 5 tumans per kharvar of 100 mans; by horse or mule, in summer 4 tumans and in winter 6 tumans per kharvar; by cart, in summer 4 tumans and in winter 7 tumans per kharvar.

B. Quchan-Mashad—about 25 farsangs.

Length of journey—by camel 8 to 10 days; by horse or mule 5 to 6 days; by cart 4 to 5 days.

Freight rate—by camel, in summer 3 to 4 tumans per kharvar; by horse or mule, in summer 3.5 to 4.5 tumans per kharvar; by cart, in summer 4 to 4.5 tumans a kharvar.

The Ashqabad-Mashad road concession is held by Aqa Riza, the Head of Merchants [*Rais al-tujjar*], and is used by droshkys, carts, and caravans. The concessionaire levies a toll of 1.75 krans on each camel; under the terms of the concession, he is also entitled to one tuman on every droshky or cart, but since he has not kept the road up properly this toll is not paid.

Travelers on this road can use the four following means of transport:

i. By droshky post—from Ashqabad to Bajigiran, 6 to 9 hours, for 10 rubles; from Bajigiran to Quchan, 12 to 18 hours, for 12 to 18 tumans; from Quchan to Mashad, 20 to 28 hours, for 28 to 30 tumans; from Ashqabad to Quchan, 2 days, for 40 to 50 rubles; from Ashqabad to Mashad, 3 days, 43 to 60 tumans.

ii. By cart post—from Ashqabad to Mashad, 3 to 6 days, 51.25 krans per person.

iii. Ordinary droshky—from Ashqabad to Quchan, 3 to 4 days, 40 to 50 rubles per droshky; from Quchan to Mashad, 5 to 6 days, 30 to 40 tumans per droshky.

iv. Ordinary cart—from Ashqabad to Quchan, 3 to 4 days, 15 to 20 krans per person; from Quchan to Mashad, 5 to 6 days, 20 to 25 krans per person. Transport of merchandise on this route is made through the Bureau des Transports Persans, which groups the following: Kavkaz i Merkurii [see 4:1,2], Vostochnoe Obshchestvo, Russkoe Obshchestvo, and Nadezhda. In addition goods can be carried by *charvadars* and private droshkys....

10. Quchan-Sabzevar—22 farsangs.

Length of journey (for merchandise)—by cart 4 to 5 days; by caravan 4 to 5 days.

Freight rate—by cart 4 to 5 tumans per kharvar of 100 mans, by caravans 35 to 45 krans per kharvar....

17. Baghdad-Tehran, via Kermanshah.

A. Muhammarah-Basra-Baghdad by river, [see EHME, pp. 146–53].

B. Baghdad-Kermanshah via Qasr-i Shirin—about 50 farsangs.

Length of journey–13 days (Baghdad-Qasr 6, and Qasr-Kermanshah 7).

Freight rate—about 11.3 tumans (12 *majidiehs*) a bale of 50 mans; 2 krans and 250 dinars a man; sometimes, in exceptional circumstances, the rate rises and may reach 22.6 tumans (24 *majidiehs*) per 50 mans.

C. Kermanshah-Tehran, about 85 farsangs (330 miles).

Length of journey—20 to 25 days.

Freight rate—by cart, 20 to 22 tumans per kharvar, and each bale 10 to 13 tumans.

The above-mentioned roads have been described solely from the point of view of trade and the transport of merchandise. In addition, travelers and tourists can use, on almost all the roads mentioned above, post carriages and droshkys and coaches [*dilijan*], which can convey them to their destination three times as fast as by caravan. Moreover, in the last few years the following paved roads have been built:

1. Enzeli to Tehran, via Rasht and Qazvin; and from Qazvin to Hamadan.

2. Tehran to Qum and Sultanabad.

3. The Bakhtiari way (Muhammarah-Shushtar-Isfahan).

We shall return to this subject in later chapters.

## Hackney Carriages in Tehran

The growth of Tehran to a city of around 100,000 by the 1890s made it necessary to set up some form of public transport. The service described in the following selection constituted a first step and was soon followed by a horse-drawn streetcar line, crossing the town from east to west.

A notice, issued in French and distributed to all European residents of Tehran (enclosed in the dispatch), described the conditions of the service. Cabs were to stand in four places: Maidani Topkhaneh, Sabze Maidan, outside the British Legation, and Sar Cheshmeh-i Maidan. They could be hired for the journey or by the hour. In winter the rates were: for the journey (which was not to extend beyond the city walls) 1 kran 5 shahis; by the hour 2 krans 10 shahis within the walls or 3 krans outside; for the journey to Shimran the rate was 4 krans. Cabs were to stand in public squares from sunrise to three hours after sunset; those wanting a cab at a later hour could hire a livery carriage from the company's offices, in Amirieh street.

Unlike most big cities, Tehran, has never had electric streetcars; motor buses have, at first very inadequately but in recent years in sufficient numbers, provided mass transportation for the rapidly expanding metropolis.

(See also works by Bémont, and Lockhart, *Persian Cities*, listed in the bibliography.)

### Selection 13. Hackney Carriages in Tehran, 1891
[De Balloy to Ribot, 15 December 1891, AE, Correspondance Commerciale, Téhéran, vol. 4]

In my dispatch no. 24, of 25 June 1890, I announced to Your Excellency that the Persian government had granted to one of its nationals, His Excellency Mirza Javad Khan, a concession for the establishment of hackney cabs and omnibuses in the city of Tehran. The concessionaire did not have the right to transfer his privilege, but was authorized to set up a company to exploit it. Mirza Javad Khan, who is a high official in the Ministry of Foreign Affairs, succeeded after much groping in setting up a company, over which he presides and whose members are Messrs: Denis, director of the [Shah Abdal-Azim] Railway; Lemaire, the shah's chief bandmaster; Meriness, who has the match concession; Muavin al-Mulk, the minister of foreign affairs' son; Jafar Quli Khan; Ardel Bashi; and Misbah al-Mulk, from the Ministry of Foreign Affairs.

As soon as the required capital had been raised, Mirza Javad Khan sent his brother to Kazan to purchase some thirty carriages, which reached Tehran in November. On the fifth of this month, the service was inaugurated by the presentation of all the carriages—with the horses in harness—to the shah. So far, the service seems to be working well and meets a real need of the population. The twenty-three cabs standing in the public squares are constantly out on business and the seven used as livery carriages are in great demand.

The company has not yet put any omnibuses in service, and I doubt whether it ever will, since the tramway would present too serious a competition. . . .

# 5

## *Agriculture*

It is extremely difficult to give even a rough picture of Persian agriculture in the nineteenth century, or to indicate any but the most general developments that took place in it. For, on the one hand, the government made very few studies of rural conditions, and kept practically no statistics other than tax returns; and on the other, most foreign observers had little interest in, or understanding of, the changes that were taking place in the villages.

Throughout Iran's history, irrigation has had a predominant influence on agriculture (see 5:1). But in contrast to the huge irrigation systems that were set up in Egypt and India—or even to the modest works built in Turkey and Iraq—almost nothing was done in this field until well after the First World War. In the other countries, practically all irrigation schemes were financed and implemented by the state, but in Iran expenditure on—or even interest in—such schemes seems to have been negligible. In the 1840s, Prime Minister Mirza Aghasi "revived the cultivation of the mulberry-tree in the Kirman region, to feed silk worms; and he envisaged the diversion of the waters of the River Karaj for Tehran's water supply."[1] His successor Amir-i Kabir showed more enterprise in this as in other fields (see 6:6), repairing minor irrigation works in various parts of the country (Yazd, Gurgan, etc.) and building the Nasiri dam on the Karkheh river, in Khuzistan; it is interesting to note that, for the latter, he employed an Iranian engineer trained in England.[2]

After that, little seems to have been done by the government. "In a report written in 1300/1882 eleven dams in Khuzistan, ruined or otherwise, are enumerated."[3] The author of that report, Mirza Abd al-Ghaffar Najm al-Mulk, described by a British official as "an engineer of some reputation," presented a detailed scheme for the development of the Karun River, including navigation (see 4:6)

[1] Avery, p. 46.
[2] For details see Adamiyyat, pp. 227–30.
[3] Lambton, *Landlord*, p. 214.

and irrigation. Building a new dam at Ahwaz, of the same size as the ruined one (900 *zer* , of 3 feet 6 inches each), was estimated to cost 78,339 tumans or, at the rate of 6/-, £28,000 [*sic*]; clearing the two irrigation channels commanded by the dam would add 81,600 tumans more. Clearing three other channels, restoring the Bendeghe dam, and other minor works brought total estimated costs to 346,015 tumans, or £123,500 [*sic*].[4] No action seems to have been taken on these proposals.

In 1888, the shah set aside 150,000 tumans for the restoration of the old Ahwaz dam, but this did not lead to any results.[5] Nor did the appointment of a Dutch engineer in 1902, since he received no backing from the shah, although irrigation was one of the items of development mentioned during the discussions on the first Russian loan of 1900.[6] In 1909 the Prime Minister signed a document addressed to the Dutch ambassador (who had sheltered him during the disturbances of 1907/8), promising an exclusive concession for the irrigation of 500,000 hectares in the vicinity of Ahwaz to any company designated by him; but this too remained fruitless.

But it was not only that the government failed to implement any irrigation schemes. Its inability to maintain law and order, and its extortionate tax policy, removed the inducement for private enterprise to do so, and indeed often led to the abandonment of existing works. As regards the first, much damage was done by the tribes—Turkoman, Arab, Bakhtiari, and others—in many parts of the country, particularly in Khuzistan.[7] Oppression by local officials or landlords was hardly less harsh, and the above-mentioned engineer, Najm al-Mulk, stated that "because of this no one dared develop the land" in Khuzistan.[8]

As for taxation, there was short-lived reform by Amir-i Kabir; "as a result dead lands were brought into cultivation and irrigation works carried out." But after his death extortion began again. "The return of prosperity was thus cut short, and when in 1286–88/1869–72 there was a series of famine years much *khaliseh* and *arbabi* land again became dead land." Other examples of the adverse effects of taxation on the extension or maintenance of irrigated areas are given by Professor Lambton.[9]

Along with the neglect of irrigation, the complete indifference to improvement of agricultural techniques[10] and the very high cost of transport, the system of land tenure, by depriving farmers of incentive to improve methods or expand

[4] FO 60/448; summary translation of report dated 2 July 1882.
[5] Litten, p. 86.
[6] Ibid., and Jamalzadeh, p. 91.
[7] Lambton, pp. 157–58, 170.
[8] Ibid., p. 157.
[9] Ibid., pp. 153, 165, 170.
[10] In the published and unpublished British and French records I consulted, there was only one reference to any interest taken by the Iranian government in any aspect of agricultural technique. A letter from the secretary of the Horticultural Society, Regent Street, to the Foreign Office, dated 12 December 1826, reads: "A present of various roots and seeds having been prepared by the Horticultural Society in consequence of an application from you, for His Majesty the Schah of Persia, I beg to inform you that they are now ready for despatch and await your orders. The collection is packed in several boxes about 9 inches square each" (FO 60/29).

output, was a strong drag on economic development. Essentially, Iran's traditional land tenure relations (see 5:2–5) remained unchanged in the period 1800–1914. The three agents—state, landlords and tribal leaders, and peasants—continued to perform their customary roles. But new factors were operating to modify these relations. First, there were shifts of power between the government and the landlords and tribal leaders. Second, the increasing adoption of European ways in warfare, administration, and mode of living strengthened the need of both government and landlords for income. And, third, the growing profitability of cash crops for export (see 5:7–13) made landownership more attractive than before. This meant, on the one hand, that there was a powerful inducement for the crown to extend its holdings of *khaliseh* land, at the expense of the large land-owners, and to seek to collect taxes directly, rather than through the assignment of *tuyuls* (for these and the following terms see 5:2).

But, for the same reason, the landlords also sought to convert both *vaqf* land[11] and *tuyuls* into private estates (*arbabi*), and, wherever possible, to increase their control over their peasants or take over their land. Moreover, merchants, officials, religious notables, and other rich city dwellers once more began to acquire land.[12]

Crown and state lands were extended in many ways. Some were acquired by purchase, for example, in Mazandaran by Aqa Muhammad, the founder of the Qajar dynasty. Much more was confiscated, or abandoned by its owners in times of famine or other catastrophes, as in the neighborhood of Isfahan under Fath Ali and his successor, Muhammad Shah, and in Sistan and Baluchistan under Nasir al-Din. Other lands were seized for arrears of taxation under various monarchs. And Riza Shah also added large estates in Mazandaran, Khuzistan, and elsewhere.[13]

But at the same time a great part of the *khaliseh* was being transferred to large landowners. In the first place, according to Malcolm,[14] the government was always ready to dispose of wasteland, particularly if it was to be built on or to be planted as a garden. In such cases a hereditary lease would be given, subject to a small ground tax, and it can be presumed that such leases were often gradually transformed into private estates. Under Nasir al-Din and his successor Muzaffar al-Din, the monarch's urgent need for cash, and the belief that land would be better developed if it were in private ownership, led to large-scale sale of *khaliseh* land.[15] This policy was continued during the Constitutional Period, for example, in Kirman. And under Riza Shah laws were passed, in 1931, 1934, and 1937, to sell such land on instalment; another set of laws was designed to transfer *khaliseh* land to tribes that had been forcibly resettled. Further moves were made under the present monarch, in 1946.[16] It should be added that, in the Constitutional and

---

[11] Ibid., p. 155.
[12] Ibid., pp. 140, 261–62; see also examples given in chap. 2, sel. 5.
[13] Ibid., pp. 147–48, 154, 238, 242, 244–45, 253, 256–57.
[14] Cited in ibid., p. 153.
[15] Ibid., pp. 154–55.
[16] Ibid., pp. 238–44.

Pahlavi periods, it was hoped that the transfer of crown lands could be used to extend peasant ownership, but in fact by far the greater part has passed to large landowners. Data for nearly one thousand villages analyzed by Lambton show that, around 1880, the greater part of the land belonged to large landlords.[17] This process continued until the land reform of 1962. The *tuyul* system was abolished in 1907 (see chap. 8, introduction), and Riza Shah confiscated several large estates, but the position of the landlords was strengthened by the Civil Code of 1929 and the general economic development of the country. On the eve of land reform a little over half of the agricultural area was owned by large landowners and a little over a tenth by small proprietors, the balance consisting of tribal holdings, crown lands, public domain, and *vaqf* (see epilogue).

While the structure of land ownership was thus being slowly modified, relations between landlords and peasants were also changing, in a capitalist direction. Money transactions began to assume increasing importance in the village, replacing barter. The expansion of such crops as silk, opium, cotton, and tobacco evidently favored cash payments, since they were processed and sold outside the village in which they were grown. So did the increase in the proportion of wheat and rice that was either exported abroad or sent to the towns to meet the needs of the growing urban population (see 2:2,3). This had three further consequences: the peasant's need for credit increased; there may have been a tendency for the landlord to take his rent in cash rather than in kind and for the government also to demand tax payment in cash; and there was a direct investment of capital in plantations.

As regards the first, an outstanding example is silk growing in Gilan. The use of imported silkworm eggs, starting in the 1860s, meant that the farmer had to purchase such eggs on credit. This was supplied either by foreigners—Greeks, Armenians, and others—or by Persians who in turn often borrowed from such foreigners[18] (see 5:3–6). Another example is given by the British consul in Mashad:

Formerly the peasant knew that if his stock failed there was no hope of replenishing it. He would have to go without his Nauroz festivities. That made him careful. But now things are altered. He knows that a week or two before the festival the Russian speculators will commence to appear on the scene and to offer the proprietor advances of money to sow cotton for them, the seed of which they provide, or to buy up in advance the best part of his crop of wheat. The ignorant peasant is led to agree to bartering a part of his share too, and when the harvest is over he finds he has not enough corn to carry him through the winter.

The report goes on to state that the export of wheat had greatly raised its price, inflicting much hardship on the poor.

---

[17] Ibid., pp. 155–57.

[18] Abdullaev, p. 15, citing Russian archives. Rural indebtedness goes much further back in time. In his Report on Gilan for 1865, the British consul stated: "In many districts of Gilan the peasantry are heavily in debt to their landlords, who exact an usurious rate of interest, from 24 to 40 per cent being the lowest figure upon such loans. Money thus lent is frequently lost. A succession of bad crops plunges the labourer into difficulties, he is unable to pay, and when reduced to great straits deserts the village to elude the pursuit of his creditors." A and P 1867, 67, p. 109.

The Shah is constantly issuing the most stringent orders prohibiting the export of wheat, but nobody in the north pays any attention to them. Strings of 50 or 100 camels laden with corn may be seen crossing the frontier daily after the harvest by the main road.[19]

The second hypothesis is not easy to demonstrate. A sharp rise in land rents seems undoubtedly to have taken place—an Armenian observer, writing shortly before the First World War, goes so far as to state that rents had risen tenfold in the previous thirty years, which may have been true of particular localities but can hardly be taken as representative of the country as a whole.[20] Moreover, landlords showed increasing interest in extracting as much as possible from their peasants. As the British consul in Isfahan reported:

These lands [crown lands, sold by the government for "want of money"] have been mostly bought by the rich nobles and the Ulema, who are enabled to store their grain and even buy the superfluity of their peasants. In the old days, the peasants paid into the Government their rent in kind, it was resold at low rates, and what grain the peasants held above their requirements for food and seed, they sold at once at the best price they could command in the open market, and so the price current in the bazaars was kept normal, whereas now the big grain-holders are able to set the price by holding up their grain. The peasants, in place of having an easy task-master in the State are now ground down to the very last penny by their landlords.[21]

There is also some indirect evidence that, whereas previously rents on major crops were paid in kind and only those on minor crops in cash, an increasing amount came to be collected in cash. Similarly the government's revenues show a rising proportion of cash payments.[22]

As regards the third point, two interesting developments may be noted. In 1895–96, Prince Kashif al-Sultaneh established tea plantations in Gilan; lack of funds limited expansion, but his annual output of 800 to 1,000 lbs. found a ready market in Iran. In 1902 the Yuzhno-Russkoe Company planted jute and kenaf, also in Gilan, and exported over 4,000 pouds (65 tons) of fiber to Russia. All three crops were grown by hired labor.[23] Last, it is worth noting that there was a considerable amount of purchase of land in Astarabad, Gilan, and Azerbaijan by Russian subjects; in some places this resulted in settlement in the second half of the nineteenth century; for example, in 1911 there were 192 families in Azerbaijan, owning or holding on long leases land valued at 5,400,000 tumans.[24]

A few general remarks may be made on the changes that took place in agricultural production. Naturally, no statistics on area under cultivation or output are available, and tax returns provide a very inadequate basis for estimation. But one

[19] A and P, 1894, 87, p. 5. A similar observation had been made twenty years earlier by the consul in Rasht, regarding rice: "The continued export throughout the year of this important article, the staple food of the people in Ghilan, can alone account for this enormous rise in price"—A and P 1872, 68, p. 1187.

[20] Atrpet, cited by Abdullaev, p. 26.

[21] A and P 1899, 101, p. 13.

[22] See Lambton, *Landlord*, pp. 127, 145–48, 165, 169, 173. Cash rents have been used on a small scale for several hundred years; thus Chardin reports such rents in the neighborhood of Isfahan.

[23] Abdullaev, p. 22.

[24] Ibid., pp. 27–28.

can state with confidence that, during the period under review and more particularly in its second half, total output must have increased considerably. For, on the
one hand, population seems to have grown appreciably (see 2:2,3) which, even
if there was some reduction in levels of living (see 2:5), probably implies greater
domestic consumption. And, second, the quantum of exports increased severalfold
(see 3:19 and 20) and some three-quarters of exports consisted of agricultural
produce.

As regards the pattern of agricultural production, the most striking change is
the rapid growth of cash crops. It is impossible to say whether total output of
bread grains increased: the rise in total domestic consumption would indicate an
increase, but it seems probable that this was partly achieved by converting an
export surplus into a small import surplus.[25] But production of the main cash
crops—silk, cotton, opium, rice, and tobacco—increased severalfold (see 5:7-13)
and, judging from the large growth in exports, that of another important item,
fruits and nuts, also must have risen substantially.

Two other cash crops may be briefly mentioned. An early attempt to introduce
tea in Gilan, in 1875, failed.

Owing to the great similarity of the climate of these shores with that of the foot of the
Himalaya, where a fair quality of tea is produced, it has been supposed that this plant
would succeed here, and I have applied for some tea seed from that part of India to try
it. Unfortunately the person who had first suggested this idea, and who had made overtures to the Persian government for the establishment of a tea plantation in Ghilan, has
been obliged to quit the country on account of ill health, and this notion has apparently
been abandoned.[26]

As was noted earlier, tea plantations were successfully established in 1895, but the
expansion of production came only in the 1930s.

The olive tree has been widely grown in Gilan for several hundred years, and
in the 1890s the number of trees was put at 100,000 to 130,000 by various British
consuls, and the crop at about 6,000,000 pounds.[27] The primitive methods used
for pressing resulted in a very poor quality oil, fit only for the making of soap,
and from the 1840s on various unsuccessful attempts were made by Europeans to
introduce modern presses.[28] In 1890 a Greek firm (Koussis and Theophilaktos),
under Russian protection, was granted a twenty-five-year monopoly for "the
purchase and working of all the olives in Northern Persia" and by 1895 it had
installed a modern factory. But the very sharp rise in customs duties on olives and
olive oil imported to Russia forced the firm to suspend business.[29]

---

[25] Blau, writing in the 1850s, put bread grains among the leading exports and did not list them among imports
(see 3:19). Curzon (Persia, 2:496) stated: "The growth of wheat is already in excess of the needs of the home
population, and grain is exported in some quantity to Turkey, the Caucasus, India (from Bunder Abbas) and
even to England (from Bushire)." This is confirmed by Stolze and Andreas, p. 10. On the eve of the First World
War, however, Iran's imports of wheat flour somewhat exceeded, in value, its exports of wheat.

[26] "Gilan," 1874 and 1875, A and P 1876, 76, p. 1496.

[27] "Note on Olive Cultivation," A and P 1897, 88.

[28] Stolze and Andreas, p. 13.

[29] "Note on Olive Cultivation," A and P 1897, 88.; Abdullaev, p. 131, citing Russian archives.

In 1890 the same firm was also granted a monopoly for the exploitation of the northern forests. Boxwood had been exported to Russia and England (through Russia) at least as early as the 1870s, and shipments to England alone were worth about £30,000.[30] By the beginning of this century, the firm's investment in lumbering was estimated at 500,000 rubles or over. In 1900 its monopoly was extended, but after 1907 other firms, including a Russian firm and a Franco-Austrian one, entered the lumbering business.[31]

Little can be said about a very important branch of the economy, animal husbandry. Presumably livestock numbers fluctuated violently, as they still do, in response to drought, cold, and epidemics, but it is possible that the trend was upward, since exports of live animals and livestock products do not seem to have diminished. The importance of livestock raising in the economy may be judged from the fact that, as late as 1958, it was estimated to account for about one-third of the total agricultural product and to contribute one-third of exports other than petroleum.[32] As regards the Caspian Sea fisheries, which were exploited by a Russian concessionaire, the increase in output was very substantial (see 5:15).

## Irrigation

Like other parts of the Middle East, most of Iran suffers from a severe shortage of water.

Iran's most obvious hydrographic problems are compounded of the disadvantages of scanty and highly seasonal precipitation, and a surface configuration which tends to concentrate moisture on the periphery of the country, leaving its vast heart an area of irreconcilable sterility. South of the Alburz mountains there is no hope of rain during the summer months, when streams wither and the land is parched. Frontal precipitation occurs between October and May, its distribution and quantity being conspicuously related to elevation and exposure. Mountainous areas in the north and west may receive as much as 80 in. of precipitation, while many interior stations show a statistical average of less than 3 in. annually. Precipitation at all levels decreases in a south-easterly direction.[1]

As in other parts of the Middle East, this shortage has necessitated the development of an elaborate system of irrigation. The latter fulfills four functions, which are combined in practice but can be distinguished analytically. First, as the author of the following section—a French engineer with considerable experience in Iran—points out, it supplies water for drinking and for garden crops to villages and towns, a service performed in more humid climates by rain and rivers. Second, it makes cultivation possible in areas which do not receive enough precipitation.

[30] Churchill to Morrison, 11 November 1875, FO 60/375; "Gilan," 1874 and 1875, A and P 1876, 76, p. 1496.
[31] Abdullaev, pp. 131, 142, citing Russian archives; Litten, pp. 191–93.
[32] For an interesting account, see Thomas R. Stauffer, "The Economics of Nomadism in Iran," *Middle East Journal*, Summer 1965.
[1] T. M. Oberlander, in CHI, 1:264–65.

Third, whether used alone or in combination with rainwater, it greatly raises the yields of crops; thus in central Iran wheat yields on irrigated land are three to five times as high as on rain-fed land.[2] Last, irrigation allows the introduction of new crops, which could not otherwise be grown.

In other Middle Eastern countries, irrigation has centered on rivers. Very recently, deep wells, worked by petrol or electric pumps, have been used to irrigate extensive areas, as in Pakistan and Syria. But for the reasons given below, there has been little in Iran to compare with the vast hydraulic works of Egypt, Mesopotamia, or India. However, as Goblot points out in another article,[3] several minor works were undertaken at relatively early dates. Those he mentions include three Achaemenian gravity dams; a gravity dam and three Sasanian dams (at Shushtar, Dizful, and Paipul) with movable gates—which he claims to be the oldest of their kind; and an arched masonry dam at Kebar, near Qum, also apparently the oldest in the world, since it seems to have been built in the early Mongol period. Following the Second World War, a set of large dams has been built in various parts of the country (see epilogue).

Wells, worked by one, six, or eight oxen, have been widely used from early times.[4] More recently, there has been a proliferation of deep wells, worked by petrol or electric pumps. The relatively small capital outlay on such pumps can often be amortized in only a few years, thanks to the increase in output.[5]

But Iran's most original contribution to hydraulics is the *qanat*, or *kariz*, described in the following selection. The *qanat* is sometimes designed primarily to supply the village with water for drinking and garden farming, the main field crops depending entirely on rain. Or it can be used as the main source of water for the field crops, or as an auxiliary source; in the latter case the lag between the seasonal rainfall cycle and that of the *qanat*—which reaches its peak distinctly later, sometimes in the summer, when it is most needed—helps to ensure a steadier supply of water the whole year round.[6]

Before the Arab conquest, *qanats* spread from Iran to neighboring lands and countries under Persian rule, for example, the oasis of Siwa in Egypt. In the Islamic period the technique was carried to North Africa, where they are known as *foggaras*.

Iran's *qanats* vary greatly in length and depth. "Some are only a few hundred metres long, and do not go deep down, but there are some in the Yazd region which are over 43 kilometres in length and others, near Gunabad, which reach down to more than 300 metres. A length of 5 to 10 kilometres, with a depth of the order of 100 metres, is a common average."[7] The cross section is some four feet high

---

[2] H. Bowen-Jones in ibid., p. 571. citing *First National Census of Agriculture* (Tehran, 1960).
[3] "Le rôle de l'Iran dans les techniques de l'eau," *Techniques et Sciences municipales* (Paris), February 1961.
[4] Lambton, *Landlord*, pp. 227–28.
[5] Ibid. and D. J. Flower in CHI,. 1 : 606–10.
[6] For an excellent account see English, *Origin*.
[7] Goblot, "Le rôle de l'Iran."

and $2\frac{1}{2}$ to 3 feet wide.[8] The flow also varies, but discharge rates of 30 to 100 liters per second are common; the longest, the Shahrud or "Royal River," has a discharge of 900 liters per second.[9]

Naturally costs also vary widely, depending not only on the length and depth of the qanat but also on the nature of the soil through which it flows and the amount of upkeep. Demin gives an "average" of 2,000,000 rials, or $27,000.[10] Beckett, writing in 1953, put the capital cost of a qanat near Kirman, capable of irrigating 130–200 acres, at £30,000 or $84,000.[11] Paul English states that an eighteen-mile qanat to Kirman, completed in 1950, cost $213,000 and estimates the average cost per kilometer in the 1960s at $10,000.[12] Lambton quotes an average cost in the Qazvin area, for qanats 3 to 5 miles long and about 100 feet deep, of 2,000,000 rials or $27,000.[13]

The rent paid for qanat water varies accordingly.[14] The use of such water is strictly regulated by local custom, but as in all arid countries tensions and disputes tend to arise in periods of shortage.[15]

(See also works by Goblot, Lambton, CHI, English, Bémont, Caponera, Keen, and Worthington, listed in the bibliography.)

[8] Lambton, *Landlord*, p. 217.
[9] Goblot, "Le rôle de l'Iran."
[10] Demin, p. 94.
[11] Cited by Bowen-Jones, p. 583.
[12] English, *Kirman*, p. 140.
[13] Lambton, *Persian Land Reform*, p. 283.
[14] Lambton, *Landlord*, pp. 221–22.
[15] Ibid., pp. 222–26, CHI, pp. 600–606.

## Selection 1. Irrigation

[Henri Goblot, "Le problème de l'eau en Iran," *Orient*, 1962, no. 23, pp. 46–55]

### WATER RESOURCES OF IRAN

... Egypt has the Nile, which brings down considerable quantities of water falling over the rainy equatorial regions of Africa, and the river has made it possible to compensate for an almost total lack of rain and thus to support a dense population in its valley and delta. Mesopotamia, slightly less arid, has the Tigris and Euphrates, which bring to it water from the mountains and plateaus of Anatolia and Armenia. These "foreign" waters, coming to these deserts, made possible the creation of the first empires. Iran, on the other hand, has to live on what falls on its own territory. The flow it can use from the Arax, which forms the border between it and USSR, is about equal to the amount drained from the Iranian catchment area into that large river.

There is, near Zabul, the delta of the Helmand, whose catchment area is almost entirely in Afghanistan, but the latter country wants to use almost all the water of that river. Difficult negotiations are under way between the two governments, and anyway the matter concerns only a small region of Iran.

I have before me three complementary maps: a physical map, showing relief and altitude; an isohyet map—that is, curves linking points of equal rainfall, measured in millimeters per year; and a map of catchment areas. A comparative study of these maps is most instructive. One can see where precipitations come from, what their magnitude is, where the water is concentrated, and where it flows to. Naturally, it is not within the scope of this article to go into the details of these complex questions. I should point out in passing, however, that equal precipitation does not mean similar conditions: one must take into account the seasonal distribution of rain and the mean temperatures as well as maxima and minima, etc. Two learned and detailed studies of these questions have been made by H. E. Ahmed Hossein, an agronomist, who has served several times as minister of agriculture and who was president of the Higher Council of the Plan Organization; these studies, *Climats de l'Iran*, and *Régions climatiques et végétation en Iran*, earned the author a high distinction from the monarch.

The bulk of precipitation—at least the densest relative to the surface watered—comes from the Caspian Sea. Rainfall is abundant along the coastal plain, especially in its western part, and also on the steep slopes of the high Elburz chain, which still bear magnificent forests, unfortunately partly devastated by irrational exploitation. In winter, some of the clouds cross the chain and water its southern slopes. Last, the remains of the great Atlantic and Mediterranean cloud systems, after having passed over the Syrian desert, are stopped in turn by the parallel mountain chains of the Zagros, the chain separating Iran from Iraq and continuing along the Persian Gulf. The little that remains is captured by the lower mountains on the Central Plateau. Eastern Iran is completely outside the monsoon zone.

The greater part of the country lies within the two-hundred-millimeter isohyet, which does not allow the growing of crops and at best provides meager pastures for camels and sheep. A very small part lies within the three-hundred-millimeter isohyet, and in it rather poor crops of winter cereals can be grown under "dry farming"—that is, when the conditions of temperature and relief make this possible and when, moreover, a neighboring source provides the water required by a village. Except for the Caspian plain, a few narrow valleys in the Elburz, and the western Zagros valleys, more abundant precipitation is to be found only on mountain slopes, where neither cultivation nor habitation is possible.

A rough calculation allows me to put the total amount of precipitation falling over the whole territory at between three hun-dred and four hundred milliard [i.e., thousand million] cubic meters, and this figure may be too high. Part of this—surely a large part, but it is impossible to say how much—evaporates immediately in this country, where even in winter the air is very dry. Another part seeps into the surface layers and is absorbed by the roots of a vegetation which is more or less sparse; after having played its part as carrier of nutrient matter, it disappears in turn into the atmosphere through evapotranspiration. Yet another part penetrates deeper into the ground, below the zone where it can be absorbed by plant roots; there it fills the empty spaces in the subsoil and constitutes an underground pool of water.

At this point a factor very favorable to Iran makes its appearance. The big and wide depressions between the open Zagros chains, and also the central plateau, are full of quaternary alluvial soil; these are particularly porous at the foot of chains formed of big blocks, pebbles, shingles, and of finer elements, muddy and clayey, as one moves away from the slope—and it is precisely where almost no rain falls that the soil becomes nonporous. Moreover, these porous quaternary alluvial soils often rest on pliocene gravel, more or less gently folded but of great thickness, which in turn contains underground pools whose importance is increased by the fact that their potential zone of impregnation extends beyond that of the quaternary alluvium. Not only does the water that falls on the impregnation zones filter down to them, but also water that flows down the steep slopes.

Because of the configuration of the land, these pools generally rise again near the surface, in depressions where their water forms a *kavir*—a kind of marsh similar to the *shatt* (*chott*) of North Africa—from which it evaporates. Sometimes their course is less lengthy, and Mr. Asfia has brought out two very distinct zones of evaporation of the water that flows under Tehran; these zones are crossed by the Tehran–Varamin highway and can be clearly distinguished from the air.

There is another zone which is well suited to infiltration, and precisely in a region where rain is relatively abundant: the great blocks of fissured limestone which stretch, in a central band, along almost the entire length of the Zagros mountains. The water which infiltrates them comes out in numerous *vauclusian* springs, on which very ancient human settlements—the oldest known in Iran—have taken place.

Last, part of the precipitation flows through torrent and river beds into the Persian Gulf, the Caspian Sea, and the inland depressions on the plateau. Frequently the wide beds of these rivers, which are filled with porous alluvium, are saturated with water—which the Anglo-Saxon hydrologists call *underflow* and which their French colleagues have christened by the vile name of *inféroflux*. These flows, in turn, enrich the underground pools. These rivers are often of little importance, with an extremely small summer and autumn discharge; sometimes they dry up completely.

Given the size of Iran, the catchment areas of these rivers and the amount of water flowing in them are tiny—not only because precipitation is scanty but also because, in addition to heavy evaporation, seepage plays a much more important part than in other regions.

For example, the biggest of these rivers, the Karun, drains 60,000 square kilometers in the Zagros region and discharges into the Shatt al-Arab, at Khurramshahr, about 24 milliard cubic meters, or an average flow of 750 cubic meters per second; the Karkheh, which drains a basin northwest of that of the Karun, with an area of 43,000 square kilometers, discharges only 3.5 milliard cubic meters. Including the other rivers flowing into it, this sea [Persian Gulf] must surely not receive more than 30 milliard cubic meters per annum from the Iranian territory. The Safid Rud is the only river draining part of the plateau and crossing the Elburz chain, in the gorges where the big Manjil dam has been built. Draining an area of 57,000 square kilometers, it brings to the Caspian between 4 and 6 milliard cubic

meters. The small rivers flowing down the Elburz to the Caspian drain about 21,000 square kilometers and contribute some 3.5 milliard cubic meters. As for the main river flowing into the inner depressions, the Zayandeh Rud, which waters Isfahan, it drains only 30,000 square kilometers and has a total flow of the order of only 250 million cubic meters, even though some of this comes from the Zagros. It is unnecessary to continue this enumeration of the meager rivers flowing into the depressions on the plateau; their total contribution is certainly under 10 milliard cubic meters.

A large number of seasonal small rivers and torrents end, at the plateau, in alluvial fans, more or less spread out, in which their water disappears; this water feeds the underground pools, thus forming saturated zones suitable for tapping. Last, there are huge areas, in the center of the plateau, which are not drained—because there is nothing to drain!

Thus only some 18 to 20 percent of the Iranian territory is drained by the flow of rivers and streams, which carry at most 50 milliard cubic meters, or between an eighth and a sixth of the total precipitation falling over the whole country; the remainder evaporates or infiltrates. Over half the total river flow is contributed by the Karun, although it accounts for only one-fifth of the drained area.

A large part of the water flowing in the rivers has been used for a long time. The Karun irrigates magnificent palm groves, the delta of the Safid Rud gives rise to fine rice plantations, and, above all, the small rivers are very often exploited, and also *saqias* [small canals] are used to divert torrents, at their exit from steep to gentler slopes. But it is obvious that irrigation works would make it possible to utilize these flowing waters much more efficiently.

However, it is not river water which today plays the main part in irrigation, or which will play that part in future; it is, and will remain, the water in the underground pools, with which Iran is so well provided, thanks to the favorable circumstances I mentioned earlier.

I reckon that of the 6,000,000 cultivated hectares, half are irrigated by *qanats*; moreover, many crops under dry farming on the plateaus or the slopes would not be cultivated if, in the neighborhood, it had not been possible to set up a village and start market gardening by means of a *qanat*. But for this genial invention, made nearly 3,000 years ago, as I have said, the economic bases of the powerful Persian empires of ancient times would not have existed, and many of the ancient satrapies could not have come into being. But for *qanats*, the towns of Tabriz, Hamadan, Qazvin, Saveh, Tehran, Kashan, Yazd, Kirman, and Shiraz would never have been founded.

How many *qanats* are there in Iran today, and how much water do they provide? Students of this question put the number of *qanats* at between 30,000 and 50,000, and their total flow at between 500 and 750 cubic meters per second. I accept the figure given to me by Mr. Asfia a few years ago: 40,000 *qanats* with a total discharge of 600 cubic meters per second, or 15 liters per second per *qanat*, a reasonable figure. During a large part of the year, this flow is entirely used, to the last drop. This is almost equal to the discharge of the Karun at Khurram-Shahr, almost equal to the discharge of all the other rivers of Iran; for purposes of comparison, it is the mean flow of the Garonne at Bordeaux, or three times the low-water flow of the Seine. It is like a large river divided into thousands of canals, precisely at the place of use—an almost incredible phenomenon.

The main current projects based on the utilization of flowing water by means of dams will always deal with discharges smaller than the amount of water derived from underground pools by means of *qanats*, and with areas smaller than those irrigated by the latter. Still better, as I shall try to show, more can doubtless be expected from the untapped, or underutilized, water pool than from any other source.

What then are these celebrated *qanats*? Many travelers, and even foreigners who have lived long in Iran, imagine that they

are "subterranean aqueducts" constructed to transport underground—in order to protect it from evaporation—a visible and disposable amount of water from a point where it cannot be well utilized to another where it is more useful. This is completely false. It is true that in some exceptional cases the *qanat* technique has been used for aqueducts: for instance, the canal diverting the Karaj river toward Tehran, which was built in 1930, is partly underground—solely because of the lie of the land; examples have also been given where the underground conveying section of the *qanat* has been prolonged, precisely to reduce evaporation, as in the neighborhood of Yazd. But this is really accidental. The *qanats* are mining installations, using galleries called cross-cuts [*travers-bancs*] to extract a useful and expensive mineral hidden in the depths of the earth, namely, water in the underground pool, just as seams of coal are exploited by means of cross-cuts or shafts.

Not only does the digging of the shafts and cross-cuts pertain to mining technique; the search for the *qanat* and the determination of its site—especially the mother-well—are carried out by excellent hydrogeological methods, obviously more or less "unformulated" but not in the least using the dubious methods of the water-diviners. Careful observation of the conditions that have led to success and the logical deductions which have been drawn from them for research truly witness to what one may call a scientific spirit.

The *muqannis* are *qanat* specialists, who usually belong to families in which knowledge of the craft is transmitted—it is even said that there are *muqanni* villages. It has often been said that their work is particularly dangerous, that many accidents, often fatal, occur and that it would desirable if this profession were to disappear. I am not sure of this, and as there are no statistics it is difficult to know. At any rate, the *muqannis* I have questioned do not complain of danger and attribute accidents to clumsiness or carelessness rather than to the "job" itself. Obviously, I understand our fright at seeing the miner go down and up in the primitive windlass which all tourists have seen; we also exaggerate the risks of the gallery's crumbling.

One should point out a factor which partly explains the extraordinary development of *qanats* in Iran and, in identical geological conditions, in Baluchistan and Afghanistan. The "ground" is particularly favorable for the digging of both wells and galleries, by the simple methods and tools used by the *muqannis*. The gravel of which it is composed crumbles easily under a pickaxe with no need for explosives or—for a normal pace—of extraordinary efforts. But at the same time caving in is rare; what happens is limited "crumblings" of the ceiling and walls rather than the caving in of large fractured blocks. This same factor makes upkeep relatively inexpensive and allows the use of simple techniques, namely, oval ceramic pipes which fit into each other and which are brought down, through the wells, to the sectors which show a tendency to cave in.

When dealing with solid minerals, extraction is necessary. The *muqannis* have taken care to give the galleries a gentle slope, which assures the flow of the water and at the same time avoids erosion of the canal; in the porous parts, a casing of lime mortar is enough to prevent water seepage. Thus, once the *qanat* is built, its utilization costs nothing except upkeep, which is minute compared to the value of the product. The flow of water continues uninterruptedly from the impregnated zone in the water pool which the *qanat* has penetrated as deeply as possible, through the dry or conveying section, to the mouth where a network of open canals distributes the water in the cultivated area.

Who has not observed in the neighborhood of Tehran, along the Shimran roads, those trenches in the gravel? Often several meters high, vertically, they stand remarkably well and suffer only from slight crumbling after several years. This is precisely the kind of ground in which *qanats* are built all over the country. Those I have

seen in the neighborhood of Marrakesh are located in much less favorable conditions.

*Qanats* have drawbacks, which it is important to point out.

1. Water flows the whole year round. It is thus wasted during the rainy season, and also when irrigation is not required. Obviously, a small part serves domestic needs and the ingenuity of Iranians has allowed them to find some uses, which are, however, minor. Where it freezes in winter, that is, almost all over the plateau, ice is made by allowing water to spread in the shade of walls lying east and west, and the ice is kept in cellars until the autumn. Spreading water on some crops kills parasites, by freezing. But these are only palliatives and a large part of the water accumulated in the underground pool is simply wasted, flowing beyond the cultivated areas and ending in a *kavir*, where it evaporates. Ingenious experiments carried out by Mr. Asfia may perhaps obviate this drawback in new *qanats*.

The loss may not be too serious for a single *qanat*, taken in isolation—even if it is a new one—provided the production it renders possible covers its costs and amortizes it rapidly. But the inconvenience becomes serious where a group of canals overutilizes the pool and lowers the water table. In such cases there is a "regional," and therefore a "national" loss, since overall use is being kept below the natural potential of the region. In such circumstances, it is no longer private individuals who are hurt but the managing authorities. As we shall see, the drilling of wells does not have this drawback—but it has others, which mainly concern private individuals. We shall discuss this point in the "program" that follows.

2. In the course of his excavation in the saturated zone, the *muqanni* is hampered by water seeping from the floor, the sides, and finally the ceiling, even if it flows down the duct. He is therefore stopped before penetrating deeply into the water pool, which is often several meters, or even several tens of meters, thick. The table is therefore only

skimmed in its upper part, all that lies below being lost.

3. It is naturally impossible to reach layers below the usable water pool that has first been struck. Anyway, such layers are often at such depths that it would be impossible to make them flow to the surface.

4. The irrigation area commanded by the mouth of the *qanat* is limited by the configuration of the land. The *qanat* can serve only zones lying below its mouth.

The drilling of wells does not suffer from drawbacks 2 and 3, and although it is subject to 4 it makes it possible to reclaim zones lying downstream of the limits served by the *qanats*.

Drawbacks 2, 3, and 4 point out a very important fact. Where they exist, the *qanats* exploit only a small part of the water pool that could supply the region, and increasing the available water in those regions could be very significant. I am sure it would exceed the flow that could be obtained from all the dams that are economically and technically feasible.

In addition, there are large regions where the usable underground water has not been touched. In the course of my travels across the country, I have often noted virgin zones offering excellent possibilities, in which no attempt has been made to tap the water. Besides, borings made to supply water to towns, to factories, and, more seldom, to farms have demonstrated the existence of unexplored underground pools.

Indeed *qanats* have constituted a perfect solution for farmers who had no mechanical means of lifting water above a few meters. (There are some regions where shallow water pools are trapped by primitive means of raising water, for example, in Fars, but

the flow thus obtained cannot, in all, exceed a few cubic meters per second; this may have local importance but is minor compared to the output of the *qanats*). The Chinese invented drilling precisely to obtain water, but their method implies the laborious lifting of infinitesimal quantities. The situation is completely different with modern means of well drilling and pumping.

In pools not too deep below the surface, the Renney or Felman processes have been used with excellent results. . . .

OUTLINE OF A WATER POLICY

Iran therefore has the means to increase its agricultural water supply, partly by means of dams regulating the flow of rivers and streams and partly by drawing on the underground water, which is far from being fully tapped.

Professor E. Feylessoufi, who is one of the leading experts in this field, reckons that about a fourth of the *qanats* are out of use or abandoned; if those which are being used were properly taken care of and those that are unproductive were restored—which can almost always be done—the total flow could be tripled. Such a flow would be several times as great as that of the Karun, at its point of confluence with the Shatt al-Arab, and almost equal to that of the Nile in Cairo; this would transform the 18,000 villages (out of a total of 45,000) irrigated by *qanats*, which could then supply more than half the country's agricultural output.

Without being quite as optimistic, it is certain that the results that could be obtained by exploiting underground water would be considerable, and far beyond what is imagined by those who have not given much attention to this problem. . . .

## Land Tenure

The following four selections show some aspects of the system of land tenure in Iran. The first is a sketch of general conditions prevailing until the land reform of 1962 (see epilogue). The second describes agricultural practices, tenure, and taxation in the growing of cereals and other crops in Fars, in the 1870s. The other two deal with the silk-producing area of Gilan, in 1844 and in 1870.

In all countries land tenure is a complex subject, but in Iran it is more so than in most. The size of the country, the great variety of natural conditions, the co-existence of nomadic and sedentary communities, and repeated invasions by foreign peoples—Arab, Turkic, Mongol—each of which brought with it different concepts of property, have combined to produce a diverse and highly complicated system of land property and tenure. To this should be added the developments of the last hundred and fifty years: the increasing involvement of Iran in the world market led, as in other parts of the Middle East, to the growth of capitalist relations in agriculture, and modification of the ones previously existing between government, landlord, and peasant.

Thanks to the pioneering efforts of Professor Lambton, whose works constitute almost the only serious study on the subject, the rough outlines of land tenure in Iran may be discerned. Legally, the position changed comparatively little until the Constitution of 1906 and the Civil Code of 1929. Muslim law recognizes freehold property (milk), but in practice this was, with few exceptions, confined to built-up areas in towns and villages and to immediately adjacent lands. For the rest, which covered the bulk of agricultural land, ultimate ownership resided in the monarch (crown lands: khaliseh, khass) or in the whole Muslim community; the persons who actually farmed the land enjoyed only rights of usufruct and had to pay land tax (kharaj). A fourth category was constituted by land put in trust or mortmain (waqf, vaqf); here, the donor irrevocably transferred the ownership to God, the actual beneficiary being a religious or charitable institution, though the device was often used to preserve real estate in the donor's family.

Actual relations varied widely over time and place but, at the risk of over-simplification, the following general remarks may be made. First, throughout Iran's history, the basic rural unit remained the village, with a headman (kadkhuda) who represented it in its dealings with landlord and government: "The basis of the village is the peasant holding. This is reckoned in two main ways, by plough-land or by a share of water."[1] The former varied in area from locality to locality—and also within each locality, depending on the quality of land—but in principle equaled the amount that could be cultivated by a yoke of oxen (juft, zauj, khish). As in other parts of the world at comparable stages of development, equalization of shares was frequently reinforced by periodic redistribution of lots. Under the second form, which tended to prevail where irrigation water rather than cultivable land was the limiting factor, "the available amount of water is normally divided into a varying number of shares of equal duration in time and apportioned to the land"; here "periodic redistribution is not usual."[2]

At the apex of the social pyramid stood the monarch, the owner of crown lands (khaliseh, khass) and, for all practical purposes, also of state lands (divani), the two categories often not being clearly distinguished. These lands were constantly being

[1] Lambton, *Landlord*, p. 4.
[2] Ibid., p. 7.

enlarged by confiscations, but also diminished by usurpations. They were cultivated by peasants on terms that were generally not too dissimilar from those prevailing in landlord areas. But the monarch's interest in land went further, since, until very recently, it was not only the main form of wealth and the chief producer of national income but also the principal source of government revenue. Since the bulk of government expenditure went to the upkeep of the armed forces, there was a constant temptation to grant the military, on a lifetime or hereditary basis, an assignment of land, or of land taxes, in lieu of salary. These assignments were known under various names (*qatia* and *iqta* in the early Muslim period, *tuyul* and *soyurghal* under the Safavids and Qajars) and covered a wide variety of rights.[3] As was noted before, a constant theme of Persian history is the weakening of a dynasty once the original tribal impetus that brought it to power has been spent, the assigning by the monarch to military and civilian officials of fiscal and other rights which made them increasingly independent of the central government, and the conversion of such rights into either political sovereignty or hereditary private property (see Background).

The third party, standing between government and village, has always been the landlord. Large landownership (*arbabi*) has sprung from many sources, but in the last few hundred years the main one has been the *tuyul* and *soyurghal*. Particularly after the Mongol invasion had weakened the traditional and Islamic restraints on the holders of such assignments, their power seems to have grown at the expense of both the village community and, except for short periods, the central government.[4] This seems to have been the dominant trend in the last and present centuries, and to have been reversed only by the land reform of 1962 (see introduction and epilogue).

(See also works by Lambton, Petrushevskii, Keddie, EHME, and McLachlan in CHI, listed in the bibliography.)

[3] Idem, "The Evolution of the Iqta."
[4] Idem, *Landlord*, pp. 175–76.

## Selection 2. Land Rents, 1950s
[A. I. Demin, *Selskoe khozyaistvo sovremennogo Irana* (Moscow, 1967) pp. 44–50]

### BASIC FORMS OF LAND TENURE

Forms of land tenure based on labor rent never played an important part in the agricultural economy of Iran, because of the particular nature of the country's socioeconomic development. Semifeudal landlords—as well as the state and religious institutions—did not directly manage their land [*ne imeli svoei zapashki*], and they ran their farms on the basis of different kinds of rent. Labor rent was usually a supplement to rent in kind or money rent, and did not directly affect the sphere of production of the main crops. Directly related to the specific conditions of life of the Iranian village, it found expression in the fulfillment by the peasant of such obligations as the construction and repair of irrigation canals, care of the garden belonging to rich owners, provision of fuel to them, and so on.

The main form of land tenure in Iran was métayage (sharecropping). In 1960, according to official figures, 54 percent of all cultivated land, was based on it.[1] It was most widespread in eastern and western Azerbaijan, and also in Kurdistan, which are grain-growing regions. In these regions, 72.86 and 76 percent, respectively, of the land was cultivated under the *raiyati*, a sharecropping system. But in Khurasan, an [important] center of agricultural production, sharecropping was practiced on only 38.3 percent of the land.[2] However, these figures need substantial adjustment, since in Iran lands leased under other forms are distinguished in a separate category from those under the *raiyati* system. These lands include fairly large tracts leased from the state, religious institutions, landlords, and *khans* which, basically, were operated under a sharecropping system.[3] This was particularly true of Khurasan, where there were vast estates belonging to the mosque of Imam Riza. It is on this sharecropping basis that the principle inherited from the Safavids stands: dividing the crop between landowner and peasant according to the participation of each in production or, rather, according to ownership by each of its main component elements: land, water, draft animals, seeds, and labor.[4] With time this principle has suffered change, but its essence remains as it was before. Such a division of the crop, on the one hand, presupposed the separation of the peasant from the means of production and his transformation into a hired worker. But on the other, such a division of the product, in the circumstances arising from Iran's economic backwardness and the monopoly by the semifeudal landowners of the basic means of production, gave the landlords leeway for maneuver, was a means of tying the peasant to the soil, and hindered the development of capitalist relations in the Iranian village. The last-mentioned con-

sideration accounts for the fact that, although Iran has already for a long time been drawn into the orbit of the world capitalist market, its sharecropping system has, in the course of centuries, undergone only insignificant change; one can say that it has faithfully and truly served the medieval mode of production from which it was born.

Sharecropping is a convenient screen for hiding the ruthless exploitation of peasants by the semifeudal landowners. Outwardly it would appear that one side, for instance, contributed to production capital—in the form of land, water, and seeds—while the other contributed draft animals and labor, and that the product was divided accordingly. The prevailing circumstances explain the appearance of the theory that sharecropping is the most advantageous form of production in the Iranian village. According to the defenders of semifeudal landownership, it safeguards the interests of both the landlord and the peasant, for both are partners in production.[5] This theory, which was intended to deceive public opinion, does not deserve serious criticism, for the facts of the ruin and immiserization of peasants and of the reduction of yields per unit area prove that sharecropping has outlived its usefulness and constitutes an obstacle to the development of agricultural production. Nevertheless, as the very embodiment of the economic backwardness of the country, it continues to be the most widespread form of land tenure in the Iranian village.

The main change that occurred in sharecropping over the centuries has been in the division of the crop. This was affected by such important factors as the kind of land (irrigated or rain-fed), the crops grown, and so on. As a result the basic elements of production took on a somewhat different meaning, and their specific gravity increased or diminished. In addition, in arid regions where irrigation is carried out through underground canals, part of the crop is often assigned to the clearing and repair of the canals, and in those regions where fertilizers

[1] Shahpur Rasekh and Jamshid Behnam, "Jamie shinasi rustai Iran," *Sukhan* (Tehran), 1342, no. 1, p. 38.
[2] *Tehran Economist*, 3 November 1962, no. 483, p. 18; 17 November 1962, no. 485, p. 19; 1 December 1962, no. 487, p. 19; 9 February 1963, no. 497, p. 22.
[3] Rasekh and Behnam, p. 41.
[4] Muhammad Ali Ibadi, *Islahat-i arzi dar Iran* (Tehran, 1340), p. 15.

[5] *Tehran Economist*, 1961, no. 409, p. 20; 1962, no. 453, p. 13.

are used, to a greater or smaller extent, part of the crop is given to their owner. As a result systems of crop division based on 6, 7, 10, 12, 15, or 20 elements arose, in which each element of production had its place, strengthened by local traditions and customs and confirmed in sharecropping agreements.[6] But whether under one form or another, the social significance of share-cropping remained what it had been; as a rule the peasant obtained only the very minimum necessary for the reproduction of his labor power. In the collective work edited by H. H. Vreeland, it is stated that even in the most favorable circumstances, when the peasants contribute seed and draft power and receive three-fifths of the crop, they cannot maintain their families at an adequate level of living. After meeting their debts, so little is left in the hands of peasants that they are forced to resort to supple-mentary work.[7]

The forms and modes of crop division in Iranian villages are diverse. This fact, re-inforced by the shortage of published data and their frequent contradictions, makes it impossible to present an accurate picture of crop sharing. However, the evidence at our disposal allows us to perceive the basic law-conforming nature of the process, which is fully sufficient to elucidate the socio-economic content of sharecropping and, in this respect, its function as a distinctive regulator of agrarian relations on the estates of semifeudal landlords.

Analysis of the forms and modes of crop sharing shows that the view that the division of the crop was based on the specific weight of the fundamental elements of production is, to a certain extent, unfounded. The land-owners, who exercised almost uncontrolled power on their estates, often divided the crop at their own discretion. In some cases they took not only their share but also part of the peasant's, and in others they received nothing for the elements of production belonging to them. Thus in the fertile lands in the neighborhood of Isfahan, peasants

contributing draft animals and seed took only one-third of the crop. At the same time, the same share accrued to peasants in the poor lands of Baraan, in the same region, although draft animals and seed belonged to the landlords.[8] Such an action on the part of landlords was facilitated by the fact that sharecropping agreements—at any rate in the regions under the main crops—were often concluded orally, which provided a fertile soil for abuse.[9]

In this way, while analyzing the forms and modes of crop sharing, one can limit oneself to examining the final results of the division of the crop, which are directly dependent on the factors of agricultural production enumerated above: kind of soil, method of irrigation, etc. Rates of rent payments varied sharply, and ranged between 10 and 80 percent of the crop. However, in all cases, the share of the peasant did not usually exceed the amount required to provide his family with the minimum means of sub-sistence. The peasant's share was regularly higher in rain-fed land than in irrigated land, and the difference between rents attained imposing proportions. This is shown, for various regions, by data on the most common rates of rent payment pre-vailing in the sharing of grains other than rice:[10]

| | IRRIGATED LANDS | RAIN-FED LANDS |
|---|---|---|
| Isfahan | 1/3–2/3 | 1/3 |
| Fars | 1/3–1/2 | 1/5–1/10 |
| Arak | 1/3–2/3 | 1/5 |
| Kashan | 1/2–2/3 | 1/5 |
| Kirman | 1/2–3/4 | 1/10 |
| Kurdistan | 1/3–3/5 | 1/5 |
| Khurasan | 2/3 | 1/10 |
| Iranian Azerbaijan | 1/3–1/2 | 1/5 |

These rates reflect, at least to a certain extent, the share of landlords and peasants in the provision of the means of production on rain-fed and irrigated lands. In this connec-tion, the results of investigations regarding three forms of such participation are of

⁶ Rasekh and Behnam.

⁷ *Iran*, pp. 194–95.

⁸ Sh. M. Badi, *Agrarnye otnosheniya v sovremennom Irane* (Moscow, 1959), p. 44.

⁹ Rasekh and Behnam, p. 1183.

¹⁰ Ahmad Human, *Iqtisad-i kashavarzi* (Tehran, 1334), I, 320–22; Ibadi, pp. 15–17; *Andishe va hunar* 1962/63 no. 6, pp. 387–99.

interest. In the first the tenant provided only labor, in the second labor and draft animals, and in the third labor, draft animals, and seed. In irrigated zones, twenty-five farms out of one hundred were operated under the first form, seventy-four under the second, and one under the third; in rain-fed lands the corresponding figures were three, thirteen, and eighty-four.[11] This division of the means of production reflects above all the effort of rich landowners to seize the greater part of the product in irrigated areas, where crops enjoying high market demand are grown.

At the same time, the peasants' share in irrigated lands was, in absolute terms, generally not lower—and in many cases was higher—than their share in rain-fed lands, for yields on the former are always much higher than on the latter. Thus, in 1957, the average wheat yield on irrigated land was ten quintals per hectare and on rain-fed land five quintals.[12]

For rice, technical crops, and fruits and vegetables, which are grown mainly under irrigation or in regions with relatively high rainfall, rents usually range from one-third to two-thirds of the crop. But there are often deviations from this rule. In Kirman, for instance, where irrigation is mainly through underground canals and landlord oppression is particularly great,[13] rents for cotton land are up to 80 percent of the crop.[14] In general, however, the cotton crop is shared equally between landlord and peasant.[15] In Isfahan, owners of fruit trees take 75 percent of the crop.[16] At the same time, in Gilan and Mazandaran, in rice cultivation, rents are sometimes as low as one-tenth for rain-fed land and one-seventh to one-eighth for irrigated land.[17] These rates, and other similar ones which are low by Iranian standards, were designed to stimulate the production of such labor-intensive crops as rice, for which there is a great demand on the market. But here, too, the rich landowners were none the worse off. In the end the peasants, burdened by debts and cut off from the market, were often compelled to sell the crop to those same landlords, and at lower prices; this undoubtedly compensated the latter for the "losses" and "concessions" made on their share of the crop.[18]

Tenants often did not get the full share of the crop to which they were entitled because of the imperfect methods of crop estimation used, which provided a fertile soil for abuse. The crop was estimated in two ways: on the threshing floor and on the stalk [na gumne i na kornyu]. Especially in the second case, the results of the estimate depended largely on the representatives of the administration, who determined the size of the crop in the presence of the village officials. But both the administrator and the officials who carried out this important act were under the influence of the landlords and did not neglect their interests, diminishing the already small share of the peasant.

Along with sharecropping, fixed rents were fairly widely used in the Iranian village. This kind of rent provides for the conclusion of special agreements in which specified payments (in cash or kind) are set for the cultivation of one crop or another. . . .

[11] B. Khalatbari, "Die Agrarfrage in Iran," *Deutsche Aussenpolitik*, Berlin, 1962, H. 9, p. 1077.
[12] *Majalle-i rasmi-yi vazarat-i kashavarzi 1960/61*, nos. 9–10, p. 29; a quintal is equal to 100 kilograms.
[13] *Facts about Iran*, 30 May 1963.
[14] Lambton, *Landlord*, p. 316.
[15] *Cotton in the Middle East* (New York, 1952), p. 126.
[16] Hasan Abidi, *Isfahan az lihaz-i ijtimai va iqtisadi* (Isfahan, 1334), pp. 177–80.

[17] Ibadi, pp. 16–17.
[18] *Keyhan* 10 November 1958. According to *Keyhan International* of 26 July 1964, peasants often sold rice at 12 riyals per kilogram and had to buy it, for their own consumption, at 20 rials.

## Land Tenure in Gilan

Many nineteenth century observers noted that in the Caspian provinces peasants were distinctly better off than in most other parts of Iran, and the same seems to be true today. Several factors contributed to this. The abundance of rain not only eliminated the hardships caused by drought in other parts of the country but also made it relatively easy to reclaim new land; this could be done, as in Europe and America, by individuals' clearing the forest, whereas in other parts of the country costly irrigation works were necessary, which only a rich landlord or the government could afford. The proximity of Russia encouraged large-scale emigration to that country (see 2:5), which meant not only an additional source of income but often also the acquiring of new skills and attitudes by the emigrants. But another factor is that natural and market conditions favored the growing of tree crops, and such crops by their very nature demand land tenure arrangements more favorable to the tenant than do annual field crops like grain; this has been noted in other parts of the Middle East, for example, in Lebanon.

The information provided in the following two selections may be supplemented by the account given by the British consul in Rasht a few years later.[1] This, incidentally, confirms that the prohibition of the musaliseh system referred to in chapter 5, selection 4 was only temporary.

In Ghilan, one of the richest and most productive districts of Persia, where, on account of its rich vegetation, almost every plant or tree will grow, the lower classes have no reason to be unhappy. Few of them it is true, possess land, but the arrangements they make with the landowners are all to their advantage. If they engage to clear a piece of jungle, they divide the produce of the land with the owner of the ground. If mulberry trees are planted, the seedlings are purchased by the landowner, and when after a few years silk is produced, the peasant rears the worms and gets a third of the produce for his trouble, one half of the remainder going to the landowner and the other half to the speculator who furnishes the silk-worm eggs. As little supervision can be at all times exercised over the villager, he naturally contrives to secure for himself a good portion of the crop. The advantages the peasant derives from his agricultural vocation are not inconsiderable. He can cut down wood in the jungle—that is, the neglected part of his landowner's estates—and sell it on his own account. His cows and sheep can browse freely in those parts that are not under cultivation; he can make charcoal without let or hindrance; he can produce vegetables around his hut, and reap all the benefits arising therefrom; he can rear poultry and sell it on his own account; and last, but not least of all, he can dispose of the fruit which grows in abundance on the estate without consulting the owner of the land. The principal profits of the latter are his portion of the silk crop, the value of the mulberry leaf when sold, and his share of the rice produced on the estate. He also gets, out of courtesy, the fruits of the land brought to him as an offering by his tenants.

When the silk crop fails, the burthen falls principally on the landowner, who has to pay the land tax assessed years ago, irrespective of what the land may now produce. The peasantry and speculator, together with the landowner, lose their profits.

The taxes are not farmed out in Persia as they are in the Ottoman Empire, and the officers employed by Government in collecting the revenue are not, as a rule, exacting. Here and there cases do occur in which complaints are made to the superior authorities, but they do not constitute a system of oppression. As a matter of course in collecting the maliat (taxes), the collectors contrive to extract from the taxpayers some 10 per cent. or 20 per cent. more than they are entitled to, but so long as they do not exceed

[1] "Rasht," A and P 1878, 74, p. 701.

these limits everybody feels satisfied. When the tax-gatherer grows rich he is pounced upon by the governor, who makes him disgorge.

In his turn the governor is called upon by the Shah either to pay large presents on his appointment or heavy fines for reported malversations. The revenue in Ghilan is collected one half towards the end of August, by which time the silk crop, which constitutes the principal produce of the district, has been brought to maturity; the other half is collected towards the end of the financial year.

### Selection 3. Organization of Silkworm Breeding in Gilan, 1844
[K. E. Abbott, "Report on Journey to Caspian," 29 June 1844, FO 60/108]

. . . The Young Trees are raised from Seed and are very cheap, costing from 1 Sahib Kurran to 2½ Ditto or from 1/- to 2/6d per 1,000, according to their age. The Season of planting them and the following one pass without any profits to the owner. The 3rd year the leaves are gathered for the food of the Worms, but the quantity is small and therefore little Silk is obtained, until the 4th or 5th Season.—The reason of so great a quantity of Young Trees being required is that besides numbers of them getting destroyed by Wild animals the plantations must be closely set otherwise of course a longer time would pass before they yielded a sufficient supply of leaves. They are afterwards thinned as they increase in size—and they are not allowed to grow above the reach of a man's hand so that an old Plantation consists of an ugly set of stumps from the tops of which the Young branches sprout and are cut off with their leaves each season for the supply of the worms. These Plantations last a long while—the Tree is of the white Mulberry species. . . .

. . . Estates are farmed in Several ways. Sometimes the Landowner, paying all Expenses and Government claims, hires Labourers whose reward is ½ of the Produce whether of Silk, Rice or other Articles—this appears a very fair arrangement but unfortunately it is not a general one. Frequently the Landowner lets his Estate to the Peasantry for a fixed Amount of Produce—the remuneration to the latter is always very small but should the Season be unfavourable the poor Peasant has to make good any deficiency in the stipulated quantity so that he is sometimes actually a loser by this method. Occasionally the Proprietor farms the land himself hiring Labourers but this mode answers only for those who are resident on the spot and will not generally speaking prove advantageous to the Resident in town who cannot overlook the Work. When the Property belongs to the Peasant the Governor of the district exacts almost what he pleases or is able to get from him, for at present the poor man has no one to appeal to for redress—he therefore often finds it more advantageous to be without than with landed Property of his own and accordingly makes the best bargain he can with his Chief for the disposal of it and in this way much property has changed hands from the poor to the rich man. After the Plague also a great deal of land which had become almost untenanted was purchased by the wealthy Inhabitants and in these two ways the landed Property of the Province in the Possession of the Upper classes has increased probably to 8/10th of the whole. . . .

### Selection 4. Organization of Silkworm Breeding in Gilan, 1870
[Abbott to Thomson, 5 April 1870, FO 60/328]

I have the honor to report, with reference to the concluding paragraph of my despatch No. 3, that the Minister for Foreign Affairs, shortly before leaving Resht, adopted a measure which was calculated to be most detrimental to the welfare of this Province. This was the abolition of Musaliseh, a system fraught with equal benefits to Silk speculators, landed proprietors and the peasantry, affording at the same time one of the best means that could be devised for the development of the staple industry of this Province which has been reduced to a state of great impoverishment, in consequence of a disease of long standing amongst the silk worms.

By the terms of the arrangement called Musaliseh, Armenian Merchants of Persian or Russian Nationality were permitted to distribute silk worms eggs amongst the land-owners and to aid them with small loans or advances on the crops, free of interest; and the landlords, in their turn, were thus enabled to assist the ryots in a similar manner. After the crops, the profits were equally divided between the speculator, the proprietor and the peasant, one third being allotted to each of the parties; and if there was a very bad crop—or none at all, as is now not unfrequently the case in many localities—the people were not pressed for immediate payment and ultimately reduced to penury, as they would have been in the hands of the usurer.

It will thus be seen that the System of Musaliseh offered great advantages to the landlords who were not required to disburse any funds for seed and to the peasant who had not to resort to the Moneylender whilst it insured the introduction of healthy seed into the Province, it being obviously in the interest of the speculator to procure the best quality he could and to devote every care to the proper rearing of the worms.

The late Governor and his predecessor were alive to the advantages of this arrangement and wisely sanctioned it because they knew that the Government was never likely to come to the aid of this Province by furnishing Seed for the Silk crops, whether for the landlord proprietors, who had not the Means of procuring it themselves, or for the crown lands.

I am informed that the Minister for Foreign Affairs was influenced in great Measure by the Chief Priest Hajee Mollah Reffee in abolishing Musaliseh under the pretext that it caused embarrassments to the Government and deprived the landlords of a great part of their crops; but I think

His Excellency will eventually discover that the interdiction of the system will create more serious embarrassments than the continuance of it was ever likely to produce.

It has been reported to me on good authority that the Minister, whilst at this place, announced that he had two hundred batmans of seed at his disposal for distribution amongst such landed proprietors as might be in want of it and that His Excellency even called upon the latter to furnish him with written requisitions for it; but it soon became apparent that these promises, like others, were not made for the purpose of fulfilment. No seed was forthcoming and the landed proprietors as well as the cultivators of the Crown lands were ultimately given to understand that if they wanted it they must find it themselves as best they could. . . .

## Selection 5. Land Tenure and Taxes in Fars, 1878

["Report on Bushire," A and P 1880, 73, pp. 250–55]

### CULTIVATION IN KAZEROON

The land in Kazeroon is private property. If the cultivation be undertaken by the landowner himself, he has to provide seed for an area of one "gao"[1] of cultivation, viz., 1,000 lbs. wheat and 1,000 lbs. barley, and pay about 14 krans for the labour of ploughing and sowing. He pays in kind 11 per cent of the yield of his harvest to Government, and 20 per cent. to the reapers, who have to undertake all the duties appertaining to the collection of the harvest and the carriage into the stores of the landlord. The landowner also pays 2 to 4 per cent. for threshing or treading the corn.

Other than a landowner undertaking a cultivation has to pay to the landowner 9 per cent. in kind from the out-turn of his harvest as rent for one "gao" of ground, and 14 per cent. to Government as tax; his other expenses are the same as above.

The agriculturalists of Kazeroon are of

[1] The extent cultivable with one ox.

two classes, viz., the "ryot-i-padishah," and the non-ryot, the former being always looked down upon by all classes, and subjected by Government to more oppression than the others. The ryot cultivator thus not only pays more taxes to Government, but has to pay his taxes in cash instead of in kind, and at 30 per cent. above market value. He is also obliged to give a certain quantity of straw to Government officials whenever required.

A ryot, when a landowner and cultivating his own grounds, has to pay $15\frac{1}{2}$ per cent. on his harvest in cash, and at the above enhanced valuation.

A poor ryot pays about 60 krans annually in cash to Government. There is another class of ryots who are obliged to buy at 30 per cent. above market value a certain portion of the produce received by Government as taxes. A wealthy ryot is entirely at the mercy of the authorities, a sum of about 1,000 krans being annually levied from him. The value of one "gao" of land is from 100 to 600 krans, according to the locality.

To start a cultivation an expense of about 15 tomans is necessary, viz:—

|  | KRANS |
|---|---|
| One ox, valued at | 50 |
| Seed, valued at | 60 |
| Labour, about | 14 |
| Straw and cotton seeds | 16 |
| Sundries | 10 |

One donkey is also maintained by a ryot when undertaking four or more "gaos" of cultivation.

About 2,000 lbs. of grain is sufficient for cultivating one "gao" of ground at Kazeroon.

In the case of "saifee" (summer) cultivation no distinction is made by Government between a ryot and a non-ryot.

"Saifee" sowings are always undertaken by proprietors of water and agriculturists conjointly, the proprietor providing the water and ground and the agriculturist finding the seed, labour, implements, &c.

Should the water owner, however, not be a landowner as well, any other landowner would be but too glad to permit his lands to be used for "saifee" cultivation gratis, inasmuch as the soil becomes enriched by manuring, which the "saifee" cultivation necessitates.

The time taken up for "saifee" sowing is about seven months, the following being cultivated:—Tobacco, water melon, marsh melon, vegetables, cotton, sesame-seeds, lentils, rice, gram, &c.

A tax of 20 per cent. *ad valorem* on the out-turn is levied by Government, three-fifths of which is payable by the proprietor of the water and two-fifths by the cultivator, and the balance is equally divided between the proprietor and cultivator.

Rice and gram, however, form an exception, and are cultivated under the following conditions:—

The agriculturist recoups himself for the quantity of seed supplied by him after harvest. He then goes into equal shares with the water owner, who alone pays Government taxes as follows:—If a ryot, he pays three-fifths of his share to Government; if a non-ryot, he pays only half, the agriculturist paying no tax on his share.

In all cases the Government share of the produce is to be carried to Government stores at the cultivators' expense.

The approximate value of the produce on the spot is—

|  | PER KAZEROON MAUND | |
|---|---|---|
| Wheat at | 40 to 60 cents | |
| Barley | 25 | 30 cents |
| Gram | 50 | 80 cents |
| Sesame | 70 | 100 cents |
| Maithee | 15 | 20 cents |
| Dhall | 15 | 20 cents |
| Cotton | $2\frac{1}{2}$ | 3 krans |
| Rice 9 | 50 | 80 cents |

The expenses of a ryot cultivator in Kazeroon, supposed to have one wife and two children, are 10 tomans per annum.

The yield of wheat and barley is from tenfold to twelve-fold in a good year, and three-fold to four-fold in a bad one.

Rice in a bad year yields twenty-fold, and in a very good year sixty-fold; cotton five-fold in a bad year, and ten-fold in a good year.

Irrigation in Kazeroon is generally conducted by means of kanats, and the water thereof should in all cases be allowed free passage across grounds, even though not belonging to the proprietor of the kanat.

Should the proprietor of a kanat not wish to undertake any "saifee" cultivation he would still be made liable by Government to such taxes as may be due by the cultivator.

The land in Kazeroon is sown every alternate year. The portions remaining fallow are ploughed.

No taxes whatever are levied by Government on gardens at Kazeroon.

In the cultivation of the poppy at Kazeroon the proprietor provides the land, seed, and expenses of sowing; the cultivation is then made over to the ryot, who undertakes all the labour necessary for the tending of the crop till the season of cultivation, when the proprietor pays for the labour of incision, say 1 kran per man per day. The out-turn is then equally divided between the landowner and ryots. No taxes are levied by Government on the cultivation of opium at Kazeroon.

There are large tracts of land in Fars with plentiful supply of water, but owing to the perennial growth of rank grass, cultivation is impeded to the ruin of landowners and that of the ryots, who are obliged by compulsion to stay permanently in those spots.

A good deal of water is wasted in Persia owing to the long distances it has very often to travel before reaching a land eligible for its security against raids, &c., and to damages constantly sustained by watercourses, which, owing to the social conditions of the country, it is very often beyond the reach of the ryot to travel out of the jurisdiction of his village to repair.

There are also large tracts of fertile land which remain waste owing to their proximity to the main roads, as no village having cultivators on such spots can possibly prosper or enjoy the least immunity from the pestering visits of Government officials, and thefts and robberies committed by the "Iliyat"

tribes on their passage along the country thoroughfares.

MEMORANDUM ON CULTIVATION OF A VILLAGE IN ONE OF THE BOOLOOKS (DISTRICTS) OF SHIRAZ

A village with an area of land sufficient for sowing 18,000 to 20,000 maunds of grain is valued at 60,000 krans. Government taxation on such a village would be about 2,500 krans per annum, which is considered to be more or less reasonable.

This area is divided into three parts, of which one part only is cultivated during the year, the other two parts being allowed to remain fallow, awaiting their turn for cultivation in subsequent years.

The "shatwee" or autumn sowings for the year in such a village necessitate the outlay of seed in the following proportion:—

|  | MAUNDS |
|---|---|
| Barley . . . . . . . . | 2,000 |
| Wheat . . . . . . . . | 4,000 |

"Saifee" or spring sowings are proportioned as under:—

|  | MAUNDS |
|---|---|
| Rice . . . . . . . . . | 400 |
| Maize . . . . . . . . | 200 |
| Cotton . . . . . . . . | 200 |
| Sesame, &c. . . . . . | 100 |

The out-turn of "shatwee" sowing is ten-fold in a good year and five-fold in a bad one; rice, thirty-fold during a prosperous year, and ten-fold during an unfavourable one; maize, fifty-fold during a good year, and twenty-fold during a bad year.

Irrigation may be natural, such as by rivers and springs, or artificial, by means of kanats. A kanat is invariably private property appertaining to the village and involving an annual expenditure of 500 krans to keep it in repair.

If the village happen to be irrigated by a river, the proprietor of that village has to pay for his share of the watercourse leading to his lands. If irrigated by a spring, disputes very frequently arise on account of proprietors of other villages attempting to draw away more water than is their due. This is due to the insufficiency of water supplied by a spring. An outlay of 600 krans is necessary towards obtaining a favourable or just decision.

Such a village should entertain 40 ryots, irrespective of their families and strangers, and have 20 bands (pairs) of beasts of burden, or 40 oxen. The ryots find themselves altogether. The out-turn is divided into three parts—one-third for the ryots and two-thirds for the proprietor; if the proprietor should wish to bring his share of the produce to town, he must defray the expenses of the carriage.

All taxes on the land and water are paid by the proprietor, the amount of which in most cases varies in proportion to his position and influence, for he either manages to pay the taxes as per ancient Government "toomar" (tariff), which is generally on a low scale, or contrives to lessen a certain amount from the new and higher rate of taxation, the deficiency in which latter case is burthened on the revenues of a neighbouring village whereof the proprietor may be less influential.

Taxation on villages is very irregular, and in most instances extremely oppressive. Wealthy and prosperous villages worth about 50,000 krans are known to pay only 300 to 500 krans per year, whereas smaller and less prosperous villages are subjected to a payment of 10,000 to 12,000 krans per year. In the latter case the owner necessarily is a ruined man and always in trouble with Government, whose officials become liberal with the bastinado and imprisonment for default of payment. It is not at all a paying thing in the end to be a farmer in Persia, unless, however, the proprietor is a really influential man, or a "moola" or a "mojtehid." The difficulties experienced by a proprietor are as follows:—Want of protection against the robberies of the ryots; the heavy Government taxation, ordinary and extraordinary; and the constant and false claims set up against the property. This last is a characteristic feature in Persia, especially as there is no law for the punishment of a false claimant. Many *bonâ-fide* landowners therefore have been utterly

ruined. Such false claims are always tolerated both by the Government and priesthood, as it constitutes a sure source of income to them.

The taxes are paid in kind on the "shatwee" sowings and in cash on the "saifee" sowings.

There are two classes of ryots, viz., one called the "ryot-i-padishah" who pay only "sarmardy" or poll-tax, and no change of residence to however great a distance from his original place of abode will exempt him from the levy of that tax; the ryots of Dashty are in this category. The other class pays no "sarmardy," but a sum of about 20 krans is annually taken from each ryot towards the maintenance of Government sowars, &c., but in many instances where the "kedkhoda" or the landlord possesses any influence, this payment is successfully resisted, the actual taxation on the land and cultivation however being payable by the owner.

The proprietor provides for the seed; labour during cultivation up to collection after harvest is undertaken by the ryots.

Education is totally neglected, but each village is bound to have one person able to read and write.

A "motesadee" (overseer) is entertained by the proprietor, receiving as his salary 3 per cent. on the produce. A kedkhoda is also appointed by the proprietor, taking 5 per cent; this person is obliged to entertain the proprietor whenever he should call at the village, as also all persons deputed by Government that may be passing there on duty. The kedkhoda is expected to have one mare at least.

The expenses incurred by the kedkhoda for the occasional entertainment of the owner and his servants may amount to 30 tomans annually, his own (kedkhoda's) private expenses not exceeding that amount. It is not customary for the proprietor to make a long stay in his village, and there are landlords who have never seen their property.

A systematic spoliation is carried on by the ryots both during the season for sowing and gathering in the harvest; and in no instance has a farmer been able to check these robberies or to ascertain the exact quantity of his harvest, notwithstanding the motesadee and kedkhoda are pretty often administered the bastinado.

The value of the produce on the spot may be quoted as under:—

| | PER MAUND |
|---|---|
| Wheat . . . . . . . . | 25 cents |
| Barley . . . . . . . . | 12½ cents |
| Rice . . . . . . . . . | 50 cents |
| Cotton . . . . . . . . | 1.50 krans |
| Maize . . . . . . . | 10 cents |
| Sesame, &c.. . . . . . | 70 cents |

The value of the 40 oxen varies from 30 to 100 krans, thus averaging about 6 tomans per head.

As a rule the oxen are bought and maintained by the ryots themselves; but in cases where the ryots are unable to do so the proprietor provides the cash, and reimburses himself after the harvest.

The annual cost for the maintenance of an ox is about 15 krans, but no cash is laid out for that purpose, as the food is grown on the land itself, cotton-seeds forming the principal and most nourishing part of it.

The agricultural instruments principally in use are the following:— Khish (plough), borré (a machine consisting of sharp-edged discs, used for separating grain from husk), aubsee (winnowing fork), daus (sickle), khooré (sack), beel (spade), two or three sieves, jawal (pannier), and ropes. A supply of at least 50 krans worth of implements being required for each "gao," is furnished by and appertains to the ryots.

Two hundred krans may be taken as an approximate estimate of the annual expenses of a ryot and his family.

In no case does the value of the furniture of a ryot—consisting of copper utensils, a couple of inferior carpets, a few earthen jars, beer or soda-water bottles—exceed 20 tomans.

A proprietor is often obliged to construct a wall round the village, with a gate and a tower or two. The ryots build their own quarters and at their own expense.

Every ryot invariably undertakes a small amount of cultivation on his own private account, which is called "khássee," and in which the proprietor has no share whatever.

## Silk Production

The sharp contraction of Iran's output of silk in the eighteenth century (see Background) was followed by a steady and rapid increase in the first half of the nineteenth. In the 1840s most estimates put the Gilan crop, which accounted for about five-sixths of total output, at over 1,000,000 pounds and its value at around £500,000; and a peak of 2,190,000 pounds, worth £1,000,000 was reached in 1864.[1] An important factor in this expansion was the activity of various Greek and other firms, notably Ralli Brothers (see 3:11), who advanced the necessary funds to growers, directly or through small merchants, many of them Armenians.

In 1864 the muscardine disease which had been ravaging European crops reached Iran, and by 1873 Gilan's output had fallen to 210,000 pounds, with a value of £135,000.[2] The effect on the province was disastrous: "Some fifteen years ago the annual silk crop of Ghilan represented a native capital of two millions sterling—a capital which has since decreased to one-third of that amount; but the province is still assessed at the same rate for the *maliat*, or land tax, as it was then."[3] However, successful efforts were made by Ralli and other firms to combat the

[1] See table in Curzon, *Persia*, 1:367.

[2] Ibid.—for details see annual reports on Gilan in A and P 1866 to 1874; a wealth of information, including a set of figures which often differ from those given by Curzon, is to be found in Stolze and Andreas, pp. 20–22.

[3] "Gilan," A and P 1871, 65.

disease by introducing silkworm eggs from Japan, and by the mid 1870s crops began to improve again.[4] In 1890 another Greek firm, Pascalidis Brothers, brought in eggs from Bursa, which also proved successful, and by the beginning of the present century output had regained or surpassed the previous peak.[5] But the competition of Japanese and other silks kept prices down, and the value of exports did not exceed £400,000.[6] Most of these exports went to France and Italy.

(See also works by Curzon, Stolze and Andreas, Fateh, and Jamalzadeh, listed in the bibliography, and *EI*(2) s.v. "Filaha" and "Harir.")

[4] "Rasht," A and P 1873, 68, and "Gilan," A and P 1874, 67.

[5] Jamalzadeh, p. 27. Of course the introduction of better varieties of eggs encountered many obstacles. Thus when, in 1873, it was discovered that Sabzevar eggs produced better results than Japanese, some merchants bought poor eggs in Gilan and sold them to merchants in Sabzevar, who resold them—as Sabzevar eggs—in Gilan. The government did nothing to discourage such practices, nor indeed did it make any attempt to remedy the situation except for prohibiting the export of Persian eggs. (See dispatches of 25 September 1873 and 28 October 1876, AE Téhéran, vol. 2).

[6] A table showing the quantity of exports of cocoons from Gilan in 1893–1909 and 1921–25 is given in *Severnaya Persiya*, p. 50.

## Selection 6. Silk Production and Trade, 1812

[Ouseley to Court of Directors, 5 August 1812, FO 60/7]

*Tabriz*

Having been applied to by the Hon^ble Company's Resident at Besheher on the subject of the silk to be procured in the Northern provinces of H. Persian Majesty's Dominions, I have sent people into Gilan and to Resht on the Caspian to bring me samples as well as particular information respecting the quantity collected in that province, the prices etc. etc. etc.

As however, it may be of some importance to the Hon^ble Court to be furnished with the substance of what I have been able to collect on this subject, without loss of time I have the honor to acquaint you that in the Province of Gilan alone, 40,000 Shahi Maunds of about 15 lbs. each are annually collected of three sorts, varying seldom a Tuman per Maund each Year. The best sort from 9 to 10 Tumans per Maund—the second from 6 to 7—the third from $3\frac{1}{2}$ to $4\frac{1}{2}$.—Of this quantity I cannot at present give you any idea how much is exported to Russia, how much consumed in Persia, and what surplus remains in the Market, but this I know that the Hon^ble Company may safely reckon upon every preference & every advantage that the strong influence which that Body now enjoys here can insure.

The inland Transportation is the business of greatest moment. A mule load 20 Shahi Maunds, of 200 Tumans value, could not be delivered at Busheher under 5 Tumans, or for shortness $2\frac{1}{2}$ per Cent. But it strikes me that if you could arrange with the Levant Company and the Turkish Government a great saving might be made both in time & Freight by having it shipped for you at Trebizond on the Black Sea. The land carriage would also be 1 p. cent less— and you might receive the Cargo in London three months after its purchase in Resht: however ere long I hope to be enabled to give you more satisfactory elucidations on this subject. On a rough calculation it appears that considering the Tuman at 17^s6^d and the Shahi Maund at 15 lbs. the silk would stand the Hon^ble Company at the rate of 8^s6$\frac{1}{4}$^d per lb. in Busheher or 8^s5$\frac{1}{4}$^d at Trebizond, at equal quantities of all 3 kinds, exclusive of the charges of purchase which, need not be certainly at all heavy.

At Sheki & Shamakhi on the left bank of the Arras & Kur Rivers a great quantity is collected annually but I can not speak at present as to its being monopolized by the Russians or not.

Of the Quality of either Kinds I am no judge, and therefore must refer you to the Samples which in the Course of a Couple of Months I hope to have the honor of forwarding to you.

### Selection 7. Silk Production, 1842
["Report on the Silk Trade of Ghilan," 5 May 1842, FO 60/90]

*Ghilaun*

In conformity with the instructions which I received last year from Her Majesty's Government and with the approval of Her Majesty's Minister at Tehran, I proceeded from that City on the 15th February on a visit into Ghilaun.

I experienced great difficulty this time in eliciting information from the people whose suspicions were aroused by my repeating my visit to Ghilaun, they seemed to be apprehensive lest the information I sought should be turned to their disadvantage and there was consequently the greatest reluctance shown in answering my questions, or they were frequently replied to in a way which convinced me that no reliance could be placed on the information given. I stated generally that my wish was to acquaint myself with the state of the Silk Trade of the Province and to endeavour to induce the people to adopt an improved method in the preparation of their Silk by which it would be rendered considerably more valuable to them and better suited to the English Market—that with this view I had taken pains when in England to inform myself on the subject and had brought with me samples of different kinds of Silks, such as are esteemed in Europe, to distribute in Ghilaun. I explained that I had no other motive in view than the prosperity of the Province and of the trade— that as regarded our own merchants they would, generally speaking, prefer receiving Silk in exchange for their merchandize, to being paid for it in coin, provided the Silk were of the description they required— it therefore was obviously for the benefit of both Countries that improvements should be adopted. The Samples were received with every appearance of satisfaction and were much admired for their fineness and even thread. Some were in return produced of the Silk of the Province, which really appeared to me to approach very nearly to, if not equal in quality, the fine Silk of Turkey, but the quantity produced of this description is too insignificant to be otherwise worth noticing.

Knowing the apathy and dullness of Asiatics in matters of this kind, I should be slow in placing faith in the many assurances I received from people of their readiness to adopt the required alterations—there are besides serious difficulties to any plan for rendering the Silk of Ghilaun more valuable than at present, as an Export to England. Still, I would hope that what is really so requisite to the prosperity of our trade with this Country, may sooner or later be accomplished.

The objections to what I urged are principally these. The Persian skein of Silk is too long for general use in England, and the thread is usually uneven and knotty. The people are unwilling to alter their machinery (simple as the operation with them would be) in order to remove the first objection, on the score of its being less difficult to wind off the Silk on a large than on a small hand-wheel—and that it is more expeditiously and therefore more advantageously performed with the former. As regards the second point, the uneven quality of the thread of the Silk, it is stated that to remove this objection, so much more labour and time would be required that it would not be practicable on a large scale, because, on account of the excessive dampness of the climate the Cocoons became injured if not quickly wound off. These would at first appear reasons sufficient to remove the hope of any improvement ever being effected, but that it is probable the difficulties have been much exaggerated and that should the example once be set obstacles which at first appear great to an indolent people would probably vanish when they had distinctly before them the prospect of advantage—at least such has been the case elsewhere in the East.

It may be objected that the Silk wound into short skeins would be adapted only to the manufacturers in England and France, of those countries which are interested in the article, and that those of Russia would still require the long skein and this I believe is the case. Also it may be said that as the quantity of Persian Silk which England receives is inconsiderable, the subject is one of small importance, but it is my decided opinion that the ameliorations I have pointed out would, if adopted, lead in time to a very sensible improvement in our Commerce with this Country, and were it properly prepared no quantity of Silk which Persia could ever offer us would fail of a market in England. Persia takes from us annually to the amount of about £500,000 worth of manufactured goods, but besides silk she has no article of any value to offer us in return—of this at present she exports to Europe through Constantinople a quantity probably amounting in value to no more than Two Fifths of the above sum, and her other exports consist of articles of small value. Thus the balance of this Trade is much against Persia and there is consequently a continued drain on her currency. Could she offer us good Silk instead of an article which even in small quantities is of difficult sale in England, the exchange would, I am convinced, lead to a rapid increase of the trade on both sides. The short reel would enhance its value and bring the article into more general use in England even if the quality of the silk was not improved.

I feel convinced that the length of reel is the point first to be attended to and when that difficulty has been overcome other improvements it may be hoped will follow in course of time.

My information leads me to believe that the Silk Trade of Ghilaun continues to prosper—that notwithstanding the general misrule common to all parts of Persia, the injustice and exactions of each successive Governor the wealth of the Province is great and increasing. The clearance of the Forest to make way for the cultivation of the Mulberry Tree is becoming each year more extended and the riches of the Province are evidently limited only by a deficiency of population.

At present the value of the Silk produced in Ghilaun is by no means inconsiderable as may be shown by the following statement of the quantity which paid duty at Resht during the year ending 21st March 1842, to which is added the manner of its distribution and the Revenue derived from it under the form of Custom Duties.

| IN WHAT PARTS | NUMBER OF PACKAGES | WEIGHT IN MAUNS SHAHEE | PRICE | VALUE IN TOMAUNS | RATE OF DUTY | AMOUNT OF DUTY |
|---|---|---|---|---|---|---|
| To Russian Possessions . . . . | 2,200 | 15,400 | T°13 | T°200,200 | at To. 3 per Package | T° 6,600.–. |
| To various parts of central & Southern Persia for consumption and to Baghdad . . . . | 3,010 | 18,060 | T°12 | T°216,720 | at Ks. 2½ per Maun | T° 4,515.— |
| To Tabreez for Constantinople & the Russian Provinces for local consumption . . . . . | 7,000 | 42,000 | T°12 | T°504,000 | at Do. Do. | T° 10,500.— |
| Consumed in Resht. . . . . . | 34 | 200 | T°12 | T°2,400 | at Do. Do. | T° 5.— |
| Packages of 6 or 7 mauns each. . | 12,244 | 75,660 | | T°923,320 | | T°21,620.— |
| English lbs. | 1,008,800 | | | £461,660 | | £10,810 |

The Custom Houses of Lahijan and Fomen derive also something from duties on Silk, and a good deal is carried out of the Province without paying any Customs dues, so that I think the whole produce of Silk wound into Skeins may fall nothing short of 90,000 mauns Shahee or about 1,200,000 lbs. value Tomauns 1,080,000 or about £540,000. Besides there is Waste Silk in great quantities—in fact I believe that for every maun of Silk wound into Skeins there is an equal quantity of waste silk, some of which is spun into yarn and sent with the rest chiefly to Baghdad. It is not very valuable—the yarn may be reckoned, on an average, at Two Tomauns per maun of which there may be about 7,000 mauns, and the other which is not at all worked up in Ghilaun may be taken at Eight Sahib Kurauns per annum of which there would probably be about 80,000 mauns—value of the two Toms. 78,000 or about £39,000 and the value of the whole produce of Silk in the Country Toms. 1,158,000 or about £579,000.

This is a large amount for so small and so thinly peopled a Province, containing probably not more than Fifteen hundred square miles more than half of which may be mountain land where the Mulberry Tree is not cultivated, and the population of the whole of which, it is thought, does not exceed One Hundred Thousand souls.

Add to this amount of exportable wealth, the produce of the Sturgeon, Salmon and other fisheries from which the Government certainly derives but a small revenue com-pared with their value, and it will be acknowledged that independently of its Geographical position, Ghilaun is a tract of country indispensable to Persia—that the loss of it would prove most disastrous to her, and that for ages the source of great wealth to the Government and Empire, it is deserving of the utmost attention and care of the Sovereign—but neither the one nor the other is bestowed on it—the system of financial Government is becoming every year more vicious than before, the people obtain no redress for wrongs and the utmost dissatisfaction exists throughout the Province. . . .

### Selection 8. Silk Production, 1900s
[F. Lafont and H.-L. Rabino, *L'industrie séricole en Perse* (Montpellier, 1910), pp. 28–30, 44, 48–50]

OUTPUT OF THE VARIOUS PROVINCES OF PERSIA
. . . Gilan has always been, and still is, the province that produces by far the largest quantity of silk. If one can accept the figures given by Chardin, in 1670 Gilan accounted for 1,269,000 kilograms of silk, out of a total Persian output of 1,900,000.

In 1865, 1887, 1890, and the last few years, production of raw silk was distributed roughly as follows (in metric tons).

| PLACE | 1865 (Duseigneur) | 1887 (Rondot) | 1890 (J. Rabino) | PRESENT |
|---|---|---|---|---|
| Gilan. . . . . . . . . . . . . | 220 | 251 | 210 | 450 |
| Mazandaran and Astarabad . . . | 8 | 16 | 15.8 | 30 |
| Khurasan . . . . . . . . . . . | 16 | 10 | 7.3 | 45 |
| Azerbaijan . . . . . . . . . . | 4 | 15 | 14.7 | 15 |
| Center (Yazd, Kashan) . . . . . | 32 | 8 | 6 | 10 |
| | 280 | 300 | 253.8 | 550 |

. . . Silkworm eggs are sold either directly by importers, or through agents, to Persian landowners (or their bailiffs), in one of three ways:

1. The seller of eggs advances to landowners a small sum, for example five francs on every box sold; no interest is charged on the amounts advanced, but the price per box is set at one franc below the ruling price, and the landowner undertakes to deliver to the supplier of eggs a certain quantity of cocoons at about 10 centimes per kilogram below the price prevailing in the market at such and such a date during the [coming] season. This mode of sale, which was especially popular between 1899 and

1906/7, is less and less used nowadays; however, newly established importers, or those who want to advertise their goods and who have sufficient funds, make use of it to gain clients.[1] It presents much risk for the seller, who has to use all sorts of methods and wait patiently for several years to recover his loans. Occasionally, too, landowners who have undertaken to deliver their crop to him secretly sell their cocoons to other people, in order to get slightly more, or else hand over to him only their worst cocoons.

2. The landowner pays for the eggs at harvest time, in cocoons. Formerly, he gave one-third of the crop as the price of the eggs (the so-called *musaliseh* contract); then, because of increasing competition among importers, this gave way to one-fourth (*murabieh*), one-fifth (*mukhamiseh*), one-sixth (*musadiseh*), one-eighth, and one-tenth of the crop. At present, the seller of eggs usually receives two to three kilograms of fresh cocoons per box. The *musaliseh* and *murabieh* were especially prevalent from 1894 to 1899.

In both the above-mentioned forms of sale, the two parties draw up a contract.

3. Sales are made against cash payment; this method, which is the most correct one, is still little used but is becoming more widespread.

Sale prices in the Gilan markets are very volatile;[2] in 1894, some boxes were sold at 7.50 to 9 francs apiece; in 1899, at 4.50 to 5.25 francs; in 1900, at 3 to 4 francs. In 1906, most of the importers formed a union [*syndicat*] and undertook not to sell below 4.50 to 5 francs; at the end of the season, 30,000 boxes remained, which were destroyed in order to maintain prices. In 1908, several importers sold at 5 to 6 francs, but owing to excessive imports prices fell sharply and in April some boxes were sold in the bazaar for a few sous.

At a sale price of 5 francs, importers make substantial profits.

Almost all importers of eggs are also buyers of cocoons, and the most distinct profits are generally those made on the sale of eggs and on the advancing of money at high interest; hence, when they buy fresh cocoons from a landowner, the egg merchants try to obtain a written undertaking that he will buy from them the eggs he needs for the following season.

Since 1906, it would seem that cash sales have been exclusively used; in fact, advances are still made but the amounts lent are variable and smaller than in the past. . . .

The silk trade is carried on by native peddlers called *tavvafs*, who go through the villages immediately after the cocoons have been gathered and ensure their purchase by advancing to the peasants 50 francs for every ten kilograms of dry cocoons. Ten or fifteen days later, the *tavvaf* returns, takes delivery of the silk, and pays for it at a rate of 2 krans below the market price prevailing that day in Rasht, keeping the 2 krans as a commission.

The small *tavvafs* hand over the silk they have picked up here and there to bigger *tavvafs*, who in turn sell it to silk merchants on six-month credit; no interest is charged for the first three months, but for the last three a rate of 12 percent of the value of the goods is paid.

For some time, in the various markets of Gilan, sales have been made only on a cash basis. The buyer has the right to take two *dirhams* on sales of silk and floss, constituting what is called *tavfi-i-mil*, or difference of the scales (in France this is known as "la montre").

---

[1] The advancing of money on future and uncertain crops is very widespread in Persia, especially for export products such as cotton, tobacco, opium, etc; should the crops fail, claims may rise to a disquieting extent and, consequently, the larger European firms increasingly abstain from such operations. Greek and Armenian merchants, long established in the various localities, are more fit for this kind of speculation and manage, with patience and skill, to recover their loans on favorable terms.

The Banks advance loans to those importers of eggs who do not have enough funds to finance their operations and, in such cases, a large part of the profit accrues to the banks, which charge a fairly high rate of interest.

[2] The centers for the sale of eggs are: Rasht and Lahijan in Gilan; Barfurush and Sari in Mazandaran; Bujnurd, Sabzevar, and Turbat in Khurasan; and Kashan and Yazd in the central provinces.

The unit of weight in silk sales is the *dirham* (30.16 grams).[3] Silk is sold the whole year round, but especially in summer, from harvesting time (end of June) to September or October.

The *tavvafs* usually have a capital of 15,000 to 25,000 francs for their transactions, which consist exclusively of spot [*sans terme*] purchases and sales. Some, however, export raw silk or knubs and take in exchange cloth coming by way of Baghdad or Tabriz. All the silk merchants of Rasht have their offices in the street known as *Rasteh Tavva-fha*.

Silk is produced in all the places where silkworms are raised. The best kind comes from the town and vicinity of Rasht (*mawazi-i-Rasht*), followed by that of the villages near the Safid-Rud river (*Kenari Safid Rud*), especially Rashtabad, Fushtum, Ibrahim Sera, and Chulab on the left bank and Bazeki-Gurab, Kisum, and Astaneh on the right bank. Next comes the silk of Shaft and Fomen; the least valued are those of Langrud, Gaskar, and Talish. The rank we have indicated is not immutable—it may be changed by various causes, notably by the quality of the crops.

The various kinds of native silk have the following names; they are ranked, roughly, by value:

*Sharbafi* (meaning "for weaver")—this is the best silk; much is sent to the central part of the country, for weaving in Yazd, Kashan, and Isfahan.

*Ala*—second quality silk.

*Tajiri* (meaning "merchant's")—third quality silk.

*Tai*—third quality silk.

*Alaghbandi* (meaning "for lace").

*Duvil*—silk from double cocoons, for rough silks.

*Kaj*—silk made from knubs or floss, for rough silks.

In Rasht a considerable amount of twisted silk is made for embroidery, sewing, lace, and rich trimmings; for this *tai* silk

[3] The *dirham* equals 6.40 *mithqals*, of 4.64 grams each.

and the first quality of *alaghbandi* silk are used.

As in Europe, silk prices fluctuate, in response to demand by the factories and the abundance or scarcity of the commodity in the market.

In 1840, extra Gilan silk known as *milani* (which was made especially for Tabriz) fetched 28 to 32 krans per kilogram, *sharbafi* silk 25 to 27 krans, *ala* 21 to 22 krans, *tajiri* 20 to 21 krans, and knubs 4 to 5 krans; at that time the kran was worth about one franc.

In the summer of 1857 prices in Rasht were:

> 1st quality, bought by natives
>     54 to 58 francs a kilogram
> 1st quality, bought by Ralli Brothers
>     45 to 50 francs a kilogram
> 2d quality
>     42.50 francs a kilogram
> 3d quality
>     40 francs a kilogram
> 4th quality
>     22.75 francs a kilogram

In 1859, Mackenzie stated that prices had shown little variation during the previous thirty years.

In 1864/65 prices held at up to 50 francs a kilogram and in 1865/66 they reached 65 and even 70 francs, since crops in Europe were becoming smaller and smaller.

After that, prices fell considerably and stood at:

| | |
|---|---|
| 1866/67 | 19 francs a kilogram (*bassinés*) 5 francs |
| 1871 | 12.50 to 25 francs[a] |
| 1872 | 14 francs[a] |
| 1878 | 13 francs[a] |
| 1905 | 33 to 42 francs |
| January 1907 | 33.30 francs—for Amin az Zarb silk |
| | 24 to 26.60 francs—Sharbafi silk |
| | 24 francs—for Tajiri |
| | 21.60 francs—for Tai silk |
| | 20 francs—for Alaghbandi silk |
| | 13.30 francs—for Duvil silk |

[a] silk obtained from Japanese eggs; silk from native cocoons was dearer, but scarce.

In the summer of 1909, prices in Rasht were:

| *Sharbafi khaili ala* silk: | KRANS |
|---|---|
| for Europe and Yazd . . . . . . . . . . | 48 |
| from Astareh, Lahijan, and neighborhood, for Milan . . . . . . . . . . . . . . . | 47 |
| from Lahijan, for Constantinople and Tabriz | 47 |

| Sharbafi silk for Baghdad: | KRANS | | no. 2 . . . . . . . . | 42 |
|---|---|---|---|---|
| du ala bab baghdadi quality . . . . . . . . | 42 | | Tajiri silk (known to Baghdad merchants as | |
| Baghdadi-alaghbandi-ala quality . . . . . . | 38 | | alaghbandi) . . . . . . . . . . . . . | 40 |
| Alaghbandi silk | | | Tai silk for Rasht . . . . . . . . . . | 38 |
| durusht-nakh (thick thread) for Hamadan. . | 38 | | Tai silk for Tehran . . . . . . . . . . . | 39 |
| vasat for Hamadan . . . . . . . . . . | 36 | | Duvil silk from Lahijan, for Tehran, Hamadan, | |
| zard-bab for Kashan no. 1 . . . . . . . . | 43 | | Tabriz . . . . . . . . . . . . . . . | 26 |

## Opium Production and Trade

Opium has been used in the Middle East, for medical and other purposes, since ancient times, and is mentioned in many classical and Islamic texts.[1] The opium poppy has been cultivated in Iran "from the end of the eleventh or twelfth centuries,"[2] but both production and consumption were small until the middle of the nineteenth century;[3] however, a small amount was exported from Bushire by the end of the eighteenth century.[4] The two following selections describe the development of the opium trade in the 1820s and 1860s.

Already in 1867 the British consul in Tehran was reporting that "opium seems to be in good demand, and it was expected that about 10,000 shah mauns (130,000 lbs.), or three times the usual quantity, will be exported this season to China" ("Tehran," 1866, A and P 1867–68, 68). Two years later his successor put production at 540,000 pounds and exports at about 250,000 pounds. ("Persia," A and P 1867–68, 69). In his report on the Trade of the Persian Gulf, 1873 (A and P 1876, 74), the political resident in the gulf expressed his fears: "It is said that adulteration is now extensively practised as to bid fair to check the trade with China, unless the Persian authorities take measures to prevent fraud." Shortly after, the consul at Bushire reported: "A few years ago the profits of the opium attracted the attention of the Persians, almost all available or suitable ground in Yazd, Isfahan, and elsewhere, was utilized for the cultivation of opium to the exclusion of cereals and other produce ... [this], combined with drought and other circumstances, resulted in the famine of 1871–2" ("Persian Gulf," 1873–78, A and P 1880, 73).

But output and exports continued to rise rapidly. This is brought out very clearly in the "Report by Mr. Baring on Trade and Cultivation of Opium in Persia" (A and P 1881, 69), which contains valuable and detailed information. Output in 1859 was put at 300 cases (of 195 pounds each) and exports in 1861 at 1,000 cases. In the 1870s, exports from the Persian Gulf ports rose severalfold, from 870 cases worth 696,000 rupees in 1871/72 to 7,700 worth 8,470,000 in 1880/81. These figures covered "nearly every pound of the drug" sent to China. A further, very small, amount was sent to Baghdad from Kermanshah. In addition, a small quantity was consumed locally, and total production was estimated at around 8,000 cases.

[1] See Neligan, pp. 1–11.
[2] Petrushevsky in CHI, 5:502.
[3] Adamiyat, pp. 230–32.
[4] Kelly, p. 44.

As regards quality:

It appears that adulteration is not carried on to the extent that it used to be in former years. The Persians lost heavily in the first years of the export trade by sending to China badly prepared and adulterated opium; when they found that, by improving the quality, they could realize good profits, they paid attention to preparation, and also decreased the adulteration.

At one time a chest of Persian opium only fetched in China from 280 dollars to 350 dollars. In 1879 good Persian opium was in demand in Hong Kong at from 450 dollars to 520 dollars the "picul," whereas I am informed that a chest of last year's crop sells at 539 dollars. The chest contains 137 lbs., but, by the time it reaches China, the deficiency caused by drying up makes it about equal to the "picul" of 135 lbs.

The route taken changed repeatedly.

When opium was first exported from Persia it was sent by sailing vessels to Java, and there reshipped by steamer to Singapore and Hong Kong. The Dutch authorities, however, prohibited the importation, and an attempt was made to ship to China direct from the Persian Gulf. Owing, however, to very high freights, this direct route was abandoned, and shipments were made by the regular gulf steamers to Aden, where cargoes were transhipped for China. As soon as Government levied a transhipment duty of 10 reis a chest, the course of trade was again changed, and the transhipment was effected at Suez, where no dues were levied. As, however, no dues are levied in Ceylon either, and as the Suez route was naturally found circuitous, the Persian Steam Navigation Company undertook that their ships should touch at Galle whenever a sufficient quantity of opium was collected at Bushire to make it worth their while. In order to avoid the transhipment dues at Bombay, the greater part of the Persian opium is now sent by Ceylon and Suez, but last April one vessel, the "Himalaya," was sent direct to China.[5]

The cultivation of opium was very profitable: "It is said that grain nets about a third of what the opium harvest would yield on an equal space of ground." Middlemen also made large profits. But exporters "complain that they have of late made little or none," and a detailed "average invoice" for 1880–81, based on a purchase price of 2,510 krans for a case of crude drug weighing $136\frac{1}{2}$ pounds and a sale price of $539 in Hong Kong, shows a small loss. "The exporter has, however, little choice in the matter; with him the export of opium is pretty well a matter of necessity, being his principal means wherewith to balance the import trade."

After that, production seems to have leveled off, while rising consumption began to reduce the quantity exported—and this notwithstanding the fact that "Persian opium now competes successfully with other descriptions (Turkey, Asia Minor etc.) in London and Hong Kong" ("Persia," 1887, A and P 1887, 85). In 1904 production was estimated at 7,000 cases of $140\frac{1}{2}$ pounds, consumption at 2,000, and exports at 5,000 cases, or 700,000 pounds, worth about £500,000.[6] In 1914/15 exports amounted to 875,000 pounds, worth £815,000.[7]

[5] In 1878 a considerable quantity of opium "was shipped direct from Persia to England for the first time," Kelly, p. 555.
[6] H. W. McLean, "Report," A and P 1904, 95.
[7] Neligan, p. 40.

In 1910 the Majlis passed an Opium Act, designed to restrict, within seven years, the use of the drug to medical and scientific requirements (see 8:6), but the war and postwar disruptions prevented effective control and by the mid 1920s exports had risen to over 1,000,000 pounds, worth £1,500,000. In the interwar period there were further prohibitions, and opium was subjected to a government monopoly. On the eve of the Second World War exports amounted to about 132,000 kilograms, worth 15,000,000 rials. In 1947 the government began to restrict and in 1955 it banned the cultivation and use of opium. The prohibition seems to have been effective, and exports dropped sharply. The impact on the main producing regions was also great. Thus in Kirman, where "opium had been the principal cash summer crop ... replacement crops such as potatoes, sugar beets, alfalfa, and to a lesser extent cummin seed and saffron, were cultivated."[8] Thus opium has lost the important role in Iranian agriculture and trade which it acquired in the nineteenth century.

(See also works by Gorelikov, Djourbatchi, El (2) s.v. "Filaha," listed in the bibliography.)

[8] English, *City*, p. 105.

## Selection 9. Opium Production and Trade, 1824
[Stannus to Willock, 3 June 1824, FO 60/24]

*Bushire*

... The importation of Chinese goods is very considerable, but there is no direct trade carried on with that Country, although it appears by no means improbable that a communication may shortly be opened with the Ports to the Eastward for the Purpose of introducing Persian opium into the Chinese market;—an experiment on the advantages of this new species of Export has already been made on a small scale by Sheikh Abdul Rasool Khan who has lately sent about 20 chests to Duman from whence it has been conveyed to Macao, and is expected to hold forth good encouragement to future speculators. It is strange indeed that the exportation of Opium should not earlier have attracted the attention of the Persian Merchants, as this drug may be made with common attention to its cultivation and package fully equal to any produced in India, and can be procured in Bushire for one third of the price at which the best Malwa Opium sells in Bombay ...

## Selection 10. Opium Production and Trade, 1869
[R. Thomson, "Memorandum on Opium Trade of Persia," 6 March 1869, FO 60/321]

*Tehran*

1. Of late years the manufacture of opium in Persia has increased considerably, and the quantity now exported from the country may be reckoned at double what it was in 1860. The Merchants have lately discovered that instead of sending it through Central Asia at great risk and cost they can forward this drug at a comparatively small expense to China by sea without touching at any British port and that consequently large profits may be realized in the trade. The result has been that the poppy is now cultivated in most of the Provinces of Persia, where the climate appears generally to be extremely favourable to its growth. Near Tehran for instance and in many other districts where it was formerly almost unknown, large fields are at present under

cultivation with this plant and there is every reason to believe that a steady increase in the production of opium throughout the Kingdom will now annually take place.

2. During the year 1868–69 the quantity produced in Persia and imported from Herat was 15,500 Shah Mans—and each Man weighing 13½ lbs. It will be seen from the following statement that Yezd and Ispahan are the districts where the largest quantity is obtained, though the quality is inferior to that manufactured in the other provinces.

Opium produced in Persia in 1868–69.

| | SHAH MANS |
|---|---|
| In Kerman and districts | 150 |
| Cashan and villages | 250 |
| Yezd districts | 7500 |
| Khorassan and Tubbus | 1400 |
| Tehran villages | 200 |
| Ispahan Districts | 5000 |
| Imported from Herat | 1000 |
| | 15,500 |

3. Of the 15,500 Mans about 600 or 700 Mans were last year consumed in Persia and the rest was exported from Bender Abbas and the other ports in the Persian Gulf mostly to Batavia for reshipment to China. A small quantity found its way to the Toorkoman desert, having been purchased by agents from these tribes in various parts of Khorassan.

4. The quality of this opium varies in the different Provinces where it is produced. In the North, near the Caspian Sea, where the climate is exceedingly damp it is dark in colour and very inferior in quality—Natives explain its relative quality thus. The strength of that manufactured in Kerman and Cashan is given at 12°—that from Khorassan at 10°—from Tehran at 8°—and from Yezd and Ispahan at 7°. About 1000 Shah Mans are also imported annually from Herat, but it is said to be of very inferior quality and is of less value than that pro-

duced in Ispahan. Kerman and Cashan are the two districts where the best opium is obtained in Persia. Agents have on two occasions been sent from France to analyze and report on the value of this drug and they found that when unadulterated it contained a larger proportion of Morphine and was altogether inferior [sic] to that produced in Turkey and better also than the average quality prepared in India. Of late however some difficulty has been experienced in the Provinces in procuring opium in a pure state, as the Persians frequently while preparing and manipulating the drug, mix raw sugar and other substances with it.

5. The price of unprepared opium at the beginning of last season was 18 *Tomans* (£6.18.6), the Shah Man, but the rates advanced somewhat later to 24 tomans. Manufactured and in a pure state, it fetched not less than 30 tomans for the same quantity in the Persian market. As already stated, many of the native dealers are in the habit of adulterating the opium intended for exportation and several chests were returned from Batavia last year in consequence.

6. About 15 years ago, opium of the best and purest quality was sold in the bazars here at from 10 to 12 tomans the Shah Man. The entire amount exported from Persia was sent by Herat to Bokhara whence it was forwarded through Tartary to the Chinese frontier. This route was however so unsafe and the expense of transport was so heavy that it was abandoned 12 years ago and most of the produce was then sent in a half prepared state to Constantinople. That route has now been almost entirely discontinued, the Persian traders having found that it was cheaper and more expeditious to charter a vessel for the purpose of conveying their consignments from the Gulf direct to Batavia.

## Rice Production and Trade

The following selection describes the methods used in rice cultivation in Gilan in 1844. In that province rice and silk were the basic crops, and in Mazandaran, rice and cotton.[1] In a report on his second journey to the Caspian, written in

[1] Bartold, p. 53.

1848, Abbott stated:

Rice yields the most productive crops throughout the Southern Coast of the Caspian. In Mazenderan 10 killehs or 20 Tabreez mens ($\frac{1}{2}$ a kherwar) of seed are sufficient to sow one jereeb[2] of land and the produce will be from 15 to 40 kherwars or from 30 to 80 fold. The usual estimate, however, between the Government and the Farmer is only 20 kherwars or 40 fold though I believe this is generally much under the average rate of the crops.

The removal of the Husk from the Rice by the rude process described in my former report occasions a loss of 3 to 4 and sometimes $4\frac{1}{2}$ Parts of the 9 of the original weight. The grain is separated from the straw by the tread of horses.[3]

As far as can be judged from the available evidence, no significant change took place in the techniques used in rice cultivation during the period under review. Nor did the tenure arrangements change:

The price of the peasant's labour is in most cases one-half of the produce, be it rice or silk. Under this arrangement, called *menasifi*, the peasantry who work upon the estates of silk proprietors have to furnish the seed or silkworm eggs, but in rice plantations the seed is provided by the landlord.[4]

But there was a considerable expansion of cultivated area and output. In 1865, the British consul estimated the area planted to rice in Gilan at 11,800 acres, which, at an average yield of 1,100 *batmans* or 13,750 pounds, gave a crop of some 12,000,000 *batmans* or 150,000,000 pounds.

The rice of Gilan is considered to be superior to that of Mazandaran, the latter province, however, produces a far greater quantity, whereas the rice produce of Gilan is only sufficient for domestic consumption.[5]

By 1872 the same consul was reporting:

The rice crops were abundant throughout Ghilan, and have trebled of late years. Since the failure of the silk crops became chronic, the people began to sow rice in larger quantities. In 1865 the annual produce of rice was estimated at 12,000,000 *mauns* (150,000,000 lbs.); it may now be put down at 30,000,000 *mauns* (392,500,000 lbs.) [*sic*]. The price paid in 1865 for $12\frac{3}{4}$ lbs. of rice was $7\frac{1}{2}$d; but 2s. $3\frac{1}{2}$d. is now the cost of the same quantity. The continued export throughout the years of this important article, the staple food of the people in Ghilan, can alone account for this enormous rise in price.

By the following year, however, the price had fallen to a more normal level of 10d.

In 1877 the consul reported that "since the repeated failures of the silk crops

---

[2] In Mazandaran the *jarib* was equal to 100 *arij*. "The arij is the length of the arm of a man of common stature, from the elbow to the top of the middle finger. But the length and breadth of the land being ascertained instead of multiplying one by the other and ascertaining the square measure contained in the area, the custom is to take a quarter of the measure either of length or breadth and make it a multiplier of the other sum. The product is the amount required. Thus instead of determining the real superficies of the area the people make their calculation on only one quarter of it and I sought in vain for an explanation of this."

[3] Report on Journey to the Caspian, November 1847–February 1848, FO 60/141.

[4] "Gilan," 1865, A and P 1867, 67, p. 108.

[5] Ibid.

the peasantry of Ghilan have applied themselves to clearing away the jungle and sowing rice."[6] And in 1879 he stated:

It is calculated that there are upwards of thousand villages in this province, and that 50,000 *kutis* are produced by each village a year, which makes 2,560,000 cwts, or 128,000 tons, representing a money value of 576,000 l.; and as only 65,000 l. worth of this commodity was exported, there remained 512,000 l. worth for the consumption of the country.[7]

Until the 1880s, the bulk of the crop was absorbed domestically, and exports to Russia, although significant, remained small. But Persian rice, like Persian cotton (see 5:12), benefited from the imposition by the Russians of a high duty on other rice:

Formerly the Black Sea ports were supplied with rice from the East Indies, but the present duty of 85 gold copecks per pood on cleaned rice has effectually stopped that trade, and deprived the Russian Customs of an important item of revenue, which is by no means compensated for by the 5 per cent *ad valorem* duty levied on the Asiatic frontiers and consequently, on Persian rice.[8]

A further stimulating factor was the completion of the Transcaspian railway, enabling Iran to supply Turkistan.[9] As a result, exports to Russia from Rasht, which had averaged about £25,000 in the 1870s, rose to £234,000 in 1892/93. This increase was partly due to a doubling of the price from 4 krans to 8–10 per *kuti*,[10] implying a three- or fourfold increase in real terms.[11]

This progress continued until the First World War. Lord Curzon stated that "the export of rice from Mazandaran and Gilan to Russia was given to me as 3,600,000 *pouds*, or 58,064 tons per annum; value from 1,000,000 to 1,100,000 *tomans*, or £285,700 to £314,000."[12] The British consul in Rasht reported: "740,671 cwts., valued at 268,973 l., having been exported to Russia during the twelve-months [1902/3] against 658,154 cwts, value 164,900 l. in 1894."[13] In 1904–08, total rice exports averaged £500,000 a year.[14] And Entner states that "by 1913 [Russia] received up to 4.8 million puds [77,000 tons] a year, from about 97 to 99 per cent of the export, or by value almost 14 per cent of Persia's trade with Russia."[15] Figures given by Rabino[16] indicate that, on the eve of the First World War, rice was grown on 103,000 hectares, in 1,400 villages in Gilan, and that the total production of that province had risen to 185,000 tons.

---

6 "Gilan," 1871, A and P 1872, 58, p. 1187; ibid., 1876, A and P 1877, 82, p. 754.
7 "Gilan," 1878, A and P 1878–79, 70, p. 471.
8 "Persia," A and P 1889, 77.
9 Entner, p. 75.
10 This was, however, partly offset by a decline in the rate of the kran from 25 to 33 per pound sterling.
11 "Gilan," 1892–93, A and P 1893–94, 95.
12 *Persia*, 2:496.
13 "Gilan," 1902/3, A and P 1904, 100.
14 "Persia," 1908/9, A and P 1910, 101.
15 Entner, p. 75.
16 Cited by Jamalzadeh, p. 21–22.

Rice was also grown in many other parts of Iran, but almost solely for domestic consumption (see 5:13).

In the interwar period rice cultivation expanded and by the outbreak of the Second World War stood at about 700,00 tons. In recent years, thanks to the large irrigation schemes, area and output have risen sharply, and at present some 700,000 hectares are planted to rice and annual output is nearly 1,000,000 tons, some four-fifths of which is grown in the Caspian provinces.

(See also works by Polak, Rabino, Gorelikov, Fateh, *Economic*, OCI, and Djourbatchi, listed in the bibliography.)

## Selection 11. Rice Production and Trade, 1844

[K. E. Abbott, "Report on Journey to Caspian," 29 June 1844, FO 60/108]

... Some particulars regarding Rice, the great article of Produce. There are four qualities of it grown in Mazanderan and distinguished as follows

| | |
|---|---|
| Gherdih or Zerekh worth . . . . . . . . . . . . . . | s.k. 2/15 or 2s. 9d. per 10 Tabreez Mauns or 67 lbs. |
| S            b h . . . . . . . . . . . . . . | s.k. 2/15 or 2s. 9d. per 10 Tabreez Mauns or 67 lbs. |
| Shahek of a long grain produce small . . . . . | s.k. 2/15 or 2s. 9d. per 10 Tabreez Mauns or 67 lbs. |
| Amberboo . . . . . . . . . . . . . . . . | s.k. 3/- or 3s. |

Rice is sown at the Vernal Equinox. It is first raised in a heap and 20 or 30 days afterwards when the plants are of a sufficient size they are separated and planted by women in the fields which have already undergone the necessary ploughing and saturation. The plants are placed at a few inches apart from each other and each one yields several stalks—in about 100 days the Crop is ready for Harvest.

To remove the Husk the Rice is placed in a large wooden receptacle or mortar—a beam of wood crooked at one end, fixed on a pivot and armed with blunt iron Spikes at its crooked end is raised by a water wheel and drops into the mortar. The iron spikes by continually falling on the Rice remove the husk without much injuring the grain but still a good deal of it gets pounded by this rude process. Two Kherwers or 80 Tabreez Mauns of Rice in the Husk yield generally only 40 Mauns of clean Rice in the Grain—but when the latter is of good and full quality the result will be as far as 48 Mauns.

As no account is kept of the produce of this or indeed of any other Article in the Province it is impossible to say what it may be. The Government in its nominal Tax of a Quarter of the Produce receives about 107,000 Kherwers of Rice or their equivalent in money at the rate of 4 Saheb Kurrans per Kherwer of that article in the husk or as it is called in the language of the Country "Sheltook." This amount four times multiplied would give 428,000 Kherwars of 40 Tabreez Mauns of 267 lbs. each or a total of 114,276,000 lbs. English—value in Tomans at the price of the Country Tom. 171,200 or about £85,600. Sterling, only— but the quantity taken by Government is an old established rate which I believe is not altered according to the Harvest of each year or any increase or decrease in the cultivation, so that it may be less or more than one Fourth of the Actual Produce.

A Person informed me it is reckoned that for 3 months in the Year 1,000 Horseloads of Rice are sent daily into Arâk—this would give 4,500,000 Mauns or 112,500 Kherwers exported during 3 months, only to one part of the Country. . . .

## Cotton Cultivation

Since its introduction, probably in Achaemenid times, cotton has been grown in many parts of Iran, especially in Khurasan, supplying the raw material for an important branch of the textile industry (see 6:2). After the 1840s, the decline of the cotton handicrafts, under the impact of foreign competition, may have led to a shrinkage in cotton cultivation in Iran, as for example occurred in Syria, but no evidence is available to support such a hypothesis.

Although burdened by very high transport cost, Persian cotton seems to have been exported in significant quantities to Europe, by way of Smyrna and other places, until the general breakdown in the eighteenth century.[1] After that, exports dried up and the extensive list of Persian exports through Trebizond in the 1840s given by Gödel does not mention cotton,[2] and Blau put the total going through Trebizond in 1857 at only 100 bales. Nor is cotton mentioned in the various British consular reports on the trade of the Persian Gulf; indeed Milburn lists cotton as an import to Bushire at the beginning of the nineteenth century.[3]

Around 1852, Sea Island cotton was introduced in the Urumiya region, presumably by American missionaries.[4] The "cotton famine" resulting from the American Civil War, and the consequent sharp rise in prices, stimulated British efforts to find alternative sources, and led to a rapid increase in production in Egypt, Syria, and Turkey (see EHME). The following selection shows that a similar interest was taken in Iran. During the war and its aftermath, cotton exports from Iran increased significantly, and then fell off again. Shipments of raw cotton from the Persian Gulf to Bombay, which had been nil in 1844/45 and 19,200 rupees' worth in 1860/61, rose sharply to 1,614,060 rupees in 1863/64 and 6,793,845 in 1864/65, and then dropped back;[5] the British consular agent in Isfahan reported that in 1866 no cotton was exported to India.[6] Similarly, exports of cotton from Tabriz, apparently mainly to Marseilles, rose from a negligible amount to 13,000 bales (of about 200 pounds each) in 1866 but fell off to 4,500 the following year.[7]

In the meantime, a much more important customer had appeared—Russia. Already in 1855 a report on the Nizhni Novgorod fair had noted that significant amounts of raw cotton were being imported from Persia and Bukhara.[8] Thereafter progress seems to have been swift. In 1866, exports from Tabriz to Russia were put at 7,800 bales and in 1870 at 54,000. After that they fell to practically nothing, but that was because a new source of supply had been opened, through the Caspian.[9] In 1866 the British consul in Rasht reported that about 6,300,000 pounds of cotton had been exported from Mazandaran to Russia; in 1881 that "Russian and Armenian merchants exported to Moscow, via Resht and the

[1] Blau, p. 83.

[2] Gödel, pp. 17–25.

[3] Milburn, p. 129.

[4] EI (2) s.v. "Filaha."

[5] Report by Col Pelly, A and P 1871, 51, pp. 1, 7. In the 1880s, annual shipments to Bombay were about 15,000 to 20,000 bales (of 3½ hundredweight each). See Curzon, *Persia*, 2:496.

[6] "Tehran," 1866, A and P 1867/68, 68, p. 301. A later report ("Bushire," 1873, A and P 1880, 73, p. 242) states that at their peak, annual cotton exports from the gulf totaled 100,000 bales.

[7] "Tabriz," 1867, A and P 1867/68, 68. Exports to Marseilles in 1870 were 26,000 bales—"Tabriz," 1870, A and P 1871, 65.

[8] Quoted by Blau, p. 83.

[9] Reports on Tabriz for 1866, 1870, and 1873, A and P 1867–68, 68; 1871, 65; and 1875, 75.

Caspian, about 4,284,000 lbs. of this article, the produce of Casvin, Zenjan, Taroom and Khorassan"; and in 1874, 2,500,000 pounds, the produce of Mazandaran; cotton exports to Russia through Gilan were valued at £35,000 in 1877 and £56,000 in 1878.[10]

A further stimulus was given to Persian production by the increase, in 1887, of the duty paid by cotton entering Russia over the European and Black Sea frontiers to 4 rubles 15 kopeks a poud, whereas Persian cotton paid only 40 kopeks, that is, a differential of 3.75 rubles (sic) a poud (over $2\frac{1}{2}$ pence a pound) or about 10 percent of the landed price. At the same time, Russian and Armenian merchants advanced money to Persian cotton cultivators, stimulating both an expansion in output (partly at the expense of opium) and an improvement in quality.[11] A Russian consular report stated that, between 1900 and 1905, the area planted to cotton in Khurasan doubled.[12] By the turn of the century, Persian cotton exports were over 250,000 cwt. (12,500 tons), and those to India about 10,000 cwt. And on the eve of the First World War total cotton exports were about 25,000 tons, worth about £1,500,000, of which 97 to 98 percent went to Russia.[13] The total area under cotton at that time was estimated at 110,000 hectares and total output at 33,000 metric tons.[14]

During the First World War, cotton cultivation was seriously disrupted and output fell to negligible figures. But the prewar level was recovered in the 1920s and by the outbreak of the Second World War the crop had passed the 40,000 ton mark. Again there was a sharp decline during the Second World War, as in other parts of the Middle East, because of the loss of export markets and the need to grow more food at home. In the last twenty years the advance has been swift, and at present the country produces some 150,000 tons of ginned cotton; of this some 100,000 tons are exported and the rest is consumed by the local textile industry.

(See also works by Stolze and Andreas, Curzon, Gorelikov, Fateh, Economic, OCI, and Djourbatchi listed in the bibliography.)

[10] A and P 1867–68, 68; 1872, 58; 1874, 68; 1878–79, 70.
[11] "British Trade," A and P 1889, 77; "British Trade," A and P 1904, 95; "Khurasan," 1904, A and P 1908, 114; Entner, pp. 73–74.
[12] Cited in Abdullaev, p. 13.
[13] "Persia," A and P 1910, 94; Entner, p. 73.
[14] Gorelikov, p. 192.

### Selection 12. Cotton Cultivation, 1863
[Abbott to Russell, 20 February 1863, FO 60/277]

Tabreez

I have the honor to transmit to Your Lordship a Bag containing Specimens of Cotton, the growth of this and of the neighbouring Province of Arak. The in-closed Proforma account of the purchase at this place shows at what price it might be laid down at Trebizonde on the Black Sea.

I should have sent these Specimens at an earlier date had I not learned from the European Merchants here that the quality of the Cotton grown in the North of Persia is of so inferior a kind as not to bear the expense of land transport to the Black Sea.

Recently, however, I have heard that a Specimen of Persian Cotton sent to England had been approved of. I therefore no longer delay sending the accompanying Samples.

It is uncertain to what extent Cotton is grown either in this province or indeed in Persia generally, as no statistics exist of this production—but it is probable that some Million of pounds might be purchased here in the Course of the Year whether of the growth of this or of the neighbouring Province. Cotton is produced throughout the plain, inhabited Country of Persia and the quantity cannot be inconsiderable when it is considered that the extent of Persia is equal to about twice and a half that of France. Much of it is required for local wants—the Manufacture of coarse twist—coarse Calico—Canvass and rope—and other minor purposes—and it finds its way in the raw state to Russia and Turkey. The great obstacle to the exportation abroad is the cost of land transport from the more distant inland parts and which from this to Trebizonde would amount, at the present high rate, Three Halfpence per English Pound.

At this moment there are some 800 Bales of Cotton awaiting the means of conveyance to the Black Sea.

The Specimens I am now sending consist of the Raw Cotton as taken from the Pod and that which has undergone a partial cleansing by beating on the Bow-String—which process costs 16 Shahees per Men or nearly $1^d$ per lb. The present price of Azerbaijan Cotton is Kerans 6 8/20th and that of Arak, Kerans 6 12/20th per Men of 1000 Miscals, equal to about $5\frac{3}{4}$ d. and 5 8/9 d. per English Pound. Its ordinary value has been only about $3\frac{1}{2}$ to 4 Kerans or about 3 2/3th d. to $4\frac{1}{4}$ d. per Pound.

## Tobacco and Other Cash Crops

Both the smoking and planting of tobacco came to the Middle East from Europe at the end of the sixteenth century, and spread rapidly in spite of attempts at suppression.[1] "By 1622 the Persians had already invented the art of smoking through water"[2] and Shah Abbas's prohibition on imports resulted only in local planting in the south.[3] Olearius, who visited Iran in 1637/38, mentions tobacco growing in Gilan. By the beginning of the nineteenth century tobacco was grown in many parts of Iran and had become one of the leading export items—indeed, Gödel, writing in the 1840s, mentions it as the leading export and states that it was sent to India, Constantinople, and Egypt.[4] Blau estimated the crop in the 1850s at 50,000,000 pounds, of which some 22,000,000 were exported, but these figures are probably exaggerated.[5]

After that, output seems to have risen in various parts of the country. In 1869 the British consul in Tabriz reported: "A large quantity of tobacco is grown in Azerbijan, around the lake of Urumiah, but it is in little request out of the province, being much too mild to be in general favour."[6] In Gilan, in 1875, "the governor, Nasir-ul-Mulk, who is both enlightened and enterprising, has at my

[1] Gorelikov, p. 196; EHME, p. 60.
[2] *Cambridge Economic History of Europe*, 4:283; water pipes are mentioned by a British traveler in India as early as 1616—H. Yule and A. Burnell, *Hobson Jobson* (London, 1903) s.v. Hubble-bubble.
[3] Gorelikov, p. 196.
[4] Gödel, p. 20.
[5] Blau, p. 82.
[6] "Tabriz," 1870, A and P 1871, 65, p. 240.

suggestion written to Constantinople for a large supply of Yenija and Latakieh seed." The experiment was successful. "This has encouraged the natives to turn their attention to this branch of industry. . . . A company has been formed with this object in view, and special tobacco growers have been induced to come to Resht to undertake its proper culture." By 1878, upward of 2,000 cwt. (100 tons) were raised; "Under proper management it can be produced at about 20s. the poud of 36 lbs., which gives a profit of 22s. the cwt." A strong encouragement was provided by the fact that "the export duty on this article, together with the import duty in Russia, does not exceed 10 per cent, while that levied on Turkish tobacco is considerably higher."[7]

Production and exports also increased in the south. In 1882 the British consul in Bushire reported, "A considerable export trade in Persian tobacco has sprung of late years and is increasing. The tobacco is largely shipped to Syrian and other Turkish ports since the prohibitive tariff has been removed"; and two years later, "Tobacco exportation is on the increase, and is of some importance."[8] Another report put the production of the Isfahan district at 80,000 bales of $7\frac{1}{2}$ shahmans each, that is, about 4,000 tons, of which about 60,000 bales were exported by "English and Persian houses to Bagdad, Beyrouth, Aleppo etc. . . . and also about 20,000 bales to Tabreez. A certain quantity is also sent by way of Kermanshah to Bagdad . . . the quality of Ispahan tobacco is inferior to that of Shiraz."[9] At this time Lord Curzon could say, without too much exaggeration: "The tobacco of Persia is known in every town and village in the Western half of the Asiatic continent; and greatly to be commiserated is the European traveller or resident who, when either passing through or sojourning in that land, is guilty of indifference to the exquisite solace of the Persian waterpipe or *kalian*." He quotes an official estimate of total output of 52,230 tons, but adds "the figures supplied to me represent the total production as only one half."[10] The figures given in the following selection indicate a total crop of about 20,000 tons.

The attempt to give a British company a concession for a tobacco monopoly, mentioned in the selection, caused a major political crisis, which has been very well analyzed by professors Kazemzadeh and Keddie. In return for an annual payment to the government of £15,000, plus 25 percent of net profits after payment of a 5 percent dividend to shareholders, the company was granted a complete monopoly over all tobacco transactions. It was given the right to buy the entire crop from the cultivators "at prices agreed upon by buyer and sellers [cultivators]," disagreements to be solved by compulsory arbitration.[11] All sales were to be made through the company's agents. The last provision aroused the opposition of the merchants, who were supported by both the *mullahs* and the Russian embassy.

[7] "Gilan," 1874 and 1875, A and P 1876, 76, ibid., 1876, A and P 1877, 82; ibid., 1878, A and P 1878–79, 70.
[8] "Bushire," 1882, A and P 1883, 74,; ibid., 1884, A and P 1888, 78.
[9] "Trade and Industries," A and P 1887, 85.
[10] *Persia*, 2:497–98.
[11] Kazemzadeh, *Russia*, p. 248.

This forced the cancellation of the concession, the company receiving a compensation of £500,000.

No further attempt was made to regulate the growing or sale of tobacco until 1929, when a government monopoly was established. Output may have risen considerably by 1914, but the estimate of 58 crores of Tabriz mans (nearly 90,000 tons) given by Jamalzadeh seems far too high.[12] Exports remained at the low figure of about 1,500 tons, worth around £15,000, mainly it would seem because the Ottoman tobacco monopoly bought only small quantities from Iran, as is mentioned in the following selection. Output at the outbreak of the Second World War was 13,000 tons, and today stands at some 22,000 tons.

(See also works by Polak, Stolze and Andreas, Kazemzadeh, Keddie, Gorelikov, and Djourbatchi, listed in the bibliography.)

[12] Jamalzadeh, p. 34.

## Selection 13. Tobacco and Other Cash Crops, 1890s
[M. L. Tomara, *Ekonomicheskoe Polozhenie Persii* (Saint Petersburg, 1895), pp. 8–17]

### RICE

... Although rice grows in many parts of Persia—in Azerbaijan, Khurasan, Fars, Isfahan—the main center of cultivation is the Caspian coast. ...

The greater part of the rice crop is consumed within the country, but part of the Mazandaran crop goes to Russia (Baku). The best kinds of Persian rice grow not in the Caspian provinces but in Fars (the *shahri* and *champa* varieties, the latter of Indian origin). The price of rice in Isfahan in the spring of 1894 was 2 to 3 krans per shahi man (1.10 ruble to 1.60 ruble per poud). In Mazandaran during the year 1894 prices fluctuated between 22 and 33 krans per khalvar of 7½ pouds (from 60 to 90 kopeks per poud) [A poud equalled 16.38 kilograms].

Exports to Russia, which are subjected to the same restraints as those on wheat, are indicated by the following figures: in 1891 they were 2,549,000 pouds and in 1892 2,464,500 pouds, almost exclusively from Mazandaran and Astarabad.

### COTTON

Cotton cultivation is spread all over Persia; it is a particularly important occupation for the inhabitants of Azerbaijan, Khurasan, eastern Mazandaran, and the central districts of Isfahan, Yazd, Kashan, and Qum; much cotton is also grown in Kirman. Sowing takes place, according to locality, at the beginning or end of April—in Mazandaran earlier and in other provinces later. In the hottest and dampest parts of the Caspian coast, harvesting begins in August; in drier places or those lying at higher altitudes, in the neighborhood of Shiraz and in Azerbaijan, cotton is not harvested before October. The quality of cotton is not good; the fiber is short and breaks easily. Experiments with American seeds in various places (Mazandaran, Khurasan, Azerbaijan, Isfahan) have proved successful, but so far large areas have not been sown with such varieties because of the inhabitants' conservatism and distrust. The preparation of cotton for marketing, its ginning and pressing, are carried out either by hand or with the most primitive instruments. Because of this, and the dishonesty of the Persians, cotton is almost always delivered without being cleaned of seeds and is mixed with stones, earth, and sometimes nails. Recently some Armenian exporters introduced their own machines, ordered from Russia, for the proper processing of cotton, and offered them for general use for a stated payment. In this respect, much could be done by enterprising

Russian businessmen who could distribute American cotton seeds among farmers, buy their crop, and process it on their own machines.[1] If this were done, Persian cotton would be a powerful competitor of American and Egyptian cotton imported to Russia.

Cotton prices in Persia are not high; in Mazandaran in 1893 they stood at 14 to 17 tumans for 7½ pouds or 3.50 to 4.50 rubles a poud, depending on quality, degree of cleanliness, etc. In Isfahan, where cotton of higher quality is sold (some varieties are not inferior to Egyptian in toughness and length of fiber) prices are lower, thanks to abundant supplies from other places such as Kashan and Hamadan, and, for the 1893 crop, stood in the spring of 1894 at 5 krans 5 shahis per shahi man, or 2.80 rubles a poud.

Persian cotton is exported across all the Persian frontiers: to Russia from Khurasan (through the Transcaspian region), from Mazandaran, Astarabad, and the Qazvin and Hamadan regions (through Astrakhan and Baku) and from Azerbaijan (through the Caucasus). The breakdown by frontiers is:

| | | |
|---|---|---|
| From Khurasan | 1890 | 155,609 pouds |
| From Khurasan | 1891 | 166,515 pouds |
| From Khurasan | 1892 | 258,151 pouds |
| From the northern and central provinces | 1890 | 364,335 pouds |
| From the northern and central provinces | 1891 | 313,057 pouds |
| From the northern and central provinces | 1892 | 401,253 pouds |
| From Azerbaijan. | 1890 | 41,642 pouds |
| From Azerbaijan. | 1891 | 17,901 pouds |
| From Azerbaijan. | 1892 | 20,786 pouds |

Cotton is exported, in small quantities, to Europe and India through Trebizond (Azerbaijan cotton) and Basra (Kirman and Hamadan cotton), but mainly from Bushire (principally, from Shiraz, Isfahan, and Kashan) and Bandar Abbas (from Kirman, Birjand, and Yazd).

| Exports | | about |
|---|---|---|
| From Bushire | 1890 | 250,000 pouds |
| From Bushire | 1891 | 135,000 pouds |
| From Bushire | 1892 | 100,000 pouds |
| From Bandar Abbas | 1890 | 82,000 pouds |
| From Bandar Abbas | 1891 | 40,000 pouds |
| From Bandar Abbas | 1892 | 33,000 pouds |

## TOBACCO

Three kinds of tobacco are grown in Persia; the first, known as *tumbak*, is for smoking in water pipes, the second, *tutun*, for pipes, and the third can be used for making cigarettes. The geographical distribution of the various kinds is as follows: water-pipe tobacco is grown in southern Farsistan and partly in the Isfahan region; in Kurdistan and Kermanshah tobacco is grown for pipes which, like water pipes, are widespread in the East; cigarette tobacco —very tough and of low quality—is grown in Gilan, in the vicinity of Rasht.[2] The sowing of tobacco takes place at the end of March and harvesting is done in November; sales are not made before winter, and sometimes not until spring.

The extent of cultivation in 1891 is brought out fairly accurately by the Tobacco Monopoly, which at that time had exclusive rights of sale; its figures were as follows:

| | | |
|---|---|---|
| *Tumbak* crop 1891 | 4,881,700 | Tabriz mans (up to 900,000 pouds) |
| Pipe tobacco crop 1891 | 1,550,000 | Tabriz mans (up to 300,000 pouds) |
| Cigarette tobacco crop 1891 | 200,000 | Tabriz mans (up to 40,000 pouds) |

Prices in 1891 were, apparently, exceptionally high and fell appreciably in subsequent years. Prices, in krans per Tabriz man, in 1891 and 1894 were as follows:

| | 1891 | 1894[3] |
|---|---|---|
| *Tumbak*—Shiraz variety. | 1.80 | 1.30 |
| *Tumbak*—Isfahan variety | 1.06 | 0.75 |
| *Tumbak*—Kashan variety | 0.96 | 0.60 |

| | | |
|---|---|---|
| *Tumbak*—Yazd variety | 1.10 | 1.00 |
| *Tumbak*—Gulpaigan variety | 1.00 | 0.85 |
| *Tumbak*—Nihavand variety | 1.15 | 0.875 |
| *Tutun*—Urumia variety | 6.50 | 5.25 |
| *Tutun*—Kurdistan variety | 1.20 | 0.90 |
| Cigarette tobacco—Rasht variety. | 3.98 | 2.90 |

[2] The seeds of this tobacco were brought from Adrianople.

[3] These are prices paid to producers; in towns they are much higher, for instance in Isfahan the Tabriz man of Kashan *Tumbak* was 2 to 3 krans, the best kind of Shiraz *tumbak* was up to 5 krans, and of *tutun* up to 7½ krans.

[1] The Imperial Bank of Persia is at present carrying out experiments with Indian cotton, which may be more suitable for Persia, although less profitable.

As regards the above-mentioned tobacco monopoly, a concession was given by the shah in the autumn of 1890. The company (Imperial Tobacco Corporation of Persia) was constituted with a capital of £650,000 sterling and received for a fifty-year period the right to a monopoly of purchasing, processing, and sale of all kinds of Persian tobacco. The company conducted its affairs very unskillfully, irritated and antagonized the people by its haughty and captious treatment of producers, and, above all, did not succeed in drawing to its side the very powerful clergy. The latter therefore began preaching in the mosques that the tobacco produced by infidels was impure and should be destroyed. There followed a popular riot and the crowd wrecked the tobacco shops and broke the water pipes. When, in addition, the highest clergymen—those in Karbala, the holiest town for Shii Muslims—came out with statements against the enterprise, the shah was compelled to renounce the concession and to ask the company to move out of Persia, compensating it—with the help of the Imperial Bank of Persia—for its losses, estimated at £500,000 sterling.

The shock due to the events arising out of the formation and subsequent abolition of the tobacco monopoly caused significant fluctuations in the export of tobacco. To this were added the restraints on the import of tobacco to Turkey, the main consumer of Persian *tumbak*, namely, that a monopoly on imports of this product was granted to the *Société du tombac*, which sharply reduced purchases of *tumbak* by Turkey, in order to raise the price.

The main demand for Persian tobacco comes from Turkey, Egypt, Arabia, and Transcaucasia. The bulk of exports to Turkey comes from the adjacent regions of Arabistan, Kurdistan, and Azerbaijan, through small points of passage, and it is impossible to estimate the volume of such transactions. But some data are available on the most important channels of export, and exports of tobacco were (in pouds):

|  |  | FROM BUSHIRE | FROM BANDAR ABBAS |
|---|---|---|---|
| 1889 | up to | 80,000 | 10,000 |
| 1890 |  | 95,000 | 10,000 |
| 1891 |  | 90,000 | 6,500 |
| 1892 |  | 110,000 | up to 14,000 |

Exports from Azerbaijan were (in pouds):

|  |  | To TREBIZOND | To TRANSCAUCASIA |
|---|---|---|---|
| 1889 | about | 80,000 | 358 |
| 1890 | up to | 65,000 | 456 |
| 1891 | up to | 70,000 | 436 |
| 1892 | up to | 30,000 | 203 |
| 1893 | up to | 8,500 | ... |

Exports from the Caspian Sea ports were 3,003 pouds in 1889, 4,291 in 1890, 4,126 in 1891, and 1,672 in 1892.

OPIUM [see 5:9]. ...

SUGAR

The warm and damp regions of Mazandaran and the banks of the Karun are well suited for the growing of sugarcane, which was in fact grown there in the past and met the inhabitants' sugar consumption. At present sugarcane cultivation has been almost wholly given up and only a small amount of cane is grown in Mazandaran. The sugar consumed in Persia is supplied by other countries—Russia and France for beet sugar, India and Mauritius for cane sugar. Insignificant quantities of Mazandaran sugar are exported to Russia, thus in 1891, 2,165 pouds were exported and in 1892, 948 pouds.

In Persia itself the growing of sugar beets is fully possible and not long ago a Belgian company was founded for the cultivation of beets and the manufacture of sugar in the vicinity of Tehran, but the attempt was hardly crowned with success [see 6:10]. Not having the right to purchase land, and consequently being compelled to undertake beet cultivation indirectly, the company was forced to distribute seeds to the peasants and take the beets from them. This way of doing things, given the ignorance and natural carelessness of Persian farmers, could not produce good results and the experiments carried out last year, although they prove that beets yield huge amounts of sugar, corroborate the opinion given above. In future, however, if farmers get accustomed to this kind of work and understand their own interest, a very serious danger may threaten the sale of Russian sugar in Persia.

SILK [see 5:6–8]. . . .

FRUITS AND GRAPES

Fruit growing plays an important part in the national economy of Persia, constituting one of the main sources of food for the people and one of the foremost items of export. Persian towns are always surrounded by vineyards and orchards in which all kinds of fruits grow: plums, apricots, figs, oranges, lemons, peaches, pomegranates, quinces, nuts, almonds, and pistachios. The last three also grow wild in the forests of Mazandaran and Kurdistan. The widespread occurrence of orchards makes it difficult to designate the richest fruit-bearing regions, but common opinion points to the western and northern provinces, that is, Azerbaijan, Kurdistan, Hamadan, Karagan, Ardalan, Mazandaran, and Khurasan. Grapes, which grow in abundance in these provinces, are sold mainly in the form of raisins, *kishmish*; in central and southern Persia, however, they are used for making wine which cannot stand transportation and is therefore consumed on the spot.

In the extreme south, on the coastal belt of the Persian Gulf, the most widespread fruit is the date, which is eaten by the inhabitants and exported in large quantities, especially from Arabistan and Laristan.

A more detailed study of exports of each kind of fruit indicates the relative productivity of the different provinces.

1. Exports to Russia over the Caspian–Caucasian borders, through Astrakhan (from the Caspian provinces, and the Qazvin and Karagan regions) and to the Transcaspian region from Khurasan, amounted in 1892 to:

| | |
|---|---|
| Fresh fruit, other than oranges, etc. . | 14,065 pouds |
| Oranges, lemons, and bitter oranges[4] . | 31,945 pouds |

[4] Almost exclusively from Gilan and Mazandaran, the main growing centers.

| | |
|---|---|
| Dried fruits and raisins . . . . . . . | 402,343 pouds |
| Nuts and stones of peaches, apricots, etc., *khoshkebar* . . . . . . . . . | 38,502 pouds |
| Almonds and pistachios. . . . . . . | 48,325 pouds |

2. Over the Russo–Persian border (from Kurdistan and Azerbaijan) in the same year:

| | |
|---|---|
| All kinds of fresh fruits . . . . . . | 10,493 [5] pouds |
| Dried fruits and raisins. . . . . . . | 767,134 pouds |
| Nuts and fruit stones . . . . . . . | 8,785 pouds |
| Almonds and pistachios . . . . . . | 50,982 pouds |

3. Over the Transcaspian border (from Khurasan):

| | |
|---|---|
| All kinds of fresh fruits . . . . . . . | 1,932 pouds |
| Dried fruits and raisins . . . .about | 170,000 pouds |
| Nuts and fruit stones . . . . . . . . | 7,860 pouds |
| Almonds and pistachios. . . . . . | 8,670 pouds |

Exports to Europe through Trebizond (mainly from Azerbaijan and Kurdistan) consisted, in the same year, of 39,140 pouds of all kinds of dried fruits.

Exports of fruits through Bushire (from Shiraz and Isfahan, mainly almonds) amounted in 1892 to 70,000 pouds, and through Bandar Abbas (from Kirman and Yazd, almonds) to 300,000 pouds. Exports of dates in the same year from Bushire amounted to 35,000 pouds, from Bandar Abbas up to 400,000 pouds, and from Muhammarah up to 80,000 pouds. . . .

## Selection 14. Two Iranian Villages, 1910
[P. M. Sykes, *Report on the Agriculture of Khorasan* (Calcutta, 1910)]

A PERSIAN VILLAGE

One great difference in a Persian village compared with one in the Punjab is that any villager can do any work. Consequently, he has not to keep parasites to skin his cattle and perform other work, which it is forbidden him to do by religion or custom.

The centre and club of a village is its bath, *hammam*. This is frequently built by the landlord or, in other cases, is subscribed to and built by the villagers, who pay a fixed amount of grain per family. In the case of small villages, three or four subscribe together for a bath.

[5] (Of which oranges, lemons, etc., 22 pouds).

A Persian village is frequently enclosed inside a high mud wall as Mahmudabad in which case the houses are small and squalid. Generally speaking, however, they occupy a good deal of room and some walled gardens are also a pleasing and profitable feature.

The large majority of villagers, in a *rayati* [peasant-owned] village, are peasant proprietors but there is also a number of landless men termed sitters in the sun, *aftab nishin* who are engaged as labourers and look after the bath, etc. The barber is drawn from among them: but there is nothing whatever in the way of caste.

To exemplify Persian villages, I have taken (a) an *Arabi* [landlord-owned] village, Mahmudabad, situated in the agricultural district of Turbat-i-Haidari and (b) the *rayati* orchard hill village of Jaghark.

NOTES ON MAHMUDABAD. *Vide* PLAN.

The village is situated on the southern slopes of the Koh-i-Mazar range, in the Turbat-i-Haidari district. It lies about six miles to the north of Turbat-i-Haidari town. Its elevation is 5,040 feet.

The village consists of 32 domed houses, built of sun dried brick. It possesses no mosque, bath, or caravan sarai. The site occupies 1 acre of ground; and two walled gardens, which adjoin the village, and grow fruit trees, vines, willows, etc., have together an area of 1½ acres.

The following is the population, all being Persians:—

Men . . . . . . . . . . . . . . . . . . . . . 20
Women . . . . . . . . . . . . . . . . . . 15
Children (unfit for agricultural labour) . . . . . 15

Total    50

The following is the live-stock owned by the village community:—

Horses . . . . . . . . . . .    1
Mules . . . . . . . . . .    Nil
Camels . . . . . . . . .    Nil
Donkeys . . . . . . . .    14
Oxen and cows . . . . . .    20
Goats and sheep . . . . . .    150
Fowls . . . . . . . . . .    50

The total cultivated area is 946 acres. Of this 346 acres receives *kanat* irrigation, and the remainder is dependent upon rainfall. The quality of the soil is good.

There is one *kanat* only, which is the property of the owner of the village (see next paragraph). The owner keeps it in a proper state of repair. Should any work on it be necessary, the villagers are employed for the purpose and receive a small wage for their labour. The *kanat* is two miles in length. Each villager receives water every tenth day for about six or seven hours.

The village valued at £5,000 is the property of a rich merchant, a resident of Turbat-i-Haidari, and the land is let to tenants-at-will. The owner has a representative, named Ghulam Hussain, resident in the village, whose duty it is to superintend the distribution of water, collect his master's rent and generally to act as steward, *Sahib Kar*, of the property. For this he receives a monthly payment of Ts. 3 from the proprietor and also realizes a small share of the crop from the tenants on his own account. There is also a *dashtban*, who receives Ts. 10, 2 *kharwars* of wheat and 10 *man* of cotton annually.

The tenants bear all the expenses of cultivation and provide their own seed-grain. The water is provided free by the proprietor who, on both irrigated and un-irrigated land, takes half the crop as rent. It is taken in kind in the case of grain crops and in cash, calculated at the market rate, in the case of crops which cannot conveniently be divided.

The tenants are 10 in number, and the average area in their holdings is 94 acres. They own 8 yoke of oxen.

The chief crops grown are wheat, barley, oil-seeds, opium and lucerne; also cotton with turnips and other root crops in the autumn.

The proprietor is alone responsible for the payment of the Government taxes. They are collected in two instalments, at the time of harvesting the spring and autumn crops. As a rule the taxes are paid in cash, but the proprietor may be called on to pay in kind or partly in cash, partly in kind. The revenue assessed on the village is Ts. 430, but the amount actually collected is rarely less than Ts. 700 per annum.

The surplus produce is usually transported to Turbat-i-Haidari town where it is sold.

A small income is derived by the villagers from the sale of brushwood which they collect in the desert and sell for fuel. Hides are disposed of in Turbat-i-Haidari. A few foxes are trapped during the winter months and their skins sold at from *krans* 5 to 10 each. Horns and bone of dead cattle have no commercial value and are thrown away. Wool is sold at the rate of about *krans* 4 per sheep yearly.

The breeding of poultry yields a small profit. The women of the village weave a coarse cloth and also make sacks (jowals), but only in sufficient quantities for their own use.

The following is the average weight and value of crops harvested yearly:—

|  | KHARWARS |  | TOMANS |
|---|---|---|---|
| Wheat . . . . . . | 550 | value | 2,500 |
| Barley . . . . . . | 250 |  | 500 |
| Cotton . . . . . . | 75 |  | 750 |
| Lucerne. . . . . . | 200 |  | 200 |
| Oil seeds . . . . . | 10 |  | 30 |
| Opium . . . . . . | 1 |  | 1,000 |
| Fruit . . . . . . . |  |  | 200 |
| Total | 1,086 |  | 5,180 |

In the Punjab, revenue is, I understand from Captain Grey, assessed at about 1/6 of the gross produce: but, in this case, even with the enhanced revenue, less than 1/7 is taken, and the owner makes about 10% on his property.

A HIGH VILLAGE

I have taken Jaghark, with which I am well acquainted, as typical of the hill villages of Khorasan although, owing to its being on the summer route from Meshed to Nishapur, it draws much profit from pilgrim and other traffic. The valley is some fourteen miles in length, of which perhaps one-half is cultivated, mainly on terraced plots. Its stream is divided into twenty-six irrigation channels, of which only twenty-two are now used.

In the valley are three villages of which Jaghark, with an altitude of 5,000 feet, is the highest up. Below comes Amberan and Turkobei is much the most important village with larger and more fertile lands.

In Persia, the usual custom is for the village that controls the water-supply to have the right to use as much as it requires: but, in the case under observation, this custom has been broken and other regulations, now at least a century old, have been substituted.

Roughly speaking, the present division is that Jaghark and Amberan each receive 5/20ths and Turkobei 10/20ths of the water. The actual arrangement is that Jaghark has the right to take water from eighteen of the twenty-two channels, the other four remaining dry during these five days. Then, until their turn comes round again, one of these four channels may be kept running as a special concession.

During the last four years, water has been abundant; but, in years of drought, disputes take place, which frequently culminate in bloodshed.

The Jaghark land being higher up the valley has smaller plots and thus the land for this and other reasons dries up much more quickly than at Turkobei and is less valuable.

The Jaghark valley contains 1,675 *jaribs* or acres of cultivable land, apart from many square miles of grazing ground in the hills. This is divided as follows:—

|  | JARIBS |
|---|---|
| Endowed land. . . . . . | 40 |
| Waste land . . . . . . . | 135 |
| Orchards . . . . . . . . | 1,500 |
| Total | 1,675 |

There are 300 families in Jaghark and adjacent hamlets or 1,500 souls. Of these, one hundred families are *Saiyids* and poor men who pay nothing. One hundred families pay a head-tax, *sirshumari*, of *tomans* 40, and 100 families owning land pay the revenue. A census would show:—

| | |
|---|---|
| 100 families | land-owners |
| 30 families | shop-keepers |
| 10 families | carpenters |
| 50 families | shawl-weavers |
| 50 families | carriers |
| 40 families | labourers |
| 20 families | elders and *katkhudas* |
| Total | 300 families |

The people are of Arab descent and are very well off as, owing to the caravans being accustomed to halt at Jaghark, there is an excellent market for much of their produce close at hand. Indeed, they import forage largely and retail it at high prices to travellers, who also purchase some of the dried mulberries, which are highly esteemed.

The revenue of Jaghark is *tomans* 350 in cash and 10 *kherwars* of grain in the proportion of two-thirds wheat and one-third barley. In addition, *tomans* 25 and 1 *kharwar* of grain is paid to the *katkhudas* and another *tomans* 25 is paid for the food, etc., of *mamurs* or Government officials.

There is practically no grain grown in the valley and so 880 *kharwars* are purchased on account of revenue. Half of the balance is raised from the only mill and three hamlets pay 60 *man*, thus making up the 10 *kharwars*.

The sale of fruit and timber forms the main source of income: but lucerne, potatoes, turnips, beans, etc., are grown in small quantities. A good deal of honey too is produced and 65 lbs. of caraway seeds are collected annually; silk too is grown. Poplar poles are sold to the value of *tomans* 3,000 annually: other timber is, generally speaking, sold as fuel.

| | |
|---|---:|
| Sheep, about . . . . . . . . . . . | 1,000 |
| Cattle . . . . . . . . . . . . . | 50 |
| Horses and mules, about . . . . . | 25 |
| Donkeys, about . . . . . . . . | 100 |

A shawl termed *safid abi* is woven, which is chiefly exported to Tehran, and there used for making *yal* or jackets. It costs *tomans* 6 per piece of 4 feet, and so is expensive.

## Caspian Fisheries

Fishing for sturgeon has for many centuries been carried on in the rivers flowing into the southern part of the Caspian and the famous Russian, as well as the Persian, caviar comes from fish caught in Iranian waters. As the following selection shows, at least as early as the 1840s the government granted a concession for the fisheries to a Persian subject, and small amounts were exported to Astrakhan. But since many kinds of fish were regarded as "unclean" by the *mullahs*, Muslim interest was restricted, and the development of the industry was achieved mainly by Russian Armenians.[1]

Already in the report on his second visit to the Caspian, made in 1847–48, Abbott stated:

The Sturgeon fishery at the mouth of the Tedjou, the River which flows near Saree, is still held by the Russian Armenian whom I found there in 1844 although the lease formerly granted to him is expired. I believe he now pays 240 Tomans a year for it—and about 160 Tomans more for the fishery of the Harraz, Baboul, Tailar, and two or three other streams in the vicinity. The produce is said to fetch 8,000 Tomans in the Astracan market, from which however there must be heavy expenses to deduct.[2]

And in 1873 the consul mentioned that Lianozov "an Armenian merchant of Russian nationality" had rented, at the rate of 41,000 tumans per annum, all the fisheries "from Enzellee to the river Atrek," all expenses to be borne by the concessionaire. The previous year they had been rented by a Persian subject

[1] Other Iranian concessionaires are mentioned in Abdullaev, p. 142.
[2] Report on Journey to the Caspian in November 1847—February 1848, FO 60/141. Entner, p. 77, mentions Armenians and other Russian subjects who operated the fisheries in 1837–40.

(who sold the fish to Lianozov) for 60,000 tumans "the working and maintenance of the fisheries being at the government charge." The consul judged that the government would benefit from the change, since the fish could now be considered as foreign produce and therefore subjected to an export tax[3]—but in fact no such tax was levied.[4]

By 1875 the consul was reporting that "the produce of these fisheries exceeds 200,000 tomans a year" and that the "expense of catching, salting, packing and shipping cannot come to much less than 100,000 tomans a year."[5] The following year, in a lengthy report, he stated that during the fishing season (December to March) Lianozov employed "about 1,100 men, the greater part of whom are Russian subjects of Bakou and Lenkoran. Out of this number 350 are employed at Enzelee, and the remainder along the Sefidrood, where sturgeon is mostly caught, and along the coast. At Enzelee the establishment looks quite a Russian settlement, with its shipwrights and blacksmiths, its glove and bootmakers, its huts for the men to sleep in, and its comfortable wooden house, constructed in Astrakhan and brought out in pieces for the manager."[6]

The concession was renewed, at a very slowly rising rent—400,000 francs a year (£16,000) in 1888–1901, 460,000 francs in 1901–10, and 480,000 in 1911–19. At the outbreak of the First World War, the capital invested by Lianozov was estimated at 3,380,000 francs, or £135,000.[7] Modern equipment was installed, including a telephone system and an electric power station, but the methods used were regarded as exploitative and led to much friction with the local population, including a short-lived boycott in 1910.[8] The quantity and value of the catch increased rapidly, from around 600,000 rubles (about £60,000) in the early 1890s to between 900,000 and 1,000,000 by 1906 and around 2,250,000 in 1907–13.[9] A British estimate for 1908/9 put the amount of fish exported to Russia at 10,911,000 pounds worth £40,000, but these figures, obtained from Persian sources, are probably too low.[10] Lianozov's net profits in 1913 were estimated at 510,000 rubles.[11]

The Bolshevik revolution and the fighting in the area disrupted the fisheries, but the Soviet government's interest in them was reflected in Article 14 of the 1921 Soviet-Iranian Treaty. After prolonged negotiations, the Soviet government bought Lianozov's rights and in October 1927 an Irano-Soviet Fisheries Company, with a twenty-five-year concession, was set up.[12] In the 1930s, annual exports of caviar were about 500,000 kilograms and of fish 8,000 to 9,000 tons with an

[3] Abbott to Granville, 29 May 1873, FO 60/354.
[4] "Gilan," 1874 and 1875, A and P 1876, 76.
[5] Ibid.
[6] "Gilan," 1876, A and P 1877, 82.
[7] Litten, p. 169; see also Kazemzadeh, *Russia*, p. 207.
[8] Abdullaev, pp. 143–49; Kazemzadeh, p. 569.
[9] Entner.
[10] "Gilan," 1908/9, A and P 1910, 101.
[11] Abdullaev, p. 158.
[12] Avery, p. 238.

aggregate value of 10 to 20 million rials. In January 1953, the concession lapsed and the fisheries were taken over by the Iranian government.

(See also works by Abdullaev, Litten, Entner, Fateh, and OCI, listed in the bibliography.)

### Selection 15. Caspian Fisheries, 1844
[K. E. Abbott, "Report on Journey to Caspian," 29 June 1844, FO 60/108]

... The Season commences in the early part of March and lasts till the end of May but the fish are caught all through the Year in small numbers. In April the greatest quantity is taken and I am told that then, for 15 to 20 days the number is from 3,000 to 3,500 daily. The fishery for a Year produces about 125,000 Fish—one person reckoned the number at 150,000. Seven or eight vessels are employed in carrying the Produce to Astracan. The fish is not weighed here, I therefore could not ascertain what the quantity in Mauns or Poots might be, but probably 15 lbs. each when dried and Salted would be a fair average though I am speaking at hazard. The Roe or Caviare is thrown into large troughs containing Salt and water, and stirred about—when it has become properly Salted it rises to the surface. It is then strained through a net work to remove from it any Skin or fleshy matter, and after being pressed, to draw off the water, it is wrapped in matting and finally packed in Casks. It is of two kinds, dark and white but the latter is seldom obtained. The whole may amount to 250 or 300 Barrels of 40 Poots each and the Isinglass which is a membrane of the inside of the fish, to about 250 Poots, in the Year. Salmon and Mâhee Seffeed are also taken in this stream. Some opinion may be formed of the value of the fishery from the following figures—the prices being those which I understand are obtained at Astracan, on the average—but I do not pretend to accuracy.

| | |
|---|---|
| Sturgeon and Ispil—125,000 Fish at 15 lbs. each. 1,875000 lbs. or 52,083 Poots of Russia at s.k. 4/- medium price. . . | Ts.20,833.-.- |
| Caviare—275 Barrels of 40 Poots = 11,000 Poots at s.k. 20/- medium price . . . . . . . . . . . . . . . | Ts.22,000.-.- |
| Isinglass—250 Poots at 32½ Tomans per poot . . . . . . . . . . . . . . . | Ts. 8,125.-.- |
| *or about* £25,479 | Ts.50,958.-.- |

It may appear extraordinary that so great a fishery should be rented for the trifling sum of 2,500 Tomans or about £1,250, which is what I understand Meer Abou Taleb Khan pays for it—and doubtless this is much less than the Government might derive from it—but there are heavy expenses to be added to the rent—such as the wages of the Fishermen, cost of Salt, erection of Stores etc., fishing apparatus, Casks and the expense of the Shipping employed in the conveyance of the Produce to Market. I cannot pretend to estimate what these may amount to but doubtless, though heavy, there must still remain a handsome profit to the Amer of the Fishery. ...

# 6

## Industry

Under the Safavids, Iranian crafts reached an artistic and technical level which, in several respects, was hardly below that of the most advanced countries. But even then Chardin had been struck by the "softness" and laziness of the crafts- men and their lack of desire to innovate or even to imitate.[1] Hence there is no reason to believe that, even under moderately favorable conditions, Iran would have been any more successful than were other Asian countries in effecting the transition from handicraft production to modern factory industry. Instead, the country was subjected to civil wars and devastating invasions, which had par- ticularly adverse effects on such leading handicraft centers as Isfahan, Kirman, and Shiraz.

Thanks to the restoration of order by the first Qajar kings, most crafts recovered and—presumably helped by the reduction in European exports caused by the Napoleonic Wars—once more began to supply domestic and foreign markets (see 6:1). But with peace, greater security in the Persian Gulf, improved transport, and increased trade, a new danger arose—that of machine-made European goods.[2] All contemporary accounts agree on the damage to Persian handicrafts.[3] Three quotations, from reports by the very well informed British consul K. E. Abbott in the 1840s, illustrate this process (see also 6:2, 3):[4] In 1844 "a memorial was presented to His Majesty the Shah by the traders and manufacturers of Cashan praying for protection to their commerce which they represented as suffering in consequence of the introduction of European merchandize into their country."

In 1848 he stated: "The manufactures of England have in a great measure superseded the use of the Cotton and Silk fabrics of this country, owing to their cheapness, the superiority of the style and execution of the designs, and the greater

---

[1] Chardin, 3:97–99.
[2] Writing in 1838, Gagemeister stated that "no cotton yarn is sent to Persia"; see Glukhoded, p. 38.
[3] For the impact on other Middle Eastern countries see EHME, pp. 41–59, 220–47, 452–58.
[4] 30 September 1844, FO 60/117, Trade of Tehran, FO 60/141, and Trade Report FO 60/165.

variety of patterns, which both enabled people to make a more frequent change of dress and to satisfy their taste for novelty of patterns—and even the higher classes have often preferred European chintz to the more expensive silk dresses of their own country."

And again, in 1849, he reported from Kashan: "The manufactures have however rapidly declined for some time past in consequence of the trade with Europe which has gradually extended into every part of the Kingdom to the detriment or ruin of many branches of native industry."

A little earlier, the merchants of Tabriz had petitioned the crown prince to prohibit imports of European manufactures "on the ground principally of the ruin Persian manufactures are reduced to by the constant and immense importation of foreign goods."[5]

No action was taken by the government on the petitions—not surprisingly in view of its general weakness and ignorance of economics, the provisions of the commercial treaties it had signed with the major powers, and the prevailing climate of economic thought (see 3:1). Some measures were attempted by the reforming minister Amir-i Kabir, but their effect was transient (see 6:2, 6). With constantly improving communications and growing trade, the pressure on the crafts steadily increased, and their decay entailed the weakening of the ancient guilds (see 6:5).

However, the decline of the crafts, although considerable, should not be exaggerated. Available data show that in many branches the number of producing units was still high at the beginning of the century. A few crafts managed to retain their domestic and even their foreign markets (see 6:8). Taking cotton, woolen, and silk cloth alone, exports in 1912/13 amounted to nearly £100,000. And if foreign trade hurt those crafts that competed with imports, it stimulated the ones connected with exports and led to the establishment of workshops processing leather,[6] opium, henna, silk, and other export products (see 6:7). But by far the most important craft benefiting from expanded foreign markets was carpet weaving, which attracted a substantial amount of foreign and domestic capital and by 1914 was exporting goods worth £1,000,000 (see 6:9).

In some other Middle Eastern countries foreign demand also led to the growth of the mining industry, but huge distances and poor transport precluded such a development in Iran and minerals continued to be exploited on a small scale and by primitive techniques (see 6:2, 4, 7). With the very important exception of petroleum, the only mineral exported on a significant scale was iron oxide, from the islands of the Persian Gulf.

---

[5] Dispatch by Bonham, 28 June 1844, FO 60/107.

[6] Largely as a result of increased demand from Russia, the leather industry expanded and underwent structural change. Writing in 1913, Sobotsinskii (pp. 228–29) pointed out that "leather production, which until now was in the hands of a large number of enterprises, standing halfway between cottage and handicraft industry and employing 5–10 workers, is changing into manufactories. Thus already in 1909, in Mashad and Hamadan, there were 8 workshops, with up to 40–50 workers each. The small handicraft shops were unable to withstand the competition of the large enterprises, and rapidly declined. . . . In Hamadan, in 1912, there were 300 small leather shops, compared with 400 in 1909, and in Mashad 50 compared with 200."

As regards factory industry, even by Middle Eastern standards Iran remained backward. The reasons for this are not difficult to find. There was, first, the dispersion of the population over vast areas and the absence of water or mechanical transport, which between them prevented the growth of a national market. The effects of this were reinforced by the low productivity and poverty of the rural population, and the fact that most of them lived in a subsistence economy and had little contact with the market. The expensiveness of fuel and the absence of power added greatly to costs,[7] as did the lack of labor familiar with the operation and maintenance of modern machinery, and of supervisory personnel. Capital was scarce and little inclined to venture into fields where returns were slow in coming in and where investments could not be easily liquidated. Industrial credit was nonexistent. In many parts of the country insecurity prevailed. Last, foreign competition was intense and the government had neither the inclination nor the means to give effective protection and assistance to industry. The following pessimistic judgment, made by a British mission in 1905, is a fair assessment of the situation:[8]

It is hopeless for any Indian or English manufacturer to think of establishing works in Persia at present. If he embarks on such an enterprise, he will but add another item to the long list of industrial ventures that have failed in that land. The difficulties that stand in the way of such enterprises are at present too great. There is first the Government. No foreigner is allowed to own land or house in Persia, except under very stringent rules, and if he becomes a Persian landholder he must, as a rule, first become a Persian subject. If he becomes a Persian subject, he must expect continually to be "squeezed." Then there is the cost of transporting machinery, which is prohibitive, and at present no heavy machinery could be got up at all. Labour, too, in Persia while fairly cheap (though dearer than Indian) is inefficient and undisciplined to a degree hard to conceive.

Lastly, any factory setting up would have to be on a small scale, only large enough to use local supplies, for once you have to carry raw material any distance the present cost of transport renders it prohibitive. This means hopelessly expensive working, as having small factories scattered all over the country would make the cost and task of supervision prohibitive.

A few efforts to introduce modern industries were made as early as 1820, when the Persian ambassador in London was instructed to engage a superintendent of iron works, two furnace men, a glass worker, two miners, and a cloth manufacturer, and when a steam engine was sent from England to Iran.[9] The Tabriz arsenal was also put under the supervision of an Englishman and produced good

[7] Both coal, from the Elburz and other mines, and oil from Russia and the Persian Gulf were very expensive in the main consuming centers, owing to high transport costs. Electric power was generated and used by Anglo-Persian Oil Company and the Caspian Fisheries. Electricity was, by the early years of this century, also available in Tehran, Tabriz, Rasht, Mashad, and Shiraz, but seems to have been used only for lighting—see Aubin, p. 39; Foreign Office Handbook, *Persia*, p. 105; and chap. 6, sel. 11.

[8] Gleadowe-Newcomen, p. 12; for an equally gloomy Russian analysis, see Sobotsinskii, pp. 59–69. In 1888, under British pressure, a decree was issued protecting property rights in Iran (see "Correspondence," A and P 1888, 109), but it seems to have had little effect.

[9] Mirza Abul Hassan Khan to Castlereagh, 9 January 1820, and Ouseley to Planta, 23 November 1820, FO 60/19.

cannon and ammunition.[10] In 1849, thanks to the efforts of Amir-i Kabir, textile, paper, glass, and pottery works were established, but these enterprises ended in failure (see 6:6). Equally unsuccessful were a private spinning mill, glass factory, and gasworks set up in the 1850s to 1870s.[11]

Starting in the 1880s, several larger factories were established by foreign or private capital, but here too success was limited (see 6:10, 11). However, in the years immediately preceding the First World War it looked as though industrialization might at last get started. Not only did local entrepreneurs increase their activity (see 2:5), but foreign capital began to set up various enterprises. The British established the Anglo-Persian Oil Company and the Russians several small petroleum refineries and cotton ginneries, as well as the Caspian Fisheries. As for the Germans, either alone or in partnership with Persian capital, they founded a carpet factory, a spinning mill, a brick factory, and other firms.[12]

However, the very limited extent to which Iran had been industrialized on the eve of the First World War is well brought out by the following estimates of employment.[13] Only 1,700 persons worked in modern factories, of whom 400 were employed in cotton ginneries and 300 in the sugar plants. Some 7,000 to 8,000 were employed by the Anglo-Persian Oil Company and 5,000 Russian subjects worked in the fisheries, road construction, and other Russian enterprises in Iran. As for the handicrafts, they are estimated to have employed about 100,000 persons, of whom 65,000 were in carpet-making and 20,000 in weaving.

Like other Middle Eastern countries, but to a still greater degree, Iran had to wait till the 1930s for its first serious efforts at industrialization, and, except for petroleum, did not develop a really significant manufacturing and mining sector until the 1950s and 1960s (see epilogue).

## The Melville Papers

Sir John Malcolm, a senior official in the East India Company's service, wrote the report from which the following extract is taken after the completion of his mission in Iran in 1801. His dispatches to Dundas, together with some other dispatches, were edited by Sir A. T. Wilson and published in a pamphlet, under the title *The Melville Papers*, by the Royal Central Asian Society in London, in 1930. The pamphlet is described as consisting of reprints of three articles published in the journal of the society in 1929 and 1930, but in fact the second of these

---

[10] Campbell to Grant, 10 October 1833, FO 60/35.
[11] For details see Jamalzadeh, pp. 93–94, and Abdullaev, p. 125. "The factory near Tehran for spinning cotton has been lately repaired under the management of two able English machinists, and is again in operation. But the chief of the establishment has told me that if it pays its expenses it will be all that is expected. Raw cotton is brought to it from Isfahan, whither, after being spun, it is re-transmitted and sold to the weavers. It would seem that it might answer better were weaving establishments set up at Tehran and the expense of re-transport to Isfahan saved. The chief of the factory said that he had thought of such a plan and would try to carry it out"— "Tehran," A and P 1867–68, 68.
[12] For details see Abdullaev, pp. 125–60.
[13] See details in ibid., pp. 199–212.

articles—from which the following selection was taken—although scheduled to appear in the January 1930 issue, never was published in the journal.

(See also works by Hambly, Fraser, Malcolm, Ouseley, Porter, Dupré, Drouville, and Joubert, listed in the bibliography.)

## Selection 1. Industry and Foreign Trade, 1800
[John Malcolm, *The Melville Papers*]

COMMERCIAL STATE OF PERSIA

HOME TRADE

To give any detailed account of the internal commerce of Persia is foreign to my present purpose. I shall therefore confine myself to very general remarks on that subject.

The manufactures of Persia that are in demand over all that Empire, are silks of various kinds, coarse cotton cloths, plain and coloured, carpets, Nummuds,[1] cotton cloths, Kirmaun shawls, gold cloths, etc., swords and other military weapons, saddles and horse furniture, leather, glassware, sheep and lambskins, iron work, gold and silver articles and enamelled work.

The towns in Persia at which these manufactures are chiefly produced, are Isfahaun, Yezd, Cashaun, Shirawz, Hamadaun and Resht. Cazveen and Kirmaunshauh, though equal in population to any one of those cities, except Isfahaun, are neither of them much celebrated for any manufacture. Cazveen owes its prosperity to its being from situation the mart of all the commerce of the Caspian, and Kirmaunshauh to its being that of a great part of the trade between Turkey and Persia.

Teheraun has yet no manufacture of consequence except that of sheep and lambskins, which form an essential article of Persian dress. It will no doubt soon have many if it continues to be the capital, a circumstance that I should doubt, as the reasons that made the late King chuse it as a residence, will probably soon cease to exist, and the Court will most probably be re-

[1] A thick felt used for sitting and sleeping upon.

moved to Isfahaun, unless Russia should make any attack on Persia, in which case it will be more than ever necessary to keep the capital on the Northern part of the Empire.

Isfahaun, though fallen from its former greatness, is still the first city in Persia. Its manufactures are gold brocades, which are lately brought to great perfection, lambskin caps, coarse cotton cloths, plain and coloured, saddles, swords, and other arms, all utensils in gold, silver, iron, steel and brass, besides which it has lesser manufactures that are, as well as those I have already stated, exported from it to every part of the Empire, and occasion its still retaining a commercial importance.

Yezd has enjoyed more tranquility than any city in the Persian Empire, and commerce has of course flourished there more than anywhere else. Its chief manufactures are silk, carpets, nummuds, shawls made of Karmania wool, and coarse cotton cloth, besides these some new manufactures have lately been tried at this city that appear likely to meet with much success. One made of Karmania wool and silk, which is denominated the Yezd shawl, is the principal; the others are imitations of English damasks, and velvet, and when to these productions we add that in the vicinity of this town there are lead mines which are now worked and that there are also beyond a doubt rich veins of copper and iron, we may conjecture the importance that it will in all likelihood reach if the Government of Persia continues settled.

The chief manufactures of Shirawz are guns, pistols, swords and other military arms, glassware, sheep and lambskin for caps, articles of gold and silver, enamelled work and coarse cloths, all of which are exported to other parts of the Empire. The trade of this city has much decreased since it ceased to be the Seat of Government. It will, however, always maintain some importance as a place of trade, while Bushire is the chief port in the Gulph, as it must from situation while that is the case be a great mart of Indian commerce.

Cashaun is famous for its silk and carpet manufactures. The silk produced at Cashaun is only second to that of Resht, and its carpets are hardly inferior to those manufactured at Tubbus and other cities in Independent Khorassaun. Imitations of velvet and some other manufactures of Europe are made with tolerable success in this city, the inhabitants of which are both ingenious and industrious.

The chief manufacture of Humadaun is leather, which is dressed better in this city than in any other in Persia. It forms the principal article of export, though not the only one, Hamadaun having also manufactures of Nummuds, saddles and coarse cloths.

The silks manufactured at Resht, are more esteemed than any other in Persia. They bear a higher price than those of Cashaun and Yezd, and their consumption is therefore not so great. This town is also celebrated for making the best saddle cloths and coverlids, articles of very general use in Persia. These are made of English broad cloth and cashmere, the various colours of which are curiously wrought on each other with much labour, and a considerable degree of tastes.

Independent of the manufactures I have stated, which form the chief branches of the internal commerce, grain of all kinds is an article of trade from one province to another, as it is in demand.

Tobacco in great quantities is always exported from Fars to the other provinces of the Empire, a circumstance owing to that plant being there produced of a very superior quality.

There are in the province of Mazinderaun several iron mines which are worked, the metal is not so much esteemed as the iron of Europe, probably from the ignorance of those who prepare it.

Near the city of Musennan in Independent Khorassaun which fell into the possession of the King of Persia last year, there is a very celebrated copper mine, which was worked till the death of Naudir Shauh, and a few years before that I find on the Gombroon Records, quantities of copper received from the Hon'ble Company's Factory from Yezd, which I have every reason on enquiry to believe was the produce of that mine.

FOREIGN TRADE OF PERSIA

Persia carries on a trade with India and Arabia by the Gulph, with Russia by the Caspian, and with the Turkish Empire, the Kingdom of Caubul, and that of Bokharra, on land by Caffilas [caravans]. That with Independent Khorassaun, I shall not mention as that province has most productions in common with the other parts of the Persian Empire, of which it ever has till the death of Naudir-Shauh been an actual part.

INDIA

The imports from India to Persia do not exceed the gross sum of twenty-six lacks of rupees, the chief articles are:

FROM BENGAL

Sugar, muslins, piece goods, indigo.

FROM MADRAS

Chintz and piece goods, indigo.

FROM BOMBAY

European articles, china ware, sugar, sugar candy, camphire.

FROM THE COAST OF MALABAR

Wood for building vessels, coir rope for rigging, black pepper, ginger, turmeric, cardamums, etc.

FROM SURAT

Gold cloths (kumkhaubs), coarse piece goods, indigo, coarse chintz, cotton cloths, cotton thread, handkerchiefs.

FROM BATAVIA

Sugar and spices.

DEVAIL SCIND

Coarse chintz, leather, oil and cotton.

Independent of these imports are the staple articles of the Hon'ble Company's broad cloth, perpetts, iron, steel, lead and tin. Supposing the latter to amount to five hundred bales of broad cloth, eight hundred of perpetts, 1,500 cwt. of iron, 620 cwt. of tin, 300 cwt. of lead, and 150 cwt. of steel, the greatest extent to which they are ever likely to reach, the amount of their sale will not be found to exceed four lacks of rupees, which added to the import before mentioned, makes the whole import to Persia from India thirty lacks of rupees.

The exports from Persia to India, are silk, pearls, brimstone, assafatida, carmania wool, dried fruits of all kinds, carpets, gall nuts, rose water, drugs, salt fish, wheat, myrrh, saffron, tobacco and cummun seeds. All these do not amount to more than fifteen lacks of rupees. The remaining half is sent in specie to the great distress of the country, and the loss of the Persian merchant who always suffer by the exchange.

## ARABIA

From the Red Sea there is imported to Persia annually about a lack of rupees in specie, Abysinian slaves and a small quantity of coffee, to an amount of one lack and twenty thousand rupees. And from the Southern shore of the Persian Gulph, pearls and some coarse cloths to an amount of two lacks of rupees.

To the Red Sea, Persia annually sends carpets, wheat, tobacco, dried fruits, drugs, dried roses, rose water, cummun seeds and red dye. And to Bahrien, wheat, tobacco and red dye.

The pilgrims from Persia to Mecca may be calculated at three hundred, and independent of merchandize these cannot carry in specie on an average less than two hundred rupees each, which makes an annual export of six lacks of rupees in specie from Persia to Arabia.

## RUSSIA

Persia imports from Russia specie in gold and silver, iron, cutlery of all descriptions, glassware, looking glasses, stationery, broad cloth and cashmeres, a cloth or hair list, called in Persia Beigress, Russian leather of different kinds, spirits, gold lace, and gold thread, furs of all descriptions, fine lambskins, called Kozaukee, cochineal, coarse cloths, printed and plain, of different sorts, European dimittys and chintzes, velvet, clocks, watches, guns and pistols, oil, iron, brass, steel, lead and sea horse teeth.

This import, the amount of which I have never been able correctly to ascertain, but which I am inclined to think does not at its most flourishing epoch exceed twenty lacks of rupees, annually, is answered from Persia by exports of raw and manufactured silks, cotton, cotton thread, coarse lambskins, rice, fox skins, gold cloths of Isfahaun, pearls, coarse cloth and coarse chintz of Persia, naphta, saffron, sulphur, gallnuts and some cloths and chintzes of India.

## TURKEY

Persia imports from Turkey, golden coins and bars, jewels, tabbies, velvet, French and Venetian woolens, and other European stuffs, Damascus and Aleppo stuffs, glassware, painted glass, coral, amber, hardwares, wood for dyeing, vermelion, white lead, looking glasses, opium, iron, steel, lace and gold thread.

To answer this import, which I have good grounds to estimate at the gross sum of thirty-five lacks of rupees, Persia returns silk, cashmere shawls, Indian indigo, coarse printed cloths, gum ammoniac, tobacco, lambskins, cotton, cochineal, rhubarb, saffron, gold cloths, printed and flowered cloths of Isfahaun.

On a moderate calculation of the specie annually brought to Baghdad and its vicinity by Persian pilgrims to the Sacred Tombs near that city, it is found to amount to the sum of ten lacks of rupees.

Within two or three years a great quantity of jewels, received at Baghdad from Constantinople, have found a sale in Persia, and have lessened the export of specie from Turkey, and thereby rendered the trade less unfavourable to that country than it was before.

This is however a very temporary branch of commerce, and an accident to the present King of Persia, who is the only purchaser of jewels in his dominions, would probably occasion near the whole lately sent to Persia, to find the same road back to Europe, or to go to Caubul and India.

CAUBUL

Persia imports annually from the kingdom of Zumaun Shauh indigo, cashmere shawls, coarse chintz, drugs and rhubarb. This import, which amounts to the gross sum of forty lacks of rupees, is answered by an export of European cloths, sattins, velvets, silks, lace and gold thread, diamonds, rubies, emeralds and pearls. Isfahaun gold cloth, brocades, coarse cloth, of different colours, saffron, hardwares, Yezd and Cashaun silks, and manufactures of karmania wool, to an amount equal to thirty lacks, the remaining ten lacks is sent in specie.

The imports from Bokharra and the country of the Oosbegs is at present very confined. It consists chiefly of black lamb-skins, cotton thread and gold dust. This import does not exceed five lacks of rupees. It is answered by an export of gold cloths, brocades, coloured lambskins, coarse cloths, dyed of different colours, pearls, silk, coral, amber and painted glass.

GENERAL OBSERVATIONS ON THE TRADE OF PERSIA

The annual amount of the imports and exports of Persia do not (if this statement is correct) much exceed two millions and a half sterling; and when it is considered that at least one half of this only passes through that kingdom on its way to others, it will probably be judged but a trifling trade in proportion to the extent of the Empire. This commerce might perhaps be trebled if the country was to remain settled, and the Government to encourage arts and manufactures, but even then it would bear no comparison with that of many other kingdoms of not half its extent.

Persia enjoys a delightful climate, and is a plentiful country, but not a rich one, and

there seems to be strong natural objections to its ever becoming so. There is not a navigable river,[2] or canal in the whole kingdom, and rivers of any description are very scarce. Wherever they are, the utmost exertions have been formerly, and are still made to turn every drop of their waters to the cultivation of the country. From the deficiency of water, there is also a great scarcity of wood in Persia. Except the gardens near towns, and a few planted avenues in the vicinity of the largest cities, no plantations, or forests, are to be seen on the level grounds. Some of the mountains produce quantities of low wood, but good timber is almost unknown. The Persians have in consequence little ability; if they had the inclination, to build vessels on either the shores of the Gulph, or the Caspian; on those of the latter this would be most practicable, as the province of Mazinderaun has more good wood than all the rest of the Persian Empire.

Wheel-carriages are unknown in Persia, though roads would in most places, with very little repair, admit of their use. The scarcity of timber is perhaps one cause of their not having been introduced. The build of their towns, all the streets of which are too narrow for their admission, may be another, but the chief is ignorance of the advantage from this improved stile of conveying merchandize.

The population of Persia is below mediocrity, and more than one half of the inhabitants are *Illiauts* or wandering tribes, who live in tents, and remove from province to province as the seasons change.

I do not think above one seventh of the land in Persia is now cultivated, and perhaps one fifth is the utmost that could under every encouragement be made usable; most of the rest is fine pasture land, and the wealth of Persia will be found, if ever the Government of that country is permanent, to depend as much on the increase and excellence of her flocks of herds, as on the produce of her soil.

[2] The Kurroon, that which passes Shushter, cannot be called navigable till it enters Arabia.

The actual riches of the Persian Empire, and the great value of her commerce, have generally been overrated, the martial habits of her inhabitants having often enabled her Sovereigns to bring the riches of foreign conquests into their native country, which has, from the temporary accession of such spoils, obtained a credit for wealth beyond that she actually possesses.

By the statement given of the commerce of Persia, it appears that that nation must annually export to make up the balance of trade and to pay the expense of her pilgrims, a considerable sum in money beyond that which she receives, and as she has no mines, that export must in time drain the country of specie, unless that is occasionally brought from other kingdoms. The last great influx of wealth to Persia was on Naudir Shauh's return from India, and the wealth then obtained is far from being yet all dissipated.

If the Government of Persia was to continue settled and agriculture and manufactures to be encouraged, (an event to be wished than expected) that Empire would soon be able not only fully to answer her imports by her exports, but to turn the balance of trade in her own favour.

The certain sources of opulence that Persia possesses, are the following.

1st. Silk.—Which though no longer in the great demand it was when produced in few or other parts of the world, is still an article that will meet a sale in any quantity that is made.

2nd. Karmania Wool.—This valuable article which is found only in Persia, is in constant demand in Europe. It might be increased to any quantity. Nothing is required but attention to the goats of that province and taking every means to propagate the breed.

3rd. Iron, Copper and Lead.—The mines of these metals that are in Persia would not only meet the consumption of the Empire, but prove, if paid attention to, a valuable source of wealth in its commerce with neighbouring nations.

4th Wheat.—This is always a certain export to the Red Sea, Bussorah, and the Southern shore of the Persian Gulph, and not unfrequently one to Surat and Bombay.

5th Wine.—If religious prejudices did not operate, wine might be produced in Persia of excellent quality, and in a sufficient quantity to prove a valuable article of export.

6th. Dried Fruit.—If Persia remains undisturbed, this article of export from that kingdom will increase of itself to much beyond its present amount, which is, however, very considerable.

7th. Brimstone.—Any quantity of which can be exported from Persia.

8th. Carpets.—Which are made in Persia equal to any in the world.

9th. Tobacco.—Which is produced particularly in the province of Fars, in the greatest abundance and from its superior quality is always in demand over all Turkey and Arabia.

10th. Gall Nuts.—Great quantities of which are now exported to Russia and Turkey.

The trade by the Gulph with India, is of all others the most important to Persia. It is also the one least liable to be disturbed, and therefore, that which is most likely to increase.

The importance of this trade to Persia proceeds from two causes. 1st. Because the articles of greatest necessity come into Persia by that route. And 2ndly. Because Persia can obtain by it, whenever necessary, almost all the articles she receives from other quarters, such as the European commodities now imported from Russia and Turkey, and the cashmere shawls and indigo received from Caubul. The shawls at present not unfrequently find their way down the Indus, to Surat, and are from that sent to Persia, and as to Indigo, that made in Bengal has within these four years been imported into Persia, where it is already more esteemed than any brought from the higher parts of India by the way of Caubul and Candahar, and I should hope that in a very few years, the supplies of this article from India would turn into a new channel this great branch of trade.

On a calculation which I have reason to think correct, the value of indigo annually brought to Persia from Caubul, is thirty three lacks of rupees, two thirds of which is again exported to Turkey.

If Cochineal is brought to perfection in India, it will always meet with a certain and advantageous sale in Persia, as it is the dye of the greatest demand at all the silk manufacturers of that kingdom.

JOHN MALCOLM,
*Envoy*

BUSSORAH,
10*th April*, 1801

**Handicrafts**

The following selection, taken from a book by a German physician who spent several years in Iran and knew the country well, gives a detailed account of the processes and products of the main industries. The decline of the crafts under the impact of foreign competition, noted by the author, continued throughout the period under review.

Naturally, there are no overall figures on production, equipment, or employment, but some data relating to the middle and end of the century are available. In 1849–50, K. E. Abbott visited central, western, and southern Iran and gave the following information:[1]

*Kashan*—30,000 inhabitants; 27 caravanserais, 770 shops, 130 merchants; European cotton and woolen goods worth £4,000 were sold in 28 shops; 80 coppersmiths, 800 silk looms; "a great deal" of cotton twist was spun, 1,500 mule-loads having been sent to Astrakhan alone in 1848.

European competition had greatly injured the crafts, and the town was said to have formerly had 8,000 silk looms.

*Isfahan*—28 caravanserais, 340 traders; 200 silk looms, "the manufacture of cotton goods is carried to a great extent, and affords occupation to many of the inhabitants of the town and surrounding villages"; here too industry "had been impaired by an unrestricted trade in foreign productions."

*Yazd*—35,000–40,000 inhabitants; "a thriving trade with India"; 40 to 50 shops selling foreign goods; imports of cottons from India were worth about £60,000–65,000 and from Turkey and northern Iran about £65,000; 300 to 350 silk looms, 1,300 cotton looms, also in decline.

*Kirman*—25,000 inhabitants; 250 merchants; 17 shops selling foreign goods; imports of English manufactures about £98,000; 2,200 shawl manufacturing looms, 220 woolen looms, producing £40,000–45,000 worth of goods, "exclusive of that of about 325 looms belonging to 9 villages around, valued at Tomans 15,000 (£7,000) more."

*Bushire*—Imports from India and Java £500,000–600,000; exports including specie £400,000–480,000.

*Bandar Abbas*—imports for Kirman, Yazd, and Isfahan, £300,000; imports for

---

[1] "Notes on the Trade, Manufactures and Productions of Various Cities and Countries of Persia," FO 60/165; the report also contains much valuable information on trade and agricultural production.

other districts, unknown; exports from Yazd and Kirman £35,000–40,000; exports of specie, unknown.

*Shiraz*—1,200 shops, 100 of which sold English textiles; 80,000 pieces of plain and dyed British cottons, worth £65,000, imported from India, through Bushire; "3,000 or 4,000 pieces of plain cottons, and a few cloths and silks, worth £40,000 more are imported from Tabriz," via Yazd; manufactures of hardware and cutlery.

*Kermanshah*—5,000 inhabitants; 16 caravanserais; imports 500 horse-loads of English manufactures, worth about £25,000, sold in 40 shops.

*Hamadan*—about 6,000 families; 13 caravanserais; 68 shops selling British goods; numerous tanneries and production of leather, felt, cotton goods.

Ten years later, a consular report put the number of traders and handicraftsmen in Tabriz at 3,114, of whom 2,676 were in the town itself and 438 in the suburbs.[2]

In 1889, according to Curzon, there were in Mashad 650 silk looms and 320 shawl looms and in Tabriz 166 caravanserais and 3,922 shops, many of them "deserted fabrics"; in 1870, Kirman had 80 cotton factories and 6 "really good carpet factories" and in the middle of the century had had "as many as 1,800 silk factories, employing 9,000 hands ... this has, however, declined for reasons elsewhere displayed."[3]

Figures for the end of the nineteenth century or the beginning of the twentieth include 1,000 shawl looms in Kirman, with an annual export of 300,000 tumans; 200 woolen looms in Nain and 300 in Kirman; 200 silk looms in Kashan with a monthly output of 400 pieces, 400 workshops with 2,000 looms in Yazd, 100 shops with 200 looms in Mashad, and 16 shops with 3 to 4 looms each in Nishapur. As for cotton weaving, in Yazd there were 800 workshops, with 2,000 looms producing cloth worth 100,000 tumans, in Isfahan 2,000 looms and in Kashan 100 workshops.[4] It will thus be seen that although the crafts had been hurt by foreign competition, their output was still considerable.

[2] Report by Dickson, 14 February, 1860, FO 60/253.
[3] Curzon, *Persia*, 1:167, 521, and 2:242, 245; see also Tomara, pp. 26–27.
[4] Abdullaev, pp. 87–98.

## Selection 2. Handicrafts, 1850s
[Jakob Polak, *Persien, das Land und seine Bewohner* (Leipzig, 1865), 2:165–90]

Persian industry, although it cannot be compared with that of most European states, is, taken as a whole, not insignificant and meets domestic needs. When one considers that nothing is done by the government to raise the level of industry, that on the contrary an irrational tariff system encourages the import of foreign goods to the detriment of domestic products, that roads and means of communication are lacking, that metal deposits lie buried in the womb of the earth and that all iron must be brought in from abroad, at high prices; when one contemplates the imperfection of tools and machines, the shortage of capital, the high rate of interest and the lack of development of credit facilities—one must truly wonder how many domestic products manage to compete with foreign.

For two centuries, since Chardin visited the country, Persian industry has made no progress—rather it has gone backward. In the face of ever increasing European competition, the manufacture of many goods no longer pays and it is profitable to sell the raw material. Moreover, long internal wars have hit the centers of industry—Isfahan, Yazd, Kirman—particularly hard. With the workers has disappeared their craft, for nowhere as much as in Persia are certain industries as firmly tied to individual towns; this is mainly attributable to the differences in the quality of water in the different localities.

Until recently, *cotton* (*panbeh*) was, in most parts of the country, made into a rough, strong material, known as *kerbas*,[1] which was used for clothing by the middle classes, like linen in our country, but mainly as tent covering. In Qum, Simnan, and Abadeh near Shiraz, *Kerbas* is made by craftsmen, but in addition every household weaves enough to cover its needs. The piece (*tub*) is six to eight meters long. Better cloth, similar to nanking (*gadek*) is made in Isfahan, Yazd, and Kashan and, in smaller quantities, also in Bushire; this cloth is closely and evenly woven, and holds its color very well and is therefore very popular for summer clothing among city people in Persia and in the Caucasus. Formerly, the natural yellow cotton (*gadek-e shudreng*) was used for this purpose but, because of its brittleness, it is difficult to spin it into equal threads, and people prefer to weave *gadeks* out of English yarn imported through Bushire. As a result, the price has been reduced, but the quality has also worsened. The so-called *Indiennes* or *Pars* (*qalamkar*, pen-designs) are highly valued—fine weaves with patterns of arabesquelike, interlaced flowers, or many-colored calicoes. Their manufacture is very laborious and costly, for the colors have to be printed separately, by hand, and then covered with resin (*Sakkesharz*) to prevent them from mixing together. The most widely used calicoes in Persia (*chit*) are usually supplied by Manchester factories, where goods are made to suit Persian taste and for sale in the Orient. The merchandise comes either directly from England,

through the Greek firm of Ralli Brothers [see 3:11] or through intermediaries in Constantinople, Trebizond, and Tabriz [and is then considered] as a German, French, or Swiss product.

The Persians make shawls, carpets, felt, flannels, and flannel goods out of sheep wool (*pashm*), mohair (*murgus*), or camel hair (*kurk*).

For shawls, only the finest mohair is used. The main centers of shawl-making are Kirman and Mashad (*shal-i kirmani* and *mashhadi*). Persian shawls, which are usually 3 meters long and $1\frac{1}{4}$ broad, are comparable in design and color to those of Kashmir, but are far inferior in suppleness and closeness of weave. Good quality shawls usually cost 20–30 ducats,[2] whereas Indian shawls fetch twice to three times as much. Mashad makes shawls for 8–10 ducats, and Kirman fine shawls, a quality similar to European cashmere cloth (*shal-i kusse*) costing 5–6 ducats. Different kinds are distinguished, according to pattern and color, under the following names: *laki, lajeverdi, butei, shahi-i gevezn, ahrami, tirmeh, zengari*. A significant amount of Persian shawls is exported to Constantinople and Alexandria. At home, shawlcloth is cut into narrow strips (*hashieh*) and much used for the bordering and trimming of clothes. Some years ago, shawl-making in Persia showed a marked recovery because of the encouragement given by the grand vizier Amir [see 6:6]. Shawls worth 50–60 ducats were woven, a price seldom fetched by Indian ones. But after his death this industry retrogressed once more so that now a great part of cashmere wool, whose price has risen sharply, is sold to India in raw form.

Persian carpets (*farsh*) are distinguished less by liveliness of color than by durability and closeness of weave. The bigger ones (*qali*) are six meters long and three wide; the price of such carpets is between 12 and 40 ducats. This industry, too, is in decay. Carpets woven two hundred years ago excel present ones by far in splendor of

---

[1] The *karpas* of the Bible (Esther, chap. 1).

[2] The reference seems to be to the Dutch ducat, worth about 9s. 4d.

design and freshness of color. A smaller kind (*qaliche*), used mainly for prayer, costs 4–10 ducats. The most beautiful rugs come from Farahan province, near Kermanshah. Second quality rugs are made by nomads in Kurdistan, Hamadan, and Mianeh, at fairly low prices; by giving their rugs a light brown background made out of camel wool, they know how to produce a very pleasing appearance. If the rug should have a defect (*gis*), it is sold at half-price, for such defects cannot be repaired and the material will soon be rubbed down and lose its fluffiness.

The durability of Persian carpets is truly amazing. During the second year of my stay in Tehran I wished to buy there beautiful, but used, carpets from a Persian. As the price demanded seemed too high, I told the owner that they were already old. He replied: "That is not so, for I bought them first sixteen years ago." We concluded the deal and after eight years' use I resold them at the same price. Sales of carpets abroad, to the Caucasus and Constantinople, are not considerable, for their heavy weight makes transport costly; moreover, except for those who, like the Persians, demand durability, their price may seem too high; last, their size is not suitable for all rooms. Carpets of any dimension and design can be made to order, but in such cases one must wait at least eight months, for the work advances extremely slowly.

One can learn to judge the value of a shawl or a rug only after much practice in seeing and touching. For Persians, as is related elsewhere, it is a matter of good breeding to estimate accurately the value of a horse, a shawl, or a carpet. Europeans, however, cannot trust their own judgment, but should address themselves to a reliable merchant or broker. One needs a very practiced eye and touch to distinguish between an Indian and a Persian shawl.

The Persians show much skill in the making of felt (*nemet*) of various kinds, embroidered with beautiful figures and inscriptions of colored wool. These made in Yazd, although over $1\frac{1}{2}$ inches thick, show extraordinary flexibility and elasticity; the small ones made of goat hair in Hamadan feel exactly like silk. Felts are used for covering floors, for headgear, for jackets, for horse rugs, etc. Because of their great weight, they are not suited for export.

Some nomadic tribes, especially the Kurds, weave many-colored, thin, light, and yet tough covers for use by men and horses called *gelim, kurdi, simpushta*. They cost 2–6 ducats apiece.

In Kirman, a thicker, more durable, and yet very supple flannel cloth (*patu*) is woven, and made watertight by fulling. I have carried such a *patu* for eight years in all my travels—in tents, in the desert, on mountains—I have slept on it and then brought it back, in a fully usable condition, to Europe, where it can serve me as a carpet for at least another ten years. Every traveler in Persia is advised to take a *patu* with him; for its amazing lightness, relative to its volume, makes it of the greatest use. Wrapped in a *patu*, one is sufficiently protected against dew and rain. In color, *patus* come in natural brown, blue, green, or red. Their price is 3–6 ducats.

Another, also very supple, flannel cloth (*berek*) is woven out of camel hair. Soft, warm, and durable, it is used by Persians like woolen material [*Tuch*]. The best kind, made by the Hazareh tribe, comes from Afghanistan, but fine qualities are also produced in Khurasan. A kind of cloak, similar to the Arab *aba*, is made of camel hair in Kirman and Isfahan. It is usually adorned, at the shoulders, with golden thread; all varieties are light, perfectly watertight, and durable. They cost 3–8 ducats. They are worn in summer and winter, are very practical for traveling—more so than our traveling cloaks, for they protect against sun and rain, heat, and cold.

The famous Persian stockings are also made of wool; for elasticity, liveliness of color, and beauty of design, they come close to Kashmir shawls. The most highly priced are those of Shiraz and Khoi, near Ararat.

Besides the fabrics made of sheep wool and goat and camel hair, the use of woolen cloth (*mahut*) is widespread. The Persians do not know how to make such cloth; a factory in Azerbaijan, built some thirty years ago, soon had to be closed. All such cloth comes from abroad, being imported by Persian merchants from Constantinople through Trebizond and Tabriz [see 3:10]. Most of it is of Austrian make, although it is sold under the name of Dutch cloth (*mahut valendis*). When buying such cloth, Persians look less at price than at quality, for they expect woolens to last at least six to ten years; one hears many complaints about the deterioration of European fabrics, as regards durability. For a cloak, $3\frac{1}{4}$ meters of cloth are used; Europeans who bring with them such a piece of cloth, especially in blue, chamois, or olive green, can make themselves very much liked by giving it as a present, and can get in return many valuable services.

The making of *silks* (*abrishum*) is spread throughout the whole land, but has fallen off considerably since Chardin's time [see 5:6]. The most important silk factories are in Kashan, Yazd—which makes the most beautiful fabrics—Isfahan, Tabriz, and Mashad. Ten years ago, four hundred looms were still active in Kashan, but since then business has declined because much raw silk is exported to Europe owing to the rise in prices there. In general, Persian silks are durable and lively in color; by binding the skeins during dyeing, they produce delicately shaded, flaming designs; in brilliance and evenness of color, however, they do not measure up to European varieties. The best plain taffetas (*tafteh, kanavis*) are made in Mashad and Kashan; colorful, checkered-design bed covers in Yazd and Isfahan; and door-curtains (*pardeh*) in Gilan. Moirés (*kharah*[3] and *darah*) are in every respect inferior to European products. Atlas (*gatni*) is produced only in Kashan; however, it is not made of pure silk but has a cotton woof. In the same place, brocades (*zarbafi*) are made with inwoven golden flowers, which however hardly

compare any longer with the once so famous Persian brocades. Velvet (*makhmal*) is inferior to French in softness and brilliance of color, but not in strength; there are some shades, especially blueblack, which the Persians do not manage to produce, and they are most successful at orange and poppy red. Yazd produces some silks under the name of *shal abrishum*; like Indian shawls, they are interwoven with palms and wreaths, with delicately patterned borders, and are the only kind exported—to Russia and Constantinople. On the other hand, exports of silk constitute one of the country's main resources. The only silk fabrics imported are of Ionian make, especially damask and brocade, and only in small quantities.

*Linen* is little used, only for handkerchieves and winding sheets (*Leibbinden*). Linen growing is confined to a few small areas in Mazandaran.

The *dyestuffs* used are partly produced within the country—for example, madder, safflower, indigo, pomegranate peel, gallnuts, iron and copper vitriol, acetate of iron, etc.—and partly imported from India. Cochineal is brought from Europe, but is often replaced by *porphyrophora hamelii*, from Ararat. By the addition of an Indian bark, *luter*, the intensity of cochineal dyes is increased. Nomad women are engaged in the preparation of dyestuffs, according to ancient recipes; for acids they use lemons and sulfuric acid, laboriously made by burning sulfur; for alkalis they use cow urine. In view of the great variety of concentration of the agent, it is naturally very difficult to produce a given shade, and in rugs and shawls one often notices slight color deviations in certain spots, since preparation takes a long time, usually six months. On the other hand, the colors are throughout pure and withstand the Persian sun better than the ones used in Europe. All large manufacturing centers have their own dyers (*sabbagh*), most of whom work in only one color. Similarly, bleaching grounds are to be found everywhere; in Isfahan, for example, I saw the banks of the Zayenderud covered, far and wide, with yarn and cloth.

[3] The *khur* of the Bible (Esther, chap. 1).

*Leather* production is greatest in the little town of Hamadan. Beautifully colored morocco (*cherme hamadani*) is made there from excellently tanned sheepskins; excellent shagreen leather (*saghri*) is also made from wild ass skin, with lustrous green color, produced by dyes made from copper oxide; its grainy excrescences, made with amaranth seeds, last unspoilt as long as the leather.

Only in Kirman is chamois leather produced, from the skins of wild goats and rock sheep; in other parts of the country, the skins of stags, roebucks, gazelles, rock sheep, wild goats, and ibex are thrown away, as being useless. Imports of leather are insignificant, for foreign leather is regarded by Persians as ritually unclean. Religious law also forbids the use of the skins of animals that have died a natural death. A small amount of stag leather, blackish brown in color (*jir*), is sold to Caucasian tribes for their equipment. Exports of sheep and goat skins are somewhat greater.

*Furs* are made only from sheepskins, in Shiraz and Qum. Originally black in color, they are given a dark black sheen by means of dyes made from iron acetate and pomegranate peel. The well-to-do classes wear lambskins from Bukhara (*pust-i bukhara*), or miniver or mink imported from Russia. On the other hand, there is a fairly extensive export of the unclean skins of lions, tigers, leopards, foxes, wolves, jackals, hyenas, Indian leopards, otters, and martens, which somewhat offsets those imports. The fur trade is carried on exclusively by Armenians, because Muslims may not touch unclean skins. In consequence, a great part of the skins, and more generally the members of ritually unclean animals, cannot be put to use.

In richness of *metals*, especially *copper*, I hardly know of any country that measures up to Persia. Almost every district has a copper mine (*maden-i mis*), and on the northern slopes of the Elburz, near Tehran, one can count twenty, and as many more in the vicinity of Qazvin. The most productive mine is at Karadagh, near Tabriz.

But the Persians are very backward in the art of mining, and they do not know how to use the machines ordered from Europe. The rich mines of Khurasan produce very little ore, for operations are interrupted and disturbed by frequent Turkoman raids. If a Persian, who by dabbling in alchemy has acquired some elementary knowledge, undertakes to exploit a mine, he either loses the capital he has invested in it or else, as soon as the business begins to pay, it is seized by the governor, who then neglects it out of ignorance and is soon forced to stop operations. Because of all this, and notwithstanding its rich ore deposits, the greater part of the copper used in Persia comes from Russia; and since most vessels used for cooking or for industrial operations are made of copper, the demand for this metal is very great. Some copper implements are to be found in the hut of the poorest people, and a common saying to indicate the excessive oppressiveness of a governor is: "He pushed things so far that two cottages had to use the same copper pot." The coppersmiths of Zanjan and Kashan enjoy wide popularity; in the summer of 1859 I found six hundred workers employed in the workshops of the latter town. The vessels coming from there are distinguished by the strength of their rivets, the elegance of their forms, and their graceful engravings, and find buyers all over the country. I have seen there cups and bowls decorated with arabesques, figures, and Arabic sentences which could truly claim to be works of art. Tin and ammonia, which are required for the production of copper, have to be imported from India, for the ammonia made in the country (*nishadur*), which is moreover impure, is not sufficient to cover consumption. Borax (*bureh*) is produced from the lakes of Media.

The country's rich *iron* mines are also neglected, like the copper mines. Only insignificant quantities are supplied, by those of Mazandaran and Khurasan. All the remaining iron (*ahen*) comes to Persia from the Urals, by way of the Volga, and the Caspian Sea; only the southern and southeastern parts of the country get part of their supplies from India. Persian iron-workers were once very famous and the damascene blades of Shiraz and Mashad still enjoy a good reputation; but they cannot be compared with old blades and gun barrels, especially in the beauty of the gold inlay in the steel. In the arsenals of Isfahan, Shiraz, and Tehran, firearms, especially rifles and pistols, are made on European models, and are very close to the originals, including even the factory trade-marks. Cutlery, also copied from European models, is less successful, for example, the Isfahan penknives which are put on the market. Persians are very keen on having good penknives; they show their own to Europeans and ask them if they are truly of English make. Often when I visited the minister, he would take a penknife out of his shawl purse, to let me instruct him on its quality and value. In the novel *Hajji Baba*, an ambassador, asked by the king to describe the characteristics of the various European nations, says of the English: "That is the nation which makes penknives."

Owing to the high price of iron, the use of tools and implements is naturally very restricted, which has an unfavorable effect on the whole of industry. It is true that the present shah has made many attempts, by bringing in Europeans, to smelt iron ore; but although great sums were swallowed up in the process, the experiments proved fruitless, so that he at last despaired of ever having iron smelted in his kingdom. "I will give its weight in gold" he said at that time "for the first *man* ($5\frac{1}{4}$ pounds) of iron made from Persian ore." So little did he know that Mazandaran and Khurasan produced any iron at all!

*Brass* and iron sheetware, especially the popular Russian samovar, are almost entirely imported from Russia. The metal trade is almost exclusively in the hands of the Russian–Persian Company, which has factors in the various harbors.

*Lead* (*surb*), is also produced, amply covering domestic consumption and leaving a small surplus for export. Most of the ore is supplied by Kirman and has a high silver content.

*Zinc* (*ru*), which is often made into drinking vessels (*tunge-ru*), is imported solely from Russia.

*Cobalt* (*shak-i lajevert*, lapis lazuli ore) of excellent quality is found in the village of Gamsar, near Kashan. The mine belongs to a family prominent in the silk business. Apparently, fairly large quantities of cobalt ore are sent to Russia. Good lapis lazuli comes from Turkistan, and less pure kinds from Azerbaijan.

*Arsenic*, in *Auripigment* and realgar, is available in large quantities in Kurdistan and in the vicinity of Qazvin; exports to Constantinople are not insignificant.

*Manganese* ore (*mugl*), used as an additive in molten glass, is produced in Kirman.

*Sulfur* (*gugird*) is abundant in the various parts of Persia and, if encouraged by improved means of communication, could constitute an important item of export to Europe. The best hyacinth-red sulfur crops up below the peak of Demavend, where it is gathered during the summer by the inhabitants of the little town of Ask. It is known in the trade as *gugird-i ahmar*, or *demavendi*, to distinguish it from bar-sulfur, or *gugird-i farsi*.

Kitchen *salt* and Chili saltpeter, exuded in the form of crystals, are so abundant that all one needs to pay for them is transport cost. In addition there are numerous deposits of rock and crystal salt (*namak-i turki*). Some saltpeter is, I was told, being exported to India. Persia is so rich in kitchen salts and other salts, which form the basis of sulfuric and nitric acid, that it would be in a position to supply the whole world.

Owing to the lack of roads and the absence of industrial demand, there has been no prospecting for *coal*, which is sometimes found in open seams. As Persians say, one cannot use coal for one's water pipe! The coal seam of the northern slope of the Elburz chain near Tehran shows up already below Qazvin, in the village of If, dips into the valley of the Laar, especially in a side valley called Divasia, and comes up again in the vicinity of the little town of Ask, by the Heras river. In general, the coal formations seem to be very rich.

As regards *precious stones*, Persia produces only *turquoise* (*firuz*), and as the formerly rich mines are no longer accessible, because of flooding, work is restricted to going over the old layers. Since then, the price of turquoises has risen sharply, and only small stones, or those of earlier times, are put on the market. The king's treasury has the most valuable turquoise; it is pure, deep blue in color, is free from all defects or spots (*baraz*, i.e., Lepra), and, although hardly as big as half an almond, is estimated at 600 ducats. There are bigger stones, but they are not so pure, being full of spots and veins and hence of relatively slight value. The second quality, known as *shirbam*, also comes from the old mines but is closer to white than to blue; the stones are sent mainly to Baghdad, where the Arabs pay a good price for them. The third quality is extracted from recently discovered mines, (*maden-i nau*) and at first is blue but with time changes into a greenish color. Such stones are disdained in Persia, and regarded as completely valueless. Persian turquoises are brought over to Russia for sale, especially to the fair of Nizhni Novgorod, for they are greatly esteemed by the Russians; but in recent times the total amount exported has been unimportant. The Persians seem to have learned how to cut and polish precious stones from the Indians and like the latter make very little use of emery (*sumbadeh*) in the process. In Isfahan, Shiraz, and several other towns diamonds are polished with wooden discs; they also know, in these places, how to polish stones which, because of their knotty structure (like knots of a piece of wood which makes planing difficult), could not have been mastered by European craftsmen (?) [question mark in original].

*Glass* making (*shisheh, balur*), introduced by an Italian some 250 years ago, has in recent times made some progress. Ordinary glassware, like drinking glasses, flasks, and mirrors, is very well made. Almost every

town of any importance has a glass furnace, meeting local needs. The glassware of Qum and Shiraz is considered to be the best. However, Persians can make window glass only in plates of considerable thickness. For lye, they use Barek (*qaliab qumi*), which is derived from the *solsolapflanzen* (*ushmun*) of the desert by calcination and sintering. Imports of mirrors and crystal glass from Constantinople and Russia are very considerable and cost the country large amounts of money each year.

*Porcelain* is made in small amounts and low quality; the most commonly used vessels are those of Qum (*kase qumi*). Hence real Chinese porcelain (*chini*), brought in by way of India, is highly prized. English and Russian wares, especially tea and coffee sets, also find eager buyers. Earthenware (*kashi*) is somewhat better made; the glazed tiles on which portraits, hunting scenes, landscapes, etc., are set together, are famous. The picture which it is desired to represent is first laid, in fire resistant colors, on a clay surface, which is then cut up into tiles. The tiles are baked and fastened together, with cement and mortar, to form the picture. Such mosaics serve to cover the walls and cupolas of mosques, *madrasas* [mosque-schools], baths and other public buildings. But this art, too, is in decline. Persians can no longer produce the beautiful colors which one sees on the lining of old buildings in Isfahan. The best colored tiles are at present made in Kashan, hence their name, *kashi*.

Porous *alkarazzas* are made of clay: they are drinking vessels in which water keeps cool and which also serve to filter the water. Persians like to adorn them with figures and arabesques; the ones made in Qum (*kuze qumi*) are particularly distinguished by their elegant shapes. When baking, they are not put directly in the fire, but are covered with a clay envelope so that the heat penetrates them slowly and in moderation. Before Persians put an *alkarazza* to use, they pour into it some rose water, the scent of which remains noticeable for several weeks. In addition to the elegantly shaped *alkarazzas*, there are roughly made and badly glazed clay jugs, which remind us of the earliest beginnings of the industry and compare very unfavorably with the potsherds which can be found in the ruins of the city of Rages (Ray).

Good and cheap *soap* (*sabun*) is made out of (Barek), especially in the town of Qum. In the Caspian provinces, soft soap is produced from olive oil.

*Ivory* and *metal mosaic* (*khatem sazi*) is one of the crafts that have been transplanted from India or China to Persia; it is used to adorn tables, chairs, frames, etc. The Shirazis and Isfahanis make graceful objects of this kind at amazingly low prices. They make, in particular, symmetrical figures of long ivory or metal bars which are screwed together and cut through with a saw, horizontally; the thin plates are then inserted into the wood of the furniture. I have admired beautifully inlaid doors, chairs, etc. in the royal palace in Tehran.

In Isfahan there is a guild of *painters* (*naqqash*), which paints exclusively such objects as cardboard work, pocket mirrors, inkpots, book bindings, etc. These miniature pictures of flowers, tendrils, and groups of animals and men are very elegant and true to nature, except for perspective, whose laws the Persians, like the Chinese, do not appear to have learned. Covered with a varnish (*rugan-i kemun*) made of (*Sandarak*), linseed oil, and naphtha, these miniatures keep their lively colors fresh and bright. The price paid for such pictures varies according to the reputation of the master and often reaches fabulous sums, for example, 50 ducats for a pocket mirror; such treasures are eagerly shown to Europeans, and in such cases it is tactful, and expected, that the viewer burst out in enthusiastic wonder at the work of art.

In order to check the continuous outflow of money, the present shah—as I have stated in several places—has made repeated efforts to set up the European type of factories. The government tried particularly hard, at the time of the English–Persian disputes, to free the country from the English market. Senseless hopes were indulged in. They thought that, with a small spinning mill, they would soon be able to dispense with English yarn. When a paper mill was established and was still under construction, the shah asked its manager whether it was possible to produce paper in it, to which the quick reply was "Yes—may I be your sacrifice—in a few years we shall deliver so much paper abroad that in the whole of Frangistan [Europe] not a sheet will be made." Naturally the results of these isolated attempts, in which such large sums were sunk, did not in the least correspond to those dreamed of. I often had the occasion to express my views on this subject to the shah, but all I earned was ingratitude and slander; for they suspected me, as a European, of wanting to impede the industrial development of the country and later, when things had worked out as I had foretold, they were too proud to do me justice.

My reasons for believing that a factory industry suddenly imported to Persia from outside could not thrive were the following. First, there was total lack of the necessary labor force. The sparse population is far from being in a position to till all arable land; it would therefore be necessary to withdraw from agriculture part of an already insufficient working force. If an attempt were made to remedy this deficiency by bringing European workmen, the latter would either soon die because of the climate and the strange way of life or, owing to the isolation forced on them by Oriental customs, take to drink and collapse physically and morally. Moreover, it would be impossible to prevent a huge amount of embezzlement and fraud on the part of the management of the enterprise. When even in European countries factories run with state money do not succeed, what can one expect in Persia! Last, the importation of machines and equipment, as well as spare parts, from such distant places and over the country's unpaved roads, is faced with almost unsurmountable difficulty and in any case involves such high costs as to greatly reduce the prospects of a profitable return on investment.

The government could—so I advised—encourage and strengthen private industry. Its main target should, however, be to lift up agriculture, to discover and exploit its great natural resources. Persia could then exchange its domestic products for European industrial goods and in time build up a balance of trade. In this matter my advice was not followed, as I have stated. Russian and French craftsmen and mechanics were called in and several factories were established.

1. A *stearin candle factory*. In view of the cheapness of tallow, it was thought that stearin could be produced at a lower price. A lead vessel was set up for the preparation of sulfuric acid, but the acid it produced was no stronger than lemonade; the clumsy hands of the workers ruined the mechanism of the presses; and after the outlay of 8,000 ducats, a few pounds of candles were happily produced with Persian stamp and the royal arms. Wicked rumor had it that the stearin used in the candles came from Europe, but be that as it may, the European director received a robe of honor from the shah.

2. A *paper mill* was built close to the city wall of Tehran, where water power was insufficient; some Russian workers were assigned to it. Unsuccessful attempts to make paper out of rags lasted many years, and at last a few sheets of rough paper, produced out of pure cotton, made their appearance. In the meantime, some of the foreign workmen died, the others pined away, and the enterprise closed down. Of the paper industry which had flourished in Khurasan in the thirteenth and fourteenth centuries, nothing remains except for a few establishments in Isfahan which make cardboard.

3. Two excellent workers were brought over from France for a new *glass* factory. However, they were unable to put their knowledge to use, particularly since no success was obtained in finding fire-resistant, refractory clay. However their short-lived activity had one favorable effect: the Persians observed many of their ways and transferred them to their own methods of production.

4. The greatest efforts were made to put up a spinning mill of the European type. Steam engines and other machines had to be brought over from Russia, with unimaginable trouble: whole villages were conscripted and provided the human power needed to drag the machines over the impassable roads; so the total outlay was not less than 150,000 ducats. A few pounds of yarn, which were shown to the king, were and remained the only fruits of all the effort and cost sunk in this enterprise.

5. A *sugar refinery* miscarried, as has already been mentioned, chiefly because the producers were forced to deliver moist sugar without payment, and therefore the planting of sugarcane was gradually given up.

After such large sums had been wasted senselessly and aimlessly, my advice was at last heeded and a number of young men were sent to Europe—first of all to France—to acquire practical knowledge of the various branches of industry. If they return to their country equipped with real knowledge, one can expect from them rather more in the way of development of domestic industry, although the general condition of state relations is increasingly a hindrance rather than a help.

The *handicraftsmen* (*usta*) working individually in the bazaar generally show diligence and industry, and often work at night, but their efforts are directed not toward improvement but only toward meeting their daily needs. They confine themselves to imitating European products, without developing their own inventive spirit. After a few months' apprenticeship, the young craftsman establishes himself, gets married, and after that works purely mechanically, to gain a livelihood for himself and his family. The most intelligent are the craftsmen of Isfahan and Kashan, who often migrate to other towns, but having found profitable employment are soon sucked into the usual routine. I have never known any craftsman who had achieved a moderate degree of material well-being. As for real mastery of the craft, the only ones who could lay claim to it were the engravers (*hakkak*) and possibly the gold and silver enamel workers of Shiraz. The king has many artistic enameled gold vessels of recent make, especially water pipes; the peacock throne, which was recently restored, has very elegant inscriptions and arabesques in gold enamel.

Usually, each craft has its own bazaar, which bears its name—for example, the Shoemakers' Bazaar, the Haberdashers' Bazaar, etc. Full freedom to choose one's occupation exists, and there is no compulsion to join the guilds, but the masters in each craft choose from among themselves a head, known as *bashi*, to manage their common interests [see 6:5].

The towns which stand out in respect of their workshops (*karkhaneh*) and industries (*sanaet*) are: Isfahan, Kashan, Yazd, Kirman, Shiraz, Hamadan (for leather), and Tabriz. Rasht, on the Caspian Sea, processes some silk and makes neat and artistic embroidery on cloth. Tehran, a residential city, does not have any extensive industry; its craftsmen hardly manage to meet the city's own needs.

With few exceptions, *trade* (*tijarat*) is in the hands of Persian merchants. Merchants enjoy more respect than any other social class; their property is very seldom touched and the government is afraid to inflict on them the vexations with which the other subjects are relentlessly burdened. Not once during my nine years' stay did I hear of a trader whose property had been confiscated. Saadi says: "Three things cannot exist without three other things: the State without Justice, Knowledge without Discussion, Wealth without Trade." Only the last of these three rules is kept in Persia, for the state exists without undue justice, and there is much discussion but little knowledge.

The Persian *merchant* lives very simply. Even if he is very rich he does not display any signs of luxury, for if he did so he would lose his credit with his fellow merchants. He goes through the streets without attendants, takes only one wife, shuns intercourse with great personages, and keeps to his equals. He willingly boasts "*kasebam kisb mikunam*," that is, "I am an industrialist, I carry on a trade." He is busy working the whole day. His midday meal usually consists only of bread and cheese. But in spite of the simplicity of his behavior, he is given an honorable place in society and truly deserves the respect which is shown to him. Thoroughly honest in their business dealings—although on occasion not scorning somewhat excessive profit—extremely punctual in meeting their obligations, merchants, unlike other classes, keep strictly their pledged word. Although they are cautious and mistrustful, Persian traders show no little enterprise; they travel not only through the whole of Asia, especially India, China, Afghanistan, Turkistan, and the Caucasus, but also Turkey, Russia, and Egypt. In general, they are quick to find their bearings and to turn things to their advantage. The government uses them for making payments at home and abroad, and governors and other great persons secretly entrust a merchant with their ill-gotten gains, sure that if they should fall, or be put to death or exiled, he will return to their family the sum entrusted to him.

Interest on loans is prohibited by Muslim law, but it goes without saying that this prohibition is often evaded. The legal rate of interest is fixed at 12 percent, but when money is tight it reaches 18–30 percent. Sound traders seldom pay less than 10 percent (and still more seldom over that amount) discount on their bills of exchange (*barat*). The latter are drawn with specification of capital (*ras al-mal*) and interest (*tanzil*) and paid off against receipt (*qabs*). Only very seldom do traders protest their bills (*vershikestan*), and in such cases they always take refuge in a sanctuary until their affairs are once more in order. In view of the number of sanctuaries available and of the possibility for people to spend there, unchallenged, the money they have brought with them, it is surprising that there are so few bankruptcies [see 3:11].

At the head of the merchants of each city stands a chief elected by them (*malik-i tujjar*), whose function is to protect the interests of the corporation in general; to smooth disputes between its members, to make tardy debtors pay, and to ascertain the causes of bankruptcies. A few years ago the government appointed a minister of commerce (*vazir-i tijaret*), Mahmud Khan Karaguzlu, who also took over the functions of *malik-i tujjar*. But there were soon so many complaints from merchants about oppression and arbitrariness that the old state of things was restored.

Foreign merchants who trade in Persia are Russians, Frenchmen, Swiss, Greeks, Turks, and Armenians. The Russo–Persian Company, although subsidized by the Russian government and disposing of steamers on the Caspian Sea [see 4:1], has not so far made any profits because of the incapacity and inefficiency of its agents. The Russian–Caucasian merchants, mostly Armenians, are notorious for their dishonest and usurious ways and for starting lawsuits; however, the Russian minister at present in Tehran, Anichkov, an honest and incorruptible man, does not support their unjust claims, which has significantly reduced their objectionable activities.

Most European merchants live in Tabriz and Rasht, on the Caspian, and only a few in the capital, Tehran. Tabriz is the most important commercial emporium of Persia; second-class trading towns are Isfahan, Shiraz, Rasht, Balafrush [Barfurush], and Yazd; the last-named carries on trade with the East Indies through the Zoroastrians (Parsees). Mashad serves as a market for goods intended for Afghanistan and Turkistan. Foreign goods come (1) from Constantinople, by the caravan route, through Trebizond, Erzerum, and Khoi to Tabriz; (2) from Nizhni Novgorod down the Volga, across the Caspian Sea, to the port of Enzeli, and from there by land to Rasht and Tehran, or to the port of Mashtiser [Mashad-i sar] and from there to Balafrush—small amounts of goods go to Mashad, by land, through Astarabad, to which the Turkomans bring in exchange lambskins, silks, salt, etc.; (3) from Bombay to Bushire and Shiraz, or from Muscat to Bandar Abbas; (4) through Baghdad to Isfahan. Tehran is not at all a commercial town; only a few branches of Tabriz firms have been set up there, for petty trade.

As regards *customs duties*, foreign merchants whose governments have concluded treaties with Persia pay 5 percent; native traders pay less, but have, on the other hand, to pay duties at every town through which their goods pass [see 3:2]; so that, in this respect, they are unbelievably worse off than foreigners and therefore find themselves compelled to procure goods through foreign firms, which gives rise to constant friction and lawsuits. One can hardly think of anything more absurd from the point of view of the national economy. Many Persians have settled abroad, for example in Constantinople, Trebizond, Erzerum, Tiflis, Moscow, Cairo, and Bombay. They carry on from there export and import trade with Persia, China, and India and are known as sound, enterprising, and able merchants.

Various European states have consulates in Persia, and Persia likewise has consuls, for the protection of its trade, in Tiflis, Erzerum, Trebizond, Constantinople, Bombay, Baghdad, and Cairo, and temporarily also in Smyrna, Alexandria, and Jaffa. Before the outbreak of the Anglo–Persian War, there were British consulates in Tabriz, Tehran, and Bandar Bushire; after the conclusion of that war Britain opened a consulate in Rasht and consular agencies in Isfahan, Shiraz, and Mashad. Naturally, in these distant places, the political functions of these agents cannot easily be separated from the commercial. Russia has established consulates in Tabriz, Rasht, Tehran, Balafrush, and Astarabad, and will probably do so in Mashad and Shiraz, in order to keep an eye on British influence. Turkish consulates are to be found only in Tabriz and Tehran. France thought of appointing consuls in Bushire and Tabriz, but French commercial relations with Persia are so weak that they do not require consular representation [see 3:22]. . . .

## Crafts in Isfahan

The following selection is taken from a manuscript edited by Dr. Manuchehr Sutudeh and published by the Institute for Social Research of Tehran in 1963. Its author was Mirza Husain, son of Ibrahim Khan, the *tahvildar* (cashier) of Isfahan, who states that he started writing it in A.H. 1294 (1877). The book gives a general geographical account of Isfahan, beginning in the traditional manner with a description of the soil, climate, and water and passing on to its rivers, monuments, streets, and flora and fauna. A section on population (p. 65) puts the number of inhabitants at not over 50,000—in contrast with more than 700,000 under the Safavis, and as many as 250,000 in the reign of Fath Ali Shah and 170,000 in that of Muhammad Shah.

The passages selected show very clearly the decline of the handicrafts in Isfahan —of which 199 are described by the author. Three forces were at work, and are noted: the change in tastes and fashions, which led consumers to prefer foreign styles to native; the competition of cheap imported goods in both export and domestic markets, which drove craftsmen out of business; and the attraction of the expanding market of Tehran, which caused many craftsmen from Isfahan to migrate to the capital.

### Selection 3. Crafts in Isfahan, 1870s
[*Jughrafiya-i Isfahan*, (Tehran, 1342), pp. 93–104]

22. Qadak [a blue-colored cotton cloth] *Dyers' Guild.* This is a large guild; it used to be larger, but now its number has been reduced to less than one half. Its long bazaar consists of units linked to one another; it has a high, arched ceiling and comprises 136 shops. Each shop is like a big house with a courtyard and a neat and pleasant-looking building with living and sleeping quarters for summer and winter. There are ponds, wells, and cisterns with equipment for dyeing and pounding. Some of the shops belonging to the guild masters cost more than 1,500 tumans. Formerly merchants and public officers who were acquaintances of the notables of the guild or had dealings with them spent their rest period during the day in their shops. Besides the two bazaars, located next to the Maydan-i Shah-i Naqsh-i Jahan, there are various dye shops in other bazaars and districts. . . .

25. *Printed Cotton Cloth Makers' Guild.* This is a big industry. In the past it was in great demand and had many workers. Now it has considerably declined. They made gilded *qalamkar* [a kind of flowered chintz] which was better and more expensive than the *sadris* (?) *qalamkar*. Since there was no demand for it, it was given up. They have four interconnected bazaars; one of the gates opens to the Dahana-i Qaysar on the Maydan-i Shah. In the middle of the bazaars there are five carvanserais and inns, one of which is the Saray-i Shah. All these are chintz makers' shops, comprising 284 shops, offices, and workshops. Their merchandise still goes to all provinces of Iran. European textiles have taken over their market; not half of the guild has now survived. . . .

35. *Engravers' Guild.* In the past Isfahan's engraving was in demand and most of the work went to Turkey (Rum), Egypt, and India. There were well-known craftsmen such as Aqa Muhammad Tahir and others. Today also there are competent and skilled artisans like Shaikh Hakkak and Haji

Muhammad Jafar and others. They are not known because of the slackness of the market. . . .

36. *Turners' Guild.* Isfahan turners are better than those of any other town except for those in Rasht who make wooden parts of water pipes. At present most of the turners of Isfahan are working in Tehran.

46. *Hat Makers' Guild.* They have a special bazaar next to the Maydan-i Shah-i Naqsh-i Jahan. Their business is slack and their guild has declined.

50. *Guild of Makers of Georgian Shoes.* Such shoes are worn by women; formerly they were also worn by men, but this fashion has been given up.

51. *Shoemakers' Guild.* It has many members and is a new guild which did not exist in the past.

52. *Leatherwork Guild.* They make leather shoes. Formerly they had a good market and the majority of the *mullas*, the merchants, and the dealers wore such shoes. Now some of the *mullas* and most of the merchants wear them.

53. *Bootmakers' Guild.* Their work was very much in demand in the past when the soldiers wore boots and the province had more people and more officials; now it is slack.

54. *Shagreen Guild.* Formerly the notables of Isfahan, men and women, wore shagreen shoes. Now very few follow the old way. . . .

56. *Embroiderers' Guild.* In the past this guild had a large membership. They embroidered garments for men and women and their merchandise was very much in demand. All existing designs in the art of drawing were copied on white cotton cloth or other solid color cotton cloths, then embroidered with colorful pure silk, cotton, or woolen (?) threads. The price varied according to the design. A piece of such material which would be sufficient to make a pair of trousers for an army uniform, or ladies' tight underwear, as used in those days, cost from about six or seven to forty tumans and lasted about sixty to seventy years. Those worn less frequently would last more than two hundred years and wore well. The rich wore the finest and the middle class those of medium

quality. They were also used as shelf covers, cradle covers, baby wrappers, covers on cupboards, covers on large cushions (placed against the wall opposite the entrance), on pack-saddles, etc. This merchandise was mostly bought by Egyptians, Indians, Turkestanis, and Afghans; a small part of it was sent to Europe. Since the time of the purified Shah an Shah [Muhammad] till now it has been in gradual decline and obliteration. Special merchants called embroidery traders dealt with this merchandise. They formed a prosperous community and were all influential; not many of the community have survived, excepting Haji Muhammad Husain, son of the late well-known Haji Ibrahim, and a few more who are engaged in other trades. . . .

65. *Weavers' Guild.* In former days when foreign fabrics were not widely used, everybody from the upper to the lower class—even the high state officials and the lofty princes—wore *qadak*. Therefore, choice *qadaks* were made, of which both warp and woof were spun of Isfahan cotton; from 8 to 30 *chele* were woven in Isfahan. When to it was added the tincture of Isfahan dye it acquired the elegance of *darai* [a kind of silk stuff or shawl]. It never lost its stiffness because of wear. It would become like broadcloth; the more it was spun the fluffier and the brighter its color would become. The poor could manage with one gown every two to three years. Which European cloth can hold its stiffness and color? For the past few years, the cheap red and yellow European fabrics have been popular. Whenever their textile fabrics have had a new design and have appeared different to the eyes, the people of Iran have given up their body and soul and have pursued the color and scent of the others. In doing this they have incurred losses which they do not realize. Especially now, they are crazy about inexpensive clothes which, looked at wisely, are not at all economical or lasting. On the other hand, when the merchandise of the weavers' guild lost the market, it began imitating European wares. Weavers paid more attention to appearance than to

quality. It was for the sake of elegant appearance and easy handling that they employed European yarn in weaving *qadaks*. Their work became ugly and, as a result of mixing European and Iranian materials, it became progressively defective and tore and went to pieces while worn; it also lost its stiffness, fluff, and durability. Spinners lost their jobs and gradually perished. Russia stopped buying. Iranians turned away from their own products, and the weavers' guild suffered a tremendous loss. Consequently, other guilds began to face deficits and loss. At least one-tenth of the guilds in this city were weavers, of whom not even one-fifth has survived. About one-twentieth of the needy widows of Isfahan raised their children by spinning thread for the weavers; they all have perished. Likewise other large guilds, such as dyers, carders, and laborers in the bleaching houses, which were related to this guild, have mostly disappeared. Other guilds also have felt the effect of this loss; especially the farmers suffered loss because the price of their cotton fell. Several years ago when this condition became known, the price of cotton rose and foreign buyers began importing it [see 5:12]. As a result the price of every merchandise went up and all benefited from it. No use, "it shone well but the fortune was a passing one." Each merchandise and each person exerts an effect on other goods and other persons, and they are all related. The particles in the world have the same relation with one another as the members of the human body. "If one member should suffer at any time, other members cannot enjoy rest" [Saadi]. And if there is profit its beneficial effect will multiply and preserve the species.

66. *Silk Weavers' Guild.* This guild works with silk and is close to the guild that works with cotton. It had many workers and workshops who in their revenues were no less than the cotton weavers. All that has been said about the latter holds true for this guild as well. Their merchandise had both domestic and foreign markets. Their decline has been even more serious than the others;

they have practically vanished; very few have survived. The [splendor of the] period of the Safavid sultans has been exaggerated. In the reign of the pardoned Khaqan [Fath Ali] there were 1,250 workshops; in the period of the purified Shah an Shah [Muhammad] 486; at the beginning of the reign of the present king [Nasir al-Din] 240; and at the present time it has come down to 12. The products of the above-mentioned guild consisted of *qanaviz* (damask) in various colors; *darai*, of all kinds; Aleppo cloth, linen cloth (*qasab*), *alajeh*, shawls, and the like. In the past, besides Iran, it had buyers from Turkey and Russia, but now there is no demand for it. . . .

72. *Cloak Weavers' Guild.* Formerly this guild was small and weak, but now it has become numerous and strong. Its merchandise goes to every province of Iran.

73. *Cotton Carpet Weavers' Guild (Ihrami baf).* In the past they wove good and durable cotton carpets and had several workshops in this city. When foreign articles came here, their market declined, and their workshops were reduced to two, which are always crippled and idle. . . .

76. *Bankers' Guild (Sarraf).* This consists of two groups, both with many members; they have their own bazaar in the interior section facing south of the Maydan-i Naqsh-i Jahan, which is the whole section of the Jeloy-i Khan-i Qaisariya plus half of the width of the Maydan and on both sides are the shops of the *sarrafs*. In the old Maydan and the bazaars of the Bid Abad and Chahar Suq-i Shiraziha districts, etc., there are numerous *sarraf* shops. This used to be a large guild, and still is. Formerly, when the province was populous, all lived in Isfahan. Now half of them have their business in Tehran, Tabriz, and other cities and occasionally come to Isfahan to visit their families.

77. *Book Binders' Guild.* In the past, because of the numerousness of the cities, good manuscript books, Qurans, and prayer books were written by calligraphers on Khanbaleq [Peking] and cashmere papers, and the like. Good book binding such as the

arrangement of the body of the text and the margin on papers, making covers, making portfolios, head bands, and other crafts in book binding were prevalent. This guild had a good market for its goods; well-known craftsmen used to help each other out. For some years because of the abandonment of the manuscript books and the advent of print and typography, the above-mentioned guild has been declining and diminishing. . . .

82. *Slipper Makers' Guild* (*Rassaf*). In Isfahan in the past when shoes were not in style, there were many *giveh* [light cotton shoes] makers and dealers. A good many nobles wore fine *giveh* just for the fun of it and many orders were taken at three tumans a pair. It is said that a special order, the work of Ladan Lanjan, was carried out for the famous Haji Ibrahim, the former *kadkhoda* [district chief] for the pardoned monarch [Fath Ali]. They weighed twelve mithqals and cost twenty-four tumans. Ambassador Istaji took some of this merchandise [as rarities] to Europe. In the past the *giveh* of Isfahan went to every province of Iran, now not one-tenth of the former amount is used in the city itself and in other cities put together. Very few members of this guild have survived.

## Mining

Not surprisingly in a country as large and as geologically diversified as Iran, a wide variety of minerals exists in large or small deposits.[1] Several of these have been worked for thousands of years, whereas others have only recently been discovered. The list of minerals available in significant quantities includes, in addition to petroleum: coal, iron, copper, lead, zinc, chromite, bauxite, arsenic, sulfur, cobalt, nickel, gold, silver, and many others.

As regards the nineteenth century, scattered accounts of mines and mineral deposits in various parts of the country are given in consular reports and travel books.[2] Perhaps the most systematic description is that by Curzon.[3] Among the mines he lists as being in operation were copper, iron, and coal in Azerbaijan; iron and coal on the northern and southern slopes of the Elburz mountains; turquoise, copper, coal, and salt in Khurasan; iron and marble in Kirman; and rock salt and iron ochre in the Persian Gulf area. The figures on output given by Curzon and other sources show that exploitation was on a very small scale. In the words of the British consul:

The Persian authorities have hitherto allowed these mines [in Azerbaijan] to be worked by anyone who paid them a per-centage on the profits, but the great difficulty of transport and the great expense of fuel has prevented them becoming remunerative to the undertakers, and at present they are all abandoned.[4]

A report prepared in 1888 by Nicholas, of the French Legation, on the turquoise

[1] For a detailed account, with excellent maps, see J. V. Harrison, "Minerals," in CHI, 1:489–516.
[2] See, for example, Abbott's "Report on Journey to Caspian," FO 60/141; "Tabriz," A and P 1872, 58; and chap. 6, sels. 2 and 7.
[3] *Persia*, 2:510–22.
[4] "Tabriz," A and P 1872, 58. Around the middle of the century coal was mined by local peasants in Shimshak and carried by pack animals to Tehran, where it was used for heating and, later, by such establishments as the mint and sugar factory. Nasir al-Din granted a monopoly of the mines to an Iranian, but no significant change in methods of mining seems to have been introduced—see Gorelikov, p. 252.

mines of Nishapur gives some interesting information.[5] These mines had been farmed, in 1882, for fifteen years, to four Persians who paid an annual rent of 18,000 tumans. Two hundred persons were employed, miners being paid, on average, 5 krans and cutters 2 krans a day. The value of output at the mine was estimated at 25,000 tumans, but the turquoises ultimately fetched three times as much. The concessionaires seem to have subcontracted the mines to the local inhabitants (who until 1882 had farmed them directly from the government) and to have received payment in kind.

The unfavorable factors that limited the activity of Iranians also discouraged foreigners from investing in mining. "In 1836, Sir H. Lindsay-Bethune brought out a steam engine and a number of skilled workmen from England, and sank a very large sum of money in the attempt to work both the copper and iron mines of Karadagh [in Azerbaijan], apparently without any satisfactory results."[6] In 1890, The British-owned Persian Bank Mining Rights Corporation was formed, with a capital of £1,000,000, to

acquire and work the mining rights conceded to the newly established Imperial Bank of Persia by the Royal firman of the preceding year [see also 4:7]. These rights included the monopoly of all such iron, copper, lead, mercury, coal, petroleum, manganese, borax, and asbestos mines as belonged to the State and had not previously been ceded to other persons.[7]

The concession was for sixty years, and 16 percent of net profits was to be paid to the shah. The company immediately proceeded to survey the country but does not seem to have engaged in any mining operations and soon found itself in financial difficulties.[8] However, it did acquire the Hotz oil wells in the south and was instrumental in starting Iran's petroleum industry (see chap. 7).

In the north, a Russian received, in 1908, a concession covering all minerals except gold and silver in the Karadag region, and the Julfa-Tabriz railway concession granted to Russia in 1913 (see 4:8) included the right to mine coal and petroleum within sixty versts on either side of the line.[9] But here, too, no actual exploitation took place.

Last, in the Persian Gulf area, iron oxide deposits in Hormuz island were worked by the British firm of F. C. Strick and Co., who exported some 3,000 to 4,000 tons a year,[10] and those in Abu Musa by the Wönckhaus firm until the famous Anglo-German incident of 1907.[11]

In recent years mining has greatly developed, and now plays a significant part in the country's economy (see epilogue).

[5] AE, Téhéran, vol. 3; see also Curzon, *Persia*, 1:264–65, and chap. 6, sel. 2 for further information on turquoise mining.
[6] Curzon, *Persia*, 2:512.
[7] Ibid., pp. 513–14.
[8] Litten, p. 90, and Sobotsinskii, p. 44.
[9] Litten, pp. 145–46 and 158–67.
[10] MacLean, "Report," A and P 1904, 95.
[11] For details, see Litten, and EHME, pp. 350–55.

### Selection 4. Iron Works, 1847
[K. E. Abbott, "Report on Journey to Caspian," 28 April 1848, FO 60/141]

ACCOUNT OF A VISIT MADE TO THE IRON WORKS IN THE DISTRICT OF NOOR [NEAR AMUL]

The Iron ore is procured chiefly from the bed of the streams, or, when the supply there fails, it is dug from near the surface in the sides of the Ravine. It consists of stones from the size of a mere pebble to one of many pounds weight—of a brown or reddish brown colour and close grain. I was told, but consider this an exaggeration, that 100 Parts of ore yield about 40 of Iron.

The ore is first heated in a furnace with charcoal in alternate layers, after which it is broken with a hammer into small pieces and thrown into a second furnace with Charcoal as before in the proportion of one men of ore to 3 of charcoal. A blast is effected by means of a large bellows worked by a water wheel and when fused the metal is allowed to run out in a pool and is taken up in long wooden ladles and poured into shot moulds, or it is run into short bars. The Cannon shot are sold by the villagers at 30 Tomans per 1,000 of 4 sizes, namely 6, 9, 12, and 18-Pounders, and 100 6-Pounder Shot or 50 of the above four sizes can be cast daily at each furnace. Iron for common use is sold at Amoul for 15 to 20 Sahib Kerans

per Kherwar of 40 Tabreez Mens and when Russian Iron is scarce there at 25 to 30 Kerans even.

There are 16 Shops or Furnaces scattered over the district on the three streams I have already mentioned and the names of the villages at which they are found are:

| | |
|---|---|
| Alesherood . . . . . . . | possessing 4 Furnaces |
| Anessitoorood . . . . . | possessing 1 Furnace |
| Nâpelâ . . . . . . . . | possessing 2 Furnaces |
| Vâz . . . . . . . . . | possessing 2 Furnaces |
| Lavejerood . . . . . . | possessing 3 Furnaces |
| Goolunderood . . . . . | possessing 2 Furnaces |
| Meeanbund . . . . . . | possessing 1 Furnace |
| Kherse . . . . . . . . | possessing 1 Furnace |

The furnaces each require 20 or 22 Men and are worked only during 6 to 9 months of the Year. When I visited Nâpelâ in November it was just the season for resuming the work after the return of the Inhabitants of the Villages from their Summer quarters but having been oppressed by the Chief of the district they had abandoned the works and were proceeding in a body to lay their complaints before the Prime Minister. They stated that during the preceding year they had cast 175,000 Cannon Shot for the Government.

I did not find that Coal has been discovered near any of the Iron works but a seam is reported to exist at the village of Yâloo in Yâlrood, three days journey from Âmoul. . . .

## Guilds

The description of the Persian guilds given in the following selection shows that they had many features in common with those of other Middle Eastern countries at that time, and indeed some in common with medieval European guilds.[1]

The decline of the crafts throughout the nineteenth century may be presumed to have weakened the guilds. No less important was the growth in the power of the central government, working through a bureaucracy that was very slowly being modernized—for, as the selection shows, the guilds had many administrative duties. The following extract, from a United States Legation report,[2] gives further

[1] See "Elias Qudsi's sketch of the Guilds of Damascus in the nineteenth century," translated by Y. Ibish, *Middle East Economic Papers, 1967* (Beirut), and Gabriel Baer *Egyptian Guilds in Modern Times* (Jerusalem, 1964).
[2] McDonald to Gresham, September 21, 1893, DSP, 1894, p. 483.

information on this subject:

The word trade as used in its general sense hardly expresses the term used in the Persian Government circular, which formed the subject of Mr. Sperry's dispatch. "The trades" would be the more correct form, meaning thereby such kinds of occupation as carpentry, tailoring, blacksmithing, shoemaking, hatmaking, drapery, etc. Wholesale exporters and importers are exempt from these taxes, on the ground that they pay their proportion of the general taxation in customs duty. Men engaged in professions, such as doctors, lawyers, and the priestly class generally, are also excluded.

The taxation of the trades is one of the oldest methods of raising revenue, and dates from about the time of the Mohammedan conquest of Persia, or upward of one thousand years ago; and, notwithstanding revolutions and the changes of dynasties, the amount collected from each trade has been rarely altered. Each trade is taxed according to some general computation of the profits gained in the course of the year. For instance, all the shoemakers of Teheran pay a tax of 12,000 krans, or about $1,500 a year; the sellers of native medicines (herbs), who also keep in their shops a few other articles, such as sugar, tea, tobacco, etc., pay a tax of 6,000 krans, or about $750 a year. The payment of these taxes has to be made during ten months of the year—two holy months of Ramazan and Muharram are excluded. The levying and collecting the taxes are somewhat peculiar, although they secure to each person a certain degree of protection from unjust exactions. Once in six months a meeting of all the members of the trade is called at some appointed place, when the position and standing of each individual is inquired into, and the amount that each person is to pay is determined by themselves, in such proportion as to make up the full amount due to the Government. One person, generally the chief of trade, is appointed, with an officer on the part of the Government, to collect the tax from each individual according to his assessment. Thus, it appears, that no one engaged in any trade is taxed without his having first had an opportunity of being heard on the subject.

I have not yet heard of any claim being made against an American citizen for the payment of these taxes, and I do not think that any will be made.

However, the continued existence, if not the vitality, of the guilds in the present century is shown by the fact that when, in 1305 (1926/27) under the Law of 20 Adhar, the Majlis abolished the tax on guilds, an annex to the law listed those which paid the tax at that time, and enumerated no less than 267 organizations.[3]

[3] *Mudhakarat-i majlis-i shurai milli*, 4th majlis, pp. 121–24; I owe this reference to Dr. E. Abrahamian, of Columbia University; further information on craftsmen and guilds in the 1920s is available in Z. Z. Abdullaev, *Formirovanie rabochego klassa Irana* (Baku, 1968) pp. 48–64.

### Selection 5. Guild Organization, Early Nineteenth Century

[N. A. Kuznetsova, "Materialy k kharakteristike remeslennogo proizvodstva v iranskom gorode XVIII–nachala XIX veka," *O genezise kapitalizma v stranakh vostoka* (XV–XIX vv.) (Moscow, 1962), pp. 336–60].

. . . In most Iranian towns, handicrafts and trade were not leading sectors of the economy. Handicraftsmen could not assure their subsistence by these activities alone and had to seek additional employment in market gardening and truck farming. Even in large towns like Tabriz, such agricultural activities were widespread. At the beginning of the nineteenth century, Tabriz had a population of around 50,000. In it was concentrated trade with Russia, through Tiflis, and with western Europe, through Trebizond. Tabriz was not only a "warehouse for local goods" and a transit station, but also an important center for handicrafts. The *bayaz* (white cotton cloth) made in Tabriz, its *burme* (blue cloth), *kadak*, and calico (printed cotton cloth), its shawls (of the cashmere type, but with large designs) and its silk cloth, *kanaus*, found eager markets in Transcaucasia and were exported to Russia. According to Yu. A. Gagemeister, a mid-nineteenth-century Russian economist, Tabriz exported, in the 1830s, 3 to 4 million rubles worth of goods. Vasili Borozdna reports that Tabriz had, at the beginning of the nineteenth century, "silk production," "a dyeing plant," "a silk reeling plant," factories for silk stuffs, cotton textiles, soap plants, a leather workshop, a factory making native ("Asiatic") porcelain (plain and gilded), a small powder factory, and a factory for making clay pipes and forges. But with all that, the majority of the population worked in truck farming.[1] Similar conditions prevailed in other towns. Market gardening and truck farming held first place in Shiraz, one of the main Iranian centers for trade and handicrafts. Its population not only worked in trade and handicrafts (textiles, perfumes, glassware, firearms, and other weapons, etc.) but raised fruits, vegetables, flowers, tobacco, and opium poppies.[2] In small towns agriculture played a still greater part. . . .

Handicraftsmen were known by various names: *asnaf*, *ahali-ye kasb*, etc. The material and social conditions of craftsmen differed. Most of them were, legally, free. Craftsmen in general, notwithstanding their union in guild organizations, leased space from the owners of the bazaar buildings, rows of stalls, or caravanserais, and paid them rents. An annual tax, whose rates were not always uniform, was levied on craftsmen and its proceeds went to the government. Those craftsmen who were also engaged in farming paid an additional garden tax to the *mubashir* [bailiff].

According to Egiazarov, the main tax on the urban population was the "chimney tax"[3]—levied on families with an *ochag* [hearth], and also in villages. In addition, craftsmen paid the *boniche* tax on their shops. Chardin states that receipts from craftsmen held a not unimportant place in the shah's revenue: "On each handicraft shop 10 sous and on each dealer 20 sous. This is known as *boniche*, or handicraft tax."[4] Du Mans also mentions the same subject.[5] At the beginning of the year, the *naqib* [head of guild] called together the elders of each guild. By mutual consent, they fixed the *boniche* for each guild, "in accordance with law, right, common sense, and the customs and regulations of the state." The apportionment of the tax was set in a special document, *tumare*, which was kept by the *kalantar* or governor of the town. The latter confirmed the decision of "the meeting of all the guilds" regarding the tax on handicrafts. The vezir, *kalantar*, and *mustawfi* formally registered this financial document."[6]

Handicraftsmen also paid indirect taxes, whose sum often exceeded that of direct taxes. One of these was, for example, the levy on merchants and craftsmen for the capture of thieves. The executioner's assistants took from "Merchants and shopowners (craftsmen) a few pence when they captured a thief."[7]

Forced labor ordered by the authorities—construction work, the restoration of ruined buildings, bridges, etc.—constituted a great burden on craftsmen. If such work was not

[1] D. Kaftarev, *Istoricheskie, geograficheskie i statisticheskie svedeniya o Persii* (Saint Petersburg, 1829) p. 50; A. Z. Podrobnoe opisanie Persii (Moscow, 1829), p. 39; V. Borozdna, *Kratkoe opisanie puteshestvia Rossiskogo imperatorskogo posolstva v Persiyu v 1817 g.* (Saint Petersburg, 1821), pp. 103, 151; Yu. A. Gagemeister, "O evropeiskoi torgovle Turtsii i Persii", *Zhurnal manufaktur i torgovli* 1838, no. 1, p. 105; Platon Zubov, *Kartina poslednoi voiny Rosii s Persiei 1826–1828*, (Saint Petersburg) 1834, p. 91.

[2] *Fars-nameh*, pp. 61–165.

[3] S. A. Egiazarov, *Issledovanya po istorii uchrezhdenii Zakavkazia*, part 2, (Kazan, 1891), p. 248.

[4] J. Chardin, *Voyage du chevalier Chardin* (Paris, 1811), 5:399.

[5] Du Mans, *Estat de la Perse en 1660 par le père Raphael du Mans* (Paris, 1890), p. 30.

[6] [V. Minorsky] 'Tadhkirat al-muluk', pp. 81–83; J. Chardin, 1:405.

[7] Wills, p. 277.

paid for, the craftsmen obtained tax relief. Those who suffered most from such forced labor were men in the building trades: masons, carpenters, joiners, and others. For the construction of the shah's palaces, of bridges, and even of whole towns (for example Sultaniyeh, built on the orders of Fath Ali Shah, by craftsmen and peasants from the surrounding areas forcibly put to work for ten years) was achieved by the tax-paying classes' fulfilling their labor obligations. These obligations were very heavy and all craftsmen who had the means to do so bribed officials in order to get exempted.[8]

The forced labor of craftsmen on construction work was paid for. A case is known where a group of craftsmen, not having received payment from a certain Karim Khan, complained to Abbas Mirza [crown prince in the 1820s], who ordered the military authorities of Nakhichevan to exact the required sum from the property of Karim Khan and pay it to the craftsmen.[9]

Work in the shah's arsenals and military workshops also partook of the character of forced labor. For instance Abbas Mirza, in the course of preparing for war with Russia and reorganizing his army, set up in Tabriz and Tehran military workshops and arsenals for the production of gunpowder, casting of guns, etc., designed to supply his army with the necessary projectiles, arms, and ammunition. Equipment was delivered from England, and English foremen were sent for, who were obligated to teach those Iranian craftsmen who had been engaged in the workshops and arsenals. These craftsmen did not have the right to leave the workshop or to refuse to work.

Some of the handicraftsmen served directly the needs of the court and were regarded as, so to speak, government employees. They were not members of guilds, being subject to one of the court departments, dwelt in the shah's or khan's court, received their food and clothing, and did not have the right to engage in any other work. This was the most privileged group of craftsmen. This institution was widespread in Central Asia and Iran in the fourteenth and fifteenth centuries and survived until the nineteenth, although the term *darbasteh*, designating craftsmen belonging to a court department, fell into disuse. Once a year the work of the craftsmen was judged, confirming their right to receive wages from the treasury. According to the author of *Tadhkirat al-muluk*, they seem to have even been granted "vacations."[10]

A small part of the urban craftsmen was in fact in serflike dependence on feudal lords. Feudal economy in the West-European sense did not exist in Iran. The khans, beys, and mulkdars did not have dominion over land (*gospodskogo khozyaistva ne veli*), but merely received rents from peasants, craftsmen, and nomads. At the courts of the khans lived craftsmen who had migrated from rural areas. Their dependence on the feudal lords was complete: they dwelt in the place assigned to them, were subject only to their authority (they were not under the jurisdiction of the town authorities), and worked only to the orders of their master. This situation of craftsmen was regarded by the ruling dynasty as right and lawful, and was supported by its decrees. In 1822 Abbas Mirza issued a decree supporting the rights of a certain Muhammad Sultan against some people who had migrated from his villages to a town. In that decree, the governors, *mubashirs*, and *kadkhudas* of the town were ordered not to demand any taxes from the said people of Muhammad Sultan as from the beginning of 1822 and thereafter. It was decreed that "from several households, both Armenian and Muslim, which he (i.e., Muhammad Sultan—N.K.) brought over, not even one dinar should be demanded or exacted and no attempt should be made in that direction and no difficulties should be caused to them, so that they may find work (*kasb kardan*,

[8] Chardin, 1:354, 4:405–7, 5:120.
[9] *Nakhichevanskie rukopisnye dokumenty* (Tiflis, 1936) document no. 21.

[10] A. M. Belenitskii, "Organizatsia remesla v Samarkande XV–XVI vv." *Kratkie soobscheniya Instituta istorii materialnoi kultury* 1940, vyp. VI, p. 45; *Tadhkirat al-muluk*, p. 49.

i.e., be employed in some handicraft trade—N.K.) for the above-mentioned."[11]

In the late Middle Ages, slave labor did not, in fact, exist.

Thus in Iran, at the beginning of the nineteenth century, there were three categories of handicraftsmen. One group worked freely in the bazaar, on [customer's] orders; the second were attached to the courts of the shah or the khans or were employed in arsenals or military workshops; and the last belonged to individual feudal lords. "Free" master craftsmen constituted the majority. As a rule, in large towns they combined in unions; that is, in guilds. In small towns they formed a federation of various crafts, or worked individually. . . .

The *asnaf* (guilds) were not only fiscal-administrative units in the government of Iranian towns. They constituted, at the same time, religious unions of masters and apprentices belonging to the same craft and played an outstanding part in the productive life of the craftsmen.

In his studies on the *hamkars* (guilds) S. A. Egiazarov seeks to demonstrate the democratic character of these guilds, based on the ideas of equality and mutual aid, which limit the possibilities of exploitation within them. But in fact this was not so. The structure of the craft guilds shows profound inequality in the property and rights enjoyed by their members.

Craft guilds were marked by strict hierarchy. At the head of the guild stood the spiritual head, *naqib* or *ustabashi*. It is not known whether, in Iran, the post of *naqib* was elective, hereditary, or filled by the authorities. Chardin says only that attempts were made to keep the post within the same family: the *naqibs* handed over their functions to their sons, on the pretext of sickness or old age. It seems probable that the function of *naqib* was elective, as in Central Asia and in the Akhaltsikhski guilds.[12]

Among the duties of the heads of guilds were to see that the guild traditions were observed, to perform ceremonies, to supervise the morals of guild members, and to carry out judicial functions. They were responsible for ensuring that all rules were observed in the initiation rites by which an apprentice became a master, read and preserved the authoritative prayer, *fatiha*, said the *takbir* ["God is greatest"] and read and preserved the legends about the origins of the craft and its *pirs* or patron saints.

Regardless of whether the *naqib* was elected or succeeded by right of birth, his authority in the guild was great and was consecrated by the customary rules and religious beliefs of the craftsmen. Among them the belief was widespread that the craft was a sacred duty, and that one could rise to the higher rank of old master who knew the "secret" of the craft only through ritual consecration. The *naqib* had great power: he exercised direct influence on the material condition of the members of the guild; together with the town authorities, he fixed the amount of tax to be raised from the guild; and after that, together with the *kadkhuda*, he determined the sum payable by each craftsman. The assigning of customers' orders to individual craftsmen in certain cases, the organization of sales of goods, the supervision of fluctuations in the bazaar, the setting of prices for goods, negotiations with neighboring guilds regarding the right relations between prices—all this, also, fell within the jurisdiction of the *naqib*.

Besides the *naqib*, an important part was played by the elders. They saw to it that the master craftsmen gave proper instruction to the apprentices and took an active part in discussing candidacies for the rank of master; in the latter case, the decision rested with the elders and the *naqib*. The elders, together with the *naqib*, appraised the work of apprentices or journeymen (*podmaster*). But their main role was in financial matters:

---

[11] *Nakhichivanskie* . . . , document no. 20.
[12] *Tadhkirat al-muluk* p. 83; Chardin, p. 120; E. M. Peshcherova, "Iz istorii tsekhovykh organizatsii v Srednei Azii," *Kratkie soobshcheniya Istituta etnografii AN SSSR,* 6:(1949) 34; L. Zagurskii, "Poezdka v Akhaltsikhskii uezd v 1872 g.", *Zapiski Kavkazkogo otdeleniya Russkogo geograficheskogo obshchestva,* (Tiflis, 1874) 8:25.

they were in charge of collecting taxes, sometimes together with the *naqib*. This is what a Russian author wrote about the condition of the craft elders at the end of the 1820s:

Each guild has two elders, who oversee work and collect the taxes that each guild must pay into the treasury of the King or *Beglerbey*. To this post are usually elected the oldest and most honest persons. They are responsible for the sums paid by the persons listed in their registers, and if someone has a need to claim something back, it is only through these elders that such requests reach the government, or even the Ruler, depending on the circumstances.[13]

It is possible that, in this case, the word "elders" covers both elders and the spiritual heads of guilds. It should also be remembered that not all guilds had a *naqib* and that the elders sometimes fulfilled the functions of spiritual head of the guild.

Because of their social position, the craft elders were often buyers-up: they took orders from merchants for the making of specified goods and divided them up among the masters. The finished product was then delivered to the merchant, the elder keeping the difference between the cost of the product and the price at which he delivered it to the merchant. At the beginning of the nineteenth century almost all craft elders served, to a greater or lesser extent, as intermediaries between craftsmen and merchants.

The heads of the guilds had the right, in certain circumstances, to take a specified percentage on the sale of goods. Thus, according to Chardin, the *zargarbashi*—the head of all gold and silver craftsmen—kept for himself 2 percent of the value of the jewels delivered to the court and 1 percent of jewels sold in the town. He took a still higher percentage on sales to foreigners.[14]

Almost every guild had its treasury, into which were paid the amounts collected from craftsmen, for example, entrance fees, etc. But [the sum in] the guild treasury was not great and, consequently, not every guild had the post of treasurer, *khazinedar*. Usually, this function was performed by the *naqib* or one of the elders.

The mass of craftsmen consisted of the masters, *ustad*. Masters were the mainstay of handicraft production in Iran. Taxes were fixed according to the number of masters in each guild. Masters had the right to make goods which had no connection with their guild. Monopolization by guilds was not allowed in Iran and the guilds did not prevent their members from engaging in any occupation. But, in order to limit competition, each master worked and sold his goods in a strictly defined place, did not have the right to entice customers, "outbid for an order," praise his goods, or decry those of others. The rent paid collectively made the masters largely interdependent; if a master committed an offense—such as making shoddy goods, cheating a customer and thus undermining the authority of the whole guild, insulting another master, stealing, and so on—his shop could be taken away and given to another master.

Only masters had the right to have apprentices, teach them their trade and prepare them for initiation as masters. The number of apprentices working for each master was not fixed. Usually, each had one or, more seldom, two apprentices. The proportion between masters and apprentices in Erivan in the first third of the nineteenth century was approximately as follows:

|  | MASTERS | APPRENTICES |
|---|---|---|
| Shoemakers (*bashmachniki*) | 10 | 15 |
| Potters | 11 | 19 |
| Masons | 25 | 70 |
| Blacksmiths | 20 | 45 |
| Horseshoe smiths (*podkovshchiki*) | 12 | 10 |
| Tailors | 18 | 20 |
| Bootmakers | 60 | 150 |
| Silversmiths | 6 | 21 |
| Metalworkers | 40 | 3 |
| Joiners and Carpenters | 49 | 150 |
| Saddlers | 8 | 19 |

According to Egiazarov, the members of all the *hamkars* of Erivan, consisted of 722 masters with 667 apprentices.[15] On the average, each master had one apprentice, but some had none. Bakers and coppersmiths had no apprentices, whereas

---

[13] A. Z., *Podrobnoe*, pp. 102–3.
[14] Chardin, 5: 355–56.

[15] Egiazarov, appendix.

carpenters, bootmakers, and masons had four or five each. The relative numbers of masters and apprentices varied from one Iranian town to another. Masters who did not belong to guilds had fewer apprentices. This is shown by figures for Erivan, Nakhichevan, and Ordubad: in Erivan 143 masters had 43 apprentices, in Nakhichevan 109 masters had 41, and in Ordubad 140 masters had 128 apprentices.[16]

The elders, who constituted the guild council, did not usually interfere in relations between masters and apprentices. Only when masters committed an abuse, such as deliberately delaying the raising of an apprentice to the rank of master, did the council have the right to confer mastership on the apprentice without the consent of his master. . . .

The master's work could be easily controlled, for each master had his mark, *nishan* or *tamgha*, which he put on his products.[17] This mark was approved by the council of masters, or in a full meeting of members. In each guild such marks were not numerous. If the master died without posterity, his mark could be transferred to another master by decision of the council and general meeting. The marks make it possible to distinguish the schools of various masters, for apprentices used the same mark as their masters, with minor changes. . . .

Usually the master came to an oral agreement with the parents of his future apprentice regarding conditions of instruction. Sometimes these discussions took place before witnesses—guild elders, two or three masters, a *mullah*. More seldom, such agreements were formalized in a written document. The illiteracy of the majority of craftsmen favored the oral form and customary standards guaranteed that each side would fulfill the obligations it had taken upon itself. Analogous conditions prevailed when masters not belonging to a guild took on apprentices. Masters tried to take as apprentices their closest relatives, so as to keep in their family the secrets of their craft.[18] According to Chardin, in the *karkhanes* sons of masters were taken on as apprentices at the age of 12–15.[19]

Iranian crafts did not include the rank of journeyman (*podmaster*), although some students of the subject, such as Egiazarov, identify the *kargare* (worker) with the journeyman.[20] Chardin was very well acquainted with the structure of European guilds, which in the seventeenth century were still very powerful; in them journeymen played an important part in production and carried a stubborn fight against the masters for the rights enjoyed by the latter; he could not therefore have failed to notice the presence of journeymen in Iran. And yet he mentions only masters and apprentices.

In the Iranian guilds there was no need for journeymen. The number of masters in a guild was not limited, for anyone who had learned the craft could freely rise from the rank of apprentice to that of master. It is also known that, in Iranian towns, not all handicraftsmen belonged to guilds—many masters worked on their own. Having acquired his training, the apprentice could immediately set up as a craftsman on his own, and not work as a journeyman. If, for some reason, the apprentice was not raised to the rank of master, he could move to another town and start working there. The *muzdvar* (which means "one who is paid," "hired worker," "day laborer") or *kargar* was not a journeyman in the generally accepted meaning of the word; he was a hired worker. Various masters had hired workers, if the nature or scale of their work demanded this. Thus in Erivan there were 6 grain merchants, who did not have apprentices but hired 42 workers to transport and load the grain. Nor did the bakers have apprentices, but the 18 masters hired 50 workers. There were 52 perfumers, *attar*, who had neither apprentices nor workers.

[16] *Sbornik statisticheskikh svedenii o Kavkaze* (Tiflis, 1856), I: 31–32, 48, 53–54.
[17] V. A. Gordlevskii, *Dervishi Akhi Evrana i tsekhi v Turtsii," Izvestia AN SSSR*, series 6, 1927, no. 15–17, p. 1187.

[18] Wills, p. 224.
[19] Chardin, 7: 333.
[20] Egiazarov, p. 277.

The 10 master shoemakers had 5 hired workers and 15 apprentices. The 11 potters had 23 auxiliary workers and 19 apprentices, and the 25 masons had 18 and 70 respectively. The 8 leather craftsmen had 30 workers and no apprentices. The 6 silversmiths had 8 hired workers and 21 apprentices, the 8 saddlers had 12 and 19 repectively, and the 49 joiners and carpenters had 90 and 150 respectively. Blacksmiths, coppersmiths (tin-smiths), horseshoe smiths, candlemakers, metalworkers, braid-makers, slipper-makers and wool-workers did not have a single hired worker. In all likelihood, in such crafts the concentration of capital was minimal; mastercraftsmen worked alone, with one or two apprentices. The kind of craft in which hired labor was employed indicates the birth of capitalist enterprises in them and not the presence of a guild hierarchy.[21]

But craftsmen did not always hand down their craft to their descendents. For instance, in a treatise on calligraphers and painters, some biographical data are given on the best-known masters in these fields. The father of Amir-Sayyid Ahmad Mashhadi was in the candle business; the father of Maulana Mir Husain was a saddler in Tabriz; Hakim Rukna came from a family of physicians. . . .[22]

In the eighteenth and early nineteenth centuries, the guilds were still important as fiscal-administrative units. In Iran, the amount of taxes levied on a district or town was not based on the number of its inhabitants, since accurate population figures were unavailable not only to the central authorities but even to the local ones. In these circumstances, the guild represented a taxable unit. In the guilds, as in village communities, there was a collective responsibility. The elders collected the required sum from the craftsmen and handed it to the town's fiscal officials; in assessing the amount due from each master, however, account was taken of his income, and craftsmen who understated their income were punished or even expelled from the guild. Even those town officials who were in charge of guild affairs did not usually interfere unless they received a request to do so or a complaint;[23] however, the internal management of guilds in Iran was not always free from interference by government authorities. When the shah's authority was very powerful, it put pressure on the craft organizations; under the Safavids, the heads of guilds in Isfahan were nominated by the shah.[24]

The interference of town authorities in the lives of handicraftsmen and merchants can also be seen in the fixing of prices. This was seldom done by the guilds themselves, and prices were determined by demand and supply. However in exceptional circumstances—such as famines, epidemics, wars, etc.—the price of goods was set by the government or by the local governors. Price regulation was not always practiced, and not in all towns. Sometimes the elders of crafts or merchant unions negotiated with each other regarding price regulations in the bazaar. Such price regulation had been known in Iran for a long time. . . .

Wills[25] reports that, during the famine of the middle of the nineteenth century, grain prices rose sharply but bakers were ordered by the *beglerbegs* to continue selling bread and other products at the old prices. In order to avoid losses, bakers adulterated their bread. This angered the population, so the *beglerbeg* of Isfahan called for the elders of the bakers and demanded that they sell bread without admixture.

No less important were the functions performed by the guilds in connection with the preservation of order in their quarter of town. They hired special guards for keeping the peace at night; during the day order was kept by the guild elders and, more generally, by all the masters.[26]

Guild organizations played an important

---

[21] *Sbornik*, pp. 28–32.
[22] Kazi Ahmad, *Treatise on Calligraphists and Artists*, pp. 144–77.
[23] There is some evidence that the good quality of products was sometimes confirmed by the stamp of a special official. Most likely, such stamps were used for goods made in *karkhanes*.
[24] Chardin, 4:93.
[25] Wills, p. 45.
[26] Egiazarov, p. 291.

part in times of civil war and struggles between the various feudal groups for the throne. In such circumstances, they had the responsibility of maintaining order in the town, preserving the rights of craftsmen, ensuring normal living conditions etc.

Guilds also had a certain jurisdiction. The highest court of first instance was constituted by the spiritual head of the guild, the *naqib*. Together with the guild elders, the *naqib* judged minor suits between masters; his sentence was executed on the spot and was not subject to appeal. Little recourse was had to the highest police official of the town, the *daruge*, or to the religious court, for this involved appreciable expenses whereas the guild court was free. Only in cases of major offenses, lying outside the jurisdiction of the guilds, did masters turn to the religious or secular courts. . . .

## Amir-i Kabir

Mirza Taqi Khan, or Amir-i Kabir, as he came to be known, was one of the few statesmen of stature of the Qajar period. The son of a cook, he rose rapidly in government service thanks to his ability and the protection of the prime minister, Abu al-Qasim Qaim Maqam. Journeys to Russia and Turkey broadened his views and impressed on him the urgency of reform, and the example of such contemporary modernizers as Muhammed Ali of Egypt and Sultan Mahmud II probably acted in the same direction. Having helped to secure the accession of Nasir al-Din to the throne, in 1848, he was rewarded with the premiership. His three-year tenure of office was marked by reforms in many fields: administration, education, language, and economics. In 1851, however, he was dismissed from office and soon after murdered at the command of the shah.

The following account of his attempts to promote the industrial and mining development of Iran is taken from the excellent biography by Feridun Adamiyat.

(See also works by Avery, Polak, Binning, Shiel, and Watson, listed in the bibliography.)

### Selection 6. Attempts at Development, 1850
[Feridun Adamiyat, *Amir-i Kabir wa Iran* (Tehran, 1334), pp. 218–26]

DEVELOPMENT AND EXPANSION OF INDUSTRY

Amir believed that factories should be established in Iran to produce modern European manufactures; in other words, that the new material means of contemporary European civilization should be made within the country. Hence, he made the encouragement of national industry one of the main issues in his economic plan. Binning, the English author whom we have often mentioned in this book, states, "Mirza Taqi-Khan shows special interest in shutting out of Iran all foreign industrial goods by encouraging national industries. This policy, arising from short-sightedness, cannot in any way promote the advancement of commerce and civilization."

Binning's statement is at variance with the actual measures taken by Amir, for we see that he was a patron of modern industries in Iran. What induced Binning to make such a statement is that Amir did not wish Iran's imports to include all the new industrial goods and products, and consequently convert our country into a market for the sale of foreign goods and thereby subject it to exploitation. On the contrary, he considered it necessary to make Iran an industrial country and promote commerce and modern civilization. Thus through his efforts many factories were established, namely:

Two sugar refineries were founded in Maidan-i Ark of Sari and Barfurush, which refined Mazandaran sugar and produced refined granulated and lump sugar. Before the foundation of these two plants, Ustad Abd al-Hamid Qannad had been in charge of refining Mazandaran sugar. Since the task proved successful, he sent a sample of the refined sugar to Tehran. It was found of good quality and orders were issued to expand sugarcane cultivation; following that, these two plants were established. In the month of Shaban 1268 [1851], refined sugar produced from brown sugar was obtained and offered for sale for five krans a man. Each month ten kharvars of the product of this plant were sent to Tehran; thus the sugar consumption of Iran that was formerly met by India, was, to a certain extent, covered.

A four-story sixty by sixty zar spinning factory was founded in Tehran; iron was used in the roof of the fourth floor and implements and instruments were imported from Europe.

A calico-weaving factory on the road from Tehran to Shemiran and a silk-weaving factory in Kashan are among other industrial establishments set up by Amir.

Mirza Taqi-Khan encouraged and supported artisans and craftsmen, charged them with the management of the above-mentioned factories and demanded steady progress.

In order to increase the availability of European industrial goods in Iran and establish larger factories, in 1267 [1850] he dispatched a group of artisans and craftsmen to Moscow and Saint Petersburg under the supervision of Haji Mirza Muhammad Tajir-i Tabrizi to work in factories there and learn new industries such as confectionary, crystal making, casting metals, carpentry, and smithcraft. He asked the Russian government to supervise and watch over the craftsmanship of the Iranian student artisans.

In 1270 [1853] this skilled body of men returned, bringing back numerous implements, and undertook the establishment of new factories. Among them was Aqa Rahim Isfahani, who established a cut-crystal factory in Tehran and a papermill in Isfahan; the ruins of the latter can still be seen in the Pain-i Darvaze district in Isfahan. Likewise, in addition to the sugar refinery, the previously mentioned Haji Muhammad Tajir Tabrizi set up a cast-iron workshop and carpentry in Sari. Moreover, Amir sent two of the silk weavers of Kashan to Istanbul to learn new methods of preparing silk. Owing to Amir's special interest in silk, Gilan and Kashan silk in his time became, as we shall see, in demand.

Following Amir's precedent of sending craftsmen abroad, in the year 1275 [1858] a number of student artisans were sent to France. Eighteen of them studied the making of broadcloth, china, paper, and other useful industries. Hasan Ali-Khan Amir Nizam Garusi, the Ambassador of Iran in Persia, supervised them and looked after their welfare.[1]

Amir took a special interest in the establishment of a broadcloth factory. To this end in a letter to John David, who was charged by Amir to hire teachers from Austria and Prussia, he instructed him to hire two master craftsmen in broadcloth weaving to teach the craft of making broadcloth, which is much used in Iran, and settle their salaries at 600 to 800 tumans and also to purchase and bring to Iran the implements and instruments of a broadcloth factory....

As already mentioned, Mirza Taqi-Khan endeavored to have foreign industrial goods produced in Iran. Through his efforts, samovars and carriages were manufactured and spread in Iran, as described below:

From the Safavid period on, consumption of tea became more or less customary in Iran, but at that time it was not commonly used.[2] In the Qajar period, with imports of

---

[1] "Notes of Hasan-Ali Khan Garusi."

[2] A well-known orientalist, Krenku [F. Krenkow], quoting from the unpublished *Kitab al-Saydalah* of al-Biruni [died around A.D. 1050] states that travelers coming from China relate that in that country there is a substance by the name of "shay" which is brewed and consumed, and also that there are places, evidently the tea-houses, in which people get together and drink "shay." (This information has been obtained from Mr. Iqbal Ashtiani.)

samovars from Russia, tea drinking little by little came into general use. Two sets of gifts sent to Amir, one by the French court and the other by the leading Russian merchant, stimulated Amir's desire and interest in starting the propagation of the art of samovar making. . . .

For the development of samovar making in Iran, Amir Kabir summoned a group of craftsmen from Isfahan and handed them the samovar he had received from Russia so that they would make one like it. One of the craftsmen undertook to carry out the task; he succeeded and met with Amir's appreciation and encouragement. Then, on behalf of Amir, he was given a certain sum to produce numerous samovars. With great enthusiasm, the craftsman began preparations and set out to work. But before long, Amir was ousted from the premiership and thus ended the enterprise of the master samovar maker.[3]

As for the carriages, it was under Shah Abbas the Great that for the first time carriages, presented as gifts to the Persian court by the government of Russia and the king of England, were brought to Iran. Apparently the gifts did not impress the shah; consequently, they remained unused and rotted.[4]

In 1227 [1812] when Sir Gore Ouseley came to Iran as ambassador, among the gifts he presented to the Persian court on behalf of the King of England were several good carriages, which impressed the shah and the courtiers. When they were brought into the presence of His Majesty, Fath Ali-

Shah got into one and began smoking a hookah. Morier, who has spoken at great length about this topic, writes, "what more than anything else caused wonder and admiration on the part of the Prime Minister was the fact that the carriage could move both forward and backward."[5]

After that, carriages were made in Iran, but they were not prevalent. They were used only by the king, high officials, and nobles and were brought from Russia. On his journey to Isfahan, Mirza Taqi-Khan issued orders to produce there, for the first time, a number of carriages. The first three sets were shown to Amir; since they were of excellent quality, Amir was pleased and received their makers with kindness and appreciation. After that carriage making became prevalent in the city.

In Tehran also—by Amir's orders and through the efforts of Husain Ali-Khan Muir al-Mamalik son of Dust-Ali Khan Bastami, and the well-known Hasan Amal Quli Beg—carriage-making workshops were established in Qurkhana. From then on riding carriages became customary and popular among the masses. The leveling and paving of Ark Avenue and other streets was due to this.[6]

Not only did Amir Kabir develop in Iran the production of foreign manufactures, but he had an unlimited interest in the expansion and propagation of national industries. He personally encouraged the development and spread of domestic industries; he favored artisans and craftsmen and made an effort to encourage them; he kept them assured of his assistance and kindness and never refrained from any material or moral support. It was owing to this policy of Amir that Persian handicrafts developed greatly; Kirman woolen textiles were as choice as those from Kashmir, so that even experts were unable to differentiate between the Kirman woolen textile, which was and still is known as Amiri cashmere, and that made in Kashmir. For instance, one day a piece of Kirman textile was shown

---

[3] It is said that after Amir, in the time of Aqa Khan-i Nuri, the Isfahani samovar maker was summoned and asked to return the sum given to him by Amir. The Isfahani master craftsman was unable to pay back the entire amount. The government officials, while torturing and hitting him on the head, paraded him through the bazaars of Isfahan in order to induce others to donate, through kindness and compassion, something to assist this helpless and indebted artisan to liquidate his debts to the oppressive, antiscience and antiart advancement government which was then in charge of affairs. This skilled craftsman, who was once a protégé of Amir Nizam, under the heavy blows pounded on his head, became blind in both eyes and spent the rest of his life as a beggar in the Masjid Shah of Isfahan. How well was he rewarded for his craftsmanship!

[4] Tavernier, *Voyage en Perse* (Paris, 1930), p. 107.

[5] J. Morier, 2: 197–98.
[6] See *Waqay-i Itfaqiyyah*, nos. 26, 38, 39.

to a couple of woolen textile experts who, taking it for Kashmir product, offered a price of 80 tumans. With all their experience and perceptiveness they could not tell whether it was from Kirman or Kashmir.[7] Consequently, the market for woolen textiles from Kashmir slackened in Iran in favor of the Amiri textiles. In feasts, or on the occasion of presenting a robe of honor, Amiri cashmere was given.

The Mazandaran woolen cloaks, made especially for the local population, thanks to Amir's endeavors and the efforts of Mahdi Quli Mirza, governor of Mazandaran, gained such popularity and increase in the volume of production that they were used, instead of broadcloth, for the uniforms and garments of the soldiers and were sold at four krans a roll.[8]

When Amir learned of the difficulties facing the weavers in Isfahan, he arranged for them to prepare and deliver to the government officials 50,000 uniforms annually. Thus, by giving them financial assistance, he endeavored to stimulate their market.

With such support and encouragement from Amir, the artisans and craftsmen took an interest in their work and showed initiative and inventiveness. For instance, in Kashan Haji Muhammad Husain-i Kashani produced from cotton and silk [reading *kaj* for *gach*] a good and durable fabric similar to broadcloth and presented it to Amir. Mirza Taqi-Khan liked it as an army overcoat and gave him a sum of 900 tumans to prepare, from that material, and deliver about 2,000 army overcoats. And a certain Ustad Hasan Tabrizi made the safe for the treasury, which is very sturdy and weighs about one kharvar, and is as good as the safes manufactured in Europe.[10]

Likewise, when a lady artisan from Tehran by the name of Khorshid made a sample of officers' shoulder straps, which were formerly imported from Austria and the Ottoman Empire, and presented it to Amir, she was received with much kindness and warmth. Through financial aid, Mirza Taqi-Khan had the necessary equipment prepared for her and hired numerous assistants. For five years she was put in complete charge of making officers' shoulder straps.[11] This act of Amir is truly remarkable. A hundred years ago, he assigned government jobs to professional women.

In view of the above developments, when thanks to Amir's efforts the foundation for a great industrial revolution was laid, it was resolved to establish an exposition of the arts and crafts in which to display a few specimens of Iranian textile and other manufactures.

To this end, with the help of the previously mentioned Muir al-Mamalik, an industrial fair consisting of several pavilions was set up in Ark. There samples of all the manufactures were displayed, such as carriages, clocks, guns, officers' shoulder straps, embroidery in filigree work, gold embroidery, and even exquisite paintings, each representing a different aspect of Persian art and talent.[12]

This exposition, founded through Amir's encouragement, was not, unfortunately, opened during his lifetime.

## MINING

During his short term of office, Mirza Taqi-Khan took useful steps toward industrialization, naturally in accordance with the practices of his times. For instance, he did not neglect mining in Iran. Toward this end he exerted the utmost effort and utilized the assistance of artisans, introducing them to dealing with economic affairs, and thereby put to work dormant capital and increased internal productivity. He issued a decree allowing unrestricted operation of mines in Iran and put mining affairs in the hands of the previously mentioned Mirza Jabbar Nazim al-Muham. Under this decree, first, all subjects of Iran were given, with the permission of the government, the right to

[7] Ibid., no. 6.
[8] Ibid., no. 2.
[9] Ibid., no. 21.
[10] *Muntazam-i Nasiri*, 3:214.

[11] *Waqaya-i Itfaqiyyah*, no. 2.
[12] Ibid. no. 111.

work the mines and, second, for five years, they were exempt from all taxation.

One of the important and interesting points in this decree was that the right of working mines was granted exclusively to citizens of Iran. In other words, foreigners were deprived of this right. Another point was the five-year exemption from taxation, so that those less inclined to undertake productive activities would be encouraged to put their capital to work and thereby promote economic advancement and increase the volume of the country's output.

The policies and procedures of Amir in the development of mining were very effective and operations became profitable. Among them was the operating of the mines of Qarache Dagh in Azerbaijan. Since it is an important political episode, it is necessary to recount its history briefly.

Among the English officers who in year 1809 came to Iran was Captain Monteith, who in 1815 was commissioned by Crown Prince Abbas Mirza to investigate the copper and iron mines in Qarache Dagh; the result of his investigations was extremely interesting. Then Sir H. Lindsay Bethune obtained from Fath-Ali-Shah a decree to operate, at his own expense, the mines of Qarache Dagh. In 1252 [1836], during the reign of Muhammad-Shah, Sir Henry Lindsay Bethune brought from England a steam engine and a number of workmen and began work there. But, owing to the dispute between Iran and England in the times of Muhammad-Shah, he abandoned work, left Iran, and filed a complaint with his own government. This was among the grievances raised by Lord Palmerston against Muhammad-Shah and Haji-Mirza-Aqasi and has been fully treated in the *Safar-nama* of Mirza Husain Khan Ajudan-bashi.[13]

Mirza Taqi-Khan, drawing on the ex-

perience he had gained from the Qarache Dagh mines, set out to produce metals and charged Mirza-Aqasi-Khan with this enterprise. Mirza-Aqasi-Khan showed much interest in this matter and organized operations. The copper produced was, for the most part, used in cannon casting.

From then on, until Mirza Husain-Khan Sipahsalar entered the political scene of Iran, the question of Qarache Dagh remained dormant. As was pointed out by Rawlinson, the British minister, to resolve the important issues which had long existed between Iran and Britain, such a sympathetic person toward Britain was appointed prime minister. With a stroke of the pen he offered to the English Baron Reuter the entire right over the mines and other resources of Iran [see 4:7]. This strange act of concession, which even the English themselves avoided implementing because of the difficulties involved, included, of course, the mines of Qarache Dagh. However, we shall leave this question aside, since it falls outside the scope of the topic under discussion.

Under Amir the Masule mines of Gilan began operating. Since the iron obtained from there was softer than that formerly imported from Haji-Tarkhan, it was used for gun-barrels and other arms. The mines in the district of Nanich, in Mazandaran, also began to be worked. Tar, formerly brought from Russia for use in cannon making, was—thanks to the efforts of Mirza Ali Akbar, the arsenal officer—prepared in Rahmat Abad in Gilan. The volume of production increased steadily, so that there was a surplus over domestic consumption.

In addition to what has just been said, Amir had also other plans for the production of precious minerals in Iran. As a matter of fact, Rishard-Khan was commissioned by Amir to investigate the mines in Kurdistan and explicitly writes, "... I had been out of Tehran for two months. Amir sent me to Kurdistan to investigate the mines there."[14]

---

[13] Lindsay, who was called "Linzy Sahib" in Iran and was known among the masses as "Rustam-i Dastan" because of his tall stature, died in Tehran on Wednesday, 17, Rabi al-Thani, 1267. By Amir's order impressive obsequies were performed; as a result the British government extended an official appreciation to the government of Iran.

[14] "Various Notes of the late Dr. Alam al-Daula-i Thaqafi"—Rishard-Khan's letter to one of his friends in Erzerum.

Amir intended to develop the mines of Iran according to the new scientific rules, and that Iranian teachers be trained for this purpose. He therefore instructed Monsieur John David in regard to the employment of a mineralogist from Austria or Prussia in this manner (Muharram 12, 1267) [1850]: "As has already been written to that Exalted one in a separate letter, a number of learned and experienced teachers are needed for the Royal School which has been founded in the Dar al-Khalafa of Tehran. That Exalted one is, therefore, authorized to hire, according to the list, knowledgeable teachers from Austria or Prussia for a term of four to five years." Amir then gives the list of the teachers needed and states: ". . . One expert mineralogist who has had experience with all metals; two mine workers to work in the mines. . . ." Similarly, in another letter he writes to him: ". . . As for the expert mineralogist, make sure that he has full experience with all metals especially gold and silver; God willing, you must soon bring those teachers and not delay any longer; I do not wish to emphasize any further." From these instructions the extent of Amir's interest in mining, especially gold and silver, is evident.

Let us not omit that among the gifts sent by Louis Napoleon for Nasir al-Din-Shah after his accession to the throne there were several smelting furnaces. I quote their description from the documents belonging to that period:

Sample furnace for separating lead from silver, one unit,
Furnace for smelting copper, one unit,
Furnace for smelting lead brought from the mine, one unit.

From the above account, it is evident that under Amir the operation of the mines gained strength and stature, but after Mirza Taqi-Khan it was not pursued. Instead of encouragement and reward to those engaged in the working of the mines, heavy tax loads were put on their shoulders to make them quit; when the governor of Astarabad decided to operate the coal mine of Shahrud, the central government opposed his pro-

posal.[15] In any case, negligence and lack of interest shook the very notion of reform to its foundation and made it collapse.

## Selection 7. Manufactories, Late Nineteenth Century
[Z. Z. Abdullaev, *Promyshlennost i zarozhdenie rabochego klassa Irana v kontse XIX-nachale XX vv.* (Baku, 1963), pp. 115–22.]

. . . At the end of the nineteenth and beginning of the twentieth centuries, manufactories existed only in a limited number of Iranian industries. The main branches were: carpet weaving, leather, workshops for the preparation of opium and henna and, to a very small extent, some fields of mining, shoemaking, etc.

The constantly increasing demand in the world capitalist market for Persian carpets necessitated extension of the production of that salable commodity. The demand for carpets was so great that workshops based on simple capitalist cooperation were no longer in a position to satisfy it. The demand from merchant capital necessitated the further extension of carpet making, which steadily led to the appearance of carpet workshops, of the manufactory type. P. Averyanov, describing the condition of the carpet industry in Azerbaijan in 1899, stated: "until recently there were no carpet factories (i.e., large enterprises—Z.A.) in the whole of Azerbaijan, the work being done exclusively by women, at home."[1]

Workshops with a large number of hired workers constantly carried the division of labor further. In large carpet workshops, for instance, the following basic operations existed. . . .

Apart from this immediate division of work on the loom, in some large carpet workshops there were specialists who dyed the yarn, which apprentices gathered in skeins. Often large merchants who owned carpet manufactories bought up raw wool and put it out for spinning into yarn at

[15] Eastwick, 2:81.
[1] P. I. Averyanov, *Otchet o poezdke po severnomu Azerbaidzhanu*, (Tiflis, 1900), chap 1., p. 50.

home; later this yarn would be dyed in specialized dye-works also belonging to the same merchant. This form of production was interwoven with another: the merchant owning a large carpet workshop also put out raw wool to carpet weavers, who worked at home. In the latter case the house of the carpet weaver was transformed into an external section of the manufactory, which was a characteristic phenomenon of manufactory production: manufactories were closely tied to home work. Often the owners of carpet manufactories were foreign firms, or merchants from Transcaucasia. Around the carpet manufactories gathered large capitalists, who bought the raw material and sold the finished product.

In his account of the appearance of large carpet-making enterprises in Tabriz, Averyanov dwells on the "factory" of a merchant from Elizavetpol (Ganje), a Russian subject by the name of Ganjiev (Mamedov), in which up to 1,500 workers were employed.[2] This enterprise was a large manufactory, consisting of several brick buildings, in which were workshops for carpet making and a dye-house. Mamedov also had his own bakery, in which ten thousand loaves were baked each week for his workers. In the large workshop, about one hundred carpets were in process at any one time. Very expensive woolen and silk carpets were made, mostly based on European designs. The products were mostly exported to America and England. Annual turnover was 500,000 rubles [about £50,000]. We have not come across any other carpet-making enterprise of that size, but establishments with up to one hundred workers and over were to be found in several carpet-making centers. Such enterprises often belonged to representatives of foreign capital.

The larger the workshop the further advanced was the division of labor. The workers received only wages, and controlled neither the raw material nor the finished product. In the workshops of the manufactory type, the mass of workers were hired

laborers, "although this relation never attains in manufactories the completeness and purity which is peculiar to factories."[3]

The example of carpet making clearly illustrates the process of the union of merchant and industrial capital. This interweaving comes about in many ways and the dependence of the worker on the entrepreneur takes many forms and shades —beginning with hired work in someone else's workshop, domestic work for a "master," and ending with dependence in the purchase of the raw material or sale of the product.[4]

Apart from carpet making, manufactories were most widespread in the leather industry. In Hamadan, the center of leather preparation and the production of morocco, there were relatively large workshops where labor was divided in definite processes. In contrast to carpet making, all processes were, as a rule, carried out in the same workshops, which frequently had the appearance of a dirty and dark pit. In this industry, the manufactories had no links with domestic work. In his book, L. Sobotsinskii gives some information which is of interest for study of leather manufactories. Writing about the production of morocco in 1909–12, the author concludes that: "It was until now in the hands of a large number of half-cottage industry half-handicraft [*polukustarnykh, poluremeslennikh*] establishments with 5–10 workers, but is now moving on to the manufactory form."[5] According to him, in 1909 there were in Mashad and Hamadan, the main centers for the production of morocco, some eight manufactories, with forty to fifty workers. The author directly emphasizes the impossibility of the small enterprises' meeting the competition of the large workshops, which often led to the liquidation of the small firms.

Among other branches in which production took place in manufactories, mention may be made of the preparation of opium, which was a seasonal operation. According

[2] Ibid., pp. 50–52.

[3] V. I. Lenin, *Sochineniya*, 3:381.
[4] Ibid.
[5] Sobotsinskii, p. 288.

to established practice,[6] the fresh opium juice passed into the hands of a merchant or buyer, who was also often the owner of the workshop. The buyer determined each time the quantity of each kind of opium that should be mixed together in order to obtain a homogeneous product, satisfying the demands of the ultimate buyer. After that the prepared dough was carried for packing. The leader of the workers' artel—the head foreman—cut it up into pieces (*chuneh*) weighing one pound avoirdupois each. . . . For local use, opium was prepared in the form of small pills or sticks.[7] There is evidence that, in Mashad, the preparation of opium was carried out by the excise administration, which hired for that purpose up to fifty persons who worked in the courtyard of that administration.[8]

The preparation of henna also took place in manufactories. As is well known, in the period under study the Kirman district was the only producer of henna not only in Iran but in the whole of the Near and Middle East. The raw material, in the form of dried leaves, was taken for processing to Yazd where, in 1907–08, there were some sixty enterprises engaged in that activity. In these establishments, the leaves were pulverized and the powder was then sifted through pieces of cloth of different thickness. After that, the product was poured into canvas bags of 1.8 pounds weight, which were then stamped with the seal of the firm. The finest powder was regarded as the best kind, and was known in the trade as *jawhari*.[9]

Evidence on the existence of manufactories in the mining industry is very scanty. In a document in the archives,[10] the representative of the Discount and Loan Bank in Sabzevar, A. Kassis, provides interesting data on a copper mine near the Dagan Siah mountain, not far from Sabzevar, which was worked at that time. In the course of the preceding years this mine, together with other copper mines of Khurasan, had been leased to Muhammad Ismail Arbab, who died in 1915 and whose business passed on to his son, Mirza Muhammad Ali Arbab.[11] The holder of the mine built on the Dagan Siah a six-room house for the older employees, a stable, and other buildings. In addition, huts were built for the workers. The source states that Dagan Siah was situated far from the town and was located in desert surroundings, unfit for irrigation because of the absence of water.

Arbab's business was particularly good until 1910, when the ore yielded 20 to 30 percent of pure copper. At that time the number of workers reached 250 to 300. A special grocery was set up at the mines, catering to the workers. In 1912–13, the lower parts of this rich mine were flooded, which made it necessary to cease work on the lower layers and turn to the upper, which did not yield more than 5 to 7 percent of pure copper.

Kassis also gives interesting information on Arbab's other mines, scattered in Zanglou, Kuh Gomai, Chund, Rivand, and Abbas Abad. Arbab began to work the Kuh Gomai mine in 1900. At the time of Kassis's visit, fifty persons worked in the mine and extracted each day one hundred *mans* of ore, yielding twelve *mans* of copper. Arbab also put up there a well-built house and laid out a large orchard, yielding an annual income of about 150 tumans; there was also a separate farm, a *kalat*. Both Kuh Gomai and Dagan Siah had a workshop. In Chund, which was near the town, ten persons were employed and daily output was thirty *mans*; the high quality ore extracted there was taken to the town, where it was processed. Rivand was a completely new mine, with a high copper content. Because of frequent Turkoman attacks, the Abbas Abad mine was not being worked at the time of Kassis's visit. The daily output of the four mines was 580 *mans*, which gave 54 *mans* of pure copper. Arbab paid 500 tumans a month as rent for the mines.

---

6 Ts. G.I.A.L., f. 600, op. 10, d. 767, l. 9 ob.
7 SKD, 1908, vyp, II, p. 293.
8 Ts. G.I.A.L., f. 600, op. 10, d. 1003, ll. 8 ob.–9 ob.
9 SKD, 1908, vyp. II, pp. 294–95.
10 Ts. G.I.A.L., f. 600, op. 10, d. 321, l. 15–16.

11 Ts. G.I.A.L., f. 600, op. 10, d. 321, l. 15.

The account given by Kassis makes it possible to affirm that in these regions work proceeded the whole year round. As regards Zanglou, he merely states that "in winter, when the cold is intense, some of the workers go elsewhere in search of employment." According to the author, the first extraction was achieved by shattering with gunpowder the layers of rock containing ore, after which other workers sorted out the stones which had broken away from the rock. The workers then carried the ore-bearing stones to the workshop, which was half a *verst* away from the pit. This contained specially large furnaces (*falaka*), in which the ore was deposited on wood that had previously been put under it. In this way, the ore was melted down and a dense, dark substance, *sang-i sukhta*, was obtained. This was carried to another workshop, close to the first, where it was further processed: it was melted down again and, thus purified from foreign matter, part of the substance was transformed into ingots, known as *kauchuk*. The remaining part, which was of less value and was known as *rubar*, was mixed with fresh ore and again sent for melting in the furnace (*falaka*). The *kauchuk*, on the other hand, was sent to a workshop in the town, where the final processing, into pure copper, took place.

As may be seen from the preceding description, processing was divided into at least six separate operations; in other words, there was a great division of labor, characteristic of manufactory industry.

The absence of relevant material and data does not allow us to affirm the presence of manufactories in other branches of Iranian industry. In all likelihood, production in some other branches took the form of manufactory industry, even if on a dwarf scale and in imperfect forms. The dominance of feudal relations prevented the passage to manufactory production. The absence of appropriate conditions for the normal development of national industry, on the one hand, and the beginning of the decline and degradation of handicraft production, on the other, under the impact of the increasing penetration of foreign capital and goods, constituted the main obstacles to the development of handicrafts into manufactories.

The study of manufactories in Iran shows that they developed essentially only in those branches of industry that produced for the world market. Although the appearance of manufactories at the end of the nineteenth century and the beginning of the twentieth constituted a definite progress, their development only in branches connected with export produced a deformed, one-sided, national industry. This placed Iranian industry, especially its more advanced branches and those with better prospects, in still further dependence on foreign capital. These branches, as a whole, were subjected to the will of foreign enterprises. Besides, manufactories represented the most profitable way of exploiting workers. . . .

## Export of Textiles to Russia, 1880s

For many centuries Iran supplied the Caucasus and Central Asia with handicraft products, especially textiles, and this trade continued after the Russian conquest. But in the 1880s both streams began to dry up. In 1877 Russia increased the protectionist effects of its tariff by nearly 50 percent by insisting that duties be paid in gold, not paper, rubles, and this presumably affected Iranian goods as well as the European ones against which it was primarily directed.[1] Still more important was the rapid expansion of Russian industry, which by the 1890s was growing at 8 percent a year, a rate higher than that of the United States and all European

[1] Peter Lyashchenko, *History of the National Economy of Russia* (New York, 1949), pp. 557–58.

countries.[2] Hence, Russian manufactured goods, especially textiles, began to displace Iranian. Exports of Iranian textiles to Russia, which had averaged 649,00 rubles in 1875–78, fell to 197,000 in 1885–87, and declined still further during the 1890s,[3] at a time when total Iranian exports to Russia were advancing very rapidly (see 3:21).

[2] Alexander Gerschenkron, *Economic Backwardness in Historical Perspective* (Cambridge, Massachusetts, 1962), p. 129.
[3] Glukhoded, p. 23.

## Selection 8. Cloth Weaving, 1877
*Report on Trade of Tabriz in 1877* (AE Correspondance Commerciale, Tauris, vol. 2, 15 September 1879)

... In the Caucasus, Persia has an outlet for the cloth made at Yazd, Kashan, and Isfahan, which it should try to keep. The market for this article is still Tabriz which, as I said in my previous annual report, is where transactions involving the sale of native cloth and the purchase of English manufactured products takes place.

These native cloths, which are badly made and woven out of inferior quality cotton, are appreciated in a poor country like the Caucasus because of the low price at which they can be delivered. I believe that Persia can easily keep this market, and even expand it by developing its own production. The cotton varieties grown in Azerbaijan are far from having the qualities of Egyptian or American cotton. Exports of cotton to Europe are insignificant, the estimated annual average never exceeding the 40,000 kilograms taken by Russia. At one time the figure may have been higher, but the increase was due to abnormal circumstances, namely, the cotton crisis which forced England to turn to all producing countries for the supply of its factories [see 5:12]. The development of native clothmaking, which I suggest as a way of keeping the Caucasian market, is actually taking place: this year, the provinces of Urumiya, Salmats, and Tabriz itself have played a fairly large part in such exports. Faced with the impossibility of marketing their cotton, the inhabitants of these districts have understood that only the weaving of cloth would enable them to take advantage of that crop, and they have succeeded. It is to be hoped that this success will serve to encourage them. ...

## Carpet Weaving

Carpets have been woven in Iran from early times by nomads, villagers, and townsmen, and for several centuries have enjoyed a high reputation abroad. But high transport costs severely limited exports, and it was not until the last quarter of the nineteenth century that growing affluence in Europe and the United States began to create a large foreign demand.[1] This led not only to increased production from traditional sources but also to the establishment, mainly by foreign enterprise but also by Tabriz[2] and other merchants, of workshops or factories such as the one described in the following selection.

In a report written in 1874, the British consul at Tabriz pointed out that "the demand for Persian carpets has increased considerably during the last two years,

[1] As late as 1903, Whigham (p. 301) estimated that transport to Europe added 30 percent to the original cost.
[2] "Tabriz," A and P 1899, 101.

and the export has doubled within that period."[3] He went on to state, "Carpets are manufactured all over Persia, but the following districts are more especially renowned for the beauty and durability of their fabrics—Feregan, Sultanabad, Sarabend, and the villages about Meshed and Gawin; in Kurdistan, Sennah, and the neighbouring villages; in Azerbijan, the district of Karadagh, Bekshaish, and Heriz"—to which he could have added Kashan, Kirman and Fars. Whole regions specialized in carpet weaving: thus there were some 5,000 looms, employing about 10,000 persons, in 150 villages near Sultanabad; the Sennah district in Kurdistan had some 5,000 looms; the neighbourhood of Kainat 2,000 looms with 12,000 workers. As for the towns, Kirman had 1,000 looms and Mashad 150 shops, some employing up to 100 workers,[4] and in Tabriz, in 1907, there were about 100 workshops with 1,200 looms.[5]

The 1874 report from Tabriz put exports of carpets from that town (through Trebizond) at £28,000 in 1872 and £25,000 in 1873, but there were other exporting centers; thus "Feregan and Sultanabad supply the greater quantity exported to Europe and Turkey, to the value of about £50,000 annually. Carpets are here made expressly for the European markets, in sizes varying from 2 yards square to 14 yards by 10."

By 1879, export of carpets from Tabriz had risen to £65,000 and "an agent from the Maison du Louvre in Paris is despatched annually to Persia for their purchase; but besides being in fair demand in the principal markets of the European continent, they are now exported hence to the United States."[6] In 1889, Curzon estimated total exports of carpets at £90,000–100,00 and by the turn of the century, they were around £500,000; the main exporting centers were Tabriz, through Trebizond or Erivan; Shiraz and Kirman, through the gulf; and Mashad by the Transcaspian railway or across the Caspian.[7] By 1914, exports had risen to about £1,000,000, accounting for almost one-eighth of Iran's total trade. The greater part of exports went to Russia, and also to Turkey, for reexport to the United States, Britain, France, and other countries.

As regards methods of production:

The bulk of the carpet industry is carried on in the weavers' homes, the women and children doing the weaving. The so-called manufacturer supplies to the weaver the design and the quantities of wool in different colours required for one carpet (this latter, to insure the same shades being employed throughout). He also advances sums to account of the price arranged, the balance being paid on delivery of the finished article. The practice has the usual disadvantages of home employment, slovenly and dilatory work, with little progress towards skill and finish, as the looms, scattered over a wide area, cannot be constantly inspected. The vast majority of weavers, however, living in small

[3] "Tabriz," A and P 1875, 75.
[4] Abdullaev, pp. 58 and 78, citing various sources; by the 1920s the number of looms in Kirman had risen to 5,000—see English, p. 29.
[5] Aubin, pp. 42–43.
[6] "Tabriz," A and P 1880, 73; both this and the 1874 report quote prices for some kinds of carpets.
[7] Curzon, *Persia*, 2:525; MacLean, "Report," A and P 1904, 95.

isolated villages, and having also household duties, can work only in this way. The untrustworthy weaver sells the good wool entrusted to him and substitutes inferior wool, and sometimes even sells the finished work and sets up a new piece, to be delivered long after contract time.

There is only one European (British) house now competing with Persians in carpet weaving. Their method of business is as indicated above. They usually employ some 3,000 looms, on which, perhaps, 10,000 hands are kept at work. Much local experience is needed in placing out work according to the skill and trustworthiness of the weaver. They purchase and dye in their own premises all the wool employed in their carpets.

Of course, the wholesale and export traders buy great numbers of carpets made for small capitalists, or by weavers who can afford to lie out of the cost of material and labour till finished.

A manufacturer with long experience of the industry in Sultanad considers that it would not be difficult to get women weavers to attend at a properly appointed factory, and that the economy of material, and increased skill and finish of supervised work, would enable such an undertaking to prosper.

In Tabriz, where carpet making is quite a recent industry, the weaving is done by boys who attend at the factories. Wages are about krs. 12 per month, and the midday meal say another krs. 12 per month. There is a foreman, say at krs. 50 per month.

A carpet of 9 feet by 12 feet with 15 by 15 stitches to the square inch will employ say five boys and an overseer. The rate of progress will depend on the intricacy of the design, say about 18 square feet per month. The Tabriz carpets have attained a reputation for good workmanship, but the local wool coming chiefly from Khoi, Urmiah, and Souj-bulak is of a hard texture and makes the carpets stiff and unpliable. The quality depends greatly on the number of stitches. The coarsest qualities turned out have about 8 by 8 stitches to the square inch. The average quality of Tabriz carpets runs about 15 by 15 stitches, and a fine carpet 20 by 20. Silk carpets contain from 15 by 15 to 22 by 22 stitches. It does not pay to produce the coarsest qualities in Tabriz, the high cost of wages and wool making them nearly as expensive as the fine qualities. As regards price, so much depends on workmanship, design and colour that only general indications can be given. Kerman and Tabriz woollen carpets cost from krs. 100 to krs. 150 per square zar (about $1\frac{1}{2}$ square yards). Meshed carpets a little lower, and the common Ferahan from krs. 20 to krs. 25. Ziegler's krs. 25 to krs. 35. Silk carpets from krs. 300 to krs. 500 per zar. Aniline dyes are constantly used, but the carpets made with them are for the most part disposed of in the eastern markets, Russia and Egypt.[8]

The aniline dyes referred to began to enter Iran in the 1870s, with the growing demand for carpets. In 1882, the government prohibited the importation of such dyes, and in 1885 that of threads dyed with aniline,[9] but it was unable to stop smuggling, and consequently a large quantity of garish carpets continued to be produced during, and after, the period under review.

In 1912 a carpet factory was founded by the Sharq company. It had 150 looms, in two buildings. The raw wool, after preliminary preparations, was put out to women, working in their own homes, for spinning into thread.[10]

---

[8] *Ibid.* However, an earlier report mentioned "a wealthy Russian subject, who employs some 2,000 men and boys, working at 200 looms"—"Tabriz," A and P 1899, 101. Whigham (p. 229) stated that "in the Sultanabad district women workers were paid $\frac{1}{2}$ kran a day," "with an occasional cup of tea thrown in."

[9] See dispatches of 2 December 1882 and 26 May 1885, FO 60/474.

[10] Glukhoded, p. 41.

### Selection 9. Carpet Industry, 1894
[Report on Ispahan, A and P, 1894, 87, pp. 57-58]

... There are about 800 houses containing some 1,200 looms where carpets are woven.

The town and district of Sultanabad has been practically made by carpet weaving. In past times this district was always noted for its weavers, but they were to be found in Faraghan, and the carpets were known as Faraghan carpets. This is a small district about 20 miles to the north of Sultanabad.

Nearly 20 years ago Messrs. Ziegler, of Manchester, who have representatives in Tabreez, Tehran, Ispahan, &c., finding that exports from Persia did not afford them sufficient means to return their capital to Manchester, looked about them for additional ways of exit for their money and conceived the idea of developing this carpet trade. Mr. Alpiger, one of their employés in Tabreez, was deputed to work the question up, and it is due to his quiet persistence and never-failing courage that the trade has become the important one it is. With no assistance from Government and without any concession, but simply by good honest work and assiduity, in face of many difficulties and much opposition from the native merchants and dealers, bit by bit was the business built up, so that at the present moment we have nothing like it in Persia.

In no town of Persia have I seen such evidence, not of wealth quite, but of well-doing and of well-being. The people are all comfortably dressed and look contented and happy; they all live on the carpet weaving—its good effects are evidenced in the whole community. In my life in Persia, I have seen most of its more important towns, but no place impressed me so much as Sultanabad.

Messrs. Ziegler and Co. do not mean to allow the good work they have commenced here to slip from their hands. To enable them to keep even with the times and to feel the taste of the European and American carpet markets, they have built large premises just outside of the town, covering about 40,000 square yards, at a cost of some 6,000l. It is so large and imposing that the townspeople have given it the name of the Kal'ah, or the Fort. Here they have the dwelling-houses of their employés, their offices, store rooms, and most important of all, their dyeing rooms. It is thus by means of the latter that they are able to get true colours, in proper harmony and in accordance with modern taste. No weaver is allowed to use, as they much prefer to do, wool of his own dyeing unless they are absolutely sure of his honesty and of the trueness of his dyes, so that by this means they prevent any carpets with colours liable to fade getting into the market.

Their store rooms of dyed wool are a curiosity, acres of almost every colour conceivable are there seen—it is a very galaxy of colour. With quiet and order the various shades of wool are sorted out, weighed and given to the weaver, and at the same time a paper stating the amount of wool, the pattern of the carpet and its size; the same details are entered in a book, so that when he comes with the carpet his account is quickly made up. If he has made it true and well he gets a small reward, and if he has committed faults he is put under penalty. It is curious to watch the gentlemen employed in receiving and assessing these carpets as they are exposed in the office, one glance of the eye is sufficient to detect everything that is wrong with the carpet under inspection.

It unfortunately happened that the day after my arrival in Sultanabad one of Messrs. Ziegler's people, who had only arrived a few days before from Manchester, died of small pox caught on the road. This, naturally, had a very depressing effect on everybody; and, although they did what they could for me in showing me all that was to be seen, yet it probably prevented me learning with profit much I might otherwise have done.

I have written at some length about Messrs. Ziegler's enterprise here only with justice, I think, as they are the pioneers of the work; but, at the same time, I must not omit to mention the other firm, which is represented at Sultanabad, namely, Messrs. J. C. P. Hotz and Son, of London, Bushire, Ispahan, &c. They were not slow to see the usefulness of this trade opened up here, nor are their eyes closed to its general advantages. They have prospected about in other places in Persia to develope a similar one. About 10 years ago they also started at Sultanabad, and entered into keen competition with Messrs. Ziegler's. They also have gone ahead, and have established their own dye works; they send out young men who have carefully studied the carpet trade, and, in fact, they do all they can to keep it at its present high level of excellence.

Besides these two firms, there are the various native dealers and traders, including Jews. I am sorry I cannot speak for them in the same terms as I have of the two European firms. For the sake of an insignificant saving in dyeing, they use almost entirely aniline colours. Whilst using some one of the lovely old Persian designs, a carpet of great merit as to weaving will be utterly disfigured and rendered valueless for the European market owing to its glaring staring reds, greens and blues, all made from aniline dyed wool. In other cases, a well woven carpet will not only be disfigured by these aniline dyes, but its design may be some hideous thing taken from a Manchester print of days long gone by. Most of these carpets find their market in Persia or in Turkey, but it is a matter of wonderment that the Persian who has known, and is so proud of the lovely artistic carpets, the production of the looms of his countrymen of past generations, can tolerate such utter anachronisms as the carpets above referred to. Aniline dyes have been prohibited entry into this country by the Shah, but yet they do find a way in; they come chiefly from Germany, I am told, and are smuggled in from Baghdad in boxes of sugar, and from the Caucasus in tins of petroleum.

Mr. Alpiger, Messrs. Ziegler's manager, told me that when he first came to Sultanabad, nearly 20 years ago, he found in the town only about 40 looms; now there are at least 1,200; and in the various villages about there are certainly another 1,500. I do not think I should be overstating it if I said that, altogether, some 3,000 looms are in work all over this country, involving an annual output of 5,000,000 krans worth of carpets. . . .

## Modern Factories

The few, and largely unsuccessful, attempts at setting up modern factories in Iran are described in the two following selections. The first, taken from what is probably the best overall study of the economy of Iran written before the First World War, relates the failure of some Belgian schemes. The second gives a list of the main enterprises that were established. In addition, mention should be made of several small refineries set up to process crude petroleum imported from Russia and, more important, many ginneries built in the northern part of the country to prepare Iran's growing cotton crop for export or internal marketing.[1]

[1] See details on these and other enterprises in Abdullaev, pp. 122–60.

**Selection 10. Modern Factories, 1890s**
[Eteocle Lorini, *La Persia economica* (Rome, 1900) pp. 159–63]

. . . After railways, the Belgians succumbed to the seduction of glass. Glass-making offered all the mirages of a gold rush. In Baron D'Erp's report of 1891, marvelous things were described. Glass, which was monopolized by French trade, had a wholesale cost of 4.5 to 5 krans (3 francs 33 to 4 francs 70 [sic]) per sheet of 55 by 37 centimeters. When shipped in crates containing eighty sheets, only one-third arrived in good condition. Hence, the local price was more than *ten times* the cost of production. On the other hand, demand was intense, since Persians live in houses with many doors and windows—looking just like lanterns. Their passion for glassware, and for mirrors, is extraordinary. All that remained, therefore, was to get down to work, in order to make immense profits.

Our Belgians did, indeed, soon get going. Three and a half million francs were put together, in the form of a joint stock company *pour la verrerie en Perse*. The machinery arrived over the Karzan route which I have described. No less than thirty German mechanics also came, accompanied by assistants and employees of every kind, all highly paid. The laboratories, storehouses, crucibles, ovens, and so on were built. And all was ready to start. But no one had thought of a trifle, which however did have a certain importance: the difficulty of finding the raw material, silicates of calcium and aluminum, as well as coal, which was very expensive and, in addition, was made still dearer by clever speculation. Things continued thus for a certain time. Each of the superintendents owned a horse—and the Persian plains called for gay rides in the warm hours. From the factory issued a product full of knots, threads [*fiele*], and glass salts, and at a cost higher than the best merchandise brought over from Marseilles. Thus the *verrerie* of Tehran resulted in a solemn fiasco, an irremediable fiasco; for the defects in the original aims were not capable of being healed, especially the lack of raw material, for which more millions would have had to be spent, with no apparent desire on the part of the shareholders! Hence, everything remained as it was, and when I was in Persia an attempt was being made to salvage part of the inauspicious enterprise by putting the burden on the shoulders of a French engineer, trying to make hollow glassware [*gobeleterie*]. Unless, of course, the object was simply to *gobelotter*, or to tipple. What is certain is that, at the

first attempts, it was found impossible to produce little bottles at less than 12 shahis apiece, that is, two shahis more than it would have cost the pharmacist to have them brought directly from Paris.

The good Belgians were not, however, discouraged and went on from glassmaking to gaslighting, founding a new company, *Compagnie générale pour l'éclairage et le chauffage en Perse*. Gas meters were installed in Tehran and all the requisite work was done, at a total cost of about a million. The company undertook to supply at least one thousand street lamps to the government to light up the streets of the capital, whose very white nights would finally pass (to the disgust of stray dogs) from the pallid light of the moon to the life of gas light, like London or Paris. But here too not enough thought had been given to the raw material, and its high price. However, in view of the government's obligation, they did not let themselves be discouraged and, in the manner of great industry, set up an auxiliary industry, close to the main one. They began to exploit directly the mines of Lalun. In 1893 another hundred thousand lire, approximately, was spent on preliminary work and rent, only to realize that "the nature of Persian coal," said the report read by the directors to the general assembly in Brussels on 19 June 1894, obliged them to "wait for more efficient means of purification before seeking to develop private lighting (*sic*), so that only a suitable product should be supplied to private consumption" [in French in original]. I omit from my account comments on and a description of the fuel, which was full of carbonic and sulfuric acid, which they tried to put on the good Persians. What is certain is that, when I arrived in Tehran, the company and the government were accusing each other of not having observed the terms of agreement, and while the gas works remained silent, the directors galloped by day and played cards in the European Club at night while, outside, the streets of the white capital were placidly illuminated by the classical and silent moonlight.

But the last, and most solemn, Belgian

experiment was the *sucrerie*, which I dedicate to the new makers of beet sugar in Italy. Baron D'Erp wrote reports which were in the nature of apologias: he was at the height of his Persophile autosuggestion. At current prices, sugar represented another gold mine. A *Comité des études industrielles en Perse* (it is clear that Persian title-mania is fatal also for Europeans who are more practical and calculating) was set up in Brussels, rue d'Arenberg. In 1891 it obtained a monopoly of sugarmaking, assuring H. M. the Shah 15 percent of net profits. Privileged shares were issued, at 500 francs a share, and a promise was made that work would begin in the winter of 1893, but installation of the factory was delayed until 1895. Meanwhile, Messrs. Pellet, Krechel, and Raeymaeckers arrived in Tehran, charged with studying, summarizing, and referring. It is hardly necessary to add that no miracles resulted, but only words. In volume 81, pages 53 ff. of the *Collection of Belgian Consular Reports*, a complete and accurate analysis of the enterprise is published, in which what remained to be done, and what could be expected in the way of returns, was shown down to the last penny. An estimate was made of domestic demand, reckoned at minimum figures. The population of Tehran was put at 250,000, and hence its consumption at at least 4,380,000 kilograms of sugar. Indeed—or so it was said—the Ziegler firm imported some five million kilograms a year into Persia, and the *Société russe pour le commerce et l'industrie* another four and half million. Hence the new factory would certainly have a steady annual demand in the capital and its surroundings, of 200,000 kilograms. In view of the nature of the demand, it was deemed necessary to make crystallized sugar, *shakar*, loaf sugar, *qand*, and sugar candy, *nabat*. The price, at 5 krans, 4.70 krans, and 4.50 krans, respectively, per kilogram, seemed to be amply remunerative. So much so, that in addition to competing with the sugar of Russia—which had already beaten India and France thanks to its transit duties and the bonus of one ruble per *poud* given to exporters—one could, with a good

output produced in the very heart of the empire, make further profits on transport costs, tariffs, and labor costs. Experiments on the spot showed that the agricultural zone around Tehran was favorable for beet cultivation. Thus M. Bouvin, a Belgian agronomist who had been brought over, stated in writing, after a few experiments, that the physical nature of the soil promised a beet crop "surpassing in weight and sugar content the finest crops of the European beetroot region"! [in French in original].

Plans were made for a yield of 45,000 to 75,000 kilograms of beet per hectare (!), at an average cost of 18 lire per ton. And the bold assurance with which the experts spoke was such that, in Tehran, perhaps only Captain Picot, the military attaché at the British Legation, did not venture to delude himself regarding the future of the *sucrerie*; in his report to the minister, Greene, he predicted its outcome for reasons which, today, are still quite valid.

All that remained for these gentlemen was to put up the factory, install the machinery, and start work. At the same time this company had acquired in the vast plain of Varamin, near Shah Abd al-Azim—where good means of transport and communications already existed—an estate which was well suited by the silicone-clay nature of its soil to serve as an excellent model farm and to supply the raw material required for starting production. But a new difficulty arose—the coal needed for the machinery was very expensive, because it had to be brought from the Lar sediments, in the Elburz chain, between Tehran and Qazvin; it cost 18 krans per kharvar, or 39 lire a ton. But, wrote Baron D'Erp, "The question of coal does not raise any difficulties" [in French in original]. The *sucrerie* joined another Belgian company, that of gas and railways, in an attempt to exploit together the above-mentioned Lalun mines.

But when Badhim married Badher they produced Badtheirs! For a new difficulty soon cropped up. When the juice was treated for removal of impurities—to eliminate the acid which prevented crystallization and spoiled the sugar—it was noticed that the juice itself warmed up rapidly at a temperature of 60°C. and it was realized that what was needed was to add about 50 grams of lime for every hectolitre of juice. And where in Persia can one find such lime, which has to be of good quality if it is to react quickly when put in contact with ammonia salts? Holy providence of Allah, help!

Stone from Bibi Shah-Banu was analyzed and, fortunately, turned out to consist, according to the reports sent to Brussels by the local experts, of excellent lime. But another question, neglected till then, arose and seemed very serious: who was to supply the raw material, the beet? Was there a sufficient rural population? Never fear, replied Baron d'Erp. When it will be known that there is a demand for working hands, the hands will appear; for their scarcity is only apparent, and "because the workers' remuneration is not sufficient" [in French in original]. He himself had seen, during his stay in Persia, whole populations migrate in mass, in the spring, in search of work—as at Nihavand, between Tehran and Kermanshah. But where are the landowners who are ready to introduce this new crop in their fields, and who can teach the laborers how to grow beets? To make a long story short, everything had been studied, everything had been provided for, but one thing—a trifle which yet had a certain importance—had been forgotten: to ensure that the area under cultivation would be sufficient to provide the required raw material. It is as though someone had set the table, and analyzed the state of the stomach and the kind and quality of the dishes to be cooked and eaten, and then, at the lunch hour, had forgotten to provide the necessary food. Ditto for the establishment which had been built, and which after all these studies remained without beets, except for the small amount in Varamin, which was incapable of supplying juice for the hoped-for 200,000 kilograms of sugar per annum. Besides, the only buyers of beets were the Belgians; and

as they wanted to set conditions and impose prices on sharecroppers, the latter preferred to revert to their grains, to barley, and run the risks of the free market—the more so as the owners made it clear that they would have nothing to do with new crops, still less to use their money to effect the desired shift. Moreover, in fact it turned out that the natives do not know how to grow beets, sometimes watering them too much, sometimes too little, and so on. Thus the *sucrerie* remains with an empty belly, the sweet champion of European enterprise in Persia . . .

## Selection 11. Modern Factories, 1850–1914

[Muhammad Ali Jamalzadeh, *Ganj-i Shaigan* (Berlin, A.H. 1335) pp. 93–96]

ENTERPRISES

In the last half century, several factories of various kinds have been established in Iran, by both Iranians and foreigners, and in addition several commercial enterprises have been founded. But, because of lack of experience and perseverance, and especially because of competition from and other difficulties created by our two inauspicious neighbors [Russia and Britain], the anticipated results have not been achieved. The following is a list of some of these enterprises.

A. FACTORIES

1. Spinning mill in 1275 (1858/59). This was built close to the Qajar palace, near Tehran. A steam engine and the other necessary equipment was bought in Moscow, at a cost of 95,000 tumans, through Mahmud Khan Nasir al-Mulk. After working for some time it ceased operations and the buildings were used first as a storehouse for ammunition and then as a government unit. The steam engine and other machinery were sold, through Mirza Alinaqi Khan Hakim al-Mamalik, for 10,000 tumans.

2. Rifle factory in Tehran in 1267 (1850/51). This factory produces 1,000 rifles a month.

3. Paper factory in Tehran [see 6:2].

4. Sugar factory in Mazandaran.

5. Calico weaving factory in the neighborhood of Tehran.

6. A glass factory was set up in Tehran, around the year 1285 (1868/69) and under the management of M. Villange (?) produced high quality glass but later had to close down for lack of the necessary materials. In 1305 (1887/88) Haj Muhammad Hasan Amin al-Zarb, opened another factory. In 1309 (1891/92) the *Société anonyme belge des verreries nationales en Perse* built another factory, which also had to close down [see 6:10].

7. A porcelain factory belonging to Haj Muhammad Hasan Amin al-Zarb in Tehran, and another belonging to Hajji Abbasali and Hajji Riza in Tabriz, which had to close down because of Russian intrigues and cost the above mentioned close to 130,000 tumans in losses.

8. A candle-making factory in Tehran [see 6:2].

9. Paper making—in Isfahan and Tehran.

10. Arsenals in Tehran and Isfahan.

11. Factory for weaving linen in Isfahan, which the troops of Masudi Zill al-Sultan use to make uniforms.

12. Silk reeling factory in Gilan, belonging to Haj Muhammad Hasan Amin al-Zarb. This factory was completely equipped with machinery from Lyons, in France, and sent by the Berthaud firm to Iran.

13. Silk reeling factory in Birikadeh, near Rasht, was founded with Russian capital with the instrumentality of Muhammad Muhsin Rashti, but because of political considerations and poor management ceased working some time later.

14. Gunpowder factory, driven by a European steam engine, belonging to the state.

15. Percussion cap factory, which was set up in 1278 (1861/62).

16. Gasworks which were established in 1297 in Tehran at a cost of £30,000 and under the direction of Hajji Mirza Husain Qazvini Sipahsalar. Because of the lack of coal, operations stopped and a few years later the installations were bought by an Iranian and in 1309 (1891/92) resold to *Compagnie générale belge pour éclairage et chauffage en Perse*. But although this company brought in more machinery, no progress was made and the works were closed down.

17. A third Belgian company, *Société anonyme belge pour la fabrication du sucre en Perse*, established itself, with a large capital, in Iran and in the winter of 1313 (1895/96) began to process beets. But high costs of raw materials and unexpected expenses forced it to suspend operations in 1317 (1899/1900). This factory is located at Kahrizek, southwest of Tehran.

18. A match factory was set up in 1308 (1890/91) in Kharrazin, near Tehran, with an initial capital of £20,000, under the auspices of a Russian company. However it could not meet Austrian and Swedish competition and closed down.

19. A spinning mill was established in 1312 (1894/95) by the late Murtada Quli Khan Sani al-Dawlah. It used very inexpensive machinery and at first produced high quality goods but could not compete with cheaper foreign goods and closed down.

20. A spinning mill in Tabriz. This was built, around 1326 (1908/9), by Haj Rahim Aqai Qazvini, the son of Hajji Fathali and is still operating.

21. Two cotton ginning plants, belonging to Hajji Mirza Alimuhammad Isfahani, in Sabzevar, and to Posnansky, in Nishapur, respectively.

22. An electric power plant in Tehran, belonging to Haj Husain Aqai Amin al-Zarb. This plant is still operating and is used for lighting the main streets and shops of Tehran. It was bought, around 1322 (1904/5) in Germany, brought over to Iran by *Allgemeine Elektrizitäts-Gesellschaft* and started working in 1325 (1907/8); it can light up to 4,000 lamps.

23. Another small electric plant in Tehran, in Ark street, used for lighting government buildings.

24. An electric power plant in Mashad. This was brought from Russia in 1320 (1902/3), at a cost of 8,000 tumans, by the

late Hajji Muhammad Baqir Milani, known as Rizaiov, on behalf of Muzaffar al-Din Shah. It was used to illuminate the shrine of Hazrat-i Riza and in addition lights up part of the street known as Bala, which lies between the plant and the shrine.

25. Electric power plants in Rasht and Tabriz. The Tabriz plant was brought over by Qasim Amir-i Tuman, the son of Ali Khan Vali, and has a capacity of 125 horse-power.

26. A brick-making plant, near Tehran, belonging to Haj Husain Aqai Amin al-Zarb, and no longer operating.

27. A calico-weaving plant near Tehran, dating from the time of Nasir al-Din Shah.

28. A brick-making plant in Urumiya; this was fitted with a steam mill in 1332 (1913/14), installed by Germans.

29. A toilet-soap-making plant in Tehran, the concession for which was given, on 14 Dh'l Qada 1328 (1910), to Rabi Zadeh and Partners, and which produces excellent soap.

30. A brewery in Tehran, around the years mentioned above.

In addition to the above, between the beginning of the twelfth century A.H. and now, several other factories were installed in Iran. Thus, around the middle of that century, Nadir Shah set up, near Amul, an iron foundry, which produced cannonballs and shells and horseshoes and attempted to make ships' anchors. After Nadir, Abbas Mirza Naib al-Saltaneh, in the first half of the thirteenth century, when he was governor of Azerbaijan, attempted to introduce a new military system in Iran. When he received 4,000 rifles from the British he decided to bring two craftsmen skilled in gun making to Iran to work in the main arsenal and produce rifles. At one time 20,000 rifles were made by Iranian craftsmen. . . .

# 7

## *Petroleum*

The development of the Iranian oil industry can be understood only in its Middle Eastern context, which in turn must be set against the growth and rivalries of the international oil industry.

Although oil seepages have been known in the Middle East for thousands of years and have been put to a variety of uses (see 7:3), and although small amounts of oil were extracted in Rumania and Galicia in the first half of the nineteenth century, the modern petroleum age is usually regarded as having begun with Colonel Drake's drilling in Pennsylvania in 1859. Thereafter progress was swift, and world output rose from one million tons in 1872 to 10 million in 1890 and passed the 100 million mark in 1921 and the 1,000 million mark in 1960.

At first petroleum was valued mainly for the kerosine it yielded; indeed for some time the other products distilled by refineries together with kerosine were simply thrown away. But the invention of the internal combustion engine in the 1860s, and the development of the automobile industry toward the end of the century, rendered another product, gasoline, increasingly valuable. However, until the First World War, kerosine was by far the most important oil product moving in international trade. And as early as the 1860s over half the kerosine produced in the United States was exported.

By 1880 the Standard Oil Trust had acquired a dominant position in both the United States and the world market. But its position came under increasing challenge, especially from the rapidly developing Russian industry based on the oil fields of Baku. Thanks to its proximity to the main markets of Europe and Asia and its consequent low costs of transport, Russian oil was able to compete very successfully with American, and at the turn of the century Russia replaced the United States, for a few years, as the world's leading producer.

Another center of competition emerged in Indonesia, based on the oil fields of Sumatra and the outstanding ability of Henri Deterding, who grouped together Standard's main rivals and in 1907 founded the Royal Dutch-Shell. This company, formed with Dutch and British capital, was able for twenty years to fight success-fully against the Standard Trust and, after the dissolution of the latter in 1911, against its main successors, notably Standard Oil Co. (New Jersey).

Still another, and at first very minor, competitor was Burmah Oil Company, which enjoyed a tariff preference in the then important Indian market and soon came to an agreement with Shell. Thanks to its investment in D'Arcy's company in 1905 (see 7:1) Burmah Oil became one of the founders of Anglo-Persian Oil Company.[1]

The Middle East had a twofold attraction for these rival groups: as a market and as a potential producing area, indicated by the oil seepages of Mesopotamia, Iran, and other places. As regards the first, nowhere was Russian oil more favor-ably placed, with respect to transport costs, than in northern and central Iran—being close to Baku and protected by the rugged terrain and lack of modern transport against any rival oil coming through the Persian Gulf. Although the ambitious project for a pipeline carrying kerosine from Baku to the Persian Gulf did not materialize (see 7:3), Russian oil steadily pushed further south in the Persian market. In his report on the trade of Isfahan in 1894/95 (A and P 1896, 88) the British consul stated: "Kerosene oil is imported entirely from Baku, via Resht and Kasvin. It sells here at $5\frac{1}{4}$ kran per 3 lbs. weight, or $1\frac{1}{4}$ gallons at 2 s. $2\frac{1}{2}$ d. Leakage is generally made good by filling up the tins with the crude stuff from Shustar; hence the oil here is not very good." At the same time the consul in Yazd reported: "Certain articles, such as petroleum and iron, naturally come from Russia" ("Yazd," 1894/95, ibid.).

A few years later the consul in Khurasan reported; "The import of Russian Kerosene into Persia is on the increase; it is said to be carried as far south as Kirman. Kafilas [caravans] returning to Bandar Abbas are often in want of a return load, and kerosene has been found to conveniently supply this want" ("Khurasan" 1899/1900, A and P 1900, 95). And in his report on Isfahan in 1910/11 (A and P 1911, 94) the British consul stated: "The whole of the import [of oil] is Russian. The trade is in the hands of Persian merchants and of the Russian 'Nobel Company,' which established an agency in Ispahan in December 1909, about one-half of the import being now in the hands of the latter."[2]

It was only in the Persian Gulf area that Russian oil met any serious competition—from oil brought directly by sea. In his report on Bushire in 1907/08 (A and P 1909, 97) the British consul referred to competition from American oil "and also a Hungarian brand, which was introduced to the market for the first time. This

[1] For details see Ralph W. Hidy, *History of Standard Oil Company (New Jersey)*, 2 vols. (New York, 1955–56); Carel Gerretson, *History of The Royal Dutch*, 4 vols. (Leiden, 1953–57); Federal Trade Commission, *The International Petroleum Cartel* (Washington, 1952); and Edith T. Penrose, *The Large International Firm in Developing Countries* (London, 1968).

[2] Nobel Brothers started operations in Iran, in 1908, by renting storage tanks (*sklady*) in Rasht. Soon after, they built two large storage tanks, in Enzeli and Rasht, with a 16 kilometer kerosine pipeline. Other Russian subjects had large storage tanks in Persian Astara, as well as a workshop in which they made boxes and drums for oil out of metal imported from Russia—See Abdullaev, pp. 141–42, citing Russian archives.

competition has lowered prices considerably." And in the report on Kirman in 1910/11 (A and P 1911, 94) it is stated:

The number of cases of American kerosene oil imported has fallen from 1,000 cases in 1909–10 to 600 cases in 1910–11, while the importation of Russian oil has increased from 5,000 to 7,000 drums. Russian oil is inferior to American, but the enormous reduction in its price threatens almost to drive the superior product out of the market . . . freights are important and the improvement of communications between Kerman and the coast would do much to enable American oil to compete on more even terms with Russian oil.

However, even in the gulf area, American oil was soon faced by still stronger competition. "Since last year the oil and other products of the Anglo–Persian Oil Company have been placed upon the market. . . . The Gulf market seems to be supplied almost entirely by the local article; the Standard Oil Co. sent a ship-load of 175,200 cases to the gulf at the close of the year under report, but they do not appear to have disposed of their stocks, the only place where any quantities were sold being Baghdad, where unexpired contracts remained" ("Arabistan," 1912/13, A and P 1914, 93). APOC products gradually spread northward, but it took them another twenty years to drive Russian oil out of the Persian market. However, well before it had completely taken over the Iranian market, Persian oil had begun to flow in significant amounts to neighboring markets, notably India and the Middle East.

As regards production, the Middle East began to attract international attention rather early—around 1870—but no oil was actually produced until shortly before the First World War. Interest was shown mainly by British firms, and until the 1930s all the oil produced in the region was exclusively British-owned. Serious United States attempts to enter the Middle East date from the 1920s, and it was only in the 1950s that American interests became predominant in Middle Eastern oil.

In Egypt, a concessionaire struck oil at Gemsa, at the mouth of the Gulf of Suez, in 1869, and his unsuccessful attempts to develop the field were followed, in 1885, by those of the government. After 1904, various British interests took over the search and, after oil had been discovered in commercial quantities in 1909, the Shell group organized production, through Anglo-Egyptian Oil-fields.

In Iraq a German mission reported favorably on prospects in 1881, and the reforming governor, Midhat Pasha, made some efforts to develop the seepages at Mandali and even built a small refinery at Baquba, which, however, soon closed down. This drew the attention of the sultan to the oil seepages and led to attempts at developing them and to the amendment of the Mining Law so as to encourage exploration. Several concessions were granted to Ottoman subjects and to foreign firms. Among the latter, Standard Oil Company of New York prospected in northern Anatolia and Palestine and some British companies prospected in Syria and Anatolia. But the most important concession was the one given, in 1888, to the Ottoman Railway Company of Anatolia, controlled by the Deutsche Bank. This covered Iraq, an area which soon attracted various British groups, including Shell and D'Arcy, and some American firms. In 1911–12 the German and British interests coalesced to form the Turkish Petroleum Company, which Anglo-Persian Oil Company joined in 1914. But the outbreak of war interrupted further progress and the shift in power resulting from it led to intensive diplomatic activity regarding the ownership and scope of TPC, with first France and then the United States insisting on a share. It was not till 1925 that the matter was settled, with 23.75 percent ownership to each of: Shell, APOC, Compagnie Française des Pétroles, and a group representing various American companies; the remaining 5 percent were held by Calouste Gulbenkian. Oil was struck in 1927 and, with the completion of pipelines to the Mediterranean in 1934, began to flow in large quantities.

No attempt was made before the First World War to secure a petroleum concession in any part of the Arabian peninsula. But in 1910 seepages of oil were discovered in Bahrain. And the presence of oil in Kuwait was suspected at about the same time. Thus a map attached to a Foreign Office memorandum of 21 July 1914 on Anglo-Russian Relations in Persia indicated "reported oil shows" in two spots in Kuwait, as well as in various parts of Iran.[3] And a "Memorandum on Recent British Enterprises in the Persian Gulf and Others Impending or Suggested," written in May 1914, suggested experimental boring for oil in Kuwait as well as Qishm.[4] Such considerations explain the undertakings given by the Shaikh of Kuwait in 1913, and the Shaikh of Bahrain in 1914, not to grant an oil concession to any party without the consent of the British government. They also explain the fact that when the interests that formed the Turkish Petroleum Company agreed, in 1914, to refrain from seeking concessions in any part of the Ottoman Empire, except as a group, Kuwait was specifically excluded from the provisions of the agreement. Except for a small production from Bahrain starting in 1933, the development of Arabian oil dates from the 1940s.[5]

But the most important developments were those in Iran; indeed, until the 1950s Iran remained by far the largest producer of oil in the Middle East. Here, too, interest began early, with the first Reuter concession of 1872 and the revised concession of 1889 (see 4:7). The subsequent history of Iranian oil is related in this chapter, and in the epilogue. Selections 1 and 2 were written by a British orientalist and an Iranian economist, both with long experience in the Persian oil industry.

By 1914 the position of Anglo-Persian Oil Company was secure. Large quantities of oil had been discovered and output was running at over a quarter of a

---

[3] FO 371/2076.
[4] FO 371/2075.
[5] For fuller details on the history of oil concessions in the Middle East, see the books by Longrigg, Shwadran, and Issawi and Yeganeh, listed in the bibliography.

million tons a year. Net profits for the financial year 1913/14 were about £60,000.[6] As pointed out, APOC had already acquired a substantial share in TPC. And in the summer of 1914 the company's position was greatly strengthened, as regards both availability of capital and market outlets, by the British government's acquisition of a 51 percent interest through subscription of £2,200,000 to its share capital. This transaction has recently formed the subject of a thorough study by Dr. Marian Jack,[7] whose conclusion is that:

The new evidence shows in fact that arguments of strategy or prestige were put forward by the Company and accepted by the Foreign Office, but were not accepted by the India Office, whom they more closely affected, and were accepted only later by the Admiralty and then as a rationalization for a change of policy made on other grounds.

These grounds were the rebates on oil delivered to the admiralty which were specified in the agreement and which, after the war, made APOC oil very much cheaper than that from any other source.[8]

When this deal was announced, Sir Edward Grey gave the Russian ambassador "my own idea on the matter. We were not contemplating any steps in the neutral zone different from anything that we had done so far. We were certainly not going to develop at present oil wells north of the one already in use." If, as seemed morally certain, all the required oil was found in the south, "I felt it would be to our interest at any rate to lease the part of the concession in the north to some other company, which might be an Anglo-Russian company," since this would bring in income and reduce the "risk of having to send troops into the interior of Persia."[9] The war and its aftermath put an end to this possibility.

The D'Arcy concession excluded the five northern provinces of Iran, which lay within the Russian sphere of influence. No attempt was made to secure a concession until 1916, when one was granted to a Russian subject, A. M. Khoshtaria. This agreement was later regarded as invalid by both the Persian and the Soviet governments but in 1920 APOC bought Khoshtaria's rights, for £100,000, and organized a subsidiary, North Persia Oil Company, with an authorized capital of £3,000,000. But this attempt by APOC to extend its activities, a bid for a concession by Standard Oil (New Jersey), a project for joint operations by both these companies, and a more sustained effort by Sinclair Consolidated Oil Corporation, were rendered fruitless by the opposition of the Soviet government, the unavoidability of shipping northern oil through the Soviet Union, and the insistence of the Iranian government on a large loan to be floated by the concessionaire. A similar fate awaited the concession granted to Amiranian Oil Company in 1937 and the bids for concessions by Socony and Sinclair in 1944.

---

[6] A letter from APOC to the Foreign Office, dated 11 December 1914, stated that the royalties due to the Persian government for the year ending 31 March 1914 were: £6,554 on behalf of the First Exploration Co. and £3,350 on behalf of the Bakhtiari Oil Co. The Foreign Office estimated net profits at about £60,000, presumably on the basis that the above sums represented 16 percent of net profits. FO 371/2079.

[7] *Past and Present*, October 1968.

[8] See figures in ibid., p. 166.

[9] Grey to Buchanan, 22 July 1914, FO 371/2077.

And the agreement signed in 1946 for establishing a joint Soviet-Iranian company was not ratified by the Majlis, which was opposed to further concessions to foreigners and was preparing to act against Anglo-Iranian Oil Company in the south. Iran's northern oil still awaits development.

For further details, see the books mentioned above and those by Elwell-Sutton, Fateh, Lisani, and Fatemi, listed in the bibliography.

### Selection 1. The Emergence of the Anglo-Persian Oil Company, 1901–14
[Laurence Lockhart]

Although Persian petroleum was well known and, in a very primitive way, exploited in ancient and medieval times, it was not until a competent geologist named W. K. Loftus visited southwest Persia a little over a century ago that anything approaching a modern assessment of its possibilities was made.[1] Little or no interest, however, was aroused in the matter until Baron Julius de Reuter (the founder of Reuter's News Agency) obtained from the Persian government, in 1872, a concession giving him the exclusive right to prospect for and to exploit certain minerals, including petroleum, as well as various other privileges. The Russian government, alarmed at the potentialities of such a wide-ranging concession, exerted such strong pressure on the Persian government that it had to cancel this concession [see 4:7]. Some twelve years later, a partner in the firm of Hotz and Company of Bushire, obtained a concession of limited extent to exploit the area of Daliki, forty miles northeast of Bushire, where there were extensive seepages. A shallow well was sunk, but no oil was found.

The next development of any importance was Baron de Reuter's second concession which was granted in 1889, which was for a term of sixty years, gave him certain exclusive mineral rights including the authority to search for and exploit petroleum and other minerals, as well as permission to

found a bank. In this bank were to be vested the aforesaid mineral rights. In this manner the Imperial Bank of Persia came into being.[2]

As it was, however, provided in the concession that the bank was not itself to exercise its mineral rights, de Reuter and his associates formed the Persian Bank Mining Rights Corporation which was to acquire these rights from it and then take steps to exploit them. During the next three years the corporation carried out prospecting work in a number of areas. It had taken over the small Hotz concession at Daliki, where it drilled two wells, but the results were abortive. It also drilled a well some seven-hundred feet deep on Qishm island, but here again no oil was found. The corporation's operations had been carried out in an inefficient and extravagant manner, with nothing tangible to show for its efforts, and early in 1894 it went into voluntary liquidation.

In the meantime, in February 1892, a French geologist and archeologist named Jacques de Morgan, after visiting the oil seepages at Kend-i-Shirin in western Persia, published his conclusions in a Paris periodical.[3]

De Morgan regarded the petroleum indications in this region as of great importance. Being anxious to turn his discoveries to useful account, he enlisted the aid of a M. Cotte, who had been Baron de Reuter's secretary, and General Kitabgi, a Persian of Caucasian extraction, who had been largely instrumental in obtaining the second

---

[1] Loftus's article, which was entitled "On the Geology of portions of the Turco-Persian Frontier and of the Districts adjoining" was published in the *Quarterly Journal of the Geological Society* 11 (part 3): 247–344. Among the areas described was that of Masjid-i-Sulaiman, in the Bakhtiari country in southwestern Persia.

[2] In 1948, when this bank's charter expired, its name was changed to the British Bank of the Middle East. Four years later, the intransigent Musaddiq regime forced the bank to withdraw from Persia.

[3] "Notes sur les Gites de Naphte de Kend-e-Chirin (Gouvernement de Ser-i-Pol)," *Annales des Mines* (February 1892), pp. 1–16.

de Reuter concession. It so happened that de Morgan, Cotte, and Kitabgi were all acquainted with Sir Henry Drummond Wolf who had not long before been British minister at Tehran. Cotte and Kitabgi went to see Sir Henry Drummond Wolf in Paris and explained the matter to him.

Sir Henry, it turned out, was acquainted with a Mr. W. K. D'Arcy, a Devon man who had recently returned to England from Australia with a large fortune that he had made in the Mount Morgan gold mines in Queensland. As D'Arcy was, in fact, looking for some promising venture in which to invest some of his money, he became very interested. The consequence was that in March 1901 D'Arcy sent his secretary, Mr. A. L. Marriott, together with General Kitabgi and Cotte, to Tehran to negotiate for the concession.

Immediately on reaching Tehran, D'Arcy's representatives began their negotiations with the Persian government. These negotiations, which seemed to be going smoothly at first, entered a difficult phase when the Russian minister at Tehran lodged most vehement protests. Foreseeing that Russian opposition would certainly prove serious, D'Arcy had at the very outset decided to exclude the five northern provinces from the concession area. The exclusion of this large area from the proposed concession did not however, allay Russia's objections. Several times it seemed that her opposition would render the negotiations nugatory. However, in the end the shah was induced to sign the D'Arcy Concession on 28 May 1901.[4] Under the terms of this concession, the holder was to have for sixty years the right to find, exploit, and export petroleum. The area covered was 480,000 square miles (out of a total of 628,000). There were exclusive rights to build pipelines. The royalty payable to the Persian government was to be 16 percent of the net profits. The concessionaire was to form within two years a company to carry out the work of the concession; the concession was to be rendered void if this company was not formed within this period (it is important to note that this was the sole provision for cancellation in the concession). When this company was formed, the concessionaire was to give the Persian government 20,000 fully paid-up shares of £1 each in it as well as £20,000 in cash.

While the negotiations for the concession were in progress in Tehran, H. T. Burls, a geologist employed by D'Arcy, was examining oil indications in the Zuhab district in western Persia and also the extensive seepages at Naft-i-Safid and elsewhere some three hundred miles southeast.[5]

Acting on the advice of Sir Boverton Redwood, the eminent geologist, D'Arcy decided to test the northern of these two areas first, at a place called Chiah Surkh, situated nine and one-half miles out of the town of Qasr-i-Shirin, and at that time seven miles east of the Mesopotamian frontier.[6] All the plant required for the drilling operations had to be sent by sea from England to Basra and thence overland through what was then Turkish territory to the Persian frontier near Qasri-i-Shirin and thence to Chiah Surkh. Much delay occurred through transport difficulties and the dilatory ways of the frontier officials. The man whom D'Arcy chose to be in charge of the drilling operations was G. B.

---

[4] Sir Arthur Hardinge, in his book *A Diplomatist in the East* (London, 1928), pp. 278, 279, alleged that the grand vizier sent to the Russian embassy a description of the D'Arcy concession written in the difficult *shikasteh* script at a time when he knew that the oriental secretary, the only person in the embassy who could read this script, was away on leave. The result was that this description lay unread in the Russian legation until after the concession had been signed. Mr. Marriott, when questioned subsequently regarding this story, said that there was no foundation whatever for it.

[5] Naft-i-Safid ("white oil") was so called because the oil from the seepages there had, before coming to the surface, to pass through a natural filter-bed, thus making it suitable for burning in lamps without having to undergo any refining process. For many centuries the local inhabitants had exploited this oil, which was much in demand throughout Persia.

[6] Chiah Surkh is situated in one of the two areas which Persia subsequently transferred to Turkey in consequence of the findings of the Turco-Persian Frontier Commission of 1913–14. The Turkish government and, subsequently, its successor, the government of Iraq, recognized the D'Arcy concessionary rights over these two areas. See Longrigg, p. 66.

Reynolds. He proved to be not only a good engineer and organizer, but also an excellent liaison official with the local tribal chiefs.

The first well at Chiah Surkh was "spudded-in" during November 1902. Operations during the following summer proved to be particularly trying, owing to the great heat (the temperature rose to 120°F. and over even in the shade). Conditions of life under canvas in such conditions (there were as yet no permanent buildings) were almost intolerable. There were several cases of sunstroke, but fortunately none proved fatal. There was also much illness caused by the bad water; it was so impregnated with salt that the tubes of the boiler of the drilling plant became corroded. Moreover, the state of the water became even worse when myriads of locusts fell into the pools in the river and were drowned.

Nevertheless, despite these severe hardships and difficulties, the drilling went on, and some oil was struck in the late autumn of 1903. Soon afterward, there was an encouraging oil show in the second well, which had been started only a short while before. Unfortunately, the elation caused by these two strikes of oil was of short duration, since the flow in both wells soon dwindled to little more than a trickle. It then became obvious that this meager yield of oil was quite insufficient to justify the high cost of a pipeline some three hundred miles in length through difficult country to the head of the Persian Gulf. Moreover, D'Arcy was already finding that the cost of the enterprise was getting beyond his means. If drilling operations were to be transferred to southwest Persia, he would have to find some associates with the will and the means to continue with the enterprise.

Although D'Arcy had the friendship and support of Admiral Sir John (later Lord) Fisher and of Mr. E. G. Pretyman, the civil lord of the admiralty,[7] he had great difficulty in finding the financial aid that he needed. Eventually, however, after meeting with a number of rebuffs and disappointments, D'Arcy was, through the good offices of the admiralty Petroleum Standing Committee, put in touch with the Burmah Oil Company, with which, in May 1905, he signed an agreement. This agreement provided, inter alia, that the Concessions Syndicate, which the Burmah Oil Company and Lord Strathcona and Mountroyal had formed a few days earlier, should repay D'Arcy all that he had spent on the concession up to that time and that it would, within certain limits, bear the cost of the endeavors to prove the existence of oil in commercial quantities in southwest Persia. Should this quest meet with success, a major company would then be formed which, after taking over the concession and all its rights from D'Arcy and the Concessions Syndicate, would exploit the oil in conformity with the terms of the concession.

Meanwhile, all operations at Chiah Surkh had ceased by the end of June 1904.

Reynolds, before going on leave to England in 1903, had visited a number of areas in southwest Persia where there were oil indications. He was particularly struck with the potentialities at a place called Maidan-i-Naftun,[8] in the rugged Bakhtiari tribal country 60 miles northeast of Ahwaz and 130 miles north of the head of the Persian Gulf. In this area is a ruined building known as the Masjid-i Sulaiman ("Solomon's Mosque").[9]

---

*Argyll* were designed to burn coal and oil, while the Tribal class destroyers, which were then being laid down, were to burn oil exclusively. Fisher's zeal on behalf of oil fuel earned him the nick-name of "The Oil Maniac." He maintained that if one Dreadnought type of ship were entirely oil-fired and another ship of the same class were to burn oil and coal, the former would be three knots faster, and he concluded "speed is everything." See his *Records*, (London, 1919) p. 194.

[8] "Maidan-i Naftun" means "the field (or place) of oil."

[9] It was for long thought that this building had been a Zoroastrian firetemple, but Professor Ghirshman, the eminent French archeologist, considers that it had probably served as a gathering point for the local inhabitants in the distant past. There is a similar building

---

[7] It is noteworthy that at this time the British navy was in process of converting its ships from coal to oil. Already, in 1903, the battleships *Hannibal* and *Mars* had been fitted to burn oil, but only as an adjunct to coal. In 1905 the battleship *Prince George* and the cruiser

Notwithstanding Reynolds's preference for Masjid-i Sulaiman (as Maidan-i Naftun soon came to be known) and the fact that Sir Boverton Redwood also thought well of it, the syndicate's geologists decided that a site at Mamatain, sixty miles to the east of Ahwaz, offered better prospects of success.

The drilling plant and all other supplies for Mamatain had to be sent by sea to Mohammerah, at the confluence of the Karun river with the Shatt al-Arab, and thence up the Karun to the rapids at Ahwaz. There everything was unloaded and taken across very difficult country to Mamatain; the journey took about ten days. Reynolds had previously had to make arrangements with the Bakhtiari khans not only for the right to drill in their country, but also for the guarding of the syndicate's personnel and plant. Under the terms of the D'Arcy Concession no such arrangements should have been necessary, since it was the duty of the Persian government to allow operations to take place anywhere in the area of the concession and to provide for the protection of the concessionaire's personnel anywhere within that area. However, under the weak Qajar régime, Reynolds had to make such arrangements with the Bakhtiari khans; he had had to take similar action at Chiah Surkh.

The Concessions Syndicate drilled two wells at Mamatain, but progress was very slow owing to the hardness of the strata and also to the inefficiency and occasional bad behavior of the Bakhtiari guards. As time went on Reynolds became very pessimistic regarding the prospects of success at Mamatain because he considered the strata overlying the hoped-for oil-bearing

limestone to be very thick. The syndicate, however, did not agree with Reynolds, but they later sent a well-known geologist named Cunningham Craig to Persia to confer with him. Cunningham Craig, on visiting Masjid-i Sulaiman, upheld Reynolds's views as to the good prospects there as compared with those at Mamatain. The syndicate thereupon decided to cease all operations at Mamatain and to test Masjid-i Sulaiman instead. By this time, however, the syndicate's funds were becoming alarmingly low, and it seemed very doubtful whether they would suffice to enable the new area to be properly tested. The operations at Masjid-i Sulaiman were indeed to be the final effort.

The first well was "spudded-in" at Masjid-i Sulaiman in January 1908, and the second well there a little later. On 26 May, when the syndicate's funds were on the point of exhaustion (indeed, according to some accounts orders to shut down were already in transit from England), a copious flow of oil occurred at the first well, at a depth of 1,180 feet. Ten days later, another copious flow of oil occurred at the second well. When other wells in the vicinity also proved successful, it became clear that a major oil field at last had been discovered.

This extremely fortunate discovery solved, as Longrigg has stated,[10] the immediate financial problems of D'Arcy and the Concessions Syndicate and led to the formation of the Anglo-Persian Oil Company on 14 April 1909. Just before the company came into being, the admiralty was shown a copy of the prospectus. It then proceeded to make some changes in the wording relating to the possible conclusion of contracts for the supply of oil fuel for the British navy. Moreover, it was on the advice of Mr. McKenna, the then first lord of the admiralty, that Lord Strathcona and Mountroyal, who was aged eighty-nine, agreed to become chairman of the APOC. D'Arcy was given a seat on the board which he retained until his death in 1917. Other

---

at Bard-i Nishan Deh, a few miles away. Another misconception regarding the building at Masjid-i Sulaiman was that the Zoroastrian priests had used oil or gas emanating from the gound there as their "eternal fire." Geologists, however, maintain that there have never been such seepages at that place. This erroneous idea was, no doubt engendered by the fact that there was, until late in the nineteenth century, a temple with such fires in the midst of the Baku oilfields. See Colonel C. E. Stewart, "Account of the Hindu Fire Temple at Baku" in the *Journal of the Royal Asiatic Society,* 1897, pp. 311, 312.

[10] Longrigg, p. 19.

directorships were given to members of the Burmah Oil Company. The APOC had an initial capital of £2,000,000.

On the formation of the new company, the Concessions Syndicate was wound up and all responsibility for the exploitation of the concession was assumed by the APOC.

As the APOC was the sole company entitled to operate at Masjid-i Sulaiman, it was able to carry out what has become known as "unit development," that is to say, there was a complete absence of competitive drilling, which had proved so wasteful in Mexico and the United States. As a well-known authority on petroleum put it, "the holdings in Persia ensured the working of a dome as a unit; and the wells could be spaced and the yields regulated to ensure a maximum of efficiency".[11] It is noteworthy that the Masjid-i Sulaanim oil field is still in production, though sixty years have now elapsed since its discovery.

In another respect, Reynolds and his men were fortunate in that the Masjid-i Sulaiman oil field is one of relatively low pressure. Had oil been struck at that time at such a field as Pazanun, with the primitive appliances then in use, the drilling rig of the discovery well would have been blown sky-high, with disastrous consequences for the driller on duty and his assistants. It would also have proved extremely difficult, if not impossible, to cap the well.

Having acquired what was evidently a major oil field, the APOC now had to provide the means to get the oil to seaboard and thence to the markets of the world. A plot of land was acquired at what was then a small place called Abadan on the Persian side of the Shatt al-Arab, some 40 miles from the mouth of that river. The construction of a pipeline to Abadan was attended with much difficulty, owing to the extremely difficult terrain for much of the way. This pipeline, which was 140 miles in length, had an initial capacity of 400,000 tons a year.[12]

Although completed in June 1911, it could not be used to anything like its full capacity until nearly a year later because of delays in the construction of the refinery and storage tanks at Abadan. It was not until after two years had elapsed that the refinery was completed and the pipeline could work to its full capacity. Along with these developments, the production of oil at Masjid-i Sulaiman was increased proportionately.

The first shipment of Persian Oil was made in August 1912, when some 2,200 tons of crude oil were sold to the Asiatic Petroleum Company and were shipped from Abadan in one of that company's tankers. This sale was made by virtue of a contract which the APOC had made with the Asiatic Petroleum Company in April 1912. The directors of the APOC, however, had had from the very outset a strong desire to come to an agreement with the admiralty for the supply of oil fuel to the British navy; this desire was indicated in the prospectus of the APOC which was issued (after being shown to, and amended by, the admiralty) early in 1909. An ardent advocate of such an association between the APOC and the admiralty was Mr. Charles Greenway,[13] who was one of the original directors of the APOC. Seldom absent from the minds of Greenway and his colleagues on the board of the APOC was the fear that they might have to acquiesce in a "takeover" by the large and formidable Royal Dutch-Shell combine. It was largely for this reason that Greenway and his fellow directors were so anxious to come to terms with the admiralty. The APOC's fears were increased when it learned that the Royal

---

[11] A. Beeby-Thompson, *Oil Pioneer* (London, 1961), p. 404.
[12] For a technical description of the construction of this pipeline, see A. C. Hartley's paper entitled "The

Anglo-Persian Oil Company's Pipeline in Persia," which he read to the Institution of Engineers and Shipbuilders in Scotland on 21 November 1933.
[13] Mr. Greenway, after spending some years in India in a firm which had close relations with the Burmah Oil Company, became associated with the Persian oil business in the latter part of 1908. He, as stated above, was one of the original members of the board of the APOC. He was a staunch imperialist in his views. After Lord Strathcona's death in 1914, Greenway became chairman of the APOC. For his services, he was made a baronet in 1919; in 1927 he was elevated to the peerage with the title of Baron Greenway of Stanbridge Earls. He died in 1934.

Dutch-Shell group was endeavoring to obtain the Mesopotamian concession from the Turkish government, a project in which first D'Arcy and later itself had for long been keenly interested.[14] The APOC feared that if the Royal Dutch-Shell group succeeded in obtaining the Mesopotamian concession, they might start a price war in the Middle East and so bring such pressure to bear on it that it would have to acquiesce in a merger.[15]

Although the Foreign Office supported the APOC, the India Office (with which the company had for long been trying to come to terms for the supply of fuel oil for the Indian Railways) was indifferent. In October 1911 Mr. Winston Churchill became first lord of the admiralty. He was at first unenthusiastic regarding the question of oil fuel for the navy as he was at that time a "Little Navy" man. Nevertheless, when he became aware of the ominous growth of the German navy and, moreover, came under the influence of Admiral Lord Fisher, the "oil maniac," his views underwent a sudden change. Instead of paying scant attention to the pleadings of Greenway and his colleagues, he adopted a more favorable attitude.

In June 1912 the Royal Commission on Oil Supply was established under the chairmanship of Lord Fisher. In the autumn of that year Greenway began negotiating actively with the admiralty; that department had by this time become irretrievably committed to the use of oil fuel instead of coal for the navy.

In November 1912 Greenway was invited to attend a meeting of the Royal Commission on Oil Supply, on which occasion Lord Fisher and his colleagues proved to be most sympathetic.

In the following January, the German government asked the APOC to give a quotation for fuel and to provide samples. On this matter being referred to the admiralty, that department replied that it had no objection to such a contract being signed so long as the offer to supply such fuel to the British navy was not withdrawn. Practically at the same time the admiralty signed a contract with the APOC for the supply of 30,000 tons of fuel oil for delivery between September 1913 and the end of June in the following year. This contract with the admiralty was not of sufficient importance to satisfy Greenway and his colleagues; what they wanted was something far more fundamental. This further requirement was a substantial advance of capital.

On 17 July 1913 Churchill made an important speech in the House of Commons when the navy estimates for 1913/14 were under discussion. Churchill said that the country's stake in oil-burning warships was such that it had become essential to obtain adequate supplies of oil fuel at a steady price; unless prompt and effective steps were taken to obtain such supplies, the admiralty would become a forced purchaser and might be grossly overcharged. He added that the navy's oil supplies should be drawn as far as possible from sources under British control or under British influence.

In the following month the admiralty decided to send a commission to Persia to examine the APOC's oil fields and installations there. This commission consisted of Rear Admiral E. J. W. Slade, Professor John Cadman,[16] Dr. E. H. Pascoe, of the

---

[14] The rival endeavors of the Royal Dutch-Shell, the Deutsche Bank, and the D'Arcy group (the APOC) to obtain the much coveted Mesopotamian concession having led to a complete stalemate, there was a fusion of interests which resulted in the so-called Foreign Office agreement of 19 March 1914. Under the terms of this agreement the D'Arcy group was given 50 percent of the interests, while the Deutsche Bank and the Anglo-Saxon (Royal Dutch-Shell) group each received 25 percent. The D'Arcy and the Anglo-Saxon groups each undertook to give Mr. C. S. Gulbenkian a $2\frac{1}{2}$ percent beneficiary nonvoting interest in the Turkish Petroleum Company. The Turkish government, on being notified of the conclusion of this agreement, promised to grant the Mesopotamian concession to the TPC on terms to be subsequently arranged. The outbreak of the First World War, however, rendered this agreement nugatory and it was not until some time after the conclusion of peace that the question was finally settled. See Longrigg, pp. 27–32, 42–46, and 68 ff.

[15] See Jack, p. 142.

[16] Professor Cadman then held the chair of mining at the University of Birmingham. He was also petroleum

Geological Survey of India, and Mr. J. C. Clarke of the admiralty.

The members of the commission reached Persia late in October 1913. They visited Abadan, Mohammerah, Masjid-i Sulaiman, Ahwaz (where drilling was then in progress), Naft-i-Safid, Qishm island, and other places in the Persian Gulf. The commission returned to England on 25 January 1914. It subsequently reported on the APOC's activities and potentialities in favorable terms, stating that the existing field (at Masjid-i-Sulaiman) was capable with proper development of supplying a large proportion of the admiralty's requirements for a considerable time, while the whole concession, if worked in a judicious manner, would probably safeguard the navy's fuel supply.

In consequence of this favorable report, rapid progress was made with the negotiations between the APOC, the admiralty, and the treasury. On 20 May 1914 the admiralty, the treasury, and the APOC signed an agreement which provided, inter alia, for:

1. The issue by the APOC of 2,000,000 additional ordinary shares of £1 each and £199,000 in debenture stock.
2. The subscription by the treasury of £2,000,000 for these additional ordinary shares, of £199,000 for debenture stock, and of £1,000 for 1000 preference shares.
3. The appointment by the government of two ex officio directors to the board of the company. These two directors had a power of veto which they, however, would only exercise if the other members of the board were proposing to take action which would be or might be harmful to the national

interest or which might endanger fulfillment of the APOC's contract with the admiralty (which was signed the same day). It is of interest that this power of veto has never been exercised.

The government's shareholding interest gave it a majority of voting rights in the company; this majority of voting rights had always been maintained until 1967.

On the same day that this agreement was made, the admiralty signed a contract with the APOC for a period of twenty years or longer if deemed necessary for 6,000,000 tons of oil fuel at a fixed price of 30/- per ton f.o.b. Abadan or any other convenient port in the Persian Gulf. There was provision for a reduction in price if the company's profits exceeded 10 percent on the ordinary shares, after all advances, payments of dividends on preference shares and interest on debenture stock had been made.[17]

The conclusion of the agreement of 20 May 1914 with the British government and the signing of the long-term contract with the admiralty on the same day put the affairs of the APOC on a firm basis at last and were largely instrumental in enabling the company to withstand the trials and tribulation that the 1914–18 war was to bring in its train.

## Selection 2. Early History of Oil Industry in Iran
[Mustafa Khan Fateh, *Panjah sal naft-i Iran* (Tehran, n.d., pp. 250–65)]

### 3. BEGINNING OF OPERATIONS AND RAISING OF CAPITAL

A few months after the signing of the concession, D'Arcy hired some Polish drillers and sent them, along with the necessary equipment, to Chiah Surkh, north of Qasr-i Shirin. At that time Chiah Surkh was part of Iran, but in 1913 it was transferred to Turkey, following a rectification of the frontier between Iran and the Otto-

---

adviser to the Colonial Office. Later, he was appointed chief technical adviser to the petroleum executive. After filling with distinction other government appointments, he was made a K.C.M.G. in 1918. Three years later, he became technical adviser to the APOC and subsequently joined the board. In 1926 he succeeded Sir Charles Greenway as chairman of the APOC. He became Baron Cadman of Silverdale in 1937. He died in 1941.

[17] For further details of the APOC's agreement with the government and the contract with the admiralty, see Jack, pp. 162–64.

man Empire which, after the First World War, became the international boundary between Iran and Iraq. The engineer whom D'Arcy chose to head operations, G. B. Reynolds, had served for many years in the Ministry of Public Works in India, and was an exceptionally persistent and persevering man. The expedition was sent to Chiah Surkh by way of Basra and Baghdad, began operations and, from the start, encountered various difficulties.

The lack of security in that part of the frontier and the numerous demands made by the tribes and communities living on both sides of the border and the threats posed by them slowed down the work, but Reynolds's constant firmness contributed greatly to the advance of operations.

In the summer of 1903, gas was struck at a depth of 507 meters, and after that a small amount of oil was found. A few months later, a second well struck oil at a similar depth; its daily output was at first thirty tons but then diminished to twenty-five. By then it was clear that, in view of the great distance between Chiah Surkh and the Persian Gulf (about 1,000 kilometers) and of the smallness of the output, the continuation of operations in that place would be unprofitable. Hence D'Arcy decided to leave Chiah Surkh and to transfer his excavation further south.

In accordance with Article 16 of the concession, D'Arcy had constituted, in 1903, a company with a capital of £600,000, the First Exploitation Company. He had delivered the shares which he had undertaken to provide, as well as £20,000 in cash, to the government of Iran. By then D'Arcy had spent nearly £300,000 out of his own pocket and was not prepared to continue disbursing such sums from his own capital; hence he decided to secure outside aid and assistance.

A number of German financiers proposed to reimburse D'Arcy for all the expenses he had incurred till then and also to pay a large sum for the concession provided he withdrew and transferred it to them. An American oil company and some French financiers also proposed buying the concession from D'Arcy, and were even prepared to take him on as a shareholder. There is some evidence that, in view of the great expenditure incurred and the failure to secure the desired results, D'Arcy was inclined to conclude such a transaction and recover his outlay, but he showed no desire to have any dealings with foreigners.

Meanwhile, an event occurred that confused the plans drawn by D'Arcy and those who sought to acquire his concession. The first lord of the admiralty, Lord Fisher, after many years' service in the British navy and long advocacy of a switch to oil as fuel for British warships, had in 1904 been put in command of the British navy and had immediately set up a committee to study the means of securing sufficient quantities of oil for it. E. G. Pretyman [secretary to the admiralty], was appointed chairman and the other members were also specialists or diplomats with wide knowledge of this subject. Fisher had learned that D'Arcy had obtained an oil concession in Iran and that he was discussing the possibility of its sale to foreign financiers; he therefore gave orders that the said concession should, by whatever means, be secured for the British government.

At that time public opinion in England—which was a leading capitalist power and strongly opposed to government interference in commercial matters—would not have allowed direct government purchase of a concession or purchase of the shares of a company holding such a concession. Hence the persons in charge deemed it best to prevent, at any cost, the transfer of D'Arcy's concession to foreign hands and at the same time to provide him with sufficient funds to pursue his operations, while awaiting the time when public opinion would gradually be prepared for direct government participation in petroleum affairs.

The committee began work without delay and Mr. Pretyman's first act was to request Lord Strathcona's aid. Strathcona had amassed a large fortune in Canada, and was the founder of the Canadian Pacific Railway; by then he had given up business activity because of old age and had gone into retirement. Ten years later, in a speech before the House of Commons concerning his meeting with Lord Strathcona, Pretyman said:

Lord Strathcona, whom I saw personally—I think it was characteristic of him—only asked me one question. He asked is it in the interest of the British Navy that this enterprise should go forward and that I should take part in it? I said, 'It is,' and Lord Strathcona, without any further questions, agreed to do what he had been asked.

In another part of his speech he said:

Really, the gratitude of the House, if this concession does turn out a valuable asset to the Navy, is due not so much to the Government and not so much to us who originated the idea, but to Lord Strathcona, to Mr. Wallace, who is the vice-chairman of the company, and to the directors of the Persian Oil Company who, knowing the origin of the formation of that company to have been national and not commercial, have, in spite of the total neglect of the Admiralty of this question for some six years, stuck to the concession and finally held on to it long enough to give the Government an opportunity to get it in the end.[1]

Pretyman also got in touch with Burmah Oil Company, a purely British firm engaged in oil production in Burmah, asked it for help and was favorably received. As a result of these negotiations, in 1905 a new company was formed, Concessions Syndicate, in Glasgow, which acquired the original shares and concession and had sufficient capital to continue operations in Iran. The main stockholders of this company were Strathcona, Burmah Oil, and D'Arcy.

One of the first things the new company did was to stop operations at Chiah Surkh and transfer all equipment to Mamatain, near Ramhurmuz and north of Ahwaz. Two exploratory wells were sunk there, by Canadian drillers under the supervision of Reynolds. The first well reached a depth of 661 meters and the second of 591, but neither struck oil. The absence of a good road and other local difficulties greatly increased expenses and soon after those in charge of the new company were also seized by anxiety.

[1] The above account, taken from Parliamentary Debates, Commons, 1914, 63: 1190–91, is slightly fuller than that in the Persian text.

Sir Arnold Wilson, in his book *South-West Persia* (p. 24), states:

The Foreign Office and Simla deserve credit for sending a detachment of troops as a foretaste of what will follow if the local tribes try to stop work by a British Company working under a proper concession which, if successfully exploited, will benefit Persia and local tribesmen beyond imagination.

When Wilson wrote that book he was British vice-consul in Ahwaz and commanding a detachment of Indian soldiers; it is therefore clear that the British sent Indian soldiers—put by Wilson at twenty men—to ensure the safety of the company's employees.

Since work at Mamatain had not produced any results, it was decided to sink another well in a place then known as Maidan-i Naftun. The French archeologist de Morgan had mentioned in a report this spot, in the Bakhtiari hills; he had stated that on the road from Mal-i Amir to Shushtar there was a place called Maidan-i Naftun where signs of oil could be seen and also the ruins of a fire temple known to the inhabitants as Masjid-i Sulaiman. The drillers and equipment were therefore transferred from Mamatain to Masjid-i Sulaiman. But by the middle of 1908 the capital of Concessions Syndicate was approaching exhaustion, the Masjid-i Sulaiman well had not yielded oil and many were of the opinion that oil would not be found there in commercial quantity. As is well known, the directors of the company, after deliberation, decided to instruct their chief engineer, Reynolds, to stop operations and send the equipment and workers out of Iran; it is even said that this order reached Reynolds who, however, owing to his extraordinary confidence in the possibilities of Masjid-i Sulaiman, did not follow it, but continued work. At any rate, operations continued at Masjid-i Sulaiman until on 26 May 1908 a drill pierced the rock capping the famous deposit of Masjid-i Sulaiman and oil gushed out under great pressure. It was then certain that Iran had valuable oil deposits and that a bright future lay before it. The depth of the first well was 360 meters and that of the second—which yielded oil the following day—307 meters, and it was ascertained that the depth of the cap rock covering the oil at Masjid-i Sulaiman was 300 meters.

The discovery of large oil deposits quickly solved the financial problems, and a few months later, in April 1909, the Anglo-Persian Oil Company was founded in London with a capital of £2,000,000, half of which was paid up. As successor to Concessions Syndicate, APOC transferred to Burmah Oil Company 970,000 shares (worth one pound each) and sold 30,000 more on the market. One should add that by this transaction Strathcona and D'Arcy became shareholders of Burmah Oil Company. Moreover, 600,000 preference shares of one pound each and 600,000 debenture stock at 5 percent, also of one pound each, were offered to the public and were bought up with extraordinary speed. Lord Strathcona, who by then was eighty-nine years old, was elected chairman of the board, and a British merchant with extensive commercial connections with India and also with close relations with Burmah Oil Company, Charles Greenway, was elected managing director. D'Arcy was also elected to the board and served until his death in 1917.

## 4. Progress of Operations until the First World War and Participation of the British Government

The expansion of operations proceeded, with utmost speed, from 1908 to 1914, when the First World War began. By then thirty wells had been dug in the Masjid-i Sulaiman area, housing had been built for the oil workers, oil pipelines had been laid down, drinking water had been brought in by pipeline from the Karun, and a workshop, a warehouse, a hospital, a clinic, a club, and other installations had been provided.

A pipeline between Masjid-i Sulaiman and Abadan was completed in 1912. Its diameter varied between ten and fifteen centimeters, and its carrying capacity was 400,000 tons a year. Four pumping stations were set up at Tumbi, Mulathani, Kut-i Abdallah, and Dar Khavin, providing enough pressure to transport the oil to Abadan. At first all materials were carried by ship from Khurramshahr to Ahwaz and from there, owing to the absence of a highway and modern transport, by camel to Masjid-i Sulaiman; later small boats were used between Ahwaz and Dar-i Khazineh, and modern transport from there to Masjid-i Sulaiman.

The question of obtaining land in Masjid-i Sulaiman, and securing it, at first raised great difficulties.

Most of these lands were pasture grounds used by the Bakhtiaris and, according to ancient custom, belonging to all the members of the tribe. But the khans claimed ownership for themselves and would not allow the company, under the terms of its concession, to deal directly with the real owners. Moreover the Bakhtiari Il-Khans and Il-Begs regarded themselves as the representatives of the central government and would undertake to assure security only on receipt of payment. One of the first employees of the company, who came to Iran in 1909, was a physician, Dr. M. Y. Young. Within a short time he learned Persian and, thanks to his medical work, soon became popular among the company employees and local inhabitants. The company benefited from his knowledge of Persian, medical work, and general information, and carried out its dealings with local agents through him.

In order to put relations between the company and the Bakhtiari khans on a proper footing, three different agreements were concluded with them, which considerably facilitated the company's work. The first concerned the company's shares, making the khans shareholders. For this purpose, a subsidiary company was formed, the Bakhtiari Oil Company, whose operations were confined to one square mile in Masjid-i Sulaiman. Its capital was £400,000, of which 3 percent, that is 12,000 one-pound shares, were given free to the Bakhtiari khans. Four persons, two representing the Haji Ilkhani family and the others representing the Ilkhani, were designated to collect the annual income from the shares and distribute it among the others. Later on the Bakhtiari Oil Company was dissolved and incorporated in the First Exploitation Company and the 12,000 shares held by the khans were replaced by shares of the latter. The second agreement dealt with the purchase of land. Each year the company would be allowed to purchase from the khans and begs, for designated sums, the lands it needed in Bakhtiari country and the Il-Khani and Il-Begi, representing the state, would see to it that the purchase price reached the real owners.

The third agreement concerned security. One of the younger khans would be appointed chief of guards and provided with riflemen. The company would pay allowances to him and to the riflemen, who would be responsible for security, as well as £3,000 a year to the khans. This chief became the virtual local governor and in all cases applied the old Bakhtiari laws and customs. This third agreement prevailed as long as the authority of the central government was not firmly established in Khuzistan; when, however, the local administration and police force gained control, it gradually ceased to be operative, but the annual payment of £3,000 continued.

In 1909 the company concluded an agreement with Shaikh Khazal, under which it bought one square mile of land in Abadan for the construction of a refinery. The following year work began on the refinery, which was finished three years later. Its initial capacity was 120,000 tons a year, but it was gradually expanded. Under another agreement with Shaikh Khazal, he became responsible for the security of Abadan, in return for payment.

In 1912 the first crude oil extracted from Iran was exported—43,000 tons. The following year exports rose to 81,000 tons and in 1914 to 274,000. . . .

### Russian Pipeline Projects

Britain's interest in Persian oil arose from the desire to control reliable sources which would make it independent of the American oil industry. But Russia had within its borders a more than adequate supply—indeed around the turn of the century Russian production actually exceeded American. As the following selection, shows, Iran drew Russia's attention not as a source of production but as a market and as a transit country to the Asian markets.

For centuries, oil from Baku has been burned in lamps, mixed with paints, and put to other uses.[1] In a report on his journey to the Caspian dated 29 June 1844 (FO 60/108), Abbott stated that "small Craft and Boats bringing Naphtha from Baku and other parts of the coast are numerous," and mentioned among the imports of Barfurush from Baku, "Naphtha—2 or 3 single masted vessels of 80 or 100 kharwars of 100 Tabriz Mauns—worth at Barfurush 16/- per kharwar of 36 Mauns"; he included naphtha in lists of imports of other towns and stated that a duty of 5 percent was levied on such imports. In the British consular report on Gilan (A and P, 1867, 67) it is stated that "several boats are also employed in bringing salt and naphtha from the Turcoman coast to Enzellee."

With the development of the Russian petroleum industry, kerosine and crude oil were shipped to Iran in steadily increasing quantities. As mentioned below,

[1] See Lockhart, "Persian Petroleum"; LeStrange, p. 181.

some refining was, for several years, undertaken in Iran, but this ceased for the reasons given by the British consul in Resht (A and P 1898, 97):

In a note on the tables of imports contained in my last Commercial Report (No. 1833 Annual Series), I noted the decrease of £14,255 in the imports of petroleum; the import of that article in 1894 having attained the figure of over £21,000 as against £6,800 in 1895. This I reported, was due to the fact "that no export duty being levied in Russia on raw naphtha it is imported and purified in Persia, thus saving the heavy excise on the purified article." Since then the Russian Government, in view of the increasing proportions of this trade in the raw article, have withdrawn the export duty on purified petroleum for Persia, and thus forced the small refining factories in Enzelli to close their establishments, it being quite impossible for them to compete with the Baku refineries without the aid of this above-mentioned excise duty. This explains the decrease of £2,200 on the imports of raw naphtha in 1896, which will gradually disappear entirely from the list, and the increase of over 50 per cent. in imports of petroleum in the year under review.

Ananich seems to imply that Russian oil was soon driven out of the Persian market by the Anglo-Persian Oil Company. In fact, however, kerosine and other products competed very successfully until the end of the 1920s. After that, the withdrawal of the Soviet Union from world oil markets, owing to greater internal demand, together with improved transport within Iran, left the Iranian market to the Anglo-Persian Oil Company.

Russia's attempts to secure oil concessions in 1916 (the Khoshtaria concession) and again in 1946 did not materialize. However, a pipeline for pumping natural gas from Iran's southern fields to the Soviet Union was opened in 1970.

(See also works by Avery, Elwell-Sutton, Fateh, Issawi and Yeganeh, Longrigg, and Shwadran listed in the bibliography.)

### Selection 3. Russian Projects for Pipeline through Iran, 1884 and 1901
[B. V. Ananich, "Rossiya i Kontsessiya d'Arsi," *Istoricheskie zapiski* 66 (1960): 278–90.]

When at the turn of this century, at a time when the economic rivalry between England and Russia in Persia was in full swing, the petroleum question came to the surface, it became clear that the interest shown in it by each of the rivals sprang from different causes. England's interest was aroused, in the first place, by the Persian oil deposits, while Russia was powerfully attracted to the Persian petroleum market.

The oil industrialists of Baku were little interested in exploiting the oil riches of Persia; in addition, they feared the competition of Persian oil in Middle Eastern markets and, above all, in Persia itself where, starting already in the early 1870s, Russian petroleum products made their entry. Thanks to the low costs and proximity of the Baku oil fields, Russian petroleum acquired a dominant position in the Persian market. This oil came from Baku either by water, through the Caspian ports, or overland through Krasnovodsk to Ashkabad in northern Persia and from there went to other parts of the country.

Until 1896 trade consisted mainly of crude petroleum, since kerosine destined for export paid excise duties equal to those on kerosine consumed within Russia. In the early 1890s, a few small plants for distilling Russian oil were set up in Persia, providing the market with fairly cheap, although poorly refined, kerosine and successfully competing with the Baku refineries.[1] In order to make it easier for the Baku oil industry to meet this competition, the Russian government, starting in 1896, refunded export duties on refined petroleum sent to Persia. This led to a sharp rise in exports of Russian kerosine to Persia which soon, like crude petroleum, acquired a dominating position.

By the early 1900s Russian kerosine was being delivered in the farthest and most inaccessible regions of the country. "Our kerosene meets no competition, since there is no other kerosene in Persia," reported the Russian consul in Sistan, A. Miller, to Saint Petersburg, "and its consumption in Sistan and adjacent lands is growing rapidly."[2] The British consul in Khurasan and Sistan also wrote to his government that Russian kerosine, brought in through Ashkabad, was in constant demand, yielded high profits, and constituted a Russian monopoly in the whole of Khurasan.[3]

It would, however, be incorrect to overestimate the significance of the Persian oil market for Russia, for Persia's consumption of kerosine at the end of the 1890s and beginning of the 1900s was relatively small.[4] As a market for kerosine India, for example, was no less important, and there Russian kerosine, according to the journal *Neftyanoe Delo*, accounted in 1901 for nearly 90 percent of all local consumption and successfully competed with American.[5] "Russian kerosene is totally excluding American kerosene from the country," wrote the Bombay weekly *Times of India* in 1901, "and its import amounted last year to over 22 million gallons while that of America was

less than one million."[6] At the same time India was an essential transit point for the conveyance, by sea, of Russian oil products to other markets in Asia and the Far East. Incidentally, not only in the Persian Gulf but also in the regions of Persia bordering on India, Russian kerosine was for long brought over from Bombay, to which it went by sea; from Bombay it made a long journey over the Indian railways to Quetta and from there reached Sistan, by camel from Nushki.[7]

The efforts of Russian petroleum industrialists to export oil to India and through it to other Asian countries strengthened their interest in Persia as a country through which lay the shortest land route to those markets. It is not accidental, therefore, that at the dawn of the development of the Russian oil industry, in 1884, a project appeared in Russia for the construction of a kerosine pipeline across Persia, from the Caspian Sea to the Persian Gulf. The author of this project was the well-known Russian engineer S. E. Palashkovskii; it deserves attention as a document reflecting the aims and plans of Russian oil industrialists in opening and developing Asian oil markets.

In his memorandum on the construction of the pipeline, Palashkovskii pointed out the enormous significance for Russia of the markets lying "near the Indian and Pacific Oceans."[8] For the sake of these markets, the author of the memorandum proposed that the traditional Near Eastern policy of the struggle for the straits be abandoned and that efforts should be directed toward a breakthrough to the coasts of the Persian Gulf and Indian Ocean. "Would it not be simple to leave aside Constantinople, which is jealously guarded by our European friends," he wrote, "and turn our efforts where the aim is both nearer and easier to attain. In Turkey we have to deal with the whole of Europe but in Persia, where we can easily reach the ocean through the Gulf

[1] Ts. G.I.A.L., f. 574, op. 4, d. 410, ll. 7–12.
[2] Ibid. f. 560, op. 28, d. 526, l. 42 ob.
[3] *Diplomatic and Consular Reports*, Persia, no. 2921 F.O. Dec. 1902, p. 7.
[4] According to official figures, in 1901 total exports of Russian oil products were 95,079,017 pouds while exports to Persia amounted to 2,136,090 pouds—see *Obzor vneshnei torgovli Rossii za 1901 god*, Saint Petersburg, 1903, table 4, pp. 76, 78. [A poud equaled 16.38 kilograms or 36 pounds.]
[5] *Neftyanoe Delo*, 1908, no. 8, p. 58.

[6] *Times of India* (weekly edition) 2/11, 1901, p. 12.
[7] Ts. G.I.A.L., f. 560, op. 28, d. 526, l. 42 ob.
[8] Ibid., f. 1222, op. 16, d. 1, l. 12 ob.

of Oman, we will have to deal only with England."[9]

In Palashkovskii's project, a leading part in the opening of the Asian markets was to be played by a pipeline to the Persian Gulf, from which cheap Russian kerosine would be delivered by ship to India, Indochina, Australia, and other countries. According to the author of the project, the sale of Baku kerosine in these countries would, in the first few years, give annual profits of up to 10 million rubles and in subsequent years up to 100 million, which in his opinion would have a beneficial effect on the general state of Russian finance.

In February 1884, Palashkovskii's project was discussed at a special conference (*v Osobom soveshchanii*), which resolved to "take no action."[10] The conference found that the significance of the pipeline for Russian trade had been overestimated in the project, that the project did not include financial data which were essential for estimating the cost of construction, and that from the political point of view "it would hardly be opportune for the government to guarantee the progress of an enterprise established in foreign territory... without confidence in the continuing favorable attitude toward it on the part of the Persian government."[11]

In contrast to Russia, England strove directly to exploit the Persian oil deposits, which for long had attracted the attention of British businessmen. Already in 1872 the British subject Baron de Reuter, with the help of the British minister in Tehran, Drummond Wolff, had succeeded in acquiring from the shah a concession for the monopolistic exploitation of the natural resources of Persia, including petroleum [see 4:7]. ...

Nineteen years later Reuter renewed his efforts to exploit the natural resources of Persia. For this purpose, in 1891 the English Imperial Bank of Persia in Tehran formed a company, the Persian Bank Mining Rights Corporation, with a capital of £1,000,000. The company started exploration for oil in the Bushire region and on one of the islands in the Persian Gulf. But in spite of the large capital and great number of experts at its disposal, the company did not succeed in discovering any oil deposits and by 1893 it had practically stopped its exploratory work.

More success attended the search of the French archeological expedition of Jacques de Morgan, who investigated natural oil wells on the Turco-Persian border. In 1893 de Morgan published a report on his work, in which he suggested that important oil resources were to be found in Persia.[12] This report renewed England's interest in Persian oil. The British government, in pursuit not only of economic but of political objectives, helped a British subject, the Australian William Knox D'Arcy, to obtain from the Persian government the right to exploit oil deposits in southern Persia. ...

However, Saint Petersburg was disturbed not so much by these fabulously advantageous conditions as by the sixth point of the agreement, which defined the limits of the concession. According to this point, D'Arcy's rights as concessionaire extended to the whole of southern Iran, that is, excluding the northern provinces of Azerbaijan, Mazandaran, Gilan, Khurasan, and Astarabad. In addition the Persian government obligated itself not to give to anyone permission to build petroleum pipelines leading to the southern rivers and southern coast of Persia.[19] These conditions in the concession agreement constituted insurmountable obstacles to the Russian plans for the marketing of Baku oil through the Persian Gulf.

The fact is that, in August 1901, in the Russian Ministry of Finance the project for the construction of a kerosine pipeline from the Caucasian border to the Persian Gulf, first raised in 1884 and since forgotten, was taken up again. The question of building a kerosine pipeline through Persia was directly

[9] Ibid., l. 68.
[10] Ibid., l. 6.
[11] Ibid., f. 1222, op. 16, d.1, l. 6 ob.

[12] L. Elwell-Sutton, *Persian Oil.*
[19] Ts. G.I.A.L., f. 560, op. 28, d. 247, l. 37.

connected with the crisis in the Baku oil market which began in 1901. In January 1901 a sharp drop in petroleum prices began. By the end of the year, prices fell to a level which had not been seen in the Baku oil market since the end of 1894. In 1902 there was no improvement in the situation—on the contrary, the crisis deepened and prices continued to fall. In 1900 the average annual price of crude petroleum at the place of production was 15.7 kopeks per poud; by 1901 it had fallen to 8.11 kopeks, and in 1902 it was still lower, at 6.72 kopeks, the lowest point, in January 1902, being 4.6.[20] The crisis in the domestic market was aggravated by the unfavorable economic conjuncture prevailing at that time in both Russian and foreign oil markets.

One of the main factors impeding the development of Russian oil exports was the absence of suitable means of communication. In order to reduce the costs of transporting kerosine, which was carried mainly on the Transcaucasian railway, the government started to build the Batum-Baku pipeline. By 1910 pipes had been laid over a total distance of 214 versts, up to the village of Mikhailovo, but they could not even take over the load of the Transcaucasian railway. Even if the Transcaucasian pipeline had been completed and put into operation it would not have represented a significant improvement. For the Batum line would have been advantageous mainly for trade with the Mediterranean and Europe, whereas the Baku oil industrialists were interested above all in exporting to the Far East and India, where Russian kerosine could successfully compete with American and where there was a chance of significantly extending the market for kerosine in the future.

This served as one of the main arguments in defense of the project of constructing a kerosine pipeline through Persia which was presented to Nicholas II at the end of August 1901. Three months after the signing of the D'Arcy concession, the author of the project, alluding to the crisis in the Baku oil

industry and to the "inadequacy" of the Baku-Batum railway, proposed laying a kerosine pipeline through Persia either as a complement to the Transcaucasian pipeline or, in the last resort, instead of the latter, and making use of the material prepared for it.[21] According to his preliminary calculations, the cost of transporting a poud of kerosine from Baku to the nearest Indian port—assuming the Transcaucasian pipeline to be operating over its whole length— would amount to seventeen kopeks, whereas it would be only six kopeks by kerosine pipeline through Persia, or three times cheaper. In the view of the author, the construction of this kerosine pipeline would open immense possibilities for the Russian oil industry in the markets of Asia, where Russia would "occupy a brilliant position" and not in any way fear American competition.[22]

The project also addressed itself to the political significance of the Persian line: "The laying and operating of the kerosine pipeline," he wrote, "would in any case create in the Persian Gulf real Russian commercial interests, which no Power would have the right to ignore . . . it would therefore serve to increase our influence in Persia and on the shores of the Indian Ocean."[23]

Nicholas II expressed his attitude toward the project with a fairly vague decision: "The question is of great importance and should be considered seriously."[24] The task of "considering it seriously" was taken up by S. Yu. Witte [the minister of finance]. Receiving the project and the czar's instruction, on 22 September, Witte transmitted a copy to Lamsdorf [the minister of foreign affairs] with the request that he give a definite decision as to whether there were, from the political point of view, any objections to negotiations with the Persian government regarding the granting to the

---

[20] *Obzor bakinskoi neftyanoi promyshlennosti za 1902 g.*, Baku, 1903, part 1, p. 389.

[21] The author of the project is unknown . . . [reasons are given for concluding that it was again, Palashkovskii].

[22] Ts. G.I.A.L., f. 560, op. 28, d. 247, ll. 13–16.

[23] Ibid., l. 15 ob.

[24] Ibid., l. 13.

Russian Discount and Loan Bank in Persia of a concession for the construction of an oil pipeline, and the sending of a group of technicians for the necessary surveys.[25]

Apparently, Witte almost simultaneously gave corresponding instructions to Tehran, since the Russian minister, Argyropoulo, knew of the project before receiving Lamsdorf's official communication to the manager of the Discount and Loan Bank, who, following the directions of the minister of finance, in September 1901 began negotiations for a concession with the Persian prime minister.

It should be mentioned that the Russian minister turned out to be an opponent of the project. In his reports to the Ministry of Foreign Affairs, he decisively argued the impossibility of implementing the concession. He mentioned the serious political consequences, the high cost of constructing the pipeline, and its fantastic character due to the high risks involved. In the future it would not, in his opinion, be secure against "the attempt of any voluntary or bribed malefactor who, on a dark night and in a remote place, would put under it a small packet of dynamite or gunpowder."[26]

However, the opposition of the minister had no influence on the course of events and merely drew reproaches on him from Witte, who irritatedly wrote to Lamsdorf on 10 December 1901 that he deemed it "highly important" for Russian interests in Persia that a concession be obtained and deeply regrettable if "such a kind of concession were to be granted to the English without the knowledge of our minister." "Evidently the English," said Witte, angrily and sarcastically, "when they strove for their recently obtained concession for the exploitation of the oil riches of Persia, did not have in view the considerations expressed by Privy Councillor Argyropoulo and did not fear the political consequences of the laying of an oil pipeline through Persia—otherwise they would not have

sought this concession and would not have obtained it."[27]

Witte's irritation had been aroused not so much by the position of the minister as by the lack of success of the Russian-Persian negotiations regarding a concession, in which, as was to be expected, the sixth point of the D'Arcy agreement proved to be a stumbling block. The Persian premier categorically refused to accept the Russian demands, quoting the obligations given to the English concessionaire. For its part, the Russian side continued to press for a concession, negotiations for which became intertwined with those for a loan, which had been begun on the initiative of the Persian government.

Although not more than one year had passed since the first Russian loan of 22.5 million rubles, the Persian government found itself once more on the eve of a financial crisis [see 8:7]. . . .

In connection with the decision of the conference, the question of the concession was temporarily put aside and at the end of December [1901] the Persian government received, through the Discount and Loan Bank, another 1,000,000 rubles with the understanding that this would be subsequently covered by the proceeds of the loan.

The broken negotiations were resumed only in January 1902, after the Russian jurists in Saint Petersburg and the Belgian jurisconsult at the Persian Ministry of Foreign Affairs in Tehran had given an official opinion that the English concession could not serve as an obstacle to the granting of permission for the construction of the pipeline.

At the end of January the Russian-Persian negotiations showed an evident progress. On 23 January, Grube cabled the Ministry of Finance that the Sadr-i Azam [prime minister] had at last accepted the Russian demands and that, within three days, the assent of the shah to the granting of a concession for a kerosine pipeline would be

25 Ibid., l. 17.
26 Ibid., f. 560, op. 28, d. 247, l. 49.
27 Ibid., l. 51.

made known "in spite of the strong opposition of the English minister"; there was however the reservation that in case of protest by D'Arcy responsibility for the violation of the English concession would be undertaken by the Russian government.[33]

Thus the question of the kerosine pipeline seemed, in principle, to have been settled and all that remained was an agreement regarding provision for the losses borne by the English concessionaire. However, at that very moment the British government hastened to intervene in the negotiations. On 31 January, the British ambassador in Saint Petersburg, Charles Scott, handed to Lamsdorf a memorandum in which he drew the attention of the Russian government to the fact that the concession requested by the Discount and Loan Bank would, if granted, violate the rights of a British subject, in corroboration of which the text of the sixth point was quoted.[34] Simultaneously the English increased their pressure on the shah, to whom a decisive protest was made against the granting of a pipeline concession to the Russians.

The results of the British intervention soon made themselves felt. On 26 January, the shah had agreed to the granting of a concession to the Russians and already on 3 February Argyropoulo informed Lamsdorf that "the Persians feared not only the financial consequences but the displeasure of England" and that the Sadr-i Azam "urgently requested, in the name of the Shah and on his behalf, the softening of the terms of the loan and the postponement, for some time, of a decision regarding the pipeline."[35] Within a few days the Sadr-i Azam again told the minister that if the Russians did not withdraw their demands he would have to hand in his resignation immediately.

In the meantime, the Ministry of Finance in Saint Petersburg continued to work on the concession agreement, as though nothing had happened. The declaration of the British ambassador evidently did not disturb

Witte, who advised Lamsdorf to reply to Charles Scott that the pipeline concession

having been requested by a private institution, the Discount and Loan Bank of Persia, the Russian government was in no position to give any precise explanations regarding its contents; however, as far as was known to the Ministry of Finance, that concession, since it referred exclusively to the import and transit of Russian oil, could not violate the rights of d'Arcy who, according to the sense of his agreement with the Persian government, received a monopoly only regarding indigenous oil.[36]

After preliminary discussion of the draft agreement at a meeting in the Ministry of Finance on 4 February, it was finally decided to lay a pipeline only for the transport of kerosine, in order that the refining of the oil and its by-products should remain "in Russian hands." The meeting decided that, if orders were placed in Russia, it would be possible within four years to pay for a kerosine pipeline with an annual capacity of 60 million pouds. According to the calculations of E. K. Ziegler, the cost of the whole enterprise would be 80 million rubles if the outlet were at Bushire and 110 million if it were on the Indian Ocean; amortization of this outlay would require twenty years.[37]

Rough estimates of receipts from the pipeline operations promised huge benefits. According to them, even in the first year, assuming the pipeline to work below capacity (with a throughput of 30–40 million pouds) it would (assuming the outlet to be at Bushire) reduce the cost of delivering kerosine to the Far East by 14.5–20 kopeks a poud, compared to sea transport through the Suez Canal. "Construction of the pipeline," pointed out Ziegler, "would significantly lower the price of our kerosine and thus give us great advantage in competition with America"; and "the cheapening of the product would greatly stimulate its consumption both in the Far East and, to a certain extent, in Persia itself."[38]

But although the Russian government strove stubbornly to obtain the concession, it did not intend to begin construction of the pipeline immediately. This is evident from

[33] Ibid., ll. 66 and 71.
[34] Ibid., l. 78–78 ob.
[35] Ibid., l. 106.

[36] Ibid., f. 560, op. 28, d. 247, l. 79.
[37] Ibid., ll. 98–101.
[38] Ibid., l. 98.

the very text of the agreement, the drafting of which in the Ministry of Finance ended in the middle of February 1902. Regarding the time schedule of construction, it was stated that the Discount and Loan Bank should keep the concession secret and not start work for two years. Within two years, the bank would announce to the Persian government whether or not it intended to implement the concession. It would obligate itself to start construction of the pipeline not later than three years from the time of that announcement and to complete it within fifteen years of receiving the land required for construction.

It should be added that the draft concession was put in fairly general terms and, in particular, did not specify exactly the direction of the future pipeline—the question of whether it would debouch on the Indian Ocean or the Persian Gulf remained open. Nevertheless, the draft was approved by the minister of finance on 16 February 1902, and on the following day was sent to Grube in Tehran to present it to the Sadr-i Azam.[39]

The draft was sent to Tehran at a moment when little chance for success remained, although the Russian representatives in Tehran made every effort to obtain the concession. Already on 12 February, Grube had urgently cabled Saint Petersburg that "the English concessionaire of the southern pipeline +[40] paid up to 50,000 tumans, receiving concession" and requested from Witte permission "to promise similar recompense" if the requested concession were granted.[41] Witte immediately replied: "You may promise 50,000 tumans."[42]

However the Persian government had become much less complaisant. On 13 February, that is, three days before the sending of the draft agreement to Tehran, the Sadr-i Azam had received a cheering communication from his ambassador in

Saint Petersburg, saying that the loan had been put through without any conditions regarding the pipeline.[43] Where the Persian ambassador had got that information it is difficult to say. Hardly from the Ministry of Finance. Most plausibly it came from the Ministry of Foreign Affairs, for around the middle of February the Russian Foreign Ministry had, apparently, already refused to support the project of the Persian pipeline. In a letter dated 15 February 1902, addressed to Witte, Lamsdorf expounded (admittedly, in a fairly vague way) his point of view on this question. He began by saying that he deemed it necessary to continue negotiations with the Persian government and that, from the political point of view, it would be inconvenient to renounce the suggested conditions, especially "in view of the intervention of the British government in this question," and concluded that it was necessary all the same to "keep in view the probability of our consenting to the softening of some of the conditions of the loan and even to the exchanging of the above-mentioned concession, later on, for some other conditions."[44]

Nevertheless in Tehran no new instructions were sent through the channels of the Ministry of Foreign Affairs, and negotiations continued until 20 February, when suddenly and unexpectedly it was learned that the Persian government was engaged in secret negotiations with the English concessionaire regarding a loan. On that day Grube and the minister simultaneously informed Saint Petersburg that D'Arcy had made an offer to the shah, through his retinue, of a loan of £200,000 (on the twenty-first Grube cabled that the sum was 300,000 and not 200,000) at 5 percent. To this Grube added the supposition that D'Arcy would simply "seem to be, in this case, a strawman."[45] It turned out that the Persian government had already for long carried on loan negotiations with D'Arcy and that the shah, dreaming only of his new trip to Europe, was trying

[39] Ibid., ll. 127–30 ob.
[40] The + sign means that one of the ciphers in the text of the telegram had not been deciphered.
[41] Ibid., f. 560, op. 28, d. 247, l. 114.
[42] Ibid., l. 115.

[43] Ibid., l. 125a.
[44] Ibid., l. 124.
[45] Ibid., ll. 136, 138.

to obtain a loan as soon as possible. This new information decided the matter: the Russian government was forced to give up the concession for construction of a pipeline. On 2 March 1902, the Persian government received an advance of 1 million rubles, on account of the forthcoming loan, and on 22 March a 10-million loan was issued on terms analogous to those of the 1900 loan (duration of 75 years, interest rate of 5 percent and half-yearly payment of interest and amortization). No new attempts were undertaken by the Russian government to obtain authorization to lay a pipeline to the Persian Gulf.[46] ...

By undertaking the exploitation of the oil riches of southern Iran, England dealt a serious blow to the economic interests of Russia in the Middle East and Asia. However, Russia had begun to lose its former position in the Asian petroleum markets even earlier. The exploitation of oil deposits in the Dutch Indies, Assam, and Burma, the critical situation of the Baku oil industry, and other causes had compelled Russia already in 1907 to give way in the Asian markets under the pressure of its competitors. The journal of the Baku oil industry, *Neftyanoe Delo*, in a leading article at the beginning of 1908 summing up the results of the oil trade in the previous year, stated

that "after a long and bitter struggle, the Russian oil export trade was compelled last year to acknowledge the futility of struggling against the conquest of world markets by its chief rival, the American petroleum trust, and its impotence to pursue the struggle further."[52]

Simultaneously, Russian kerosine was ousted from the ports of the Persian Gulf. In that same year, 1907, the Bombay weekly *Times of India*, reported that a large American oil company, taking advantage of the difficulties of Russian exporters, had delivered a big consignment of American kerosine directly from New York to the ports of the Persian Gulf which had hitherto taken Russian kerosine.[53]

It is true that in northern Persia Russian kerosine long kept its monopolistic position. In 1910–11 Russia exported to Persia 2,266,269 pouds of kerosine with a value of 1,147,769 rubles. According to the Persian consul-general in Saint Petersburg, L. A. Sobotsinskii, Russian kerosine constituted 96.2 percent of total consumption in the country, and was cheaper than English or American.[54] Nevertheless, the oil markets close to Persia were finally lost to the Baku oil industrialists. The Anglo-Persian Oil Company, formed in 1909 for the exploitation of the newly discovered oil deposits, soon took possession of these markets and began to play the leading political and military-strategic role in Great Britain's colonial policy, not only in Persia but in the whole Middle East.

---

[46] [According to the author, the matter was taken up again in the Ministry of Finance in 1906. N. A. Notovich submitted a project for highways, motor transport, and an oil pipeline to the Persian Gulf, to be financed by a group headed by a Persian bank. This scheme was held up pending the conclusion of negotiations with Britain (September 1907), after which Notovich went to Tehran but engaged in financial affairs and carried on negotiations with the Persian government regarding the establishment of a Russian Commercial-Industrial Bank.]

[52] *Neftyanoe Delo*, 1908, n. 3, p. 47.
[53] *Times of India* (weekly edition) 11/5, 1907, p. 2.
[54] Sobotsinskii, p. 203.

# 8

## *Finance and Public Finance*

The main financial development during the nineteenth century was the sharp depreciation of the Iranian currency, and the consequent rise in prices. The last decades of the period under review also saw the beginnings of modern banking in Iran, and a small amount of foreign investment took place. In the field of public finance, government expenditure rose much more rapidly than revenues and a steadily mounting foreign debt was incurred.

The depreciation of the currency, whose exchange rate with sterling was, by 1914, a fifth or less of what it had been in 1800, was partly due to the fall in the value of silver relative to gold—a phenomenon that affected the Indian, Chinese, and other currencies as well. But a no less important factor was the debasement of the currency by the successive issue of coins of lighter weight or lower fineness, an abuse that continued until close to the end of the period under review (see 8:1, 3, and appendix). This depreciation was, naturally, accompanied by a rise in prices—a trend that can be observed in different parts of the country but which cannot be measured with any degree of precision. A few rough indications for some essential foodstuffs in Tehran show rises of four to eight times between 1847 and 1914 (see 8:1). Iran shared this experience with other countries (for Egypt see EHME, pp. 449–51) opened up to world trade and starting with a rather low level of internal prices.

But the penetration of Iran by foreign capital was far smaller than that of its Middle Eastern neighbors, India and other countries. At the outbreak of the First World War, its banking system was still rudimentary, and was entirely controlled by British and Russian interests (see 8:3). Except for petroleum, it had failed to attract long-term investment in any large volume, though a certain amount of Russian capital had been invested in transport and the Caspian fisheries (see 8:4).

As in other preindustrial societies with a long and eventful history, the public revenue system of Iran was extremely complex and variegated. But its main features stand out quite clearly, and are thus described by Lord Curzon:[1]

The revenue of Persia may be divided into two headings: the Maliat, or fixed revenue, and the Sursat, or irregular revenue. The fixed revenue is derived from four sources: (1) regular taxation; (2) revenues of Crown lands; (3) customs; (4) rents and leases. The irregular revenue is derived from three sources: (1) *sadir* or public requisitions; (2) presents (*pishkesh*) on the festival of No Ruz (March 21, the Persian New Year's Day), and on the Prophet's birthday (Aid-i-Molud); (3) extraordinary *pishkesh*, arising from presents, fines, bribes, confiscations, etc.

The main source of revenue was the land tax, paid in cash or kind.

Formerly the Crown only claimed one-tenth [of the produce]; but this proportion was doubled by Fath Ali Shah. In practice it is found that the assessment frequently amounts to thirty per cent., and twenty-five per cent. may perhaps be taken as a fair average. The system, however, varies absolutely in different parts of the country, and even in different parts of the same province. . . . A further anomaly arises from the fact that the taxes are levied sometimes from the proprietor, sometimes from the cultivator, local custom again being the determining cause [see 8:5].

The central government raised land taxes,

in lump sums from villages, towns or districts, the taxes being, in fact, farmed out by the Government for a fixed money payment, and the allocation in subordinate areas being left to the arbitrary decision of local governors, chiefs, or head men. Frequently the owner of a property farms his own taxes from the Government, so as to escape the visists of the official assessor.

Assessments were "in the main wholly obsolete in date and character," and were not adjusted for changes in output. "Some districts, therefore, are heavily over-taxed, others ludicrously under-taxed. . . . Such a thing as a scientific or periodical revision of assessment has never taken place, and would cause a thrill of horror to run through every class of Persian society above the peasant."

Farmers and nomads also paid a tax on animals (see 8:5). The tax on craftsmen sometimes took "the form of a capitation, or poll-tax; elsewhere I have heard it estimated as a 20 percent impost on the profits of trade." Taxes on rents of houses, shops, etc., were "rarely exacted." The right to levy customs duties was farmed to the highest bidder, who usually made a profit of "from 20 to 25 per cent. which he puts into his own pocket"; customs provided about a fifth of regular revenue (see 3:2–4). The balance of such revenue came from rents on crown lands and various concessions, for example, fisheries, mines, mints, and quays.

In addition to being grossly unjust and inefficient, such a system had a very low elasticity of yield with respect to income. In 1836, government revenue was put at 2,461,000 tumans and in 1869 at 4,912,000 tumans; it is not clear whether

---

[1] *Persia*, 2:470–91; see also Mochaver, pp. 110–27, and Stolze and Andreas.

these two estimates are comparable (see 8:5) and it should be borne in mind that in the interval the currency had depreciated by 25 percent (see 8:1).[2]

In 1876, revenue was 4,750,000 tumans, or £1,900,000, and in 1886 5,500,000 tumans, or £1,670,000,[3] and Curzon gives a detailed breakdown for 1888/89 with a total of 5,537,000 tumans, or £1,653,000.[4] In other words, revenue expressed in tumans had risen very little between 1867 and 1888 and in sterling had actually declined, at a time when the real national product of Iran had probably increased appreciably.

The expenditure of the central government, in 1868, was 4,250,000 tumans. Of this, the army took 1,725,000 tumans, "Salaries of Princes, Ministers, and Government employés" 725,000, "Pensions to Priesthood and Syeds" 250,000, the shah's private expenses 500,000 and "Extraordinary Disbursement" another 500,000, leaving a surplus of 500,000.[5] No significant change took place until the constitution of 1906. Thus in 1884/85, out of a total expenditure of 4,750,000 tumans, the army took 1,900,000, the court absorbed 900,000, "pensions to priests, nobles etc." 750,000, the Foreign Office another 750,000, "other departments" 150,000, colleges 30,000, "and the remainder for Royal buildings, purchase of stores abroad for the army, purchase of the steam-ships 'Persepolis' and 'Susa'."[6]

The central government did not handle all fiscal receipts and disbursements. Each province had its own budget, the *kitabcheh*, prepared by financial officials known as *mustawfi*. From its revenues the province retained the amounts needed for local expenditure, and transferred the balance to the central government. Thus, in 1888/89, the provinces kept 263,000 tumans out of a total of 5,537,000.[7] These revenues were raised, from the various localities or *buluks*, by provincial officials who, in addition to the sums specified in the *kitabcheh*, demanded further amounts known as *madakhil* and which, according to Curzon, were sometimes as much as two-thirds of the specified sum.[8] As was mentioned before, "villages were assessed in a lump sum, the division of this among the individual peasants being made by the local authorities and in the peasant proprietor areas by the village elders. This group assessment was known as *bunicheh*."[9]

[2] The following figures are also given by Jamalzadeh, pp. 118–19: A.H. 1255 (1839), 3,453,000 tumans; A.H. 1270 (1853) 3,367,000; A.H. 1293 (1876) 5,070,000; A.H. 1302 (1884) 5,080,000; A.H. 1308 (1890) 6,000,000; A.H. 1325 (1907) 8,000,000; 1331 (1912) 13,069,000 tumans. The first three seem to have been taken from Rabino (see 8:3).

The figures given by Blau, pp. 6–7, showing a total revenue of 7,000,000 tumans in the 1850s are difficult to reconcile with the estimates given above.

Last, if Gardane's figures are to be trusted, central government revenue in 1807 was well over 2,000,000 tumans (see 1:1).

[3] "Persia," A and P 1886, 67.

[4] *Persia*, 2:480–81.

[5] "Persia," A and P 1867–68, 69.

[6] "Persia," A and P 1886, 67. See also a more detailed breakdown for 1888/89 in Curzon, pp. 482–83.

[7] Curzon, pp. 482–83; for details see Demorgny, Mochaver, pp. 130–154, and Jazairi, pp. 54–55. Of course, in times of disturbances provincial revenues were often withheld from the government, for example, those of Isfahan and Mashad in 1849 (Sheil to Palmerston, 26 January 1850, FO 60/150).

[8] Curzon, p. 439. It should be added that, like their counterparts in other Middle Eastern countries, the *mustawfis* formed a tightly knit, and often hereditary, group. They kept their accounts in a very complicated form, using a script unintelligible to other people and designed to make outside control almost impossible—see Demorgny, and Shuster, pp. 245–50.

[9] Lambton, *Landlord*, p. 165.

No serious attempt was made to reform this system before the 1906 Constitution. In 1885 a decree was issued, aimed at eliminating some abuses and tightening the control of the central government, but its effect was negligible.[10] One change introduced during this period made things worse. Owing to the government's growing need for cash, landowners were allowed to convert their taxes in kind into cash payments, at specified rates, *tas*$^c$*ir*. But with the rapid rise in prices (see above), conversion at the old rates meant a sharp reduction of the amounts paid by landowners and received by the government; alternatively, when peasants were forced to sell their crops for cash payment of taxes, they received only the fixed, low prices.[11]

The National Assembly, convened in 1907, however, carried out drastic financial reforms (see 8:6).[12] The most important were the fixing of a civil list for the shah; the elimination or sharp reduction of pensions paid to princes and notables; the centralization of the budget; the abolition of the conversion rates, *tas*$^c$*ir*, to the great advantage of the government; and the removal of some of the abuses in the collection of taxes. In addition, *tuyuls* (see chap. 5, introduction) were abolished, but the effectiveness of this measure depended on the relative power of the central government and the large landowners.[13] Over the next few years, with the help of American and other financial advisors, the Ministry of Finance was reorganized and some modern taxes were introduced (see 8:6). But the increasing loss of control by the government over the country, aggravated by growing Russian intervention in the north and British in the south (see chap. 1), made it very difficult to collect revenue and draw up realistic budgets. Thus in 1912, the treasurer general, M. Mornard, drew two lists of revenue, a minimum one totaling 7,000,000 tumans (of which customs were 3,200,000, land taxes and rents on *khaliseh* 2,500,000, and excise duties on opium and alcohol 500,000) and a maximum of 10,700,000 tumans (3,500,000, 5,000,000, and 750,000 respectively).[14] On the expenditure side, debt service amounted to 2,581,000 tumans, absorbing a quarter to a third of revenues.[15] Various draft budgets for this period are also available, but it is not clear to what extent they were implemented.[16] Their most striking features were, on the one hand, the high military expenditure—3,886,000 tumans in 1910/11—and, on the other, the tiny amount allocated to economic and social development; the Ministry of Trade and the Ministry of Education, Vaqfs, and Public Works received between them just under 100,000 tumans. Total estimated expenditure in that year was 19,000,000 tumans. It was not until after

---

[10] See text in Demorgny.

[11] See Lambton, *Landlord*, p. 179, and Mochaver, pp. 159–61.

[12] See also Mochaver, pp. 210–34.

[13] Lambton, *Landlord*, pp. 178–79.

[14] A breakdown of revenues actually collected in 1912/13 shows a total of 5,807,000 tumans, excluding customs. The main items were land tax (*maliat*) 3,984,000 tumans; excise duties 798,000, and *khaliseh* 636,000—see Demorgny, pp. 94–95.

[15] Mochaver, pp. 289–90.

[16] Jamalzadeh, pp. 157–66.

the First World War that Iran acquired a flexible and responsive tax system and began to invest heavily in development (see epilogue).

Like other Middle Eastern and North African countries, Iran began to contract foreign debts in the second half of the nineteenth century. In those countries the need for money arose from three sources: royal extravagance, rising military expenditure entailed by the modernization of the armed forces, and the payment of indemnities to foreign governments or individuals. All three operated in Iran, but the first seems to have been the most important. Iran's first public debt was incurred in 1892 and by 1913 the total stood at about £7,650,000 and debt servicing amounted to over £500,000 (see 8:7). Both these figures are very small compared to either Egypt or Turkey (see EHME, pp. 94–106 and 430–45); they represented a far lower level of indebtedness per capita and probably formed a much smaller proportion of national product. But expressed as a fraction of government expenditure, the Iranian figure—one quarter—was not greatly below that of Turkey—one third—or even that of Egypt—one half. And Iran had even less to show for its debt, in the way of new assets or productive enterprises, than did Egypt or Turkey. Fortunately for Iran, the fact that borrowing began nearly forty years later than in those countries prevented the accumulation of a huge debt and made it relatively easy to pay off the greater part of the debt after the First World War.

Iran was also fortunate in its direct capital investment. Relatively small amounts were invested in various sectors, notably petroleum, transport, and banking, by private individuals or by enterprises combining private and government funds (see 8:4). On the whole, such investments proved beneficial to the country, developing resources and providing the government with both revenue and foreign exchange, but their main impact did not make itself felt until after the First World War (see epilogue).

## Exchange Rates and Prices

The table in the following selection has been compiled from numerous consular reports. In the first half of the period, the source was usually a statement of expenses incurred in Iranian money, with the equivalent amount given in either sterling or sicca or Bombay rupees. In the latter half, the consular reports give either the average rate prevailing in their district during the year under review, or the range of such rates.

Over the whole period, the exchange value of the kran fell to under a fifth of what it had been at the beginning of the century. Until around 1860, the main factor depressing the kran was the reduction in its weight and fineness (see appendix). After that, the rapid fall in the price of silver, relative to gold, operated even more powerfully (see 8:3). Consequently, whereas it had taken over fifty years for the exchange rate to fall to one half of what it had been in 1809, a further drop of one half was recorded in only thirty more years. Between the mid 1890s and 1914, there was little further depreciation.

One would expect such a decline in the exchange value of a currency to be accompanied by a rise in the price level, and all accounts agree that prices did indeed advance sharply. But it is extremely difficult to get enough data to make quantitative estimates. In view of the great variety of conditions in the country, and in view of the fact that very high transport costs prevented the emergence of a national market, comparisons between prices in various towns are almost meaningless—as is brought out in the following table. For the same reasons, prices in any given place fluctuated sharply from year to year, depending on crops. Uncertainty regarding the quality of the goods referred to is also considerable. Last, the consuls tend to stress advances in prices, since they could use this to back a claim for higher salaries, while ignoring periods of decline.

PRICES, MARCH 1900
(krans per batman of 5.088 kgs.)

| COMMODITY | TEHRAN | TABRIZ | RASHT | YAZD | HAMADAN | ISFAHAN | SHIRAZ | BUSHIRE |
|---|---|---|---|---|---|---|---|---|
| Barley . . . . . . . . . | 3 | 2.55 | 2.5 | 1.75 | 2 | 1.4 | 0.6 | 0.85 |
| Wheat . . . . . . . . . | 5.2 | 3.2 | 2.5 | 2.5 | 2.65 | 1.9 | 1.7 | 1.45 |
| Bread . . . . . . . . . | 4 | 1.8 | 3.2 | 2.2 | 2.25 | 1.8 | 1.35 | 2.65 |
| Rice . . . . . . . . . . | 8 | 10.05 | 6.5 | 5 | 8 | 3.8 | 2.65 | 3.5 |
| Meat . . . . . . . . | 13 | 8.65 | 9 | 8 | 8 | 6.55 | 5.65 | 5.25 |
| Sugar . . . . . . . . | 11 | 11.2 | 6.5 | 10 | 10.5 | 11.4 | 8.55 | 7.5 |
| Tea . . . . . . . . . . | . . . . | 42.2 | 45 | 30 | 28 | . . . . | 53.4 | 42 |
| Charcoal . . . . . . . | 2.27 | 1.4 | 0.5 | 10.8 | 1.65 | 2.1 | 2.65 | 1.5 |
| Kerosine . . . . . . . | 5.7 | 5 | 1.6 | 6.5 | 5 | 5.9 | 6.4 | 5.8 |

SOURCE: Conget to Delcassé, 14 May 1900, AE Téhéran, vol. 5.

Some interesting conclusions may be drawn from this table. Not surprisingly, the capital generally showed the highest prices, and was usually followed by the second center of activity, Tabriz. The southern, and less developed, half of the country had the lowest prices. The cheapness of kerosine and sugar in Rasht is accounted for by proximity to Russia and in Bushire by access to other sources of supply (see 7:3 and chap. 3, introduction). The very high price of charcoal in Yazd was due to the aridity of the surrounding land.

Three lists of prices, for Tabriz in 1845 (Abbott, November 1845, FO 60/117), Tehran in 1847 (Abbott, 15 July 1847, FO 60/233), and Mazandaran and Astarabad in 1847/48 (Abbott, "Journey," FO 60/141) are available. Some of the more important commodities listed are as follows:

*Tabriz, 1845*

(a) Wheat bread—5 shahis per *man* of 1,000 *mithqals*, or 10$\frac{5}{12}$ pounds; this was equivalent to 0.25 pence per pound. However a note adds: "This is very cheap— in ordinary times it is 20 to 40 and 60 percent dearer; 5 years since it was 300 percent dearer on account of bad harvests."

(b) Wheat—4$\frac{1}{5}$ shahis per *man*, equal to 1s. 1$\frac{1}{5}$d. per bushel of 60 pounds.

*Tabriz, 1847*

(a) Wheat bread—26 krans 13½ shahis to 31 krans 13⅓ per *kharvar* of 100 Tabriz *mans* or about 650 pounds; this was equivalent to 0.47 to 0.56 pence per pound.

(b) Wheat—19 krans 13 shahis to 21 krans 15 per Tabriz *man*, or 1s. 9d. to 2. per bushel.

(c) Rice—1 kran 18 shahis to 3 krans 8 shahis per Ray *man*, or 26 pounds; this was equivalent to 8 to 14 shillings per cwt. (112 lbs).

(d) Mutton—1 kran 3 shahis per Tabriz *man*, equivalent to 2d. per pound.

(e) Cotton—6 krans 10 shahis to 7 krans per Ray *man*; this was equivalent to 2.8 to 3 pence per pound.

*Mazandaran, 1847/48*

Rice—in Amul, 5 to 8 krans for 30 Tabriz *mans*; in Barfurush 4 to 5 shahis per Tabriz *man*.

The wheat and bread prices recorded in Tehran and Tabriz were distinctly lower than those in Britain at that time. Between 1840 and 1850, the price of wheat in England and Wales ranged between 40 and 70 shillings an imperial quarter, or 5 shillings and 8s. 9d. a bushel, and that of bread between 1¾ and 3d. per pound.[1]

The next thirty years saw a sharp rise in prices in Azerbaijan. In 1857 the British consul reported that in the previous year or two bread had gone up by 70 percent, barley by 50, candles by 66 and charcoal by 30 percent, but that the price of meat had remained unchanged (Abbott to Clarendon, 14 November 1857, FO/223). In 1861 the consul reported that "in consequence of the late scarcity in this part of the country" prices had increased between 1854–55 and 1861 as follows: bread 100 percent, meat 140 to 200, rice 144 to 154, fowls 277 to 357, eggs 50, butter 25, milk 20, charcoal 75 (FO 60/259—see also prices for 1860 in Report on Azerbaijan, FO 60/253). And in 1872, the consul stated[2] that the "present price" of bread was 1 kran 8 shahis per 10 pounds, compared with an "ordinary price" of 8 shahis; for beef the figures were 2 krans and 1 kran 4 shahis, respectively, for rice 3 krans 10 shahis and 1 kran 8 shahis, and for mutton 5 krans and 1 kran 16 shahis. As to grains, wheat cost 160 krans per 1,000 pounds, compared with an

[1] Lord Ernle, *English Farming* (London 1961), p. 489, and B. R. Mitchell and Phyllis Deane, *Abstract of British Historical Statistics* (Cambridge, 1962), p. 498.
[2] "Tabriz," A and P 1872, 58. The general accuracy of the figures is confirmed by the following table from a French consular report (AE, Tauris, vol. 2, 10 August 1873):

PRICES PER BATMAN OF ABOUT 5½ KGS., TABRIZ
(krans and shahis)

| Commodity | 1872 | March 1873 |
|---|---|---|
| Wheat | 2.10 to 2.15 | 0.18 to 1.2 |
| Butter | 10 to 12 | 6 to 7 |
| Meat | 2.10 to 3.15 | 2 to 2.10 |
| Coffee | 11 to 13 | 11 to 13 |
| Barley | 1.7 to 1.8 | 0.12 to 0.14 |

"ordinary price" of 40, and barley 135 compared with 25. It will be noticed that even the "ordinary price of bread was 60 percent higher than in 1845 and that of wheat 80 percent higher."

In Rasht, the price of sheep rose from 7 krans per head in 1874 to 50 in 1897/98, and that of oxen from 50 to 160; rice rose from 1 kran per *man* of 12¾ pounds to 12 krans per *quti* of 60 pounds (7 krans in 1893) and raw cotton from 5½ krans to 12 krans per *man* of 13 pounds. The rise was particularly sharp after 1892/93, and in 1898 the British consul estimated that the "purchasing value of sterling" had risen 25 percent but that expenses had increased by at least 100 percent during the previous five years.[3] For Mashad, the following table is available:[4]

PRICES IN MASHAD
(krans and shahis per *man* of 6½ pounds)

| COMMODITY | 1897/98 | 1898/99 | 1904/5 | 1905/6 |
|---|---|---|---|---|
| Mutton . . . . . . . | 2.0 | 4.5 | 5.35 | 5.5 |
| Bread. . . . . . . . | 0.45 | 0.55 | 1.50 | 1.35 |
| Ghee . . . . . . . . | 6.0 | 11.0 | 15.0 | 17.75 |
| Rice . . . . . . . . | 2.0 | 3.0 | 5.0 | 4.95 |
| Milk . . . . . . . . | 0.6 | 1.0 | 2.0 | 2.0 |
| Charcoal[a] . . . . . | 25.0 | 50.0 | 75.0 | 69.0 |
| Firewood[a] . . . . . | 12.5 | 23.0 | 35.0 | 35.0 |

[a] Per 100 *mans*.

In 1891/92, the price of bread had been 1¼ shahis a pound and of mutton 5 shahis—figures slightly below those of 1889/90; wheat cost 14 shahis a stone (14 pounds) and barley 10 shahis, against 17 and 10, respectively, in 1889/90.[5]

As regards Tehran, a memorandum by Eastwick dated 4 April 1861 (FO 251/39) refers to a table (unfortunately missing) with 1843, 1855, and 1861 prices and concludes: "On a general average it appears that prices have risen from 70 to 150 percent but the most important articles, wheat and barley, charcoal and mule hire etc. are thrice as dear as they were at the time of Sir J. McNeil and Sir J. Sheil."

Last, some prices in Tehran in 1898 and 1914 may be compared with those given earlier for 1847. In 1898, bread cost 1 kran 7 shahis a Tabriz *man*, or about 500 percent of 1847, and mutton 18 shahis a *sir* (1⅔ pounds) or about 300 percent.[6] In 1914, the cost of bread per Tabriz *man* was 2 krans, or nearly 800 percent of 1847, of mutton 8 krans or about 350 percent, and of rice 4 krans or 500 to 800 percent.[7] Other food may have risen in similar proportions, but this may have been partly offset by the decline—or smaller rise—that presumably took place in the price of such imported manufactured goods of mass consumption as cotton textiles, sugar (which was heavily subsidized—see chap. 3, introduction) and kerosine.

[3] "Rasht," A and P 1876, 76; ibid., 1893, 95; ibid., 1898, 97; a list of prices in Tabriz, Rasht, and other towns for 1875–77 is given in Stolze and Andreas, pp. 84–85.
[4] "Khurasan," A and P 1906, 127.
[5] "Mashad," A and P 1890, 76; and ibid., 1892, 83; see also Curzon, *Persia*, 1:167.
[6] Lorini, p. 392.
[7] Jamalzadeh, p. 185.

## Selection 1. Exchange Rates, 1800-1914 [Charles Issawi]

### RATE OF POUND STERLING IN KRANS

| Date | Place | Rate | Source |
|------|-------|------|--------|
| 1800 | | about 10 | Malcolm |
| 14 Dec. 1809 | Tabriz | 11.0 | FO 60/2 |
| 5 Aug. 1812 | Tabriz | 11.4 | FO 60/7 |
| 1 Feb. 1814 | Tehran | 12.5 | FO 60/9 |
| 30 Nov. 1814 | Tehran | 12.9 | FO 60/9 |
| 15 Feb. 1815 | Tehran | 13 3 | FO 60/10 |
| 30 Nov. 1815 | Tehran | 12.9 | FO 60/10 |
| 22 June 1816 | Tehran | 12.9 | FO 60/11 |
| July–Sept. 1816 | Tehran | 12.9 | FO 60/11 |
| Jan.–March 1817 | Tehran | 12.9 | FO 60/12 |
| Apr.–June 1817 | Tehran | 12.9 | FO 60/12 |
| July–Sept. 1817 | Tehran | 13.0 | FO 60/12 |
| Oct.–Dec. 1817 | Tehran | 12.9 | FO 60/12 |
| Jan. 1817 | Tehran | 13.0 | FO 60/13 |
| April 1817 | Tehran | 13.2 | FO 60/13 |
| 3 March 1820 | Tehran | 11.3 | FO/60/19 |
| 26 Nov. 1824 | Tehran | 13.6 | FO 60/24 |
| 1 Dec. 1824 | Tehran | 13.5 | FO 60/24 |
| July–Sept. 1825 | Tabriz | 17.6 | FO 60/25 |
| Oct.–Dec. 1825 | Tabriz | 17.6 | FO 60/26 |
| Jan.–March 1826 | Tehran | 17.1 | FO 60/26 |
| Apr.–June 1826 | Tehran | 17.1 | FO 60/26 |
| July–Sept. 1826 | Tehran | 17.2 | FO 60/26 |
| 7 Dec. 1826 | Tehran | 17.6 | FO 60/26 |
| 23 Sept. 1834 | Tehran | about 20.0 | FO 60/34 |
| 5 March 1839 | Erzerum | 20.0 | IO LP & S/9 vol. 64 |
| 5 May 1842 | Tehran | 20.0 | FO 60/92 |
| 29 June 1844 | Tehran | 20.0 | FO 60/108 |
| 25 Oct. 1844 | Tehran | 20.8 | FO 60/107 |
| 1 July 1845 | Tehran | 22.0 | FO 60/117 |
| 27 Nov. 1845 | Tehran | 22.0 | FO 60/117 |
| 30 Dec. 1845 | Tehran | 21.6 | FO 60/117 |
| 7 March 1846 | Tabriz | 21.7 | FO 60/126 |
| 13 Nov. 1846 | Tabriz | 21.5 | FO 60/126 |
| 18 May 1847 | Tabriz | 21.0 | FO 60/133 |
| 21 June 1847 | Tabriz | 21.5 | FO 60/133 |
| 25 Oct. 1847 | Tehran | 21.8 | FO 60/141 |
| 21 Feb. 1848 | Tehran | 21.5 | FO 50/141 |
| 28 March 1848 | Tehran | 22.0 | FO 60/141 |
| 30 June 1848 | Tehran | 22.5 | FO 60/141 |
| 22 Oct. 1848 | Tehran | 22.5 | FO 60/141 |
| 31 Dec. 1848 | Tehran | 22.5 | FO 60/141 |
| 1848 | Tabriz | 21.0 | FO 60/147 |
| 1851 (average) | Tabriz | 22.1 | FO 60/166 |
| 1852 (average) | Tabriz | 21.5 | FO 60/174 |
| 1853 (average) | Tabriz | 21.5 | FO 60/186 |
| 5 Sept. 1854 | Tabriz | 22.3 | FO 60/197 |
| Nov. 1856 | Tabriz | 22.0 | FO 60/211 |
| 1857 (average) | Tabriz | 22.8 | FO 60/223 |
| 2 March 1858 | Tabriz | 22.8 | FO 60/234 |
| 1859 (average) | Tabriz | 22.0 | FO 60/253 |
| 1859 | Tabriz | 21.8–22.4 | FO 60/253 |
| 1860 (average) | Tabriz | 22.4 | FO 60/253 |
| May 1861 | Tabriz | 22.4 | FO 60/259 |
| 30 Sept. 1861 | Tabriz | 22.5 | FO 60/259 |
| June 1862 | Tabriz | 22.6 | FO 60/271 |
| Sept. 1862 | Tabriz | 22.5 | FO 60/271 |
| 20 Feb. 1863 | Tabriz | 22.5 | FO 60/277 |
| March 1864 | Tabriz | 22.5 | FO 60/286 |
| Jan.–March 1866 | Tabriz | 23.5 | FO 60/300 |
| Apr.–June 1866 | Tabriz | 23.5–24.0 | FO 60/300 |
| July–Sept. 1866 | Tabriz | 24.0–25.0 | FO 60/300 |
| Mar.–June 1867 | Tabriz | 25.0 | FO 60/307 |
| July–Sept. 1867 | Tabriz | 25.0 | FO 60/307 |

| Date | Place | Rate | Source |
|---|---|---|---|
| Oct.–Dec. 1867 | Tabriz | 25.0 | FO 60/307 |
| 29 Apr. 1868 | Tehran | 25.0 | A and P 1867–8, 69 |
| 30 May 1870 | Rasht | 26.0 | A and P 1871, 65 |
| 31 January 1871 | Tabriz | 25.0 | FO 60/337 |
| 1871 (average) | Tabriz | 26.0 | FO 60/338 |
| 1869/70 (average) | Rasht | 26.0 | FO 60/345 |
| 1870/71 (average) | Rasht | 26.0 | FO 60/345 |
| 1871/72 (average) | Rasht | 23.5 | FO 60/345 |
| 1869/70 (average) | Tehran | 26.0 | FO 60/345 |
| 1870/71 (average) | Tehran | 25.0 | FO 60/345 |
| 1871/72 (average) | Tehran | 23.5 | FO 60/345 |
| 25 Nov. 1872 | Tabriz | 25.5 | A and P 1873, 67 |
| 1872/73 (average) | Tabriz | 24.0 | FO 60/354 |
| 1872/73 (average) | Rasht | 22.0 | FO 60/354 |
| July–Sept. 1873 | Rasht | 23.5 | FO 60/354 |
| 31 Jan 1874 | Rasht | 25.1 | A and P 1874, 67 |
| 1873/74 (average) | Tabriz | 24.0 | FO 60/366 |
| 1873/74 (average) | Rasht | 23.5 | FO 60/366 |
| 1874/75 (average) | Rasht | 23.5 | FO 60/375 |
| 1875 (average) | Rasht | 25.0 | A and P 1876, 76 |
| 1876 (average) | Rasht | 25.0–27.0 | A and P 1877, 82 |
| 1876/77 (average) | Tehran | 26.0 | FO 60/400 |
| Apr.–June 1876 | Rasht | 25.0 | FO 60/401 |
| July–Sept. 1876 | Rasht | 25.0 | FO 60/401 |
| Oct.–Dec. 1876 | Rasht | 27.0 | FO 60/401 |
| Jan.–March 1877 | Rasht | 26.0 | FO 60/401 |
| End 1876 | Tabriz | 27.0 | A and P 1878, 75 |
| 1877/78 (average) | Tabriz | 29.0 | FO 60/415 |
| 1877/78 | Tabriz | 28.0–31.5 | A and P 1878, 75 |
| 1878/79 (average) | Tabriz | 27.5 | FO 60/425 |
| 1878/79 (average) | Rasht | 26.0 | FO 60/425 |
| 1878 (average) | Rasht | 26.0 | A and P 1878–79, 70 |
| 1879/80 (average) | Tabriz | 27.0 | FO 60/431 |
| 1878/79 | Tehran | 27.0 | FO 60/440 |
| 1879/80 | Tehran | 27.0 | FO 60/440 |
| 1880/81 | Tehran | 27.0 | FO 60/440 |
| 1881/82 | Tehran | 26.8 | FO 60/448 |
| 1879/80 | Tehran | 27.6 | A and P 1886, 67 |
| 1880/81 | Tehran | 27.5 | A and P 1886, 67 |
| 1881/2 | Tehran | 27.9 | A and P 1886, 67 |
| 1882/83 | Tehran | 28.6 | A and P 1886, 67 |
| 1883/84 | Tehran | 29.0 | A and P 1886, 67 |
| 1884/85 | Tehran | 31.0 | A and P 1886, 67 |
| 1883 | Tabriz | 29.0 | FO 60/457 |
| 1883/84 | Rasht | 28.0 | FO 60/464 |
| 1883/84 | Tehran | 29.0–31.0 | FO 60/463 |
| 1885 | Tehran | 31.4 | A and P 1887, 85 |
| 1889/90 | Mashad | 35.1 | A and P 1890, 76 |
| 1890/91 | Mashad | 34.0 | A and P 1892, 83 |
| 1892 | Rasht | 36.0 | A and P 1898, 97 |
| 1892/93 | Rasht | 38.0 | A and P 1893–94, 95 |
| 1894 (average) | Rasht | 50.0 | A and P 1904, 100 |
| 20 June 1894 | Tabriz | 50.0 | A and P 1894, 87 |
| 1897 | Kermanshah | 50.0 | A and P 1899, 101 |
| 1898 | Rasht | 49.0–50.0 | A and P 1898, 97 |
| 1898 | Tabriz | 53.5 | A and P 1899, 101 |
| 1897 (average) | Tehran | 51.2 | A and P 1904, 95 |
| 1898 (average) | Tehran | 50.9 | A and P 1904, 95 |
| 1899 (average) | Tehran | 52.0 | A and P 1904, 95 |
| 1900 (average) | Tehran | 51.1 | A and P 1904, 95 |
| 1901 (average) | Tehran | 52.5 | A and P 1904, 95 |
| 1902 (average) | Tehran | 55.5 | A and P 1904, 95 |
| 1903 (average) | Tehran | 55.7 | A and P 1904, 95 |
| 1899 (average) | Rasht | 51.8 | A and P 1904, 100 |
| 1900 (average) | Rasht | 50.4 | A and P 1904, 100 |
| 1901 (average) | Rasht | 52.5 | A and P 1904, 100 |
| 1902 (average) | Rasht | 55.0 | A and P 1904, 100 |
| 1903 | Rasht | 51.0–55.5 | A and P 1907, 91 |

| Date | Place | Rate | Source |
|---|---|---|---|
| 1904/5 | Mashad | 55.0–64.0 | A and P 1906, 127 |
| 1904/5 | Muhammerah | 57.0–63.0 | A and P 1906, 127 |
| 1905 | Bushire | 51.5–64.8 | A and P 1906, 127 |
| 1905/6 | Kermanshah | 55.0–64.5 | A and P 1906, 127 |
| 1905/6 | Mashad | 58.0–64.5 | A and P 1906, 127 |
| 1906/7 | Isfahan | 53.0–59.0 | A and P 1908, 114 |
| 1906/7 | Yazd | 52.8–58.5 | A and P 1908, 114 |
| 1906/7 | Kermanshah | 52.8–59.0 | A and P 1908, 114 |
| 1907/8 | Kermanshah | 48.5–50.0 | A and P 1908, 114 |
| 1906/7 | Mashad | 51.0–57.0 | A and P 1908, 114 |
| 1907/8 | Mashad | 46.0–50.0 | A and P 1908, 114 |
| 1906/7 | Lingah | 50.5–52.5 | A and P 1908, 114 |
| 1907/8 (average) | Sistan | 51.4 | A and P 1908, 114 |
| 1910/11 | Tehran | 54.0 | A and P 1910, 94 |
| 1900/1 (average) | Bushire | 52.8 | A and P 1910, 101 |
| 1901/2 (average) | Bushire | 54.4 | A and P 1910, 101 |
| 1902/3 (average) | Bushire | 57.5 | A and P, 1910 101 |
| 1903/4 (average) | Bushire | 57.3 | A and P 1910, 101 |
| 1904/5 (average) | Bushire | 60.2 | A and P 1910, 101 |
| 1905/6 (average) | Bushire | 60.1 | A and P 1910, 101 |
| 1906/7 (average) | Bushire | 55.5 | A and P 1910, 101 |
| 1907/8 (average) | Bushire | 51.3 | A and P 1910, 101 |
| 1908/9 (average) | Bushire | 54.5 | A and P 1910, 101 |
| 1909/10 | Kerman | 52.0–55.0 | A and P 1910, 101 |
| 1907/8 | Bandar Abbas | 48.8–52.5 | A and P 1910, 101 |
| 1908/9 | Bandar Abbas | 51.0–56.3 | A and P 1910, 101 |
| 1909/10 | Bandar Abbas | 54.8–57.8 | A and P 1910, 101 |
| 1909/10 | Kermanshah | 52.3–57.3 | A and P 1910, 101 |
| 1908/9 (average) | Muhammerah | 53.5 | A and P 1910, 101 |
| 1909/10 (average) | Muhammerah | 56.7 | A and P 1910, 101 |
| 1909/10 | Mashad | 53.0–55.0 | A and P 1910, 101 |
| 1909/10 | Bushire | 54.3–58.8 | A and P 1910, 101 |
| 1910/11 | Muhammerah | 53.8–56.0 | A and P 1912/13, 98 |
| 1908/9 | Rasht | 50.5–56.5 | A and P 1912/13, 98 |
| 1909/10 | Rasht | 51.5–57.0 | A and P 1912/13, 98 |
| 1910/11 | Rasht | 53.5–54.5 | A and P 1912/13, 98 |
| 1910/11 | Isfahan | 52.8–54.1 | A and P 1912/13, 98 |
| 1911/12 (average) | Tehran | 54.5 | A and P 1912/13, 98 |
| 1911/12 | Kirman | 49.5–52.0 | A and P 1912/13, 98 |
| 1911/12 | Mashad | 54.0–56.0 | A and P 1912/13, 98 |
| 1911/12 | Kermanshah | 54.5–56.5 | A and P 1912/13, 98 |
| 1911/12 | Sistan | 54.3–56.0 | A and P 1912/13, 98 |
| 1909/10 | Lingah | 51.7–56.8 | A and P 1912/13, 98 |
| 1910/11 | Lingah | 51.8–54.7 | A and P 1912/13, 98 |
| 1911/12 | Lingah | 54.5–56.1 | A and P 1912/13, 98 |
| 1909/10 | Bandar Abbas | 54.8–57.8 | A and P 1912/13, 98 |
| 1910/11 | Bandar Abbas | 52.5–55.5 | A and P 1912/13, 98 |
| 1911/12 | Bandar Abbas | 52.5–56.3 | A and P 1912/13, 98 |
| 1912 (average) | Tehran | 55.1 | A and P 1912/13, 98 |
| 1911/12 | Isfahan | 52.7–54.4 | A and P 1913, 71 |
| 1911/12 | Yazd | 49.3–53.8 | A and P 1913, 71 |
| 1911/12 | Tabriz | 53.5–56.0 | A and P 1913, 71 |
| 1911/12 | Bushire | 51.3–56.0 | A and P 1913, 71 |
| 1913/14 | Kermanshah | 55.0–56.5 | A and P 1914/16, 74 |
| 1913/14 | Lingah | 53.8–57.0 | A and P 1914/16, 74 |
| 1911/12 | Bandar Abbas | 52.5–56.3 | A and P 1914/16, 74 |
| 1912/13 | Bandar Abbas | 52.5–55.0 | A and P 1914/16, 74 |
| 1913/14 | Bandar Abbas | 52.5–55.5 | A and P 1914/16, 74 |
| 1913/14 | Bushire | 55.8–57.8 | A and P 1914/16, 74 |
| 1911/12 (average) | Muhammerah | 54.0 | A and P 1914/16, 74 |
| 1912/13 (average) | Muhammerah | 56.8 | A and P 1914/16, 74 |
| 1913/14 (average) | Muhammerah | 57.0 | A and P 1914/16, 74 |
| 1913/14 (average) | Mashad | 55.0 | A and P 1914/16, 74 |
| 1913/14 (average) | Kirman | 55.1 | A and P 1914/16, 74 |
| 1913/14 (average) | Tehran | 55.0 | A and P 1914/16, 74 |
| 1913/14 | Isfahan | 53.5–55.3 | A and P 1914/16, 74 |
| 1913/14 | Yazd | 55.0–55.5 | A and P 1914/16, 74 |
| 1913/14 | Sistan | 56.0–56.8 | A and P 1914/16, 74 |

## Banking in Iran

Although the business of the *sarrafs* (money changers) seems to have expanded in the course of the nineteenth century, the need for modern banking began to make itself increasingly felt. A first attempt was "made in 1866, when the Paris house of Erlanger applied for a concession to establish a bank in Tehran. The negotiations were broken off when the Iranian government refused to guarantee the inviolability of deposits against arbitrary seizure by the authorities—a pledge required by the Erlangers."[1] The abortive Reuter concession of 1872 (see 4:7) included the right to found a bank, and various schemes, including the one described in the following selection, were put forward from time to time. Of these, perhaps the most interesting was the proposal made by a Persian business-man, Muhammad Hasan Amin az-Zarb in 1879 (see 2:5).

The first establishment actually opened—in 1888—was the branch of the New Oriental Banking Corporation, with headquarters in London, which opened offices in Tehran, Mashad, Tabriz, Rasht, Isfahan, and Bushire. The following year, the Imperial Bank of Persia, a British firm, was founded, with a paid-up capital of £1,000,000, in settlement of the Reuter claim. Its shareholders included members of some of the leading British firms in Iran, such as Hotz and Sassoon.[2] Among its privileges was the exclusive right, for sixty years, of issuing bank notes. In addition to undertaking ordinary commercial transactions, it made loans to the Persian government and delivered bar silver to the mint for coinage. In 1890, it took over the agencies of the New Oriental Banking Corporation and opened new branches in Qazvin and Sultanabad. By 1913 its note issue stood at £962,000 and its deposits at £906,000, and it paid regular dividends to shareholders and a small amount to the Iranian government. But as a result of its competition, many of the leading sarrafs went out of business.

The First World War set back the bank, but after that the upward trend was resumed. In 1931, the note issue stood at £1,881,000, and deposits at £2,895,000. However, under the agreement of 30 May 1930, the note issue rights of the bank were transferred to the government-owned Bank Melli Iran, which had been founded in 1928. In 1948, it changed its name to British Bank of the Middle East and continued its commercial activity in Iran until 1952 and still operates in some other parts of the Middle East.

A Russian bank was bound to follow the British one. In 1891, Poliakov received, in compensation for his railway scheme which had also been frustrated (see 4:8), the right to found a bank and established the Banque des Prêts with a capital of 1,875,000 gold rubles. In 1899 its shares were taken over by the Russian government, its capital was raised to 30 million rubles, and it became a branch of the Russian State Bank; in 1902 its name was changed to Banque d'Escompte de Perse. It, too, opened branches in various parts of Iran, especially in the north.

[1] Ronall.
[2] Tomara, cited by Glukhoded, p. 20.

Like the Imperial Bank it made loans to the Persian government, delivered silver to the mint, and engaged in commercial activities, including the handling of real estate. The bank was liquidated in February 1921, under an agreement with the Soviet government.

Attempts were also made by Iranian nationalist circles, in 1906–10, to attract a German bank. First the Deutsche Orientbank and then the Deutsche Bank showed some interest. However, like the German railway projects with which they were connected (see 4:9) these schemes were not implemented. Nor did any success attend the effort made during the constitutional period to found a national bank, and the Bank Melli was not opened until 1928.

(See also the works by Bank Melli Iran, Lorini, Nayyeri, Ronall, and Yaganegi, listed in the bibliography.)

### Selection 2. Banking Project, 1885
[Souchard to Freycinet, AE, Correspondance Commerciale, Téhéran, vol. 3, 14 July 1885]

At present, there is some talk in Tehran of founding a bank under the name of "Banque de Perse et d'Afghanistan," which would be used for centralizing all movements of funds between Persia and Europe.

While not denying the great advantages which such an institution would provide in a country desiring to advance resolutely on the road of progress and civilization, I find myself compelled to state to Your Excellency that, in view of the insecurity of commercial operations in Persia, such a project can serve only to enrich the promoters of the enterprise, at the expense of those investors who are sufficiently trusting to provide the funds needed for constituting the bank. I feel it the more incumbent on me to point out to the department this state of things, because the founders of this company (three Armenians from Constantinople, Messrs. Kitabji, Charles Bazirgian, and Mirza Yusuf, backed by H. E. Muhsin Khan, ambassador of Persia in Constantinople and Hajji Mehmet Khan, consul general of Persia in Egypt and brother-in-law of Muhsin Khan) claim to have secured the cooperation of the Ottoman Bank in this enterprise and to be certain of finding

in Paris the capital they need. It would be deplorable if French money were thrown away in such an adventure which, I am sure, will bring back memories of the Turkish or Egyptian loans.

Under the farman granted by the shah, the bank will have the sole privilege of issuing—under government supervision—banknotes which will be accepted by all government departments [*caisses publiques*]. But what will be the bullion backing which every bank must hold if it has to cash its notes at sight? At present, in the whole of Persia, the gold tuman—whose initial value was about 12 francs—can no longer be found. In Azerbaijan—in Tabriz—only Russian coins of 15 and 20 kopeks are in circulation; in Tehran, silver coins of one and two krans which, because of their high lead and copper content, are hardly more than counterfeit coins; and in the countryside, only copper coins of one and two shahis. As for banking operations proper, how can they be seriously undertaken seeing that the natives almost never pay bills due at the specified date? Under one pretext or another, one is put off to the next day, or the day after that. The government itself resorts to such means: treasurers hold on to the money received for payment of salaries and lend it, at interest, in the bazaar. The only person who has any money is His Majesty, but once money enters the vaults of the imperial treasury it never comes out again, but accumulates without producing anything. Last, should the bank advance loans secured by houses or real estate, it would be very difficult for it to liquidate its security; for its debtors would raise so many difficulties and would enter into such plots with the *mujtahids*, who are supposed to dispense justice according to the Quran, that it could never recover its loans.

In such circumstances, Your Excellency will surely acknowledge that the project for founding the Banque de Perse admits of only two explanations: it is either a harebrained scheme or a vulgar swindle. Fortunately, this business may end as so many others have done in Persia; that is, it will never be implemented and the farman granting the concession will, because of the shah's whim or for some other reason, lapse and become inoperative. . . .

## Selection 3. Currency and Banking

[Joseph Rabino, "Banking in Persia," *Journal of the Institute of Bankers*, 13, January 1892]

. . . *Currency:* The story of Persian currency, like that of all eastern countries, is a story of depreciation, and in great measure of debasement.

When I had the privilege of addressing you upon Egyptian currency matters,[1] I pointed out that the Egyptian piastre, now worth $2\frac{1}{2}d.$, is no more than the Maria Teresa dollar, reduced to $\frac{1}{20}$th of its value. Etymology gives us in Persia also a lesson in economic history: I have spoken frequently of a toman, which is actually a piece of money of ten silver krans, worth about 5*s.* 9*d.* Now toman is a word introduced into Persian by the Mongols, under Jenghiz Khan, in the 13th century. It signifies "ten thousand," and, amongst other applications, was used to mean ten thousand dinars. The dinar, as we saw,[2] was a gold coin of 52 grains, equivalent, therefore, to a fraction,

[1] "On a Proposed Reform of the Egyptian Currency," *Journal of the Institute of Bankers*, 8, part 1, January 1887.
[2] Ibid.

more than half-a-sovereign; consequently a toman was worth about £5,000.

With the Sefavieh dynasty, during the 16th century, the toman ceased to be equivalent to 10,000 gold dinars, and under Abbas the Great, a toman of money was equivalent to 50 abbassis—a silver coin weighing about 130 grains, and the value of the toman was about £3 7*s.* 0*d.* The abbassi was divided into four shahis—weighing each 18 grains of silver, and worth about 4*d.* The toman, as it does to day, still figured in accounts as 10,000 dinars, but the dinars became a mere money of account without any coin to represent it.

The weights of the silver coinage were soon reduced, and in 1678, one toman (or 50 abbassis) was worth £2 6*s.* 8*d.* At the beginning of the 18th century, under Shah Sultan Hussein, the abbassi weighed only 84 grains, and the toman was worth about £2 4*s.* 0*d.*, and under Nadir Shah, some years later, the abbassi were reduced to 72 grains, and the toman was worth £1 18*s.* 0*d.*

In Sir John Malcolm's "History of Persia," published in 1815, the toman is put down at £1. Under Fath Ali Shah, who died in 1835, krans, each weighing 142 grains, were first coined, and a kran was equal to five abbassis or 20 shahis, and was the tenth part of a toman, which was worth 15*s.*

The Shahis ceased to be silver coins, and with a further reduction in the weight of the kran, silver abbassis were also abolished. The kran experienced several reductions in weight; already in 1839, ten of them, or one toman, were worth only 10*s.* $9\frac{1}{2}d.$, and now, 1891, as we have already said, the toman is worth about 5*s.* 9*d.*

The abbassi, or one-fifth of a kran, is worth less than $1\frac{1}{2}d.$, and the shahi is a copper coin weighing 77 grains, and worth a quarter of that amount.

It is tolerably certain that the people had to bear the weighty burden of these tamperings with the standard, and, as in other countries, the decrease in weight or fineness of coin was no more than an indirect and very severe tax.

Of the copper coinage we are told, for

instance, that it was considerable, that each town had its own coinage, and that it was re-minted every year at a reduction, and that the old coin was forcibly bought up at par with the new coin of lesser weight.

In the seventeenth century, one pound of copper was coined into 46 kasbeks, worth 1s. 4d., giving a profit of 15 per cent.

The Shah, in 1672, received a royalty of 2 per cent. on the mintage.

Three inferences may, I think, be drawn from the fragmentary notices we have of currency matters, viz: that the riches of the country have greatly decreased; that the circulating medium has for ages been below the wants of the country, and that one of the causes of this lack of coin is the hoardings of the Government, and doubtless also of the people.

As to the country's wealth, Contarini, Venetian Ambassador in Persia, from 1474 to 1476, says: "The Persians are a very pompous nation, and their camels are so well caparisoned, that it is a pleasure to look at them. Few are so poor as not to possess at least seven camels."

Another evidence we have in the notices of travellers, as to prices generally, Giosafat Barbaro, who was in Tabriz in 1474, says: "Bread costs a little more than at Venice; wine, four ducats the Venetian quarter (29 pints); meat, 1¼d. per lb." In the same year, Contarini, who was at Isfahan, gives the same price for wine, and says that "Bread is reasonable; meat dearer than in Venice; wood, a ducat a camel load; fowls, seven for a ducat."

Pietro della Valle, writing in 1620 from Isfahan, quotes fowls five or six for a piastre. Although these indications are too vague to be a trustworthy guide, it is clear, from the comparative value of the precious metals, that prices were higher than during this century.

Of the scarcity of coin, we have very evident proof.

In 1471, Vincentio d'Alessandri says that importers of silver gain 20 per cent., of gold 14 to 15 per cent., of copper 15 to 20 per cent.

In 1644 the export of gold and silver was prohibited.

All the authors of the seventeenth century speak of the scarcity of gold, the coinage being principally copper.

In 1739, Monsieur Bourdarde de Beaumont, French Resident at Bender Abbas, says:—

I have the honour to send you an inventory of this house, and of the warehouses wherein are the company's goods which would have been sold by this time if I had been able to arrange with the merchants the kind of payment, the scarcity of copper having led them to propose payment in silver *which cannot leave the country without loss;* If the merchants insist upon buying against silver, I shall be forced to acquiesce for fear the goods should be further damaged, and in the hope of exchanging my silver for copper or gold when opportunity arises. . . .

Of the state of the currency in recent times, we shall speak later.

The examples of hoarding show that the present condition of things has long existed in the country.

Teodoro Balbi consul of Syria 1578–82 says the resources of Persia were 4 to 4½ millions ducats—Vicentio d'Alessandri, in 1571, put them at 5 millions. He adds that Shah Tahmasp, who died in 1576, after a fifty years reign, left in his treasury gold, silver, and jewels, incredible as it may seem, to a value of 80,000,000 ducats, of which 17,000,000 coined in gold medins. He also left horses, mares and camels to a number of 100,000.

Olearius in 1637, puts the revenues at 20,000,000 florins, and Chardin, in 1672, at 700,000 tomans or £1,631,000. He estimates at £2,000,000 the value of the Shah's gold plate, and states that he receives daily 1,200 tomans, and spends 1,000, the net revenues going into the Royal treasury, "a perfect abyss, for all is lost in it, "and very little comes out."

In 1739, Nadir Shah brought into Persia an immense treasure arising from the looting of Delhi. Sir John Malcolm says: "the march of Nadir Shah from India was literally encumbered with spoil. The amount of plunder that he carried from that country has been estimated variously. The highest calculations makes it upwards of seventy millions sterling; the lowest is considerably more than thirty. A great part of this was in precious stones."

Political fears, and want of means of employing funds, are probably the cause of the hoarding by king and people which has continued to our days. . . .

To what extent these remarks are applicable to Persia, the following table will show:—

SILVER KRANS[a]

| YEARS | AVERAGE EXCHANGE ON LONDON (Krans per) £ | AVERAGE PRICE OF SILVER PER OZ. STD. | LEGAL WEIGHT (Grains) | LEGAL FINENESS | AVERAGE WEIGHT | AVERAGE FINENESS | INTRINSIC VALUE OF KRANS, CALCULATED ON LEGAL WEIGHT AND FINENESS | DEPRECIATION OF KRANS, MEASURED ON EXCHANGE | DEPRECIATION OF KRANS MEASURED ON PRICE OF SILVER |
|---|---|---|---|---|---|---|---|---|---|
| 1863 | 21.2 | $61\frac{3}{4}$ | 77 | 900 | 76.30 | 820 | 25.05 | ..... | ..... |
| 4 | 21.2 | $61\frac{3}{4}$ | 77 | 900 | 76.30 | 820 | 25.05 | ..... | ..... |
| 5 | 21.95 | $61\frac{1}{16}$ | 77 | 900 | 76.30 | 820 | 25.18 | 0.75 | 0.13 |
| 6 | 24.70 | $61\frac{1}{8}$ | 77 | 900 | 76.30 | 820 | 25.15 | 3.50 | 0.10 |
| 7 | 25 | $60\frac{9}{16}$ | 77 | 900 | 76.30 | 820 | 25.39 | 4.80 | 0.34 |
| 8 | 25 | $60\frac{1}{2}$ | 77 | 900 | 76.30 | 820 | 25.41 | 4.80 | 0.36 |
| 9 | 25 | $60\frac{7}{16}$ | 77 | 900 | 76.30 | 820 | 25.44 | 4.80 | 0.39 |
| 1870 | 25 | $60\frac{9}{16}$ | 77 | 900 | 76.30 | 820 | 25.39 | 3.80 | 0.34 |
| 1 | 22.65 | $60\frac{1}{2}$ | 77 | 900 | 76.30 | 820 | 25.41 | 1.45 | 0.36 |
| 2 | 23 | $60\frac{5}{16}$ | 77 | 900 | 76.30 | 820 | 25.49 | 1.80 | 0.44 |
| 3 | 24.50 | $59\frac{1}{4}$ | 77 | 900 | 76.30 | 820 | 25.95 | 3.30 | 0.91 |
| 4 | 25 | $58\frac{5}{16}$ | 77 | 900 | 76.30 | 820 | 25.37 | 3.80 | 0.32 |
| 5 | 26.56 | $56\frac{7}{8}$ | 77 | 900 | 76.30 | 820 | 27.03 | 5.30 | 1.98 |
| 6 | 27 | $52\frac{1}{4}$ | 77 | 900 | 76.30 | 820 | 29.15 | 5.80 | 4.10 |
| 7 | 27.80 | $54\frac{13}{16}$ | 77 | 900 | 76.30 | 820 | 28.05 | 6.60 | 3 |
| 8 | 28 | $52\frac{9}{16}$ | 77 | 900 | 76.30 | 820 | 29.25 | 6.80 | 4.20 |
| 9 | 28 | $51\frac{1}{8}$ | 71.065 | 900 | 70.60 | 895 | 32.50 | 6.80 | 7.45 |
| 1880 | 27.75 | $52\frac{1}{4}$ | 71.065 | 900 | 70.60 | 895 | 31.88 | 6.55 | 6.83 |
| 1 | 27.50 | $51\frac{15}{16}$ | 71.065 | 900 | 70.60 | 895 | 32.07 | 6.30 | 7.02 |
| 2 | 28 | $51\frac{13}{16}$ | 71.065 | 900 | 70.60 | 895 | 32.15 | 6.80 | 7.10 |
| 3 | 29 | $50\frac{5}{8}$ | 71.065 | 900 | 70.60 | 895 | 32.91 | 7.80 | 7.86 |
| 4 | 30.75 | $50\frac{1}{4}$ | 71.065 | 900 | 70.60 | 896 | 32.72 | 9.55 | 7.67 |
| 5 | 32.10 | $48\frac{9}{16}$ | 71.065 | 900 | 70.60 |  | 34.19 | 10.90 | 9.14 |
| 6 | 33 | $45\frac{3}{8}$ | 71.065 | 900 | 70.60 | 895 | 36.60 | 11.80 | 11.55 |
| 7 | 32.75 | $44\frac{5}{8}$ | 71.065 | 900 | 70.60 | 895 | 37.21 | 11.55 | 12.16 |
| 8 | 34.75 | $42\frac{7}{8}$ | 71.065 | 900 | 70.60 | 895 | 38.73 | 13.55 | 13.68 |
| 1889 | 36.25 | $42\frac{11}{16}$ | 71.065 | 900 | 70.60 | 895 | 38.85 | 15.05 | 13.80 |

[a] Total fall on Silver 30.61 per cent.
Total depreciation of Krans, measured by exchange, 41.50 per cent.
Total depreciation of Krans, measured by price of Silver, 35.52 per cent.
Average appreciation of Krans, compared with exchange, for the whole period, 8 per cent.

In order to bring the lessons of this table more clearly before you, the diagram here shown has been drawn.

The depreciation of the standard of value in Persia has been, as we see, continuous; the only break being during the years 1871–73, when funds sent from London to relieve the famine, temporarily disturbed the movement of the exchange.

In 1889, the depreciation reached its maximum, whilst in 1890, the rise in silver and—much more than that—an abnormal export of fruit, with a rise of price in the north and a large export of opium in the south, sent the exchange down to a lower point than it had touched for eight years.

The fall in silver is clearly only one of the causes of the depreciation of the kran, the others being the unfavourable trade balance and the deterioration of the currency.

Statistics of Persia, however carefully compiled, I look upon as practically valueless; but such as they are, they point to an excess of imports over exports. In "Consular

Report 113, April, 1878, Persia," the figures given are:—

Imports . . . . . £5,250,000
Exports . . . . . 4,000,000

In the Hon. Geo. Curzon's valuable letters in the *Times*, the amounts given are in still greater contrast.

The constant drainage of silver, principally from Tabriz,[3] whence it is exported to Central Asia where, as in Persia, the kran circulates at a fictitious value, is another proof of this theory.

The danger to which a bank which imports capital into Persia is exposed is three-fold:—

*First:* The depreciation of the capital by the fall in silver, and the gradual rise in exchange due to the excess of imports over exports.

*Second:* The narrowness of the Persian markets rendering the return of any considerable amount of funds an extremely difficult and tedious operation.

*Third:* The fact that capital is always imported at a loss, inasmuch as the intrinsic value of the krans is considerably below their exchange value.

An Anglo Persian Bank, founded in 1861, would, therefore, at the end of 1889 have lost about 41½ per cent. of its capital, presuming the improbable case of being able to remit any large sums at all, consequently, it is clearly the proper policy to obtain as much local money as can be employed, and to import capital with great caution, and always with a view to its return.

The ideal situation of an English bank trading with the East, is when its capital remains in gold, whilst its operations are conducted in silver by means of its deposits.

The situation in Persia is peculiarly favourable to this manner of working. The difference between the intrinsic and the exchange value of the kran, notwithstanding the constant demand for exchange as shown in the diagram, is very remarkable. During almost the whole of the period embraced by our tables there has been a constant appreciation of the Persian currency. This can only be due to the great dearth of silver of which we have ample evidence in the commercial centres of Teheran, Tabriz and Isfahan, and one of the causes of this dearth is the universal custom of hoarding. This habit we have seen was prevalent in the middle ages, and has come down to our own times. Now, as then, large sums are yearly engulfed by the Royal Treasury; now, as then, those who have money hide it, even to their own loss. The government hoarding is due to political pre-occupation, that of the people to the absence of any trustworthy organisation for the safe custody of private moneys.[4]

The first function of a bank is to attract these funds and render them once more fruitful to the country generally. The vivifying of these stagnant moneys is as useful an operation as importing silver from abroad, and a much sounder one, as such silver would have to be paid for sooner or later.

Experience has shown—even the experience of a mere twelvemonth—that this is perfectly possible, and, with patience, by no means very difficult.

Persians are beginning to see the advantage of becoming depositors in a bank offering European guarantees and conducted upon European principles, and persons competent to form an opinion, predict that before many years all the money required for trade purposes and more perhaps, will be found in the country.

The second function of a bank in Persia is: *The distribution of funds, that is the providing of funds when and where required in or out of the country.*

---

[3] Consular Report 69, 1886, Persia. Trade of Tabriz (1885) speaks of "the constant drain of specie outwards, arising from the yearly recurring excess of imports over exports."

[4] General Maclean, Consul General at Meshed, says: "If the new bank decides to open a branch at Meshed, it will be looked upon as a great boon by many, and will, probably, do a very large business, especially if it issues notes. *There is plenty of money lying idle and hidden away.* . . ." "Diplomatic and Consular Reports on Trade and Finance, 1890," 753. "Persia: trade of Khorassan."

The movement of funds is an operation of considerable difficulty in a country so destitute of means of communications as Persia is.

A Scotch bank could easily send a million of pounds from its London office to Edinburgh between the hours of the closing of its doors in the evening, and the re-opening of them the next morning.

But the distance between Tabriz and Teheran, the two most important trade centres of Persia, is considerably less than that between Edinburgh and London and the post which is bi-weekly and takes, when all goes well, five days for the journey, will only carry £1,000 of specie at a time for one establishment. Any large sum, by which I mean £5,000 to £10,000, for to send more would be impracticable, must be forwarded by caravan, which takes from 16 to 24 days to accomplish the distance.

The following table is more eloquent than any explanation that can be given on this subject:—

## TABLE B

| FROM TEHERAN TO | DISTANCE IN MILES | DAYS' JOURNEY BY POST | DAYS' JOURNEY BY CARAVAN | OBSERVATIONS |
|---|---|---|---|---|
| Tabriz . . . . . . . . . | 350 | 4 | 17 | During winter and |
| Resht . . . . . . . . . . | 200 | 3 | 10 | bad weather, times |
| Meshhed . . . . . . . . | 558 | 8 | 24 | much in excess for |
| Isfahan . . . . . . . . | 245 | 4 | 12 | letters, and in cara- |
| Shiraz . . . . . . . . . | 530 | 8 | 27 | van column, days |
| Bushire . . . . . . . . . | 700 | 13 | 37 | of stoppages not |
| Yezd . . . . . . . . . . | 412 | 8 | 21 | added. |
| Kerman . . . . . . . . . | 640 | 12 | 32 | |
| Hamadan . . . . . . . . | 200 | 3 | 9 | |
| Kermanshah . . . . . . . | 330 | 5 | 14 | |

The conditions just pointed out render it necessary to foresee any abnormal scarcity of funds, and to provide for it by forwarding specie to the locality threatened, in order to come to the help of trade.

For instance, from June to September, the opium crop absorbs all the floating capital of the provinces, of which Isfahan and Yezd are the centres; the money goes into the villages, to the great inconvenience of those towns.

Again, the export season of fruit, silk, &c., from the province of Azerbaijan is from August to November, and at this time exchange falls abnormally low, testifying to the extreme scarcity of money, and greatly hampering trade.

Internal exchange is a very important part of a bank's business in Persia, for besides trade requirements, there is a normal and constant demand for remittances to the capital for Government requirements.

The following figures have been given me, of the revenues of Persia:—

1839-40 { Cash and value of payments in kind } krs. 34,026,150 at 12.95d.   £1,835,994

1853-4 { Cash and value of payments in kind } krs. 33,685,580 at 10.90d.   £1,153,163

1876-7 { Cash and value of payments in kind } krs. 50,700,000 at 9.25d.   £1,950,800

1888-9 { Cash and value of payments in kind } krs. 54,487,630 at 7.06d.   £1,602,580

The last figures may be thus decomposed:—

Customs, cash . . . . . . . . . . . . . . . . . . . . . . . . . krs. 8,000,000
Taxes, cash and kind . . . . . . . . . . . . . . . . . . . . . . krs. 45,295,850
Post, telegraphs, mint, mines, various concessions . . . . . . krs. 1,191,780

Krs.   54,487,630

Of which krs. 2,633,500 are absorbed by local government charges and collection of revenues.

Of the revenues, about ks. 35,000,000, say, £1,000,000 pounds, have to be remitted to Teheran, the rest being spent in the provinces, for government purposes, such as pensions, army, &c.

This is a considerable volume of business for a country, financially, so underdeveloped as Persia.

Intimately connected with internal exchange is foreign exchange, which is, to a large extent, the instrument enabling internal exchange to be worked at a profit.

The arbitration of foreign exchanges is the key to profitable banking in the country, and is, at the same time, the most interesting occupation of a banker.

Arbitration of exchanges consists, as the members of the Institute know, in profiting by a break of level in prices, as the engineer seeks his water power in any sudden fall of a river bed.

Steam and electricity bring prices everywhere to the same level with great and increasing rapidity, so that profits are yearly diminishing and becoming more difficult to make.

With the continent, and even with India, genuine arbitration without speculation is now almost impracticable, on account of the perfection to which communications have been brought.

Not so in Persia, where the services a bank can render to trade are so considerable, that although transactions are very limited and irregular, a fair remuneration is still obtainable without speculation.

The exchange of Persia upon London is specially affected in the north by the value of the rouble, in the south, by that of the rupee. Of these two influences, that of the rouble is the more important and the more constant, Tabriz, the Persian centre of the Russian exchange, approaching much nearer to a regular market than any other place in the country.

At times it is possible to profit by the two exchange currents, as in the following case:—the rupee exchange being dependent entirely upon the price of silver, whilst the Russian exchange obeys quite other influences.

In Isfahan, there was last year a great dearth of silver for moving the opium crop, and a consequent fall in the price of bills upon India, drawn against or in anticipation of shipments. Silver indeed was scarce everywhere, and yet could only be imported at a loss, but there was a certain individual demand of gold for hoarding. Gold was, therefore, brought in and paid for in London; the silver received for the gold was sent by caravan to Isfahan, where rupee bills were bought upon Bombay, whence remittances were sent to London.

The breaks of level were Teheran, where gold was accidentally above its value, through demands of a private individual, and Isfahan, where rupee bills were below their exchange value, through the want of money to purchase opium.

The links of the operation go through two continents, and the duration of it was about three months.

But markets are so small in Persia, that such operations are few and far between, and the slightest miscalculation or unforeseen accident may change a profit into a loss.

It is scarcely possible to conceive the difficulty of working in a country where exchange may for months be unobtainable, whilst at other times money cannot be procured, no matter at what sacrifice. Forecasts of movements, based as elsewhere upon general causes, become consequently valueless.

Another operation later, consisted in forwarding silver to Tabriz, where cable transfers were bought on Odessa for the purpose of remittances to London from this last place.

And when operations of the kind are profitable to a bank, they are necessarily still more to trade. Thus the purchases of rupee paper in Isfahan and rouble transfers in Tabriz, furnished money to merchants, and each transaction tended to raise the price of bills, diminish the margin of profits to the bank, and the consequent cost of procuring funds with which to move the crops.

The third function of a bank in Persia is:—

### THE IMPROVEMENT OF THE CIRCULATING MEDIUM

Any one who has examined a handful of old Persian coin, i.e., coin minted before 1877, will understand the difficulty there is in counting (for weighing is out of the question) and examining any considerable sum. A thorough and well thought out reform is, therefore, of great urgency, as a first step to the economic regeneration of the country.

Unfortunately, to bring about such a reform, the Persian Government must give up all its old ideas of administration and its profits obtained by farming out the mint; in fact it must submit to be absolutely guided by European theory and practice.

Attempts have been made of late years to attain this object, but they have failed, on account of the public weal having frequently given way to temporary profit.

In 1863, Monsieur Davoust was invited to Teheran to take charge of the mint, but the resistance, active and passive, he encountered, was so great, that seven years later he left the country without having been able to accomplish anything.

In 1875, Herr Pechan, an Austrian mint official, was entrusted with a reform of the currency, and initiated one which would have been efficient had he been allowed full powers and the requisite means for carrying out his ideas. He no sooner had begun his work, however, than he was ordered to coin large quantities of copper, and to leave silver minting for a future occasion. When he attempted to coin a standard silver kran, and asked for the funds necessary for raising the quality of the piece, he was met by a refusal, and by a suggestion as to alloy, which it was impossible for him as an Austrian official to accept.

Herr Pechan furnished the following table, showing the result of his assays of coin in circulation in 1877. It must be stated that at that time the governors of provinces had each a local mint, for working which they paid a yearly royalty.

### TABLE C

| PROVINCES | YEARS | | WEIGHT IN GRAMMES | FINENESS PER 1,000 | VALUE IN FRANCS |
|---|---|---|---|---|---|
| | A.H. | A.D. | | | |
| Hamadan . . . . . | 1293 | 1877 | 4.95 | 760 | 0.836 |
| Tauris . . . . . . . | 1290 | 1874 | 4.90 | 820 | 0.8926 |
| Kashan . . . . . . | 1282 | 1865 | 5.03 | 820 | 0.91658 |
| Isfahan . . . . . . | 1293 | 1877 | 5.02 | 840 | 0.937 |
| Kerman . . . . . . | 1293 | 1877 | 4.90 | 840 | 0.9146 |
| Mazanderan . . . . | 1292 | 1876 | 4.97 | 840 | 0.9277 |
| Meshed . . . . . . | 1293 | 1877 | 4.90 | 840 | 0.91 |
| Kermanshah . . . . | 1282 | 1866 | 4.97 | 880 | 0.9719 |
| Resht . . . . . . . | 1280 | 1864 | 4.80 | 890 | 0.9493 |
| Teheran . . . . . . | 1292 | 1876 | 5.02 | 900 | 1.004 |
| Shiraz . . . . . . . | 1291 | 1875 | 4.90 | 900 | 0.98 |
| Yezd . . . . . . . | 1278 | 1862 | 4.97 | 900 | 0.994 |
| Herat . . . . . . . | 1277 | 1861 | 4.90 | 900 | 0.98 |

These figures give some idea of the irregularity of the Persian currency. Between krans of Hamadan and those of Teheran, there is a difference in value of no less than 17 per cent.; between those of other towns and of the capital, the difference is very considerable from a monetary point of view, although less than in the extreme cases quoted.

Since 1877 the currency has certainly not improved, for the old heavy krans have been re-minted, and the debased ones remain in circulation in obedience to Gresham's law.

It is evident that a reform of the currency can only be carried out in one of two ways:

*Firstly:* The Government should abandon the policy of farming out the mint for a yearly sum, and should take over the direct management of the currency. A new coinage should be struck, and the old coinage called in and re-minted at its legal standard and weight, at the expense of the State. This would be the best and soundest solution to the difficulty, but to carry it out the ideas of the Government must undergo a complete revolution.

*Secondly:* The mint might be handed over to European control for a definite period, to be worked for the benefit of the State. As the Government would probably refuse to make any sacrifices for the reform, there remains only the creation of a new system, based upon a kran, corresponding to the value of the coin actually in circulation, less the cost of re-coinage. This would enable the old coinage to be called in, and, with the dearth of the circulating medium, it is probable that the modification would affect the exchange very slightly, if at all.

On the other hand, a uniform type of kran, well executed, and circulating in sufficient quantities, would undoubtedly be a great boon to trade and to the country generally.

Meanwhile, a most valuable palliative to this monetary disorder has been introduced in the shape of bank notes.

The immense difficulty in the transmission of funds has been pointed out, and when the country has been sufficiently educated to understand the theory of a sound paper currency, and when, therefore, it has acquired a little of that confidence in a bank note, which two centuries of good government, financial security and progress, have given to the Bank of England issues, Teheran notes will circulate everywhere, and trading transactions will be greatly facilitated and hastened.

Meanwhile, the people, ignorant of the banking organizations and methods with which other countries have long been familiar, require time to understand the difference between a bank note, and a cheque which needs to be presented without delay for payment. This, of course, does not apply to the mercantile classes.

To begin with, therefore, it was necessary to have local issues of notes, payable at the issuing branches, for in a country like Persia, where movements of specie are so costly, slow and difficult, as to become impracticable, except on a small scale, the danger of issuing notes payable at more than one place, is obvious.

This mode of proceeding was adopted by the Bank of France, until the public generally was educated up to its present knowledge of that great establishment's resources, of which the London market has recently had a graceful and valuable proof.

The Bank of France formerly issued branch notes, but now, I believe only issues Paris notes, which, however, circulate everywhere as money.

The utility of notes in business, in Persia, is established by the following data:—

A street porter will carry about £300 in silver,
an ass load is about £600 in silver,
a mule load is about 800 in silver,
and a camel load is about 900 in silver,
consequently, to bring in to a bank a sum of £25,000 would take

83 men,
or 41 donkeys,
or 31 mules,
or 28 camels,

and to count and scrutinize it, an expert money changer would take about 16 days.

Of the functions of a bank in aiding trade, by giving credit and facilities to import and export traders it is unnecessary for me to speak, these being operations common to all establishments of the kind, throughout the world.

It is almost superfluous to make the observation that that spirit of free trade of which Englishmen are proud to be the apostles, must animate the management of such a bank. That its services must be at the disposal of all, that its impartiality must be unquestioned, that be a merchant Persian or European, French, Russian, Austrian or English, he must know that from the bank he will always have fair and generous treatment. That the interests of the bank are, firstly those of its shareholders, and secondly those of the country which gives it hospitality.

One service a bank may render to a country like Persia, is in diffusing sound business doctrines, and from experience I may say, that Persians are quite willing to recognize their ignorance on many points and to listen to explanations. How necessary this is, the following extract from a Consular report from Tabriz, will show: [5]

Combinations of this kind are believed in, at Tabriz. When the branch of the bank was first opened, the native merchants and moneychangers organized a boycott against it, as they had done against the New Oriental Bank Agency, and refused to sell it bills on

[5] (No. 445, 1888, Persia. Report on the year 1887–88), on the trade of Tabriz.

"As illustrative of the monetary chaos prevalent here, I may mention that the pound sterling at Odessa, in consequence of the state of European politics, went up this summer to 10.85, causing a corresponding rise in the exchanges on the Tabriz market, where, as above stated, 36 krans was obtainable for bills on London whilst the Turkish Lira and paper rouble rose in proportionate value.

"Upon this the European mercantile community, finding these rates detrimental to their pecuniary interests, as their remittances are made through Russia, endeavoured to apply a remedy, by entering into a covenant with some of the principal native merchants, fixing the rates for moneys, and the exchange for bills on Europe in this market.

"This bargain made under the auspices of the Reis-et-Tujjar (a local official delegated to settle commercial disputes) to be renewed monthly, was signed by the European, and by about 50 native merchants; the contracting parties binding themselves under heavy penalties to carry out its provisions.

"It was evident that an agreement of so unprecedented a nature could not hold for long, and it soon died a natural death.

"It was based upon false principles; the question at issue is one that would have righted itself; a mercantile minority could not control the entire local money market in opposition to the laws by which it must be ruled, Odessa, in the present instance, giving the keynote to Tabriz."

Teheran, with the result that the bank forwarded silver, to the great inconvenience of the hostile party.

As it may be imagined, the attempt was not renewed, and traders and money changers, soon found it to their advantage to be friendly.

Later, the authorities tried to put an arbitrary price on gold coin, of course perfectly uselessly.

That a bank can render inestimable services to a country devoid of banking organization and that the future of such bank, will be commensurate with such services is a simple truism; but it would be vain to imagine that a year or two will change the prejudices, the habits of thought of an oriental people with a civilization wholly different from ours, bring it up to our standard of education, and cause it to accept without hesitation or demur our cheques and bank notes, our system of doing business, which are not even understood, our habits of punctuality and exactitude, our whole financial mechanism, in fact, which is the result not of years but of ages of experience.

Nor can we be surprised at this, when we consider that so intelligent and highly cultured a nation as the French has at the present day only partially accepted the cheque system, and cannot be said to have yet acclimatized the clearing house; when we remember that so peculiarly commercial and practical a people as the English, after three quarters of a century of discussion, prefers wasting years of its children's lives and spending hundreds of thousands of pounds annually in useless clerical labour, rather than adopt the decimal system like the rest of the world. . . .

## Foreign Enterprises in Iran

The book from which the following chapters have been translated is a rich source on economic conditions in Iran on the eve of the First World War. In addition to much detailed information, it contains the English or French texts of the concessions under which the main foreign enterprises operated, as well as those of numerous laws and conventions. The author seems to have spent a dozen years in Iran before the war and wrote several books on Persian life and literature.

In addition to the Russian and British concessionaires and firms, which account-ed for the bulk of foreign enterprises in the country, the author mentions those of other nationalities (pp. 191–222).

FRENCH

On 11 August 1900 the French were granted a monopoly for all archeological excavation in Iran. This monopoly was canceled in 1930 by Riza Shah, who opened the country to German and American teams.[1] In 1905, Schneider-Creuzot supplied arms to the Iranian government, extending it a 5,000,000-franc loan (£200,000) repayable over ten years at 6 percent.

The Syndicat Franco-Iranien was founded in February 1913, with a capital of 800,000 francs, for the exploitation of coal mines of Yengi Imam, on the Tehran-Qazvin road near Tehran.

A French group took part in a study undertaken in 1912 by French, Russian, and British banks of a Trans-Iranian railway, linking Baku with Karachi. The total cost was put at 480 million francs, that of the 2,240 kilometers lying in Iran being estimated at 214.5 million. The "Société internationale d'étude de chemin de fer Transpersan" was set up in Paris in May 1912, with a share capital of 2,500,000 francs (see chap. 4, introduction).

BELGIAN

On 17 May 1888, the "Société anonyme des Chemins de fer et Tramways en Perse" was established and received exclusive rights to build railways from Tehran to Qazvin, from Tehran to Shah Abd ul-Azim, and from the latter to Qum. In fact it built a 30 kilometer line from Tehran to the quarries of Shah Abd ul-Azim and ran three lines of horse-drawn streetcars in Tehran. The company's share capital was 4,000,000 francs and in addition it issued 5-percent bonds for another 4,000,000. Its exiguous profits did not enable it to pay more than $2\frac{1}{2}$ percent interest on bonds, and no dividends were distributed. Plans for replacing horses with electric power did not materialize, and neither Tehran nor any other town has had electric streetcars, passing straight to omnibuses.

In 1889 a Belgian, Philipaert, was granted a concession for a sugar factory, established the "Syndicat des Sucreries Belges," with a capital of 5,000,000 francs, and built a refinery near Tehran (see 6:10). It operated at a loss and in 1913 was sold to a group of Zoroastrians for 125,000 francs. A glass factory set up under the same concession was also liquidated, as was a match factory. Gasworks were established in Tehran by the same group.

GERMAN

A concession granted for a Tehran-Khaniqin railway on 1 May 1898, and con-cessions for a Tehran-Shimran and Tehran-Khaniqin road failed to material-ize. So did the attempts of the Persian government, in 1898 and 1908, to raise loans in Germany or to persuade German banks to establish branches in

---

[1] Avery, p. 287; the 1900 grant confirmed earlier ones, given in 1895 and 1897.

Tehran. German interests consisted of a high school in Tehran; the Hamburg-Amerika shipping line's regular services to the Persian Gulf; a few pharmacies; several export or import houses, including the Wönckhaus firm, which also worked iron oxide deposits in the Persian Gulf area (see EHME, pp. 350–55); and a carpet-making firm, "Persische Teppichgesellschaft," founded in 1912 with a capital of 3,000,000 marks, subsequently raised to 10,000,000 (£500,000). The latter had a wool spinning and dyeing plant in Tabriz and branches in Constantinople, Sultanabad, Hamadan, Kirman, Mashad, and Shiraz and exported to Europe and the United States.

## OTHER

The author lists two Austrian trading firms, two Italian, two Dutch, one American (a branch of Singer), one Swiss, and several belonging to Turkish subjects from various minority groups: Armenians, Greeks, and Jews. The largest of these, the Italian firm of Castelli in Tabriz, is stated to have had a capital of 1,000,000 francs. Greeks also played an active part in silk growing in Gilan (see 5:6). One of the leading firms, Koussis Frères, belonged to three Greeks under Russian protection who were described as "millionaires." In addition to their silk interests, they had invested some 500,000 francs in lumbering in the Caspian provinces, where they enjoyed a monopoly until 1907.

As for American interests, in 1887 the United States legation reported that real estate owned by Americans was worth $115,000 to $120,000 "in money originally invested, its actual value being far above these figures and steadily increasing. The property in question is held almost exclusively by our missionaries, who annually expend here not less than $70,000."[2]

(See also the works by Lorini, Jamalzadeh, Kazemzadeh, and Entner listed in the bibliography.)

[2] Pratt to Bayard, 29 November 1886; DSP, 1887, p. 919.

## Selection 4. Foreign Capital and Enterprises, 1914
[Wilhelm Litten, *Persien* (Berlin, 1920), pp. 102–9, 185–90]

CHAPTER 16—SURVEY OF CONCESSIONS GRANTED BY THE PERSIAN GOVERNMENT TO BRITAIN OR BRITISH SUBJECTS AND OF AGREEMENTS CONCLUDED WITH BRITAIN OR BRITISH SUBJECTS

1. 17 December 1862—Indo-European Telegraph Department—Telegraph line Tehran—Bushire and Tehran-Khaniqin.

2. 23 November 1865—Indo-European Telegraph Department—Second line for above.

3. 11 January 1868—Siemens (Indo-European Telegraph Co.)—Telegraph Julfa-Tabriz-Tehran.

4. 2 April 1868—Indo-European Telegraph Department—Telegraph Gwadur-Jask-Bandar Abbas.

5. 2 December 1872—Indo-European Telegraph Department—Third line Tehran-Bushire.

6. 30 January 1889—Baron Julius de Reuter—Bank, mines, issue of banknotes.

7. 26 November 1889—Yahya Khan Mushir al-Dawlah—Roads Tehran-Ahwaz (Arabistan Road) and Burujird—Isfahan.

8. 6 January 1890—Imperial Bank of Persia—Roads Tehran-Ahwaz (Arabistan Road) and Burujird-Isfahan.

9. 11 January 1890—Imperial Bank of

Persia—Carting monopoly.

10. 17 June 1891—Imperial Bank of Persia—Tolls on Tehran-Qum road.

11. November-December 1898—Imperial Bank of Persia—Qum-Isfahan road.

12. 28 May 1901—William Knox D'Arcy—Petroleum monopoly in Persia excluding Azerbaijan, Gilan, Mazandaran, Khurasan, and Astarabad.

13. 24 August 1902—H. F. B. Lynch "and his Company"—Caravan routes instead of roads.

14. 1 September 1904—Government of India—Loan of £314,281-16s.-4d

15. 28 December 1906—Persian Transport Co., Ltd. (Lynch Brothers)—Tolls on Qum-Sultanabad road.

16. 27 May 1910—Imperial Bank of Persia—Consolidated Debt, £760,000.

17. 8 May 1911—Imperial Bank of Persia—Loan of £1,250,000 (Debt in 1910: £490,000).

18. 20 March 1912—Imperial Bank of Persia—Advance of £140,000.

19. 9 February 1913—Persian Railways Syndicate Ltd.—Studies for Muhammarah—Khurramabad—Burujird Railway.

20. 2 March 1913—Persian Transport Co., Ltd. (Lynch Brothers)—Prolongation of term for building of roads until 2 March 1923.

21. 10 March 1913—British government—Lighthouses in Gulf.

CHAPTER 14—"BRITISH TRADING FIRMS"
In addition to the above-mentioned, there were at the outbreak of war the following fourteen British trading firms in Persia:

1. Gray Paul & Co.—Bandar Abbas, Bushire, Lingah.

2. Livingstone, Zeytoon & Co.—Bandar Abbas, Bushire, Lingah.

3. A. & T. I. Malcolm—Bandar Abbas, Bushire, Lingah.

4. H. C. Dixon & Co.—London, Manchester, Bushire, Isfahan.

5. Shawul Morad Hayem & Son—(Representative of Jewish Indian firms)—Bushire.

6. E. David Sassoon & Co.—London, Kermanshah.

7. Sykes—Manchester, Kermanshah.

8. Forbes, Forbes, Campbell & Co.—London, Mashad.

9. Gray & Mackenzie—Muhammarah.

10. Lloyd Scott & Co.—Muhammarah.

11. Hild. Stevens—Tabriz.

12. Hoods Ltd.—London, Manchester, Tehran.

13. The Persian Art Gallery, Ltd.—London.

14. Schumann Brothers & Co.—Urumia.
Britain's total trade with Persia at the outbreak of war was about £4,000,000.

CHAPTER 17—"SUMMARY" [1]
In the course of the war, incomparably larger sums were spent in Persia as part of military expenditure.

[1] The figures given below are rough estimates and make no claim to accuracy.

|  | Invested [*Aufgewendete*] Capital (in pounds sterling) |
|---|---|
| Indo-European Telegraph Department. . . . . | 275,000? |
| Indo-European Telegraph Co. Total Capital £3,000,000 | |
| Of which in Persia . . . . . . . . . . . | 50,000? |
| Imperial Bank of Persia, share capital . . . . . | 1,000,000? |
| 1904 Loan . . . . . . . . . . . . . . . | 314,281 |
| 1911 Loan . . . . . . . . . . . . . . | 1,250,000 |
| 1912 Advance . . . . . . . . . . . . . | 140,000 |
| Persian Transport Co. (Lynch Brothers) . . . . | 100,000 |
| Anglo-Persian Oil Co. . . . . . . . . . . . | 2,747,905 |
| Persian Railways Syndicate . . . . . . . . | 3,000,000 |
| Ziegler & Co. . . . . . . . . . . . . . | 200,000 |
| Oriental Carpet Manufacturers Ltd. . . . . . | 200,000 |
| Shipping lines and trading firms . . . . . . . | 400,000 |
|  | 9,677,186 |

CHAPTER 30—"SURVEY OF CONCESSIONS GRANTED BY THE PERSIAN GOVERNMENT TO RUSSIA OR TO RUSSIAN SUBJECTS AND OF AGREEMENTS CONCLUDED WITH RUSSIA OR RUSSIAN SUBJECTS"

1. 31 February [sic] 1881—Russian government—Exploitation of telegraph line: Chikishlar—Astarabad; Russian control of Persian telegraph offices between Julfa and Chikishlar.

2. 9 July 1886—Russian government—Telegraph fees on the Julfa–Chikishlar section.

3. 12 February 1888—Stepan M. Lianozov—Caspian Sea Fisheries, 1888–1901.

4. 1890—Poliakov and Rafailovich—Pawnshop and bank.

5. 22 April 1891—Russian government—Telegraph fees on the Sarakhs section. Russian control.

6. 14 May 1891—Russian government—Prolongation of 1886 agreement.

7. 17 October 1891—Russian government—Amendment of 1891 agreement.

8. 25 September 1893—Stepan M. Lianozov—Caspian Sea Fisheries 1904–11.

9. 1 December 1891—Poliakov—Transport and insurance monopoly.

10. 7 July 1893—Cie d'Assurance et de Transport en Perse—Enzeli-Qazvin road.

11. 16 October 1893—Russian government—Telegraph fee on the Astara section. Russian control.

12. 5 November 1895—Cie de la Route d'Enzeli—Dredging of Enzeli fairway.

13. 19 December 1895—Cie de la Route D'Enzeli—Qazvin-Tehran road.

14. 19 December 1895—Cie de la Route d'Enzeli—Qavzin-Hamadan road.

15. 10 October 1896—Stepan M. Lianozov—Caspian Sea Fisheries, 1911–20.

16. 10 October 1896—Georgi Lianozov (son)—Caspian Sea Fisheries, 1911–20.

17. 28 September 1898—Gerainov and Inakiev—Karajadagh mines.

18. 1900—Russian government—Loan of 22,500,000 rubles.

19. 1902—Russian government—Loan of 10,000,000 rubles.

20. 2 April 1902—Banque d'Escompte de Perse—Julfa-Tabriz-Qazvin road; coal and petroleum mining on both sides of road.[2]

21. 1902—Russian government—Exploitation and operation of the telegraph line Mashad–Nasratabad (Sistan) and agreement with the Customs Administration regarding duty-free imports.

22. 18 May 1905—Georgi Lianozov (son)—Confirmation of previous agreement.

23. 30 March 1906—same as above.

24. 14 January 1911—Banque d'Escompte de Perse—Consolidated debt of 12,000,000 rubles.

25. September 1911—Nobel Brothers, Baku—Transport of petroleum from Enzeli to Rasht.

26. 20 March 1912—Banque d'Escompte de Perse—Advance of 945,750 rubles.

27. 6 February 1913—Banque d'Escompte de Perse—Julfa–Tabriz railway; Sofian-Lake Urumia; monopoly of coal and petroleum mining on both sides of railway. Preferential rights for all other mines in same zone and along Tabriz–Qazvin section.

CHAPTER 29—"RUSSIAN TRADING FIRMS IN PERSIA"

1. Banque d'Escompte de Perse—Julfa, Enzeli, Isfahan, Qazvin, Mashad, Nasratabad (Sistan), Rasht (representative Ter Sarkissiants Frères), Tabriz, Tehran, Barfurush, Hamadan, Kirmanshah, Sabzevar, Urumia.

2. Severian Kossych, Tehran (Retail). Sale of porcelain and glassware; annual turnover at most 100,000 rubles.

3. Bureau des Transports persans—Astara, Bandar Gez, Julfa, Rasht, Tehran, Mashad.

4. Société de commerce russo-persan—Bushire.

5. Compagnie russe de navigation à vapeur—Representative in Bushire; Firm no. 4; in Lingah Hajji Abdurahman Ben Kazem; in Muhammarah Bazil.

6. Shipping Line Kavkaz i Merkuri [see 4:1]. Representative in Enzeli: Ksenzenko.

7. Arzoumanov in Moscow—Hamadan,

---

[2] The terms of this concession, insofar as they pertain to the Julfa-Tabriz section, were annulled and superseded by the concession listed as number 22 [sic, read 27].

Tehran; export of gum tragacanth, hides, dried fruit; annual turnover 600,000 rubles.

8. Nobel Brothers—Enzeli, Rasht, Hamadan, Isfahan; import of petroleum.

9. Stucken & Co., Moscow—Mashad, Sabzevar.

10. Zenzinov Brothers, Moscow—Muhammarah.

11. K. & S. Lianozov, Astrakhan—Representative in Rasht: Ter Sarkissiants Frères.

12. Baranskii—Sabzevar.

13. Marc Benedict, Baku—Tabriz, Tehran.

14. Sociétés des Manufactures Ludwig Rabenek, Moscow—Import of printed calicoes. Annual turnover: Mazandaran 1,200 bales; Tabriz 800; Azerbaijan 700; Tehran 1,200; Isfahan 1,000; south Persia 400; Total 5,300 bales, 1,000,000 rubles.

15. Aslaniants—Tehran; import of sugar, export of lambskins, dried fruits, etc; annual turnover 800,000 rubles.

16. Rossia—Insurance Company; representative in Tehran: firm no. 2.

17. Prokhorov, Moscow—Tehran; import of printed calico and other cotton cloth; annual turnover 1,000 bales, 300,000 rubles.

18. Société I. C. Rosenblum & Co.—Tehran, Barfurush; purchase and export of cotton.

19. Société russe d'exportation, Moscow—Tehran; import of manufactures and other goods.

20. Société "Provodnik"—Tehran, Rasht, Tabriz; import of rubber goods and galoshes annual turnover 90,000 rubles.

21. Ter Mikirtirshov—Turbat-i Haidari.

22. Nicola Avaghiniants—export of lamb-

skins from Shiraz.

23. Osser and Co.—Barfurush; export of cotton.

In addition to the above, there are numerous smaller Russian firms in Persia. . . . Russia's total trade with Persia before the war amounted to about 120 million rubles a year.

CHAPTER 31—"SUMMARY OF RUSSIAN CAPITAL INVESTMENT (ANGELEGTEN) IN PERSIA (IN RUBLES)"

| | |
|---|---:|
| Telegraphs | 1,000,000 |
| Banque d'Escompte, share capital | 11,800,000 |
| Mortgages | 48,000,000 |
| 1900 Loan | 22,500,000 |
| 1902 Loan | 10,000,000 |
| Consolidated Debt of 1911 | 12,000,000 |
| Enzeli Road Company | 10,000,000 |
| Enzeli Port Company | 1,300,000 |
| Karajadag Mines | 500,000 |
| Lianozov Fisheries | 10,000,000 |
| Julfa-Tabriz-Qazvin Road Company | 4,600,000 |
| Petroleum transport, Enzeli-Tehran | 100,000 |
| Julfa-Tabriz-Qazvin Railway Company (share capital) | 4,690,000 |
| Debentures, (38.5 million francs) | 14,260,000 |
| Shares of Belgian railways held by Russians (50 percent) | 2,000,000 |
| Forestry (Greek company with Russian capital) | 500,000 |
| Shipping companies, trading firms | 20,000,000 |
| | 163,750,000 |

The above figures are only rough estimates and make no claim to accuracy. To the above-mentioned sums should be added those spent in Persia out of secret funds before the outbreak of war as well as the costs of the occupation of northern Persia by about 17,000 [men] for a year. During the war, very large amounts were spent in Persia as part of Russian military expenditures; their exact magnitude, however, escapes my knowledge.

## Government Revenue

The breakdown of revenues given in the following selection may be compared with one made in 1836: "Revenues of Persia ordered by the late Shah to be paid to the General credit of Government [IO, LP and S/9, vol. 53]." This shows a cash revenue of 2,081,532 tumans and payments in kind worth 379,217—a grand total of 2,460,749 tumans. The main constituents of payments in kind were: 163,084 kharvars of wheat, at 2 tumans each, giving a total value of 326,168 tumans; 12,850 kharvars of rice at 3 tumans, giving a value of 38,550 tumans; and 965 *mans* of silk at 6 tumans, giving a value of 5,787 tumans.

The revenue demand, in thousands of tumans, for the main provinces, in cash and kind (converted at the prices given above) was:

| | | | |
|---|---|---|---|
| Azerbaijan | 496 | Khamsa and Tarun | 40 |
| Fars | 397 | Tusurkan and Malayir | 40 |
| Isfahan | 304 | Tehran | 39 |
| Gilan | 193 | Kirman | 38 |
| Khurasan | 172 | Hamadan | 38 |
| Kizur[a] | 70 | Burujird and Sirlakhur | 35 |
| Kashan | 60 | Nihavand | 28 |
| Qazvin | 50 | Arabistan | 27 |
| Kermanshah | 49 | Qum | 22 |
| Mazandaran and Hizar Jarib | 45 | Khaar | 19 |

[a] Including the *sipahdar* contribution.

For the end of the period, figures are available in several publications. Total revenue in 1912/13 was 5,807,000 tumans, the share of the twelve leading provinces being, in thousands of tumans:[1]

| | | | |
|---|---|---|---|
| Tehran | 1,242 | Burujird | 173 |
| Khurasan | 1,185 | Fars | 167 |
| Azerbaijan | 824 | Yazd | 169 |
| Isfahan | 389 | Kirman | 161 |
| Gilan | 276 | Arak | 111 |
| Qazvin | 231 | Hamadan | 106 |

Except for the rapid rise of Tehran, the most striking difference between the tables is the relative growth of the northern provinces and the stagnation of the southern part of the country.

Some further details are also available for Azerbaijan, Gilan, and Mazandaran. In Azerbaijan, cash revenue in 1850 was put at 540,000 tumans, of which 114,000 came from customs, and 45,000 kharvars of grain; the customs receipts were sent to Tehran and the rest kept in the province (Stevens to Sheil, 7 February 1851, FO 60/166). Ten years later the total was substantially unchanged (see details in Report on Azerbaijan for 1859, FO 60/253). In 1894 its revenues were put at £250,000 ("a quarter of the revenues of Iran"), or 750,000 tumans ("Tabriz," A and P 1894, 87).

As for Gilan, in 1842 its revenue was 200,000 tumans, including customs (Abbott, Report on Journey, 10 May 1842, FO 60/92), in 1844, 204,000 (idem, Journey, 29 June 1844, FO/108) and in 1860, 345,000; of this 177,000 came from land tax, 75,000 from customs, 44,000 from fisheries, 23,000 from *sadirat* and 21,000 from crown lands; 302,000 tumans were sent to Tehran and the balance kept in the province (see details in supplement to General Report of 1860, FO 60/259). In 1866 total revenue was 389,000 tumans (see breakdown in "Gilan," A and P 1867, 67).

The revenue of Mazandaran was put, in 1844, at 90,000 tumans. A detailed

[1] Demorgny, *Institutions financières*, pp. 94–95.

breakdown, by districts, for 1848 gives a total of 96,000 tumans, raised from about 1,000 villages (Abbott, Journey, 29 June 1844, FO 60/108 and idem, Journey, 28 April 1848, FO 60/141). In Astarabad, in 1848, a sum of 16,000 to 17,000 tumans was raised from 200 villages.

The following selection brings out some of the general features of the tax system of Iran (see chap. 8, introduction). Some information on the taxes paid in the three provinces, provided in the above-mentioned reports, may be added.[2]

In Azerbaijan in 1851, villages in the Maragheh and Urumiya districts paid "in kind 2/9ths of produce of all grain," and in cash (Stevens to Shiel, 7 February 1851, FO 60/166):

|  | (Krans) | |
|  | MARAGHEH | URUMIYA |
| --- | --- | --- |
| Head and door money . . . . . . . . . . . . . . | 11.5 | 5.15 to 8.10 |
| Buffaloes and mares, each . . . . . . . . . . . . . . . | 3.0 | 3.10 |
| Cows. . . . . . . . . . . . . . . | 1.10 | 1.10 |
| Sheep and beehives . . . . . . . . . . . . . . . . . | 0.7$\frac{1}{2}$ | 0.10 |
| Asses . . . . . . . . . . . . . . . . . . | 1.10 | 1.15 |
| Fruit gardens, per kharvar measure . . . . . . . . . . . . | 40.0 | 48.0 |
| Vegetable grounds (summer), per kharvar measure . . . . . . | 40.0 | 48.0 |
| In lieu of straw, 2/9 of produce—per kharvar weight . . . . . | 5.0 | 3.10 |

In 1859, the consul reported ("Azerbaijan," 1859, FO 60/253) that, for the whole province of Azerbaijan, village taxes were: "one third of the grain produce, collected mostly in kind; one third of the straw produced, the value of which is generally paid in cash," and 8 shahis on every 10 square *arshins* (an *arshin* equaled 44 inches) on fruit gardens; 10 shahis on every 10 square *arshins* of land under vegetables, tobacco, cotton, or madder roots; a house tax of 11.3 krans per family; 2.10 krans per mare, mule, and female buffalo; and 7$\frac{1}{2}$ shahis per sheep and goat.

Two thirds of the above taxes, being the share belonging to the State, are paid to the Teeool holder, and the remainder to the proprietor of the village. In many cases, the Teeool holder is also the proprietor of the Estate.

Besides the above contributions, the villagers are bound annually to furnish, gratis, to the Teeool holder a certain quantity of lambs, fowls, eggs, milk, wood, etc., and a certain number of labourers if required.

As for Mazandaran, on *khaliseh* land planted to rice,

it appears to be in some instances 5 kherwars of 40 Tabreez mans per jereeb—in others 10 kherwars. Taking the average crops at 30 kherwars per jereeb, the above rates would be 1/6th and 1/3rd. Most of the villages in Mazenderan come under the denomination of Khaliseh.

On private property the rate is very uncertain—it has generally been fixed in remote times, I believe, and a certain sum or amount of Produce required from each village. In some instances the cultivation and produce must have increased but the same amount is all that is demanded—in others it has diminished and a remission has perhaps been

[2] For further details see Lambton, *Landlord*, pp. 164–71.

obtained. In fact the Provinces on the Caspian have generally been greatly favoured in respect of Taxation [Abbott, Journey, 28 April 1848, FO 60/141].

An interesting point, observed in Gilan in 1844, was that revenue "is now raised in money, instead of money and Produce as formerly—but the old plan is still the Standard, the only difference being that the articles for which each District was formerly rated, are now priced and the Amount is required in Cash" (Abbott, Journey, 29 June 1844, 60/108).

(See also 5:5, 14, and works by Curzon, Demorgny, Shuster, Millspaugh, Mochaver, and Lambton, listed in the bibliography.)

### Selection 5. Government Revenue, 1867

[Report on "Persia," A and P 1867–68, 69, pp. 250–55]

REVENUES

During the reign of the present Shah, the revenues of Persia have been increased by nearly 3½ crores of tomans, or 694,000*l.* They now amount to 4,361,660 tomans, or 1,744,664*l.* in money, besides payments in kind, consisting of barley, wheat, rice, and silk, valued at 550,840 tomans, or 220,336*l.*, making the total revenue of Persia, equal to 4,912,500 tomans, or 1,965,000*l.*

The following return shows the revenue demanded from each province during the present year:—

| | | |
|---|---:|---:|
| Ispahan | 420,000 | |
| Fars | 380,000 | |
| Kerman | 210,000 | |
| Yezd | 170,000 | |
| Mazanderan | 110,000 | |
| Ghilan | 440,000 | |
| Cazveen | 70,000 | |
| Khemseh | 180,000 | |
| Azerbijan | 620,000 | |
| Koordistan and Gerroso | 50,000 | |
| Khorassan, with Shahrood and Bestam | 220,000 | |
| Asterabad | 25,000 | |
| Kermanshah, with Looristan and Nehavend | 200,000 | |
| Arabistan | 215,000 | |
| Booroojird | 60,000 | |
| Gulpaigan | 60,000 | |
| Cashan | 70,000 | |
| Koom | 15,000 | |
| Tehran and adjacent districts | 210,000 | |
| Hamadan | 30,000 | |
| | 3,825,000 = | £ 1,530,000 |
| Customs, given in separate Table | 536,660 = | 214,664 |
| Persian Revenue in money | 4,361,660 = | 1,744,664 |

The income received in kind is as follows:—

| | |
|---|---:|
| 247,000 kherwars of barley and wheat, valued at | 494,000 |
| 8,500 kherwars (650 lbs. each) of rice | 25,500 |
| 58,500 kherwars of straw | 29,250 |
| 75 kherwars of nokhood (peas) | 300 |
| 71 mans of silk | 1,790 |
| | 550,840 = 220,336 |

Total Persian Revenue, in money and kind £1,965,000

The payments in kind are mostly reserved for the use of the army, the Shah's own expenses, and extraordinary disbursements.

The Shah does not, however, receive the whole of this revenue. From Khorassan, for instance, nothing is paid to the Royal Treasury, owing to the heavy disbursements made in that province for military service, and for the protection of the line of frontier by a large body of irregular troops employed in repelling the inroads of Turkoman marauders; and during the last year, in consequence of the failure of the silk crop in Ghilan, the revenue of that province has been reduced by more than 100,000 tomans. The provincial Governors, moreover, are frequently defaulters to a large amount. When appointed, they undertake to account to the Central Government for the sums specified above; but it often happens that at the end of the year's tenure of office there is a large deficit which they declare they have been unable for some reason or other to collect from their districts. A fee is then paid to the financial authorities in Tehran; and the Shah is persuaded to remit a large portion of the deficit, which has in reality been received from the peasants, and is eventually shared by the defaulter and his protector at Court.

SOURCES OF REVENUE

The revenue of Persia is derived from the following sources:—

1. Imposts on Crown lands and private landed property. These, so far as they are established and authorized by Government, may be considered on the whole fair and moderate. Two-tenths of all agricultural produce, or its value in money, is supposed to be the amount payable to the Crown by the landholders. As a general rule, however, this is somewhat exceeded, and 25 per cent. may be taken as the average assessment.

2. Duties levied on cattle and flocks, which are as follows:

Goats and sheep, 4 shahees, or 2*d.* each ⎧ –about 8 per cent.
Cows, 1½ kerrans, or 1*s.* 2*d.* each ⎨ on the value of
⎩ wool and butter yielded.

Brood mares, 5 kerrans, or 4*s.* each.
She-buffaloes, 2½ kerrans, or 2*s.* each.
She-asses, 1½ kerrans, or 1*s.* 2*d.* each.
Camels (not employed in transporting merchandize) 5 kerrans, or 4*s.* each.

3. Customs dues, which are farmed by the Government to private individuals, and produce annually a little over 1 crore of tomans, or 200,000*l.* During the present year they are farmed for the following sums:

| | TOMANS |
|---|---|
| Ispahan | 24,500 |
| Cashan | 16,360 |
| Cazveen | 7,400 |
| Khemseh | 3,200 |
| Booroojird | 7,200 |
| Hamadan | 11,000 |
| Asterabad and Barfeeroosh | 19,300 |
| Ginjan and Beejar | 1,000 |
| Tabreez | 235,000 |
| Kermanshah | 20,000 |
| Kerman | 7,000 |
| Fars | 35,000 |
| Ghilan and Fisheries | 100,000 |
| Tehran | 41,000 |
| Gulpaigan | 1,700 |
| Khorassan | 7,000 |
| Total | 536,660 = £214,664 |

4. Capitation tax, amounting to 1 kerran on each male over 18 years of age. This is not exacted from the inhabitants of towns, who may be said to be exempt from all direct taxation.

5. Rates levied upon shopkeepers, artisans, and tradespeople, which are fixed at about 20 per cent. on their annual profits and duties exacted for all provisions brought to market in the principal towns.

In theory, these are the taxes authorized by the Persian Government, but in practice, a very complicated and irregular system of taxation is pursued, the main feature of which appears to be that it is designed solely with a view to take as little as possible from the wealthy and influential classes, and to get as much as possible from the hard-working peasant. The object, indeed of all Persian Governors and their subordinates, as well as of the landowners generally, is to avoid simplicity; for the more intricate and uncertain the method for levying taxes, the greater are the opportunities afforded for extortion and all sorts of illegal exactions. Instead, therefore, of simply adhering to the above rates, by which the revenue is made to depend upon the actual produce yielded from the land, a sum, often arbitrarily fixed, is demanded from each village, without any reference to failure of crops, insufficiency of water for irrigation, disease amongst their flocks, or other losses to which the peasant may be subjected. The amount to be demanded is determined from time to time by Government assessors, "momeiyez," who are dispatched to the various districts to assess the taxes whenever the authorities may feel disposed to alter their amount. The assessor is supposed to perform this duty in accordance with the rates authorized by Government, but great injustice is done on such occasions, as he invariably demands a large fee before giving his decision, and over estimates the taxes if it is refused, or undervalues them when liberally paid. If the land belongs to an influential person, when taxed at all, the amount is made very trifling, and, in numerous instances, villages which have not been assessed for many years, continue to pay only a nominal sum, though they may have increased in size and wealth, simply on account of the proprietor's high position, while others, which have become impoverished, are compelled to pay all the taxes imposed under more prosperous conditions. Nothing can be more unfair than this system, for Persian villages undergo rapid changes, caused not infrequently by oppression, and often from the difficulty of obtaining a sufficient supply of water for irrigation. But even when, for the reasons just stated, the taxes are highly assessed, the peasants gain nothing unless they are the owners of the land themselves, for the full imposts are exacted and are ultimately paid either to the local authorities or to the proprietor of the village, or to the person who may hold it in teule or fief, if Crown property, from the Persian Government. In such cases the Government is, in reality, the loser. Under a more rational system the Persian revenues might be greatly increased, with less hardship to the peasants, whose taxes are now so irregular and uncertain that they scarcely know from year to year, what their liabilities are.

Scarcely any of the inhabitants of towns, or persons of rank, in Persia are called upon to contribute towards the expenses of the State. None of the princes, officers of state, or employés of the Government pay any direct taxes. They maintain immense establishments in town, and possess large houses and gardens in the country, and yet pay no share of the Government expenditure, nor do owners of caravanserais, baths, mills, houses, or shops contribute anything either to the Royal Treasury, or on account of municipal taxes. A deduction of 20 percent, it is true, has for some years been made on all Government salaries, but this is not so much a tax as a reduction of the public expenditure. The same may be said of a stamp duty of 21 kerrans which is exacted on all receipts given for salaries paid by the Government. Both these charges bear heavily upon the poorly paid employé and are not felt by the higher Persian officials, whose incomes are chiefly derived, not from fixed salaries, but from illicit fees and perquisites.

It is evident, therefore, that the burthen of taxation falls upon the agricultural and poorer classes, who are systematically oppressed on account of the revenues and illegal taxes, whilst not a fraction of the sums extorted from them is expended on public works, likely hereafter to benefit the nation at large, and private individuals alone profit by the present unjust system of financial administration.

It is impossible to discover what the people really do pay in excess of the fixed assessment. Some pretend that the irregular exactions amount to a sum equal to the legal assessments, and there does not appear to be any reason for supposing that this is an exaggeration. An idea may be formed of the extent to which they are carried with the connivance of the Government, from the fact that the Governor of Fars is authorized to demand over and above the usual revenue, for his own use, 75,000 tomans a year, and the Governor of Ispahan 60,000 tomans, as "Hek el Hekoomeh" or Governor's fee. The former likewise pays 60,000 tomans, and the latter 40,000 tomans under the name of "Peeshkesh," or an offering made to the King for their appointments, and by these payments they no doubt consider that they have purchased the right to reimburse themselves by means of arbitrary taxation. The same system is pursued with respect to the appointments of all the other Governors, and so long as they pay to the King's Treasury the stipulated amount of revenue and keep the inhabitants from rising in open rebellion, few inquiries are made as to how their duties are discharged.

REVENUE PAID BY MAHOMETANS

Nearly all the revenue of Persia is contributed by the Mahometan subjects of the Shah. The whole amount collected from the Christian population, Jews and Guebres, is very trifling. . . .

## Selection 6. Budgets 1907–14
[Shams al-din Jazairi, *Qavanin-i malieh* (Tehran, 1335), pp. 65–69, 79–81]

FISCAL SYSTEM AND STATE OF BUDGET IN IRAN FROM THE BEGINNING OF THE CONSTITUTIONAL PERIOD TO THE PAHLAVI PERIOD

FISCAL AND ACCOUNTING LAWS AND REGU-
LATIONS PROMULGATED IN THIS PERIOD

At the beginning of the constitutional period and the organization of the First Legislative Session [A.H. 1324–26 (1906–9)], the fiscal system, financial structure, and organization of the budget still retained their old forms. Among other changes and reforms, this system should also have been changed, a budget covering the whole kingdom presented to the Majlis [Parliament] for approval by the deputies, and authorization given to the government to undertake expenditures. But in the first legislative sessions of the Majlis, and especially in the first three, this transformation was not fully carried out, for salaries and allowances continued as in the past—that is, for life. As Mr. Taqizadeh has pointed out, the Financial Committee of the first session—whose chairman was Mushir al-Dawla and secretary Vosuq al-Dawla—spent several months looking into several thousand allowances that were in fact notifications of salaries; in the course of this examination, some allowances were discontinued or reduced. This was done in order to balance the budget inherited from the Muhammad Ali Shah period and which, according to Taqizadeh, showed a revenue of 15.5 million crores [77.5 million krans] and an expenditure of 21.5 million [107.5 million krans]. In addition, in order to balance the budget, the above-mentioned committee abolished *tasir* [conversion into cash, at fixed prices, of taxes estimated in kind]; henceforth taxes were to be paid in kind to the government which itself would undertake the sale of the produce and so derive greater revenue. Similarly, *tuyuls* were abolished by the same committee. These consisted in the assigning of government revenue rights in a given place to one person, in return for a fixed sum of money [see chap. 5, introduction and 5:2]; henceforth, revenues were to accrue directly to the government and those in charge were to receive salaries.

Thanks to the efforts of the committee, and the intense struggle it waged against recipients of salaries and allowances, it was able to strike some sort of balance in the country's expenditure.

I should mention that, in the summary of the laws passed by the First Session, I found no mention of a budget approval and, as stated before, the above information was derived from Mr. Taqizadeh. At any rate, in the list of laws passed during the First Session the only fiscal law listed as having been passed was the Pensions [*wazaif*] Law, whose preamble reads as follows: "A pension is a payment made to the survivors of those who receive salaries of any kind from the government [*divan*]." From this we can see that in this period the titles *wazife* and *mustamirri* (salary) were in use, and also the fact that salaries were given to some people not by virtue of the job they did but as a kind of retirement pension paid to survivors of someone who had previously received it.

*Second Legislative Session* [A.H. 1327–30 (1909–12)].—In this session, for the first time in Iran, a budget was drawn up by the government and presented to the Majlis. This budget was prepared by the orders of Sani al-Dawlah, the minister of finance, but by the time it was ready for presentation to the Majlis he had been assassinated, and it was presented by his successor. Examination of this budget shows that for the first time in Iran, the study and care needed for the preparation of a budget had been applied, and that those who had prepared it were not unaware of the methods of drawing up budgets used in other countries.

In the introduction to that budget, a noteworthy point is made which throws light on the financial state of the country at that time and on its revenue and debt. It also has information on salaries, allowances, and other matters. We shall therefore reproduce part of it:[1]

I present, with great pride, the budget for It-il 1328 [1910/11] to the sacred Majlis, in fulfilment of the legal procedures and representing the appropriations required by the government for the year which is about to end; and I ask for its approval of the work I have succeeded in doing and the first budget of my nation. . . .

It is clear that we are inexperienced beginners in

---

[1] Omissions in original

budget matters. Yet, to reassure those people who had doubts regarding the reforms, it was necessary for us to take the first steps in this direction, without being afraid of showing ourselves to be beginners. I have extracted some information from the confused and ill-arranged fiscal system and presented it. . . .

Iran and China were the only two countries that had no budgets, but Iran surpassed China in this respect. . . .

The lack of cooperation and activity which has so far been the outstanding feature of our governmental administration, showed itself as soon as this work was taken in hand. . . .

It would seem that the absolute power which was in the hands of the mighty Eastern and Western monarchs could not cope with the thought of preparing a budget, for this question never appeared in any country until after the nation had asked for the right of supervision over public finance. . . .

*Expenditure.* The whole amount of budget appropriations asked for totals 14,618,000 tumans and total revenue is 14,116,000; that is, there is an apparent deficit of 500,000 tumans [5 million krans]. But I should inform the honorable deputies that those figures do not represent the facts and that the real deficit—which is not very great—should not be less than 1.5 crores [750,000 tumans, or 7.5 million krans]. . . .

*Public Debt.* This increases government expenditure by 51 million krans a year, or a third of the budget. This item is a disaster, and an unfruitful burden on our finances, from which the country never derived any benefit. Yes, this debt is the legacy of a period of unbridled extravagance and the heritage of our corrupt and shameful court of older times. . . .

Here I can state with great pleasure that one of the accomplishments of the new government is the conversion of the debts of the last two monarchs into a fixed debt with a reasonable rate of interest. . . .

The third chapter, which deals with allowances, may face some criticism as regards both form and principle. We wanted to treat the matter more fully, and to divide it into several articles: first, allowances to government officials; second, allowances to heirs of government officials; third, allowances to various other people; fourth, heirs of such people. But the impossibility of making distinctions between the names of officials and nonofficials prevents the implementation of this intention. . . .

*Estimates of Revenue.* Truthfulness and honesty, which should be the guardians of our work, oblige me to keep the honorable deputies informed and alert them to the need of scrutinizing the revenue figures critically [literally, "without applying too much good will"]. This part of our work has involved much care and trouble, and yet despite this it is not as [good as] it should be. . . .

The expenditure estimates for that year were (in krans):

| | |
|---|---:|
| Majlis . . . . . . . . . . . . . . | 1,330,660 |
| Ministry of Court . . . . . . . . . . | 6,749,470 |
| Ministry of Finance . . . . . . . . . | 63,257,380 |
| Ministry of Justice . . . . . . . . . | 2,362,850 |
| Ministry of Foreign Affairs . . . . . | 4,658,870 |
| Ministry of Internal Affairs . . . . . . | 16,849,020 |
| Ministry of Education, Vaqf and Public Works . . . . . . . . . . . . . . | 3,077,660 |
| Ministry of War . . . . . . . . . . . | 37,324,470 |
| Ministry of Posts and Telegraphs . . . . | 5,540,860 |

| | |
|---|---:|
| Ministry of Agriculture, Trade, and Industry . . . . . . . . . . . . | 28,000 |
| Total . . . . . . . . . . . . . . | 136,185,240 |
| Discounts and irrecoverable sums. . . . | 10,000,000 |
| Total budget . . . . . . . . . . . | 146,185,240 |

Our intention in quoting parts of the introduction of the 1328 budget is, first, to draw special attention to the first historical budget of Iran, and to point out the care and frankness with which those who wrote it informed the Majlis of certain facts and sought to make people aware of the fiscal realities of that time. And, second, it should be noticed that although forty years or so have passed since then, the same shortcomings are still to be seen in our budget. The budget that was submitted to the Majlis this year is in many respects less perfect than the first budget of Iran. For the first was written in a beautiful hand, and has seventy-one pages of introduction which discussed the fiscal state of that time, from which every reader could gain clarification. And in the remaining sixty pages all the figures on revenue and expenditure were given item by item, according to ministries. Such clarity and detail is not to be found in our present budget.

In the fiscal enactments of the Second Session of the Majlis, however, the approval of the proposed budget of 1328 cannot be found in complete form. Only the temporary four-monthly budgets of some of the ministries, such as those for war, internal affairs, and justice were approved, as was that of the Majlis in the form of both four-monthly allocations for 1328 and annual allocations for 1329. . . .

FISCAL LEGISLATION PASSED IN THE FIRST FOUR SESSIONS OF THE MAJLIS

In the First Session, the only bill that passed was the Law on Pensions of 26 *Rabi al-thani*, 1326, which has already been mentioned. A supplement to this bill was passed in the Second Session in 1328. As was mentioned, the question of pensions was a legacy of the Preconstitutional

Period, and they were continued, and even increased, for some time during the Constitutional Period. But after the enactment of the "Supplementary Law of Pensions," some pensions were abolished, as follows: "As regards government salaries paid to deceased persons, all sums exceeding 2,000 tumans will be kept by the Treasury and only 2,000 tumans will be divided among the heirs, for fifteen years to come, in accordance with the following rules." Later on, the number of those who received monthly pensions and allowances, and the amount received by them, declined, but even today some pensions are being paid to the heirs of some officials and others, in the form of monthly allowances.

The second session of the Majlis approved the laws on Salt Tax, Tax on Means of Transport, Duties on [exports of] Casings, Supplement to the Law on Pensions, Public Accounts, Office of Accounts, Opium Restriction, Repeal of Salt Tax, and the above-mentioned Tax on Official Documents.

*Salt Tax.*—As is known, the salt tax was one of the old taxes in France, the levying of which showed many defects and which, because of the rise in rates and in the price of salt, inflicted hardship on the people of that country. In Iran too, in order to increase government revenue, the Salt Tax Law was approved during the second session of the Majlis and a fixed rate was set. But since its levying raised problems, it was abolished, in the same session, through another law.

*Law of Tax on Means of Transport.*—This was passed on 5 *Rabi al-awwal*, 1328 [1910] under the title of "City Tax on the Means of Transport" and laid the foundation of the Tax on Means of Transport which is still in force in Iran.

*Law on Sheep Intestines.*—This law imposed a tax on the slaughter of sheep and, according to its first article: "The intestines and guts connected to the intestines of all slaughtered [sheep] throughout the country belong to the government as a tax." This

law was the foundation of the tax on slaughtered animals, which is still in force. But it is raised in a different form, as we shall mention later.

*The Laws of Public Accounts and Office of Accounts.*—These laws, which constitute the most important legislation concerning accounts, were passed on 21 *Safar* and 23 *Safar*, 1329 [1910], during the Second Session. Since both these laws were amended later, we shall not discuss them here.

*The Law on Opium Restriction.*—This was passed on 12 *Rabi al-awwal*, 1329 [1911], during the second session; its first article reads: "From the date of the enactment of this law, 300 dinars will be levied on each *mithqal* of opium." This law laid the foundation of an indirect tax, the tax on opium. Under later laws, dealing in opium became a government monopoly. The tax on opium, in addition to its fiscal aspect, had an economic and social impact on our country, which we shall discuss in due course.

In the Third Session of the Majlis, because of its shortness and the suspension which caused five years of inactivity, not many laws were passed by the Majlis. But the first laws on real property taxes and tobacco tax were passed at that time.

*Real Property Tax.*—This was passed on 20 *Shawwal* 1333 [1915]; its first article reads: "A tax will be levied on all real property, including shops, stores, rented houses, warehouses, caravanserais, hotels, ice-houses, coffee houses, and public squares in cities and major towns."

This direct tax was later amended and now forms one of the constituent parts of our direct taxes.

*Tobacco Duty.*—The tobacco duty was imposed on 18 *Dhi-qade*, 1333 [1915]; its first article reads: "An excise will be levied on all sorts of pipe and cigarette tobacco produced in Iran." This duty was later sharply raised by the Law of Tobacco Monopoly and today forms one of the greatest sources of indirect taxation and will be mentioned in due course.

*Gum Tragacanth Tax.*—During the Fourth

Session of the Majlis, the Law on gum tragacanth tax was passed. It consolidated the previous taxes and duties on gum, replacing them by 4 percent of the price, taken as a tax, and levied at the border on all gum exported. . . .

## Government Debt.

Iran's first public debt was incurred in 1892, when £500,000 was borrowed from the Imperial Bank of Persia in order to pay off the compensation claimed by the Tobacco Corporation because of the cancelation of its concession (see 5:13). Before that three external transactions had taken place. First, in 1810–13, inclusive, Britain had provided an annual subsidy of 200,000 tumans, which ceased with the end of hostilities with Russia in October 1813 (see correspondence 1820, FO 60/19). Second, the Treaty of Turkmanchai of 1828 imposed on Iran an indemnity of 20,000,000 rubles (10 crores, i.e., 5,000,000 tumans). This was quickly paid off with the help of a second subsidy, of 200,000 tumans, granted by Britain, which wished to speed up the withdrawal of Russian troops from Azerbaijan; the balance of 500,000 tumans which was still outstanding in 1854 was canceled by the Russians, to ensure Iran's neutrality during the Crimean War.[1]

Until close to the end of the nineteenth century, government revenue covered expenditure and often left a small surplus, estimated in 1868 at not less than 500,000 tumans, or £200,000, a year. This was paid into the royal treasury, which at that time was believed to hold 10,000,000 tumans; half of this consisted of the crown jewels and the rest of coins and gold plate.[2] But the growing lavishness of the court, the expenses entailed by repeated royal visits to Europe, and a small increase in expenditure on the armed forces, which were being slowly modernized,[3] began to unbalance the budget. The sale of concessions having proved disappointing (see 4:7 and 5:15), Iran entered the path of foreign indebtedness in which it had been preceded by the other Middle Eastern and North African states (see EHME, pp. 94–106, 430–45). The following table summarizes the position:[4]

| YEAR | LENDER | AMOUNT | DURATION (years) | INTEREST RATE |
|---|---|---|---|---|
| 1892 . . . . . | Imperial Bank | £500,000 | 40 | 6 |
| 1900 . . . . . | Russia | 22,500,000 rubles[a] | 75 | 5 |
| 1902 . . . . . | Russia | 10,000,000 rubles | 75 | 5 |
| 1903–4 . . . . | Anglo-Indian | £300,000 ? | 15 | 5 |
| 1911 . . . . . | Russia | 60,000,000 krans[b] | 15 | 7 |
| 1911 . . . . . | Britain | £1,250,000 | 50 | 5 |
| 1912 . . . . . | Anglo-Indian | £140,000 | . . . | 7 |
| 1913 . . . . . | Russia | £200,000 | 3 | 7 |
| 1913 . . . . . | Britain | £200,000 | 2½ | 7 |
| 1913 . . . . . | Britain | £100,000 | . . . | 7 |

[a] about £2,250,000.  [b] about £1,111,000.

[1] Adamiyat, pp. 305–8; Avery, p. 39, gives a figure of £200,000 for the British subsidy. An attempt by the Iranian government, in 1834, to obtain a third British subsidy, of 200,000 tumans, was unsuccessful (Campbell to Palmerston, 23 September 1843, FO 60/34).

[2] See details in "Persia," A and P 1867–68, 69.

[3] See J. C. Hurewitz, *Middle East Politics: The Military Dimension* (New York, 1969), pp. 40–42.

[4] For a detailed account, and an excellent analysis of the diplomatic factors at work, see Kazemzadeh, chaps. 5 and 7–9; see also Mochaver, pp. 282–86; Sykes, *Persia*, 2:523; and Jamalzadeh, pp. 152–56.

In addition, as is described in the following selection, there were various short-term debts, bearing very high rates of interest.

By 1913, Iran's consolidated debt stood at £6,754,000, with an annual service charge of £537,000; the latter figure absorbed the bulk of the customs revenues, which had been pledged as a guarantee for the various loans.[5] There were also floating debts of 44,320,000 krans (nearly £900,000), owed to arms suppliers such as Schneider, banks, and Russian and British subjects claiming losses suffered during the various disturbances.[6]

During the First World War, Iran received various advances from the British government and by 1922 its debt to Britain amounted to £5,590,000. The Russian debts had, in the meantime, been canceled by the Soviet government. Thanks to rapid redemption, Iran's total consolidated and floating debt had been reduced to well under £2,000,000 by 1925.[7]

[5] Mochaver, p. 284.
[6] Jamalzadeh, p. 155.
[7] Mochaver, p. 285.

## Selection 7. Government Debt, 1909

[J. E. F., "Memorandum as to Persian Government Loans," 27 November 1912, FO 371/1711]

...46. The extent of the Persian Government's indebtedness at this time had been disclosed in the report of M. Bizot, their French Financial Adviser, dated the 15th March 1909, of which the main features were explained by Sir G. Barclay in the following words:—

"You will notice that, in M. Bizot's opinion, the need for a loan is indisputable, though he is unable to pronounce as to the amount required. In my telegram No. 152 I gave it as 2,500,000l. at the lowest estimate, independently of the small advances which would be needed for the reorganization of the Departments which most urgently call for reform, and I should mention that in this estimate I had M. Bizot's concurrence. Besides the Government's debt to the two banks, amounting in round figures to some 1,200,000l., which, bearing exorbitant interest, cries loudly for conversion, there are other creditors' claims which, according to a statement given to M. Bizot, already at the end of 1907–08 amounted to 2,751,638 tomans (550,000l.). These must greatly have increased during the year just ended. There are also the claims for postal and road robberies, &c., filed by the foreign Legations, of which it would be rash to attempt an estimate, but which must represent a very considerable sum.

"Assuming that the sum indicated above is approximately sufficient to convert the advances of the two banks, and to settle the claims of other creditors and those presented to the Persian Government by the foreign Legations, Persia's total indebtedness may be estimated at something like 6,000,000l., i.e.:—

| | £ |
|---|---|
| Russian Government's loans . . . . . . | 3,200,000 |
| British and Indian Government's loan, with arrears of interest . . . . . . | 300,000 |
| Required to pay off floating debt, &c. . . | 2,500,000 |
| | £6,000,000 |

"To pay interest on this at 5 or 6 per cent. the customs receipts would amply suffice, leaving a very substantial sum at the disposal of the Persian Government, very nearly as large a sum, indeed, as that now left over after paying the interest on the loans and advances as at present secured on the proceeds of the customs. The conversion of the 1,200,000l. owed to the Imperial Bank of Persia and to the Russian Bank, so as to reduce the interest from 12 to 6 per cent., would effect a saving of 72,000l. a year, or nearly enough to pay 6 per cent. on the sum needed to clear off the rest of the floating debt."

47. In the preceding paragraph mention has been made of the sufficiency of the customs revenue of Persia to meet the indebtedness of the country. In April 1909 Sir G. Barclay sent home the following figures (converted, for this Memo., at the rate of 5 Tomans = 1l.) supplied by the Administrator-General of Customs (M. Mornard):—

Table showing approximate Total Receipts of Customs for 1908–09 as compared with the previous year.

| | 1907–08 | 1908–09 |
|---|---|---|
| | £ | £ |
| Azerbaijan . . . . . . | 106,687 | 70,000 |
| Caspian Sea Ports:— | | |
| Astara . . . . . . . | 32,253 | 32,400 |
| Ghilan . . . . . . . . | 118,000 | 118,000 |
| Mazanderan . . . . | 28,251 | 34,400 |
| Astrabad . . . . . . | 28,888 | 22,400 |
| Khorassan . . . . . . | 53,876 | 60,000 |
| Southern ports:— | | |
| Bushire . . . . . | } 189,000 | { 100,000 |
| Bundar Abbas. . . . . | | 32,400 |
| Arabistan. . . . . . | 37,800 | 20,000 |
| Kermanshah . . . . . . | 110,806 | 110,400 |
| Parcels post (Tehran). . . | 3,559 | 4,000 |
| Total . . . . . . . | 709,120 | 604,000 |

In sending home these figures Sir G. Barclay commented on the greater extent to which British imports had fallen off as compared with Russian. The same result was shown in a table forwarded in the following October comparing the gross receipts of the customs for the first six months of 1909 with those for the same period of 1908.

48. As regards the receipts of the southern ports alone, Sir G. Barclay forwarded in September 1909 the following table:—

Comparative Statement of the Gross Customs Receipts for Southern Ports of Persia

| | 1907–08 | 1908–09 | 1909–10‡ (FIRST SIX MONTHS) |
|---|---|---|---|
| | £ | £ | £ |
| Bushire . . . | 134,517 | 101,888 | 32,000 |
| Lingah. . . . | 10,046 | 9,137 | 4,400 |
| Bundar Abbas | 44,539 | 32,535 | 11,000 |
| Mohammerah | 35,769 | 19,182 | 10,680 |
| Dizful . . . . | | | |
| Ahwaz . . . } | 2,038 | 1,896 | 920 |
| Shuster . . . | | | |
| Totals . . . . . | 226,909 | 164,630 | 59,000 |

‡ Figures approximate only.

49. In October 1909 Sir G. Barclay was supplied by M. Mornard with a statement (Appendix VII.) showing what the latter described as the "fixed charges" in the customs revenue for the previous year. These amounted to 527,900*l*., or within 80,000*l*. of the highest level reached by the customs net revenue, viz., 602,208*l*. in 1907–08. There were however certain later charges, *e.g.*, the ex-Shah's pension, which, in Sir G. Barclay's opinion, would also have to be borne by the customs, bringing up the total of such charges to 620,000*l*., or 80,000*l*. more than the previous year's net receipts, viz., 540,000*l*. Sir G. Barclay commented on the position in the following terms:—

"It is quite evident that on the basis of M. Mornard's statement no further borrowing is possible on the security of the customs, and although only the first four items are fixed charges by virtue of engagements undertaken by the Persian Government, the remaining eleven items being merely chargeable to the customs in accordance with usage, it would be difficult to relieve the customs of any of these latter. The Russian Government would doubtless object to any other security for the payment of the Cossack brigade, and it is important that the salaries of the European Government officers should be well secured. The rest of the eleven items mostly appertain to the customs administration.

"It is thus evident that a condition precedent for any further borrowing must be the conversion of the advances, &c., of the two banks, and even this would, as I calculate it, only leave sufficient margin for a very trifling loan unless it were found possible to relieve the customs revenue of some of those heads of expenditure with which it has hitherto been charged in accordance with usage.

"The advances of the Imperial Bank of Persia and the Russian Bank carry for the most part interest at the rate of 12 per cent. and over. The debt to the two banks amounts, as I understand it, to between 8,500,000 tomans (1,700,000*l*.) and 9,000,000 tomans (1,800,000*l*.), of which I would hazard an estimate that 7,000,000 tomans (1,400,000*l*.) carry interest at the rate of 12 or 15 per cent. The conversion of this debt and the reduction of the interest to 5 per cent. would effect a saving of probably 500,000 tomans (100,000*l*.), in which case, supposing that the customs receipts do not fall below last year's level—and for the first six months of this year they show an increase—there would be a margin for borrowing of 100,000 tomans (20,000*l*.)." . . .

# Epilogue

## The Iranian Economy, 1914–70

In sharp contrast to the stagnation prevailing in the period covered by this book, the last fifty years have seen rapid economic and social advance—interrupted in 1941–54 by the Allied occupation, the Azerbaijan crisis and the oil nationalization and its aftermath. Three engines of growth were at work: petroleum, the government, and investment by the national bourgeoisie; but their relative force varied at different times. In the 1950s, American aid also played a crucial part.

The First World War inflicted much hardship on Iran. Although it was officially neutral, Russian, British, and Turkish armies fought freely over its territory, while German agents raised the southern tribes. Epidemics broke out, and crop failures and the disruption of transport produced widespread famine. Thus Sykes states that in 1918 "famine conditions prevailed throughout the country, which had been denuded of supplies and livestock."[1] In Tehran province, in that year, "I found that a quarter of the agricultural population had died during the famine."[2] Then came the influenza epidemic, and in 1918 "Shiraz lost 10,000 of its 50,000 inhabitants."[3] Shortages of goods and increased expenditures by the government and by warring armies sent prices up sharply.[4]

But the war also gave Iran its great opportunity. The collapse of Russia in 1917 temporarily immobilized its most relentless adversary. And the combination of Iranian nationalist resistance, Soviet diplomatic and military aid, American antiimperialism, and war-weariness in Britain was sufficient to extinguish the last flareup of British expansionism, which had sought to secure a predominant position under the 1919 Agreement. Out of the turmoil Riza Khan emerged, and by 1925 his position was secure enough to make it possible to depose the last

[1] Sykes, *Persia*, 2:487.
[2] Balfour, p. 23.
[3] Sykes, *Persia*, 2:515.
[4] Thus, according to one estimate, taking the prewar level as 100, in 1917 the price of bread and flour stood at 900, of sugar at 1,100, of rice at 460, of cloth at 400 and of kerosine at 400—*Near East and India*, 18 February 1926, cited by Abdullaev, p. 53.

Qajar monarch. In the course of the next four years, the capitulations were abolished and a new tariff and civil code were introduced. Henceforth Iran was to be ruled by a government sufficiently powerful, and free from outside pressure, to promote the country's development.

## 1921–41

The oil industry has been studied more thoroughly than any other sector of the Iranian economy, and may be dealt with briefly.[5] Table 1 shows the growth in output and the increase in employment. Payments to the government rose rapidly, thanks not only to greater output but also to the 1933 Agreement, which raised the rate per barrel from the 12 cents level prevailing in 1926–29 to some 20–22 cents, and to the 1954 Agreement, which pushed it to around 80 cents.

TABLE 1

PETROLEUM INDUSTRY IN IRAN, 1921–68

|  | PRODUCTION OF CRUDE OIL (million metric tons) | WORKERS EMPLOYED | PAYMENTS TO GOVERNMENT (million pounds sterling) |
|---|---|---|---|
| 1921/22 . . . . . | 2.3 | 18,700 | .59 |
| 1929 . . . . . . | 5.5 | 30,000[a] | 1.44 |
| 1938 . . . . . . | 9.1 | . . . . . . | 3.31 |
| 1945 . . . . . . | 17.1 | . . . . . . | 5.62 |
| 1950 . . . . . . | 29.7 | 72,000[b] | 16.0 |
| 1955 . . . . . . | 16.3 | 63,000[c] | 32.2 |
| 1960 . . . . . . | 52.4 | . . . . . . | 101.9 |
| 1965 . . . . . . | 93.3 | . . . . . . | 190.7[d] |
| 1968 . . . . . . | 141.8 | 41,000 | 344.6[e] |

SOURCES: British Petroleum Company; Kia; Yaganegi; United Nations, *Statistical Yearbook*; Issawi and Yeganeh; *Petroleum Press Service*; NIOC.

[a] 1926
[b] 1949
[c] 1956
[d] Equal to $534 million.
[e] Equal to $827 million.

During the reign of Riza Shah almost all government oil revenues were spent on military equipment; in 1941–55, the greater part was used for budget support, but since then a rapidly growing proportion has gone to development. More generally, until the last twenty years or so, the contribution of the oil industry to the Iranian economy, though significant, was not major. In 1937/38, oil revenues accounted for 13 percent of total government receipts[6] and in 1940/41 the foreign exchange contributed by the industry in the form of payments to the government and other local expenditure constituted 62 percent of Iranian foreign exchange receipts.[7] In 1948, the value added by the oil industry was put at 10 percent of gross national product, payments amounted to 11 percent of government revenues, and foreign exchange contributions were 65 percent of the total; by 1958,

[5] For further information see the works by Fateh, Lisani, Elwell-Sutton, and Issawi and Yeganeh listed in the bibliography, and the annual reports of AIOC, BP, NIOC, and the Iranian Operating Oil Companies.
[6] United Nations, Public Finance Information Papers, *Iran*, p. 34.
[7] United Nations, *Review of Economic Conditions in the Middle East, 1949–50*, p. 63.

these figures were 15 percent, 61 percent, and 59 percent respectively, and oil financed about half the country's gross investment.[8] Figures for the late 1960s indicate that oil accounted for 15 percent of gross national product, 65 percent of government revenues and 70 percent of foreign exchange receipts.[9]

By itself, the expansion of the oil industry would not have sufficed to lift Iran from the very low level at which it found itself after the First World War. Table 2 shows the country's backwardness compared with Turkey, and still more compared with Egypt. Nothing less than the "big push" provided by Riza Shah's overall modernization program (and implemented with much friction, waste, and misdirection) could have set the economy moving.[10]

TABLE 2

IRAN, EGYPT, AND TURKEY, 1925

|  | IRAN | EGYPT | TURKEY |
|---|---|---|---|
| Population (millions) . . . . . . . . . . . . . | (12.5) | 14 | 13.1 |
| Imports (millions of dollars)[a] . . . . . . . . . | 88 | 250 | 246 |
| Railways (kilometers) . . . . . . . . . . . . | 250 | 4,555 | 4,700 |
| Automobiles[b] . . . . . . . . . . . . . . | 4,450 | 17,740 | 7,500 |
| Cement output (metric tons) . . . . . . . . | ...... | 90,000[c] | 59,000[c] |
| Refined sugar output (metric tons) . . . . . . | ...... | 109,000[c] | 5,000[c] |
| Students in schools . . . . . . . . . . . . . | 74,000 | 635,000 | 413,000 |

SOURCES: League of Nations, *International Statistical Yearbook, 1926* and *1927*; United Nations, *The Development of Manufacturing Industry in Egypt, Israel and Turkey*; *al-ihsa al-Sanawi*; *Istatistik Yilligi*; Overseas Consultants.

[a] In this and subsequent tables, only import figures are shown; exports are omitted, since both the inclusion and the exclusion of petroleum would be misleading.
[b] 1926.
[c] 1928.

At first the emphasis was on infrastructure. Poor transport constituted perhaps the greatest single obstacle to development, and, following some road construction by the British, Russian, and Ottoman armies during the war (about 1,600 kilometers),[11] many rough but usable roads were built. In 1927, a British commercial report put the length of improved roads at 1,000 kilometers, of partially improved at 2,500, and of unpaved "passable for cars nearly the whole year round, though sometimes with difficulty" at 5,000.[12] By 1938, Iran's roads were officially put at 24,000 kilometers. Most of these consisted of rough trails but their presence made it possible to expand motor transport greatly; consumption of motor fuel rose more than sevenfold between 1928 and 1937, the average duration of a journey fell to about one-tenth of what it had been before the First World War, and the cost of transport was cut by some three-quarters.[13]

[8] Issawi and Yeganeh, pp. 143–49.
[9] *Barnameh chaharom omrani kishvar, 1347–1351*; Industrial and Mining Bank of Iran, *Ninth Annual Report for the Year 1347.*
[10] For the reforms achieved in such fields as internal security, the army, administration, the judiciary, education, and the status of women, see the works by Banani, Frye, Haas, Sadiq, Upton, Wilber, and Young, listed in the bibliography.
[11] Alami, p. 156.
[12] Lingeman, pp. 25–26.
[13] Sotoudeh, pp. 113–14; Alami, p. 157.

A more ambitious project was the construction of the Trans-Iranian railway, linking the Caspian port of Bandar Shah (Bandar Gaz) with the Persian Gulf port of Bandar Shahpur (Khur-i Musa), a distance of 1,394 kilometers, much of it over very rugged terrain. Begun in 1927, the standard-gauge line was opened to traffic in 1938. Its cost of about $150 million was covered mainly by an additional import tax on tea and sugar. Work on the extension of the railway was interrupted by the invasion of Iran in 1941, when 439 kilometers of the 741-kilometer line to Tabriz and 314 kilometers of the 812-kilometer line to Mashad had been completed.[14]

Two more developments in transport and communication may be noted. Starting in 1926, flights between the main cities were carried out by the German firm of Junkers, whose regular routes covered 2,800 kilometers; in the late 1930s the Iranian government took over the service and started regular flights to Baghdad. And by 1935, telephone lines, with a total length of over 10,000 kilometers, connected the main towns, and there were some 6,000 subscribers.[15]

Neither the improvement in transport nor the other measures carried out by the government could have been achieved without a vast increase in revenues. With the help of an American mission, some order was put in Iran's chaotic fiscal system and some control was established over expenditure. The achievement of tariff autonomy in 1928 enabled the government to raise duties, mainly for revenue but also for protection, and receipts were also swollen by the expanding oil revenues. In addition, twenty-seven government monopolies were established, including tobacco, sugar, tea, matches, opium, textiles, automobiles, and others, and the wide margin between their buying and selling prices constituted an important source of government income—and, for some, of private enrichment. As a result, total revenue rose from 229 million krans in 1922 to 400 million in 1931, a substantial deficit was converted into a small surplus, and Iran's debt to Britain and India was reduced from £2,619,000 to £1,601,000—the larger debt to Russia having been canceled in 1921.[16] By 1938, total revenue was estimated at 1,376 million rials (krans) and by 1941 at 3,200 million; of this some 80 percent came from customs and excise duties and government monopolies. As regards expenditure, defense continued to absorb a large amount, but its share in the total fell from over 50 percent in the 1920s to 26 percent in 1939; correspondingly, that of public works and social services rose to 30 percent.[17]

Changes were also made in the monetary and banking systems. The rise in the world price of silver during the First World War brought with it an improvement in the rate of the kran—from 62 to the pound sterling in 1914 to a low of 34 in 1920. Moreover, during the war and immediate postwar years, Iran seems to have

[14] Peyamiras, pp. 105–14, Overseas Consultants, 4:5–6.
[15] Sotoudeh, pp. 126–31; Banani, p. 136.
[16] Yaganegi, pp. 42–43; Millspaugh, *American Task; idem, Americans in Persia;* Groseclose, pp. 149–56; Glukhoded pp. 92–95.
[17] United Nations, *Review 1949–50*, p. 80; Yaganegi, p. 15.

had a surplus in its balance of payments and imported about 94 million krans' worth of gold and silver. But the sharp fall in the price of silver after 1920, and the restoration of the pound to its prewar value, drove down the kran rate to 58 in 1929 and, in spite of the devaluation of sterling, to 112 in 1931. A law was passed in 1930 changing the basis of the Iranian currency from a silver to a gold standard and replacing the kran by the rial, but the repercussions of the devaluation of sterling and the sharp fall in the price of silver made it impossible to proceed with conversion to gold. Instead, paper money was issued in increasing quantities by the Bank Melli, a state bank founded in 1927 to perform some of the functions of a central bank. Between 1933 and 1939, the amount of notes issued by it rose more than five fold, to nearly 11,000 million rials, and paper had become the principal medium of exchange.[18]

Other banks founded by the government in the interwar period were the Bank Sepah, the Agricultural and Industrial Bank, and the Bank Rahni (Mortgage Bank). Deposits with these banks, and with the Imperial Bank of Persia (which lost its note-issuing privileges in 1930), rose from 560 million rials in 1936 to 1,320 million in 1939 and 2,000 million by the middle of 1941.[19]

Drastic changes were also made in the foreign trade system, with the introduction of monopoly in 1931 and exchange control in 1936. Both were responses to the general decline in world trade, the sharp fall in the price of Iranian exports— along with those of other primary products—and the growing import surpluses. But in addition Iran found such devices necessary to deal with the state-controlled trade of first the Soviet Union and then Germany, which between them accounted for nearly 60 percent of its foreign trade (excluding oil) in the late 1930s. Moreover, as mentioned before, the monopolies provided an important source of revenue and foreign exchange to the government. Last, these controls were used to protect Iranian industries. But there is some evidence that the Soviet Union and Germany used their strong position in the increasingly bilateral and controlled trade of Iran to Iran's disadvantage, and there seems little doubt that prices of imported goods were higher than they would have been under a less restrictive system.[20]

In addition to setting up a more adequate financial and fiscal structure and to providing transport and power, the government also intervened in the field of directly productive activities, especially industry. In 1924 imports of agricultural and industrial machinery were exempted from customs duties for a period of ten years, extended for another ten in 1934. In 1932 such machinery was exempted from the newly imposed road tax. Rebates were allowed on national products carried on the railways, premiums were granted on industrial goods, preference was given to such goods in government purchases, and a certain measure of

[18] Yaganegi, pp. 60–86; Groseclose, pp. 157–68; Nayyeri, pp. 38–77.
[19] Nayyeri, pp. 113–20; United Nations, *Statistical Yearbook;* Bank Melli, *Annual Report.*
[20] Banani, pp. 129–32; Peyamiras, pp. 124–60; Yaganegi, pp. 105–20; Alami, pp. 133–51; Sadrazdeh, pp. 12–22; and Adli, passim.

government control was imposed on industrial establishments. The Agricultural and Industrial Bank, founded in 1933, also made loans to several enterprises. In addition, from 1928 onward, industry benefited greatly from the various protective measures taken by the government—tariffs, quotas, and exchange control. Technical schools and workshops were established and provided skills. As a result, a large number of small or medium-size factories were founded by private enterprise in the 1930s, especially in textiles and food processing, though this was partly offset by a further decline of the handicrafts. Moreover, the government itself set up several plants, in sugar refining, cement, textiles, and other industries. For example, the number of textile plants rose from 5–7 in the 1920s to 22 in 1937.[21]

By 1941, Iran had 200,000 cotton spindles and 2,200 looms, producing 10,000 tons of yarn and 25,000,000 meters of cloth. In wool, there were 25,600 spindles and 700 looms, producing 870 kilograms of yarn and 2,300,000 meters of cloth. The capital invested in these and other textile industries, such as silk, jute, and hosiery, was put at 430 million rials and total employment at 30,000. The sugar refineries had a labor force of about 6,000 and an output of 25,000 tons, or a quarter of total consumption. Production of cement was 90,000 tons, with a labor force of about 500, and output of matches was over 1,000 tons. Several food, drink, and tobacco industries met a large part of domestic consumption. A steel mill and iron foundry was also under construction in 1941 and a small amount of coal, iron, copper, and other minerals was being extracted.[22]

Like Atatürk, whom he often used as a model, Riza Shah did much more for industry than for agriculture. In the latter field the main progress achieved was in the expansion and improvement of such industrial crops as silk, sugar beets, tobacco, tea and cotton, which fed the newly established industries, and in the provision of grain elevators and factories for the ginning, husking, drying, or other processing required by these crops. An agricultural college was opened in 1929 and foreign experts were hired for teaching, research, and extension. Agricultural credit was expanded and price support was extended. But very little was done by the government to provide irrigation, the chief project—in Khuzistan—being rather unsuccessful. Attempts to improve the land-tenure system resulted mainly in the acquisition of vast areas by the shah or large landlords.[23] And the measures taken to settle the tribes seem to have seriously disrupted animal husbandry. Nevertheless it is probable that agricultural production increased substantially in the interwar period, thanks to greater security, improved transport, and rising demand. No reliable figures on total output are available, but industrial crops

[21] Peyamiras, pp. 84–86; Soheily, pp. 35–48; Banani, pp. 137–41; Glukhoded, pp. 82–83; Grunwald, passim.

[22] For details see Soheily, pp. 81–93, 105–9; Kia, pp. 140–52; Naval Intelligence, *Persia*, pp. 457–70; and Z. Z. Abdullaev, *Formirovanie Rabochego Klassa Irana* (Baku, 1968) pp. 37–64, which contains information on the handicrafts.

[23] For details see Lambton, *Landlord*, chaps. 8, 10, 13; Naval Intelligence, *Persia*, pp. 423–56; Sotoudeh, pp. 183–98; Alami, pp. 61–113; Keen, passim; Sandjabi, passim.

expanded sharply and it seems likely that the production of grains kept pace with the population growth.

In summing up the results of the interwar period, one cannot fail to be impressed with the effort made by Iran and with the results achieved. The magnitude of the effort may be judged by the investment of about $260 million in railways and another $260 million in industry, over half of the latter being private investment.[24] The results may be judged from table 3, which shows that, although still lagging far behind Egypt and Turkey, Iran had somewhat narrowed the gap.

TABLE 3

IRAN, EGYPT, AND TURKEY, 1938

|  | IRAN | EGYPT | TURKEY |
|---|---|---|---|
| Population (millions) . . . . . . . . . . . . . | 15 | 16.4 | 17.1 |
| Imports (millions of dollars) . . . . . . . . . | 55 | 184 | 119 |
| Railways (kilometers) . . . . . . . . . . . | 1,700 | 5,606 | 7,324 |
| Automobiles . . . . . . . . . . . . . . . | (15,000) | 33,700 | 11,300 |
| Cement output (metric tons) . . . . . . . . . | 65,000 | 375,000 | 287,000 |
| Refined sugar output (metric tons) . . . . . . | 22,000 | 238,000 | 247,000 |
| Cereals output (million metric tons)[a] . . . . . | 3.09 | 3.63 | 6.46 |
| Cotton output (metric tons)[b] . . . . . . . . . | 34,000 | 400,000 | 52,000 |
| Energy consumption[c] . . . . . . . . . . . . | 1.55 | 2.05 | 2.18 |
| Students in schools[d] . . . . . . . . . . . . | 234,000 | 1,309,000 | 810,000 |

SOURCES: League of Nations, *International Statistical Yearbook, 1939/40*; United Nations, *Review of Economic Conditions in the Middle East, 1949–50*; ibid., *1951–52*; *al-ihsa al-sanawi*; *Istatistik Yilligi*.

[a] Wheat, barley, maize, rice—annual average, 1934–38.
[b] Annual average, 1934–38.
[c] Million metric tons of coal equivalent.
[d] 1936/37.

Of course the cost was high. There was considerable waste in ostentatious, ill-conceived, or insufficiently studied projects. The neglect of agriculture had most unfortunate consequences. Large-scale investment, high indirect taxation, and credit expansion raised prices sharply, the cost-of-living index rising by over 50 percent between 1936/37 and mid 1941; the burden of this rested largely on the poor and the salaried middle class. And political and intellectual repression took its toll. But it is difficult to see how anything less than a great—and therefore almost inevitably wasteful—effort would have sufficed to move the country from its depressed and stagnant condition.

1941–54

On 25 August 1941 British and Soviet troops invaded Iran, and a United States contingent was sent there in 1943. This occupation made it possible to transport to Russia over 4,000,000 tons of war material, which played an important part in the defeat of Germany.[25] But for Iran it was a disaster. In the north, the

---

[24] These figures have been calculated at the prevailing rates of exchange of the rial: 8.4 cents in 1928/29, 3.38 cents in 1932/33, 6.33 cents in 1934/5 and 5.45 cents in 1939/40—see, United Nations, *Economic Developments in the Middle East, 1945 to 1954*, pp. 58–59.

[25] For a detailed account, see Motter, passim.

Soviet forces prevented the government from exercising effective authority, and freely exploited the region's agricultural and industrial resources.[26] Government revenues fell off sharply, partly because of the inability to collect taxes in the northern provinces, and large budgetary deficits were incurred in 1941/42 through 1944/45. At the same time the quantum of imports was considerably reduced. Since, in addition, agricultural output declined, because of unfavorable weather and the disruption caused by the occupation, severe shortages were felt. And all over the country the Allies spent vast sums for troop maintenance and the operation of the Trans-Iranian railway and roads. Prices therefore rose sharply, the cost of living index (1939 = 100) advancing from 152 in 1941 to 756 in 1944; the corresponding figure for Egypt was 279 and for Turkey 334. As against this, Iran derived two benefits: official foreign exchange reserves increased by some $200 million, and the carrying capacity of the railways, roads, and ports was greatly expanded, though this was partly offset by the deterioration caused by the huge increase in traffic.[27]

The postwar years were dominated first by the effort to end the Soviet occupation of the northern provinces, then by the agitation leading to the nationalization of the oil industry in 1951, and after that by the disruption caused by the virtual cessation of oil production. Powerful forces were working toward restoring more normal conditions: the evacuation of all foreign troops in the course of 1946, the sharp increase in imports following the reopening of trade channels, the reduction in budget deficits, thanks mainly to rising oil revenues, and the disbursement of $37 million in United States aid up to 30 June 1952 and another $55 million in the two following fiscal years. As a result, the price level dropped appreciably in 1945 and 1946, and fluctuated with no clear trend until 1951, after which it started rising again.[28] But political uncertainty inhibited large scale investment, public or private. A Seven-Year Development Plan, prepared with the help of two American firms[29] and providing for a total expenditure of 21,000 million rials ($656 million), was approved by the Majlis on 15 February 1949. It was to be financed by the allocation of all petroleum revenues and by loans from the International Bank for Reconstruction and Development and Bank Melli. However, the nationalization of the industry cut off all oil revenues and no loans were made by the IBRD and by the end of 1954 only 4,200 million rials had been actually spent on implementing the plan.[30] And although private investment took place in industry, agriculture, transport, and, above all, housing, its extent was small.

As a result little economic progress was achieved. The cultivated area was substantially extended, but this was largely offset by a decline in yields and it seems that agricultural output failed to keep pace with population growth. However, a few

[26] For details on this and other economic aspects of the Allied occupation, see Groseclose, pp. 172–87.
[27] United Nations, *Review, 1949–50*, pp. 67–80; United Nations, *Economic Developments, 1945 to 1954*, pp 58–60.
[28] Ibid.
[29] See Morrison-Knudson; and Overseas Consultants.
[30] United Nations, *Review, 1945 to 1954*, pp. 85–88.

small irrigation schemes were carried out, agricultural credit was expanded, and a beginning was made in introducing agricultural machinery, chemical fertilizers, pesticides, and selected seeds. Industry, which, as in other Middle Eastern countries, had enjoyed expanding and protected markets during the war years but had been unable to obtain spare parts and replacements, found it very difficult to meet postwar competition. But new equipment was installed, mainly by private capital, and in some branches output expanded significantly, for example, cotton yarn to nearly 20,000 tons by 1954, sugar to 100,000 tons. Considerable progress was also registered in chemicals and in mining, but some important industries such as cement and carpets remained below their prewar peak. In 1950, the number employed in industry and mining was about 300,000. Of these, 52,000 were directly employed by the oil industry and 15,000 by contractors serving that industry; 20,000 worked in government factories and 30,000 in private factories; 130,000 were engaged in carpet making and 20,000 in handloom weaving; and the rest worked in handicrafts, small workshops, and mining.[31]

By 1954, electric power capacity had risen to 125,000 kilowatts; to this should be added 72,000 in the oil fields. Transport facilities had also been expanded, as is shown in table 4. But that table also brings out clearly the fact that Iran's position relative to Egypt and Turkey had considerably worsened since 1938.

### TABLE 4
#### IRAN, EGYPT, AND TURKEY, 1950

|  | IRAN | EGYPT | TURKEY |
|---|---|---|---|
| Population (millions) . . . . . . . . . . . . . | 19.3 | 20.4 | 20.9 |
| Imports (millions of dollars) . . . . . . . . . | 191 | 564 | 286 |
| Railways (kilometers) . . . . . . . . . . . | 3,180 | 6,092 | 7,634 |
| Automobiles . . . . . . . . . . . . | 38,300 | 77,900 | 32,600 |
| Cement output (metric tons) . . . . . . . . . | 54,000 | 1,022,000 | 396,000 |
| Refined sugar output (metric tons) . . . . . . | 69,000 | 218,000 | 186,000 |
| Cereals output (million metric tons)[a] . . . . . . | 3.09 | 3.72 | 6.74 |
| Cotton output (metric tons)[b] . . . . . . . . . | 26,000 | 364,000 | 99,000 |
| Electricity output (million kwh)[c] . . . . . . . | 200 | 642 | 676 |
| Energy consumption[d] . . . . . . . . . . . | 4.51 | 4.42 | 5.40 |
| Students in schools . . . . . . . . . . . . | 743,000 | 1,597[e] | 1,798 |

SOURCES: United Nations, *Review of Economic Conditions in the Middle East, 1949–50*; ibid., *1951–52*; United Nations, *Statistical Yearbook*.
[a] Wheat, barley, maize, rice—annual average, 1947–51.
[b] Annual average, 1947–51.
[c] 1948.
[d] Million metric tons of coal equivalent.
[e] 1949.

## 1954–69

In the past fifteen years the Iranian economy has moved forward with unprecedented speed. Over the whole period, the rate of real growth has averaged 7 to 8 percent, and the per capita growth nearly 5 percent, figures matched by

[31] For details on agriculture and industry see ibid., pp. 60–70; Morrison-Knudson; Overseas Consultants; and CHI, vol. 1.

barely half a dozen countries. In 1954–59 growth was abnormally great, as oil production was expanding rapidly after having practically ceased. In 1961 and 1962, on the other hand, there was very little increase, owing to the deflationary policy being pursued by the government. Since 1963 the growth rate has been well over 8 percent. The result is reflected in table 5, which shows that although Iran still lags behind Turkey and the United Arab Republic in certain fields, in others it has overtaken and surpassed them; particularly significant are such indicators of capital formation as steel and energy consumption and imports—which in all three countries consist largely of capital and producer goods.[32]

## TABLE 5

IRAN, UNITED ARAB REPUBLIC, TURKEY, 1968

|  | IRAN | UAR | TURKEY |
|---|---|---|---|
| Population (millions) | 27.3 | 31.7 | 33.5 |
| Per capita GDP (dollars) | 299 | 161 | 338 |
| Per capita energy consumption[a] | 478 | 298 | 450 |
| Per capita steel consumption (kilograms) | 63 | 21 | 26 |
| Per capita textile consumption (kilograms)[b] | 4.2 | 4.0 | 5.4 |
| Per capita sugar consumption (kilograms) | 24 | 15 | 18 |
| Imports (million dollars) | 1,386 | 690 | 770 |
| Railways (kilometers) | 3,645 | 5,500 | 8,162 |
| Railway freight (million tons/kilometers) | 2,225 | 3,001 | 5,245 |
| Automobiles (thousands) | 238 | 143 | 223 |
| Cement output (thousand metric tons) | 2,000 | 3,147 | 4,733 |
| Refined sugar output (thousand metric tons) | 458 | 414 | 700 |
| Electricity output (million kwh) | 5,008 | 6,735 | 6,886 |
| Cereals output (million metric tons)[c] | 5.05 | 5.55 | 13.98 |
| Cotton output (thousand metric tons)[d] | 127 | 479 | 356 |
| Students in schools (thousands) | 3,613 | 4,947[e] | 5,610[e] |

SOURCES: United Nations, *Statistical Yearbook*; United Nations, *Yearbook of National Accounts Statistics*; *Statesman's Yearbook*; Food and Agricultural Organization; *al-ihsa al-sanawi*.

[a] Coal equivalent, kilograms.　　　[d] lint, annual average 1964–67.
[b] 1964.　　　[e] 1967.
[c] Wheat, barley, maize, and rice, annual average 1964–67.

This expansion was achieved with a remarkable degree of price stability and equilibrium in international accounts. During the 1954–61 boom, inflationary pressures increased and the cost-of-living index rose by 40 percent while foreign exchange reserves fell by nearly $280 million in 1958–61. The government, following the advice of the International Monetary Fund, therefore introduced a drastic deflationary program, cutting down public expenditure and restricting credit.[33] This halted the economy in 1961 and 1962 but enabled it to resume its advance thereafter, on a sounder basis, and in 1962–68, inclusive, the cost-of-living index rose by only 1.3 percent a year, a record equaled by very few countries.

[32] For a discussion of sources and details see Issawi, "Iran's Economic Upsurge," articles by Amuzegar, Issawi, and Lambton in *Iran*, ed. Yarshater; Baldwin; and Ashraf and Mahdavy in *Studies*, ed. Cook. Much information is provided in the publications of the Bank Markazi, the Plan Organization, the Ministry of National Economy, the Industrial and Mining Bank, and the Agriculture Bank, most of which are available in English as well as in Persian.

[33] See Fatemah Moghadam, "The Stabilization Program of 1960 in Iran," masters thesis, Columbia University, 1968.

Iran also managed to avoid extensive indebtedness. In 1946–67 United States aid totaled $958 million, and sizable loans were also extended by the IBRD, the IMF, and various European countries. A considerable amount of these debts has been repaid, but in the late 1960s credits of nearly $400 million were opened by the Soviet bloc; these are being used to finance the laying of a gas pipeline from the Persian Gulf to the Soviet border, and a set of large industrial projects. Compared with its foreign exchange earnings, currently running at over $1,000 million a year, Iran's foreign indebtedness is among the lowest for developing countries, and in absolute terms is far smaller than that of Turkey and the United Arab Republic.

Three more aspects may be briefly noted. First, it is probable that the great inequality in wealth and income prevailing in Iran has been somewhat reduced, thanks mainly to the land reform and also, possibly, to a slight increase in the progressiveness of taxation: as against that, it should be noted that both the inequality of income between the urban and the rural sector and the inequality of urban incomes have increased.[34] Second, the level of living has sharply risen; this is shown not only by the national accounts but also by the marked increase in sales of such articles of mass consumption as sugar, textiles, radios (the number in use rose from 100,000 in 1948 to about 2,500,000 in 1966), and bicycles. Last, Iran has experienced development as well as increase; that is, its economy and society have become more diversified and complex. New fields of production have been opened, and new economic and financial institutions and relations have been established, thus increasing the potential for future stability and growth.

Closer analysis shows that this growth was achieved by two interrelated factors: a high rate of investment, and rapid advance in two leading sectors, oil and industry. The investment rate has risen from some 10 percent of gross national product in the mid 1950s to 19 percent in the mid 1960s and well over 20 percent in recent years; of this, foreign resources accounted for under one-fifth and domestic saving for over four-fifths. Much of the investment funds has come from the oil sector, which now accounts for 18 percent of gross national product and which in recent years has been growing at about 12 percent per annum.[35]

Industry (manufacturing and mining), which now forms 15 percent of gross national product, has also been advancing very rapidly, at over 13 percent—a figure well above that of the vast majority of both advanced and underdeveloped countries. This growth has taken place both in the older industries and in new branches. Thus, between 1955/56 and 1967/68, the output of cotton textiles rose from 74,000,000 meters to 450,000,000, of refined sugar from 75,000 tons to 320,000, of vegetable oils from 16,000 tons to 100,000, and of cement from 131,000 to 1,800,000 tons. And new industries are rapidly proliferating and include

[34] See the tables and Lorenz curves in Bank Markazi, *National Income of Iran* (Tehran, 1968) pp. 26, 94–97.

[35] In this connection, it is interesting to note that Iran is trying to widen its oil markets by concluding agreements with Rumania, Czechoslovakia, and other East European countries under which oil is to be exchanged for machinery and other goods.

an integrated steel mill; an aluminum smelter; automobile and tractor manufacturing plants; and a variety of petrochemical and engineering industries,
some in very large units.[36] Several important mineral deposits have also been
discovered, and output of some minerals has greatly increased.

As in other developing countries, agriculture, which now accounts for only 20
percent of gross national product, has been a lagging sector, growing at about
1.5 percent per annum in the 1960s. The disruptions and tensions that might have
arisen from the imbalance between the rural and urban sectors were avoided
largely because of the slack existing in the economy, a sound economic policy,
a succession of good harvests in 1965–68, and the availability of foreign exchange
oil revenues, which made it possible to increase imports and thus supplement local
resources.[37]

Pushing the analysis a step further, one can see that Iran's recent growth has
been achieved by a happy combination of government and private enterprise.
The government—that is, in effect, the shah, helped by a group of able administra-
tors and technicians trained in America and Europe—provided stability and continuity. It succeeded in somewhat improving the efficiency of the bureaucracy.
It constantly pressed the established oil companies to raise Iran's share of revenues,
and granted new concessions, on more favorable terms, to several smaller companies. It concluded a set of agreements with the Soviet bloc which both provided
it with huge loans and opened new markets for Iranian products. At the same
time it drew widely on Western capital and technical resources, both private and
public. Under the Second (1955/56–1961/62) and Third (1962/63–1967/68)
Plans, the government invested hundreds of millions of dollars in infrastructure,
extending the railways, building new roads (by 1966 there were 8,600 kilometers
of asphalt roads and 22,300 of gravel,[38] and the amount of kilometer-tons of
freight carried in 1965 was 4,500 million), developing the ports (the value of goods
other than oil passing through them doubled between 1958 and 1965 to 2,667,000
tons), and expanding the electric power capacity severalfold. Some of this capacity

---

[36] It is worth pointing out that whereas until very recently industry was heavily concentrated in Tehran, most
of the large new plants are being built in such provincial centers as Isfahan, Tabriz, Shiraz, and Arak.

[37] There is no doubt that without oil revenues, which accounted for over three-quarters of foreign exchange
earnings in the 1960s, Iran's recent development could not have taken place. But, as I have pointed out elsewhere, "The magnitude of these resources is liable to be exaggerated and should be set in its proper perspective.
In 1960/61–1964/65 inclusive, Iran's earnings from oil and exports of goods and services averaged $572 million per
annum. During the same period Egypt's earnings from exports, Suez Canal revenues and other services averaged
$801 million and Turkey's $508 million. As for imports of goods and services, which were financed by loans and
grants as well as earnings and give a truer measure of the extent to which the economy drew on outside resources, Iran averaged $579 million, Egypt $1,048 million and Turkey $672 million" (see International Monetary
Fund, *Balance of Payments Yearbook, no. 17*). "Thus on a per capita basis, Iran was slightly better off than Turkey
and distinctly worse off than Egypt. But, unlike both, it did not contract large foreign debts." P. 451 ("Iran's
Economic Upsurge").

By 1970, however, oil revenues were running at the rate of about $1,000 million, putting Iran far ahead of
Turkey and the United Arab Republic. Moreover, oil production absorbed a much smaller proportion of Iran's
manpower and natural resources than did the main foreign exchange-earning sectors of Turkey and the United
Arab Republic, e.g., cotton.

[38] But as late as 1960, 56 percent of the villages surveyed for the Agricultural Census could be reached only
by jeep or horse.

came from large multipurpose dams, like the Dez and Safidrud, which also provided irrigation. Thanks to them, to smaller dams, and to some 8,000 wells, the area under irrigation was extended to over 3,000,000 hectares in 1966. The government also helped agricultural development by encouraging the importation of tractors, pesticides, fertilizers, and improved seeds, the use of all of which increased severalfold in the 1960s, though in this respect Iran still stands well behind Turkey and the United Arab Republic. It also provided abundant and cheap credit to both agriculture and industry through its specialized banks.

But perhaps the greatest service rendered to the agricultural sector was the Land Reform of 1962. By the 1950s it was being increasingly felt that Iran's land tenure system was a major obstacle in the way of economic development. Although there are no accurate figures, it would seem that perhaps a third of the rural population was landless and that a little over 2 percent of landowners held about one-half of the privately owned area.[39] "Small landowners tended to be found in the less fertile districts round the towns. Peasant proprietors were on the whole confined to remote areas in which agriculture offered a low return, as, for example, mountain areas or the edge of the central desert."[40]

Large estates were mostly leased in small plots, under a system of sharecropping (*muzaraeh*). The 1960 Census of Agriculture[41] shows that some 16.5 percent of the cultivated area was operated by small owners (all *milki* and *milki-ijarei* holdings of less than twenty hectares); 12.3 percent by large landowners (the same of over twenty hectares); and only 2.6 percent paid a cash rent.

Such a system, in addition to its deplorable political and social results, had very adverse effects on the economy. It starved agriculture of investment and prevented technological advance. It perpetuated subsistence farming and impeded the shift to cash crops. And by slowing down the growth of output and reducing to a minimum the marketable surplus, it acted as a drag on the whole economy.

Some reforms were attempted, notably the sale of the shah's estates, starting in 1951, but most of the measures were inoperative, including the land reform law of 1960. In 1962, however, an amendment to the 1960 law limiting holdings to one village per landowner started what has probably been the most comprehensive agrarian reform in the Middle East.[42] Bold and original in conception, owing little to foreign inspiration and well suited to the peculiar conditions of the country, the reform had two main objectives: to break the power of the landlords and to bring into being a large class of peasant proprietors. Both were accomplished by the expropriation of over 15,000 villages and the redistribution, by 1968, of most

---

[39] See Farhad Khamsi, "The Development of Capitalism in Rural Iran," masters thesis, Columbia University, 1968, chapter 5.

[40] Lambton, *Persian Land Reform*, p. 24.

[41] Table 101, regrouped by Khamsi, "Development of Capitalism."

[42] For an authoritative account see Lambton, *Persian Land Reform*, and also Doreen Warriner, *Land Reform in Principle and Practice* (Oxford 1969) chap. 5; and Keddie "Iranian Village."

of them to 617,000 peasant families. Another 1,239,000 peasant families have benefited from the Additional Articles of 1963, which regulated tenancy.[43]

The land reform was accompanied by numerous supplementary measures, essential to its success, such as increased investment by the government; great expansion of agricultural credit; the setting up of cooperatives, with over 1,000,000 members; the provision of extension services; and the establishment of Literacy and Health Corps in the villages. Although it is too soon to pass a definitive judgment, it would seem that the Iranian peasant, released from his age-long dependence on landlords and provided with financial and technical help, is rapidly modernizing his farming methods and substantially increasing his output.[44]

Private enterprise took full advantage of the opportunities presented. The economic and social development of the late 1950s led to the accumulation of large amounts of capital in the hands of contractors, importers, merchants, and industrialists and to the emergence of a new segment of the bourgeoisie, with both enterprise and managerial capacity. Consequently, during the years 1959/60–1967/68, the private sector (including the oil companies) placed around 400 billion rials (over $500 million) in fixed investment, or nearly two-thirds of the total amount of fixed investment. Industry, transport, and residential housing accounted for the bulk of this, but there was also some investment in agriculture. Although, because of the great increase in government investment in industry and other branches, the share of the private sector in fixed investment will decline during the Fourth Plan (1968/69–1972/73) to 45 percent of the total, it is expected to provide some 367 billion rials. The vigorous growth of private enterprise in Iran contrasts sharply with its virtual elimination in many other parts of the Middle East.

The Fourth Plan aims to raise gross national product by 60 percent, through the investment of 810 billion rials ($1,080 million). So far the results have been very satisfactory, and although one can foresee that many strains, distortions, and tensions will make themselves felt, that shortages of skills will hold back progress in several directions, and that inflationary pressures will once more gather force, one can also confidently predict that, given political stability, the momentum of advance will be maintained. The modern economic history of Iran, related in this book, presents a gloomy picture, but the events of the last fifteen years give great hope for the country's future.

[43] Lambton, *Persian Land Reform*, pp. 219–20; and Bank Markazi, *Annual Report*, 1968.
[44] Thus the use of chemical fertilizers rose from 47,000 tons in 1962/63 to 130,000 in 1967/68 and tractors from 6,000 in 1959 to 17,500 in 1968; the index of agricultural production (1952–56 = 100) rose from 124 in 1960–62 to 160 in 1966–68. FAO, *Yearbook*.

# Appendix

## Currency, Weights, and Measures

CURRENCY

During the period under review, the main units of currency in Iran were the tuman, kran, and shahi; a tuman equaled 10 krans and a kran equaled 20 shahis.

The word "tuman" was introduced during the Mongol period and originally meant "ten thousand."[1] As a unit of account, it equaled 10,000 dinars. Under the Safavis, the dinar itself having become only a unit of account, the tuman was the equivalent of 50 abbasis; the abbasi equaled 4 shahis. Both abbasi and shahi were silver coins, weighing about 130 grains and 32 grains respectively, and during the reign of Shah Abbas (1587–1629) the tuman was worth about £3.7.0. In subsequent reigns the weight of the silver coins was steadily reduced, and under Nadir Shah (1736–47) the abbasi weighed only 72 grains and the value of the tuman fell to £1.18.0. By 1800, it stood at about £1.[2] It should, however, be added that this decline in Persian currency was far smaller than the contemporary one in the Ottoman Empire (see EHME, pp. 520–21).

Under Fath Ali Shah (1797–1834) a new silver coin was introduced, the kran, equal to a tenth of a tuman, 5 abbasis, or 20 shahis. The shahi now became a copper coin. Thus Iran had three sets of coins: gold tumans and fractions,[3] silver krans and fractions, and copper shahis and fractions, but in practice the bulk of the currency consisted of silver coins.[4] Currency was issued in several cities; Agha Muhammad (1796–97) "minted gold coins in thirteen cities of Iran and silver in twenty-two. Fath Ali Shah had twenty-five gold mints and thirty-one silver ones."[5] In addition, numerous foreign coins circulated in Iran, as in the

[1] Petrushevsky in CHI, 5:519; Lorini, pp. 293–94.
[2] J. Rabino, "Banking"; Curzon, *Persia*, 1:471.
[3] "The early coinage is almost entirely of silver, and gold does not become common till after the middle of the 18th century, as a result of Nadir's campaign"—John Allan, in Pope, *Survey*, 3:2676.
[4] At the end of the nineteenth century, the excessive issue of copper coins caused distress to trade and in 1901 they were replaced by nickel coins—see Rabino di Borgomale, p. 79.
[5] Hambly; for further details see Rabino di Borgomale.

Ottoman Empire, of which the chief were the Turkish piaster, the Dutch ducat, and the Venetian sequin. In the south, the various Indian rupees were also used, and in the north the Russian ruble.

The history of Iran's currency in the nineteenth century is one of continuous depreciation (see 8:1), due at first mainly to debasement and later to the sharp drop in the price of silver. Already during Fath Ali's reign, the weight of the gold tuman had fallen from 95 grains to 53 and that of the silver kran from 142 grains to 107. Under his successor, Muhammad Shah (1834–48), the kran fell further to 89 grains. By 1857, the tuman weighed, in principle, only 50 grains (3.225 grams) of 900 per thousand fineness, the kran 78 grains (5 grams) of 900 per thousand fineness, and the shahi 78 grains, or 5 grams.[6]

These successive debasements naturally caused much inconvenience to traders and others. Among many examples, a report sent by Campbell (envoy to the court of Persia) to the directors of the East India Company (May 1835, IO LS and P/9, vol. 52), may be quoted:

The new currency having given great dissatisfaction to the community owing to the lightness of its weight and the exorbitant demands of the Seroofs for a premium when they exchanged any coin into small pieces, and all the old silver money in consequence of its superior value in currency having been exported from the capital, the Kaim Makaum in the name of the King requested me to examine into the affair and to report upon it, in order that my decision might be final and that coin might be immediately struck to supply the wants of the people.

Campbell made various sensible suggestions, including the recalling of the old currency and the minting of new gold, silver, and copper coins, but no action seems to have been taken. Mints—farmed out to the highest bidder—continued to issue debased coins, and bad money tended to drive good out of circulation. In addition, Iran probably had a deficit in its balance of payments (see chap. 3, introduction and sel. 23), and thus may have had to export specie and bullion. Lorini also suggests that in the 1860s the relatively low price of gold, in terms of silver, in Iran encouraged its export to Europe; such exports may have been fed by the hoard of treasure brought over from India by Nadir Shah in 1739.[7]

In the 1860s, a powerful new factor began to operate: the fall in the world price of silver. For nearly two hundred years the ratio of gold to silver prices had shown little fluctuation, and in the period 1815–71 the extreme variation had been 5 percent; but between 1871 and 1889 the price of silver fell by nearly 30 percent (see 8:3). The decline continued until 1898, with a total drop of over 50 percent, after which the price of silver rose slightly, relative to gold. This greatly reduced the value of Iran's silver currency, compared with those based on gold. At the same time, debasement continued.[8] It is true that, after various mishaps, modern

---

[6] Lorini, pp. 295–96; copper coins consisted of the abbasi, equal to 4 shahis; the sanar, equal to 2 shahis; and the pul, or $\frac{1}{2}$ shahi—ibid., p. 426.

[7] Ibid., p. 297.

[8] See "Tabriz," A and P 1867–68, 68; and "Tabriz," A and P 1873, 67.

machinery arrived from Europe and in 1877 new coins began to be minted in Tehran, the mints in the other towns being closed down.[9] The kran was assigned a value equivalent to one mithqal of 900 per thousand fineness, equal to 71.04 grains or 4.6 grams.[10] But very soon the fineness was reduced to 890 or even lower,[11] and the "new" coins were worth slightly less than the "old" ones.[12] This state of affairs yielded the master of the mint a net profit of 10 percent or more![13] Naturally, it encouraged the hoarding of the better coins, or their export to neighboring countries.[14]

The consequent shortage of good coins would have had still more adverse effects on trade, had it not been alleviated by three factors. First, there was the influx of a large amount of foreign coins, especially rubles in the north.[15] Second, the merchants made extensive use of bills drawn on various foreign centers.[16] Last, foreign banks started operations in 1888 (see 8:3), and banknotes were issued by the Imperial Bank of Persia. By 1914, the amount of such notes stood at nearly £1,000,000. However, in this, as in so many other respects, Iran had to wait till after the First World War for a sound and flexible currency, and still longer for a banking system adequate to its needs.

## WEIGHTS AND MEASURES

As in other parts of the Middle East (see EHME, pp. 517–19), weights and measures in Iran were extremely diverse. They varied not only from place to place, but often also according to the nature of the object being weighed or measured.[1]

### WEIGHTS

In the nineteenth century the more commonly used weights were:
*Gandum* ("ear of wheat") or *ju* ("ear of barley"), about 0.048 grams
*Nukhud* ("pea"), equal to 4 gandum or about 0.192 grams
*Mithqal* (*misqal*), equal to 24 nukhud or about 4.6 grams
*Sir*, equal to 16 mithqal or about 74 grams
*Charak* ("quarter") equal to 10 sir, or about 737 grams
*Mann-i Tabriz* (also known as *batman*) equal to 4 charak, or about 2.950 kilograms
*Kharvar* ("donkey lead") equal to 100 mann or about 290 kilograms

[9] Curzon, *Persia*, 1:472.
[10] Lorini, p. 307.
[11] An Austrian expert, brought over in 1875, refused to issue debased coins and was therefore soon dismissed and replaced by one of the shah's favorites (Mareuil to Minister of Foreign Affairs, 25 November 1879, AE Correspondance Commerciale, Téhéran, vol. 3).
[12] Lorini, pp. 308–13; "Persia," A and P 1886, 67; and MacLean, "Report," A and P 1904, 95. See list of coins in circulation 1879–1926 in Rabino di Borgomale, p. 74.
[13] "Persia," A and P 1884, 79.
[14] "Khurasan," A and P 1908, 114.
[15] See, for example, "Mashad," A and P 1890, 76.
[16] For a detailed description, see "Tabriz," A and P 1873, 67.
[1] The following account is based mainly on Hinz, passim; Jamalzadeh, pp. 167–69; Blau, pp. 174–78; "Persia," A and P 1886, 67; Geographical Handbook Series, *Persia*, p. 600; and Lambton, *Landlord*, pp. 405–9.

Several other kinds of mann were also current; of these the most widespread were the *mann-i shah*, equal to 2 mann-i Tabriz (1,280 mithqal), or about 6 kilograms; it was used in Isfahan, Kashan, Rasht, and other places. The small *mann-i Ray* was equal to 4 mann-i Tabriz (2,560 mithqal) or about 12 kilograms, and the large *mann-i Ray* to nearly 5 mann-i Tabriz (3,000 mithqal) or about 13.8 kilograms. Other local mann ranged from 720 mithqal (Shiraz, Bandar Abbas) to 1,440 mithqal (Astarabad, Shushtar). Similarly there were variations in the Kharvar, that of Astarabad being equal to 90 mann-i Tabriz while the *asbi* ("horse") *kharvar* was equal to 20 mann-i shah.[2]

Other common units of weight were the *qirat* (carat), equal to 1/23 of a mithqal, or about 0.19 grams, and used in jewelry; the *himl* ("camel load"), which varied greatly but was frequently around 250 kilograms; and the *quti*, in the rice trade of the Caspian coast, equal to 9 mann-i Tabriz or about 26 kilograms. Liquids were sold by weight, not volume.

## LENGTH

As in other Middle Eastern countries, the ell (*zar^c* or *zira^c*, also known as the *gaz* or *arshin*) was the basic unit of measurement; Two main kinds were in use: *Zar^c-i shahi*, equal to about 1.12 meters, and *zar^c-i muqassar* ("shortened"), equal to 1.04 meters, or a little less.

The *zar^c* was divided into 4 *charak* ("quarter") which in turn were subdivided into 4 *girih* ("knot") each of which equaled 2 *bahr* ("portion"). Thus a *bahr-i shahi* was equal to about 3.5 centimeters and a *bahr-i muqassar* to about 3.25 centimeters. In the cotton textile trade, the *tob* of 6 zar^c was used. Distance was measured in *farsakh* (parasang) of about 6 kilometers, divided into 150 *tanab*, of about 40 meters each.

Areas were measured in *jarib*, which also varied widely, being often reckoned (as in other parts of the Middle East) as the amount of land which could be sown by a specified quantity of seed. The most common equaled 1,066 square zar^c, or around 1,000 square meters, but several variants were used, including the *jarib-i shah* of about 1,200 square meters and the *jarib-i rasm* of about 700 square meters, as well as larger and smaller units.[3]

In principle the jarib was divided into 10 *qafiz* (originally a measure of volume, not weight), but here the variations were even wider.

[2] For further details see Lambton, Jamalzadeh, and Geographical Handbook Series, *Persia*, p. 600.
[3] See Lambton, *Landlord*, pp. 405–9.

# Bibliography

The following are some of the more useful publications on the subjects covered in this volume. Books marked with an asterisk have good bibliographies.

Abdullaev, Z. Z. *Promyshlennost i zarozhdenie rabochego klassa Irana v kontse XIX-nachale XX vv.* Baku, 1963.

*Adamiyat, Feridun. *Amir-i Kabir wa Iran.* Tehran, 1334.

Adams, Robert McC. "Agricultural and Urban Life in Early Southwestern Iran." *Science*, 13 April 1962.

———. *Land behind Baghdad.* Chicago, 1965.

Adli, Abolfazl. *Aussenhandel und Aussenwirtschaftspolitik des Iran.* Berlin, 1960.

Afshin, Kazim. *Naft wa Khuzistan.* Tehran, 1333.

Ahrens, Peter. *Die Entwicklung der Stadt Tehran.* Cologne, 1966.

———. *Tehran.* Berlin, 1965.

Ainsworth, W. F. *The River Karun: An Opening to British Commerce.* London, 1890.

Aitchison, C. U. *A Collection of Treaties, Engagements and Sanads Relating to India and Neighbouring Countries.* Delhi, 1933.

Alami, Ebrahim K. *Le redressement économique de l'Iran.* Paris, 1939.

Amini, Ali. *L'Institution du monopole du commerce extérieur en Iran.* Paris, 1932.

Amuzegar, Jahangir. *Technical Assistance in Theory & Practice: The Case of Iran.* New York, 1965.

Anet, C. *La Perse en automobile.* Paris, 1905.

Anglo-Persian Oil Co. *The Persian Oil Industry.* London, 1927.

Anville, J.-B. de. *Mémoire sur la mer Caspienne.* Paris, 1777.

Arasteh, Reza. *Education and Social Awakening in Iran.* Leiden, 1962.

Arberry, A. J., ed. *The Legacy of Persia.* Oxford, 1953.

Atrpet. *Mamed-Ali-Shakh.* Aleksandropol, 1909.

Aubin, Eugène. *La Perse d'aujourd'hui.* Paris, 1908.

Aucher-Eloy. *Relation de voyage en Orient de 1830 à 1838.* Paris, 1842.

*Avery, Peter. *Modern Iran.* London, 1965.

Bakulin, F. A. "Ocherk russkoi torgovli v Mazendarane i Asterabade v 1871 g." *Vostochnyi Sbornik*. 1877.

———. "Ocherk vneshnei torgovli Azerbaidzhana za 1870–1871 g.g." *Vostochnyi Sbornik*, 1877.

Baldwin, George B. *Planning and Development in Iran*. Baltimore, Md., 1967.

Balfour, J. M. *Recent Happenings in Persia*. London, 1922.

*Banani, Amin. *The Modernization of Iran*. Stanford, California, 1961.

Bank Melli Iran. *Tarikhche si saleh Bank-i Melli Iran*. Tehran, n.d.

Barth, Frederik. *Nomads of South Persia*. Oslo, 1961.

Bartold, V. V. *Iran, istorischeski obzor*. Tashkent, 1928.

Baster, A. S. J. *The International Banks*. London, 1935.

Bayani, K. *Les relations de l'Iran avec l'Europe occidentale à l'époque Safavide*. Paris, 1937.

Behnam, D. *Conséquences économiques de la croissance démographique*. Paris, 1957.

Behruzi, Ali. *Shahr-i Shiraz*. Shiraz, 1334.

Bémont, Freddy. "L'irrigation en Iran." *Annales de géographie*, 1961.

———. *Les villes de l'Iran*. Paris, 1969.

Berezin, I. *Puteshestvie po severnoi persii*. Kazan, 1852.

Binning, R. *A Journal of Two Years' Travel in Persia*. 2 vols. London, 1857.

Blaramberg, I. *Statisticheskoe obozrenie Persii*. Saint Petersburg, 1853.

Blau, Ernst Otto. *Commerzielle Zustände Persiens*. Berlin, 1858.

Bobek, Hans. *Tehran*. Vienna, 1957.

Bobynin, N. N. *Persiya*. . . . Tiflis, 1923.

Bogdanov, L. *Persiya*. Saint Petersburg, 1909.

Boxer, C. R. *The Dutch Seaborne Empire*. London, 1965.

Brockway, Thomas. "Britain and the Persian Bubble—1888–1892." *Journal of Modern History*, 1941.

———. "Dollar Diplomacy and the Persian Bubble." *Royal Central Asian Journal*, 1939.

Browne, Edward. *A Literary History of Persia*. 4 vols. Cambridge, 1928.

———. *The Press and Poetry of Modern Persia*. Cambridge, 1914.

Brünner, E. R. J. *De Bagdadspoorweg*. Groningen, 1957.

Brydges, Harford John. *The Dynasty of the Qajar*. London, 1830.

Buckingham, J. S. *Travels in Assyria, Media and Persia*. London, 1829.

Cahen, C. "L'évolution de l'iqta." *Annales*, 1953.

Caponera, Dante. *Water Laws in Moslem Countries*. FAO, Rome, March 1954.

Carter, Thomas C., and Goodrich, L. Carrington. *The Invention of Printing in China*. New York, 1955.

Chabari, Sahamaddin. *Le Tapis Persan*. Geneva, 1957.

*Chapman, Maybelle. *Great Britain and the Baghdad Railway*. Northampton, Mass., 1948.

Chardin, J. *Voyages du Chevalier Chardin en Perse*. Amsterdam, 1732.

Christensen, A. *L'Iran sous les Sasanides*. Copenhagen, 1944.

Colomb, P. *Slave Catching in the Indian Ocean*. London, 1873.

Cook, Michael, ed. *Studies in the Economic History of the Middle East in Medieval and Modern Times*. London, 1970.

Coulburn, Rushton. *Feudalism in History*. Princeton, 1956.

Curzon, George. "The Karun River. . . ." *Proceedings of the Royal Geographical Society*, 1890.

———. *Persia and the Persian Question*. 2 vols. London, 1892.

Davis, Ralph. *Aleppo and Devonshire Square*. London, 1967.

Deane, Phyllis, and Cole, W. A. *British Economic Growth, 1688–1959*. Cambridge, 1967.

Dehkan, Ibrahim. *Tarikh-i Arak*. Tehran, 1330.

Demin, A. I. *Selskoe Khozyaistvo Sovremennogo Irana*. Moscow, 1967.

Demorgny, G. *Essai sur l'administration de la Perse*. Paris, 1913.

———. *Les institutions financières de la Perse*. Paris, 1915.

Dieulafoy, J. *La Perse. . . .* Paris, 1887.

Djazaeri, Chams-ed-Dine. *La crise économique mondiale et ses répercussions en Iran*. Paris, 1938.

Djourbatchi, Hasan. *La structure économique de l'Iran*. Geneva, 1955.

Drouville, Gaspard. *Voyage en Perse en 1812 et 1813*. Paris, 1825.

Dubeux, Louis. *La Perse*. Paris, 1841.

Dupré, Adrien. *Voyage en Perse fait dans les années 1807–1809*. Paris, 1819.

Earle, Edward M. *Turkey, the Great Powers, and the Baghdad Railway*. New York, 1923.

Eastwick, E. B. *Journal of a Diplomat*. 2 vols. London, 1864.

Elwell-Sutton, L. P. *A Guide to Iranian Area Study*. Ann Arbor, Michigan, 1952.

———. *Modern Iran*. London, 1941.

———. *Persian Oil: A Study in Power Politics*. London, 1955.

English, Paul W. *City and Village in Iran*. Madison, Wisc., 1966.

———. "The Origin and Spread of Qanats in the Old World." *Proceedings of the American Philosophical Society*, vol. 112 (June 1968).

Entner, Marvin. *Russo-Persian Commercial Relations, 1828–1914*. Gainesville, Fla., 1965.

Farahmand, Sohrab. *Der Wirtschaftsaufbau des Iran*. Tübingen, 1965.

Farmanfarma, Firuz. *Safarnama-i Kirman wa Baluchistan*. Tehran, 1342.

*Farman Farmaian, Hafez. *Iran: A Selected and Annotated Bibliography*. Washington, D. C., 1951.

*Farnie, D. A. *East and West of Suez*. Oxford, 1969.

Fasai Mirza Hasan. *Fars-namah-i Nasiri*. 2 vols. Tehran, 1894–96.

Fateh, Mustapha Khân. *The Economic Position of Persia*. London, 1926.

———. *Panjah sal naft-i Iran*. Tehran, n.d.

———. *Pul wa bankdari*. Tehran, 1309.

Fatemi, Nasrullah Saifpour. *Diplomatic History of Persia, 1917–1923*. New York, 1952.

Ferrier, J.-P. *Voyages en Perse. . . .* 2 vols. Paris, 1860.

Feuvrier, Dr. *Trois ans à la cour de Perse, 1889–1892*. Paris, 1895.

Flandin, Eugene. *Voyage en Perse*. 2 vols. Paris, 1851.

Foster, W. *England's Quest of Eastern Trade*. London, 1933.

Fraser, James. *Historical and Descriptive Account of Persia*. New York, 1833.

———. *A Journey through Persia, . . . in 1808–1809*. London, 1812.

———. *Narrative of a Journey to Khorassan*. London, 1825.

———. *A Second Journey through Persia, . . .* London, 1818.

———. *Travels and Adventures in the Persian Provinces on the Southern Banks of the Caspian Sea*. London, 1826.

Frechtling, L. E. "The Reuter Concession in Persia." *Asiatic Review*, 1938.

Frye, Richard N. *The Heritage of Persia*. New York, 1963.

———. *Iran*. New York, 1953.

Gardane, General. *Journal d'un voyage en Turquie et en Perse en 1807–1808*. Paris, 1819.

Ghadimy, Mochar. *Les finances publiques de la Perse*. Paris, 1923.

Ghirshman, R. *Iran*. London, 1954.

Glamann, Kristoff. *Dutch-Asiatic Trade, 1620–1740*. The Hague, 1958.

Gleadowe-Newcomen, A. H. *Report on the British-Indian Commercial Mission to South East Persia during 1904–1905*. Calcutta, 1906.

Glukhoded, V. S. *Problemy ekonomicheskovo razvitiya Irana*. Moscow, 1968.

Gobineau, Arthur de. *Trois ans en Asie*. Paris, 1859.

Goblot, H. "Le problème de l'eau en Iran." *Orient*, 1962.

———. "Le rôle de l'Iran dans les techniques de l'eau." *Techniques et Sciences municipales*. February 1961.

Gödel, Rudolf. *Ueber den pontischen Handelsweg und die Verhältnisse des europäischpersischen Verkehrs*. Vienna, 1849.

Goitein, S. D. *A Mediterranean Society*. Berkeley and Los Angeles, 1967.

Gorelikov, S. M. *Iran*. Moscow, 1961.

Gray, F. A. G. *Report on Economic and Commercial Conditions in Iran*. London, 1938.

Great Britain, Foreign Office, Historical Section Handbooks, *Persia*, June 1919.

———. *Persian Gulf*. June 1919.

Great Britain, Naval Intelligence Division, Geographical Handbook Series. *Persia*. September 1945.

Greaves, Rose. *Persia and the Defence of India, 1884–1892*. London, 1959.

Groseclose, Elgin. *Introduction to Iran*. New York, 1947.

Grunwald, K. "L'industrializzamento della Persia." *Oriente Moderno*, 1938.

Grunwald, K., and Ronall, J. *Industrialization in the Middle East*. New York, 1960.

Gulriz, Muhammad Ali. *Minudar . . . Qazvin*. Tehran, 1337.

Haas, William S. *Iran*. New York, 1946.

Hadow, R. H. *Report on the Trade and Industry of Persia*. London, 1925.

Hambly, Gavin. "An Introduction to the Economic Organization of Early Qajar Iran." *Iran*, 1964.

Hanway, Jonas. *An Historical Account of the British Trade*. London, 1754.

Harris, Christina. "The Persian Gulf Submarine Telegraph." *Geographical Journal*, 1969.

Hasan, Hadi. *A History of Persian Navigation*. London, 1928.

Hasan, Muhammad Salman. *Al-tatawwur al-iqtisadi fi al-Iraq*. Beirut, n.d.

Herbert, Thomas. *Some Yeares Travels*. London, 1665.

*Hershlag, Z. Y. *Introduction to the Modern Economic History of the Middle East*. Leiden, 1964.

Hertslet, Edward. *Treaties . . . Persia*. London, 1891.

Hinz, Walther. *Islamische Masse und Gewichte*. Leiden, 1955.

Hoskins, H. L. *British Routes to India*. London, 1928.

Hourani, George. *Arab Seafaring*. Princeton, 1951.

Houtoum-Schindler, A. *Eastern Persian Iraq*. London, 1896.

Hurewitz, J. C. *Diplomacy in the Near and Middle East: A Documentary Record, 1914–1956*. 2 vols. Princeton, 1956.

Hytier, Adrienne-Doris. *Les dépêches diplomatiques du comte de Gobineau en Perse*. Paris, 1959.

Imlah, Albert. *Economic Elements in the Pax Britannica*. Cambridge, Mass., 1958.

*Issawi, Charles. *The Economic History of the Middle East, 1800–1914*. Chicago, 1966.

———. "Iran's Economic Upsurge." *Middle East Journal*, Summer, 1967.

———. "The Tabriz–Trabzon Trade. . . ." *IJMES*, January 1970.

Issawi, Charles, and Yeganeh, Mohammed. *The Economics of Middle Eastern Oil*. New York, 1962.

Ivanov, M. S. *Babidskie vosstaniya v Irane*. Moscow, 1939.

———. *Ocherk istorii Irana*. Moscow, 1952.

———. *Iranskaya revolutsiya, 1905–1911*. Moscow, 1957.

Jack, Marian. "The Purchase of the British Government's Shares in the British Petroleum Company." *Past and Present*, 1968.

Jaeger, T. *Persien und persische Frage*. Weimar, 1916.

Jamalzadeh, Muhammad Ali. *Ganj-i Shaigan*. Berlin, 1335.

Jazairi, Shams al-Din. *Qavanin-i malieh*. Tehran, 1335.

Joubert, Amédée. *Voyage en Arménie et en Perse en 1805–1806*. Paris, 1821.

Kaempfer, Engelbert. *Amoenitatum exoticarum*. . . . Lemgoviae, 1712.

Kasravi, Ahmad. *Tarikh-i marshrutiyat dar Iran*. Tehran, 1340.

Katrak, Sohrab. *Who Are the Parsees*. Karachi, n.d.

Kazemzadeh, Firuz. *Russia and Britain in Persia*. New Haven, 1968.

Keddie, Nikki. *Historical Obstacles to Agrarian Change in Iran*. Claremont, 1960.

———. "The Iranian Village before and after Land Reform." *Journal of Contemporary History*, 1968.

———. *Religion and Rebellion in Iran*. London, 1966.

Keen, B. A. *The Agricultural Development of the Middle East*. London, 1946.

Kelly, John Barrett. *Britain and the Persian Gulf*. London, 1968.

Kia, Abbas Chamseddine. *Essai sur l'histoire industrielle de l'Iran*. Paris, 1939.

Kinnier, Macdonald. *Geographical Memoir of the Persian Empire*. London, 1813.

Korobeinikov, I. I. *Iran, ekonomika i vneshnyaya torgovlya*. Moscow, 1963.

Krusinski, Tadeusz. *The History of the Revolutions of Persia*. London, 1728.

Kukanova, N. G. "Iz istorii russko iranskikh torgovikh svyazei v XVII veke." *KSINA*, 1958.

———. "Rol armyanskogo Kupechestva v razvitii russko—iranskoy torgovli v posledney treti XVII v. v." *KSINA*, 1961.

Kulagina, L. M. "Iz istorii zakabalenia Irana angliiskim kapitalizmom." *KSIV*, 1956.

Kumar, Ravindar. *India and the Persian Gulf Region*. New York, 1966.

Lafont, F., and H. L. Rabino, *L'industrie séricole en Perse*. Montpellier, 1910.

*Lambton, A. K. S. *Landlord and Peasant in Persia*. London, 1953.

———. *Persian Land Reform*. London, 1969.

———. "Persian Society under the Qajars." *Journal of the Royal Central Asian Society*, 1961.

———. "Rural Development and Land Reform in Iran." In *Symposium on Rural Development*. CENTO, 1963.

Lavi, Habib. *Tarikh-i Yehudi Iran*. Tehran, n.d.

Le Brun, Corneille. *Voyages*. Amsterdam, 1718.

Lenczowski, George. *Russia and the West in Iran, 1918–1948*. Ithaca, N.Y. 1949.

LeStrange, G. *The Lands of the Eastern Caliphate*. Cambridge, 1905.

Lesueur, Emile. *Les anglais en Perse*. Paris, 1921.

*Lewis, Bernard, and Holt, P. M. *Historians of the Middle East*. London, 1962.

Lingeman, E. R. *Economic Conditions in Persia, 1930*. London: Department of Overseas Trade, 1928.

Lisani, Abu al-fadl. *Talai siah ya balai Iran*. Tehran, 1950.

Lisenko, V. K. *Blizhnii Vostok*. Saint Petersburg, 1913.

Litten, Wilhelm. *Persien*. Berlin, 1920.

Lloyd, Christopher. *The Navy and the Slave Trade*. London, 1906.

Lockhart, Laurence. "Khuzistan—Past and Present." *Asiatic Review*, 1948.

——. *Nadir Shah*. London, 1938.

——. *Persian Cities*. London, 1957.

——. "Persian Petroleum in Ancient and Medieval Times." In *IIe Congrès mondial du pétrole*. Paris, 1937.

Lokkegaard, F. *Islamic Taxation in the Classical Period*. Copenhagen, 1950.

Lomnitskii, S. *Persiya i persy*. Saint Petersburg, 1902.

Longrigg, S. H. *Oil in the Middle East*. Oxford, 1954.

Lorimer, J. G. *Gazetteer of the Persian Gulf*. Calcutta, 1915.

Lorini, Eteocle. *La Persia economica*. Rome, 1900.

MacGregor, C. M. *Narrative of a Journey through the Province of Khorassan*. 2 vols. London, 1879.

MacLean, H. W. "Report on the Conditions and Prospects of British Trade in Persia." A and P, 1904, 95.

Malcolm, John. *History of Persia*. London, 1829.

——. *The Melville Papers*. London, 1930.

——. *Sketches of Persia*. London, 1849.

Manandian, H. *The Trade and Cities of Armenia in Relation to Ancient World Trade*. Translated by Nina Garsoian. Lisbon, 1965.

Mandelslo, J. A. *The Voyages and Travels of. . . .* London, 1662.

Mans, Raphael du. *Estat de la Perse en 1660*. Edited by C. Scheffer. Paris, 1890.

Markham, C. R. *A General Sketch of the History of Persia*. London, 1874.

Martin, Bradford. *German-Persian Diplomatic Relations 1873–1912*. The Hague, 1959.

Masson, Paul. *Histoire du commerce français dan le Levant au XVIIe siècle*. Paris, 1896.

Mazandarani, Gh. *Iqtisad-i milli wa siyasat-i iqtisadi-i Iran*. Tehran, 1316.

Medvedev, A. I. *Persiya voenno-statisticheskoye obozrenie*. Saint Petersburg, 1909.

Mez, A. *The Renaissance of Islam*. London, 1937.

Milburn, William. *Oriental Commerce*. London, 1813.

Miles, S. B. *The Countries and Tribes of the Persian Gulf*. London, 1919.

Miller, A. *Proshloe i nastoyashchee Seistana*. Saint Petersburg, 1907.

Millspaugh, A. C. *Americans in Persia*. Washington, D.C., 1946.

——. *The American Task in Persia*. New York, 1925.

——. *The Financial and Economic Situation of Persia, 1926*. New York, 1926.

Minorsky, V. *Hudud al-alam*. London, 1937.

——. *Takhkirat al-Muluk*. London, 1943.

Mizrahi, H. *Yehude Paras*. Tel Aviv, 1959.

Mochaver, Fazlollah. *L'évolution des finances iraniennes*. Paris, 1938.

Monteil, Vincent. *Les tribus du Fars*. The Hague, 1966.

Morrison-Knudson, Inc. "Report to Iranian Government." 2 August 1947.

Motter, T. H. Vail. *The Persian Corridor and Aid to Russia*. Washington, D.C., 1952.

Moyse-Bartlett, H. *The Pirates of Trucial Oman*. London, 1966.

Mulhall, Michael. *Dictionary of Statistics*. London, 1884, 1909.

——. *Progress of the World*. London, 1880.

Murzban, M. M. *The Parsis in India*. Bombay, 1917.

Nakhai, M. *Le Pétrole en Iran*. Brussels, 1938.

Napier, G. C. *Journal and Reports on Special Duty in Persia*. London, 1876.

Navai, Hossein. *Les relations économiques irano–russes*. Paris, 1935.

Nayyeri, Mostafa. *Das Bankwesen im Iran und seine Entwicklung*. Tehran, 1964.

Neligan, A. R. *The Opium Question, with Special Reference to Persia*. London, 1927.

Ogorodnikov, P. *Ocherki Persii*. Saint Petersburg, 1878.

Ogranovich, I. A. *Provintsii Ardetilskaya i Serabskaya*. Tiflis, 1876.

Olearius, A. *The Voyages and Travels*. . . . London, 1662.

Olmstead, A. T. *History of the Persian Empire*. Chicago, 1948.

Ostapenko, S. S. *Persidskii rynok i ego znachenie dla Rossii*. Kiev, 1913.

Ouseley, W. *Travels*. London, 1819.

Overseas Consultants, Inc. *Report on Seven Year Plan*. 5 vols. New York, 1949.

Pahlavi, Mohammed Riza Shah. *Mission for My Country*. New York, 1961.

Palyukaitis, I. I. *Ekonomicheskoe razvitie Irana*. Moscow, 1965.

Pelly, Lewis. "Remarks on a Recent Journey from Bushire to Shiraz." *Transactions of the Bombay Geographical Society*, 1863.

———. "Remarks on the Tribes, Trade and Resources around the Shoreline of the Persian Gulf." *Transactions of the Bombay Geographical Society*, 1863.

Peyamiras, Parviz D. *Méthodes d'interventionnisme économique en Iran*. Geneva, 1944.

Pigulevskaya, N. V., et al. *Istoriya Irana*. Leningrad, 1958.

Pirnahad, Hassan. *Die Entstehung der modernen Volkswirtschaft in Iran*. Berlin, 1935.

Polak, Jacob. *Persien: Das Land und seine Behwohner*. 2 vols. Leipzig, 1865.

Polk, William R., and Chambers, Richard L. *Beginnings of Modernization of the Middle East*. Chicago, 1968.

Pope, A. Upham. *A Survey of Persian Art*. New York, 1938.

Popov, A. L. "Stranitsa iz istorii russkogo imperializma v Persii." *Mezhdunarodnaya zhizn*, 1924.

Porter, Ker. *Travels in Georgia, Persia, etc*. London, 1828.

Price, W. *Journal of the British Embassy to Persia*. London, 1832.

Rabino, Hyacinth. "Culture du tabac en Guilan." In *Progrès Agricole et Viticole*. Montpellier, 1911.

———. *Mazandaran and Astarabad*. London, 1928.

Rabino, Hyacinth, and Lafont, F. D. "La culture du riz en Guilan." In *Annales de l'école nationale d'agriculture de Montpellier*. Montpellier, 1911.

Rabino, Joseph. "Banking in Persia." *Journal of the Institute of Banking*, 1892.

Rabino di Borgomale, H. L. *Coins, Medals and Seals of the Shahs of Iran (1500–1941)*. Hertford, 1945.

———. "An Economist's Notes on Persia." *Journal of the Royal Statistical Society*, 1901.

Ramazani, Rouhollah. *The Foreign Policy of Iran, 1500–1941*. Charlottesville, 1966.

Riahi, Ibrahim. *Tahqiq dar tarikh-i qand sazi Iran*. Tehran, 1336.

Richard, Jean. "European Voyages in the Indian Ocean and the Caspian Sea (12th–15th centuries)." *Iran*, 1968.

Richards D. S. ed. *Islam and the Trade of Asia*. Oxford, 1970.

*Ricks, Thomas, et al. *Persian Studies: A Selected Bibliography of Works in English*. Bloomington, 1969.

Rittikh, P. A. *Otchet o poezdke v Persiyu i persidskii Beludzhistan*. Saint Petersburg, 1901.

———. *Zheleznodorozhnyi put cherez Persiyv*. Saint Petersburg, 1900.

Roberts, N. S. *Iran, Economic and Commercial Conditions.* London: Department of Overseas Trade, 1948.

Romanov, P. M. *Zheleznodorozhny vopros v Persii i mery k kazvitiyu russko—persidskoi torgovli.* Saint Petersberg, 1891.

Ronall, Joachim. "The Beginnings of Modern Banking in Iran." In *Wissenschaft, Wirtschaft und Technik,* ed. K.-H. Manegold. Munich, n.d.

Rostovtzeff, M. *The Social and Economic History of the Hellenistic World.* Oxford, 1953.

Rozhkova, M.-K. *Ekonomicheskaya politika tsarskogo pravitelstva. . . .* Moscow, 1949.

★Saba, Mohsen. *Bibliographie française de l'Iran.* Tehran, 1966.

Sadiq, Issa. *Modern Persia and Her Educational System.* New York, 1931.

Sadrzadeh, Ziya al-Din. *Saderat-i Iran.* Tehran, 1346.

St. John, Oliver. *Eastern Persia: An Account of the Journey of the Persian Boundary Commission.* 2 vols. London, 1876.

Sakharos, A. *Russkaya Kolonizatsia Astrabadskoi provintsii Persii.* Petrograd, 1915.

Sandjabi, K. *Essai sur l'économie rurale et le régime agraire de la Perse.* Paris, 1934.

Schwarz, P. *Iran im Mittelalter nach den arabischen Geographen.* Leipzig, 1896–1936.

Sée, Henri. *La France économique et sociale au XVIIIe siècle.* Paris, 1946.

Seidov, R. A. *Agrarny vopros i krestyanskoe dvizhenie v Irane, 1950–53.* Baku, 1963.

*Severniya Persiya* (Konsulskie doklady). Moscow, 1933.

Shayan, Abbas. *Mazandaran.* Tehran, 1336.

Sheil, M. L. *Glimpses of Life and Manners in Persia.* London, 1856.

Shuster, W. Morgan. *The Strangling of Persia.* New York, 1912.

Shwadran, Benjamin. *The Middle East, Oil and the Great Powers.* New York, 1955.

Simmonds, S. *Economic Conditions in Iran (Persia).* London, 1935.

Singer, Charles, ed. *A History of Technology.* Oxford, 1957.

Sipihr. *Tarikh wa juqhrafiyai Dar al Saltanah-i Tabriz.* Tabriz, n.d.

Sobotsinskii, L. A. *Persiya: Statistiko-ekonomicheskii ocherk.* Saint Petersburg, 1913.

Soheily, Hossein. *Essai sur l'industrialisation de l'Iran.* Montreux, 1950.

Sotoudeh, Hassan. *L'évolution économique de l'Iran et ses problèmes.* Paris, 1937.

*Sovremennyi Iran, spravochnik.* Moscow, 1957.

Stack, Edward. *Six Months in Persia.* 2 vols. London, 1882.

Stauff, P. "Die deutsche Bank in Teheran und der deutsch-persische Handel." *Asien,* 1908.

Stolze, F., and Andreas, F. C. *Die Handelsverhältnisse Persiens.* Göttingen, 1885.

Sventitski, A. S. "Transport Routes in Persia." *Journal of the Central Asian Society,* 1928.

Sykes, Percy. *History of Persia.* 2 vols. London, 1930.

———. *Ten Thousand Miles in Persia.* London, 1902.

Tagieva, Sh. A. "Razlozhenie feodalnogo zemlevladeniya v Irane v Kontse XIX—nachale XX v." *KSINA,* 1963.

Tavernier, J. B. *Les six voyages. . . .* Paris, 1712.

Taymuri, Ibrahim. *Asr-i bi-khabari.* Tehran, 1332.

Ter-Gukasov, G. I. *Politicheskie i ekonomicheskie interesy Rossii v Persii.* Petrograd, 1916.

Ter-Ovanesov, G. C. "Rol Sovetskogo Soyuza v razvitii rybnoy promyshlennosti Irana." *KSINA,* 1963.

Ter-Yovhaneanc, I. P. Yarutiwn. *Patmutiwm Nor Julayu u Aspahan.* 2 vols. Julfa, 1881.

"The Story of the Euphrates Company." *Near East and India,* 1935.

Thevenot, Jean. *Suite du voyage au Levant.* Paris, 1674.

Thornton, A. P. "British Policy in Persia, 1858–1890." *English Historical Review*, 1954.

Tigranov, L. F. *Iz istori obshestvenno—ekonomicheskikh otnoshenii v Persii.* Tiflis, 1905.

Tomara, M. L. *Ekonomicheskoe polozhenie Persii.* Saint Petersburg, 1895.

Toussaint, Auguste. *History of the Indian Ocean.* London, 1966.

Trubetskoi, V. V. *Bakhtiary.* Moscow, 1966.

United Nations. *Economic Developments in the Middle East, 1945–1954.* New York, 1955.

———. *Public Finance Information Papers—Iran.* New York, 1951.

Upton, Joseph. *The History of Modern Iran.* Cambridge, Mass., 1965.

Valle, Pietro Della. *Voyages. . . .* Paris, 1663.

Vreeland, H. H., ed. *Iran.* New Haven, 1957.

Warriner, Doreen. *Land Reform in Principle and Practice.* Oxford, 1969.

Watson, R. G. *A History of Persia.* London, 1866.

Whigham, H. J. *The Persian Problem.* London, 1903.

*Wickens, G. M., et al. *Persia in Islamic Times: A Practical Bibliography.* Montreal, 1964.

Wilber, Donald N. *Contemporary Iran.* New York, 1963.

———. *Iran: Past and Present.* Princeton, 1958.

Wills, C. J. *The Land of the Lion and the Sun.* London, 1891.

*Wilson, Arnold. *A Bibliography of Persia.* Oxford, 1930.

———. *Persia.* London, 1932.

———. *The Persian Gulf.* London, 1928.

———. *South-West Persia.* London, 1941.

Wishead, J. G. *Twenty Years in Persia.* New York, 1908.

Wolf, John Baptist. *The Diplomatic History of the Baghdad Railroad.* Columbia, Mo., 1936.

Wood, A. C. *History of the Levant Company.* London, 1935.

Worthington, E. B. *Middle East Science.* London, 1946.

Wulff, Hans. *The Traditional Crafts of Persia.* Cambridge, Mass., 1966.

Yaganegi, Esfandiar. *Recent Financial and Monetary History of Persia.* New York, 1934.

Yeselson, Abraham. *United States–Persian Diplomatic Relations, 1883–1921.* New Brunswick, N.J.,
  1956.

Young, T. Cuyler. "Iran in Continuing Crisis." *Foreign Affairs*, 1962.

———. "The Problem of Westernization in Modern Iran." *Middle East Journal*, 1948.

Zamudny, N. *Ekskursiya po vostochnoi Persii*, Saint Petersburg, 1901.

———. *Tretya ekskursiya po vostochnoi Persii.* Petrograd, 1916.

Zonnenshtral-Piskorskii, A. A. *Mezhdunarodnye torgovye dogovory Persii.* Moscow, 1931.

# Index of Place Names

Abadan, 27, 49, 154, 269, 320, 322, 325–26

Afghanistan, 28, 65, 71, 120, 122–24, 134, 137, 149–50, 155, 191, 195, 214, 218, 270, 277–78, 280

Africa, 7–8, 104, 124–26, 166, 188–89, 213–15, 339, 370

Ahwaz, 8, 41, 75, 157, 171, 172–73, 175, 183, 192, 195–96, 198, 201–2, 207, 318–19, 322, 324–25, 358, 372

Arabia, 85, 88, 90–1, 125, 129–30, 166, 251, 263–66, 314

Arak. *See* Sultanabad

Ashqabad, 52, 124, 139, 155, 196, 198, 327–28

Astarabad, 8, 24, 28–29, 34, 74–75, 117–18, 123, 143, 145, 154–55, 159–61, 164, 210, 235, 249–50, 278, 297, 329, 340, 359–60, 363–65, 372

Austria, 94, 99, 101, 106, 115, 134, 137, 139–40, 145, 149, 165, 178, 212, 271, 293, 295, 297, 309, 354–55, 358

Azerbaijan, 3, 8, 21–22, 24, 27, 29, 34, 40, 43–45, 51, 68, 74–75, 110, 114, 120, 128, 138, 147, 187–88, 210, 222–23, 235, 247, 249–52, 271, 273, 282–83, 296–97, 301–2, 329, 341, 347, 352, 359, 361–64, 370, 372–73

Baghdad, 3, 8, 46, 62, 71, 74–75, 85, 92–93, 95, 110, 114, 116, 119–21, 125, 129–30, 138, 153, 155–58, 165, 173–75, 189, 192, 196–98, 204, 234–35, 237–38, 248, 264, 274, 278, 305, 313, 323

Bahrein, 121, 125–27, 166, 264, 314

Baku, 51, 95, 104, 138, 145, 154, 158–59, 161–64, 198, 203, 249–50, 256, 297, 311–12, 319, 326–30, 334, 357, 360–61

Bandar Abbas, 74–75, 83–85, 122–23, 126, 137, 140, 155, 158–59, 166, 170, 174, 183, 186–87, 189, 193, 195, 197, 202, 211, 241, 250–52, 267–68, 312, 345, 349, 358–59, 372

Bandar Gez, 154, 197, 360, 376

Bandar Mashur (Bandar Shahpur), 376

Barfurush, 28, 31–32, 47–48, 130, 198, 236, 278, 293, 326, 341, 360–61, 365

Basra, 49, 83, 95, 121, 125–26, 156, 166–67, 176, 197, 204, 250, 317, 323

Birjand, 41, 197, 199, 250

Black Sea, 122, 138, 159, 164–65, 173, 232, 243, 246–47

Bombay, 23, 46, 57, 64, 77, 83, 85–87, 91–92, 119, 123, 125, 158, 166–68, 170, 175–77, 199, 239–40, 245, 263, 266, 278, 328, 334, 339, 353

Burujird, 28–29, 32, 154, 192–94, 201, 358–59, 362, 364–65

Bushire, 21, 26–28, 31–32, 34, 42, 62, 74–79, 83–90, 93, 98, 110, 122, 125–27, 130–31, 137–39, 141, 144, 146, 150, 153, 155, 165–68, 170, 174–75, 186–87, 189, 195–97, 202, 211, 227, 239–40, 245, 248, 250–52, 263, 267–69, 278, 305, 312, 316, 329, 332, 340, 345–46, 352, 358–59, 372

China, 3, 5–8, 12, 68, 71–72, 89–90, 92, 121, 123–24, 137, 149, 219, 238–41, 274–75, 277–78, 293, 335, 368

Constantinople (Istanbul), 14, 71, 74, 85, 92–94, 97–102, 104–9, 111–12, 115, 117–18, 120, 124, 130, 140, 148, 159, 165, 170, 174, 181, 197, 199, 234, 237, 241, 247–48, 264, 269–71, 273–74, 278, 293, 328, 358

Damghan, 8, 138

Duzdab (Zahidan), 159, 193

Egypt, 7, 14–17, 20, 23, 70, 119, 124, 126, 149, 152, 165, 184, 206, 213–14, 219, 245, 250–51, 277, 279–80, 292, 301, 303, 313, 335, 339, 347–48, 375, 379–85

Enzeli (Pahlavi), 42, 47, 58, 75, 138, 141, 145, 154–55, 157, 159–64, 178–79, 182, 184, 188, 197–200, 203–4, 255–56, 278, 312, 326–27, 360–61

Erzerum, 76, 93, 95–97, 101–2, 106, 110, 116, 119, 165, 173–74, 278, 296, 343

Euphrates (Tigris), 5, 14, 74, 86, 119, 156, 165, 167, 171, 173–75, 181, 183, 188, 192, 214

Fars, 6, 29–30, 34, 46, 219, 223, 227, 249–50, 263, 266, 302, 362, 364–65

France, 18, 23, 73, 89, 108, 115, 118, 120, 134, 137, 140–41, 145–49, 156, 159–60, 175, 178, 182–83, 212, 232, 234, 236, 247, 251, 264, 269, 276, 278, 282, 293–94, 302, 305–7, 309, 314, 316, 318, 323–24, 341, 347, 355–57, 369

# Subject Index

Note: To be used together with the table of contents